CW01337936

Aurelian and Probus

'A man's value is measured by his learning'
Ardashir I to his son Shapur I according to Ferdowsi/Firdausi

'All the virtues of all men are as great as they have been made to appear by the genius of those who related their deeds'
Flavius Vopiscus Syracusii, *Historia Augusta, Probus* 1.1
tr. by Magie, 335

'Aurelian… was not unlike Alexander the Great or Caesar the Dictator; for in the space of three years he retook the Roman world from invaders'
Pseudo-Victor, *Epitome De Caesaribus* 35.1,
tr. by Banchich at *www.roman-emperors.org*

'Probus, an emperor whose rule restored to perfect safety the east, the west, the south, and the north, indeed all parts of the world, is now, by reason of a lack of writers, almost unknown to us'
Flavius Vopiscus Syracusii, in *Historia Augusta, Probus* 1.3
tr. by Magie, 337

For my wife Sini, and children Ari and Nanna for their patience.

Aurelian and Probus

The Soldier Emperors Who Saved Rome

Dr. Ilkka Syvänne

Above Left: Aurelian; Above Right: Probus
Photos by author (British Museum).

Pen & Sword
MILITARY

First published in Great Britain in 2020 by
Pen & Sword Military
An imprint of
Pen & Sword Books Ltd
Yorkshire – Philadelphia

Copyright © Dr. Ilkka Syvänne 2020

ISBN 978 1 52676 750 9

The right of Dr. Ilkka Syvänne to be identified as Author of this work has been asserted by him in accordance with the Copyright, Designs and Patents Act 1988.

A CIP catalogue record for this book is available from the British Library.

All rights reserved. No part of this book may be reproduced or transmitted in any form or by any means, electronic or mechanical including photocopying, recording or by any information storage and retrieval system, without permission from the Publisher in writing.

Printed and bound in the UK by TJ International Ltd, Padstow, Cornwall.

Pen & Sword Books Limited incorporates the imprints of Atlas, Archaeology, Aviation, Discovery, Family History, Fiction, History, Maritime, Military, Military Classics, Politics, Select, Transport, True Crime, Air World, Frontline Publishing, Leo Cooper, Remember When, Seaforth Publishing, The Praetorian Press, Wharncliffe Local History, Wharncliffe Transport, Wharncliffe True Crime and White Owl.

For a complete list of Pen & Sword titles please contact

PEN & SWORD BOOKS LIMITED
47 Church Street, Barnsley, South Yorkshire, S70 2AS, England
E-mail: enquiries@pen-and-sword.co.uk
Website: www.pen-and-sword.co.uk

Or

PEN AND SWORD BOOKS
1950 Lawrence Rd, Havertown, PA 19083, USA
E-mail: Uspen-and-sword@casematepublishers.com
Website: www.penandswordbooks.com

Contents

Acknowledgements vi
List of Plates vii
List of Maps ix
Introduction x
Abbreviations xi

Chapter 1 Sources and Analysis 1
Chapter 2 The Roman Empire in 268 3
Chapter 3 Youth and Career of Aurelian and Probus until 268 29
Chapter 4 The Reign of Claudius II 'Gothicus' in 268–270 46
Chapter 5 Aurelian (Aurelianus) The Beginning of the Reign in 270–71 64
Chapter 6 Aurelian vs. Zenobia 271–272 92
Chapter 7 The Wars against the Palmyrene Rebels, Carpi and Firmus of Egypt in 272–3 127
Chapter 8 Aurelian in the West 274–5 140
Chapter 9 Aurelian, the Man with Perfect Ability in War 158
Chapter 10 Tacitus 275–6 160
Chapter 11 The Struggle for Dominance: Probus vs. Florianus 169
Chapter 12 Probus the Fireman 176
Chapter 13 Probus. The Military Intellectual 212
Chapter 14 The Reigns of Carus (282–3), Carinus (282–5) and Numerianus (282–4) 215

Appendix I: Modestus, Vegetius, and the Late Third Century Army 231
Appendix II: The Problem of Third Century Drungus/Droungos *as a Military Unit* 247
Notes 249
Bibliography 265
Index 268

Acknowledgements

I'd like to thank the Commissioning Editor Phil Sidnell and Matt Jones, Barnaby Blacker and other persons for their stellar work. Big thanks is also owed to family and friends for reasons they know well.

List of Plates

Coin of Gallienus.
Coin of Claudius.
Coin of Quintillus.
Two coins of Aurelian.
Coin of Tacitus.
Coin of Florianus.
Coin of Probus.
Coin of Carus.
Nineteenth century photos of the siege of Verona in 312 in the Arch of Constantine.
The Battle of the Milvian Bridge in 312 in the Arch of Constantine.
Coins of Aurelian.
Coin of Probus.
Coin of Carus.
Coin of Diocletian.
Bust of Claudius or Aurelian.
Busts of Probus?
A typical Germanic horseman.
A typical Germanic footman.
A Roman auxiliary soldier of Germanic origins.
Six coins of Aurelian.
Germanic clubmen attack Palmyrene cataphracts at the battle of Emesa in about May 272.
An unidentified person in the collection of the British Museum, maybe the emperor Carus.
Author's drawing of a Palmyrene horseman after a mosaic.
Praetorian cavalry performing feigned flight.
Palmyrene mounted archer after a mosaic.
Duel between Probus and Aradio in AD 269 and two coins.
Cataphract armed for both long and close distance combat.
Bust usually identified as Probus, but could be Claudius.
An unknown late third century emperor at the Metropolitan Museum.
Three Palmyrene gods in lamellar armour (first century AD).
A heavily equipped Roman front-rank fighter.
Two Roman horsemen of Dalmatian origins at the battle of Immae in 272.
Aurelian with his retinue at the Battle of Emesa in about May-June 272.
A Roman cavalry officer leading a cavalry attack.
One of the presumed busts of Claudius II at Brescia.
Author's drawing of Aurelian with aegis and bloody sword together with his coin.
Probus.

viii   Aurelian and Probus

A legionary armed for combat against infantry.
The two presumed busts of Claudius II at Brescia.
Author's drawing of Carus meeting Persian ambassadors in Armenia in 282. The narrative caption for this image is as follows: 'Come here! You have come to see me. I am Carus. Tell your young king that unless he acted wisely, he should expect that the whole of your forest and plain would be barer than my head within a single month.' After this, Carus took off his *pileus* [*a cap, which is likely to be the pileus Pannonicus, a round fur cap with a round top*], and showed his head. And then, Carus said: 'If you are hungry eat from the stew-pot with me, but if you are not in need, then leave at once!' For the source, see the text. This image shows Carus receiving Persian envoys at the beginning of his Persian campaign in the highlands of Armenia. The man holding four bowls of bean soup strengthened with bits of pork is the *comes domesticorum* Diocles (the later emperor Diocletian/Diocletianus). I have made here the educated guess that many of the so-called late Roman units were already in existence and had similar names and emblems as two years later, so that Diocles would have already been in command of the *Ioviani* (the eagle shield emblem) while the men with the horned shield emblems would have belonged to the *Cornuti*. At this time the *Ioviani* would have belonged to the corps known collectively with the name *protectores*, which served under the *comes domesticorum*. The man with the crested helmet is taken from the Ludovisi Sarchophagus and represents the *praetoriani*. Carus had been their commander before the usurpation so it is certain that the members of this corps were always close by. The man with the rectangular curved *scutum* shield belongs to the *urbaniciani*. A detachment of these often accompanied the emperors. The rectangular shield has been taken from the *Adluctio* coins of Probus. The head of Carus has been borrowed from one of his coins. I have also purposefully included among the symbols both the swastika and the Star of David to show that these could be worn simultaneously by the Romans with no problem because they did not have the connotations they have today. The Persians have been modelled after Hattenroth and extant Persian reliefs. The Persian campaign of Carus was among the greatest achievements ever achieved against the Persians and served as a model for Galerius in 297–8. It was a huge military success and similarly horrible humiliation for the Persians. Carus pillaged and torched their capital Ctesiphon and Seleucia and was ready to advance deeper into the Persian Empire to deliver the killing blow in a situation in which the Persians were divided and fighting a civil war. It was then that a disaster struck. Carus was killed by a lightning bolt. This has been quite needlessly doubted by modern historians because several Roman sources make an effort to deny its possibility, but this view does not take into account the superstitious disposition of the soldiers of the time. The death by a lightning bolt could be seen as a form of divine punishment for having advanced too deep into Persian territory, and it was this that the Roman sources attempted to hide. It was necessary to maintain that the emperor died of disease or some other cause so that the soldiers and populace would not think that the gods were against the Romans and on the side of Persia. The instance shown here belongs to the category of military stratagems. Carus allowed the Persians to go around the marching camp to demonstrate to them that he had nothing to hide. His army was far superior to that of the Persians. He also wanted to demonstrate his personal toughness and confidence to the envoys with this. The aim was to demoralize the Persians with this sight and it appears to have worked.

List of Maps

The principal legionary bases ca. 250	xii
Roman Empire in ca. 250 and its military forces	xiii
The western half of the Roman Empire	xiv
Cities and Forts in the West in the late Third and Fourth Centuries	xv
The eastern half of the Roman Empire	xvi
Byzantium (Constantinople)	xvii
The Balkans	xviii
The Environs of Verona	xix
The Environs of Rome	xx
The Enemies and Allies of Rome	xxi
Roman naval deployment	23
Probus' North African Campaign	61
Battle of Babylon in Egypt in 270	67
Aurelian's ambush against the Iuthungi in 270	72
Campaign against the Vandals and Sarmatians in 271	76
Campaign against the Alamanni-Iuthungi in 271	80
The Battle of Placentia in 271	81
The City of Rome in 271	85
Aurelian Walls of the City of Rome	87
Battle of Immae late April–May 272	102
Battle of Daphne late April–May 272	104
Legionary garrisons in the East	106
Battle of Emesa in 272 (location)	111
Antistomos difalangia	112
Left flank in the Battle of Emesa	114
Battle of Emesa (battle formations)	115
City of Palmyra	117
Aurelian vs. the Carpi, Palmyra, Firmus of Egypt, Aksum, Yemen and India in 272–3	136
European and African campaigns in 277–8	184
Siege of the City of Cremna in 278	192
The Surroundings of Ctesiphon	221
The Invasion of Persia in 282–4	223

Introduction

This book has been long in the making. It began as a project to understand the development of the Roman army and its cavalry forces of which the reigns of Aurelian and Probus formed only a small part. The first manuscript was ready in 2008 after which it was shelved until 2016. It is thanks to the encouragement of my wife and children that the book was taken out of the old files and finishing touches added. However, new illustrations were added later in 2018 and 2019 to replace some of the older ones.

Abbreviations

Amm.	Ammianus
Epitome	Epitome de Caesaribus (sometimes, probably falsely, attributed to Sextus Aurelius Victor)
Eutropius	Breviarium
Festus	Breviarium
HA	*Historia Augusta, Scriptores Historiae Augustae, Augustan History*
HA Aurel.	*Historia Augusta, Aurelianus*
HA FSPB	*Historia Augusta, Firmus, Saturninus, Proculus, Bonosus*
HA Gall.	*Historia Augusta, Gallienus*
HA Prob.	*Historia Augusta, Probus*
HA Tr.	*Historia Augusta, The Thirty Pretenders, Tyranni triginta*
HE	*Historia Ecclesiastica, Ecclesiastical History*
SKZ	*Res Gestae Divis Shapuris*
Victor	Sextus Aurelius Victor

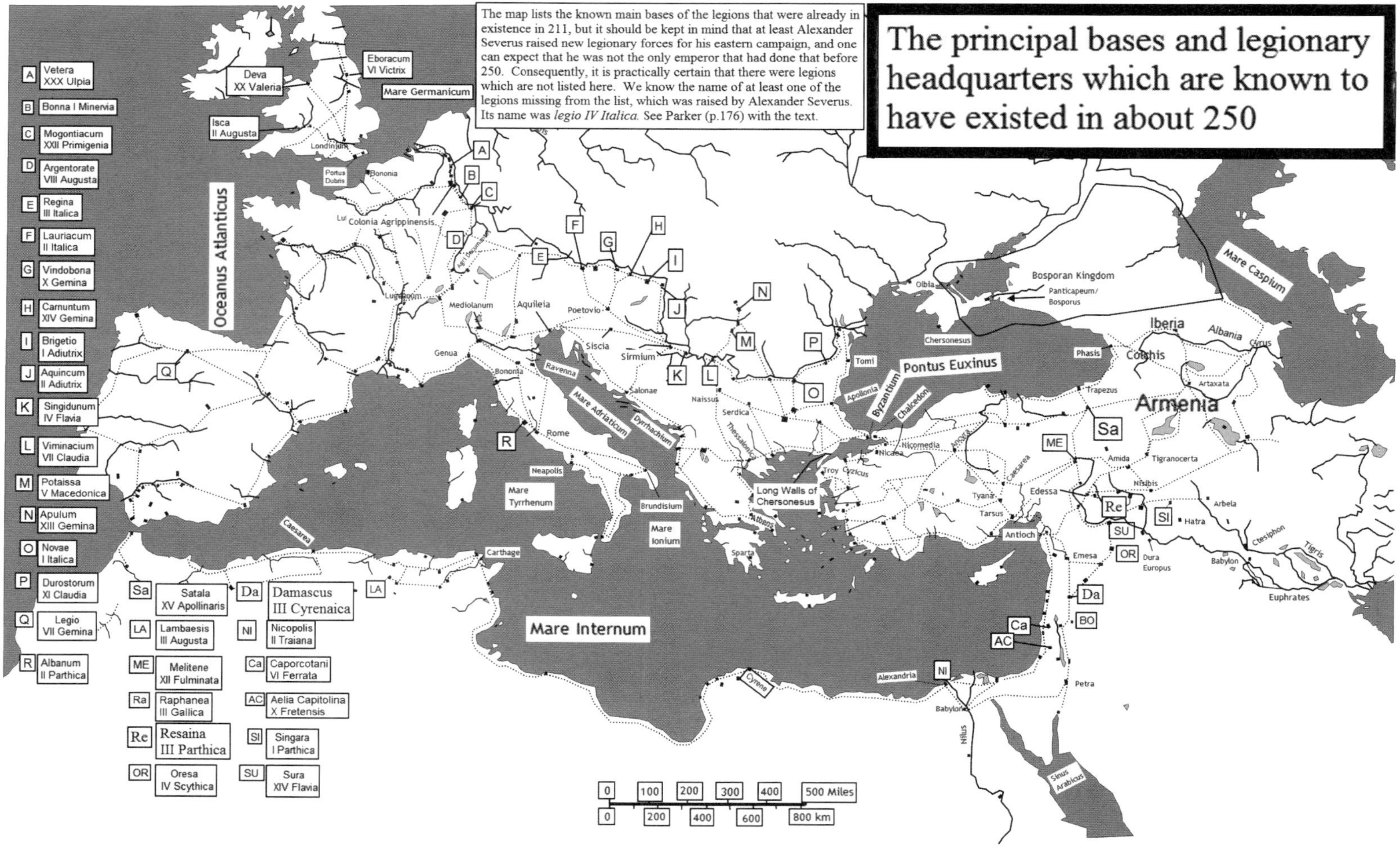
The principal bases and legionary headquarters which are known to have existed in about 250
The map lists the known main bases of the legions that were already in existence in 211, but it should be kept in mind that at least Alexander Severus raised new legionary forces for his eastern campaign, and one can expect that he was not the only emperor that had done that before 250. Consequently, it is practically certain that there were legions which are not listed here. We know the name of at least one of the legions missing from the list, which was raised by Alexander Severus. Its name was *legio IV Italica*. See Parker (p.176) with the text.
A Vetera XXX Ulpia
B Bonna I Minervia
C Mogontiacum XXII Primigenia
D Argentorate VIII Augusta
E Regina III Italica
F Lauriacum II Italica
G Vindobona X Gemina
H Carnuntum XIV Gemina
I Brigetio I Adiutrix
J Aquincum II Adiutrix
K Singidunum IV Flavia
L Viminacium VII Claudia
M Potaissa V Macedonica
N Apulum XIII Gemina
O Novae I Italica
P Durostorum XI Claudia
Q Legio VII Gemina
R Albanum II Parthica
Sa Satala XV Apollinaris
LA Lambaesis III Augusta
ME Melitene XII Fulminata
Ra Raphanea III Gallica
Re Resaina III Parthica
OR Oresa IV Scythica
Da Damascus III Cyrenaica
NI Nicopolis II Traiana
Ca Caporcotani VI Ferrata
AC Aelia Capitolina X Fretensis
SI Singara I Parthica
SU Sura XIV Flavia
Deva XX Valeria
Eboracum VI Victrix
Isca II Augusta
Mare Germanicum
Oceanus Atlanticus
Londinium
Portus Dubris
Bononia
Colonia Agrippinensis
Lugdunum
Mediolanum
Aquileia
Poetovio
Siscia
Sirmium
Genua
Bononia
Ravenna
Salonae
Naissus
Serdica
Mare Adriaticum
Dyrrhachium
Thessalonica
Rome
Neapolis
Mare Tyrrhenum
Brundisium
Mare Ionium
Caesarea
Carthage
Mare Internum
Athens
Sparta
Cyrene
Alexandria
Babylon
Nilus
Sinus Arabicus
Petra
Olbia
Bosporan Kingdom
Panticapeum/ Bosporus
Chersonesus
Tomi
Pontus Euxinus
Apollonia
Byzantium
Chalcedon
Nicomedia
Nicaea
Troy
Cyzicus
Long Walls of Chersonesus
Ancyra
Caesarea
Tyana
Tarsus
Antioch
Edessa
Emesa
Trapezus
Phasis
Colchis
Iberia
Albania
Cyrus
Artaxata
Armenia
Amida
Tigranocerta
Nisibis
Hatra
Arbela
Dura Europus
Babylon
Ctesiphon
Tigris
Euphrates
Mare Caspium
0 100 200 300 400 500 Miles
0 200 400 600 800 km

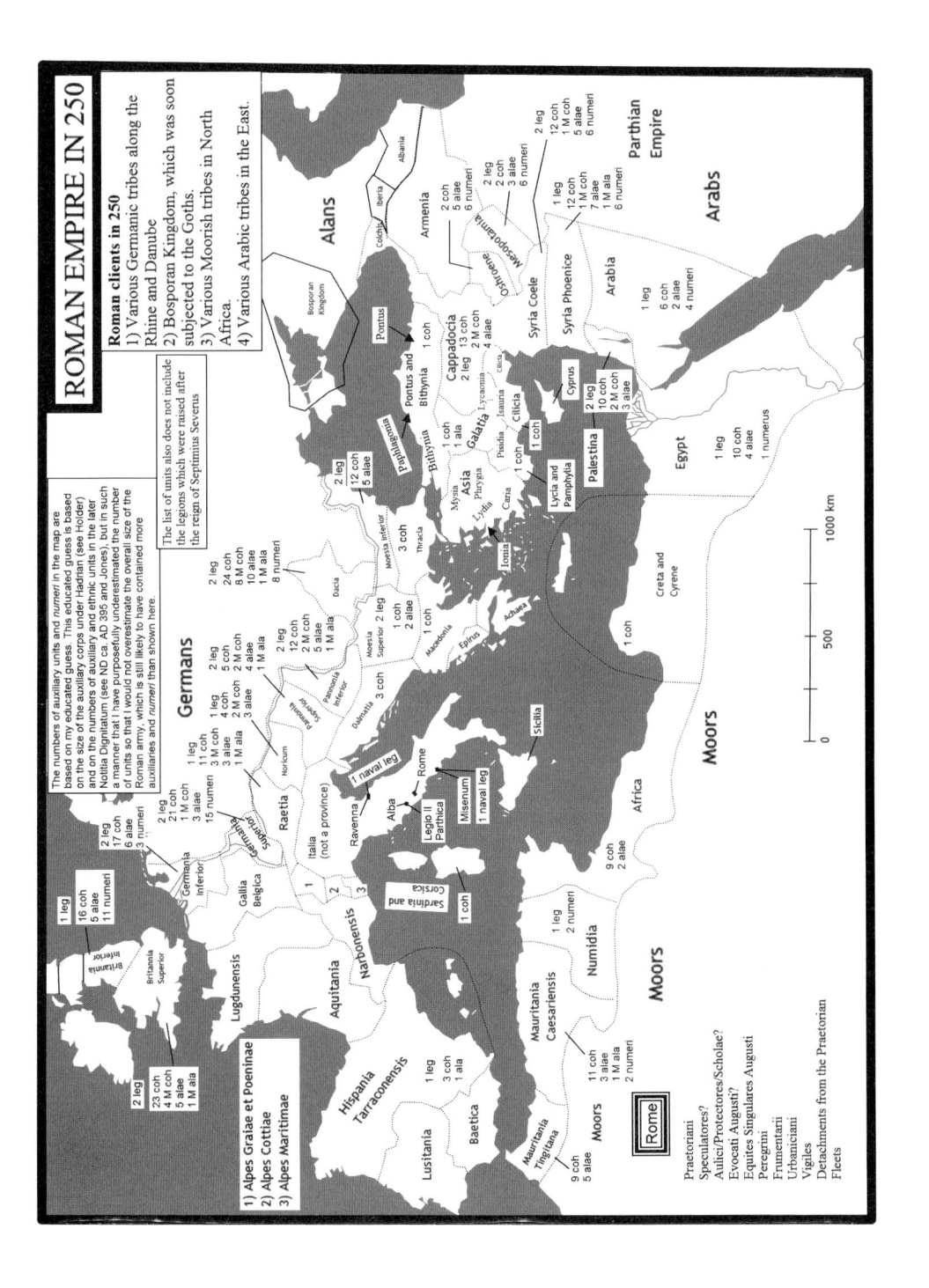

ROMAN EMPIRE IN 250

Roman clients in 250
1) Various Germanic tribes along the Rhine and Danube
2) Bosporan Kingdom, which was soon subjected to the Goths.
3) Various Moorish tribes in North Africa.
4) Various Arabic tribes in the East.

The numbers of auxiliary units and *numeri* in the map are based on my educated guess. This educated guess is based on the size of the auxiliary corps under Hadrian (see Holder) and on the numbers of auxiliary and ethnic units in the later Notitia Dignitatum (see ND ca. AD 395 and Jones), but in such a manner that I have purposefully underestimated the number of units so that I would not overestimate the overall size of the Roman army, which is still likely to have contained more auxiliaries and *numeri* than shown here.

The list of units also does not include the legions which were raised after the reign of Septimius Severus

1) Alpes Graiae et Poeninae
2) Alpes Cottiae
3) Alpes Maritimae

Praetoriani
Speculatores?
Antiles/Protectores/Scholae?
Evocati Augusti?
Equites Singulares Augusti
Peregrini
Frumentarii
Urbaniciani
Vigiles
Detachments from the Praetorian
Fleets

Britannia Inferior: 1 leg, 16 coh, 5 alae, 11 numeri
Britannia Superior: 2 leg, 23 coh, 4 M coh, 5 alae, 1 M ala
Germania Inferior: 2 leg, 17 coh, 6 alae, 3 numeri
Germania Superior: 2 leg, 21 coh, 1 M coh, 3 alae
Raetia: 1 leg, 1 M coh, 3 M coh, 3 alae, 1 M ala, 15 numeri
Noricum: 1 leg, 4 coh, 2 M coh, 3 alae
Pannonia Superior: 2 leg, 12 coh, 2 M coh, 5 alae, 1 M ala
Pannonia Inferior: 2 leg, 24 coh, 8 M coh, 10 alae, 1 M ala, 8 numeri
Dacia: 2 leg, 1 coh, 2 alae
Moesia Superior: 2 leg, 1 coh, 1 coh
Moesia Inferior: 3 coh
Dalmatia: 3 coh
Thracia: 1 coh
Macedonia: 1 coh
Achaea: 1 coh
Creta and Cyrene

Lugdunensis
Aquitania
Narbonensis
Hispania Tarraconensis: 1 leg
Lusitania
Baetica
Mauritania Tingitana: 9 coh, 5 alae
Mauritania Caesariensis: 11 coh, 3 coh, 1 M ala, 2 numeri
Numidia: 1 leg, 2 numeri
Africa: 9 coh, 2 alae

Italia (not a province)
Ravenna — 1 naval leg
Alba — Legio II Parthica
Rome
Misenum — 1 naval leg
Sardinia and Corsica — 1 coh
Sicilia

Pontus: 1 coh
Paphlagonia: 2 leg, 12 coh, 5 alae
Bithynia: 1 coh, 1 ala
Asia: 3 coh
Galatia
Cappadocia: 2 leg, 13 coh, 2 M coh, 4 alae
Lycia and Pamphylia: 1 coh
Cilicia: 1 coh
Cyprus
Syria Coele: 2 leg, 10 coh, 2 M alae, 3 alae
Syria Phoenice: 1 leg, 12 coh, 1 M coh, 7 alae, 1 M ala, 6 numeri
Osrhoene: 2 coh, 5 alae, 6 numeri
Mesopotamia: 2 leg, 2 coh, 6 numeri
Armenia: 2 leg, 12 coh, 1 M coh, 5 alae, 6 numeri
Arabia: 1 leg, 6 coh, 2 alae, 4 numeri
Palestina: 2 leg
Egypt: 1 leg, 10 coh, 4 alae, 1 numerus

Germans
Moors
Alans
Arabs
Parthian Empire
Bosporan Kingdom
Colchis
Iberia
Albania

0 — 500 — 1000 km

The western half of the Roman Empire.

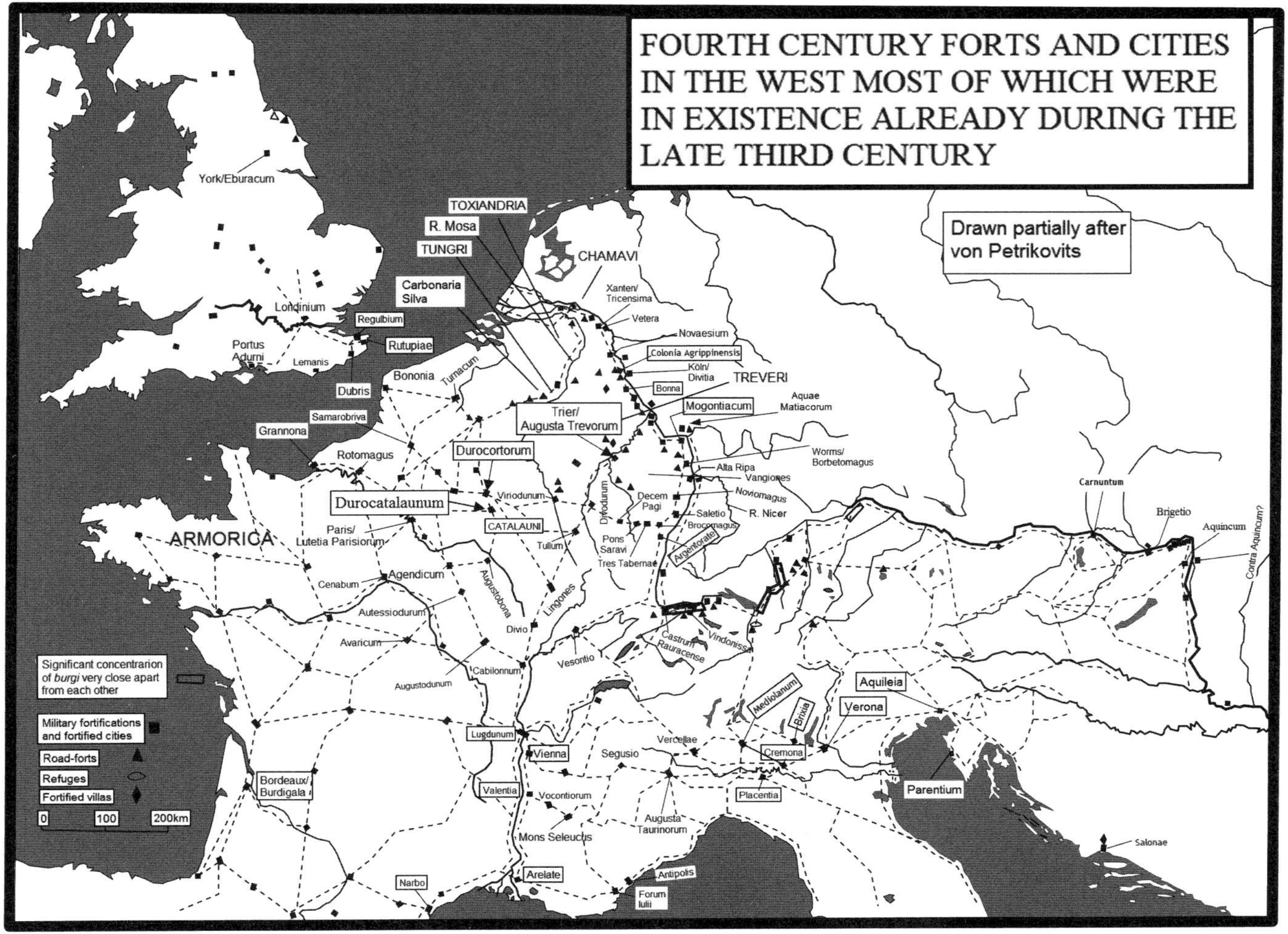
FOURTH CENTURY FORTS AND CITIES IN THE WEST MOST OF WHICH WERE IN EXISTENCE ALREADY DURING THE LATE THIRD CENTURY
Drawn partially after von Petrikovits
York/Eburacum
Londinium
Portus Adurni
Lemanis
Regulbium
Rutupiae
Dubris
Bononia
Turnacum
Samarobriva
Grannona
Rotomagus
TOXIANDRIA
R. Mosa
TUNGRI
Carbonaria Silva
CHAMAVI
Xanten/ Tricensima
Vetera
Novaesium
Colonia Agrippinensis
Köln/ Divitia
TREVERI
Bonna
Mogontiacum
Aquae Matiacorum
Trier/ Augusta Trevorum
Durocortorum
Worms/ Borbetomagus
Alta Ripa
Vangiones
Noviomagus
R. Nicer
Saletio
Brocomagus
Argentorate
Decem Pagi
Divodurum
Viriodunum
Durocatalaunum
CATALAUNI
Pons Saravi
Tres Tabernae
Tullum
ARMORICA
Paris/ Lutetia Parisiorum
Agendicum
Cenabum
Augustobona
Lingones
Autessiodurum
Divio
Avaricum
Castrum Rauracense
Vindonissa
Vesontio
Cabilonnum
Augustodunum
Carnuntum
Brigetio
Aquincum
Contra Aquincum?
Aquileia
Verona
Mediolanum
Brixia
Cremona
Vercellae
Segusio
Lugdunum
Vienna
Valentia
Vocontiorum
Placentia
Parentium
Augusta Taurinorum
Mons Seleucus
Bordeaux/ Burdigala
Arelate
Antipolis
Forum Iulii
Narbo
Salonae
Significant concentrarion of burgi very close apart from each other
Military fortifications and fortified cities
Road-forts
Refuges
Fortified villas
0
100
200km

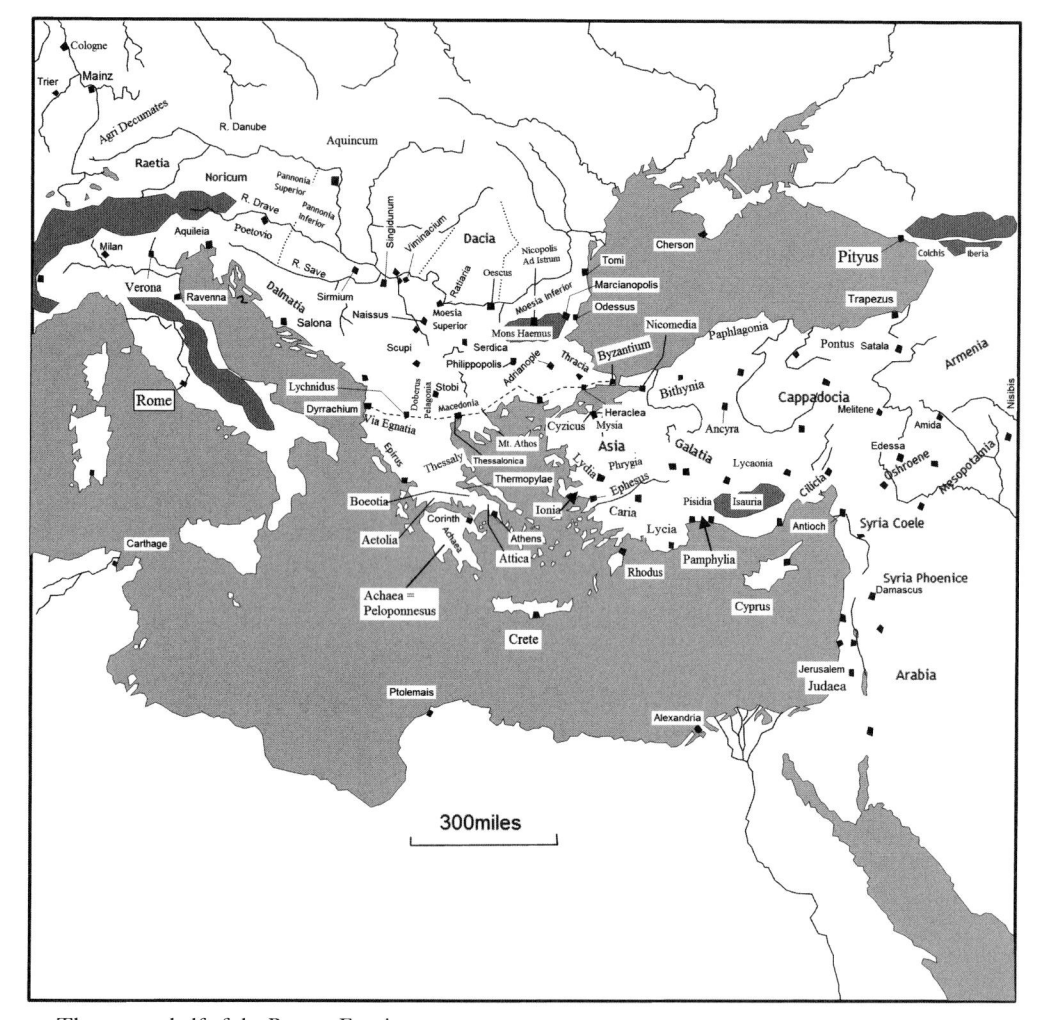

The eastern half of the Roman Empire.

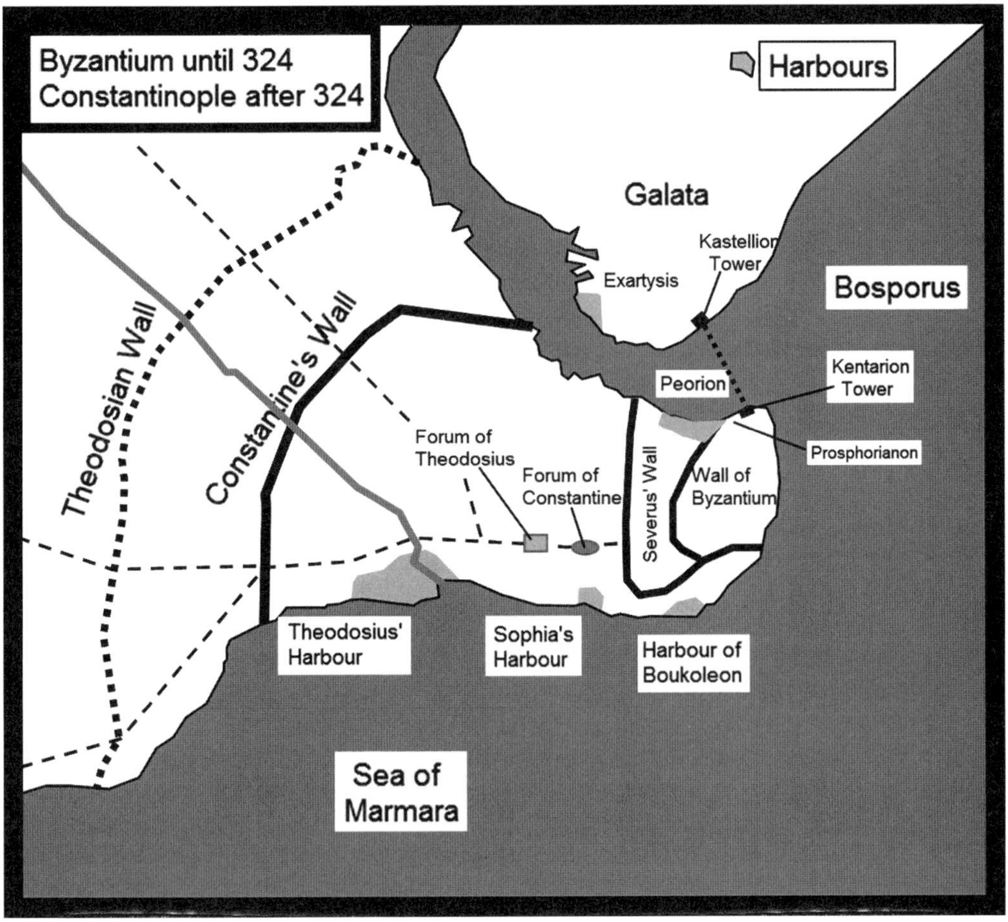

Byzantium until 324
Constantinople after 324
Harbours
Galata
Kastellion Tower
Exartysis
Bosporus
Theodosian Wall
Constantine's Wall
Peorion
Kentarion Tower
Prosphorianon
Forum of Theodosius
Forum of Constantine
Severus' Wall
Wall of Byzantium
Theodosius' Harbour
Sophia's Harbour
Harbour of Boukoleon
Sea of Marmara

The Balkans.

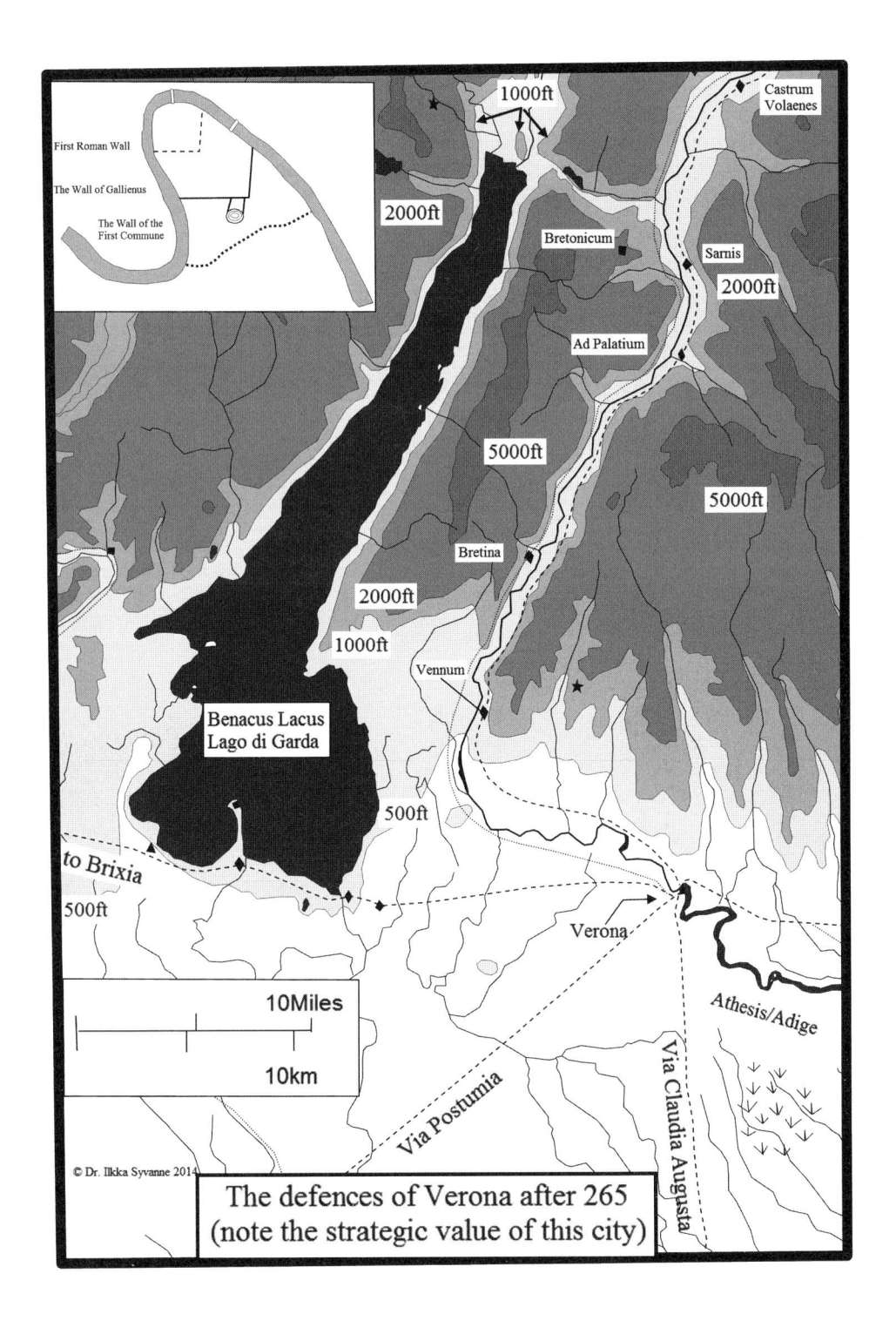

Inset
First Roman Wall
The Wall of Gallienus
The Wall of the First Commune

Map labels
1000ft
2000ft
Castrum Volaenes
Bretonicum
Sarnis
2000ft
Ad Palatium
5000ft
5000ft
Bretina
2000ft
1000ft
Vennum
Benacus Lacus
Lago di Garda
500ft
to Brixia
500ft
Verona
Athesis/Adige
10 Miles
10 km
Via Postumia
Via Claudia Augusta

© Dr. Ilkka Syvanne 2014

The defences of Verona after 265
(note the strategic value of this city)

The Neighbourhood of the City of Rome

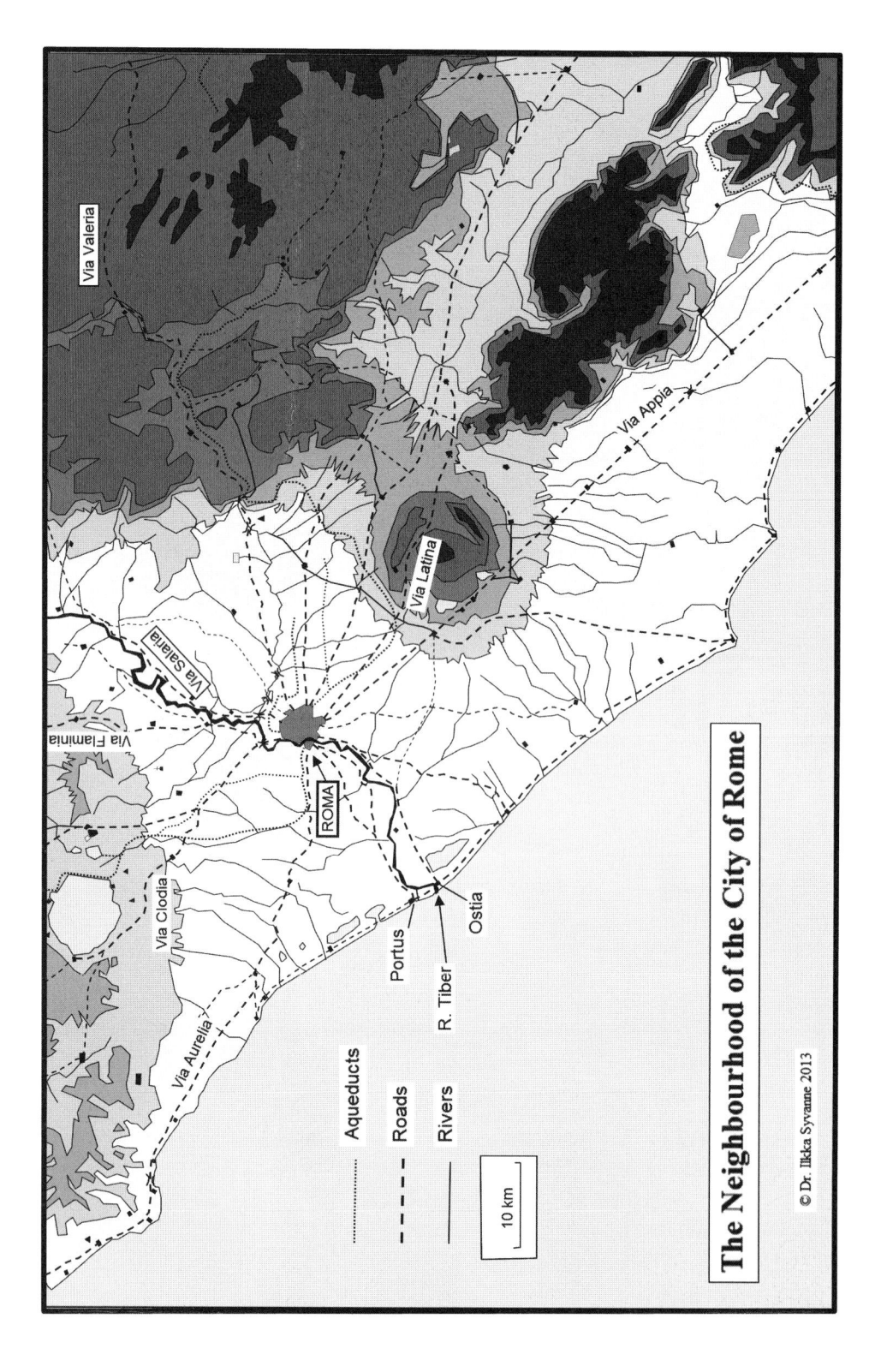

© Dr. Ilkka Syvänne 2013

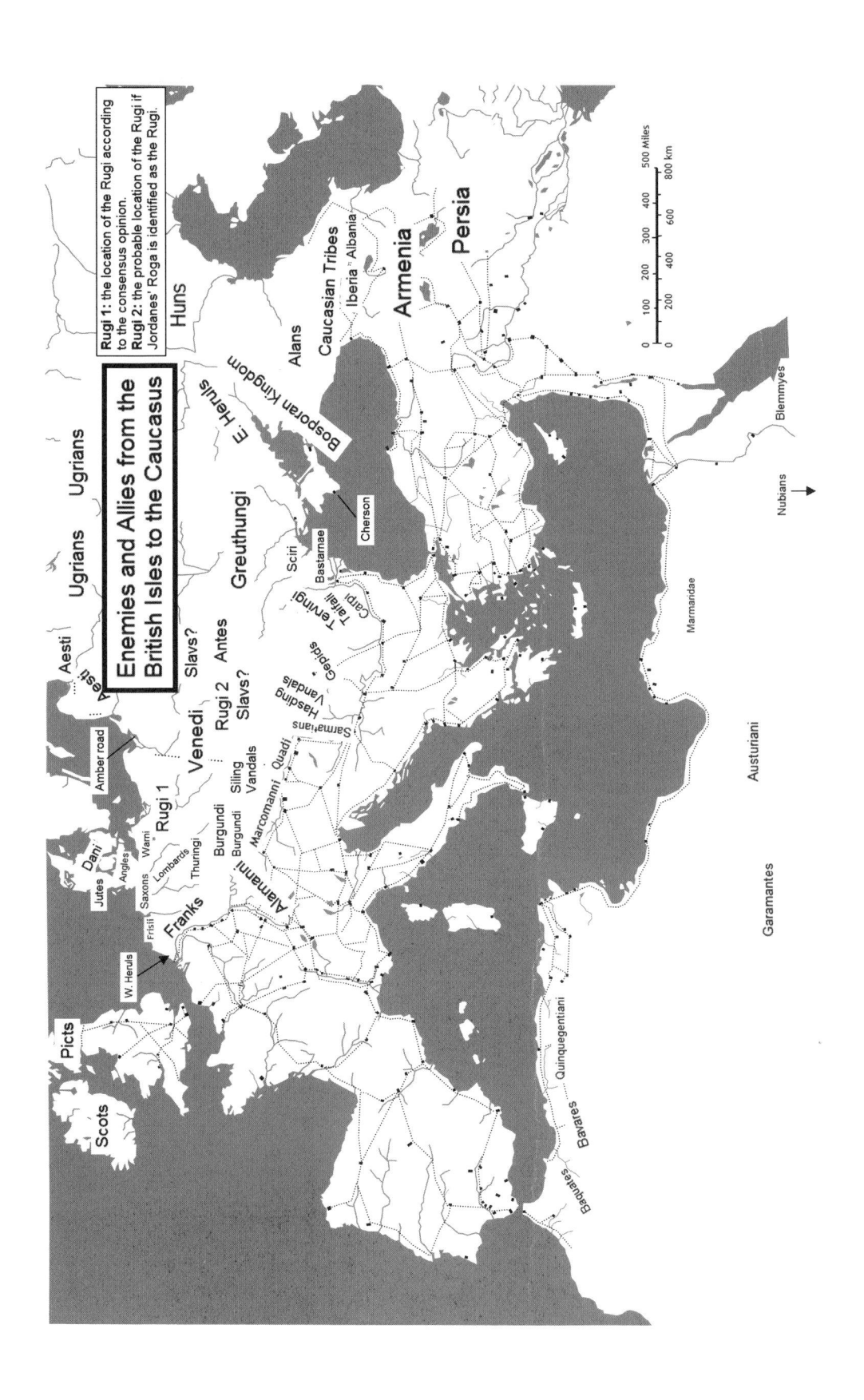

Enemies and Allies from the British Isles to the Caucasus

Rugi 1: the location of the Rugi according to the consensus opinion.
Rugi 2: the probable location of the Rugi if Jordanes' Roga is identified as the Rugi.

Chapter One

Sources and Analysis

1.1. Sources

The principal literary sources for the reigns of Aurelian and Probus are: Eusebius of Caesarea with Jerome (4–5th century), Lactantius (early 4th century), Orosius (375/80–417/8), Zosimus (early 6th century), Zonaras (beginning of 12th century), Cedrenus (11–12th cent), *Historia Augusta* (turn of 4th century and/or late 4th century, also known as *Scriptores Historiae Augusta*), Sextus Aurelius Victor (c. AD 360), *Epitome de Caesaribus* formerly attributed (wrongly) to Aurelius Victor (turn of 5th century) and hence the so-called Pseudo-Victor, Eutropius' *Breviarium* (c.369), Rufus Festus' *Breviarium* (c.370), fragments of Herennius Dexippus (a period source from the 3rd century), fragments of Anonymous Continuator of Dio Cassius now attributed to Petrus Patricius/Peter the Patrician (6th century), Malalas (6th century), George Syncellus (early 9th century), Jordanes (6th century), fragments of John of Antioch (6–7th century), and other less important sources.[1]

There are indeed many sources, but none of these includes any detailed narratives of the reigns of Aurelian or Probus, the heroes of this narrative history. Furthermore, we no longer possess any of the original period sources in their entirety. The most detailed sources are the very unreliable *Historia Augusta* and the slightly more reliable Zosimus. It is largely thanks to this that the numismatics has assumed a very important role in the analysis of their reigns, and it is the numismatic evidence that dates for example the course of the war between Aurelian and Zenobia.

In this study the sources are analyzed from the point of view of military history and military probability so that I have sought to analyze each of the sources on its own terms. In other words, I have not dismissed evidence preserved in the generally unreliable source on the basis that it is preserved in this source unless there are very strong reasons to do so. This has been done case-by-case so that each piece of evidence has been analyzed separately, not like it used to be done by the methodologically ultra-conservative Classicists roughly from the 1970s until the 2010s, who have been in the habit of dismissing the entire source as worthless with the result that they have replaced close-to-the-period evidence with their own 'must-have-beens'. This concerns in particular the use of the *Historia Augusta* (*Augustan History*/*Scriptores Historiae Augusta*), which some historians dismiss as worthless and therefore not worth even commenting on. I agree with those who are prepared to use it (e.g. Christol, Cizek, Yann Le Bohec, White, Geiger, Paul N. Pearson) and I am also inclined to accept the older and now the newer opinion that the *Historia Augusta* was indeed written by six separate authors, as it claims to have been.

The authors that concern us are as follows:

Author:	Books:
Trebellius Pollio:	*Valeriani Duo*; *Gallieni Duo*; *Tyranni Triginta*; *Divus Claudius*
Flavius Vopiscus:	*Divus Aurelianus*; *Tacitus*; *Probus*; *Firmus, Saturninus, Proculus and Bonosus*; *Carus et Carinus et Numerianus*

For the sake of clarity however, I have used the traditional *HA* to mean all of the authors of the *Historia Augusta* collectively even if I also use the supposed name of the author in an effort to avoid unnecessary repetition. In addition to this I also abbreviate the names of the books.

The following analysis of the reigns takes the account of Zosimus as its core text so that it includes several quotes from it. These quotes are then compared with the other evidence that we have to arrive at a likely reconstruction of the events.

1.2. My Analysis of the Battles

The following analysis combines the information provided by the sources and military treatises with military probability to provide an account of the likely course of action. The reason for this combination of different analytical tools and sources is the scantiness of evidence provided by the narrative sources. Therefore, if one wants to shed additional light onto the events it is necessary to analyze this evidence from the point of view of period military practices and from the point of view of military probability. It is therefore very important to place the events on the map as this provides additional insights into the thinking processes behind the decisions taken by the military commanders in each situation, and this is one of the principal methodological tools behind the concept of military probability, alongside the military doctrine of the period. It should still be kept in mind that all of these analyzes of the military situations are by nature speculative and should be seen as such. It is because of this that I will always state in the narrative when the reconstruction is based on such educated guesses and it is because of this that I include the reasons for the conclusions and long quotes from the sources with my analysis also in the text instead of presenting the events as a single narrative.

Chapter Two

The Roman Empire in 268

2.1. The Divided Empire

The period from 249 until 269, just before the rise of Aurelian on the throne in 270, is among the darkest in the history of the Roman Empire. It was then that the Goths annihilated the Roman field army together with the emperor Decius at the battle of Abrittus in 251. It was during those years that the Franks, Alamanni, Sarmatians, Goths, Heruls and many other barbarians ravaged and pillaged Roman territory in North Africa, Spain, Gaul, Raetia, Noricum, the Balkans and Asia Minor. As if this would not have been enough, the Persians under their great military king of kings Shapur I repeatedly ravaged Roman Mesopotamia, Syria and Asia Minor and even took the emperor Valerian prisoner. It was under Valerian's son Gallienus that things took a distinct turn for the worse thanks to the numerous usurpations and revolts at the same time as the empire was still threatened by the barbarians and Persians. As a result of this chaos Gaul separated itself from the Roman Empire and became the Gallic Empire led by the usurper-emperor Postumus. In the meantime, the East became the private domain of the Palmyrene royal house thanks to the fact that Gallienus was forced to rely on it to crush the Persians and the usurpers (Macriani and Ballista). At the time of his death in 268 the situation was even worse because the Goths and their allies still roamed in the eastern Mediterranean and the city of Milan was still controlled by the usurper Aureolus. In addition to this, the frantic and erratic monetary policies of Gallienus had created a situation in which the populace no longer trusted the value of their coins. However, it was also under Gallienus that the revival of the Roman Empire began, thanks to his relentless efforts to save it. Regardless, the situation was still critical at the time of his death, and it required the frantic efforts of three emperors – Claudius II, Aurelian and Probus – to restore order. All of these generals owed their initial rise to Valerian, but their rise to prominent positions was still one of the most enduring legacies of Gallienus, who clearly recognized their military talents and promoted them to higher posts.

Gallienus' emergency ad hoc reforms included, for example: 1) the re-creation of cavalry army, 2) the creation of new offices; 3) restrictions put on senatorial careers, 4) defence-in-depth; 5) the use of large regional field armies; 6) new forms of propaganda. In most of these cases Gallienus merely followed the precedents set up by his predecessors, but he was certainly prepared to go further in all of these fields than any of them, so it was under him that many of the previous exceptions became the norm. The equestrian officers had already been placed in command of several legions by the previous emperors, but under Gallienus they became the commanders of all legions. The senators, however, retained some of the governorships, with the result that they still commanded legions, each of which now had an equestrian prefect in command. The unofficial titles for the temporary generals – for example the *dux, comes, comes domesticorum, magister equitum* and *tribunus et magister officiorum* – became permanent under him. Even though the Romans had sometimes used large cavalry armies in the past, it was under Gallienus that it became the dominant arm of service when he recreated the large cavalry army previously destroyed under Decius. The Romans had also used the defence-in-depth concept in the past whenever necessary, but under Gallienus it became more widely used than ever before thanks to the many threats that he faced. Gallienus was also forced to group his forces, which consisted largely of detachments drawn from other units, into regional field armies and one personal field army. This was not a new practice and had been used for example by his father and several of his predecessors whenever there had been a need to form a large field army to meet an emergency, but the scale of this phenomenon was unprecedented under Gallienus.

2.2. Roman Military in 268

Just like any empire, the Roman Empire possessed armed forces and security apparatus. The official security apparatus consisted of: 1) the land forces (legions, auxiliaries, national *numeri*); 2) navy (Praetorian and Provincial); 3) *vigiles* (firemen/policemen); 4) *urbaniciani* (policemen, urban combat troops); 4) the imperial bodyguard units (*praetoriani; equites singulares Augusti/germani; aulici/collegia/scholae/protectores;* and *evocati Augusti*). Their strength was bolstered by: a) treaty-bound allied forces (*foederati*); and b) the paramilitary civilian citizen militias and policemen which patrolled seas and land areas. However, the division of the Roman Empire into the central Empire led by Claudius II, the forces of the usurper Aureolus at Milan, the Gallic Empire of Postumus, and the de facto Palmyran Empire in 268 means that the composition of armed forces varied in the different parts of the Empire. In the legitimate part of the Empire under Claudius II it was the cavalry – the *equites* of Gallienus – that formed the *crème de la crème* of the armed forces. In Gaul, however, it was the infantry which formed the flower of the armed forces. These consisted of those forces that had been left in the many garrisons of the area, and of the new locally recruited forces and very large numbers of German mercenaries (mainly Franks and Alamanni). The German mercenaries consisted also mainly of infantry and it was these forces that became the precursors of the late Roman *auxilia palatina*.

In normal circumstances the Imperial bodyguards and the *Legio II Parthica* (organization is given below) formed the principal mobile reserve army at the immediate disposal of the emperor. However, at the time of the death of Gallienus the situation was different because he had formed a separate imperial field army in about 257/8. The core of this force consisted of the cavalry units grouped together as *equites* under the cavalry commander (in the sources the *hipparchos* presumably meaning the *magister equitum* or *comes domesticorum equitum*) and of the infantry army consisting of the units drawn from the regular bodyguard units, legions, and auxiliaries. It is probable that the infantry had a separate commander (possibly *comes domesticorum peditum* or *magister peditum*) just like the cavalry and that the overall commander of both cavalry and infantry was *tribunus et magister officiorum* (Tribune and Master of Offices) who appears to have been Claudius II at the time of Gallienus' murder.

In normal circumstances the imperial bodyguards consisted at least of the *praetoriani* (10,240 foot, 1,920 horse?), 300 cavalry *speculatores*, a *numerus* of *statores Augusti*, *equites singulares Augusti* (2,048 horse), *frumentarii* (spies), and of the *peregrini* (spies). There are also reasons to believe that the staff of the Imperial Stables (*stratores*/equerries and grooms, the *stablesiani*, under *tribunus stabuli*) and the *evocati Augusti* also belonged to the bodyguards of the emperor. It is unfortunate that we do not possess any reliable numbers for the *frumentarii, peregrini, stablesiani* and *evocati Augusti*. Similarly we do not know the size of the bodyguard unit variously called the *aulici/collegia/scholae/ protectores/protectores domestici*. The problem is accentuated by the fact that the meaning of the names *scholae, protectores* and *domestici* changed in the course of the third to fifth centuries; but a good educated guess is that the *protectores/domestici* would have encompassed at least roughly the same number of soldiers as the *scholae* of one half of the Empire in the fifth century – a minimum of 3,500 horsemen. The reason for this conclusion is that the *scholae* appear to have been commanded by the *protectores/domestici* and at the beginning of the fourth century all those forces that were commanded by them were called *protectores*. The problem with this is that even the *protectores* proper seem to have included far more men than this before the reign of Julian.[1] The other units, which were in normal circumstances at the immediate disposal of the emperor, consisted of the Urban Cohorts (*cohortes urbanae/urbaniciani*, 4,500 policemen usable also as a military force), the *vigiles* (7,000 firemen and policemen) and of the detached naval cohorts from the two Praetorian Fleets (Misenum and Ravenna) all located in Rome and of the *Legio II Parthica* located at Alba (Albanum). The *urbaniciani* operated throughout the Empire to secure supplies for the capital on behalf of the Urban Prefect, and it was because of this that we find separate urban cohorts at least at Ostia, Puteoli, Lyon and Carthage. The soldiers on leave in Rome could also be used for military purposes, but obviously these did not count in the making of any military plans.[2]

At the end of the third century the equipment used by the legionaries and units of bodyguards was undergoing a change in fashions which then became the standard equipment of the so-called late Roman period. What remained the same was that the legionaries and bodyguards were taught how to fight with empty-handed (martial arts) techniques and with weapons such as the short sword (*semispatha, gladius*), medium to long sword (*spatha*), various types of javelins and spears, shield, and the throwing of stones by hand or sling. In addition to this, at least a third of the infantry were also taught how to use bows, presumably including in this figure the crossbows. In contrast, all horsemen were required to able to use bows and crossbows while mounted.

It is probable that the change in fashions resulted from the dominance of Illyrian soldiers in the Roman armed forces. This was the result of their better availability during the reign of Gallienus whose principal recruiting ground was in Illyricum. The main result of this was that ridge and segmented helmets started to replace the other types of helmets, while it became fashionable to use the *pilleus Pannonicus* (round Pannonian hat, often made of fur). Typical protective equipment of this period consisted of the: 1) flat (or slightly curved) oval and round shields; 2) scale and mail armour; 3) metal-made muscular armour; 4) muscular leather armour and other types of ersatz armour; 5) ridge and segmented helmets. Just like before and later, it was also possible for men to be unarmoured to increase the mobility of the unit. In short, ever fewer men used the older *lorica segmentata* type of armour and the rectangular *scutum*. However, this does not mean that the older types of equipment would not have continued in use, because we find these still in use at least until the turn of the fifth century and in some cases (e.g. pseudo-Corinthian helmets) much later still, but it does mean that these were by then relatively rare. Similarly, just like before and later, legionaries could also be equipped either lightly (no armour, small shield and light javelins or bows or slings) or with heavier equipment (armour, heavy shield, and heavy javelins or long spears) as required by the situation, which means that we should not draw too drastic conclusions from the evidence. The men fought basically in the same manner as before even if military fashions had changed. The main difference between the typical legionary and the bodyguard was that the latter often wore more expensive equipment than the former.

The number of legions, auxiliary units and *numeri* at the disposal of the various rulers is not known, but what we know is that their internal organization was based on the following models. The legions followed three basic models: 1) the old standard legions; 2) the legions based on the Parthian legions of Septimius Severus; 3) the temporary legions built out of the detachments drawn from the legions. The Parthian legions may have been based on a different unit structure and their tactics with unit depths and equipment may have been different from the standard units (see Appendix 1).

The old standard legion consisted of about 5,120 heavy infantrymen plus recruits, servants, horsemen and specialists. Such legions consisted of cohorts (quingenary 480 men and milliary 800 men), maniples of 160 men, centuria of 80 men, and *contubernia* of eight men. Each *contubernium* (tent group/file in rank and file array) consisted of eight men, one green recruit and one servant so that it in truth consisted of ten men under a commander of ten, called a *decanus*. Each of the legions had also a cavalry contingent which consisted of 500 to 600 horsemen (but typically a 512 horsemen *ala*) all of whom were taught how to use spears, javelins, swords, crossbows, shields and composite bows so that these could be used for a great variety of missions. Severus' Parthian legions differed from the above in that they had ca. 6,000 footmen and 732 horsemen. The attached diagrams show the basic structures of the various types of legions.

STANDARD LEGION

Probable command structure of the regular legion c. AD 90–260
- 1 Legate (S) until the reign of Gallienus who abolished the office; or Prefect (E) for the Egyptian and Parthian legions. After Gallienus the commanders were prefects (E); commander of the legion.
- 1 Laticlavian tribune (S) changed by Gallienus into *tribunus maior* (E); in charge of one cohort and second-in-command of the legion.
- 1 *Praefectus Castrorum* (camp, medics, siege equipment etc.) (E)
- 1 *Praefectus Fabrorum* (workmen, construction etc.) (E)
- 5 tribunes (E) each in charge of one cohort 480 men.
- 1 *tribunus sexmenstris* (in charge of cavalry?) (E).
- 5 centurions of the 1st Cohort (incl. *primus pilus* who could act as *praepositus* for the cohort).
- 54 centurions (called *centenarii* by the end of the 3rd century):
    - 5 unattached centurions who could be detailed for variety of purposes; these could be used e.g. as acting *praepositi* (commanders for the cohorts (à 480 men)).
    - 9 x 1 centurion each in charge of two centuries (2 x 80).
    - 9 x 4 centurions each in charge of one century (80 men).
    - 4 cavalry centurions each with 128 horsemen.
- 64 infantry *decani* one of whom was *optio*/second-in-command to centurion (each *decanus* part of and in charge of their 8 man file/*contubernium*, in addition to which came a *tiro*/recruit and one servant used for the guarding of the camp).

- 16 cavalry decurions (each in charge of their 32 horsemen *turma*).
- 1st cohort 800 men (5 centuries à 160 men) plus 100 recruits and 100 servants.
- cohorts 2–10 = 9 x 420 footmen (including the *decani* 480) plus 60 recruits and 60 servants per cohort.
- 496 horsemen (with the decurions 512; Vegetius may have been wrong in adding the decurions to the strength of the *turma*, because the Roman cavalry organization was based on the Greek one; however, if Vegetius is correct then these should be added to the total for a total of 512 + 16 decurions plus about 128 servants/squires.
- at least 715 artillerymen in charge of the 55 *carroballistae* (cart-mounted bolt/arrow shooters) and 10 *onagri* (single-armed stone-throwers).
- 10 *speculatores* (formerly scouts), but now couriers, police officers and executioners.
- *proculcatores* and *exploratores* scouted the roads. It is not known whether these counted as part of the cavalry or were separate from it. In practice the *mensores* could also act as scouts.
- unknown numbers of military police with the title of *stator*, and unknown numbers of guard dogs. Inside each camp there was also a police station called *statio* under a tribune. Some of the soldiers were also used as sentinels (*excubitores*) and there were also other specific guards for various things.
- in addition there were unknown numbers of other specialists and bureaucrats consisting of surveyors, *campidoctor* (Chief Instructor), *haruspex* (who read the entrails prepared by *victimarius*), *pullarius*, *actuarii*, *librarii* (*librarius a rationibus* worked also for the state post and could act as a spy), *notarii* (could act as spies on the activities of the commander), *commentariensis* (archivist under head curator), heralds, standard-bearers, *draconarii*, cape-bearers, trumpeters, drummers, engineers, workmen, artisans, hunters, carters and cartwrights, doctors, medics etc.
- the legates/prefects were also guarded by a unit of *singulares* (both inf. and cav.), which consisted of detached auxiliaries (confusingly the staff officers in training could also be called *singulares*). These bodyguards were replaced by *protectores* detached by the emperor from his staff at the latest during the reign of Gallienus as a safety measure against usurpations.
- the legion also included beasts of burden (which, depending on the units, could be horses, asses, mules, camels, oxen).

(S) = senatorial office; (E) = equestrian office

THE PARTHIAN LEGIONS CREATED BY SEPTIMIUS SEVERUS (HOWEVER, SEE ALSO APPENDIX 1).

Vegetius's Ancient Legion (Epit. 2.6ff.) with additional comments in brackets.
- 1 *praefectus legionis* formerly *legatus*; commander of the legion.
- 1 *tribunus maior*; appointed by the emperor in charge of one cohort (probably the 1st; second-in-command of the legion).
- 1 *Praefectus Castrorum* (camp, medics, siege equipment etc.)
- 1 *Praefectus Fabrorum* (workmen, construction etc.)
- *tribuni minores* from the ranks (6 tribunes? put in charge of the cohorts and cavalry alongside with the *praepositi*).
- 5 centurions of the 1st Cohort (Vegetius' list differs from the other known lists of officers and is also 100 men short of the 1,100 men he gives for the 1st Cohort)
  primus pilus in charge of 4 centuries/400 men (this probably means that there were 440 men which consisted of 4 centuries each with 110 men)
  primus hastatus 'now called *ducenarius*' in charge of two centuries/200 men (probably 220 men)
  princeps 1.5 centuries/150 men (probably 165 men)
  secundus hastatus 1.5 centuries/150 men (probably 165 men)
  triarius prior 100 men (probably 110 men)

- 5 centurions for the cavalry.
- 45 centurions of the 2nd to 10th COs each in charge of 110 men 'now' called *centenarii*.
- 1st Cohort: 1,105 footmen (this probably means that there were 720 heavy infantry deployed four deep, two in the front and two in the back of a six-rank-array, and 360 light infantry deployed two deep between the heavy infantry ranks + 10 optiones, 10 standard-bearers, and 5 centurions).
  132 horsemen (128 horsemen and 4 decurions; in truth the decurions may have been part of the 128 horsemen in addition to which came one centurion, 2 musicians and one standard-bearer; when trained to do so the 128 horsemen could form up a rhombus so that at each apex stood one decurion).
- 2nd to 10th Cohorts: 9 x 555 footmen (this probably means that there were 360 heavy infantry deployed four deep so that these formed the two front ranks and two rear ranks in a six deep formation, and 180 light infantry deployed two deep between the heavy infantry ranks + 5 optiones, 5 standard-bearers, 5 centurions).
  9 x 66 horsemen (64 horsemen and 2 decurions; as noted above the decurions should possibly be included as part of the 64 horsemen; the 64 men could be formed either as a wedge or two rank-and-file oblongs).
- artillerymen (55 *carroballistae* each with 11 men and 10 *onagri* per legion), 'squires', servants, various kinds of standard-bearers and musicians, and other specialists like clerks, medics, woodworkers, masons, carpenters, blacksmiths, painters, siege-equipment builders, armourers etc. (*aquiliferi, imaginarii/imaginiferi, signiferi/draconarii, tesserarii, optiones, metatores, librarii, tubicines, cornicines, buccinators, mensores, lignarios, structores, ferrarios, carpentarios, pictores* etc.)
- On the basis of my above hypothesis regarding the organization behind Vegetius' figures, a possible overall fighting strength of Vegetius' legion may have been: 6,100 footmen (3,960 heavy infantry; 1,980 light infantry) plus supernumeraries; 726 cavalry; at least 660 artillerymen with 55 *carroballistae* and 10 *onagri*; at least 510 recruits left to defend the marching camp together with the servants and workmen. The extra men on top of the older paper strengths may actually represent the recruits not normally included in armed strengths, but one cannot be entirely sure of that. It is possible that the cohorts were really 555 men strong because Dio's reference to 550 men does suggest this. The obvious problem with Vegetius' information and my reconstruction based on it is that we have practically no evidence to corroborate it, but at least if one presents the information in this manner it does make sense and is therefore plausible. Vegetius notes that the legion could also include several milliary cohorts, which probably refers to the Praetorians which had milliary cohorts after Septimius's reign, or it refers to the practice of Vegetius's own day to group together different units to form 'temporary legions' that were later called *mere* by the East Romans (sing. *meros*/division).

The equipment of the auxiliary forces which belonged to the 'line infantry and line cavalry' was basically the same as in the legions so that the auxiliary units typically used the flat (or slightly curved) oval or round shields, *spatha*-longsword, spears, and javelins, but other types of equipment was also used. The auxiliary units were either quingenary or milliary in size. Some of the auxiliary units specialized in a particular type of combat (e.g. cavalry cataphracts, mounted archers, foot archers, slingers), but the vast majority were required to be able to perform all types of combat either as line infantry/cavalry or as skirmishing forces. There also existed a special type of auxiliary force called *numeri*. There was no uniformity in their unit size or use in combat. In addition to this there were barbarian forces called *laeti* (defeated enemies) which were settled on Roman territory with the duty of providing soldiers when required to do so. Despite being called auxiliary forces the above-mentioned auxiliaries were actually part of the Roman army. At this time the real auxiliary forces were

The Roman Empire in 268   9

the allies who were called *foederati* (treaty-bound allies). These forces consisted of whatever type and size of force the ally could contribute for their Roman ally. The following list (based on my earlier studies) summarizes the information.

Approximate size and organization of auxiliary units:

Unit	Foot	Horse	Centuries	Turmae
Cohors Quingenaria Peditata	480		6	
Cohors Quingenaria Equitata	480	128	6	4
Cohors Milliaria Peditata	800		10	
Cohors Milliaria Equitata	800	256	10	8
Ala Quingenaria		512		16
Ala Milliaria		768 (campaign strength?)	24	
		1,024 (paper strength?)	32	
Numeri (mercenaries)	varied	varied	varied	varied
Foederati (treaty based allies)	varied	varied	varied	varied

The attached drawings and the images in the plates depict some of the types of forces employed by contemporary Romans. One of the drawings in the text (page 14) is a three-panel drawing of some of the scenes from the *Arch of Constantine* by Bellori. It gives a good overview of the different types of forces employed by the Romans from the Germanic auxiliaries (unarmoured spearmen, the *auxilia palatina* of the late Roman period) to the Meroitic foot archers (archers with arrows placed in the hair) and from the shieldless unarmoured horsemen of Constantine to the scale-armoured Praetorians of Maxentius. Note the resemblance of the latter to the Sarmatian cavalry in Trajan's column. The only differences are that the horses are unarmoured and the helmet is the so-called pseudo-Attic helmet. Readers should however be aware that Bellori has taken some artistic liberties and has drawn most of the helmets inaccurately. For a more accurate picture, see the photos in the plates. Bellori's drawing gives only a general image.

Roman elite horseman equipped with a ridge helmet and scale armour (source Arch of Galerius)

Soldiers wearing coifs in the Vatican Manuscript (drawn after Bishop & Coulston)

Aurelius Sudecentius, legionary of the *Legio XI Claudia* (first half of the fourth century AD)

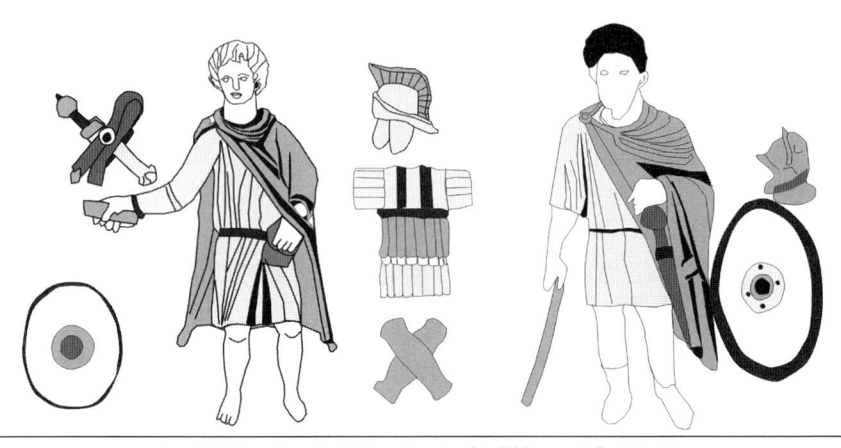

10 Aurelian and Probus

Third-century tombstones drawn after Bishop and Coulston.
Top left: Severus Acceptus, *legio VIII Augusta* (Istanbul). The "armour" in this image is actually the so-called *subarmalis*, which was worn underneath the armour, but it could also be worn as the only "armour" as in this case. The *subarmalis* or other ersatz armour could be made out of linen, felt or leather. **Top right:** Julius Aufidius, *legio XVI Claudia* (Veria)

Right: A sketch/drawing of a soldier depicted in a shield found at Dura Europos. The date is therefore before its capture in 253 or 256. Note that the Romans continued to use also this archaic style equipment at least until the seventh century when updated versions are depicted in the so-called David Plates. However, there is quite secure evidence for the persistence of these styles much later in East Rome.

Left: A sketch/drawing of a soldier depicted in the Synagogue mural depicting the battle of Eben-Ezer at Dura Europos. Date before 256. Note the scale armour coif and the six-sided shield. These continued in use at least until the fourth century.

The above funerary relief shows a Roman auxiliary charging over the enemy footman. The relief is early for this period, but it shows nicely how the Romans taught their cavalry to run over the the enemy infantry formations like lawnmovers. If the morale of the enemy held and they were in close order, this tactic was not necessarily successful because even when the horses were taught to do this, it was possible that the horse's instincts prevailed and the horse refused to charge into the solid looking enemy formation. The source of the drawing: Duruy.

The Roman Empire in 268   11

The spearman is a drawing of one of the soldiers depicted in the painted Dura Europus shields dated mid-third century.

The horse and its harness drawn partially after Mattesini

Gallic kontos (contus, hasta)

The fancy Pseudo-Attic helmet is taken from the Arch of Constantine (one of the so-called Trajanic reliefs). This means that the man belongs to the Imperial Bodyguards - in this case to the Praetorian cavalry. This is shown by the scorpion emblem in the helmet.

Lorica squamata (scale armour) typically used by the Praetorians in the 3rd century, but other types of armour were also worn.

oval scutum shield

a spatha and a composite bow in a holster behind the back

javelin-quiver

arrow-quiver

greaves

A fully equipped 2nd-3rd century officer of the Praetorian Guard in full combat readiness usable as a *logchoforos*, *kontoforos* and *hippotoxotes* (Arrian, *Techne Taktika* 34.1-44.2, *Ektaxis kata Alanon*)

© Dr. Ilkka Syvänne 2016

A Roman foot archer. He wears padded jacket for protection and is equipped with a composite bow, small shield and sword. Since the legionaries were also taught how to use bows, he could equally well be legionary or auxiliary.

Left: A so-called ADLUCTIO coin of Probus depicts him addressing the soldiers. Source: Beger 1696. The important point is that it depicts the soldiers with the rectangular curved/cylindrical *scutum* shield. This is of course a 17th century drawing, but its depiction of equipment is still accurate. See e.g. the wildwinds coins website RIC 581/Cohen 19. The works of art continue to depict this type of shield at least until the turn of the sixth century and it is very likely that it was also used at least until then. One possible reason for the continued use of this type of shield would have been the idolisation of the gladiators, and vice versa it is possible to think that it fell out from use thanks to the ending of the gladiatorial games in the fifth century.

12 Aurelian and Probus

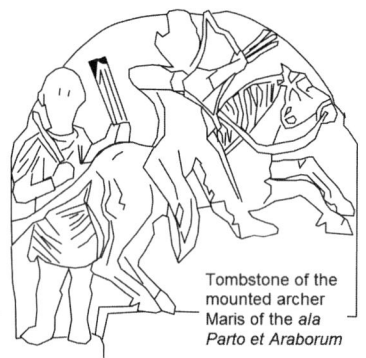

Tombstone of the mounted archer Maris of the *ala Parto et Araborum*

Note the use of the shower archer technique with three arrows on the left hand and the use of the servant behind to replenish the arrows!

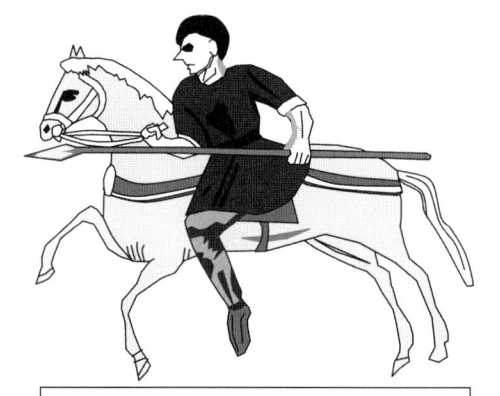

A sketch/drawing of a horseman depicted in the Synagogue mural depicting the battle of Eben-Ezer at Dura Europos. Date before 253 or 256.

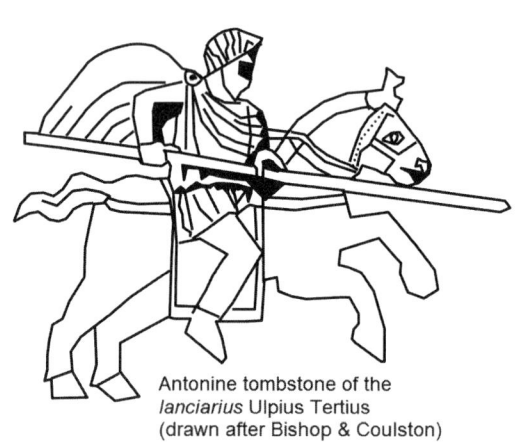

Antonine tombstone of the *lanciarius* Ulpius Tertius (drawn after Bishop & Coulston)

Constantine the Great's Elite Cavalry
The drawing on the left depicts a horseman in the Arch of Constantine. What is striking about the cavalry images is that the Constantinian cavalry has no armour or shields. Some of them do not even have a helmet, like this one, but when they do, and most do, they have the pseudo-Attic helmet which I have depicted here separately. What is also notable about these images is that many of them show both hands to make it clear to the viewer that the horseman does not carry any shield. This suggests that these men did not carry shields so that they could demonstrate their manhood in combat. Does this mean that the cavalry in question would have consisted of Herul horsemen who did not use shields or armour in combat before they had proved their manhood by killing an enemy, or does this mean that Constantine's Roman soldiers would have emulated them? Both are possible because the Arch also gives a prominent role for the *Cornuti* auxiliaries and Meroitic archers. If this is the case, then it would have been foreigners who decided the war in favour of Constantine. However, in light of the use of Pseudo-Attic helmets it is more likely that the soldiers are Roman elite cavalry who just demonstrated their superior fighting skill and spirit by not using armour and shields. Whatever the truth, the inclusion of these images implies in no uncertain terms that Constantine employed a cavalry of this type and it was this cavalry that had a decisive role in the battle of the Milvian Bridge in 312. In short, the image suggests that the cavalry of this type and the Meroitic foot archers, which are also in that image, both had a very significant role in

this battle. Did the Meroitic infantry ride pillion to the bridge? The Greco-Roman military theory (e.g. Arrian, *Techne Taktike* 4.4, Modestus 18, Vegetius 3.16) and other period evidence (see e.g. the attached tombstone and Dura Europos painting on page 10) recognized a type of cavalry that did not carry shields so it is clear that the images in the Arch must represent reality and that Constantine employed this type of cavalry to great effect. Its main advantage was speed and my assumption is that Constantine unleashed these cavalry forces in pursuit of the defeated armoured enemy cavalry at the battle of the Milvian Bridge with the result that they were unable to flee. It is difficult to know with certainty what type of spear was employed by these men because the size of the reliefs dictated the length shown, but in light of the fact that the spears are used like javelins in the images the spears cannot have been longer than about 2.5 metres or at most 3.74 metres so that the latter would have already been a *lanciarius* or *contarius*. The continuity in the types of cavalry (Arrian, tombstone, Arch etc.) suggests that the same type of cavalry forces were also used in the latter half of the third century.

These Roman soldiers drawn after the mid-third century *Ludovisi Sarchophagus* depict some of the more unusual types of shields used by the Romans at this time. In addition to this, they continued to use the sexagonal and hexagonal shields.

Soldiers from the Ludovisi Sarcophagus (mid-third century)

Above: A scene in the Arch of Constantine depicting the siege of Verona in 312. Bellori has drawn the helmets incorrectly, but the drawing still gives a good overall image of how the Roman soldiers were equipped.

Above: A scene in the Arch of Constantine depicting the battle of the Milvian Bridge in 312. Note the horsemen without armour and shields with Pseudo-Attic helmets and the Meroitic archers.
Below: Constantine's army marching.

2.3. Combat on Land

Roman military doctrine was very practical. It was based on the expectation that the generals possessed accurate intelligence of the enemy and its activities and that the logistical network provided adequate supplies for the Roman armed forces. This combination would then enable the commander to pick and choose the best time and place and how to engage the enemy.

The Romans also took safety precautions very seriously so that they employed layers of spies, scouts and patrols for the protection of their armies, and always built fortified marching camps. Combat doctrine also required that marching of the armies was done by the book so that soldiers were similarly protected by layers of spies, scouts and patrols. Typical marching formations were the hollow square/oblong array (baggage in the middle), *epikampios opisthia* (baggage behind or in the hollow), *epikampios opisthia* with the baggage train and rearguard following so that it could be formed into a hollow square/oblong, and the use of marching columns where the above were not possible. In addition to this, the Romans typically posted vanguards and rearguards that could be used both defensively and offensively. In certain conditions the vanguard could consist solely of cavalry so that it was used separately from its infantry support.

Roman combat doctrine had always been based on the combined arms concept, but from the reign of Alexander Severus onwards the Romans had depended increasingly on their cavalry to win their battles, to such an extent that we see Decius fighting only with cavalry against the Goths and Gallienus fighting mainly with his cavalry. At the time of the death of Gallienus, Roman combat doctrine was based on the use of cavalry when this was advantageous and on the use of the combined arms concept when this was advantageous, but in such a manner that the cavalry was clearly the favoured arms of service.[3]

The combined arms combat doctrine was based on the advantageous use of all arms of service, but in such a manner that the infantry formed its core. Land tactics were traditional so that the Romans could deploy their infantry in cohorts (one to four lines) or as phalanxes so that the battle line was usually divided into left, centre and right. Standard combat formations were the lateral phalanx with baggage train (with *ballistae*-carts) posted behind for its protection and the double phalanx (or two lines of cohorts) if the baggage train did not follow. Standard depths for these lines were 6 (4 ranks of heavy infantry and 2 of light infantry), 12 (8 heavy, 4 light), and 24 (16 heavy and 8 light), but in practice this could vary according to the quality of the unit, place and amount of light infantry, the number of men fit for service, and the type of unit (see Appendix 1). The cavalry was usually posted on the flanks and in reserve to protect the infantry, to outflank the enemy, or to pursue the defeated foe. The light infantry was placed where considered the most advantageous.

The Romans employed four standard ways to defeat the enemy: 1) ambushes and surprise attacks; 2) to break the enemy line with deeper formations or with a wedge array; 3) to outflank the enemy either on the left or right flank; 4) to outflank the enemy on both wings. To achieve these, the Romans employed several different grand tactical formations most of which are described by Vegetius (see the diagrams borrowed from my earlier books), but the other military treatises and narrative histories prove that the

16 Aurelian and Probus

Romans used a variety of defensive arrays like the oblong and hollow square arrays that they could also use for offensive purposes. In addition to this, the Romans could use a double front (*amphistomos phalanx, orbis*) or double phalanx (*diphalangia amphistomos*,[4] *duplex acies*) if the enemy had managed to outflank the Romans.

Basic unit orders were: 1) the open order; 2) close order with shields placed rim-to-rim in width; 3) the defensive tortoise (*testudo/foulkon*) against cavalry (front rank kneeling, shields rim-to-boss in depth and almost rim-to-rim in width), which was used to bring an enemy cavalry attack to a halt with a wall-like appearance after which the front-rankers rose and attacked if the enemy cavalrymen had advanced close enough; 4) the offensive *testudo* (shields rim-to-boss in width and depth), which could also be used defensively by having all men kneel to receive enemy missiles, but with the expectation that the men would rise to their feet to fight.; 5) the siege *testudo* (rear rank kneeling to help the 'mounting' of the formation by other men, shields rim-to-boss in depth and almost rim-to-rim in width or alternatively rim-to-boss if the shields allowed this); 6) the irregular array (*drungus/droungos*).

simplified versions of the standard infantry battle formations not specifically mentioned among Vegetius's seven tactics

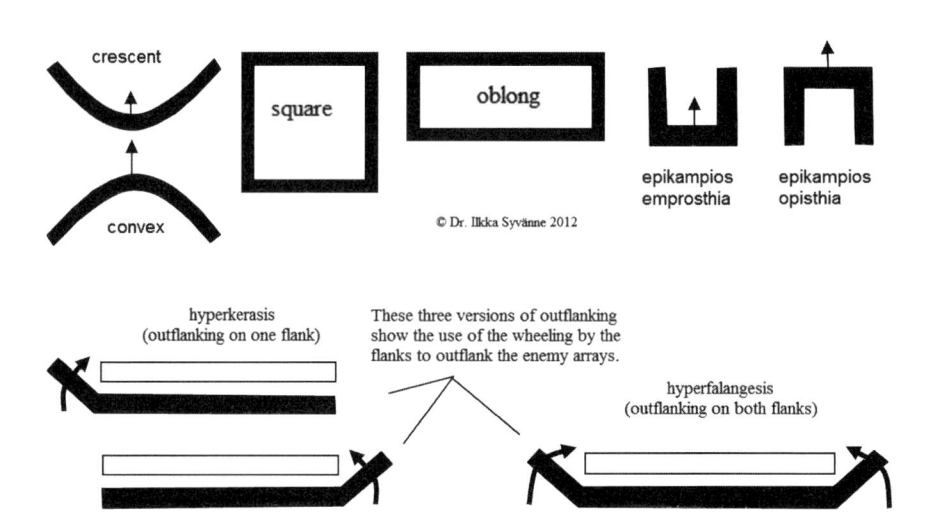

crescent
convex
square
oblong
epikampios emprosthia
epikampios opisthia

© Dr. Ilkka Syvänne 2012

hyperkerasis (outflanking on one flank)

These three versions of outflanking show the use of the wheeling by the flanks to outflank the enemy arrays.

hyperfalangesis (outflanking on both flanks)

The attached diagrams provide an overview into the different tactical concepts and formations used when the Romans used the combined arms approach. In addition to these methods, the Romans could also employ their infantry units in ways that negated the advantages posed by the enemy (e.g. by opening up their array to allow cavalry wedges, elephants, chariots etc. to pass through) and/or they could employ specialist units like the mace/club-bearers against heavily armoured opponents like the cataphracts. A good example of the use of these tactics can be found in the narrative of the battle of Emesa in 272 and these are detailed there in greater depth. Appendix 1 also suggests a possible variation to the tactics discussed when the Romans deployed two different types of legion simultaneously.

Vegetius' Seven Tactics 3.20, 3.26:

1. Oblong rectangle array was the standard array, but it was considered unsafe because the length of the line could cause a breach of the line during advance. It was also necessary to use reserves to protect the flanks. Its use was recommended only in such instances where there were enough brave troops to surround the enemy formation on both sides (*hyperfalangesis*).

2. Oblique array vs. enemy's left wing. This version of the oblique array was considered better since the attack was directed against the shieldless side. The purpose was to place the best inf. and cav. on the right and use them to surround the enemy.

3. Oblique vs. enemy's right wing. Note the wedge shape of the tip of the oblique array. It seems probable that the reason for calling Epaimenondas' array both a wedge and oblique has resulted from this. This was considered weaker than the 2nd tactics and its use was recommended only when the left wing was much stronger than the enemy's right. In that case, the commander posted his reserves on the left. The general was also to take special care that enemy wedges wouldn't penetrate the array.

4. The forward-angled array (in Greek *epikampios emprosthia*) was used to outflank the enemy suddenly on both sides when he did not expect it. When the army was 400-500 paces away from the enemy, the wings suddenly charged forward to surprise the enemy. This was dangerous tactic, if the enemy managed to hold its own, because the wings were separated from the centre.

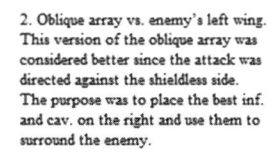

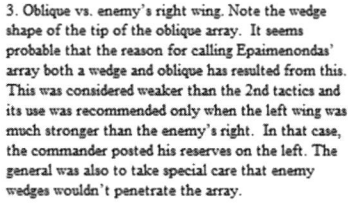

5. The fifth formation was an improvement of the fourth. In this array the light-armed and archers were placed in the front of the 1st line (*ante primam acie*: this proves that Vegetius' source envisaged the presence of at least two lines). The presence of these protected the centre from the failure of the wings. This tactic was used by Scipio Africanus at Ilipa in 206 BC.

6. Outflanking on one side (*hyperkerasis*). According to Vegetius, this array was the best formation for those who were outnumbered by the enemy. When the army advanced towards the enemy, the general suddenly sent the right wing consisting of his best cavalry and very swift infantry against the enemy, while the remaining part of the army stayed behind and lengthened the line to a straight javelin-like line. This method of attack was often used while on the march (i.e. vanguard was sent against one enemy wing).

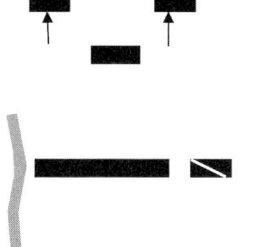

7. When the army had fewer men (including cases with fewer brave men), it was possible to even out the odds by resting one wing against a mountain, a sea, a lake, a river, a city, a swamp, or broken ground, and then by placing all the cavalry and light-armed on the opposite wing.

The principal cavalry array used by the Romans was the so-called Italian drill formation of the *Strategikon* consisting of two combat lines each of which had three divisions with wing units in front. It had three basic versions: the largest standard cavalry array for armies in excess of 10–15,000 men had four divisions in the second line with rearguards as the fourth line; the medium sized array (15,000/12,000/10,000 and more than 5,000/6,000 men) had two divisions in the second line; the smallest (2,000–5,000/6,000 men or less) had only one division in the second line. The diagrams in the *Strategikon* enable us to reconstruct these in detail. It shows that the standard large cavalry array had about 31,000 horsemen, but on the basis of the other information in the treatise we know that it also allowed the use of even larger cavalry arrays. On the basis of later evidence, I have speculated that the extra men in these cases were posted as the third line. The accompanying diagrams are from my dissertation and article, which are based on the *Strategikon*. The Ks in the diagrams (from *kaballarios*) stand for ranks of regular soldiers in the array.

18 Aurelian and Probus

Offensive unit tactics and counter-tactics:

The traditional Greco-Roman wedge consisting of the larger units like divisions deployed to initiate a grand tactical breakthrough

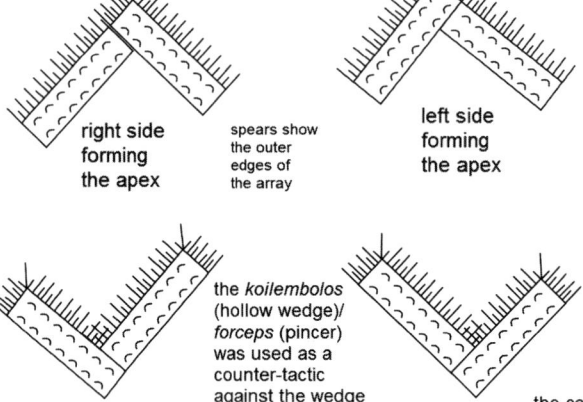

right side forming the apex

spears show the outer edges of the array

left side forming the apex

The Germanic *caput porcinum* (boar's head/*svinfylking*) consisted of 1,100 men (note the 555 men cohorts of Vegetius). The use of this array by the Romans is uncertain for this period. The likeliest date for its adoption is after ca. 267, but if Septimius' new legionary structure reflects also tactical changes, then this array may have been copied from the Germans or invented as a result of the Marcomannic Wars.

the *koilembolos* (hollow wedge)/ *forceps* (pincer) was used as a counter-tactic against the wedge

the use of the protruding wedge to initiate a local breakthrough

the *serra* (saw) array was used to protect the reorganization of the battle line when it had become disordered: the *serra* meant the use of the crack troops in front of the battle line so that they advanced and retreated to harass and confuse the enemy.

The defensive unit arrays when the enemy had managed to outflank the Romans

The *amfistomos* (double-fronted) array was used to face enemy when it had outflanked the Romans (**left**). The Latin name for this array was *orbis* because in practice the array faced all directions simultaneously (**right**) if there was a need for this.

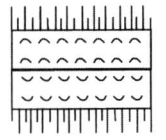

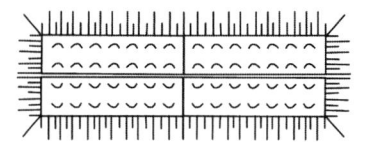

the difalangia array (double phalanx) was used to face the enemy from two directions when there was enough time to form it.

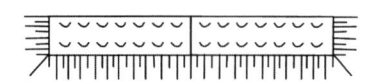

The Roman Empire in 268   19

First line

| Flank guards, 1-3 banda | Meros of Vexillations | Meros of Federates | Meros of Illyrikiani | Outflankers 1-2 banda |

Second, or support line

Meros | Tagma | Meros of Optimates | Tagma | Meros | Tagma | Meros

Rearguard | Baggage train | Reserve horses 1 | | Rearguard

Reserve horses 2

Symbol legend:
- Strategos (general)
- Merarch
- Bandon of the koursores
- Touldon
- Hypostrategos (lieutenant general)
- Moirarch
- Deputatoi (medical corpsmen)
- Bandon of the baggage train guard, if present
- Taxiarch of the Optimates
- Bandon of the defensores
- Reserve horses, if present

The diagram of the large cavalry array in the sixth century *Strategikon* (symbols show this array to have ca. 31–32,000 horsemen).

The 6,000–7,000 horsemen divisions of horse (*mere*, sing. *meros*) in their turn consisted of three *moirai* ('regiments', sing. *moira*) each with a maximum of 3,000 men. The standard way to form these *moirai* was to make the two flank *moirai* of each *meros* consist of the so-called *koursores* (runners/skirmishers). The units of these skirmishers used typically the highly mobile irregular *droungos* array when needed. The Romans placed between these skirmishers the *moira* of the *defensores* (defenders). The *defensores* were almost always deployed in the close-order so that they could protect the *koursores* when needed. The *moirai* were naturally divided into smaller units of 300–400 men (or 200–400 men; the *Strategikon* has two variants) which were variously called *tagmata*, *arithmoi* or *banda*. This means that the *Strategikon* did not envisage that the the cavalry units would have been close to their paper strengths (ca. 500–600 men), but I would not consider it

20　Aurelian and Probus

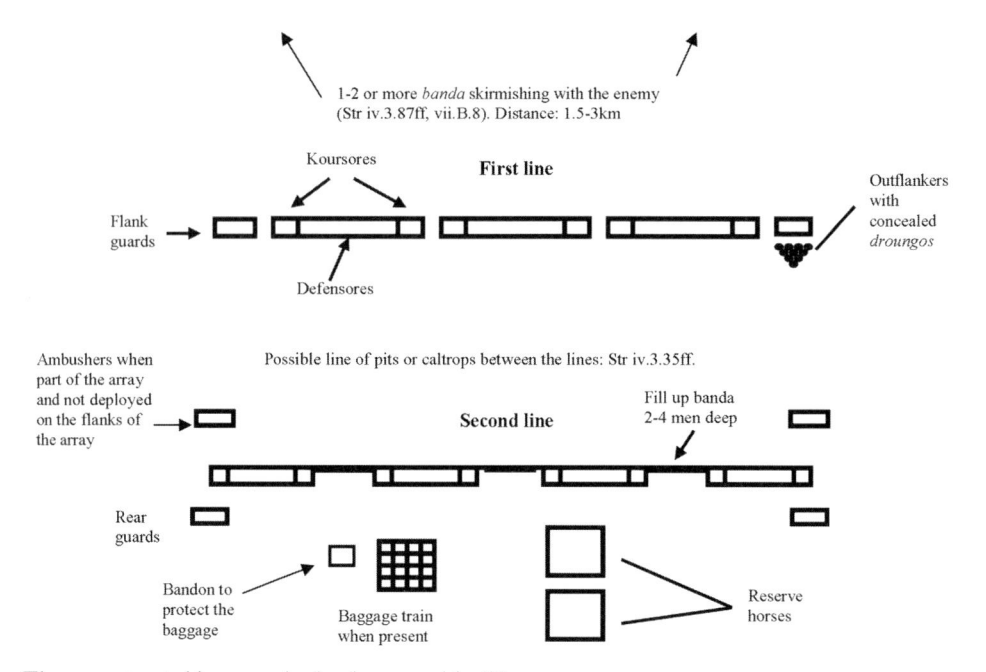

The reconstructed large cavalry battle array with all its parts.

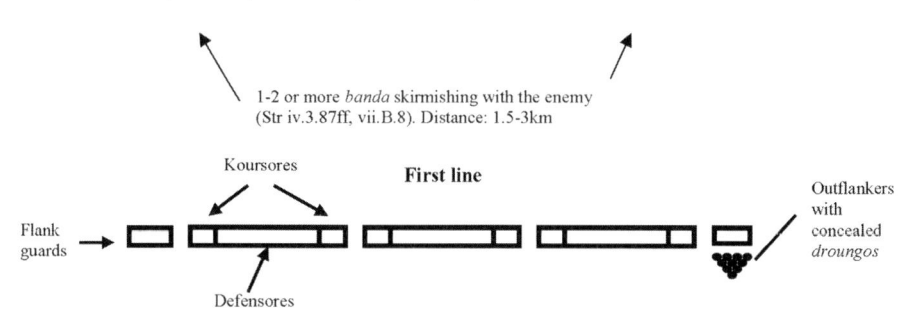

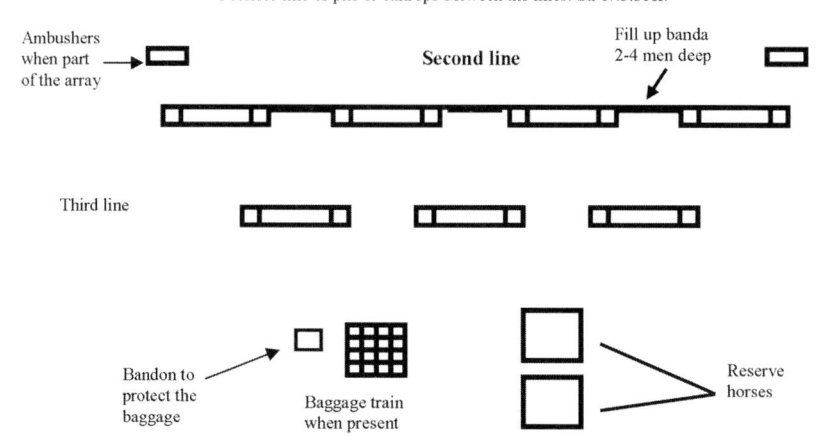

The reconstructed super large battle array for cavalry armies in excess of ca. 50,000 men.

The Roman Empire in 268   21

Medium sized cavalry army with less than 15,000/12,000/10,000 and more than 5,000/6,000 men

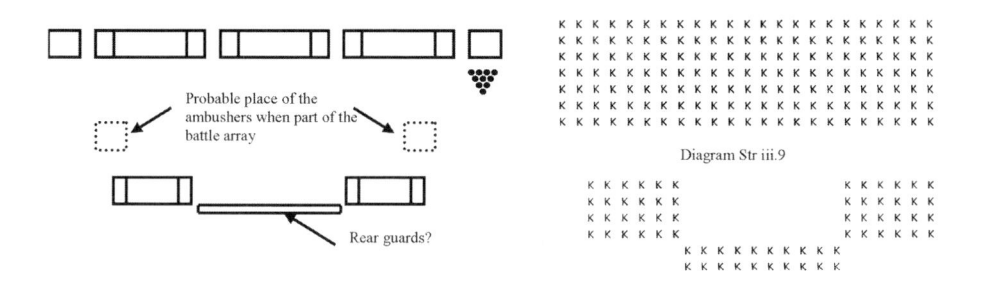

Probable place of the ambushers when part of the battle array

Rear guards?

Diagram Str iii.9

Small cavalry army with 2,000-5,000/6,000 men or less had only one division in the second line

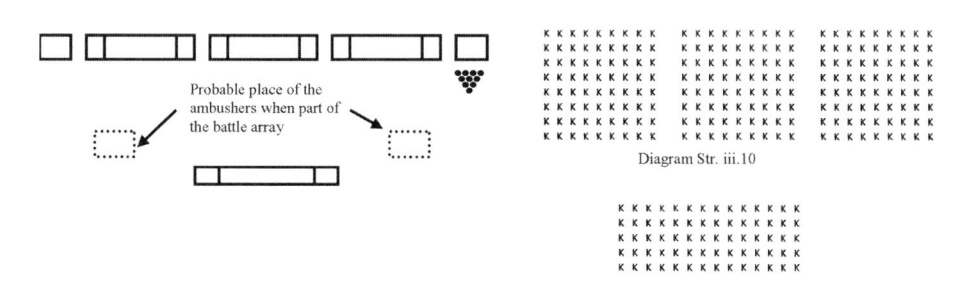

Probable place of the ambushers when part of the battle array

Diagram Str. iii.10

impossible that the units could also have been deployed in full strength. The *tagmata*, *arithmoi* or *banda* in their turn consisted of smaller units of approximately 100 men, but in practice these seem to have been deployed side-by-side to form the above-mentioned units. However, there is still every reason to believe that other combat formations, unit structures and unit formations continued to exist side-by-side with these because the Romans had not yet completely standardized the equipment, training and fighting styles of their cavalry units of different ethnic origins.

It is very likely that the Romans continued to use the tactical formations described by Arrian in his *Taktika* and *Ektaxis kata Alanôn* because they continued to use the same types of cavalry units with the same types of infantry formations. In the latter case Arrian describes a cavalry formation which he used for the pursuit of the Alans. It is probable that this same type of array was also used when the cavalry was deployed separately in front of the infantry. The Armenian *symmachiarii* formed the flanks of the front line. These Armenian units consisted of *katafraktoi* (cataphracts possibly used as a front rank), *kontoforoi* (*contarii*), and of the *hippotoxotai* (mounted archers). Between these two wings were six *lochoi* of auxiliary *alae*. These consisted of the *hippotoxotai* (mounted archers) who were also equipped with javelins, swords and shields. The two wing reserves on both flanks consisted of the legionary cavalry. The legionary cavalry in its turn consisted of units of lancers (*kontoforoi, machairoforoi*) and of units of javelineers (*logchoforoi, machairaforoi, pelekoforoi*), or alternatively these units included both types within the same units so that the *kontoforoi* formed the two front ranks and the *lonchoforoi* the next two in a formation of four ranks. In addition to this it is probable that the commander followed the cavalry line in the middle with his *equites singulares* (elite auxiliaries), and it is probable that Aurelian deployed his cavalry in this manner at the battle of Emesa in 272. See later.

The unit orders of the Roman cavalry varied according to the type of unit and situation. Standard unit formations were the square array (usually four ranks and eight files, or units with depths of five or ten ranks as Arrian recommends and which was also to become the standard during the so-called Byzantine times) and oblong arrays of various sizes up to ca. 512 men. The horsemen in these could be deployed in open order for marching or in close order for combat. In addition to this, the Romans used the wedge array (64 men or the massive regimental version from ca. 300 to 1,500 horsemen), rhombus (128 men) and irregular order called *drungus/droungos* (varied in size).

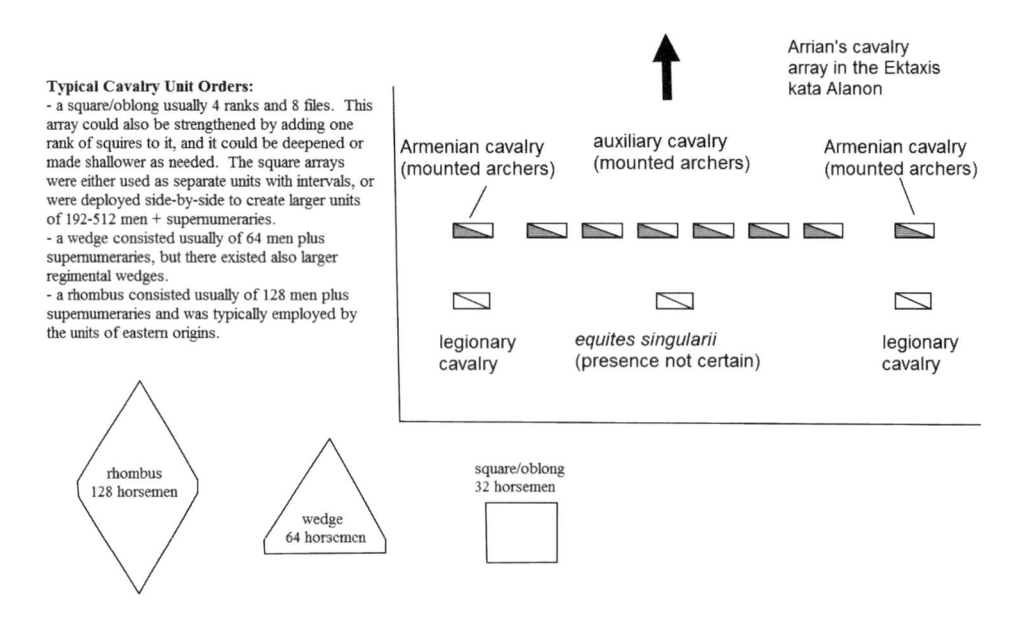

Typical Cavalry Unit Orders:
- a square/oblong usually 4 ranks and 8 files. This array could also be strengthened by adding one rank of squires to it, and it could be deepened or made shallower as needed. The square arrays were either used as separate units with intervals, or were deployed side-by-side to create larger units of 192-512 men + supernumeraries.
- a wedge consisted usually of 64 men plus supernumeraries, but there existed also larger regimental wedges.
- a rhombus consisted usually of 128 men plus supernumeraries and was typically employed by the units of eastern origins.

Arrian's cavalry array in the Ektaxis kata Alanon

Armenian cavalry (mounted archers) / auxiliary cavalry (mounted archers) / Armenian cavalry (mounted archers)

legionary cavalry / equites singularii (presence not certain) / legionary cavalry

rhombus 128 horsemen

wedge 64 horsemen

square/oblong 32 horsemen

2.4. Roman Naval Combat[5]

The Romans divided their navy into two basic categories: 1) The Praetorian Fleets of Italy; 2) The Provincial Fleet in the provinces. The two Praetorian Fleets, *Classis Praetoriae Misenatium/Misenatis* and *Classis Praetoriae Ravennatum/Ravennatis/Ravennas*, formed the core of the naval forces and served as reserves in Italy. The Provincial Fleets included at least the *Classis Alexandrina, Classis Syriaca, Classis Nova Libyca, Classis Germanica, Classis Pannonica, Classis Moesica, Classis Britannica, Classis Pontica, Classis Mauretanica* (thirteen *liburnae*), *Classis Nova Libyca*, and *Classis Africana*.[6] According to Vegetius (4.31), each of the praetorian fleets had a single naval legion attached to them. We do not possess similar information regarding the provincial fleets, but it is still clear that the provincial fleets had some sort of fighting contingents attached. Some of the provincial fleets were in the hands of the usurpers in 268. Besides their use in naval combat the Romans also used their fleets to support military operations, to protect the sea lanes, and to ship both men and supplies where needed.

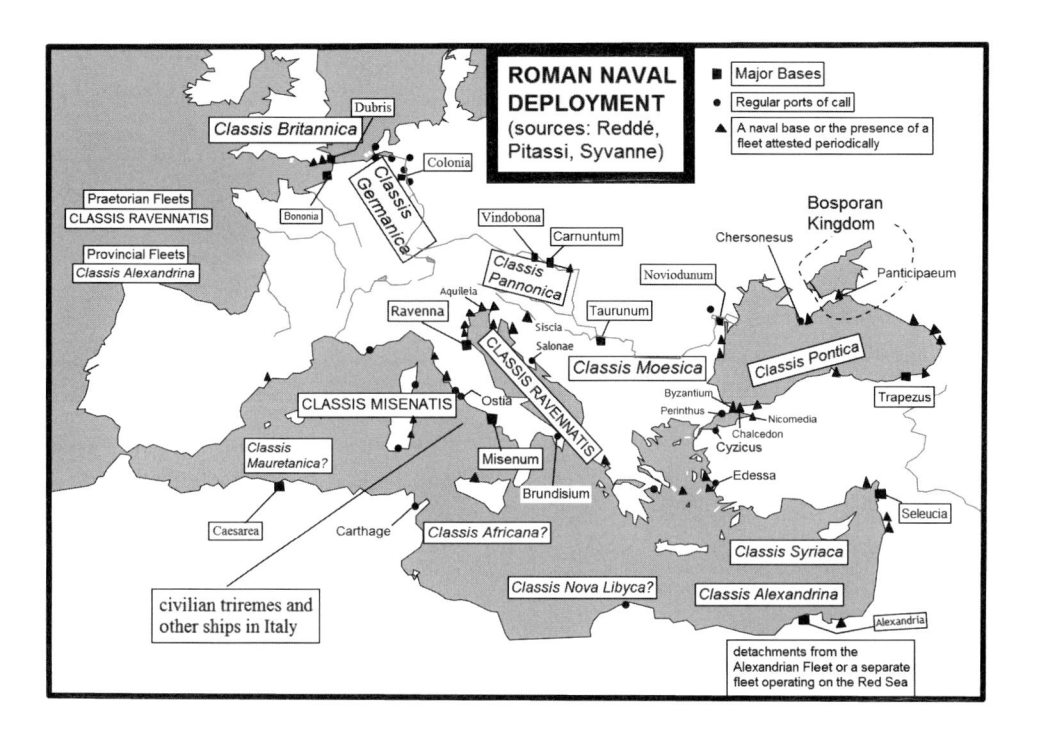

The accompanying map shows the naval deployment pattern at the first half of the third century. The situation after this is not known with certainty. On the basis of the narrative sources, it is possible but by no means certain that Gallienus may have created a separate fleet for the Aegean Sea.

The coastal defence system employed by the Romans consisted of two separate systems: 1) the passive/defensive measures (forts, towers, fortified cities and towns along the coasts and rivers); 2) the active/offensive measures undertaken by the fleets. The civilians were responsible for the basic defence (control of harbours, collection of tolls/taxes, prevention of smuggling and wrecking, guarding of the coasts against piratical attacks), but the fleets performed in most cases the active/offensive defence with the possible help of corvéed civilian ships. The Romans could appoint special officers to take control of larger sections of the coast. Civilians were also required to contribute ships and men whenever needed.[7]

Ships
The fast *liburna* (a fast galley, pl. *liburnae*) was the principal type of warship used by all fleets so that the triremes served as flagships of the provincial fleets while the fives or sixes served as flagships for the praetorian fleets. In addition to this, the praetorian fleets had significant numbers of larger ships (mostly triremes with fives and sixes serving as flagships) to secure them advantage over the provincial fleets in case of need. The fleets also possessed special types of ships, boats and rafts to enable them to transport horses, men, equipment and supplies, the numbers of which could be bolstered with corvéed civilian transports or warships.

Liburnian
c. AD 100

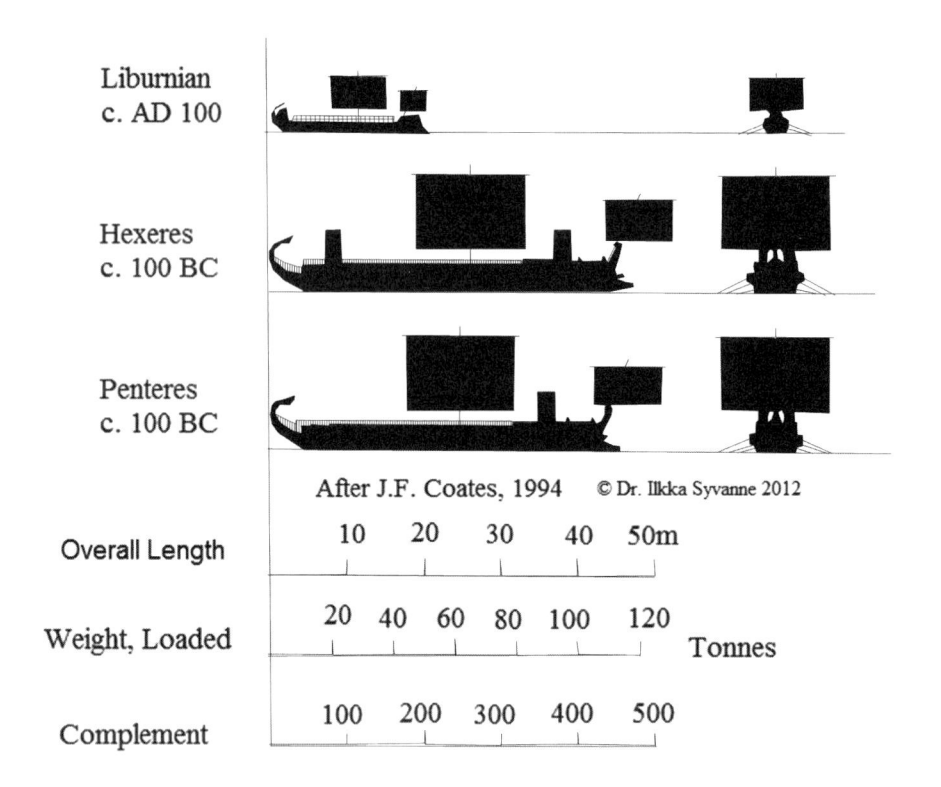

Hexeres
c. 100 BC

Penteres
c. 100 BC

After J.F. Coates, 1994   © Dr. Ilkka Syvänne 2012

Overall Length: 10, 20, 30, 40, 50m

Weight, Loaded: 20, 40, 60, 80, 100, 120 Tonnes

Complement: 100, 200, 300, 400, 500

Naval Tactics[8]

It was always considered risky to row or sail during the stormy winter season, which meant that this was usually avoided. However, the sources prove that the Romans sometimes took the risk to surprise their enemies. The Roman navy expected that its personnel would always possess good knowledge of the winds, tides, locale and signs of weather to enable it to fight in the most advantageous manner against enemies. Combat tactics on the seas mirrored those on land. At the heart of plans was the obtaining of information of enemy plans through spies and scouting boats, and then surprise the enemy with an ambush or surprise attack.

Naval battle formations used by the Romans were: a) the crescent formation with the best ships and crews posted on the wings to encircle the enemy; b) the convex array in which the best ships and crews were placed in the middle to break apart the enemy formation; c) the double convex array when there were enough ships to provide reserves; d) the line abreast with reserves behind; e) the double line abreast if there existed enough ships; f) the defensive circle. Individual ships and groups of ships were trained to perform: 1) the *diekplous* manoeuvre to penetrate into the enemy formation so that one galley ran forward into the gap between two enemy galleys where it sheared the oars of one galley after which the second galley followed it and rammed the immobile defenceless ship; 2) the outflanking of the enemy line with the *periplous* manoeuvre so that the outermost galleys extended their line to encircle the enemy line.

A naval battle consisted of several stages. When the Romans possessed larger ships, they started to bombard the enemy with the *ballistae* and bows at a range of about

300–600 metres. Next the larger ships started to employ the *onagri* (stone throwers), slings and staff-slings from about 150 metres. The stone throwers used either stones and/or fire-bombs and the *ballistae* primarily incendiary arrows. When the Romans reached within about 30–40 metres they started to use light javelins, and then at 20–30 metres they moved on to heavy javelins. At a ramming distance, the galleys either rammed, sheared the enemy's oars, or grappled the enemy vessel for boarding.

The principal foreign naval threats during this period were the Franks, Saxons, Borani, Goths, Heruls, Blemmyes, and Aksumites. Their ships were no match for the Roman ships, but when the Romans were hampered by civil wars they could still invade and raid with relative impunity.

2.5. Siege Warfare

The various methods employed by the Romans in siege warfare were the most advanced of the age. They can be divided into defensive and offensive techniques.

Offensive sieges had some standard features, which were: 1) terms of surrender offered to the enemy at first to avoid the costly siege; 2) use of surprise attacks if possible; 3) use of a traitor; 4) if the enemy had refused to surrender, assault using *testudo* formation with ladders, possibly with some protective sheds; 5) if the first assault failed, siege engines might be used, mounds built, and mines excavated; 6) if the place was considered too costly to take by other means, the defenders would be starved into surrender.

Standard defensive siege techniques were as follows: 1) scorched-earth policy to make the attack difficult if there was prior information of the enemy invasion; 2) the building of sophisticated fortifications with enough provisions placed inside to withstand a siege; 3) exploitation of defensive features like walls and towers; 4) use of siege engines; 5) the sending of a relief army against the besiegers; 6) use of diversionary invasion; 7) guerrilla warfare against the besiegers; 8) if all else failed, then the Romans offered terms of surrender.

The Romans were the beneficiaries of the revolution that had taken place in siege warfare during the Hellenistic age, but they had not merely copied the equipment they had inherited, they had improved it. The siege equipment employed by the Romans included the *sambuca* (a hollow tube to land men on top of a wall), various kinds of siege towers, various kinds of battering rams (from simple rams all the way up to the city-taker '*helepolis*'), borers, drills, flails, the 'fire hose' to spread liquids, mining equipment, various types of sheds, fire bombs, cranes, and various types of artillery (small to large ballistae, steel-spring powered artillery, repeating ballista, *onager* and possibly also mangonels/trebuchets if the super heavy stones used at the siege of Cremna are evidence for that). A sample of these is illustrated here.

26 Aurelian and Probus

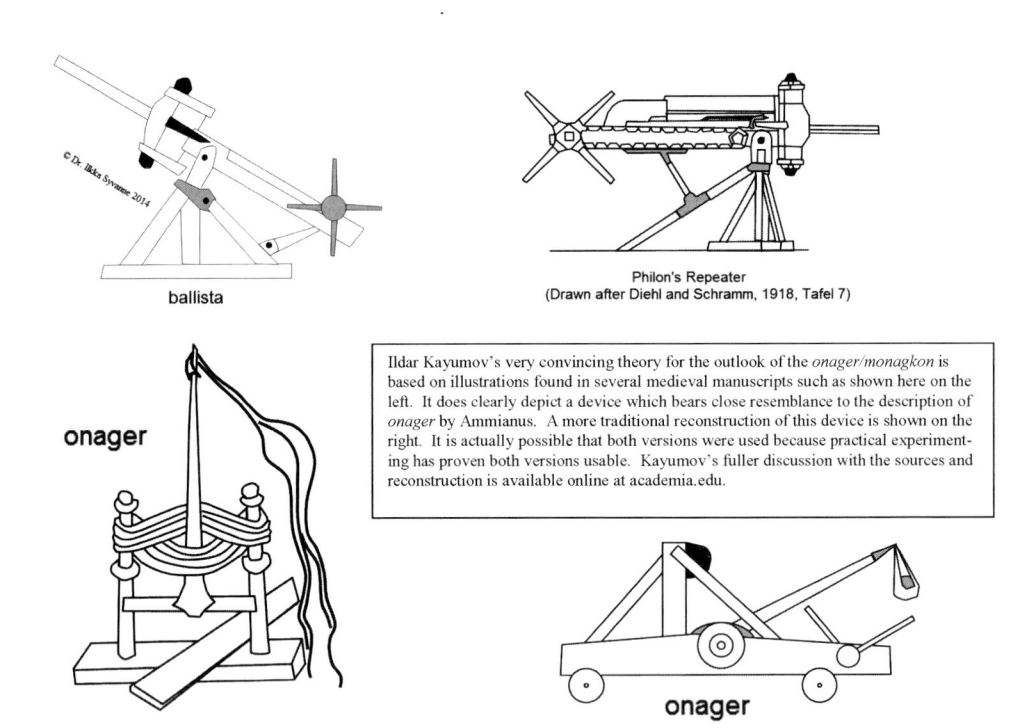

ballista

Philon's Repeater
(Drawn after Diehl and Schramm, 1918, Tafel 7)

onager

Ildar Kayumov's very convincing theory for the outlook of the *onager/monagkon* is based on illustrations found in several medieval manuscripts such as shown here on the left. It does clearly depict a device which bears close resemblance to the description of *onager* by Ammianus. A more traditional reconstruction of this device is shown on the right. It is actually possible that both versions were used because practical experimenting has proven both versions usable. Kayumov's fuller discussion with the sources and reconstruction is available online at academia.edu.

onager

2.6. Intelligence Gathering and Security

The primary concern for all emperors was their personal safety and this dictated their approach to intelligence gathering. Most effort was directed towards potential domestic foes, but obviously they did not forget external threats. The imperial bodyguard units ensured the personal safety of the emperor and were also the principal means of obtaining intelligence of internal and external threats. The principal intelligence gathering units were the *frumentarii* and *peregrini*, but other units of bodyguards or troops posted in the city of Rome were also used as secret services. The other principal units in charge of intelligence gathering were the *speculatores, protectores/scholae/aulici, evocati Augusti, praetoriani, equites singlares Augusti* and the *urbaniciani*. With the exception of *protectores*, who were commanded by their *comes* or *magister*, and the *urbaniciani*, who were commanded by their prefect, the other units were all under one or two praetorian prefects. These units combined the functions of bodyguard with intelligence gathering and other special operations which included assassinations, police operations and interrogation. However, we should not forget that in practice emperors could use anyone they trusted (for example eunuchs) as their special operatives. Even if these were the principal intelligence gathering organizations, we should not forget that the contribution of regular military units was also important, because they were also given internal and external security missions. In fact it was the frontier units that gathered most of the intelligence from across the border. In addition to this, the Romans used civilian paramilitary police forces and other civilians for the gathering of intelligence, which reported important findings to local military commanders and/or the governor of the province.[9]

The Roman Empire in 268 27

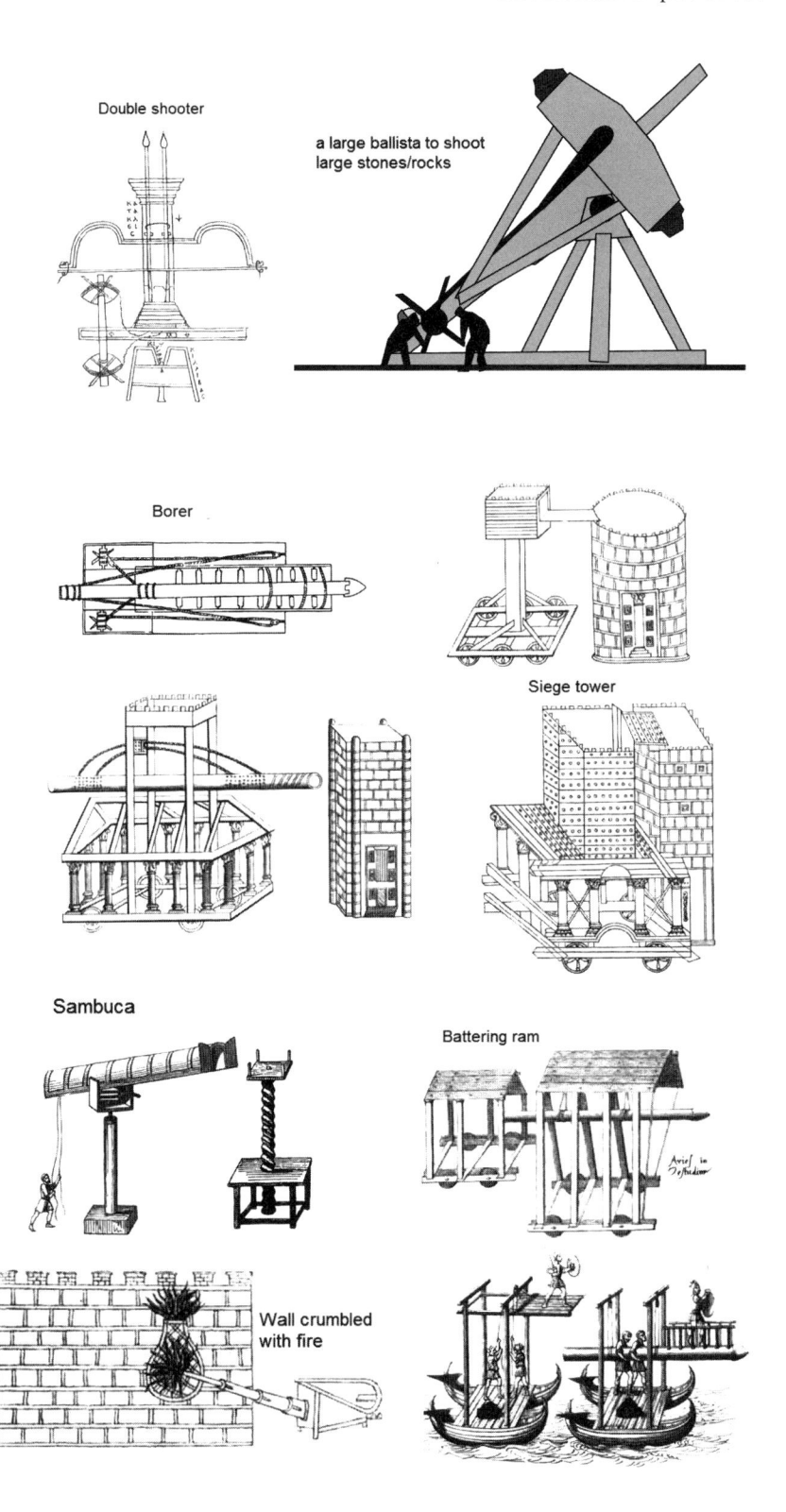

Double shooter

a large ballista to shoot large stones/rocks

Borer

Siege tower

Sambuca

Battering ram

Wall crumbled with fire

2.7. Strategy

Thanks to the limitations posed by speed of travel (feet, horses, wagons, ships) the general peacetime deployment pattern of Roman forces was defensive. The Romans simply could not transfer their forces fast from one front to another so they had to post them close to the border. These forces were then used to interfere in politics across the border so that enemies could be kept divided. It was because of this that the forces posted near the frontier conducted active intelligence gathering operations across the border. However, there were occasions in which intelligence gathering operations, diplomacy and the forces posted on the frontier proved insufficient to meet an enemy invasion. In such situations, the Romans typically sent detachments from other legions and units (or entire legions and auxiliary units) to the threatened sector. This naturally weakened the areas from which these units had been taken, and enemies opposite those sectors often exploited this and invaded. When this happened, emperors were often required to raise new legions and other units to meet the crisis.

The above-mentioned peacetime deployment pattern was changed when the emperors conducted offensive wars or when there had been a prolonged crisis like there was after ca. 251. In these cases the emperor was accompanied by the only significant field army of the Empire, which was the case for most of the time from the reign of Gallienus onwards. He created a personal field army, which formed the core of the army which also accompanied Aurelian and Probus in their campaigns. The keeping of this major field army in the field resulted in the creation of an elite fighting force, which gave the emperor the advantage over all usurpers and enemies. The withdrawal of these forces in its turn weakened the defences along the frontiers even further. However, this was still safer than giving generals such large forces that they could try to usurp power themselves. Regardless, as we shall see, the emperors were still forced to do this, and sure enough the generals did usurp power. It was therefore possible to secure only that sector of the Empire or frontier where the emperor was present in person with his personal field army. The principal threats to the Roman Empire were not the foreign enemies but the power-hungry generals. Foreign enemies could threaten the Roman Empire only when the Romans were fighting civil wars.

The combination of civil wars with foreign invasions had caused a change in Roman strategy, which was the adoption of the defence-in-depth. It has often been claimed that Gallienus was the man who invented it, but this is not true because there are instances of this strategy before him. However, it was Gallienus and Valerian who were forced to adopt this on a greater scale than ever before. They fortified and strengthened several cities in Gaul, Italy, the Balkans and Asia Minor, both for defensive and offensive purposes. Similarly, it has been claimed that Gallienus created the first real cavalry army to enable him to engage the many foreign invaders fast, but this is also erroneus because the Romans had used large cavalry armies well before him. However, it was once again Gallienus who made use of cavalry forces more than any of his predecessors with the exception of Decius.[10]

As we shall see, the stabilization of the situation under Aurelian and Probus enabled the latter to attempt to return to the strategy of preclusive security along the borders. It was because of this that Probus built or rebuilt fortifications along the borders and posted forces along those frontiers. However, there was still one major difference in this system compared to that which had existed before the 250s: Probus was always accompanied by a huge field army.

Chapter Three

Youth and Career of Aurelian and Probus until 268

The early careers of both heroes of this study are very scantily known and most of what we know is based on the information provided by the *Augustan Histories*. Therefore readers are advised to take everything that follows with a grain of salt, but in the absence of any other evidence this is all we have to go on.

Our knowledge of the career of Aurelian is based almost completely on the scattered and unreliable evidence included in the *Augustan Histories* until the year 268. Only after that are we on more certain ground. A careful analysis of these details, however, can be used to bring to light much important information when they are put into context, and I have done that already in my biography of Gallienus.

The same is true of the career of Probus, but in his case the uncertainties persist until the year 275. The reader who is interested to read a detailed analysis of his career up to the year 268 is once again advised to read my biography of Gallienus. I will provide an analysis of what we know of his career between the years 268 and 275 in this book too, but going into less detail.

3.1. Aurelian

Lucius Domitius Aurelianus, as he is named in the coins, inscriptions and papyri, was born on 5 or 9 September – the exact date of his birth is not known. According to Malalas, he was 61 years old when he died, which, if correct, would place the year of his birth at 214. He was of humble birth and even his place of birth is not known with any certainty beyond the fact that he came from the Balkans like almost all of the emperors after the reign of Gallienus. Malalas (12.30 tr. by Jeffreys, Jeffreys and Scott p.164) describes Aurelian when he was already an emperor as follows: 'Aurelian, the warrior,… was tall, slender, slightly bald, with small eyes and completely grey hair; he was magnanimous and quick moving. He wore a diadem decorated with a star.'

The *Augustan Histories* give us two alternatives for his origins: a Pannonian from the city of Sirmium (Aurel. 3.1, 24.3); a native of *Dacia Ripensis*, which he created so that he would have been a Moesian (Aurel. 3.2). Pseudo-Victor (35.1) states that he came from the area between Moesia and Macedonia, while the *Epitome* claims that he came from the province of Dacia Mediterranea (located between Dacia Ripensis and Macedonia and therefore the same as in Aurelius Victor). Eutropius (9, 13.1) also places his birth in Dacia Ripensis. On the basis of this cumulative evidence Eugen Cizek suggests that it is probable that Aurelian's place of birth was indeed Dacia Ripensis, a province which he created when he became the emperor, which would have been a part of Moesia Superior at a time of his birth.[1]

Thanks to his humble birth we know next to nothing about Aurelian's parents. According to Pseudo-Victor (35.1), Aurelian was a son of a *colonus* (tenant farmer) who farmed the lands of the *clarissimus* (a title with judicial privileges) senator Aurelius. It is more than likely that Aurelian's father was a retired soldier, because as a youth he was taught how to use weapons. This tenant farmer would therefore have married a freedwoman belonging to the family of his landlord. The mother in her turn would have received her name at the time of her emancipation so that her son became Aurelianus. Aurelian's background was therefore very humble indeed, but it did not prevent him from performing deeds of greatness later in life. The *Historia Augusta* (*Aurel.* 4.2) claims that Aurelian's mother was a priestess of the temple of Sun God (*Sol*). Various forms of sun cult were favourites of the armed forced in the Balkans so it is likely that Aurelian's father was a member of the same cult. The *Vita* (*HA, Aurel.* 4.3ff.) naturally gives a list of omens (prophecies and omens that signalled the rise of Lucius as emperor) that foretold of the great future that the young Lucius would have when he grew up. The listing of such omens formed a part of the historical genre, and it is entirely possible that many of these so-called omens took place in practice and that superstitious people interpreted them contemporaneously, while some other events came to be seen as omens only after Aurelian had already become an emperor. It is therefore possible that the ambitions of the young Aurelian were already inflamed in his youth by his priestess mother.[2]

It is perhaps no coincidence that the *Historia Augusta* (*Aurel.* 4.5–6) states that Aurelian's priestess mother made swadding clothes for her son from the purple cloak which the emperor of the time (he would be Caracalla) had dedicated to the *Sol*. We shall find Aurelian later imitating some of the policies of Caracalla and we shall also find him paying his respects to Apollonius of Tyana and *Sol Invictus* and *Heliogabalus* (the Sun-God of Emesa and not the emperor who claimed to be the son of Caracalla) just like Caracalla had done. Perhaps this is the reason why Aurelian was so opposed to adultery and why he was known as a stern man.

In my opinion, the fact that Aurelian's mother is likely to have been a priestess of the Sun God goes a long way to explain what Aurelian did later. The usual assumption among those historians who accept the veracity of this claim is that it explains Aurelian's devotion to the worship of the *Sol*, but this is likely to be only a part of the truth. The fact that Aurelian's mother was a priestess would have given Aurelian intimate knowledge of how religions worked and what methods were used by the priestesses and priests in the manipulation of their devout followers just like the emperors as high-priests (each emperor held the office of *Pontifex Maximus*) knew how to manipulate the superstitious minds of the soldiers. It is unlikely to be a coincidence that Aurelian as officer is claimed to have forbidden the consultation of *haruspices* (soothsayers) by soldiers as stated by the *Historia Augusta* (*Aurel.* 7.8) and that he clearly used the cult of the Sun with Apollonius of Tyana to improve the morale of his army. This obviously does not preclude the possibility that Aurelian himself believed in the gods and that he would have been a follower of the *Sol*. It is entirely possible for a man to believe in a god or gods and still use religion to strengthen his own position in a cynical manner.

According to Flavius Vopiscus (*HA, Aurel.* 4.1ff., 6.1ff.), the young Lucius grew up to become a tall handsome man who had a quick mind. From the very early days onwards, he was known for his bodily strength and muscular appearance. He also claims that

Lucius trained to fight with the *pilum*, bow and other arms daily, even during feast days and holidays. There is no reason to doubt this statement. This is how all modern day top class athletes have trained in their youth. The ability to reach the top requires self-discipline bordering on fanaticism, and plenty of luck. It would have been these excellent fighting skills in combination with his tall stature and muscular strength that lay behind the phenomenal rise of this man of humble birth in the military ranks. It is likely that it was Lucius's veteran father who taught his son these fighting skills and the necessary self-discipline to persist in his training. The next thing this man needed was a patron who would promote his career.

On the basis of the *Historia Augusta* (*Aurel.* 5.3ff.), the man who promoted the career of Aurelian was the emperor Valerian. On the basis of this account it is probable that Aurelian accompanied Valerian to the east in 254. The only details that Flavius Vopiscus gives us is that Aurelian was wounded in action and served as an envoy to the Persians, in the course of which he received an elephant as a gift which he then gave to the emperor. It was then that Aurelian received his nickname, Aurelian Sword-in-hand (*Aurelianus manu ad ferrum*), to separate him from his namesake who was subsequently captured by the Persians at the same time as they captured the emperor Valerian in 259.

Aurelian was always ready to draw his sword to discipline his men. He was known as a self-disciplined man who indulged in his passions of eating and drinking wine only rarely, while being feared by his men as a strict disciplinarian who punished all transgressions with the harshest severity. According to Flavius Vopiscus, Aurelian was in the habit of making warning examples so that once the soldiers had witnessed his severity they did not commit offences anymore. He gives as an example an incident in which one of his soldiers had committed adultery with the wife of the man at whose house he lodged. Aurelian had this man torn in two by bending down two trees. The second of his examples concerns an alleged letter of Aurelian to his deputy in a cavalry unit in which he instructed the man to prevent the men from looting the property of their hosts on pain of death. The officer was also to make certain that the men followed the other regulations to the letter.[3]

It is actually not surprising that Valerian promoted the career of such a man because both were conservatives by nature. Flavius Vopiscus claims that in a (probably fictitious) letter from Valerian to Antoninus Gallus, Valerian states that Aurelian was too stern and harsh for the times and that it was because of this that Valerian had joined his frivolous merry-making son Gallienus with Postumus rather than with Aurelian. The following account, however, makes it clear that Aurelian came to serve under Gallienus so that the two men met. These two men were the polar opposites of each other in character and habits. Aurelian was a lowly born disciplinarian with a Spartan lifestyle who opposed adultery, while Gallienus was an upper class dandy known for his luxurious lifestyle and libertarian habits. It was this that became one of the reasons why Aurelian became one of the principal plotters in the cabal to kill Gallienus.[4]

The next detail (*HA*, *Aurel.*, 6.3ff.) that we have of his career proves that Aurelian was transferred to the Balkans by 255 where he appears to have joined the army operating under Gallienus. According to this text, Aurelian and his 300 men defeated the Sarmatian invaders facing them. It also claims that it was in this war that Aurelian killed with his own hand 48 men in a single day and in the course of several days he slew over 950. These figures have been suspected, but the killing of 48 men in a single day by a man of exceptional fighting skills is by no means impossible. One does suspect that the figure of over 950 would be the number of men killed by Aurelian and his 300 men rather than by him alone, but one cannot entirely exclude the possibility that he did indeed kill this number in the course of several days; it would certainly explain his phenomenal rise in the ranks.

The information in the *Historia Augusta* (*Aurel.*, 7.1ff) suggests that Aurelian marched together with Gallienus to Gaul in late 255. It was then that he distinguished himself as a tribune of the *Legio VI Gallicana*[5] at Mainz where he completely crushed one of the invading parties of the Franks, killing 700 and capturing 300 whom he sold as slaves. Flavius Vopiscus claims that his soldiers then composed a song in which they sang that they had killed Franks and Sarmatians by the thousand and that they were now seeking a thousand Persians to kill. It was at this point that Vopiscus placed the above-mentioned letter of Valerian to Antoninus Gallus (*Aurel.* 8.1ff.). The implication is that Valerian did not leave Aurelian with Gallienus but transferred him to the Balkans where we indeed find him next in Vopiscus's text. If there is any truth in these allegations, it is clear that Valerian realized that Gallienus and Aurelian would not get along that well thanks to their very different character traits.

The next piece of information in the *Augustan Histories* (*Aurel.* 9.1ff.) is a (possibly fictitious) letter from Valerian to the *Praefectus Urbis Romae/Praefectus Urbi* (Urban Prefect of Rome/Prefect of the City of Rome) Ceionius Albinus who is probably to be identified with Marcus Nummius Celonius Annius Albinus who in his turn may be identical with Nummius Albinus who was the Prefect of the City in 256. In this letter, Valerian informs the prefect that he had appointed Aurelian as inspector of all camps and instructed the prefect to provide Aurelian with adequate resources as long as he stayed in the City of Rome. Aurelian had been promoted to this position thanks to his stellar performance in Illyricum and Gaul. This would obviously suggest that Aurelian had been dispatched from Gaul to Rome, but it is inherently more likely that this promotion actually belongs to the period after Aurelian's next stay in the Balkans as a deputy of the *dux* (general) Crinitus.

Following this, the *Augustan Histories* (*Aurel.*, 10.1) state that Aurelian acted as a deputy for generals and tribunes on about 40 occasions, and names as an example of this Aurelian's role as a deputy of *dux* Crinitus in the Balkans, presumably also in 255 or in 256. This shows that he was used as a deputy officer wherever needed. However, in my opinion we should interpret the 40 occasions to refer to instances of combat when holding such positions rather as separate instances of holding such positions.

The possibly fictitious letter of Valerian to Aurelian (*HA, Aurel.*, 10.1ff., 11.1ff.) refers to the period when Aurelian acted as Crinitus's deputy. In this letter Valerian ordered Aurelian to take command of the war in the Nicopolis (presumably Nicopolis ad Istrum) area during the medical leave of Crinitus presumably in 255 or in 256. Aurelian was given 1,650 light cavalry (Itureans, Armenians, Arabs, Saracens, Mesopotamian auxiliaries), 800 *equites cataphractos*, *Legio III Felix*,[6] together with the Germanic chieftains Hariomundus, Haldagates, Hildomundus and Charioviscus and their retinues. Aurelian was ordered to find out where the enemy's wagon train was, what type of enemy they were facing and what was its strength. In other words, Aurelian was sent to reconnoitre, but he acted on his own initiative and surprised the enemy in its encampment probably with a sudden cavalry attack.⁷ The invaders were the Tervingi Goths (*HA Aurel.* 13.2) presumably with their subjects and allies.

Vopiscus also claims that Aurelian restored the frontiers; distributed booty among the soldiers; enriched Thrace with captured cattle, horses and slaves; dedicated spoils in the Palace (the emperor's spoils); and brought to Valerian's private estate 500 slaves, 2,000 cows, 1,000 mares, 10,000 sheep, and 15,000 goats. In other words, Aurelian divided the booty as expected so that the emperor got his share of the loot. The details also make it clear that Aurelian did not only surprise the enemy on his own initiative, but also exacted vengeance on the enemy by crossing the Danube into enemy territory where he destroyed several enemy encampments and settlements. The grateful Valerian rewarded Aurelian with all kinds of crowns (at the time close equivalents of medals of honour) and other rewards. In fact it is this list of rewards that has enabled me to reconstruct the course of this campaign.

The list of rewards handed over to Aurelian included: four mural crowns/*coronae* (given for scaling the enemy wall first), five rampart crowns (forcing a way into the enemy camp), two naval crowns (boarding an enemy vessel first), two civic crowns (saving the life of a citizen), ten spears (*hastae*) without points, four bi-coloured *vexilla* (banners), four red tunicas of the *duces*, two proconsular cloaks, a bordered toga, a tunic with palms, a gold embroidered toga, and an ivory chair. On the basis of this list, it is probable that Aurelian engaged five enemy forces separately and destroyed their camps, quite probably when they were inside Roman territory. The naval and mural crowns in their turn imply that Aurelian crossed the Danube and boarded some enemy vessels. It is quite likely that he crossed the river using those very same boats. The tribes that possessed boats along the Danube included the Bastarnae and Peuci, but it is also possible that these were the Tervingi Goths or some of their subject tribes. The four mural crowns suggest that once inside enemy territory Aurelian destroyed four enemy settlements. The different crowns given here should probably be considered to be representative of 13 instances out of the total of 40 in which Aurelian acted as deputy, and if the spears, *vexilla*, tunicas of the *duces* and the proconsular cloaks are counted in, then this would already reach the figure of 33 out of 40. By including the other instances included in the *Augustan Histories*, the overall figure is already very close to the total of 40, so it is possible that Aurelian acted as a deputy only on one to three additional occasions which are not mentioned by the *Augustan Histories* – although it is entirely plausible that the rest of the instances also belong to the ones that were included in this text. It is probable that, while Aurelian was fighting in the eastern Balkans, Probus was fighting in the western Balkans against the Sarmatians and Quadi (*HA, Probus* 5). For this, see the career of Probus below.

I would suggest that it was thanks to this that Aurelian was then promoted to the position of inspector of army camps[8] at a meeting of officers which took place at Byzantium either in 255 when Valerian was there or passing through it or in 256. Vopiscus claims that it was then that Aurelian was adopted into a senatorial family of Crinitus and was also appointed consul (undoubtedly *consul suffectus*), and given enough money to act according to his new status.[9] This statement has been quite needlessly considered suspect by most modern historians. The claim is just as reliable as the claim that Gallienus appointed the Herulian chieftain as consul. It is clear that we are here dealing with *consules suffecti*, who were not listed in the Fasti as the *consules ordinarii* were, so there is nothing incredible in the statement.[10] The appointment to the position of inspector of army camps was particularly suitable because Aurelian had demonstrated himself to be an incorruptible man who followed regulations to the letter.

It was then thanks to this promotion to the position of inspector of camps that Aurelian disappears from the sources until the great Gothic invasion of the years 267–70. Then once again we find Aurelian in charge of men in combat. The *Augustan Histories* (*Aurel.* 18.1) refer to one instance under the emperor Claudius II Gothicus in which Aurelian was promoted to be the commander of all cavalry forces after the other cavalry commanders had acted rashly contrary to the wishes of the emperor. It is actually very probable that this example belongs to the reign of Gallienus because Aurelian became the commander of all cavalry forces under him while Claudius was promoted to become the *tribunus et magister officiorum* who was the supreme commander of all bodyguard units (*protectores*) including the cavalry *equites*.[11]

3.2. Probus

Marcus Aurelius Probus, as he was called in most inscriptions, coins and papyri, was born at Sirmium in Pannonia on 19 August 232. However, there are also other versions of his name. The *Historia Augusta* (Probus 11.5) calls him Aurelius Valerius Probus; Pseudo-Victor (*Epit.* 36.2) and coins from Ticinum call him Equitius Probus; and Malalas (12.33) calls him Aelius Probus. But it is likely that his official name was the first mentioned. The *Augustan Histories* (*HA, Probus* 3.1.ff.) claim that his mother was of nobler birth than his father, and that his private fortune was modest and his kindred unimportant. The name of his father was either Maximus (*HA, Probus* 3.1.1–2) or Dalmatius/Delmatius (*Epit.* 37.1) or perhaps Maximus Dalmatius. Dalmatius started his career as a soldier but ended up as a tribune. He died in Egypt, leaving behind a wife, his son Probus, and a daughter called Claudia.[12] This means that Probus had a slightly better start for his career than his compatriot Aurelian.[13] Flavius Vopiscus (HA, *Probus* 3) claims that on the basis of one Greek author there were many who claimed that Probus was a relative of Claudius and that the name of his sister lends support to this claim. This is all that the author says of this claim, and since the source is very unreliable, it is usually dismissed by modern authors. Considering the poor quality of the period evidence, I would not dismiss this alternative altogether. It is possible to think that Probus's higher ranking mother could have been a distant relative of Claudius, but the question is ultimately unsolvable.

According to Malalas, Probus's appearance, when he had already become an emperor, was as follows: 'Aelius Probus … was of medium height, with a large belly and straight, closely cropped hair, a bushy beard, dark skin, a ruddy complexion, good eyes and was very learned; he favoured the Green faction.' (Malalas 12.33, tr. by Jeffreys, Jeffreys and Scott p.165.) If there is any truth in this description, then it is clear that Probus allowed his physical condition to deteriorate as he grew older or that it reflected gladiatorial diet.

However, according to the *Augustan Histories* (*Probus* 3.5ff.), the young Probus was famous for his bodily strength, and because of this he caught the attention of Valerian. Valerian appointed him tribune 'almost before his beard was grown' and recommended him in a letter to his son Gallienus as a man to be imitated. This possibly fictitious letter states that Valerian had nominated Probus as a tribune and had given him command of six cohorts of Saracens together with a number of Gallic auxiliaries and Persians that Artabassis Syrus[14] (the Syrian) had handed over to the Romans. The important point in this account is that the information is once again a close fit with period circumstances just as it was with the above information regarding Aurelian. It is therefore very likely that Probus was dispatched to the Balkans at about the same time as Aurelian and the following account (*HA Probus* 5) confirms this. The same text also proves that Gallienus's elite *equites* included at least some Persian cavalry units.

It comes as no surprise that the next piece of information in the *Historia Augusta* (*Probus* 5) shows the newly appointed tribune Probus distinguishing himself in combat against the Sarmatians and Quadi in the western Balkans in about 255–6 at about the same time as Aurelian fought with success against other barbarians in the eastern Balkans. The *Augustan History* gives us a list of rewards that Probus received in front of an assembly (possibly the assembly held at Byzantium in which Aurelian also received his rewards). The rewards included: four *hastae* (spears) without points, two rampart *coronae* (crowns) (for forcing a way into an enemy camp), one civic crown (for saving a citizen), two golden *armillae* (highest grade bracelets given for bravery), and a golden *torque* (a neck-ring given for bravery). According to Vopiscus, Valerian handed over the civic crown in person because Probus had saved his kinsman Valerius Flaccinus from the hands of the Quadi. This Flaccinus is unknown and has been used to prove the account suspect, but in my opinion it is the other way around. The information is once again in agreement with the rest of the information provided, on top of which the circumstantial evidence backs it up. It has been speculated that Valerian and Decius must have been related to each other and the presence of this Flaccinus in the Balkans does indeed lend support for such speculations.

The above details make it likely that Probus engaged at least the Quadi when they were returning to their home territory with their loot, and he was then able to free Valerius Flaccinus along with the other booty. The two rampart crowns imply that Probus destroyed two separate enemy forces operating within Roman territory, which must be Quadi and Sarmatians. The absence of mural crowns and naval crowns suggest that he did not pursue the enemy across the Danube like Aurelian. Probus was rewarded with the command of the *legio III Felix* at the same time as Aurelian was promoted to the position of inspector of army camps. *Legio III Felix* had been under Aurelian, which means that Probus was transferred to Thrace so that he became successor to Aurelian in the eastern Balkans.[15]

The next piece of evidence that we have of Probus's career does indeed place him in the Balkans. The possibly fictitious letter of Gallienus to the tribunes of the armies in Illyricum in the aftermath of the revolt of some pretender and capture of Gallienus's father Valerian by the Persians in 259, states that had Probus been present there the pretender would not have dared to usurp power. Gallienus therefore ordered the tribunes to obey Probus. On the basis of this I have speculated in my biography of emperor Gallienus that Gallienus must have promoted Probus from the command he had held in the eastern Balkans into his own entourage thanks to the loyalty he had show during the revolt of Ingenuus in the western Balkans (supported by the Pannonian and Moesian legions) so that he was not present in the Balkans to crush the next usurper Regalianus, who usurped power after the capture of Valerian by the Persians. It was then because of this that Probus was made supreme commander of all of the forces in Illyricum (i.e. in western Balkans up to Thrace in the east). I have also speculated in my biography of Gallienus that while Probus was serving in the personal army of Gallienus that he served as a commander of the elite bodyguard unit *equites Mauri*, because Zonaras 12.29 notes that Probus was a friend of Saturninus the Moor and Victorinus the Moor. Service in the same unit would be the natural place for the men to befriend each other. Obviously there is no definite proof of this – it is only my best educated guess. It is possible that he could have befriended these men also during his youth or after ca. 260.[16]

The sources do not give us any secure information about the whereabouts of Probus before the reign of Tacitus. All we have to go on are general statements or information in the *Augustan Histories* which appear to have confused the two Probi – Tenagino Probus and Marcus Aurelius Probus – with each other. The generalized information we can find in the *Augustan Histories* (Probus 6.1) states merely that Probus performed great exploits as a commoner (*privatus*) under Valerian, Gallienus, Aurelian and Claudius, and that he scaled walls, tore down ramparts, killed enemies in hand-to-hand combat and received rewards from the emperors for his services. It is in fact very likely that Probus participated in some of the military campaigns conducted by Gallienus in person against the usurpers in Gaul and the Balkans and then against the Goths and others in 267–8. The reference to hand-to-hand combat shows how important it was for commanders of the period to demonstrate personal valour in combat to encourage the men. It was this that had brought great fame to Caracalla and to Gallienus. In fact, it was this readiness to fight that the assassins of Gallienus had used to murder their emperor. The fact that Probus was not included in any of the lists naming the conspirators that assassinated the emperor Gallienus can be used to prove that he indeed did not participate in that plot, and it is the probable reason why he failed to hold any high positions under the emperor Claudius.

3.3. The Military Experience of Aurelian and Probus

The above evidence suggests that the enemies Aurelian fought during his early career consisted at least of the Franks, Getae/Dacians/Carpi, Bastarnae/Sciri, Sarmatians, Heruls, Goths, Arabs, Armenians, Persians and fellow Romans. Probus had experience of facing at least the Quadi, Sarmatians, Marcomanni, Alamanni/Iuthungi, Getae/Dacians/Carpi, Heruls, Goths, Arabs, Armenians, Persians and fellow Romans. This would have given them both very well-rounded military educations against all types of enemies, and it is therefore not surprising to see both commanders excel against all types of enemies once they became emperors.

3.3.1. The Germanic Threat
The Germanic peoples consisted of three major groupings: 1) the Scandinavian tribes (Saxons and other tribes in the south of Denmark and north of Germany can be considered to belong to this group); 2) The Western tribes and confederacies (Saxons etc can also be considered part of this group, Franks, Alamanni, Suevi/Suebi, Marcomanni, Thuringians, Lombards, the western branch of the Heruls etc.); 3) Eastern tribes and confederacies (Goths, the eastern branch of the Heruls, Burgundi, Vandals, Gepids, Quadi, Taifali, Rugi, Sciri, Bastarnae etc.).

At this time most of the tribes or tribal confederacies were led by kings or high kings, but they did not possess the same authority over their subjects as the Roman emperors because the Germanic peoples valued personal freedom more than the Roman populace. The nobles and their retinues formed the military elite and were usually better equipped than all the rest. The Germanic peoples also required their entire free male population to serve in the tribal army when called to do so. Therefore the entire male population was divided into age groupings; the young ones were required to prove their manhood by fighting while the older married men were required to fight only in emergencies.

The Romans considered all Germanic tribes to be fearless warriors who preferred to fight in hand-to-hand combat. It was this that made them feared as enemies. Most Germanic cavalry forces preferred to avoid complicated manoeuvres, because they were usually not drilled in this. In practice, they often simply charged at a gallop straight at the enemy, which they sought to repeat by using spare horses if the enemy did not flee. Such a wild and impetuous cavalry attack was a frightful sight. Military men of the period expected that well trained and disciplined medium to heavily armed infantry forces would be able to withstand a cavalry attack of any kind when deployed in close order (e.g. close order or *testudo/foulkon* used against cavalry with shields rim-to-rim in width, or *testudo/foulkon* with shields rim-to-boss in width), but if the infantry force was deployed in open order, then elite forces would be required for the infantry to be able to deal with such an attack. Good examples of elite forces of this kind are the club/mace-bearers, whose specialty it was to engage cataphracts in open terrain. Green, poorly trained, and poorly disciplined infantry forces and the light infantry were not expected to be able to face such an attack. If the Romans possessed cavalry forces and they were similarly deployed in irregular order, then it was a question of morale whether the Romans could face such an attack. However, the units in close order gained moral ascendancy over those using irregular order because it made flight more difficult. Therefore it was probable that cavalry units in close order would prevail over the wild Germanic cavalry attack. However, this was always a matter of morale; many things could influence the outcome, and it was for this reason that it was important to outflank the enemy and prevent the enemy from outflanking one's own array.

All the Germanic groupings were adept in the use of the infantry phalanx/shield-wall and knew how to form a wedge for attack and circle/hollow square in defence. In addition to this, when the Germanic tribes migrated with their families they took with them wagons which were used to form wagon laagers – a specialty of the East Germanic tribes. At unit level the Germans knew how to use their infantries in close order, tortoise, and in open order so that they could deploy their forces in whatever types of terrain they faced. In short, the Germanic peoples used all of the principal combat formations and unit orders, which made them dangerous foes for the Romans.

The principal weaknesses of the Germans were: 1) poorly organized logistical services; 2) poor siege skills; 3) tribal levies were not as well trained as the Roman professionals; 4) the missile arm was relatively weak; 5) the Germanic peoples wore in general less armour than the Romans. However, there were exceptions. There were differences between the major groupings and tribes and confederacies within them. For example, the eastern and Scandinavian tribes preferred to use armour and helmets whenever the warriors or their masters possessed enough wealth to obtain them.

West Germanic Peoples

The West Germanic peoples relied primarily on their infantry to win their battles. Their standard combat formations were the infantry phalanx, used both offensively and defensively, and the wedge, used offensively. Cavalry was usually used either for raiding, for protection of infantry flanks, or for outflanking and for pursuit. Most footmen consisted of spearmen who were armed with only spears, swords and shields. All tribes possessed light infantry archers, javelineers and slingers, but their role was minimal in comparison with the spearmen. The Franks, however, differed from others in that their infantry specialized in the use of the pilum-style tactic in which footmen threw either their throwing axe, called *Francisca*, or their heavy harpoon-like javelin, after which they advanced into contact with the enemy. There were also tribes who specialized in the use of cavalry. These included the Iuthungi and Lentienses from the tribal confederacy of the Alamanni, and the Tencteri from the Frankish Confederacy. The Chatti, who may have belonged to the Frankish Confederacy and who were famous for their infantry, were considered just as good and well-organized as the Romans by Tacitus (*Germania* 30–31). The principal West Germanic threats to the Romans were the Franks and the Alamanni/Iuthungi. The following image depicting the Marcomanni from the Column of Marcus Aurelius also proves nicely that one should not underestimate the other Germanic peoples. All of them were able to put to the field large numbers of well-motivated warriors who were able to use all the basic infantry tactics.

The Marcomannic infantry phalanx/shield wall on Aurelius' Column demonstrates how disciplined the Germanic combat formations could be. Source: Bartoli 1673.

The West Germanic tribes whose lands bordered the North Sea or Atlantic Ocean posed another kind of threat to the Romans. Most of these nations possessed seaworthy ships resembling the later Viking style ships with crews ranging from ca. 12 to 60/70 men (up to at most perhaps 100–150 men). The evidence suggests that at this time the vast majority of the naval vessels belonged to the smallest category of about 12 to 16 men per boat. However, even the largest were too small to oppose the average Roman war galley. The only problem for the Romans was to guard the coastline against raids conducted by these pirates. They had five methods at their disposal: 1) placing guard towers, forts and cavalry forces along the coasts; 2) engaging the enemy; 3) paying the raiders not to invade; 4) forming alliances with tribes that could be used against the raiders; 5) raiding their territories to force the enemy to submit to their will. But it was next to impossible to guard every part of the coastline all the time.

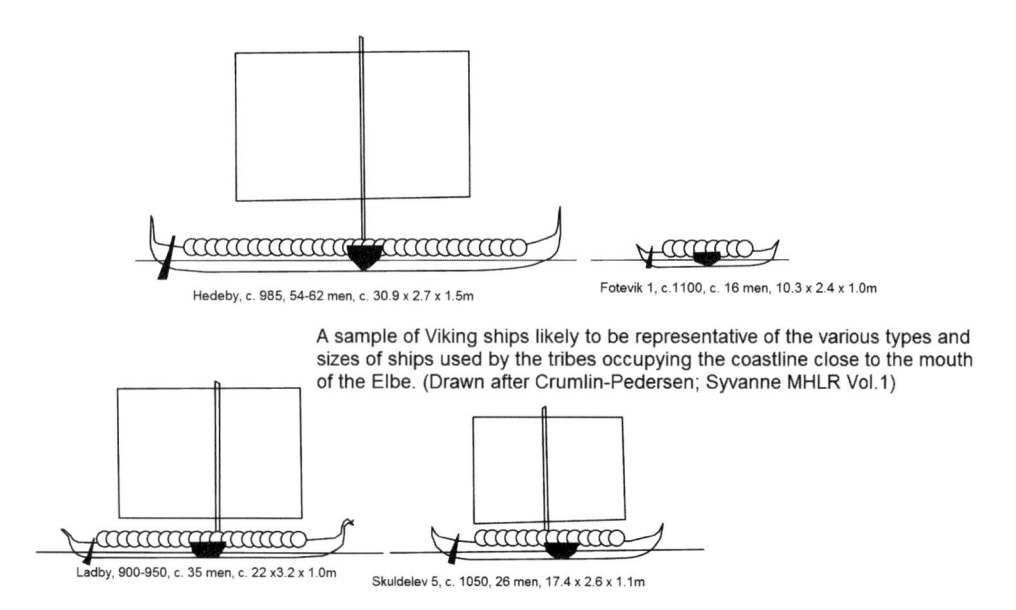

A sample of Viking ships likely to be representative of the various types and sizes of ships used by the tribes occupying the coastline close to the mouth of the Elbe. (Drawn after Crumlin-Pedersen; Syvanne MHLR Vol.1)

Hedeby, c. 985, 54-62 men, c. 30.9 x 2.7 x 1.5m

Fotevik 1, c.1100, c. 16 men, 10.3 x 2.4 x 1.0m

Ladby, 900-950, c. 35 men, c. 22 x3.2 x 1.0m

Skuldelev 5, c. 1050, 26 men, 17.4 x 2.6 x 1.1m

East Germanic Tribes

The principal difference between the West and East Germanic peoples was that the latter had adopted the use of the lancer/*contarii* cavalry and cataphracts from the Sarmatians, even to such an extent that their armies could consist solely of horsemen. There were some important tribal differences however. The Goths wore more armour than others, while the Heruls wore no armour at all; the rest were somewhere between these two extremes. The role of the infantry (spearmen and archers) among the East Germanic tribes was usually restricted to the holding of the wagon laager (*carrago*) or for the protection of the cavalry. The Sarmatian influence made itself felt also in the fact that their armies usually included mounted archers and multi-purpose troops able to use bows and mêlée weapons with equal ease. It was also typical for the East Germanic peoples to use wagon laagers/fortresses for protection.

The most powerful of the East Germanic tribes were the Goths who consisted of the Tervingi and Greuthungi and their sub-tribes or allies. The allies consisted at least of the Dacians/Carpi (mostly lightly equipped cavalry and infantry) and of the Sciri and Bastarnae (no details of their military methods is known for certain). The ancient sources claim that these and their allies (the Bastarnae, Sciri, Dacians) were able to invade Roman territory with 320,000 warriors in about 267–8; one part of the force marched on land while the other part of the force sailed in ships. In fact, the naval threat (Roman style ships provided by the Bosporans; Germanic style longships and boats; local vessels built by the peoples of the coastal regions of the Black Sea) posed by the Goths and Heruls was just as important in the 250s and 260s as the naval threat posed by the Franks and Saxons.

Gothic combat doctrine was a combination of Sarmatian and Germanic influences, but the principal tactic was the cavalry charge with lances which could be accompanied with archery, and withdrawals and feigned flights when these were thought necessary. The following diagram shows their typical battle formation on land.

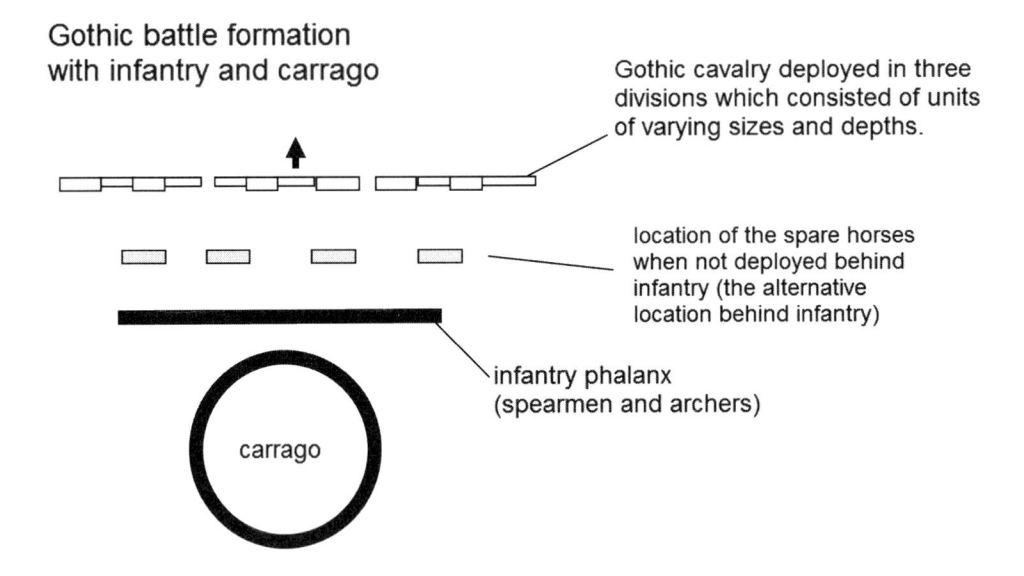

Gothic battle formation with infantry and carrago

Gothic cavalry deployed in three divisions which consisted of units of varying sizes and depths.

location of the spare horses when not deployed behind infantry (the alternative location behind infantry)

infantry phalanx (spearmen and archers)

carrago

3.3.2. The Sarmatians and Alans[17]

The Sarmatians and Alans were famed for their well-bred horses and for their cavalry charge with lancers (both *katafraktoi* and *kontoforoi*). The third century Alans were divided into three major groupings: 1) the western Alans who were subjects of the Goths; 2) the eastern Alans (the modern Ossetes) who inhabited the northern reaches of the Caucasus; 3) with Sarmatians the Alans formed the upper classes of the Bosporan kingdom (the eastern portion of the Crimea and some lands east of it).

The Romans faced the eastern Alans and their Sarmatian brethren only at such times as the 'Ossetes' or the armies of the Bosporan kingdom were allowed to pass through the Caucasus mountains either by the mountain tribes themselves or by their Georgian (the Dariel Pass/the Gates of the Alans) or Persian (the Derbend Pass) overlords. It is possible, even when the sources do not mention it, to deduce that there were units drawn from these peoples serving in the Persian armies. However, on the basis of the Georgian sources from ca. 270 onwards, some nomadic groups (possibly the eastern Alans and/or the Bosporans) appear to have fought against the Persians. This could only have happened with the tacit approval of the Alans and Bosporans, whose territories lay just west of the marching route taken by the nomads, which in turn may mean that the Romans had bribed them and the nomads in question.[18] The eastern Alans were primarily mounted archers while the Bosporians possessed Sarmato-Alan style multi-purpose lancers armed with both spears and bows, and Romano-Gothic-Greek style infantry.

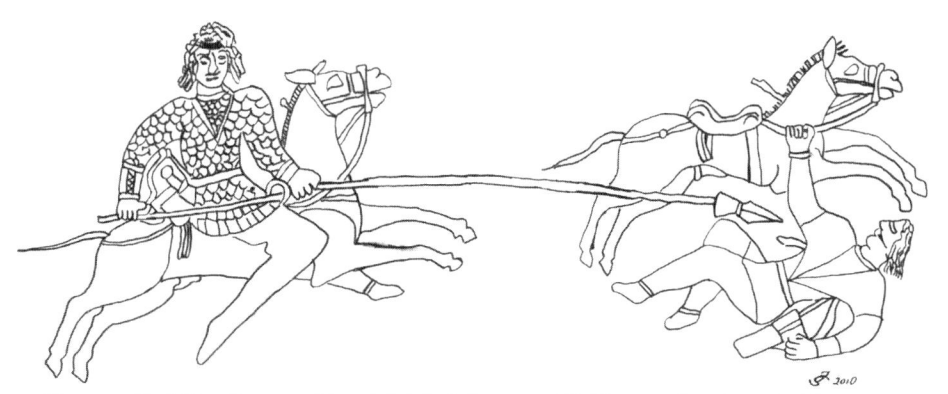

The so-called Kossika vase (Russia) 1-3rd Century AD (drawn after Brzezinski & Mielczarek, 15). It is usually thought that the men represent duelling Sarmato-Alans, but it is possible that the man on the left could be Goth and the man on the right an Alan. Note the fact that the *contus*-bearer had shot at least two arrows before he charged.

It was only the western Sarmatians and Alans that posed an actual threat to the Romans at this time. There were these in the Gothic armies, and there were the independent Sarmatian tribes between the Danube and Roman Dacia. For the former, see above. The independent Sarmatians followed their traditional fighting style: the vast majority of their forces consisted of cataphract cavalry or lancers both of which were able to use bows when necessary. The standard tactical formation was to divide a cavalry line into skirmishers and defenders such that every other division consisted of either skirmishers or defenders. Their standard tactic was to invade Roman territory when the Danube was frozen and then raid and pillage as far and wide as possible after which they fled as fast as they had arrived. The idea was to be back in their own territory before the Romans could mount a counter-attack. The principal problem for the Sarmatians was that they were no longer real nomads. Now they had dwellings and villages which the Romans could target in revenge, which meant that the Romans were able to force the Sarmatians to follow their will when the Romans did not face any other serious troubles to distract them.

3.3.3. The Sasanian Empire and its subjects

The Sasanian Empire was the most powerful of the enemies of Rome, but one should not underestimate the power of the Franks, Alamanni/Iuthungi and Goths either. The Persian realm, however, was the best organized and the only one of the enemies able to capture well fortified Roman cities. In 268 the Georgians, Armenians, Albanians and Arabs were either subjects or allies of Persia so that whenever the Romans fought against Persia they also faced these.

The military structure of the Sasanian Empire was based on the fourfold division of the Empire so that there was a *vitaxa/spahbed* (viceroy) in charge of the East, West, North and South. Persian society was feudal, kept together by strict social and religious control practised by the Zoroastrian Church. The King of Kings had to take into account the opinion of both the magnates and the Zoroastrian clergy. Sasanian military organization was hierarchial so that at the very top was the *Shahanshah* (King of Kings) himself whose second-in-command was the supreme commander of Iran, the *Iran-spahbadh*. Below them served the *vitaxae* and other generals and officers.

The Persian army (*spah*) consisted of bodyguard units (the best known of these were the 10,000 Immortals cavalry), cataphracts, light cavalry provided by mercenaries and tribal forces, elephants of the royal house, foot soldiers, navy, and logistical services. The cataphract cavalry provided by the mostly Parthian nobility formed the vast majority and the flower of the Sasanian army. The King of Kings possessed also his own units of bodyguards, which formed the crème de la crème of all forces. When not threatened by several major powers simultaneously the Sasanians had the capacity to put to the field cavalry armies of about 90,000 to 120,000 horsemen, in addition to which came the infantry and servants. However, this was not the case for most of the period after ca. 260 until ca. 285 because it was during those years that the Sasanians faced a series of enemies in the east which prevented them from placing this many men against the Romans. It is not known what number of men the Persians were able to put against the Romans during this time. Their subject nations – Armenians, Georgians and Albanians – certainly possessed the necessary numbers to bolster the Persian army to attain the maximum sizes mentioned above, but we do not possess any evidence for this. In fact, this inability of the Persians to mount any effective defence or offensives against the Romans rather suggests that the Persians feared to raise too many men from their allies during those years.

The Persian and Armenian cataphracts were the most fearsome cavalries of the era. Both of these possessed the ability to fight at long and short distances with their bows, spears and swords even if the Persian cavalry was better known for its preference to use prolonged periods of archery before engaging the enemy while the Armenians were better known for their immediate charge into contact with the enemy. The Persians delegated their infantry forces of spearmen, legionary style forces (the so-called *Murmillones*-style gladiators) and light infantry archers to secondary duties such as holding a camp or protection of cavalry (the infantry was placed behind) or for siege operations. Elite forces consisted always of cataphracts who were also dismounted for siege duties when necessary. The Georgians and Albanians usually contributed cataphract knights, but both of these nations could also provide cavalry with lighter equipment for the Persians. The Kushans and Sakas provided large numbers of mounted archers and small numbers of cataphracts. The Arabs, on the other hand, provided mainly lightly equipped cavalry lancers; these were fearsome warriors who rode camels during travel and then mounted horses for combat. Even if the Arabs preferred to raid and be gone before the enemy could mount a counter-attack, when the Arabs decided to fight, they were terrible foes to face because of their dogged determination to win.

The Sasanians were the most sophisticated of the enemies the Romans ever faced. They produced works of military theory to ensure the dissemination of military knowledge, which were copied by the Muslims later. The Sasanians combined ancient Indo-Persian military practices with Parthian nomadic cavalry tactics and Romano-Greek infantry tactics. Standard combat tactics was to use cavalry in two lines each of which consisted of outer left, left, centre, right, and outer right. If infantry accompanied the army, it was usually placed behind these in front of a fortified marching camp. Standard combat tactics were: 1) to encircle the enemy with a crescent array; 2) to encircle the enemy on one flank; 3) to place the battle formation on high ground to put the enemy under constant archery bombardment. The Persians usually closed in with the enemy only when it had been weakened enough with a prolonged archery barrage. The attack with the centre (convex array when the enemy outnumbered the Persians) and the defensive circle (cavalry dismounted or inside infantry circle) were used only in extreme emergencies.

3.4. The Assassination of Gallienus (August/September AD 268)[19]

When Gallienus had advanced against the invading barbarian hordes in the Balkans in 267, he had left Aureolus in charge of the defence of Italy, south of Gaul and Raetia, against the usurper Postumus (the emperor of the so-called Gallic Empire). Aureolus had joined ranks with Postumus in 268 while Gallienus was fighting against the Goths and Heruls in the Balkans with the result that Gallienus left Marcianus in charge of the war in the Balkans while he hastened back to Italy. Gallienus inflicted a defeat on Aureolus at the battle of Pontirolo and forced Aureolus inside the city of Milan which Gallienus then proceeded to besiege. It was then that the highest ranking military officers accompanying Gallienus formed a plot to kill him, possibly because he had abandoned the Balkans, the homeland of most of the officers, to the barbarian hordes so that he could deal with the rebel – a rebel whom Gallienus had pardoned earlier.

The three basic versions of the assassination of Gallienus in the sources are: 1) Claudius was unaware of the plot to kill Gallienus and was appointed by him to be his successor before his death; 2) Aureolus used a ruse and had a falsified letter dropped outside the walls of Milan, which indicated that Gallienus intended to execute certain officers; 3) Claudius was the man behind the assassination. The sources are also divided in their claims of how the murder was committed. The two basic variants are: 1) Gallienus was killed in his tent; 2) Gallienus was lured away from his tent and then killed.

Aurelius Victor (33.21) claims that Aurelian's (in the variant text 'Herculianus', who is presumably Heraclianus) participation in the plot resulted from a ruse of Aureolus. Aureolus had falsified in the name of Gallienus a list of *duces* and tribunes that he intended to execute, which he then threw away from the wall secretly so that the besiegers obtained it. It was then thanks to this that Aurelian formed the plan for the assassination of Gallienus, which the other men accepted because Aurelian was highly respected by the soldiers. Aurelian then sent his cavalry to perform a fake attack against Gallienus's lines in the middle of the night with the result that Aurelian's other henchmen were able to lead Gallienus out of his tent to be assassinated by one unknown assassin who threw the spear that delivered the mortal wound. When Gallienus realized that the wound was fatal, he dispatched the imperial insignia to Claudius.

The principal problem with this account is the fact that the alternate reading for the chief conspirator is Herculianus, probably a misreading of Heraclianus, who is known to have been one of the chief plotters. Therefore the role of Aurelian is not absolutely certain on the basis of this account. However, since we know that Aurelian and Gallienus were polar opposites in character (see e.g. *HA Aurel.* 6, 7, 8, 36, 39, 46, 49 with Lactantius 6), it is quite likely that Aurelian was involved in the plot at some level. Aurelian was a lowly-born conservative person with very black and white views of what was acceptable, while Gallienus was an upper class libertarian. It is unlikely to be a coincidence that Aurelian punished adultery in all forms both as officer and emperor (*Aurel.* 7.3–4, 9.4–5) while Gallienus was adulterous in public view; and it is unlikely to be a coincidence that as emperor Aurelian forbade the keeping of free-born women as concubines as Gallienus had done with Pipa (*HA Aurel.* 49.8). Aurelian was also hostile towards Christianity while Gallienus was not (Eusebius *EH* 7.30.20ff.; Lactantius 6). In sum, it is highly likely that Aurelian was either the *primus motor* behind the plot or at least a very willing participant in it.

The *Historia Augusta* (*Gall.* 14) in its turn has preserved us the version according to which the principal plotters against Gallienus were the Praetorian prefect Heraclianus and Marcianus, and that these two men used the commander of the Dalmatian cavalry, Ceronius/Cecropius, to carry out the assassination. According to this version, it was Marcianus and Cecropius who sent the word to Gallienus that Aureolus had attacked. Gallienus then duly gathered his soldiers and advanced against the imaginary foe only to be slain by the assassins, so that the man who actually killed Gallienus with the spear was Cecropius. The reaction of the soldiers was hostile because they loved Gallienus, but Marcianus bribed the men to be silent and a council of officers chose Claudius as emperor. This version has at least one thing which is likely to be incorrect, namely the participation of Marcianus in the plot, because he had been left in charge of the operations in the Balkans. One possible way to reconcile this version is to think that in this case the *Augustan History* has purposefully hidden the role of either Claudius or Aurelian behind the name of Marcianus. It is clear that whoever this man was, he had a decisive role in the rise of Claudius on the throne, because it was thanks to his bribery of the men that this was possible. The likeliest candidates are actually Heraclianus as Praetorian Prefect so that the *Historia Augusta* has confused Marcianus and Heraclianus, or Aurelian because he was loved by the rank-and-file.

The most obvious point in the above accounts is the absence of the name Claudius from the list of conspirators. The three possible explanations for this are: firstly, the Latin texts follow the senatorial line which was very favourable towards Claudius; secondly, the sources sought to flatter the House of Constantine the Great, which claimed Claudius as its ancestor; thirdly, Claudius was indeed not party to the plot.

The Greek sources give us alternative versions, which also sometimes include the name of Claudius among the plotters. According to the version preserved by Zonaras (12.25) and by the most commonly accepted reading of Aurelius Victor (33.21ff.), Aurelian was one of the chief conspirators. Zonaras states that the mighty men of the state wanted to kill Gallienus with the help of Aurelian (Aurelianus), the commander of horsemen. The mighty men could be interpreted to include Claudius, but this is not stated clearly. Aurelian then sent horsemen (i.e. Ceronius/Cecropius, the commander of the Dalmatian cavalry, who according to the *HA Gall.* 14 was the killer of Gallienus) to lure Gallienus away from his bodyguards by claiming that Aureolus had attacked. When Gallienus then mounted his horse and galloped away, the horsemen (i.e. Cecropius) killed Gallienus. John of Antioch (f.232/f.152.3) also claims that the man who then killed Gallienus was the commander of the Dalmatian cavalry, but he claims that the murder took place at a dinner in which Claudius was present.

Zosimus (1.40–41) claims that the praetorian prefect Heraclianus and Claudius were the men who plotted to kill Gallienus. These men then gave the task to the commander of the Dalmatian cavalry (i.e. Cecropius). He informed Gallienus, who was at dinner, that Aureolus had attacked. Gallienus then armed himself, mounted his horse, and rode off without waiting for his bodyguards, with the result that the commander of the Dalmatian cavalry was able to kill him.

According to the second version preserved by Zonaras, the plotters were Heraclianus and Claudius. This version, however, claims that Gallienus was asleep at the time and was woken up with the news that Aureolus was attacking. When Gallienus jumped off the bed Heraclianus struck him. John of Antioch (f.232/f.152.3) in his turn states, as noted previously, that Gallienus was killed at dinner by the commander of the Dalmatian cavalry Heraclianus while Claudius was present. It is therefore clear that John's version combines two different versions and men in the same account: commander of the Dalmatian cavalry Cecropius has become commander of the Dalmatian cavalry Heraclianus (in truth praetorian prefect). It is probable that this results from careless reading of the sources.

Synopsis Chronike (p.38) names as conspirators Heraclianus and Claudius, and states that it was Heraclianus who awoke Gallienus and claimed that Aureolus was attacking, and then killed Gallienus when he was attempting to find his arms.

In sum, while the Latin sources claim that Claudius was innocent of the murder, most of the Greek sources claim that the chief plotters were Claudius and Heraclianus, the two highest ranking subordinates of Gallienus. The only exception among the Greek sources is Zonaras who also includes the variant version which adds Aurelian to the list of plotters. The commander of the Dalmatian cavalry is not named, but we know his name from the Latin sources. If Aurelian was the commander of all cavalry forces at this time, as is very likely, then it is clear that he was the superior of Cecropius, as stated by Cizek, which in its turn makes it more than likely that Aurelian was also involved in the plot. It is indeed probable that he faked the cavalry attack against Gallienus's forces while his accomplice Cecropius informed the emperor.

The way in which the murder was committed is open to question. The evidence does not allow us to definitely conclude whether Gallienus was killed in his tent or whether he was killed while galloping against the imaginary enemy.

The reason for the murder is also not known with certainty. It is possible that it resulted from a ruse and that it was because of this that Aurelian in particular felt intense hatred towards Aureolus (see later) or that the assassination resulted from the abandonment of the war against the barbarians in favour of dealing with rebel Aureolus as implied by Zonaras's text (2.26) or that it was simply the result of personal ambition by the key plotters.

What is also notable is the absence of the name of Probus from the list of conspirators. This could have resulted from the fact that he had remained behind in the Balkans with Marcianus, or, if he had accompanied Gallienus to Italy, that he was known for his loyalty and was therefore not included in the plot; or that he was simply not important enough either to be included in the plot or named by the sources at the time.

Chapter Four

The Reign of Claudius II 'Gothicus' in 268–270[1]

Coin of Claudius II
(source: Cohen)

The reign of Claudius II is among the most difficult to reconstruct, because the reliability of the sources is suspect thanks to the fact that he was claimed to be a relative or ancestor of Constantius and Constantine the Great. It is thanks to this that many of the successful campaigns that took place under Gallienus have been placed during Claudius's reign while his failures are placed under Gallienus's. Most modern historians think that the connection between Constantius and Claudius was fabricated to create an illustrious ancestor for the emperor. Furthermore, the sources also give several versions of the family tree of Constantius Chlorus/Constantine the Great and Claudius. Constantius and therefore Constantine the Great either descended from Claudius or from his brother. However, I agree with those who, like Bray (321–4), suspect that there must have been at least a germ of truth in the claim. The reason for this is that the emperor Julian, who was himself a descendant of Constantius, is believed to be Claudius's descendant (Julian, *Oration/Panegyric* 1.6.D; *Oration* 2.51.C-D).[2]

4.1. The Siege of Milan and the Death of Aureolus in 268 or 268–9

At the time Claudius assumed power the barbarians still ravaged the Balkans and the Aegean Sea, the Gallic Empire was still in existence, Palmyra was still in the hands of Zenobia, and Aureolus was still holed up in Milan. Therefore the assassination of Gallienus did not change the military reality, but it did create some new problems. Claudius needed to secure his own position among the army and the Senate. The first of these had already been done by some unknown officer who had bribed the soldiers to accept Claudius as emperor. This would naturally have been the donative that was given to the troops when the new emperor was nominated. The second of the problems facing

Claudius was that the soldiers did not accept the killing of the relatives of Gallienus which was taking place in Rome and elsewhere.

We are actually in the dark as regards the fate of Gallienus's relatives, because the sources give us different versions of what happened. It is likely that at least Gallienus's brother Valerian (Valerianus) was killed in the camp immediately after Gallienus. The other persons who are claimed to have been killed immediately are the sons of Gallienus. Aurelius Victor claims that the Roman population and senators were elated when they learnt of the death of Gallienus and decreed that Gallienus's relatives and friends were to be thrown down the Gemonian stairs. However, he also claims that after the capture of Milan Claudius gave the order to spare those who had survived this purge, because the army had demanded it. The implication is that Claudius, who had sought recognition from the Senate with a letter,[3] was the man who had ordered the purge but was forced to cancel it when the soldiers were no longer forced to obey commands thanks to the fact that Aureolus and his soldiers were no longer a threat. Aurelius Victor's obvious intent was to demonstrate that Claudius was merciful, but when it is placed in context, as I have done here, it becomes clear that Claudius was the man behind the butchery. This proves that the soldiers had not just wanted to extort as much money as possible from the new emperor with their actions, but that they had really loved their emperor Gallienus and were therefore prepared to threaten the new emperor at the first opportunity they got, which was right after the siege of Milan had ended. Claudius was forced to placate the soldiers, so he ordered the Senate to put a stop to the killing. On top of this, he forced the Senate to declare Gallienus a god.

Trebellius Pollio (*HA, Gall.* 19.8) claims that there were still descendants/relatives of Gallienus surviving in Rome at the time of his writing. This implies that the siege of Milan cannot have lasted long because it is otherwise difficult to see how these descendants/relatives could have survived the massacre, unless of course they fled from the city immediately. The latter alternative receives support from the readiness of Aureolus to surrender which could be the result of the problems that the Gallic Empire faced or the result of new foreign invasions that would have required the Romans to cooperate. In short, it is impossible to know whether the siege was short and ended in 268, or whether it was longer and lasted until 269.[4]

There are several versions of how the siege of Milan came to an end. The only common denominators are that Aureolus negotiated his terms of surrender with Claudius, and that Aureolus was killed in the end. The Greek sources state that Aureolus negotiated with Claudius and then surrendered to him, but the latter's bodyguard killed him. The *Historia Augusta* (Aureolus, Claud., Aur.) gives us several versions: Aureolus asked terms from Claudius, but Claudius stated that Aureolus should have asked them from Gallienus, after which they fought a battle in which Aureolus was killed by his own men; Claudius fought a battle with Aureolus and killed him at the battle of Pontirolo; Aurelian killed Aureolus against the wishes of Claudius after Aureolus had surrendered; Aureolus was killed after the surrender by Aurelian because Claudius had ordered it; Aurelian killed Aureolus only after the death of Claudius. As can be seen, the name of Aurelian is present in several of these alternatives.

Let us now then analyze the different versions for their probability. It is possible that there were two separate battles of Pontirolo, but it is also possible that this is just another instance in which the successes of Gallienus are placed to have occured under Claudius. This is obviously only partially false because it is clear that Claudius would also have been present at the battle of Pontirolo that took place under Gallienus. The same has happened with the Gothic war. Claudius obtained the title 'Gothicus' because of the victories he achieved as a general of Gallienus, which were then transferred by the sources to have taken place during his reign.[5]

Let us now turn to the role of Aurelian in these events. On the basis of the above it is clear that Aurelian remained in Italy as long as the siege of Milan lasted, and if there was a second battle of Pontirolo it is probable that he participated in it. If Aurelian killed Aureolus against the will of Claudius, this implies that Aurelian probably had personal reasons for hating Aureolus. The three likeliest reasons for such a hatred would be: Claudius may have convinced Aurelian that the death of Gallienus would have been caused by Aureolus's actions (ruse or assassins); Aureolus had indeed fooled Aurelian with the stratagem given above; the sources paint Aurelian as a stern conservatively minded person who saw things in terms of black and white with the implication that it is possible that Aurelian just wanted to punish Aureolus for his disloyalty. If Claudius had ordered Aurelian or his bodyguard to kill Aureolus, the implication is that Claudius considered Aurelian to be a man who could be trusted with delicate missions. If the killing of Aureolus took place only after Aurelian had become emperor, the implication is that Aurelian was probably not a party to the plot to kill Gallienus and that he exacted vengeance on all those implicated in the murder of Gallienus when this became possible, or that he just wanted to punish all those who had betrayed their rulers. It is impossible to know which of these is true, if any.

In the meantime, very significant events had taken place in Gaul. Postumus had just defeated Germanic invaders when Vipius Cornelius Laelianus (Lollianus of the *HA*) revolted against Postumus in about 268. Postumus had reacted swiftly and had put Laelianus under siege at Mainz, where Laelianus was killed by his own soldiers (*HA TR.* 5.3) probably also in 268 or at the latest in the spring of 269. The soldiers who had suffered the hardships of the siege wanted to pillage the city of Mainz, but Postumus forbade this, presumably because Mainz was a Roman city. This was a mistake that cost him his life. The soldiers killed him. The date usually given by historians for this is the year 268, but it is possible that it took place only later in 269 because, according to the *Epitome* 34.2–3, Victorinus began his rule at about the same time as Claudius defeated the Alamanni near Lake Garda (Benacus), which must have happened in 269. A general called Marius then usurped power and it is quite possible that he had been the man behind the murder of Postumus. However, it is also possible that Marius was used as a patsy for the murders of Postumus and Laelianus by Victorinus and by his mother Victoria/Vitruvia because the *Historia Augusta* (*Tr.* 5.3) claims that Victoria was behind the enthronement of Marius and Tetricus. Whatever the truth, Marius had had a phenomenal career behind him. Marius had begun as a blacksmith and had then risen to the position of *dux* before being enthroned as emperor. This, however, was not accepted by M. Piavonius/Piaonius Victorinus, who, according to the *Historia Augusta*, was the co-ruler with Postumus. He duly organized the assassination of Marius (after he had ruled for only two days or three days or twelve weeks depending on the source). According to the *Historia Augusta* and Aurelius Victor, the power behind Victorinus was actually his mother Victoria/Vitruvia so it is possible that it was she who orchestrated the whole sequence of events. Victorinus in his turn stayed in power for two years (268–70 or 269–71), but was then killed in a conspiracy organized by *actuarius* (quartermaster) Attianus. The reason for the killing was that, although a capable general, Victorinus was a man unable to keep the loyalty of his men because he either seduced or raped many women and when he then raped the wife of Attianus, Attianus exacted his own sweet revenge against the violator of his wife. According to Aurelius Victor, it was because of the power of the quartermasters over the soldiers that Attianus was able to incite the soldiers to kill their emperor. Victoria/Vitruvia was one of the remarkable figures of the era and she used her influence and money to convince the soldiers to choose *praeses Aquitaniae* C. Pius Esuvius Tetricus as the next emperor in 270 or 271. Tetricus, however, rewarded her support by having her murdered. He did not want to be in her debt and to rely on her support. It is possible that this murder worsened his relationship with the soldiers.[6]

4.2. Claudius II overextends his hand: the Wars in the Balkans, Gaul and East, in ca. 268–9

After the siege of Milan ended, Claudius II was finally free to visit Rome to secure the support of the Senate with a personal appearance.[7] The visit was a great success. Claudius managed to gain the support of important power brokers in the city. These men included Aspanius Paternus, a sort of *éminence grise* who had been consul in 267–8 and was therefore an important figure in Gallienus's Rome. His influence ensured a relatively smooth transition of power. Now Claudius had the backing of both, the former supporters of Gallienus and his enemies. Claudius did not want to become too dependent upon the support of one party alone; he might use these two against each other in a game of power. Cladius was not a member of the Roman aristocracy and it was because of this that he needed their support more than Gallienus had.[8]

Claudius may have appointed Aurelian as commander of all cavalry forces (presumably *comes domesticorum equitum* or *magister equitum*) or he was just kept in the same office. Trebellius Pollio also claims that Aurelian was given the command of the *legio X*, which he claimed to signify that the commander was destined to become an emperor, in other words the intended successor. This *legio X* is probably not one of the known tenth legions, but a new formation. I have speculated that it had been created under Gallienus or before him, and that it was either the *Ioviani* or *Herculiani* known from the reigns of Diocletian and Maximian. The problematic part of this is that before the murder of Gallienus, Claudius had been *tribunus et magister officiorum* who would have been the superior of the *comites* commanding the *protectores*, and if Aurelian was only *comes domesticorum equitum* (or its equivalent) why had he been given command of the *legio X* and who was the new *tribunus et magister officiorum* if such was appointed? The giving of command of the *legio X* would imply that Aurelian was nominated as *tribunus et magister officiorum* or *comes domesticorum peditum* (commander of domestic infantry). However, it is also possible that Claudius did not nominate any man as *tribunus et magister officiorum* even if it is probable that he did appoint someone in charge of the infantry *protectores*. If Claudius appointed someone as *tribunus et magister officiorum*, the likeliest candidate would be the *praefectus praetorio* Heraclianus, but, as said, none of this is known with any certainty. In fact it is entirely plausible that Claudius would have also given the *praefectus praetorio* command over the commanders of the *protectores* without giving him the title that he had had.

Whatever his official title, Aurelian was dispatched back to the Balkans to take charge of operations there, with command of all of the armies posted in Thrace and Illyricum. This means that Claudius replaced Marcianus with Aurelian, the probable reason for the sacking being that Marcianus had not been party to the plot to kill Gallienus.[9]

The *Historia Augusta* (TR. 29.12, 33) has preserved us a problematic account of an otherwise unknown usurper – Censorinus – for the reign of Claudius. Trebellius Pollio claims that Censorinus was a soldier and a senator who had in him old-time dignity. He also claims that Censorinus was living on his own estates, possibly in Bologne where he was buried, at the time he was proclaimed emperor. This implies that Censurinus was in Italy at the time of his usurpation and that he probably usurped power in Rome. Pollio asserts that the usurpation resulted from a witticism of a jester who called him Claudius because he was lame in one foot as a result of a wound received in the Persian War under Valerian (*claudus* = lame).[10]

According to the *Historia Augusta*, Censorinus then made the serious mistake of trying to instill discipline among the soldiers (the Praetorians?) with severity. The result was the soldiers killed him. If there is any truth to this account, the implication is that the succession from Gallienus to Claudius was not quite as smooth as usually claimed. The likeliest date for the usurpation would be the immediate aftermath of the murder of Gallienus when Claudius was still preoccupied with the siege of Milan. This also implies that the Senate did not stand as united behind the real Claudius as the sources claim, which would indeed have made it necessary for the real Claudius II to proceed to Rome to secure his own position after the siege of Milan had ended, if the usurpation indeed took place early in his reign. The other possible dates for the usurpation attempt would be the time when Claudius was preoccupied with the war against the Alamanni/Iuthungi in 269, or when he had advanced to the Balkans in 270.[11]

According to the possibly fictitious letter from Claudius to Aurelian in the *Historia Augusta*, Claudius censured Aurelian for his lack of bold action against the Goths at some unknown point in time during his reign. Claudius hastened Aurelian on and asked why he was delaying in a situation in which the Goths were ravaging Haemimontum and Europe. Claudius ordered Aurelian to drive the Goths away from Thrace regardless of the cost. The letter also informed Aurelian that Claudius would send his brother Quintillus with reinforcements to assist him. As far as we know, he did not then send Quintillus possibly because he and his men were needed against the Iuthungi and Alamanni in 269–70, or because Claudius came to the conclusion that it was safer for him to lead the men to the Balkans in person rather than risk the possibility that Aurelian could tamper with the loyalty of the men when they were led by Quintillus.[12]

The contents of the letter ring true. The forces ravaging Haemimontum and Europe can be idenfied with the Goths besieging the cities of Nicopolis ad Istrum and Anchialus. True to its tendency to whitewash the events of the reign of Claudius, the *Historia Augusta* (*Claud*. 12) claims that it was thanks to the valour of the provincials that the Goths failed to seize Anchialus and Nicopolis when they retreated northwards. Fortunately we possess evidence from the more reliable Ammianus (31.5.16) for these events. He states that the barbarians sacked both Anchialus and Nicopolis. He adds that it was only after the death of Claudius that Aurelian drove the Goths out of Roman territory. Sextus Aurelius Victor (34.2–6) states basically the same by claiming that Claudius II consulted the Sibylline Books which stated that the first man of the Empire was to sacrifice himself to achieve a victory over the Goths, and that it was only after Claudius II had sacrificed himself like the Decii that the Goths were defeated and driven out of the Empire with no loss in Roman soldiers. Therefore it is clear that neither the locals nor Aurelian could defend Nicopolis and Anchialus. However, it is also possible that the sacking actually took place only after the death of Claudius in which case it would have resulted from the transferral of troops to the west by Aurelian who was trying to secure the throne for himself. The above-mentioned letter of Claudius to Aurelian in which Claudius censured Aurelian for lack of boldness, however, would suggest otherwise. And why was this so? Aurelian is known to be among the greatest military leaders Rome ever produced. The letter provides the answer. Aurelian did not possess enough men to defend the cities and it was because of this that Claudius promised to send reinforcements under Quintillus. And why did Aurelian have too few men for the task? The reason is that Claudius had overextended his resources by dividing his armies among too many fronts. Aurelius Victor's statement that the Goths were driven out of the Roman Empire with no loss in men explains how the war progressed after the death of Claudius II. Aurelian left the scene of combat and marched west to usurp power, and it was then that the Goths evacuated Roman territory simply by retreating northwards.

The sources prove that Claudius: 1) dispatched *praefectus vigilum* Julius Placidianus to lead an invasion of Narbonensis in 269; 2) gave Tenagino Probus the task of clearing the Aegean Sea of the pirates (Heruls, Goths and others) in 269; 3) dispatched Heraclianus against the Persians also in about 269 (see below). As if this was not enough, Claudius was himself tied in Italy because the Iuthungi and Alamanni launched massive invasions of Raetia and Italy also in 269. The probable reason for this invasion was the power vacuum left as a result of the dispatching of forces to Gaul under Placidianus, the Balkans under Aurelian, and against the Persians under Heraclianus. The situation was also aggravated by Claudius's other mistakes. The most important of these is that Claudius seems to have stopped the payment of subsidies to the Iuthungi which resulted in invasions of Italy and Raetia.[13] The most costly of the mistakes, however, was the one that led to the break-up of the relationship between Claudius and Zenobia. This means that the forces that Aurelian would have needed for the mopping up of the remaining pockets of Gothic forces in the Balkans just were not there. In addition to this, it is quite clear that he would have been forced to give some of his forces to Heraclianus when he marched through the Balkans to fight against the Persians with the result that the Goths were able to break through the cordon of Roman troops as discussed above.

Julius Placidianus's campaign, however, was a success. He was able to exploit the chaotic situation of the Gallic Empire. On the basis of the inscription at Gratianopolis (Gallia Narbonensis), Placidianus's forces consisted of both *vexillationes* and *equites* (Saxer 57–8). It is probable that in this case we should take *vexillationes* in its traditional sense to mean infantry detachments because the separate use of the word *equites* implies this. Placidianus was able to capture Narbonensis while the Spanish provinces also declared their loyalty to the new emperor.[14] Flavius Vopiscus (*HA FSPB* 9.5) claims that Saturninus, the future rebel against Probus, recovered the provinces of Spain for Rome. This would be easy to dismiss because of the source, but I see no reason to do so. Therefore, my suggestion is that once Placidianus had recovered Narbonensis, he dispatched Saturninus with some forces to recover Spain, while he himself protected the south of Gaul against Victorinus. The other possibility is that Saturninus invaded Spain from North Africa while Placidianus invaded Narbonensis, because Saturninus is claimed to have recovered Africa from the Moors. Saturninus's recovery of the provinces of Gaul is likely to mean the campaign of Aurelian in 274 rather than the campaign of Placidianus, but this cannot entirely be ruled out either. On the basis of the praise that the sources give for the military talents of the new Gallic Emperor Victorinus, it is probable that he managed to stabilize the situation after the initial losses.[15] It was partly because of these successes that when Autun revolted next year, they received no support from Claudius. Other reasons would obviously have been the troubles Claudius was facing elsewhere, the most important of which was the Iuthungi invasion and the fact that the Goths and their allies were still on the loose in the Balkans. It was then that the Palmyrenes revolted against Claudius.

4.3. The Rise of Palmyra in 268–70

The rise of Palmyra into a major power took place under Odaenathus during the reign of Gallienus. It was largely thanks to three developments. When Odaenathus had sought a peace from Shapur I, the latter had haughtily and foolishly decided to overlook his requests. Secondly, when Shapur I had defeated and captured Valerian, Odaenathus had managed to inflict a series of defeats on the Persians with the result that Gallienus rewarded Odaenathus with the title *dux Romanorum*. When the Macriani then revolted against Gallienus, it was Odaenathus who crushed their forces in the east, which earned him the gratitude of Gallienus who then gave Odaenathus the title *corrector totius Orientis*. This gave Odaenathus control over most of the Roman forces of the east for use against the Persians and others who could threaten Gallienus.[16]

Trebellius Pollio (*HA*, *Gallienus* 13.4–5) claims that the break-up in the relationship between Rome and Palmyra took place already under Gallienus after the murder of Odaenathus when Zenobia had become the ruler of Palmyra. He also claims that it was after the death of Odaenathus in about 267 that Gallienus finally gathered an army under the Praetorian Prefect Heraclianus against the Persians to exact vengeance on them for their treatment of his father Valerian, but then claims that the Palmyrenes destroyed this army in its entirety. The extant evidence proves otherwise. Coins prove that Zenobia continued to recognize Gallienus as emperor and that the break-up in relations took place only under Claudius. Furthermore, it is well known that the Praetorian Prefect Heraclianus was with Gallienus in 268 because he was one of the principal plotters against him. This means, as has already been suggested by Potter (p.266), that it is very probable that Heraclianus had actually been dispatched by Claudius in about 269 against the Persians, because the sources are in the habit of trying to place all Roman failures in the reign of Gallienus in their effort to exonerate Constantine the Great's assumed ancestor of all blame.[17] The wording and other information in the *Historia Augusta* suggests that Zenobia betrayed the Romans in the midst of their campaign against the Persians. It is probable that we should connect the negotiations between Zenobia and the Persians mentioned by the same source with this very same event. Zenobia had clearly come to the conclusion that a peace and alliance with Persia was preferable to being a subject of Claudius. This begs the question why? My educated guess is that Claudius had made the mistake of demoting Zenobia by placing her under Heraclianus in a situation in which Gallienus had accepted Zenobia as successor of her husband's position.

In short, the thing that pushed Zenobia into revolt was most likely Heraclianus's real mission, which was to place the Palmyrenes under secure Roman control, but in light of Zenobia's actions in the desert regions it is probable that she had been planning to revolt from the beginning of her rule. However, it is possible that Heraclianus had some successes against the Persians before Zenobia crushed him, because one inscription gives Claudius the title *Parthicus Maximus*. The coins and other evidence places the beginning of the revolt of Zenobia to the spring of 270 with the implication that Heraclianus's campaign against the Persians must have taken place either in 269 or in the winter of 269/70. The principal evidence for this conclusion is that the mint at Antioch was closed in the spring of 270, which dates the beginning of Zenobia's revolt against Claudius to the spring of 270. The mint resumed its minting during the winter of 270/1 by issuing coins with the joint names of Vaballathus and Aurelianus. The apparent purpose was to declare loyalty to the new emperor Aurelian and to attempt to find reconciliation between the two parties.[18]

Therefore, the evidence suggests that Zenobia took full control of Antioch and Syria during the spring of 270. It is likely that she launched an invasion of Asia Minor approximately at the same time. The Palmyrenes decisively conquered the territory up to Galatia and Ancyra, but the Bithynians overthrew the Palmyrenes when they learnt of the rise of Aurelian on the throne. The Palmyrenes invaded Arabia approximately at the same time. The Palmyrenes were commanded by the general Zabdas (Zaba, Saba). Trassus, the *dux* of Arabia, had under him at least the local *legio III Cyrenaica* and some other local troops. The latter category may also have included legions (at least *X Fretensis* at Jerusalem)[19] and other forces posted in Palestine/Judaea, but it is also possible that these surrendered without a fight or withdrew to Egypt. The case for the *legio III Gallica* which was garrisoned at Damascus is also uncertain. It is possible that it sided with the Palmyrenes, but it is also possible that it had surrendered without a fight or had withdrawn south to Bostra. The Romans were undoubtedly outnumbered but Trassus still confronted the invaders near his provincial capital Bostra. Unsurprisingly, Trassus was defeated and killed in action. Zabdas pillaged Bostra and advanced into the Jordan valley. Now that Zabdas had secured Arabia, Palestine and Judaea, he was ready to advance into Egypt.[20]

4.4. The Palmyran Enemy

Palmyra was a rich city state – the most important commercial hub of the east largely thanks to its own efforts in the promotion of trade through its facilities. One modern estimate for the size of the population of the city is 150–200,000, but I would not preclude the possibility that it could have housed even more inhabitants. Despite being an oasis, Palmyra was entirely reliant on trade because the city possessed a far larger population than the oasis was able to support. This fact dominated its politics. Its leaders wanted to protect their position as the foremost trading centre of the east, through which went a significant amount of international trade. Most of this trade was in the form of silk, spices and other luxury items. The rulers, the city administrators and the merchant and banking houses of the city all sought to facilitate the transport of goods, either by providing transport and financial services or simply by renting animals or other necessary things for others. The persons with the title *synodiarchês* (possibly the same as *archemporos*) were probably the central figures in commercial transactions. They were rich landowners who provided transport animals, raised finances for a group of merchants making up a caravan, and then organized, led and protected the caravan to and from its destination. To be able to do this, they also possessed personal military retinues that specialized in caravan protection. The Palmyran state in its turn maintained military posts along the trade routes. The Palmyran merchant houses had colonies in the most important trading centres of Persia, Mesopotamia and Egypt. The state of war between Rome and Persia endangered this traffic, because the Persians were in a position to prevent access to Mesopotamia, Syria, Asia Minor, the Persian Gulf and Arabian Peninsula. When Zenobia broke up with Rome and concluded peace with Persia, she endangered the other trade route running from the Indian Ocean to the Red Sea, from there through Trajan's Canal up to the Nile, and from there to the Mediterranean. Therefore it is not surprising that it became her goal to conquer Egypt immediately after she had revolted from Rome. It would give Zenobia complete control over all traffic from the east to the Mediterranean.[21] However, in my opinion it is probable that the actual conquest of Egypt was done on behalf of Aurelian, even if it is still likely that it had been in Zenobia's mind from the beginning, of which the best proof is her conquest of Arabia.

After the death of Odaenathus, the official head of the state of Palmyra was Vaballathus, but in practice power was in the hands of his mother Zenobia. As successor of his father, Vaballathus held officially the titles of King of Kings as an insult to the Persians, *dux Romanorum* and *corrector totius orientis*, the latter two of which had been granted to Odaenathus by Gallienus as a reward for his loyalty to him. However, as we have already seen, it is more than likely that Claudius II took away these titles when he dispatched Heraclianus with an army to take charge of the war against Persia.[22] Zenobia was unwilling to give up the position that her husband had achieved, and revolted, the result being the destruction of Heraclianus's army, after which followed the conquests of most of Asia Minor together with Arabia and that of Egypt for Aurelian.

When she revolted, Zenobia's principal aim appears to have been to create a true Palmyran Empire which controlled all trade between East and West. In fact, her diplomatic efforts appear to have been quite successful because the *Historia Augusta* names among her supporters the Persians, Armenians, Iberians, Saracens, Arabs from Arabia Felix (Himyarites), Blemmyes, Aksumites, Bactrians, and Indians. This list of names suggests that her commercial and imperial ambitions found a ready audience among all those who were involved in the silk and spice trade.

We know very little about the Palmyran army. All that we know is based on the very few descriptions of it in the sources (mainly Zosimus), some works of art, and on some extant inscriptions. The inscriptions prove that the commanders of the Palmyran army were called *strategoi* and that these were not as high ranking as the *strategoi* in the Roman army because *cohors XX Palmyrenorum*, which was a regular Roman auxiliary unit posted at Dura Europos, had two *strategoi* of archers. It is also known that the Palmyrenes did not only contribute soldiers to the Roman army, but that they also possessed a sizable regular army of their own. On the basis of Zosimus's account (see my analysis later), the most important part of this regular army was the elite *katafraktoi/cataphractarii* (cataphracts, both men and horses fully armoured) which this wealthy city possessed in abundance as we shall see. In addition to this, the Palmyrenes possessed Bedouin-style cavalry which used camels for transport and horses for combat, and probably also *kontoforoi/ contarii* cavalry, a lighter version of cataphract cavalry. In other words, their horses were not armoured and the men were also unarmoured or wore only small amounts of it. The *hippotoxotai* (mounted archers) could be either *katafraktoi* (cataphracted) or *afraktoi* (not armoured) as can be seen from one of the images preserved in Dura Europos. The extant works of art and other evidence proves that the Palmyrenes also possessed infantry forces consisting of armoured spearmen and light infantry archers. In addition to this, the Palmyrenes obviously had access to the Roman forces garrisoned in the area.[23]

The subsequent discussion proves that Palmyrenes possessed a massive number of cataphracts, so that they were able to mass together at least 70,000 of them for a single battle as they did at Emesa. It is probable that they could have massed together even more if they had acted more wisely, because this was the number of cataphracts the Palmyrenes had after they had already lost a very large number in the previous battle.

It is difficult to know which of the legions sided with the Palmyrenes in the initial stage of the conflict. When reading the following analysis, readers should keep in mind that it is possible or even quite likely that the legions mentioned here were not present in their entirety in the garrisons and that there were detachments from these forces also in Europe. The likeliest candidates to side with the Palmyrenes are the legions *I Parthica*, *III Parthica*, *IV Scythica* and *XVI Flavia Firma* because these were located in Syria, Mesopotamia and Oshroene which were under de facto Palmyran control. The case for the *X Fretensis legio* (Jerusalem), *III Gallica* (Damascus) and the possibly newly raised legion to replace the previously destroyed *legio VI Ferrata* (at Legio-Kefar Otnay/Caparcotna) is not certain. It is possible that these surrendered or deserted to the Palmyrenes, or were destroyed at Bostra or withdrew to Egypt. Similarly, it is impossible to know with any certainty what was the stance adopted by the legions *XV Apollinaris* and *XII Fulminata* when the Palmyrenes advanced into Asia Minor. It is possible that they withdrew, or that they surrendered or deserted to the Palmyrenes. In addition to these, the Palmyrenes would obviously have had in their control the auxiliaries from the areas controlled by them and the *Classis Syriaca* (Fleet of Syria) with the main base located at Seleucia. However, with the exception of Palmyrene and Arab auxiliaries, the loyalty of the rest of the Roman forces was suspect and many of them duly deserted back to the Roman side once the emperor reached the area. In fact, the list of forces serving under Aurelian in 271–2 (Asian forces from Tyana, Mesopotamia, Syria, Phoenicia, and Palestine) suggests that all of the legions and other non-Arab forces deserted to the Roman side immediately, unless these forces consisted of the detachments previously sent to the west, which is indeed quite possible. Regardless, it is still likely that at least some of the Roman forces serving under the Palmyrenes remained loyal to their new master and one may estimate that the Palmyrenes could have had at their disposal at least about 10,000–15,000 infantry, and perhaps about 10,000 cavalry drawn from the Roman sources.

In addition to these, we should include the allies which consisted of the Armenians and Persians. Unfortunately for the Palmyrenes, these did not join forces with Zenobia but fought a separate war against the Romans in their effort to save Zenobia.

The principal striking forces of the Armenians and Persians were the cataphracts, as with Palmyra, and both of these nations possessed masses of these so that one can estimate that they could put against the Romans a minimum of 50,000–70,000 cataphracts even when the King of Kings and/or his main field army was fighting in the east, as was the case at this time.

The accompanying drawings of mine show what types of forces the Palmyrenes possessed on the basis of the extant works of art. Some of the images depict men who could be equally well Romans or Persians. The image of a procession of Palmyran nobles in about 100–150 AD depicts Palmyrene or any Arab cavalry as it would have appeared when it emerged from the desert to attack the sedentary peoples. The camels were used for transport and the horses for combat. Note the bow-cases and quivers attached to the rear of the saddles and the ends of the spears between the legs shown with the grey. The men depicted in this scene were multi-purpose troops able to fight at long distance with bows and at close quarters with spears and swords.

The two graffiti from Dura Europos give us a rough image of how the third century cataphracts would have looked. They can be seen to be representative of the cataphracts employed by the Parthians, Persians, Palmyrenes and indeed also by the Romans. These two graffiti divide the cataphracts into two major types, the lancers and mounted archers, but in practice the cataphracts could be equipped with both lances and bows. My own educated guess is that these two graffiti should be interpreted to mean different ranks in the same formation so that the lancers formed the front ranks and the archers the rear ranks, in the same manner as the sixth century Romans.

The Palmyrene footman armed with the spear and sword is based on a relief of a warrior god from Dura Europos dated early third century AD. A dotted line is added to show the missing portions. It is probable that the shield was in truth larger than shown in this image, but the small size still implies that it was not as large as the legionary *scutum* – my educated guess is that it represents a round shield with a width of 45–60 cm. The footman with the coif/hood of scale is drawn after the Battle of Eben-Ezer fresco in the synagogue at Dura Europos, ca. mid-third century. It is possible that the scale-like paintings actually

The Reign of Claudius II 'Gothicus' in 268–270   57

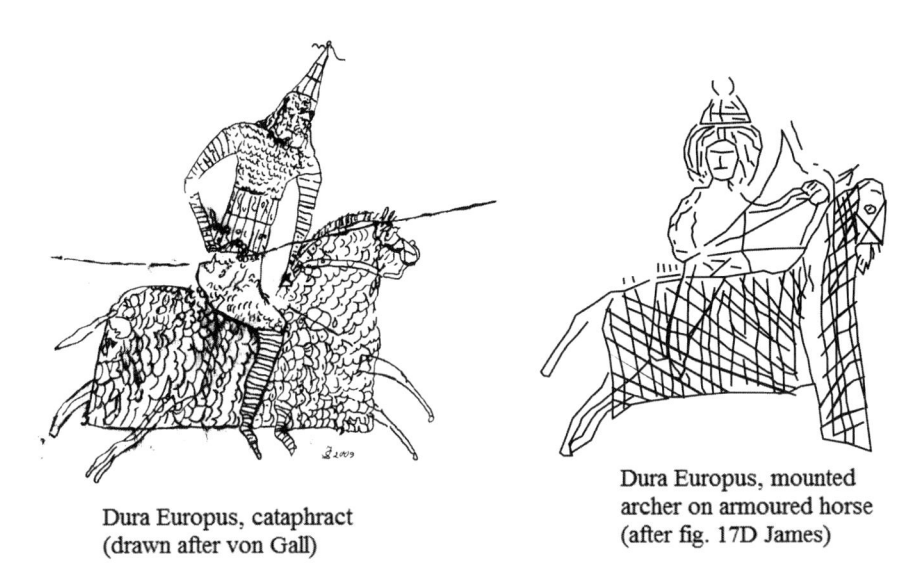

Dura Europus, cataphract
(drawn after von Gall)

Dura Europus, mounted
archer on armoured horse
(after fig. 17D James)

represent mail because they reach the wrists, but on the basis of the appearance it is still safest to assume that this represents a man equipped with scale armour. However, we know from other sources (e.g. Vatican manuscript illustration of coifs; mail attached to Sasanian helmets) that it was possible that Roman soldiers also wore mail coifs, possibly even underneath their helmets. Note also the continued use of sexagonal shields and the possible use of a strap beneath the shoe to hold the trousers in place. This soldier can be seen to be representative of both Roman and Palmyrene footmen in the region.

4.5. Zenobia's Inner Circle and Propaganda

As a ruler Zenobia relied on the support of the friends of her husband Odaenathus and on her position as a guardian of her underage son Wahballath/Vaballathus. The court consisted of Zenobia, her sons, the friends of Odaenathus, and the cultural and religious circle of Zenobia. The principal military men of the court were Zabdas, the general-in-chief, and Zabbai, the commander of Asia. Stoneman notes that these two men were two separate people and are not to be confused with each other as has often been done today just like it was in antiquity. After the conquest of Egypt this circle of military men came to include also Timagenes. Zenobia sought to endear herself with these and other military men by joining their drinking feasts and by hunting wild game with them. The most important man in the court appears to have been the philosopher and rhetorician Cassius Longinus who was officially in charge of teaching Greek to the queen and to conduct her diplomacy in the same language, but his role as an advisor and confidant appears to have been even more important than this. As well as these, there must have been other men of importance about whom we know nothing. One could have been Septimius Vorodes. Under Odaenathus he had been *procurator Augusti ducenarius*, *argapet* (a Parthian title meaning commander of a fort) and the second most important man after the king, but his fate after the death of Odaenathus is not known. Stoneman speculates that Zenobia had either purged him, or, if he was still alive, that he was still one of the most important men of the Palmyran Empire. He suggests that the name Vorodes implies a pro-Persian stance, which would have been a recommendation under Zenobia.[24]

Zenobia according to Duruy

Author's drawing of a bust supposed to represent Zenobia's deceased husband Odaenathus.

Just like Julia Domna before her, Zenobia surrounded herself with philosophers, intellectuals and religious teachers. Her aim was undoubtedly to project an image of learning. The most important of these was the already mentioned Cassius Longinus, but others may have included the sophist and historian Callinicus of Petra, the sophist Genetlius, and the historian Nicomachus of Trebizont. Zenobia is known to have supported the founding of the Neoplatonic school of Apamea. To make her rule as acceptable as possible to all the new subjects, Zenobia appears to have practised religious tolerance. She is also known to have shown interest in Christianity, just like Julia Domna, and Photius claims that Longinus converted her from the Hellenic superstition into Judaism, while some of the no-longer-extant Coptic papyri claim that she converted into Manicheanism. Her conversion to Judaism receives circumstantial support from the presence of a large Jewish community in Palmyra and from the fact that Zenobia is known to have improved their position in Egypt. If she was a Jew, as is quite possible, this would also have had important foreign policy consequences, because it would have been particularly helpful when dealing with the Jewish kings of Himyar.[25]

Zenobia's interest in Christianity also had political consequences. As has been recognized for a long time, Paul of Samosata, who was a Bishop of Antioch from ca. 260–268/9, was a supporter of Zenobia. Two church councils, in 265 and 268/9, denounced Paul as a heretic and forced him to leave his see in about 270. It is possible that it was then in 270 that the Antiochians sent an appeal to the new emperor Aurelian who duly removed Paul from office. According to Bar Hebraeus, Paul fled to Zenobia. However, I am inclined to agree with the traditional interpretation of what happened and accept the view that Zenobia then reinstated Paul to his see when she revolted against Claudius II in 270 so that Paul was not only Bishop of Antioch but also *procurator ducenarius* with a military retinue of his own. In other words, I agree with those who consider Paul of Samosata to have been a secular imperial financial officer in the service of Zenobia. The traditional view is that it was because of this that the Antiochians asked Aurelian to depose Paul when he arrived in the city in 272. However, it is possible that the appeal was already made in 270, as stated above.[26]

As a rule Zenobia sought to portray the rule of her and her son to project an image of grandeur. However, it was only in Egypt that she struck coins in her own name and it was also in Egypt that she portrayed herself as Cleopatra. In fact she claimed to be a descendant of Cleopatra. She also included the goddess Selene in her coins, but it is possible that this was a reference to Cleopatra because this was one of her names. The principal means of portraying her power was through the coins struck in the name of her son Vaballathus, and only secondarily through works of art or buildings.[27]

4.6. Egypt and North Africa from 269 until 270

Flavius Vopiscus (*HA Probus* 9.1ff.) places M. Aurelius Probus in Egypt, but the problem with this is that we know from other sources that Claudius had nominated Tenagino Probus as *praefectus Aegypti* with the mission to clear up the eastern Mediterranean of the last remnants of the Heruls and Goths. It is clear, as has been recognized for a long time, that Vopiscus has confused the two Probi with each other. However, most historians are still of the opinion that M. Aurelius Probus, the future emperor, was also present in Egypt serving under Tenagino Probus, because Vopiscus's account proves that M. Aurelius Probus was still present in Egypt later. The sending of M. Aurelius Probus to Egypt to serve under Tenagino Probus actually makes a lot of sense. Having spent his youth in Egypt, M. Aurelius Probus was familiar with the region. Tenagino Probus appears to have cleared the barbarian pirates by 269, but we do not know if M. Aurelius Probus had any role in this campaign. However, he seems to have been present as Tenagino Probus's subordinate in the next campaign against the Moors. The inscriptions and the *Historia Augusta* prove that the Marmaridae and other Moors had started raiding Roman North Africa. Tenagino Probus marched to Cyrene where he defeated the Marmaridae and founded the city of Claudiopolis.[28]

Moorish cavalry in the column of Trajan

The Moors consisted of lightly equipped infantry and cavalry, which meant that the Romans had a clear tactical superiority over them in pitched battles. The exact proportions of these depended upon the tribe. The attached eighteenth century drawing of Moorish cavalry on the Column of Trajan shows how lightly they were equipped. Javelins/spears should be added to it because these are no longer extant in the sculpture. Such tribes as the Garamantes still employed war chariots, but it remains clear that by Roman standards all of these tribes were inferior in their combat abilities. The fact that the Moors employed phalangial arrays in combat was not enough to change the situation. The Moors attempted to mitigate their comparative weaknesses through force of numbers or by avoiding contact with the Romans, which they usually did by retreating into the deserts.[29] The details given by Vopiscus, however, suggest that at this time the Moors decided to fight it out, with poor results for them. It is quite possible that the large uprisings of the Moors and Egyptians (see below) against the Romans had all been fomented by the Palmyrenes and their diplomats.

According to Vopiscus, M. Aurelius Probus continued the march to Carthage where he defeated the rebels. It was there, according to Vopiscus, that M. Aurelius Probus fought a duel with one Aradio in Africa and killed him. On the basis of this it is uncertain whether Tenagino Probus accompanied his subordinate M. Aurelius Probus or whether M. Aurelius Probus conducted the latter portion of the campaign alone. Furthermore, it is uncertain who the rebels were. They could have been local Romans and/or Moors. If the former, then the likely rebel was Galliena (see my *Gallienus*). What is clear is that most of North Africa was in flames, and that it required the concerted efforts of the two Probi to crush these. The confusion of the material in Vopiscus (*HA Prob.* 9.1–5) also allows the possibility that the campaign of Probus should be dated roughly to the year 271, so it would have predated the reconquest of Egypt by the Palmyrenes in 272. I will discuss this matter in greater detail later.

Vopiscus (*HA FSPB* 9.5) states that Saturninus, the future usurper against Probus, recovered Africa from the Moors, which makes it possible that both M. Aurelius Probus and Saturninus fought together during this war, but since he also claims that Saturninus was the man responsible for the recovery of Spain in about 269 it is possible that he refers to another war against the Moors.

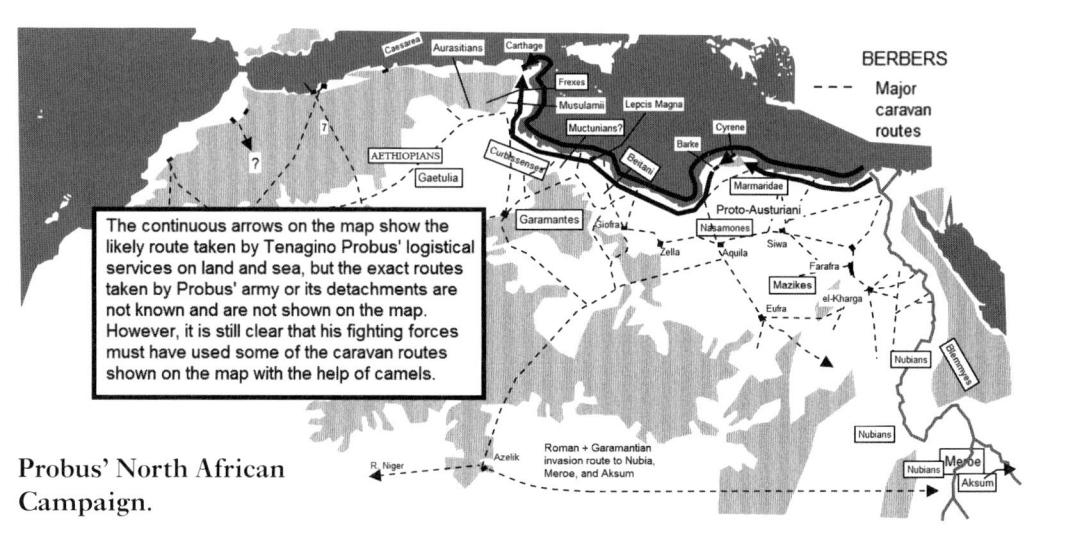

Probus' North African Campaign.

4.7. Claudius vs. the Alamanni and Sarmatians in 269–70

The revolt of Aureolus in Raetia and the subsequent transferral of a part of the army under Aurelian to Thrace against the Goths created a power vacuum in Raetia and the north of Italy, which the Alamanni and Iuthungi exploited by invading Italy during the spring or summer of 269. The situation was further aggravated by the fact that the Marcomanni/Iuthungi who had been settled in Pannonia by Gallienus formed an alliance with the Sarmatians and Vandals against Claudius. The likeliest reason for this uprising was that Claudius was considered responsible for the murder of Gallienus who had been married to Pipara/Pipa, the daughter of their king Attalus.[30] One may also assume that Pipa did not survive the murder of her husband. A fragment of Dexippus proves that Claudius had also stopped the payment of subsidies to the Iuthungi, which always resulted in the renewal of hostilities.[31]

The invasion took place when the emperor Claudius was in Rome. Consequently, he marched north where he defeated the Alamanni and Iuthungi near Lake Garda in 269.[32] See the map of Verona on page xix. The likeliest route for these invaders was either through the Brenner Pass or via the Splüngen/Septimer Passes up to Lake Garda. It is probable that the battle took place somewhere east of the lake close to the road leading north. The location suggests the possibility that Claudius may have blocked the enemy's route of retreat, so that could have protected his right flank against the lake and his left flank against the mountains. The other possibility is that Claudius pursued the retreating enemy and forced it to fight in this location. Considering subsequent events the latter is actually more likely, because the enemy renewed its war against the Romans next year with the implication that the Roman victory was by no means decisive. Regardless, the victory still enabled Claudius to take the title *Germanicus Maximus* to advertise his success.

We do not know for certain what went on in Claudius's head, but he appears to have hesitated whether he should invade Gaul or whether he should pursue the defeated barbarians or whether he should move to the Balkans against other invaders which included the Marcomanni, Sarmatians, Vandals and Goths. The situation was ripe for the reconquest of Gaul. It is quite possible, as suggested by Watson (44), that it was now that Claudius uttered his famous words that war against the usurper was his personal concern, but the war against the barbarians was the state's concern and the state's concerns should always take precedence over his own. It was now, at the latest, that Claudius dispatched Placidianus to Narbonensis, but it is probable that he had done that already after the revolt of Aureolus had been crushed.[33]

It is not surprising that the Illyrian Claudius chose to march to the Balkans against the Marcomanni, Vandals and Sarmatians (*HA Aur.* 18.1–2; Dexippus fr. 7). This left the Iuthungian war unfinished with the Iuthungi renewing their invasion the next year. Dexippus's text (fr. 6) proves that they were pillaging Italy at the time of Claudius's death. We also know that Claudius appointed his brother Quintillus to take charge of the defence of Italy (*HA Aur.* 17.5). When in the Balkans Claudius was unable to achieve anything of note because he caught the plague, withdrew to Sirmium, and died probably in August 270.

4.8. Claudius II 'Gothicus' as Emperor

The fame of Claudius as a great military commander is based solely on the claim that he was the man responsible for the defeat of the Goths and other invaders in the Balkans. This, however, has resulted from the falsification of the evidence. The two principal reasons for this are: 1) Constantine the Great and his successors claimed that Claudius

Coin of Claudius II struck after his death (Divo). Source: Cohen.

was their ancestor; 2) the senators hated Gallienus and attributed all of his successes to his successor Claudius. As I have demonstrated in my biography of Gallienus, this last claim was not entirely unfair because Claudius did have a very significant role in the defeat of the Gothic invasion. But this took place when he was still only one of the generals of Gallienus, even if he was the most important of these.

The real achievements of Claudius as emperor were far more modest. He crushed the revolt of Aureolus and defeated the Alamanni and Iuthungi near Verona. Gallienus had already inflicted the decisive defeat on the Goths and Heruls, so it was only the mopping up of the remnants of these forces that took place under Claudius. Furthermore, this was performed by Aurelian and Tenagino Probus. Claudius's main contribution to the situation was actually two serious blunders. The first of these was the stopping of payments to the Alamanni, Iuthungi and Marcomanni, which predictably resulted in wars. The second, considerably more serious, was that his high-handed policies caused Zenobia of Palmyra to revolt. Therefore Claudius's inheritance to his successor Aurelian was poisoned. His anti-barbarian policies had worsened the situation.

Top Left: A Sarmatian *draconarius* from a tombstone at Grosvenor Museum, Chester, latter half of the 2nd cent. Note the loop stirrup. Drawn after Gawronski Fig. 146. Gawronski has now proven beyond doubt that the Romans used loop stirrups during the imperial period. However, this was not decisive in combat not even from the point of view of shock combat. The latest study to confirm this is by Williams, Edge and Capwell. Furthermore, the use of loop stirrups restricted the ability of the horseman to dismount fast. It was because of this that the vast majority of the Roman horsemen chose not to use the stirrups.

Top Right: First century AD Kushan seal, British Museum. Drawn after Gawronski Fig. 145. Note the loop proto-stirrup, which according to Gawronski was probably used as a mounting aid. It is quite clear that the loop stirrups were very widely known in ancient world.

Chapter Five

Aurelian (Aurelianus)
The Beginning of the Reign in 270–71

5.1. The Empire in August 270

At the time of Claudius II's death the Roman Empire was a shadow of its former self. In the west there was the separatist Gallic Empire, which had lost Spain and a part of Gaul to Claudius's forces, and in the east there was the Palmyran Empire which had declared its independence from Claudius and was about to conquer Egypt, a major supplier of grain for Rome. On top of that, Claudius's field armies had been divided into separate armies to oppose the different invasions. In the east, in the Balkans, there were the forces placed under Aurelian who served as commander of all forces posted in Illyricum, Dacia and Thrace against the Goths and their allies, with the title of commander of all cavalry (*hipparchos*, which I interpret to mean either *magister equitum* or *comes domestici equitum*),[1] and just west of him there were the forces that Claudius had brought with him to Sirmium. In Italy at Aquileia there were forces under Quintillus, brother of Claudius, presumably meant to oppose the invading Iuthungi. In Gaul there were forces that had been brought there by Placidianus, but these proved insufficient even to threaten the Gallic Empire. At the time of Claudius's death the massive concentration of naval and land forces in Egypt and the eastern Mediterranean under Tenagino Probus were about to be annihilated by the Palmyrenes so that by the end of 270 the only loyalist forces left in Africa were their remnants and the remaining forces posted in Libya and west of Libya.

5.2. Quintillus vs. Aurelian in the autumn of 270[2]

When news of the death of Claudius II was brought to Aquileia, the troops there naturally raised his brother Quintillus as emperor, and his nomination was soon confirmed by the Senate at Rome so he became the legitimate emperor of the Roman Empire. Quintillus and the Senate, however, had not taken into account the ambitions of Aurelian and the support he had among the troops. Even though Zonaras (12.26) and Cedrenus (p.454) claim that Claudius nominated Aurelian as his successor on his deathbed at Sirmium, it is clear that this is a fiction created afterwards by Aurelian himself. Aurelian was nowhere near Sirmium at the time of Claudius's death, and it was thanks to this that Quintillus was universally recognized as emperor in all those areas where Claudius had been the nominal ruler, and the mint at Siscia was able to mint a coin in his name. Thanks to the fact that Aurelian had the command of the operations against the Goths, it is very likely that he was conducting a not-so-successful defence of the cities of Nicopolis and Anchialus, and when news of the death of Claudius reached him, he abandoned both cities to their fate and marched at the double to Sirmium to test the loyalty of the forces and their officers there before declaring himself emperor.[3] When Aurelian then got the reassurances he wanted, he had himself declared emperor by the forces present at the scene. On the basis of the rapid collapse of support for Quintillus, it is also likely that he was in some contact with the officers serving under Quintillus at Aquileia before he announced his bid for power. It is also certain that Aurelian considered himself the only legitimate successor of Claudius because he dated his reign to begin on Claudius's death. It is very unfortunate that we do not known whether Claudius had made any such promises at the time of his own accession in order to gain Aurelian's support.

Coins of Quintillus, the brother of Claudius II (source: Duruy)

The sources give different lengths for Quintillus's reign, but all are unanimous that it was short. Saunders summarises the information as follows: seven days (Cedrenus p.454; Synopsis Sathas p.39); a few days (Epitome 34.5); seventeen days (Eutr. 9.12; Jerome, *Chron.* 222b; *HA Claud.* 12.5; Malalas 12.29; Syncellus AM5763; Zonaras 12.26); twenty days (*HA Aur.* 37.5–6); seventy-seven days (*Chronica urbis Romae* p.148); a few months (Zos. 1.47); or about a year or two (Zonaras 12.26). On the basis of the abundance of extant coins, some researchers believe that Quintillus must have ruled for seventy-seven days/a few months, but as Saunders notes this is not conclusive. On the basis of the Egyptian papyri and coins, he thinks that the lower figures are more likely, but in my opinion the Egyptian evidence suffers from the same problems of not providing a definite answer. All that we know for certain is that Quintillus ruled long enough to be universally recognized and that he lost the support of the army serving under him relatively soon after the news of Aurelian's usurpation reached it. One cannot even entirely rule out the possibility that Quintillus could have been a co-ruler with Claudius so that he would have ruled for one or two years. Cizek (87) suggests an attractive solution to the above problem which is that those accounts which put the reign of Quintillus to last only days actually refer to the time that Quintillus and Aurelian reigned together as opposing emperors. My own educated guess is that Quintillus's reign lasted indeed about seventy-seven days/a few months, because the evidence from Egypt does suggest in no uncertain terms that Zenobia's invasion of Egypt was done as an ally of Aurelian against Quintillus.

There are two versions for the death of Quintillus. Most Latin sources claim that his troops killed him, but I am inclined to agree with Saunders that the Greek sources are correct in stating that the desperate Quintillus committed suicide by slitting his own veins. This kind of suicide for an emperor was a rare occurrence and therefore sounds quite plausible.

If we interpret the evidence as I have suggested above, so that Quintillus ruled for about seventy-seven days, this influences the way in which the two wars that took place during the year 270 – namely the Iuthungian invasion of Italy and the Palmyrene invasion of Egypt – have to be reconstructed. The circumstantial evidence does indeed back up this.

The Iuthungian war had started already when Claudius was alive and it was because of this that Quintillus had been posted at Aquileia. Quintillus appears to have been unwilling to risk a battle with them when he faced the revolt of Aurelian. Aurelian in his turn appears to have exploited this by demonstrating his military mettle by ambushing the Iuthungi in a situation in which Quintillus had done nothing. See below. It was this that would have then undermined Quintillus's position as the legitimate successor of Claudius.

The death of Claudius also brought a change in the relationship between Aurelian and Zenobia, which can be detected from the coins minted in the east which depict Aurelian and Vaballathus simultaneously. The implication is that Aurelian and Zenobia concluded a peace. There are two possible ways this could have happened. It was either Zenobia who sent envoys to Aurelian immediately she had heard of the death of Claudius, with the task of concluding a peace with Aurelian. The other alternative is that it had been Aurelian who sent envoys to Zenobia to form an alliance with her in a situation in which he still needed to secure his own position. None of the narrative sources mention such an alliance, but the timing of the events, as well as the official recognition that Zenobia gave to Aurelian, are highly suggestive. If it was Aurelian who suggested such an alliance, and I would suggest that he is the likelier candidate, this would have been believable because Quintillus was Claudius's brother and therefore the natural enemy of Zenobia. It is also possible that Aurelian and Zenobia had met each other in 254 when Aurelian was in the east, so there would also have been a personal aspect to the alliance. I would also suggest that it is very likely that Zenobia invaded Egypt on behalf of Aurelian with the intention of denying grain supplies if Quintillus had managed to hold on to Italy and Rome. As we shall see, Aurelian's plan was not to keep his word but to crush the Palmyrenes. His intention was clearly to act like Caracalla had acted before him and fool all the enemies he could. Zenobia, however, attempted to keep the peace to the very end because she continued to mint coins portraying Aurelian as the superior emperor/*Augustus* until the spring of 272.[4]

Coin of Vaballathus/Zenobia recognizing Aurelian as *Augustus*. Source: Duruy.

5.3. The Palmyran Invasion of Egypt in the autumn of 270

The date for the beginning of the invasion of Egypt is controversial. We know that the Romans still controlled most of Egypt in late September which is proven by the fact that the papyrus finds at Oxyrhyncus still recognized Claudius as emperor in late September, while the mint at Alexandria minted its first coins in Quintillus's name after 29 August 270, but Quintillus's series was just as shortlived as was his reign. The region south of Memphis never recognized Quintillus. Their papyri were dated according to Roman consuls from 12 October until mid-November or mid-December with the implication that the situation was volatile during those months. After this, the papyri named Aurelianus and Vaballathus jointly, which means that the Palmyrenes had conquered the area and Zenobia was attempting to reach a reconciliation with Aurelian, which she probably obtained in some form because there is no evidence for her withholding any grain shipments bound for Rome. I agree with Pat Southern that the evidence in papyri and coins does not mean that the invasion of Egypt could not have started during the reign of Claudius as implied by Zosimus, but I am still of the opinion that Alaric Watson is correct in stating on the basis of the papyri and coins that the main offensive of the Palmyrenes started in early October when Aurelian was already the emperor. The invasion apparently took place at the same time as the Probi were conducting their counter-attack against the Moors. It would be really nice to know whether Palmyrene diplomacy had played any role in inducing the Moors to invade Roman North Africa at this moment, because it certainly facilitated the Palmyrene invasion. Furthermore, we know that the Blemmyes captured Coptos in 268 and held it until 270. It has also been suggested that Palmyrene diplomacy was behind this invasion. This is a distinct possibility, but it is also possible, as suggested by Pat Southern, that one of the reasons for the Palmyrene invasion of Egypt would have been to secure the trade route by destroying such enemies as the Blemmyes who were causing disruptions to the trade networks. It is unfortunately impossible to know for sure which of the versions is correct, if any.[5]

In sum, my own educated guess, which is based on the circumstantial evidence, is that Zenobia actually fought as an ally of Aurelian against Claudius's brother Quintillus. This evidence consists of the above-mentioned dating of the coins and papyri and on the fact that Zenobia recognized Aurelian as the senior *Augustus* in her coins immediately after

Battle of Babylon in Egypt in 270.

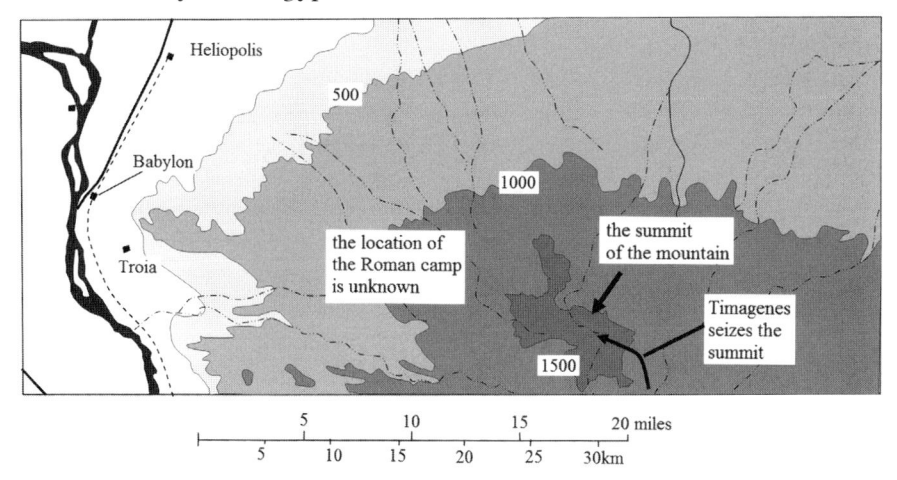

she had gained control of Egypt. This alliance also explains why Zenobia recognized Aurelian as emperor and why Zenobia did not withhold the grain shipments of Egypt.

Zosimus is our best source for the Palmyrene conquest of Egypt and it is worth quoting him at length because there are some serious misunderstandings regarding the events in modern studies of the war.

> The Scythians being thus dispersed, with the loss of a great part of their troops [*this refers to the successes of Tenagino Probus and others against the Goths and Heruls*], Zenobia began to think of extending her dominion, and therefore sent Zabdas to Egypt, because Timagenes an Egyptian attempted to place Egypt under the government of the Palmyrenians, Syrians, and Barbarians, to the number of seventy thousand, which was opposed by fifty thousand Egyptians. A sharp engagement ensued between them, in which the Palmyrenians had greatly the advantage. He [*Zabdas*] then departed, leaving them a garrison of five thousand men [*this appears to mean the garrison placed at Alexandria*].
>
> During these transactions, Probus [*Tenagino Probus*], who had been appointed by the emperor [*Claudius*] to clear the sea of pirates, having heard of the subjugation of Egypt by the Palmyrenians [*he was clearly fighting against the Moors at the time*], marched against them with his own forces, and with as many of the Egyptians as were averse to the Palmyrenians, and drove out their garrison. The Palmyrenians rallying with fresh forces [*it is probable that there were other Palmyrenes or their allies like the Blemmyes and Aksumites present in Egypt*], Probus, having levied a body of Egyptians and Africans, gained another victory, and drove the Palmyrenians out of Egypt. But as Probus was encamped on a mountain near Babylon, thereby cutting off the passage of the enemy into Syria, Timagenes, who was well acquainted with the country, seized the summit of the mountain with two thousand men, and attacked the Egyptians by surprise. Probus being taken with the rest killed himself [*this means Tenagino Probus, because Vopiscus/HA Probus 5 states quite clearly that M. Aurelius Probus managed to flee despite he too being almost captured*]. [Zosimus 1.44., 1814 tr. p.23 with changes and comments.]

Vopiscus (*HA Probus* 9.6), in his account of the career of M. Aurelius Probus, claims that after the Moorish campaign M. Aurelius Probus fought next against the Palmyrenes who had taken control of Egypt. He claims that M. Aurelius Probus fought first with success, but was then almost captured thanks to his recklessness, only to claim that he later returned with reinforcements when Aurelian had become emperor. The former describes clearly the campaign of Tenagino Probus which is also described by Zosimus. The latter campaign will be dealt with later. The other alternative is that both the reckless fighting and the renewal of the fight indeed took place during the reconquest of Egypt in 272, but the other alternative is more likely because it fits the sequence of events better.

As we have seen, the evidence for the Palmyrene conquest of Egypt is full of problems. However, what is known for certain on the basis of Zosimus, the coins and papyri is that the Palmyrene commander Zabdas with 70,000 men defeated the local Egyptian forces consisting of 50,000 men in a major battle and that the Palmyrenes gained possession of the north of Egypt after September and that the situation remained volatile because Tenagino

Probus then launched his counter-attack so that by late October or early November in 270 he was in control of Alexandria.[6] The Palmyrenes gathered reinforcements, but Probus defeated the Palmyrenes again and forced them to retreat south past the city of Babylon so that Probus pitched his camp on the nearby mountain with the idea of preventing the flight of the Palmyrene army to Syria. However, it was then that he was surprised in his camp by Timagenes, so the Palmyrenes regained control of Egypt by December when the mint at Alexandria struck coins in the name of Vaballathus and Aurelian.

5.4. Aurelian's First Challenge: The Iuthungian War in the autumn of 270[7]

As noted above, it is probable that this war took place while Quintillus was still alive, with the implication that Aurelian's decision to engage the Iuthungi was meant to be a propaganda gesture to undermine Quintillus's standing among the soldiers. However, since this is not known with certainty, it is possible that this war took place immediately after Quintillus had committed suicide. It is indeed possible that the crushing of the Iuthungi invasion was Aurelian's first challenge as sole ruler in a situation in which Aurelian had not yet even gained the support of the Roman Senate. The former alternative, however, appears more likely. This was also not to be the last of the invasions Aurelian would face.

According to the *Historia Augusta* (*Aurelian* 18.2–3), Aurelian faced a succession of invasions at the very beginning of his reign. The first of these was the invasion of the Suebi, which was followed up by the invasions of the Sarmatians and Marcomanni. What is notable about this is that the *Historia Augusta* actually preserves for us the most complete version of the events, which stands once again as a good proof of its value as a much-too-overlooked source. The archaic names mentioned by the *Historia Augusta* hide behind them a number of more recent names. On the basis of Dexippus's fragment (see below) we know that the Suebi means the Iuthungi. Similarly we know on the basis of another fragment of Dexippus (*Skythika* 7) that the Sarmatian invasion included the Vandals. However, it is also known that Aurelian faced the real Sarmatians as well because he received the title *Sarmaticus Maximus*. We can add further details into this account from the already mentioned fragment of Dexippus which refers to a separate force of Vandals, which is likely to mean that the Sarmatians campaigned separately from them. We can also identify the Marcomannic invasion of the *HA* with the invasion of the Iuthungi (Dexippus frg. 7.4), Alamanni (Victor 35.2) and Alamanni and neighbouring peoples (Zos. 1.49.1). Some historians think that this third massive invasion at the beginning of Aurelian's reign in 271 included all of the peoples mentioned, while others think it meant only the Iuthungi or alternatively the Alamanni or the Alamanni and Iuthungi. My own educated guess is that it included all of the above because these tribes lived right next to each other and it is quite easy to see that they could have formed an alliance.

These invasions were not the only troubles that Aurelian faced. He had also inherited the old problems of the breakaway Gallic Empire and the aggressively expansive Palmyran Empire to deal with. But the solving of these problems had to wait for a more opportune time. The Iuthungi needed to be punished.

Saunders (168ff.) is likely to be correct when he states that the Iuthungian invasion had begun when Claudius was still alive and that Quintillus had placed himself at Aquileia to oppose it. It is also likely that just before Claudius's death Quintillus had asked Claudius either to send reinforcements and/or to return to Italy in person because he (Quintillus) apparently felt unable to oppose the vast numbers he was facing. Saunders suggest that the Iuthungi invasion began at Augusta Vindelicum and progressed from there to Verona – Aquileia – Virunum – Lauriacum for a distance of some 694 miles. This is a plausible suggestion, but if the usual emendation to change the Rhodanus (Rhône)[8] into Epidaurus (Po) in Dexippus's *Skythika* is correct, then the invading force would have naturally marched past Verona up to the Po before starting their return journey. None of the sources mention the sacking of Verona or any other major city in Italy, which means that the Iuthungi probably did not try to attack any of the walled cities, but this is obviously an argument from the silence of the sources.

We do not know this with certainty, but it is very likely that Aurelian had immediately started to advance towards Aquileia after he had been declared emperor, because the first thing he needed to do was eliminate Quintillus and to secure the support of the forces serving under him. However, it is also possible that Aurelian advanced first against the Iuthungi and only then against Quintillus, who was duly killed or committed suicide. Still another possibility is that Aurelian advanced against the Iuthungi after Quintillus was dead and went to Aquileia only after he had defeated the Iuthungi. In normal circumstances the next thing in order of importance would have been to secure the support of the Senate of Rome, but this was now of secondary importance to the defeating of the Iuthungian invaders who appear to have been in the process of withdrawing from Italy at the time Aurelian usurped the power. Gallienus's murder proves that his officers, Aurelian included, considered foreign invasions more important to deal with than usurpations and it was thanks to this that Aurelian now prioritized the pursuit of the enemy.[9]

Due to the uncertainties of the sources we do not know when Quintillus died, or whether Aurelian marched to Aquileia before turning against the invaders. It all depends on how long Quintillus reigned. My own educated guess is that Quintillus reigned about seventy-seven days and that it was because of this that Aurelian actually engaged the Iuthungi while Quintillus was still alive. Therefore I accept as the likeliest alternative Saunders' suggestion that Aurelian marched directly to the Danube.[10] In short, my educated guess is that Aurelian did not enter Italy, but led most of his cavalry forces north-east to ambush the Iuthungi while he left his infantry behind, possibly in the Julian Alps, to block Quintillus's route to the Balkans.[11]

The reconstruction of the following events is a hotly debated issue among modern historians and is based upon their individual interpretations of the two extant fragments of Dexippus's *Skythika* (frg. 6–7).[12] It has long been recognized that fragment 6 of Dexippus's *Skythika* belongs to the very beginning of Aurelian's reign because Aurelian's speech in Dexippus's text refers only to the Roman victories over the Goths and Galmionoi (*galmionôn* of the text is usually emended to mean *alamanôn*/Alamanni) that took place before his reign and that it should be connected with the invasion of the Suebi mentioned by the *Historia Augusta*. Consequently, Aurelian was unable to continue his march to Rome to secure the support of the Senate for his nomination. Aurelian had to march north on the double to crush the Iuthungi whom he engaged and defeated and forced against the Danube (exact location unknown). It is a hotly debated topic whether these Iuthungi were the remnants of the Alamanni who had escaped the defeat of the

Alamanni at Lake Garda, or whether these were a separate force that had just exploited the absence of Claudius II or his death. What is certain is that they had a legitimate grievance against the Romans, as the Romans had discontinued the payments to them agreed by the previous emperors. I agree with Drinkwater that it is probable that the original agreement to which the Iuthungi referred had been concluded under Gallienus in about 260 and that this agreement had been broken by the Romans presumably already under Claudius II, but it is also possible that this referred to an agreement made by Claudius with the Iuthungi after the battle of Lake Garda in 269.[13] Whatever the truth, it is still clear that the result of the Roman perfidy was the invasion of Roman Raetia and part of Italy, and the immediate counter-strike by Aurelian.

Unsurprisingly given the problems with the textual interpretation of Dexippus's fragment 6, historians have interpreted the evidence in it very differently. All that is known with certainty is that Aurelian defeated the Iuthungi at the Danube so severely that they sent an embassy to ask for terms of peace. According to Gibbon (pp.306–8), the Romans were deployed on the opposite bank of the Danube in an ambush and allowed about half of the enemy force to cross the river before attacking. Aurelian advanced the two horns of a crescent over the river to enclose the enemy host inside. Saunders (168ff.) suggests there was a pursuit of the Iuthungi up to the Danube where the Romans defeated them, without attempting to interpret the details of the battle. White (65ff.) suggests that Aurelian collected an elite force of light infantry and ambushed the Iuthungi on both sides of the river.

My own suggestion is that we should interpret the battle between Aurelian and the Iuthungi as a cavalry ambush in which Aurelian had concealed his cavalry forces on the northern bank of the Danube. In other words, I interpret the battle so that Aurelian first bypassed the Iuthungi by making a circuitous march with his cavalry, so they would have marched eighty kilometres a day for four or five days to get enough time to cross the Danube and then conceal themselves on the opposite side before the Iuthungi scouts arrived on the scene. After having crossed the Danube, Aurelian would also have advanced northwards with a wide front so that the locals would have been forced to flee northwards with the result that they would have been unable to provide any warning to their fellow countrymen. Aurelian would then have returned southwards, but only as much as was necessary. He would have stayed far enough from the Danube so that the enemy scouts would not have been able to detect the ambush and he would have launched his own ambush only when his scouts informed him that substantial numbers of the enemy had crossed the river. When about half the enemy force had crossed the Danube, Aurelian launched his ambush so that his cavalry 'with all its might' overthrew all of the 'Iuthungi-Scythians' who had already crossed the Danube back to the other side, after which the survivors asked for a truce to negotiate a peace. According to Zosimus 1.49, Aurelian killed myriads of Alamanni barbarians in a battle near the Danube. The reference must be to this battle. The cavalry attack formation, however, would not necessarily have been a crescent, as it was during the audience next day, but a modified version of the regular cavalry formation so that it could be hidden inside a forest or on another suitable piece of ground hiding its presence, although it is still possible that it was a crescent to enable the wings to outflank the enemy immediately. Whatever the formation was, the decisive factor for the way in which the ambushing formation was formed would have been the lay of the land.[14]

72 Aurelian and Probus

Aurelian's Ambush vs. the Iuthungi in about September 270

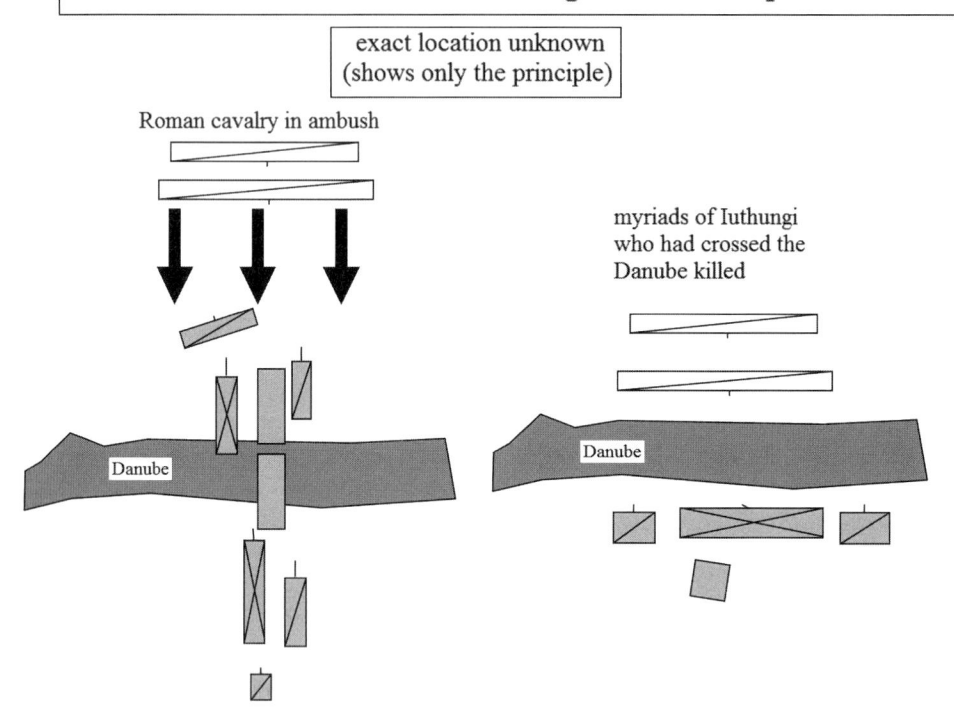

exact location unknown
(shows only the principle)

Roman cavalry in ambush

myriads of Iuthungi
who had crossed the
Danube killed

Danube

Danube

When the Iuthungi embassy arrived to negotiate terms of peace, Aurelian equipped his whole army for combat to frighten the enemy and arrayed it in a crescent. Then he took his seat at a raised platform just as Contantius II did later when receiving enemy ambassadors.[15] The leading generals ('*archas*') stood beside their horses on both sides of the emperor. Behind the emperor were the standards (and/or shield emblems '*sêmata*') of the picked army ('*epilektou stratias*'), and on silvered *xyston*-spears (standard poles) the golden eagles (the legionary standards), images/icons of the emperors, and the names of the units of the army/encampment ('*stratopedôn katalogoi*') engraved in golden letters. The inclusion of the legionary eagles does not necessarily mean that their footmen would have been present because it is entirely plausible that only the legionary horsemen were present. Furthermore, since the purpose was to amaze the enemy, it is clear that all of the unit emblems (including those that were in truth under the Gallic Empire or Palmyran Empire) were displayed, as were images of the emperors.

It is unfortunate that Dexippus fails to clarify who the picked soldiers were. It is possible that they were Praetorians (or rather their cavalry component) or *equites singulares Augusti* or the newly created bodyguard units variously called *aulici, scholae, protectores*, and *domestici* in the sources, or all of those together. My own educated guess is that the picked soldiers included all of these, and whatever other units (like the *equites Mauri*) had been included in the cavalry bodyguards of Gallienus.[16] It is also quite obvious that, as under Gallienus, the army also included the legionary cavalry and auxiliary cavalry so that the entire corps accompanying Aurelian would have been the equivalent of Gallienus's *equites* corps. Therefore it is quite possible that the *katalogoi* (= *arithmoi, numeri*) meant the auxiliary cavalry units, but it is also possible that this generic term meant all of the units accompanying Aurelian.

However, the enemy was not prepared to be impressed. On the contrary, according to the probably invented speech of Dexippus, they demanded that the tribute that they had previously been entitled to receive be reinstated to them in return for peace.[17] They also boasted that they had penetrated deep into Italy and that they had 40,000 purebred (*katharos*)[18] Iuthungi horsemen who excelled in cavalry combat ('*hippomachia*'), and 80,000 shield-bearing footmen. In other words, the Iuthungi bragged that their cavalry fought better than the Roman and that it was only thanks to the division of the Iuthungi by the river that the Romans had defeated them. The reference to the 40,000 horsemen and 80,000 shield-bearers should be seen to mean the remaining Iuthungi on the opposite side of the river. The idea was to attempt to frighten Aurelian with the size of their host. However, since we know that the references to numbers in the speech were put into the mouths of the Iuthungi envoys by Dexippus, we do not know whether this statement was ever made and furthermore we do not know how many Iuthungi there had been originally and how many were left after the battle. If the Iuthungi really claimed to have had so many men on the opposite side of the river, it is probable that this would have been an exaggeration meant to frighten Aurelian. However, one cannot preclude the possibility that they did because Dexippus may have used a period report as his source and similarly it is possible that Dexippus may have used an estimated size of the defeated overall force as his source for the figures. In my opinion, it is entirely plausible that the Iuthungi had at least the number they claimed to possess because that would explain why they had been able to raid northern Italy without any interference from the army under Quintillus.[19]

Aurelian responded by noting the recent Roman victories [see Syvänne, *Gallienus*, 129ff.] over the 300,000 Scythians (Goths) and Galmionoi (probably a corrupt reference to the Alamanni) and by stating that he could not allow them safe passage after their plundering. He left them only the choice of unconditional surrender because in his opinion the Iuthungi would have to surrender soon anyway. Unfortunately the fragment ends at this and we do not know what happened next. My own educated guess is that some sort of agreement was reached with the Iuthungi, because Aurelian was then able to continue his march to Rome. The later events (see below) suggest that the Iuthungi were allowed to return to the lands previously given to them by Gallienus with the same requirements but without the payments.

5.5. Aurelian Secures the Senate's Approval

The quick conclusion of the war enabled Aurelian to return to Italy for the purpose of obtaining the Senate's support, but as we shall see the quick conclusion of peace with the Iuthungi was a mistake. Aurelian should have eliminated the enemy force and not let it go free. However, it is easy to see why Aurelian engaged the Iuthungi before he had dealt with Quintillus. The fast victory over the Iuthungi gave him the leverage he needed to turn the soldiers of Quintillus to his side. Whatever the truth, it is clear that Aurelian still needed to secure the support of the Senate after the death of Quintillus, and it is possible that even this need would have sufficed in this case to make Aurelian prepared to negotiate with the Iuthungi. The fast end to the war enabled Aurelian to march to Italy. When Aurelian reached Ravenna he received an embassy of senators, which conveyed the Senate's declaration of loyalty for the new emperor.[20] Aurelian was ready to accept the excuses of the senators and the Senate for their initial declaration for Quintillus and their newly found readiness to declare their loyalty to him.[21] Once again, Aurelian preferred the conciliatory approach to unnecessary confrontation while his grip on power and the army was not secure enough.

Aurelian was a man who sought to rule his army and officials with an iron hand, and he sought to remove all indiscipline and corruption in the ranks. Both Zonaras (12.27) and Peter the Patrician (frg. 190, *Anonymous Continuator of Dio*, frg. 10.1) contain references to an incident that took place when Aurelian reached the city of Ravenna at the very beginning of his reign. Both of these have been conveniently translated and analyzed by Thomas M. Banchich. Aurelian convened a council of advisors at Ravenna and asked them how he should rule. One of the men advised him to gather gold and iron, and use iron against those who caused him discomfort while giving gold to those who served him well. This was a sound piece of advice, but it was also an instance of corrupt behaviour that Aurelian detested heart and soul. Consequently, the man who gave this advice was the first one to taste the iron. This was to be the first sign of Aurelian's anticorruption and anticrime policies which he pursued with ruthless brutality.[22]

It is very probable that Aurelian visited Rome after this even if this is only implied by Zosimus (1.48) when he states that Aurelian marched from Rome against the Scythians (Vandals). The length and purpose of his visit is not known, but Saunders is surely right in his speculation that Aurelian's sole purpose was to show his respect to the Senate, because he would have remembered what happened during Maximinus Thrax's reign when he had not visited Rome – namely the revolt of the Senate against Maximinus. Like him, Aurelian had humble origins. It is also possible that Aurelian stayed in Rome long enough to assume his consulship on 1 January 271, but it is equally clear that he did not linger there because the Sarmatian-Vandal invasion also took place in early 271.[23]

I would suggest that it was on his first visit to Rome that Aurelian launched his campaign against crime and corruption among the imperial officials and provincial governors, and enacted the first pieces of his legislation meant for the upkeep of public morals, which included the law against the keeping of free women as concubines as Gallienus had done. In short, his aim was to bring back the good old times by restoring law and order and the old morals. This was naturally detested by corrupt officials and senators who duly revolted against him as we shall see. It is also probable that Aurelian began his economizing immediately after assuming power, by cancelling the grandiose project initiated by Gallienus to build a colossal statue of Gallienus as Sol. If it did not take place now or during Aurelian's next trip to Rome, it certainly took place during the third visit when Aurelian initiated his project to promote the worship of Sol.[24]

5.6. The Sarmatian-Vandal War in early 271

But Aurelian could not yet rest on his laurels. The barbarians intended to take advantage of the Roman troubles. According to Zosimus, the reason for the invasion was famine, which times the invasion to the winter/spring of 270/1.

Aurelianus, having regulated the empire, went from Rome to Aquileia, and from thence into Pannonia, which he was informed the Scythians were preparing to invade. For this reason he sent orders to the inhabitants of that country to carry into the towns all their corn and cattle, and everything that could be of use to the enemy, in order to distress them with famine, with which they were already afflicted. The Barbarians having crossed the river into Pannonia had an engagement, the result of which was nearly equal. But that same night, the Barbarians recrossed the river, and as soon as the day appeared, sent ambassadors to treat for peace. [Zosimus 1.48.1–2, English tr. 1814, p.24 with some changes by the author.]

In short, Aurelian was forced to march from the city of Rome to Pannonia either in very late 270 or early 271, but before he did that he had already sent an advance warning to the inhabitants and garrisons of the impending invasion. On the basis of Dexippus's *Skythika fragment 7* we know that the invaders were the Vandals. The *Historia Augusta* (*Aurelian* 18.2) calls the first invaders Sarmatians, and it is possible that the invaders included also these, but my suggestion is that the Sarmatian invasion was a separate invasion which followed in the footsteps of the Vandal invasion at the same time as the Alamanni/Marcomanni descended on Italy. See below. Aurelian immediately sent an order for the people to take all their livestock and food supplies inside fortified cities. His strategy was to use a war of attrition to weaken the Vandals before engaging them in battle.[25] The enclosing of grain supplies inside the fortified cities and the lack of forage ensured that the Vandal horses would soon lose their stamina, while the men would begin to suffer from the effects of hunger. If the Vandals used steppe ponies, these did not suffer similarly from a lack of barley, but by harassing the enemy continually the Romans could also limit the amount of time the enemy could use for grazing, and if the Vandals used normal European horses the situation was even worse. After the enemy had been weakened through skirmishes and Aurelian had assembled his forces, he engaged the enemy in Pannonia. My suggestion for the route taken by Aurelian against the Vandals is that he passed through Aquileia and the Julian Alps after which he marched north-east so that he would have engaged the Vandals somewhere between Carnuntum and the modern Lake Balaton. According to Zosimus, the resulting battle was indecisive, but when night fell the barbarians crossed back over the river so that they placed the river between the armies, and at daybreak sent heralds to sue for peace. It is unfortunate that we do not know the exact date of the invasion, but my suggestion is that at least the battle between Aurelian and Vandals took place during the spring or early summer 271 because the river could not have served as a defence if it was still frozen.[26]

According to Dexippus (*Skythika* frg. 7), Aurelian gave his soldiers the final word in making the decision of how to respond to the peace proposal made by the Vandals. The soldiers opted for peace. Aurelian's idea was clearly to involve the soldiers in the decision so that he would not face similar problems with the officers who opposed the granting of peace to the barbarians as Gallienus had. He had evidently learnt from the mistakes of Gallienus who had been criticized for his readiness to make peace settlements with the barbarians. I would also suggest that the Iuthungi-Alamanni-Marcomanni invasion of Italy had already taken place and that it was because of this that Aurelian and presumably also the soldiers were prepared to grant peace to the invaders. The Vandals agreed to give the Romans hostages and 2,000 horsemen in return for peace and enough food supplies to reach the Danube. They also returned captives and booty. However, a war party of 500 warriors did not abide by the treaty and were duly killed by the Vandals, presumably because they wanted their hostages safely returned and because they wanted to reach the Danube safely.[27]

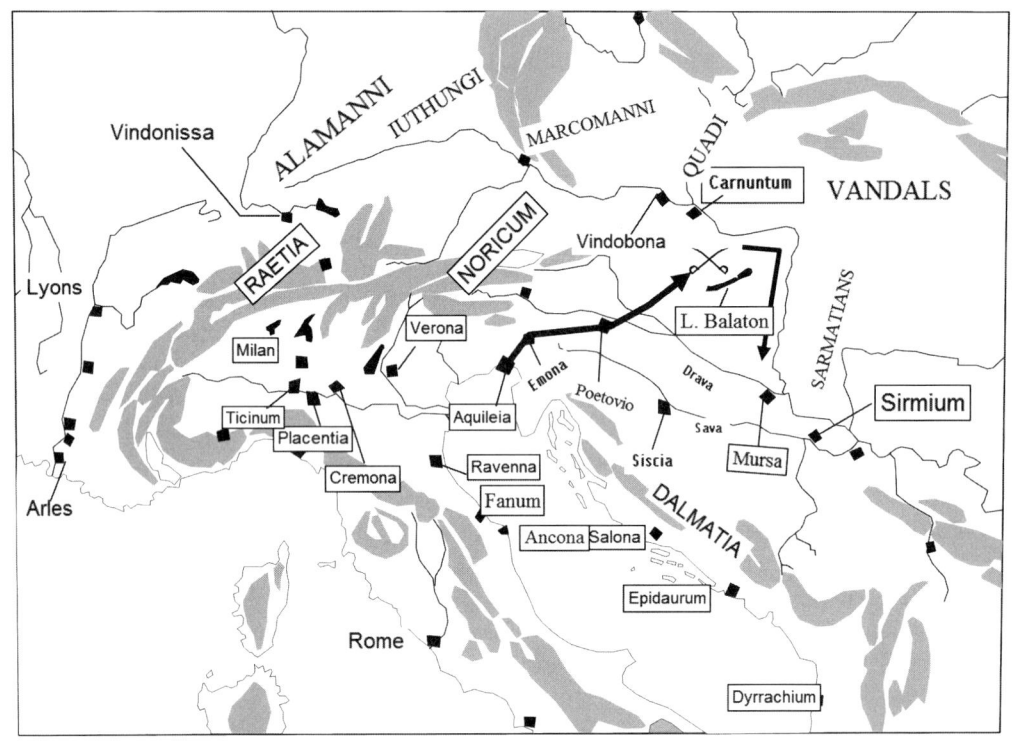

Campaign against the Vandals and Sarmatians in 271.

The following quote from Zosimus shows what happened next:

> The Emperor, hearing that the Alamanni and the neighbouring nations intended to overrun Italy, was with just reason more concerned for Rome and the adjacent places, than for the more remote. Having therefore ordered a sufficient force to remain for the defence of Pannonia, he marched towards Italy, and on his route, on the borders of that country, near the Ister [*Danube*], slew many thousands of the Barbarians in one battle [*These would be the Sarmatians of the Historia Augusta, Aurel. 18.2*]. [Zosimus 1.49, English tr. 1814, p.25 with some changes by author.]

According to Dexippus (*Skythika* frg. 7), Aurelian sent the bulk of his infantry and cavalry on ahead to Italy while he himself stayed behind with his bodyguards/Companions ('*auton taxin hetairiken*') to ensure that the Vandals followed the treaty to the letter. After that, he, together with the 2,000 Vandal retainers, marched at the double to join the main

Aurelian (Aurelianus) The Beginning of the Reign in 270–71

army. This means that Aurelian escorted the Vandals to the Danube, after which he would have marched along the Danube towards the city of Mursa. It is likely that Aurelian joined forces with those that he had sent in advance before engaging the Sarmatians somewhere north of the River Drava near the Danube. What is certain is that it was after this war that Aurelian was awarded the title of *Sarmaticus Maximus* and this in itself should be seen as evidence that the unknown invaders who were defeated by the Danube were the Sarmatians.

It is possible that it was during the above-mentioned Sarmatian war that there took place an incident described by Vopiscus which involved Probus. The reason for this is that he mentions the Alans (which could easily be Sarmatians) but it is also possible that this incident took place only later during the Gothic wars because the Alans were usually present in the Gothic armies. The latter option is likelier, but I have still included this piece of information here just in case Vopiscus was referring to this earlier Sarmatian war. It is also valuable for another reason, which is that it describes the influence Probus had in the policies of Aurelian. It is unfortunate that we do not know when Aurelian appointed Probus as commander of all *protectores/domestici* bodyguards, because this would enable us to determine Probus's position during the reign of Aurelian. A fuller discussion of this matter is included at the end of the chapter dealing with the reign of Aurelian.[28] It is possible that Probus was appointed to this position at the very beginning of Aurelian's reign after he had returned from Egypt in about January 271 because Probus had served as one of the commanders of the *protectores* probably since the reign of Gallienus and because Probus was entrusted with the important task of conquering Egypt at the same time as Aurelian marched against Zenobia, or that Probus was appointed supreme commander of the *protectores* as a reward for the conquest of Egypt. In my opinion the former is more likely in light of the fact that Probus was given the command of an expedition as important as the campaign against Egypt. This implies that Probus's influence on the policies of Aurelian was very important, as the quote from Vopiscus claims it was.

> The love of the soldiers toward Probus was always very great. He never permitted them to commit any wrong. He often prevented Aurelian from committing great acts of cruelty. [*This implies that Probus as the supreme commander of Aurelian's bodyguards influenced Aurelian's policies significantly because Aurelian pardoned several enemy leaders in the course of his reign.*] He visited the maniples, and examined their clothes and boots, and whatever booty was at any time taken, he divided it all amongst them, and reserved nothing to himself except darts and arms. Amongst other things, whether taken from the Alani or some other barbarian nation I know not, but there was a horse, which was neither handsome nor large, but the prisoners said that he was so good a runner that he would go 100 miles a day and continue it for eight or ten days together. [*This shows that the Alan horses were particularly good and that the Alans and at least some Roman cavalrymen preferred horses that had good stamina over size and appearance.*] Everyone thought that Probus should have kept this beast to himself, but Probus said that such a horse was fitter for one that was for running away than a brave man. [*Unless meant as a way to convince the soldiers to keep the horse for themselves, this implies that Probus considered sizable stallions which*

were used for a shock attack as better suited for Roman cavalry tactics, but as we shall see the Roman cavalry under Aurelian actually fought in the Alan-Sarmatian manner in which the stamina of the horse was the preferred quality.] He ordered the soldiers to draw lots for the horse. They wrote their names and put them all into an urn. Four of the soldiers had the same name as himself. But he for his part put in no name. They drew and the first name that came up was Probus. The four soldiers of the name of Probus not agreeing to which of them the horse should go because each challenged the lot, he ordered all the army to draw a second time. The lot came up the second time for Probus, and so it was for a third and fourth time… all the army, together with those of that name who had drawn the lots, dedicated the horse to their commander Probus [*The lottery was clearly fixed by the soldiers so that their commander would be forced to accept the horse. This shows how much his subordinates loved Probus*]. [Vopiscus, HA Prob. 8.1ff. tr. by Bernard with emendations, changes and additions.]

The Alamanni-Iuthungi-Marcomanni invasion of Italy so soon after the Iuthungi invasion of 270 suggests strongly that Aurelian had left the war unfinished. While Aurelian was fighting against the Vandals and Sarmatians, there was a window of opportunity for others to invade. It is probable that the previously defeated Iuthungi allied themselves now with the Alamanni and Marcomanni to exact revenge on Aurelian. It is probable that these tribes invaded immediately after the snows had melted in the early spring so that they were able to pass through the Alpine passes.[29]

5.7. The Alamanni-Iuthungi Invasion of Italy in 271

Meanwhile, the Alamanni-Iuthungi-Marcomanni (the Alamanni and neighbours in Zosimus) had managed to penetrate the Roman defences and reach Italy. It is probable that the invaders marched through the Septimier Pass past Milan to Placentia (Placenza). Another possible route they could have taken is through the Brenner Pass past Verona to Placentia (Placenza). A third possibility is that they used both passes and united their forces at Placentia because the inclusion of all three tribal groupings would have made this possible. However, the use of the Septimier Pass by all is the likeliest because the *Historia Augusta* (*Aurel.* 18.3) specifically notes that the invaders devastated the area around Milan (Mediolanum). The invaders had captured the city of Placentia by the time Aurelian arrived on the scene. In light of this, it is probable that Aurelian had committed the mistake of weakening the defences of the Alpine passes. In fact, the presence of the infantry corps with Aurelian in the campaign against the Vandals suggests that he had collected his entire field army with its separate cavalry and infantry components for the war against the Vandals and Sarmatians. This in itself suggests that he had withdrawn whatever elements of infantry he may have posted at the passes of the Alps during the first Iuthungi War of 270 with the result that the direct invasion route lay once again open in the spring of 271. Aurelian would probably have followed the route Mursa–Siscia–Emona–Aquileia–Verona–Cremona–Placentia to reach the scene as fast as possible.

Then Aurelian committed the gravest mistake of his military career. A fragment of Peter the Patrician[30] has preserved for us the initial exchange of words between Aurelian and the invaders. When Aurelian learnt of the presence of a detachment of Iuthungi inside Placentia he ordered them to surrender and treat him as their master, but if they wished to fight, he said that he was ready. The Iuthungi in their turn answered that they had no master and that Aurelian should prepare to fight against the free men tomorrow. Aurelian foolishly swallowed this bait. On the basis of the other sources, the men inside Placentia consisted of the Iuthungi, the Alamanni and Marcomanni, and hid themselves in some close by forest.

… Under him, it is true, a disaster was inflicted by the Marcomanni as a result of this blunder. For, while he was making no plan to meet them face to face during a sudden invasion, but was preparing to pursue them from the rear, they wrought great devastation in all the region around Milan. Later on, however, he conquered even the Marcomanni also. …Aurelian, however, since he wished, by massing his forces together, to meet all the enemy at once, suffered such a defeat near Placentia that the empire of Rome was almost destroyed. This peril, in fact, was caused by the cunning and perfidy of the barbarians' mode of attack. For, being unable to meet him in open battle, they fell back into the thickest forests, and thus as evening came on they routed our forces. [*This implies the use of feigned flight by the barbarian cavalry to the place of ambush and the foolish pursuit of them by the Roman cavalry.*] And, indeed, if the power of the gods, after the Books [*this refers to the consulting of the Sibylline Books/Oracles*] had been consulted and the sacrifices performed, had not confounded the barbarians by means of certain prodigies and heaven-sent visions, there would have been no victory for Rome.' [Flavius Vopiscus (HA, Aurelian 18.3, 21.1–4), tr. by Magie.]

In short, this account of the battle of Placentia by Flavius Vopiscus implies that thanks to the massing of the forces together by Aurelian, the Alamanni-Iuthungi-Marcomanni were unable to meet the Romans in open battle, and that their solution to this problem was to use an ambush. This means that Aurelian had amassed a huge force because on the basis of the previous references to the size of the Iuthungi contingents (40,000 cavalry and 80,000 infantry), it is clear that the invading force consisted at least of this number. The barbarian invaders lured the Romans with a feigned flight into the thick forest near Placentia where they then routed the Roman forces by evening.[31] It is clear that the severe defeat concerned only the cavalry portion of the Roman army because it would have been impossible for the Roman infantry to pursue the fleeing enemy cavalry at the necessary speed. The reference to the pursuit in the *Historia Augusta* (*Aurel.* 18.3) confirms this interpretation. The Romans suffered a crushing defeat. It is likely that the Alamanni-Iuthungi-Marcomanni infantry had the advantage of terrain over the Roman cavalry in the forest; the forested terrain negated the superior speed and mobility of the cavalry. The previous boast of the Iuthungi that they outshone others in cavalry combat was not entirely without basis when they used infantry to support their cavalry.

80 Aurelian and Probus

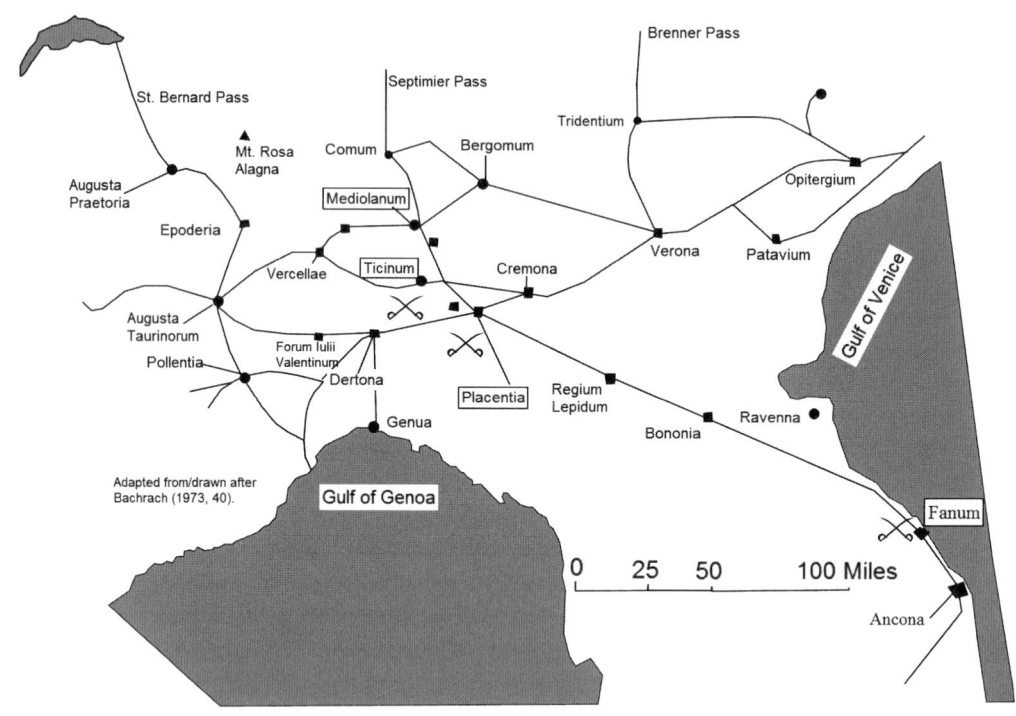

Campaign against the Alamanni-Iuthungi in 271.

It is quite probable that Aurelian squandered a very significant portion of the remaining elite cavalry forces of Gallienus in this one disastrous battle. The reason for this conclusion is that when Aurelian encountered the Palmyrene cataphracts in 272 his cavalry consisted mainly of the lightly-equipped Dalmatian and Moorish cavalry (Zosimus 1.50.1–53.3). When we combine this with the information provided by the sixth century *Strategikon* of the locations of each type of cavalry force (Dalmatian cavalry identified here with the *Illyriciani* of the *Strategikon*) and when we remember the fact that under Gallienus the Moorish cavalry had been placed in the second reserve line,[32] it becomes probable that Aurelian lost his entire left cavalry wing (the *Vexillationes* of the *Strategikon*) and centre of the first line (the *Foederati* of the *Strategikon*) with its more heavily equipped units but not his right wing units (the *Illyriciani*). The diagram opposite of the battle shows the main features of this massive disaster. The boxes have purposefully been drawn by hand to show that the cavalry lines were not straight lines.

When the news of the crushing defeat reached Rome and the provinces, it caused widespread panic. Usurpers appeared in Rome and even in Gaul and Dalmatia. According to Zosimus (1.49.2), the usurpers were Septimius, Urbanus, and Domitianus. Septimius/Septiminus usurped the throne in Dalmatia while, based on coin finds, Domitianus usurped power in South-East Gaul. Domitianus may have been Gallienus's former general. White, however, has suggested an alternative interpretation. He suggests the possibility that Domitianus could have been the son of Aurelian's sister Domitia, on the grounds of his name.[33] Domitianus II represented himself as a descendant of the Emperor Domitian and Domitilla and propagated his friendship with the military rather

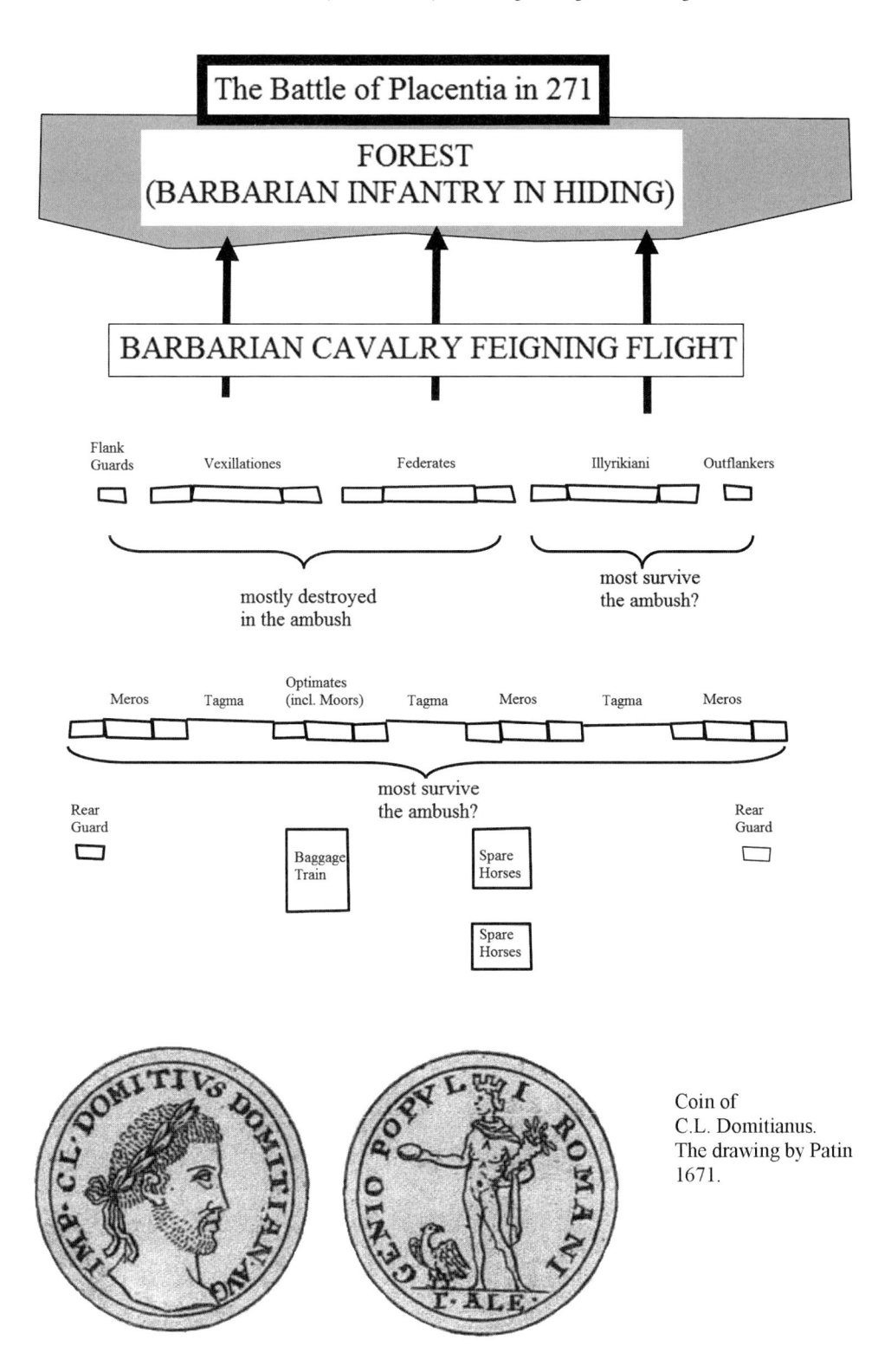

Aurelian (Aurelianus) The Beginning of the Reign in 270–71 81

The Battle of Placentia in 271

**FOREST
(BARBARIAN INFANTRY IN HIDING)**

↑ ↑ ↑

BARBARIAN CAVALRY FEIGNING FLIGHT

Flank Guards | Vexillationes | Federates | Illyrikiani | Outflankers

mostly destroyed in the ambush

most survive the ambush?

Meros | Tagma | Optimates (incl. Moors) | Tagma | Meros | Tagma | Meros

most survive the ambush?

Rear Guard

Baggage Train

Spare Horses

Spare Horses

Rear Guard

Coin of C.L. Domitianus. The drawing by Patin 1671.

than the Senate.[34] It is because of this that I am inclined to agree with those who identify Domitianus II with the general of Gallienus.

After the crushing defeat, according to the *Historia Augusta* (Aurelian 20.4ff.), Aurelian sent a letter to the Senate demanding them to consult the Sibylline Books and bring help to their *princeps* through the sacred ceremonies. He supposedly even promised that he would provide the senators and pontiffs with all the necessary expenses and would give them whatever sacrificial captives (i.e. human sacrifices) or animals that would be needed so that the gods would grant their aid. Even though it is quite plausible that the calculating Aurelianus could have sent this sort of order to the senators in his state of panic to get the aid of the gods and also to calm the restless senators and populace, one still cannot entirely rule out the possibility that it is a fabrication. Nevertheless, it is clear that the information contained in the *Historia Augusta* is believable. On the basis of this text it is easy to see that what seems to have actually happened is that the senators and the populace panicked when the news of the defeat arrived and resorted to consulting the Sibylline Books on their own accord, as was required by the ancient custom. What the senators found was that they should make human and animal sacrifices in certain places to block the routes of advance from the enemy. In their panic, they even installed their own emperor Urbanus (Zosimus 1.49.2[35]). The *Historia Augusta* (*Aurelian* 18.3–6) says there were great revolts in Rome and it was the rebels who consulted the Sibylline Books first. The *Historia Augusta* (*Aurelian* 19.4) also claims that some of the senators had previously maintained, before the arrival of Aurelian's supposed letter, that the books should be consulted because Aurelian himself revered the gods and would therefore support such an action with the implication that Aurelian's position on the question was not known. This suggests a rather different personality from the one put forward by the *Historia Augusta*. It is quite probable that Aurelian was not as religious as claimed, but rather a typical military commander who used and turned to religion only when it suited his own political purposes, and this appears to have been such an occasion. The intention of the letter to the Senate, which confirmed that their own actions were legal, would merely have been a measure meant to secure their support.[36] Aurelian even promised human sacrifices from the ranks of the captured enemies if the senators after the consultation of the Books wished this. On balance it would appear probable that the senators simply lost their wits and resorted to human sacrifices. They then revolted against Aurelian because they were well aware that they had acted without his permission and knew his severity. The letter in which Aurelian ordered the senators to consult the Sibylline Books after they had already been consulted should therefore be seen as an effort to create divisions among the senators, because this letter removed the fear that the senators would be punished for having acted without Aurelian's permission. However, this was merely a stratagem, because after Aurelian had reached Rome he started a purge of senators.[37] The senators most ready to resort to the use of human sacrifice and to the setting up of the new emperor would have consisted of those who had previously been the most vehement supporters of the traditionalist Claudius and his brother Quintillus. This would best explain why, after having defeated the invaders, Aurelian marched to Rome and unleashed his army and military police (*statores Augusti*) on the city.

The Alamanni-Iuthungi-Marcomanni sought to exploit their victory by advancing against the city of Rome itself. The fact that Rome was in the hands of Aurelian's enemies made the strategic situation very problematic for Aurelian. The invaders' planned route was to march along the Via Aemilia and then use the Via Flaminia to get over the Appenines into Central Italy and Rome. The enemy had divided themselves into several marching columns to facilitate foraging and pillaging. After Aurelian had managed to regroup the remnants of his army, he gave chase. He caught up with one of the marching columns of the enemy near Fanum on the banks of the Metaurus River. This was not difficult to achieve, since the barbarians were slowed down by the amount of booty they had amassed. The invaders were trapped against the river. This time Aurelian won the battle resoundingly. A great number of barbarians were drowned in the river in the ensuing rout. The Romans later celebrated the great victory with a pair of commemorative inscriptions. The remaining marching columns of the Alamanni-Iuthungi-Marcomanni began their homeward march while Aurelian's forces shadowed them, waiting for the right moment to strike, which came when the barbarians reached the open plains near the River Ticinus/Ticinum (Pavia). Aurelianus unleashed his army and crushed the remnants of the invading army. In my opinion the locale implies that Aurelian had preserved the decisive role for his cavalry forces because their mobility could be used to the fullest advantage only in the open plains – this would not be a surprising tactic for a cavalry general. This must have happened some time during the summer of 271. The rest of the campaign consisted of the rounding up of fugitives and the killing of those who resisted. Aurelian assumed the title *Germanicus Maximus* to celebrate his victory.[38]

Aurelian was now free to settle scores with the usurpers Septimius, Urbanus and Domitianus (Zosimus 1.49.2). The news of the defeat of the Alamanni-Iuthungi-Marcomanni seems to have taken care of most of the willingness of his enemies to resist. Septimius was killed by his own men (*Epitome* 35.3). We do not know what exactly happened to Domitianus II in South-East Gaul, but it seems likely that he too was killed by his own men or, alternatively, as suggested by Watson, Julius Placiadianus suppressed it. That leaves out Urbanus.[39]

According to the *Historia Augusta* (Aurelian 21.5), Aurelian was extremely violent by nature and now filled with rage, and he advanced to Rome in person to exact retribution for the revolts. Practically all of the extant sources claim that Aurelian was over-violent, cruel and bloodthirsty. But in truth he was a pragmatist who was moderate and lenient when he considered it advantageous to be so, and used harsh punishment and merciless cruelty when it served his and his Empire's best interests. If some unscrupulous person was stupid enough to take advantage of his clemency, he meted out merciless punishment on him or her to make it absolutely clear that such behaviour would not be tolerated under his rule. This was particularly true of cases of corruption and public morality. Aurelian did not accept any abuse of power by those holding public offices and he punished even relatively minor offences with extreme severity. It was this that brought him his reputation for cruelty.[40]

I would also suggest that Aurelian purposefully cultivated a reputation for cruelty, at least among his soldiers to keep them disciplined and united, as was later advocated by Machiavelli. Machiavelli (*Prince*, 17, tr. by Bull, 97) puts the matter thus: 'When a prince is campaigning with his soldiers and is in command of a large army then he need not worry about having a reputation for cruelty; because, without such a reputation, no army was ever kept united and disciplined.'

The sources tell that Aurelian executed the leaders of the revolt, which included a number of Roman aristocrats/senators – sometimes on the basis of information provided by only one informant. This leaves open both the possibility that the Praetorians present in the city[41] had already killed the usurper and allowed Aurelianus inside the city without fighting, and also the possibility that there was some serious fighting in the streets of Rome before the revolt was crushed, though the former appears inherently more likely. The killing of the real and supposed aristocratic plotters also had the benefit of bringing money to the imperial coffers that Aurelian could use to bribe his own troops and supporters, as previously advised by someone to his own detriment. According to Ammianus, Aurelian found the state coffers empty after the reign of Gallienus and the disasters suffered (in truth mainly under Claudius) with the result that he inflicted punishments and torture on both the guilty and innocent in order to get reinforcements and to be able to pay his troops. It was because of this that he went after money like a torrent. But this was not the entire truth. As noted by Watson, Aurelian also needed money for the forthcoming campaign against Palmyra. For the time being, however, Aurelian was ready to act as if he would accept Zenobia's and Vaballathus's position in the east. The best evidence for this is that Zenobia continued to mint coins portraying Aurelian as the superior emperor/ *Augustus* until April 272.[42]

The narrative sources state that there was a very serious and bloody revolt of the mint workers instigated by the treasurer/finance minister (*rationalis*) Felicissimus at Rome, which Aurelian also crushed. The reason for the revolt was that they had been filing off silver from the coins. It has been suggested that the coins in question were the so-called *Divus Claudius* series of coins that Aurelian issued at the beginning of his reign to claim his right to be the successor of Claudius because the coins minted in Rome were well below the silver standard of the day.[43] According to Sextus Aurelius Victor and the *Scriptores Historiae Augustae*, the mint workers gathered on the Caelian Hill and fought so fiercely that they killed about 7,000 soldiers (*militia*), boatmen (*lembariarii*), border troops (*riparienses*), castle-troops (*castrensiani*) and Dacians.[44] The rebels were massacred, but we do not have numbers. Unfortunately the sources do not state whether the revolt of the mint workers was connected with the revolt of the upper class senators or Urbanus or whether it occurred only after Aurelian had already crushed the usurper and senators.[45]

The fact that the revolt of the mint workers is mentioned separately suggests that it occurred only after the main revolt or revolts had already been crushed. The large number of soldiers killed would suggest that there would have also been other men involved in the combat besides the mint workers. However, since the reason for the revolt was the alleged corruption of the treasurer and the workers, it seems probable that their revolt followed the revelation that Aurelian would not overlook or tolerate any kind of corruption among the civil servants, which would have become obvious only after Aurelian had already retaken power in the capital. In other words, there seems to have been two revolts in Rome: 1) One led by the Senate and usurper Urbanus; 2) Another by Felicissimus and the mint workers. It is possible that Felicissimus had actively participated in the crushing of the first mentioned revolt only to find out that his embezzlement would still not be overlooked. However, it is also possible that Urbanus and his senatorial friends had armed the mint workers of Felicissimus and used them as soldiers because they were an organized body that could be used for such a purpose. After the revolt, the mint was closed.

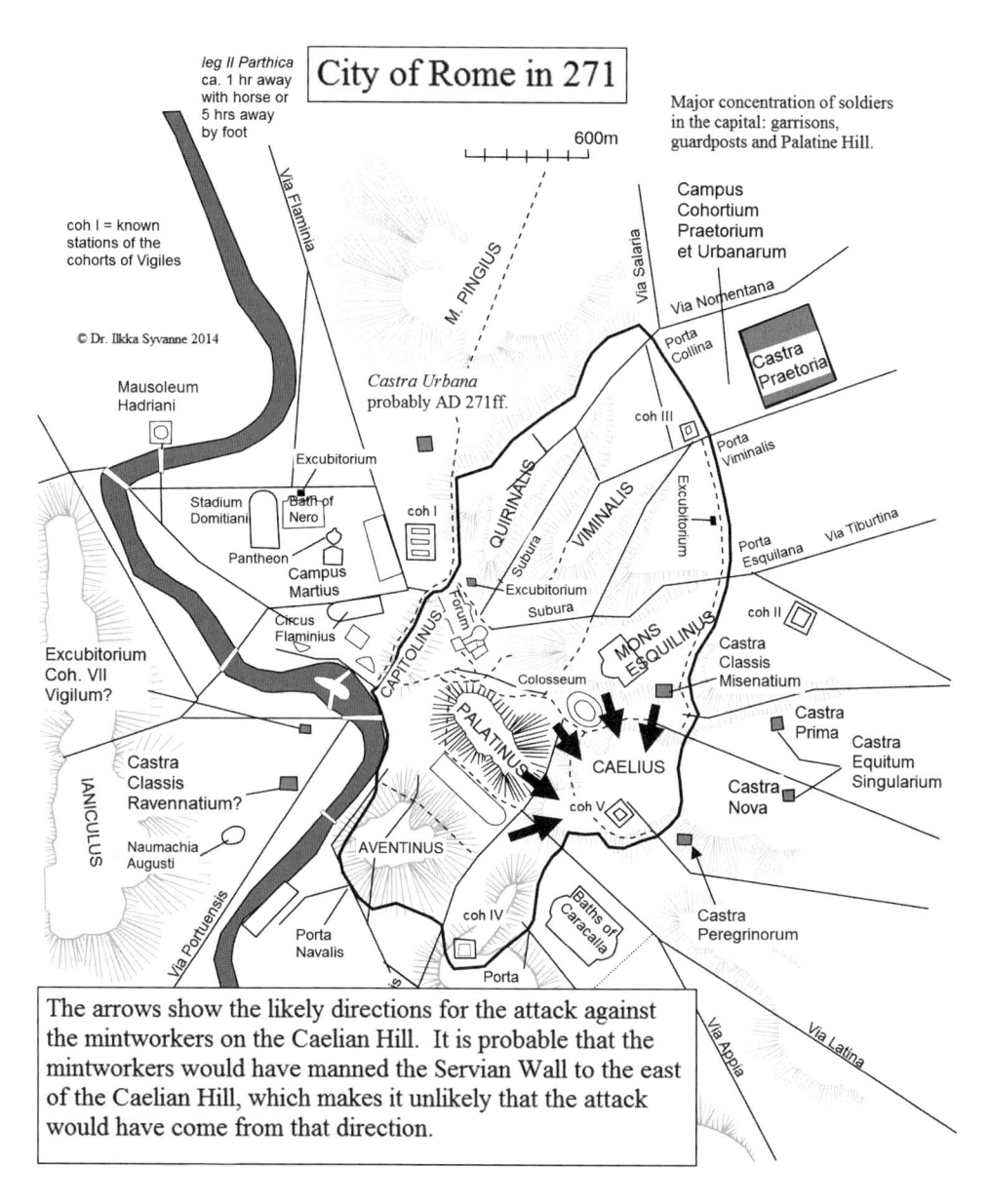

Aurelian (Aurelianus) The Beginning of the Reign in 270–71 85

City of Rome in 271

leg II Parthica ca. 1 hr away with horse or 5 hrs away by foot

Major concentration of soldiers in the capital: garrisons, guardposts and Palatine Hill.

coh I = known stations of the cohorts of Vigiles

© Dr. Ilkka Syvänne 2014

The arrows show the likely directions for the attack against the mintworkers on the Caelian Hill. It is probable that the mintworkers would have manned the Servian Wall to the east of the Caelian Hill, which makes it unlikely that the attack would have come from that direction.

It is probable that Aurelian sent his soldiers against the mint workers on the Caelian Hill mainly from the north and west (shown with arrows on the map) because it is probable that the mint workers would have occupied the Servian Wall making it difficult to approach from this direction. However, the presence of the camps of soldiers outside this wall would have isolated the mint workers from that side. It is also probable that the attack would have been supported by ballistae and onagri placed on the Palatinus Hill (the Imperial Palace complex) and on the Mons Esquilinus. The fact that the attackers lost 7,000 men proves that the fight was still very difficult. After all, the attackers were forced to attack a well prepared enemy by advancing uphill.

86   Aurelian and Probus

My educated guess is that it is possible that the *urbaniciani* (the urban cohorts) of Rome had stayed loyal to Aurelian throughout the usurpations and revolts because they now received new barracks from Aurelian, which must have been a reward, or alternatively that they had fought with particular distinction during the uprising of the mint workers. The building of the new barracks also proves that they remained important for military, security and policing purposes.

5.8. Pacification of the Capital, Reforms, and the Building of the Aurelian Walls

The bloody purge of Aurelian's real and imagined enemies among the senators, and the purge of corrupt officials cleared the table. Despite the hostility that this caused among the conservative senators, the elimination of all potential troublemakers in the capital together with the two usurpers in the provinces ensured that Aurelian did not have to fear another usurpation in the territory controlled by him for the next three years. To the dismay of the conservative senators there were plenty of other senators who were ready to lend their support to Aurelian in return for high offices and honours. It should be remembered that the purge of Aurelian's enemies created vacant posts to be filled by his friends and supporters, who were thereby rewarded for their loyalty. Though, according to the *Historia Augusta* (*Aurel.* 45.3), he did this with moderation and wisdom.

Having crushed the revolts, Aurelian wanted to make certain that the capital of the Roman Empire would be better protected in the future so that its inhabitants and senators would not feel it necessary to take action of their own or to set up their own rulers to protect them. Aurelian's solution was the building of the wall which bears his name, the Aurelian Wall.[46] The circuit of the wall was almost nineteen kilometres and it encompassed most of the fourteen Augustan regions and important buildings of the city, but not all of the inhabited parts. Defensive needs dictated the course of the wall so that the enemy would not be able to exploit any terrain against the defenders. It was extended across the Tiber to incorporate the important flour mills and the Mausoleum of Hadrian (Castel Sant'Angelo). The wall was also designed with defensive artillery fire in mind so as to position ballistae throughout the wall for the purpose of subjecting any enemy which approached the walls to a barrage of bolts.

Aurelian could not spare his soldiers for the building project so he assigned the city guilds to perform the labour. These were allowed to add the title *Aureliani* to their name as a form of thanks. The guilds worked to a preconceived plan and their work was supervised by professional engineers and architects some of whom certainly came from the ranks of the military. However, due to the inexperience of the workforce and the human tendency to build as fast as possible, the quality of the resulting work varied greatly. In my opinion, it is also likely that corruption played a role in this. However, it is still clear that haste was the primary reason for the poor workmanship because the wall was finished within six years (it was completed under Probus).

The Aurelian Wall was 6.1 metres high and 3.65 metres wide. It had a core of concrete which was brick- or tile-faced. It had two variants. The first was a solid curtain wall with a rampart walk that had a parapet 1 metre high with 60cm-high merlons. The second variant consisted of galleried curtain walls, the galleries placed at a height of 3 metres

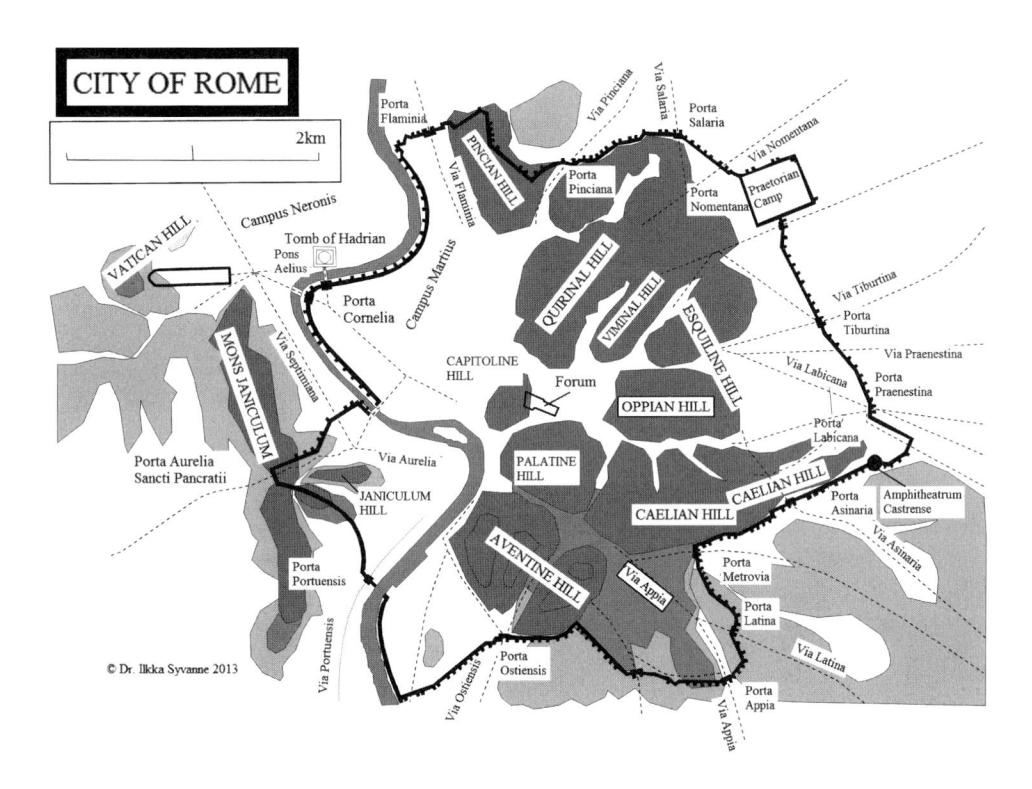

Aurelian (Aurelianus) The Beginning of the Reign in 270–71 87

CITY OF ROME

where there were windows for ballistae and archers. There were towers every 30 metres so there were 381 towers altogether. These projected 3.35 metres in front of the curtains and rose about 4.5 metres above the rampart walk. The towers along these galleried sections of the wall had similar galleries with windows placed at a height of 3 metres for the same purpose. The wall had 18 gateways and 29 entrances altogether with the postern gates included. The gateways were of four categories. The first were the four gateways (the Flaminia, Appia, Ostiensis east, and Portuensis gates) that had double archways. These had more imposing defences with round-fronted towers. The second category, with single archways (the Salaria, Nomentana, Tiburtina and Latina gates), were meant to protect roads of secondary importance. These were also flanked with round-fronted towers. The third category (Pinciana, Chiusa, Asinaria, Metrobia, Ardeatina and Septimiana gates) were those that were designed for local traffic. These did not have flanking towers. The fourth category consisted of the postern gates and doorways.

It has usually been assumed that the defences were meant solely to deter barbarian invaders long enough for a Roman relief army to arrive and that the city would not have possessed enough men able to use the ballistae so they could not be placed along the entire length of the wall which would have required at least 700 ballistae. In my opinion, the wall was indeed primarily meant to deter the barbarians with poor siege skills, but it is still clear that it actually worked well against Romans too, contary to the assumption that the walls and its defences were not strong enough to withstand an attack by skilled besiegers. The best proof of this is the successful defence of the city by Maxentius against Severus and Galerius in the next century. Furthermore, this approach overlooks the

88 Aurelian and Probus

Porta Appia (Aurelian) — drawn after Nick Fields. © Dr. Ilkka Syvänne 2018

overwhelming amount of evidence for the successful use of ballistae and stone throwers by civilians during the sieges. The likeliest place for such training would have been in the citizen militias. It is likely that most Roman youths (*iuvenes*) were trained to use such equipment.

The accompanying images show the Porta Appia (the type one, i.e. the strongest version) and the line of the Aurelian Wall on the map on page 87.

Aurelian Walls of Rome according to Piranesi

At the beginning of his reign Aurelian's internal policies can be summarized as follows: 1) securing the army, done by killing Quintillus and by campaigning against the invaders; 2) securing the capital by purging enemies; 3) looting the rich with various excuses to cover expenses and to finance his forthcoming campaigns; 4) building the wall; 5) stopping the drainage of bullion to the east; 6) preparing for the war against Zenobia.

The barbarian invasions of Italy under Gallienus and Aurelian, and the resulting problems in the capital, had brought home the lesson that the capital had to be secured with a wall and other measures when Aurelian's intention was to march against Zenobia. It was because of this that he needed to find a way to replace the bread of Egypt, now held by the Palmyrenes. In the meantime Aurelian instituted a free supply of pork to the populace. The populace had to be kept happy to make certain that unscrupulous noblemen could not exploit their unhappiness in a situation in which the Palmyrenes could cut off bread supplies from Egypt. It seems likely that it was at this time that Aurelian refused to dress in silk or buy silk for others to use, the reason being that a pound of silk cost a pound of gold. It only helped his enemies in the east if he kept buying silk and other similar items. Possibly Aurelian forbade the buying of silk for the time being even if this is not stated by the sources.[47]

Flavius Vopiscus claimed that Aurelian had records of debts due to the state burned in the Forum of Trajan. The obvious intention was to please those who owed money to the Exchequer so they would have no urgent need to revolt against Aurelian while he was away from the city. It would also have been good for the economy because the removal of debts would have given the populace more money to spend.[48] Vopiscus also states that Aurelian gave a general amnesty to those who had committed offences against the state. This measure might have the same intention if it took place now, but more importantly it would have been a very useful tool to calm fears among those who were currently serving under the Pamyrenes. If it took place in 274, its intention was to calm the fears of the Gallic nobility and soldiers that Aurelian would exact vengeance against them. My suggestion is that probably Aurelian would have promised the same amnesty in both cases, to make it easier for the Romans to surrender to him. This was actually quite easy to do in the aftermath of the purge which had removed most of Aurelian's enemies. It was also necessary, because it removed the fear of being purged from the remaining rich and made them less likely to revolt in his absence.[49]

The break-up with the Palmyrenes was not immediately apparent, since it was not in Aurelian's interest to warn them. On the basis of Zenobia's coinage depicting both Vaballathus and Aurelian, Zenobia seems to have simultaneously tried her best to stress her loyalty to Aurelian and the Roman Empire; it was not in Aurelian's interest to rock the boat before his preparations were completed.

The crushing of the revolt of the mint workers of Rome resulted in the closure of its operations until the summer of 273. Most of its workers were transferred to Milan where they operated under Gaius Valerius Sabinus who received the title *agens vice rationalis*. Sabinus became effectively the finance minister of Aurelian; it has been speculated that he was the man behind the monetary reforms of Aurelian. The first part of these reforms was the improvement of the weight standard of the billon (debased silver) coinage back to the standard it had been before the corrupt debasement of the Divus Claudius coinage by the Roman Mint. In addition to this, Aurelian tightened the general control over all the rest of the mints, so they issued propaganda designs that were uniform in their design and intent. The surviving mint workers of Rome were transferred to two new mints which Aurelianus set up in the Balkans for the forthcoming campaigns both in the Balkans and in the East. The first of the mints was set up at Serdica (Sofia) which lay on the road from Milan to Byzantium. The second was set up at some unknown place, possibly a maritime port, in the Balkans from autumn 271 until spring 273. The most likely location for the mint is Byzantium. Aurelian faced the Goths in the autumn 271 and the Palmyrenes in 272 so the coins from these mints were highly useful for keeping the soldiers paid.[50]

The accompanying images of coins of Aurelian are from Beger 1696. Note how Aurelian, like so many other emperors, used his coins as tools of propaganda, advertising his military victories, the reconquest of territory lost (*Restitutor Orientis*, *Restitutor Orbis*), loyalty of the army, *virtus*, and, most importantly, that he was the favourite of the gods who brought victories.

Aurelian (Aurelianus) The Beginning of the Reign in 270–71   91

Chapter Six

Aurelian vs. Zenobia 271–272

6.1. The Preparations

Having satisfactorily settled matters in Rome and in Italy, Aurelianus headed east against Zenobia and the Palmyrenes. Since it was of utmost importance to retake Egypt, Aurelian sent a separate naval detachment under Probus, the future emperor, to reconquer Egypt, the breadbasket of the empire. Roman Africa centred on the city of Carthage was a more important source of grain for the city of Rome at this time, but Egypt was important also for other reasons which included its revenue for the state. The aim was clearly to advance against the Palmyrenes on two fronts simultaneously so that they would either have to divide their forces or abandon the defence of one front. The subsequent timing of the attacks to occur approximately simultaneously is a sure sign of good coordination of the army corps and navies by Aurelian and Probus.[1]

6.2. The Gothic Interlude in the Balkans in 271

Aurelian's campaign against Zenobia was delayed by the invasion of the Goths under Cannabas, or Cannabaudes, who seem to have exploited the absence of Aurelian by invading both Thrace and Illyricum. Consequently, Aurelian advanced first against the Goths, whom he defeated both in Illyricum and then in Thrace. This must have happened in the course of the autumn of 271. After Aurelian had crushed the different enemy columns inside the Empire, he pursued the remnants over the Danube where he slew the chieftain Cannabas/Cannabaudes together with 5,000 enemy. This was effectively the end of the series of Gothic invasions that had begun in 238. It is quite probable that it was this war that Ammianus Marcellinus meant when he stated that the Goths were finally driven out of Roman territory after the death of Claudius.[2]

Aurelian paid close attention to intelligence gathering needs when he dealt with the barbarians and their envoys. This is a sign that he was a good commander. Aurelian knew that he needed intelligence of enemy activities to be able to response properly to them in a timely manner. The advance intelligence of the Vandal/Sarmatian invasion is a good example of Aurelian's intelligence apparatus working well. Vopiscus has preserved for us one example of Aurelian's intelligence gathering methods. He used a man called Bonosus (the future usurper) as intelligence officer, and married him to a Gothic princess:

> The emperor Aurelian said often of him [*Bonosus*] that 'He was born not to live, but to drink.' But he still held him in high honour because of his ability in war. And when any envoys arrived from the barbarian nations, it was the business of Bonosus to drink with them till they were overwhelmed with wine and drunken so that in

this condition they spilled out their secrets. Bonosus, however, always remained calm and sober regardless of how much he drank… she [*his wife*] was a woman of wit and merit, … she was a princess of royal Gothic blood, and one whom the emperor Aurelian had purposefully married to Bonosus that through her and him he might the better penetrate into all the affairs of the Goths… 'From the emperor Aurelian to Gallio Avitus, greetings. I wrote to you previously about the Gothic noblewomen at Perinthus… I wish that Hunila be married to Bonosus.' (This letter may once again be fictitious, but I would still suggest that it contains the truth that it was really Aurelian who married the Gothic princess to Bonosus, as claimed by Vopiscus, for intelligence gathering purposes.) [Vopiscus HA FSPB 12.3ff., tr. by Bernard 315ff. with emendations, changes and comments.]

There are several alternative routes that Aurelian could have taken to reach the Balkans and Byzantium for the crossing of the straits. The first led from Epidaurum/Dyrrachium along the Via Egnatia to Thessalonica, Philippi, across the Danube and then to Byzantium. The second led from Aquileia to Siscia, Sirmium, Naissus, Philippopolis, Hadrianopolis, across the Danube and then to Byzantium, or from Sirmium alongside the Danube and then across the Danube and from there to Byzantium. The third alternative route would be from Aquileia to Poetovia, Sirmium, Naissus, Philippopolis, Hadrianopolis, across the Danube and then to Byzantium, or from Sirmium alongside the Danube and then across the Danube and to Byzantium. The second and third of these alternatives seem more likely since both would have allowed Aurelian to march his army on land alongside the rivers Sava or Drava and then inland towards Thrace and Byzantium. Alternatively, it is possible that Aurelian may have marched from Sirmium along the Danube (which would have facilitated supply) to cut off the route of retreat from the enemy.

Watson (p.55) and many others have speculated that it was now that Aurelian decided to evacuate Dacia and transfer the soldiers and part of the population to the other side of the Danube. Other historians have speculated that it occurred only after the campaign against the Palmyrenes and the crushing of the invading Carpi (Free Dacians), while still others have speculated that it occurred when Aurelian was en route against the Persians in 275. None of the educated guesses can definitely be verified. However, I agree with Watson that the likeliest date for the evacuation of Dacia is the immediate aftermath of the Gothic victory, because it was then that Aurelian had defeated the enemy so he was able to evacuate Dacia from a position of strength, while also shortening the border in a situation in which he needed all available men for the war in the east. In addition, the border areas close to the Danube that had been repeatedly ravaged since the 250s needed new settlers and defenders in the absence of Aurelian in the east, which could be obtained by shortening the border. It is easy to see that Aurelian might also have wanted to shorten the border to make available resources for the eastern campaign. Aurelian created a new province called *Dacia Ripensis* for the evacuated inhabitants of Dacia so that he was able to keep up the pretence that he had not abandoned Roman territory to the enemy because Dacia still existed. Furthermore, if he was a native of this area, as suggested above, the transferral of the population made these his compatriots, which could be seen as an honour.

6.3. The Campaign against Palmyra in 271–2

6.3.1. Winter 271/2

According to the *Historia Augusta* (*Aurel.* 22.3–4), having crushed the Goths, Aurelian continued his march to Byzantium and then crossed into Bithynia,[3] which surrendered without a fight. It is clear that Aurelian must have had a navy accompanying him, which was used for three purposes: 1) it carried supplies; 2) it shipped the army into Bithynia, 3) it protected the crossing. It is in fact possible that this is the same navy that we find Probus using for the taking of Egypt in 272, if it accompanied Aurelian up to here before sailing along the Aegean Sea into Crete and from there to Egypt. This is the view adopted by Watson (p.224). Watson's view is that the fleet under Probus started its journey from Byzantium no later than the very beginning of April 272. On the basis of the silence of the sources for any presence of a fleet during Aurelian's march to Antioch this is the likeliest alternative, but we should remember that this is an argument from the silence of the sources. The other possibility is of course that Aurelian had divided his principal naval assets into four forces: 1) part of the fleet was left in Italy to protect Italy and the south of Gaul; 2) part was used to protect the shipping lanes from Carthage to Italy; 3) part was dispatched under Probus to Carthage from which it then sailed along the North African coast into Egypt;[4] 4) part was used to support the operations under Aurelian.

Whatever the truth, Aurelian apparently wintered his forces in Byzantium before the crossing, or he wintered his forces in Byzantium and Bithynia in 271–2 to secure the bridgehead in advance of the main campaign. Cizek (p.106) suggests that he spent the winter at Byzantium, and indeed this is quite possible.

On the basis of the list of units present at the battle of Emesa, which is included in Zosimus's *New History* (see the quote later), the army which Aurelian led into Asia Minor was a very substantial one. It included units from Raetia, Noricum, Balkans and Italy, as well as bodyguard units and the Dalmatians and Moorish cavalry. Zosimus also lists the eastern units present at this battle, but it is possible that these deserted to Aurelian only afterwards. Regardless, one cannot entirely exclude the possibility that there would have already been at least some detachments drawn from these units present when Aurelian entered Asia. In addition to this, Aurelian would have had new units that had been raised by him or by one of his predecessors about which we know very little. The only names that we know are the legions, *I Illyricorum* and *IV Martia*, the former of which was stationed later at Palmyra and the latter in Bosra, but it is clear that there were also other newly raised units, the existence of which becomes apparent only later under the Tetrarchs.

If we assume that Aurelian would have drawn an average about 3,000 men per legion from the west (ca. 15 legions), this would have amounted to about 45,000 men. If we add to this figure the two known new legions (*I Illyricorum* and *IV Martia*) posted in the east, the total would be 55,000 legionaries. However, since it is quite likely that Aurelian and his predecessors had created even more new legions than this, we should add at least two legions to this figure for a total of about 65,000 legionaries. If we assume that the auxiliary units would have contributed half the number then the total number of footmen would be about 97,500–100,000. If we assume that each of the legions contributed ca. 300 horsemen, these would have amounted to ca. 5,700 horse, in addition to which we should count up the Dalmatian and Moorish cavalry (9,000–10,000?), the Praetorian cavalry (ca.

2,000), the *equites singulares Augusti* (ca. 2,000) and about 2,500 *aulici/protectores/scholae*. If we assume that the auxiliary units would have contributed about twice the number of legionary cavalry, then the grand total would have been about 33,500 horsemen. I would suggest that Aurelian sent at least 20,000 footmen out of this number with Probus to retake Egypt. In addition to this, Probus would have had the marines and multi-purpose rowers/soldiers at his disposal, so his land force would have amounted to at least 30,000 footmen and marines plus the rowers/soldiers. This was quite enough for the task.

6.3.2. The Triumphal reconquest of Asia Minor in the spring of 272

The details of Aurelian's campaign in Asia Minor before he reached the city of Tyana are not known with any certainty. Stephen Mitchell (1995, 212–16) has speculated on the basis of significant coin finds from the reign of Aurelian that Pamphylia probably served as a staging area/military base from which at least part of Aurelian's forces advanced against Iconium. He has also noted that there is evidence for the existence of Roman military activities (i.e. a base) in Pamphylia from about 230 onwards so that the area became a major operational base during the 250s and 260s in response to the Persian and Gothic threat. If his speculations are correct, then Aurelian would have dispatched a part of his force in ships to Pamphylia from which it would have made a separate advance into Iconium and presumably also to other cities along the coast or close to it. The fact that the Palmyrenes did not attempt to hold the Cilician Gates against Aurelian does indeed suggest that Aurelian's forces were already in possession of the coastal areas, so it was impossible for the Palmyrenes to contemplate such an option. However, the silence of the sources regarding the navy can also be interpreted in another way, namely that Aurelian either left the navy in the naval bases at Byzantium and Cyzicus to protect the supply route, or that his fleet followed only in his footsteps so that the fleet took control of each new port and harbour along the coast of Asia Minor once it had deserted back to the Roman side, or that the fleet was indeed dispatched to take Egypt in its entirety once it had shipped Aurelian's forces across into Asia.

Fortunately we are on more certain ground when considering the route taken by the main army led by Aurelian in person. He seems to have marched from Nicomedia to Nicaea, Ancyra, Koloneia and Tyana, where he faced the first city which did not immediately open its gates to him. It is probable, however, that he also dispatched envoys or detachments of soldiers to all of the other cities of Asia Minor at the same time as his main army marched along the military road and that these envoys received the submission of the rest of the cities on his behalf. It is similarly likely that the existing Roman garrisons and military detachments in the area deserted to Aurelian's side. These would have included at least the headquarters units of the legions *XV Apollinaris* (at Satala) and *XII Fulminata* (Melitene).

The following quote from Zosimus describes Aurelian's journey from Bithynia to Antioch:

> During these occurrences in Italy and Pannonia, the emperor [*Aurelian*] prepared to march against the Palmyrenians, who had subdued all Egypt, and the east, as far as Ancyra in Galatia, and would have acquired Bithynia as far as Chalcedon, if the inhabitants of that country had not learned that Aurelianus was made emperor, and

so shook off the Palmyrenian yoke. As soon as the emperor was on his march there, Ancyra submitted to the Romans, and afterwards Tyana, and all the cities between it and Antioch. [Zosimus 1.50.1–2, English tr. possibly by J. Davis in 1814, p.25 with some additions and changes.]

Zosimus's text proves nicely how most of the Romans of Asia Minor welcomed their emperor and deserted the Palmyrenes at the first opportunity so that Aurelian was able to march unopposed up to the city of Tyana. It is worthwhile to discuss the events that took place in or around Tyana at greater length because these provide us with very important details of what went on in the Roman Empire at this time and these were harbingers of the future. The following, a slightly emended quote from the seventeenth century translation of the *Historia Augusta*, gives us a good indication of how Aurelian manipulated his men and what were his plans for the future of the Empire. It is well-known that Aurelian did indeed promote the cults of the *Sol* and Apollonius of Tyana, which stands as another instance of Aurelian imitating or following in the footsteps of the great soldier emperor Caracalla. It was not only the coins of Caracalla that Aurelian imitated but also his religious policies. Members of Caracalla's extended family were priests of the Sun God at Emesa. Therefore it is more than likely that it was actually Aurelian and his clever use of the supernatural to motivate the soldiers to do his bidding that Constantine the Great later copied even if there were earlier examples of such manipulation.

> Coming to the city of Tyana in Cappadocia, he found its gates closed against him, so he became angered and said in passion: 'I will not leave a dog alive in this place.' This made the soldiers storm it more violently in the hopes of booty, until one Heraclammon, afraid that he should be killed along with the rest, betrayed his native city. Now Aurelian immediately did two things worthy of an emperor, one which he showed an example of his severity, and the other his mercy. Like a wise victor, he put to death Heraclammon for betraying his native city. Then, when the soldiers desired total destruction of the city, according to his words that he would not leave a dog alive in Tyana, Aurelian answered them, 'It is true I have said I would not leave a dog in the city, so kill all the dogs.' [*This account is confirmed by Peter the Patrician, who also stated that Aurelian calmed down the men with this jest and he sent both tribunes and soldiers inside the city to kill all the dogs. Aurelian also stated to his men that they were there to free the cities and not to pillage them. If they did that, none would trust them. The soldiers were instructed to pillage the barbarians.*[5]] …and it was followed by …the army, because they were as much pleased with the wit of their emperor as if he had really given them the riches of the city.
>
> The Emperor Aurelian to Mallius Chilo: 'I have taken Tyana, and suffered the man to be killed by whose, as it were, good office I did it. I could not let such a traitor live. I willingly let the soldiers kill him because how could he be faithful to me, who spared not to betray his own country? He is the only one of all the besieged who had been killed. [*From the point of view of military practice the killing of the man who betrayed his city was potentially risky because the aim would usually have been to induce enemies to betray their cities. Therefore one can call such a move by Aurelian a mistake, but subsequent events prove that this actually did not prevent the desertions and*

surrenders of other cities in the future so in practice it did not prove to be a mistake. It is possible that the news of this did not travel fast enough to have an effect, and it is possible that subsequent enemies of Aurelian were just as predisposed to surrender and that the clemency he had shown in the taking of Tyana was enough to convince everyone to seek a pardon.] I cannot deny that he was rich. But yet I have given his estate to his children that none shall pretend to say that it was to get his money I killed him.'

The city of Tyana was taken in this manner. Heraclammon betrayed to Aurelian a place where there was a natural rising of the ground by which he might mount the walls undiscovered. Aurelian did so and, holding his purple cloak in the air, he showed himself to the people within and to the soldiers without, and so the city was taken as if the whole army was within the walls. [*In other words, the mere sight of Aurelian in this place was enough to convince the inhabitants that it would be impossible to defend the city if Aurelian placed his siege equipment on top of this natural siege mound. It is likely that Heraclammon was actually killed in a fit of anger because his supposedly important information was worthless. Any general would have recognized the mound.*]

I ought not here omit a thing, which is to the honour of the memory of the venerable Apollonius, who was a native of the city of Tyana. Aurelian, it is said, was furiously speaking and thinking of destroying the city of Tyana. But as he was going to his tent, that wise man of so known fame and authority, an ancient philosopher, and a true friend of the gods, Apollonius Tyanaeus, who is himself to be highly celebrated as a god, appeared to him in the form in which his image is in the temples at this day, and spoke to him these words in Latin so that a man from Pannonia could understand him: 'Aurelian, Why should you think of murdering my poor countrymen? If you would like to reign in glory abstain, Aurelian, from the blood of the innocent. Aurelian, be merciful, if you wish to live long.' Aurelian recognized the visage of the venerable philosopher because he had seen it before in several temples. He was much struck at it, and immediately returned to a better mind about his treatment of the city, and promised to erect a temple to Apollonius and to set up his image and statues. This account is what I have received from grave men, and I have also often read the same myself in the books in the Ulpian Library; to which I give the more credit; because I have great respect for the majesty of Apollonius; than whom, what man had there ever been more holy, venerable, illustrious and divine? He raised the dead to life again. [Flavius Vopiscus, *Historia Augusta*, Aurelian 22.5–24.8, tr. by John Bernard, pp.220–3 with some emendations, changes and corrections.]

Pat Southern in her biography of the empress Zenobia has aptly noted that the siege of Tyana was actually no siege at all but only a brief interlude in the campaign. Flavius Vopiscus's account makes it clear that the city surrendered when its citizens witnessed Aurelian on the hill holding his purple cloak in the air. However, the initial refusal of the citizens to let Aurelian inside had caused him to utter the burst of angry words that not even a dog would be left living inside the city. Pat Southern is surely correct in stating that the information regarding Aurelian's vision of Apollonius of Tyana mentioned in the *Historia Augusta* is likely to have a basis in truth. Aurelian wanted to maintain his policy of showing clemency to all cities that would open up their gates to him, and now there existed the danger that his soldiers wanted to put into effect his angry words. It was when the citizens had already promised to open up the gates, and Aurelian was returning back to his tent, that he came up with the masterplan of claiming to have seen a vision of Apollonius of Tyana who commanded him to avoid the shedding of blood. Southern is also correct to compare this with the situation in which Postumus had forbidden the pillaging of the city of Mainz with the result that the soldiers killed him. Aurelian was wise enough to use religion to calm the soldiers down and when they then reminded him of his own words he had the presence of mind to order the killing of all dogs inside the city, which the soldiers readily accepted as a great joke.[6]

The subsequent account of the taking of Antioch and Daphne in the *Historia Augusta* (*Aurel.* 25.1) proves that Aurelian used the vision of Apollonius of Tyana for propaganda purposes so that he claimed it was Apollonius of Tyana who commanded him to show clemency to all cities and that all cities should expect to be treated well and have no fear. It is therefore clear that Aurelian managed to compensate for the possible troubles caused by the killing of Heraclammon with the vision of Apollonius of Tyana commanding clemency. The subsequent ease with which all cities surrendered to him proves that this propaganda was highly successful. Therefore, the Apollonius of Tyana incident at Tyana and possibly also the previous consulting of the Sibylline Books in the city of Rome proved to be harbingers of Aurelian's policy of using the *Sol Invictus* and Apollonius of Tyana for the dual purpose of uniting the realm behind him while uplifting the morale and fighting spirit of the soldiers at the right moments with visions provided by these 'gods', as we shall witness in the battle of Emesa.

Above: A coin depicting Apollonius of Tyana.
Right: A bust of Apollonius of Tyana.
Source: English language version of Duruy's History of Rome

Coins and papyri prove that Aurelian was somehow able to keep Zenobia in the dark regarding his intentions until about April 272 or alternatively that Zenobia was holding onto the vain hope of finding some way to reconcile her differences with Aurelian. The coins and papyri prove that the Palmyrenes did not break up relations with Aurelian before early April 272. Saunders suggests that the likely last straw that broke the camel's back was the siege of Tyana, and that it was after this that the mint at Antioch started to mint coins in the name of Vaballathus as *C(aesar) Vhbalathus Aug(ustus)* and in the name of Zenobia with the text *S(eptimia) Zenobia Aug(usta)*. Similar coins were struck at Alexandria for Vaballathus year 5. There are milestones in Arabia which include the titles *Persicus maximus*, *Arabicus maximus*, and *Adiabenicus maximus* for *Imperator Caesar Augustus* Vaballathus. In other words, when Zenobia then revolted openly she did this as a Roman usurper to gain as much support from the native population as possible. According to the *Historia Augusta* (*Aurel.* 33.2), she even built a triumphal chariot which she intended to use when she entered the city of Rome as a victor of the civil war. This was not the first such usurpation in this area because Heliogabalus/Elagabalus had done so in 218 and Uranius Antoninus in about 253/4. It was entirely plausible for a Palmyrene to see himself/herself as a native Roman and declare usurpation.[7] This view was also adopted by none other than Trebellius Pollio (*HA Tr.* 15–16, 27–28, 30) who included the Palmyrenes among the list of usurpers.

6.3.3. *Probus Reconquers Egypt with an Amphibious Landing in about May–June 272*[8]

At about the same time as Aurelian marched through Asia Minor, M. Aurelius Probus sailed his fleet against the Palmyrenes in Egypt. The timing of the Egyptian campaign led by M. Aurelius Probus can be dated on the basis of papyri and coins struck at Alexandria. However, even this evidence has not resulted in a consensus of what happened and when. Cizek (p.106) places the reconquest of Alexandria to have taken place in August 271 on the basis of coins then minted in the name of Aurelian in Alexandria. This, however, is a mistake. I agree with Watson and Southern that the minting of coins in the name of Aurelian at Alexandria actually started in late June 272, and when one takes into account the papyrological evidence and the minted coins at Alexandria in the name of Vaballathus and Zenobia in about April 272, it becomes very likely that M. Aurelius Probus landed his forces in Egypt in May and captured Alexandria either before the end of May 272 or early in June. The local governor of Egypt, Statilius Ammianus, who had previously been accepted in this position by both Aurelian and Zenobia, appears to have negotiated with Probus because he was kept in office possibly until the end of 272 or early 273. The local Palmyrene garrison was subdued by the forces led by Probus with relative ease probably because Zenobia wisely chose to concentrate her limited resources against the main enemy.[9]

6.3.4. *The Battle of Immae and Capture of Antioch in about late April-May 272*[10]

Once Aurelian had marched through the Cilician Gates, his next object was the capture of Antioch. Aurelian was well placed to do this because, as we shall see, he knew the enemy's dispositions and he also knew the terrain intimately having spent some time there in about 253/4. It is not known with certainty why Zenobia did not attempt to defend the Cilician

Gates or the line of Issus or the Gates of Syria, but chose to concentrate her forces at Antioch. See the topographical map of the area (page 102). The likeliest answer would probably be that even after the departure of Probus, Aurelian possessed enough ships to make an amphibious landing behind the enemy. The second reason would probably be that the cataphract cavalry formed Zenobia's main strength and that she and her generals did not want to attempt to defend the narrows with infantry forces.

The sources for the subsequent campaign and the so-called battle of Immae are very sparse. Zosimus is our best and most detailed source, but he does not mention the place of the battle. The other sources which refer to the campaign are very brief. They include the *HA Aurelian*, Festus, Eusebius-Jerome, Jordanes, Syncellus, Eutropius and Malalas. These sources are listed and analyzed by Homo and G. Downey. The best modern reconstruction of the campaign to take Antioch and of the battle of Immae is the article 'Aurelian's Victory over Zenobia at Immae, A.D. 272' by G. Downey and the following analysis with its map on page 102 is based on this seminal study. Most modern historians have accepted his analysis without any criticism, but I am here making one very important emendation to his study by placing the infantry of Aurelian in a different location.

On the basis of the above-mentioned sources we know that Zenobia and her commander-in-chief Zabdas had made Antioch their headquarters and had built a camp for their main field army beside the river Orontes. There was clearly no attempt to hold the city of Seleucia, the harbour of Antioch, which makes it possible that Aurelian's fleet had taken control of it at about the same time as Aurelian marched along the coastal road from Issus to Pagrae across the Gates of Syria. It is unfortunate that we do not know the exact location of Zenobia's camp, because that would help us reconstruct what happened next. Consequently we are forced to make a series of conjectures and educated guesses. But these guesses can be made from a relatively secure position when one takes into account the geography and pays more attention to the details provided by Zosimus. His account proves that Aurelian was aware of the enemy dispositions and was therefore able to formulate his own plan accordingly when he reached Pagrae.

> There [*at Antioch*] finding Zenobia with a large army ready to engage, as he himself also was, he [*Aurelian*] met and engaged her as honour obliged him. But observing that the Palmyrene cavalry placed great confidence in their armour, which was very strong and secure, and that they were much better horsemen than his soldiers, he placed his infantry by themselves on the other side of the Orontes. [*The location of the infantry during this battle has caused most speculation. Downey has suggested that it stayed initially on the same side of the river as the cavalry and then crossed the Orontes only after the enemy had started its pursuit of the Roman cavalry. The meaning is actually not necessarily that of the crossing of the river by the infantry but that it was on the other side of the river figuratively speaking, thanks to the fact that the Orontes makes a wide turn just north of Antioch so that when the infantry marched along the road which was west of Lake Antioch it was on the other side of the Orontes.*] He charged his cavalry not to engage immediately with the vigorous cavalry of the Palmyrenians, but to wait for their attack, and then, pretending to fly, to continue so doing until they had wearied both the men and their horses through excess of heat and the weight of their armour; so that they could pursue them no longer. [*Festus 24.1 also*

refers to the thousands of Palmyrene armoured horsemen and archers at Immae.] This project succeeded, and as soon as the cavalry of the emperor saw their enemy tired, and that their horses were scarcely able to stand under them, or themselves to move, they drew up the reins of their horses, and, wheeling round, charged them, and trod them under foot as they fell from their horses. By which means the slaughter was promiscuous, some falling by the sword, and others by their own and their enemies' horses. [*Aurelian clearly knew how to neutralize the superior numbers of Palmyrene cataphracts – after all he had been a cavalry general before becoming an emperor. This was first rate generalship. The Roman cavalry defeated a numerically superior enemy force with very little effort thanks to the foresight of Aurelian.*] [Zosimus 1.50.2–4, 1814 tr. possibly by J. Davis, p.25.]

After this defeat, the survivors [*Palmyrans*] fled into Antioch. Zabdas, the general of Zenobia, fearing that the Antiochians on hearing of it should mutiny, chose a man resembling the emperor, and clothing him in a dress such as Aurelianus was accustomed to wear, led him through the city as if he had taken the emperor prisoner. By this contrivance he imposed on the Antiochians, stole out of the city by night, and took with him Zenobia with the remainder of the army to Emesa. In the meantime, the emperor was intent on his affairs, and as soon as it was day called the foot soldiers around him, intending to attack the defeated enemy on both sides; [*This 1.51.2 is the key clause for the understanding of the whereabouts of the Roman infantry. This ('…kai hekaterôthen epithesthai trapeisin êdê tois polemiois…') implies that Aurelian with his infantry had approached the city of Antioch from a different direction than his cavalry. In short, Aurelian was approaching the city of Antioch from the north along the Bagrae–Antioch road, while his cavalry forces would have approached Antioch from the east along the Antioch–Immae–Beroea road. This also means that Aurelian had with his infantry reached the vicinity of the city of Antioch just before nightfall and that his plan was to rest his infantry in a fortified marching camp and then, together with the cavalry, attack Antioch in the morning. The fact that Zenobia fled during the night spoiled his plans.*] but, hearing of the escape of Zenobia, he entered Antioch, where he was joyfully received by the citizens. [*In other words, Zenobia fled before Aurelian's cavalry forces could cut off her route of retreat.*] Finding that many had left the city, under apprehensions that they should suffer for having espoused the party of Zenobia, he published edicts in every place to recall them, and told them, that such events had happened more through compulsion rather than of their own inclination [*This appears to have been done in conjunction with the religious propaganda statement that it had been Apollonius of Tyana who had commanded Aurelian to be merciful. See above and below.*] [Zosimus 1.51.1–2, 1814 tr. possibly by J. Davis, p.25–6 with some changes and additions.]

It is worthwhile to start the analysis of the above with the analysis offered by Downey because it is in these days usually accepted as it is.[11] Downey (see the redrawn map) notes that there were two roads to Antioch from Pagrae, one which ran west of Lake Antioch and another which ran east of the lake. Downey suggests that in the initial stage of the battle the Roman infantry and cavalry were east of the lake and River Orontes so that the infantry crossed the Orontes once the Palmyrene cavalry swallowed the bait of the fleeing

Roman cavalry. When Zabdas and Zenobia had witnessed the encircling movement of the Roman cavalry, they had no alternative but to try to prevent this; because had they allowed the Roman cavalry to complete their circuitous route the Romans would have cut off the Palmyrene route of retreat. The way in which the Palmyrenes sought to prevent this, however, was in their own hands. Downey suggests that the Roman and the Palmyrene cavalry met each other at some point between Gephyra and the place where the Gindarus road left the Antioch–Beroae road, and that the Roman feigned flight was continued up to Immae which has given its name for the battle. The length of the flight must have been long enough to exhaust the Palmyrene horses and men in the summer heat. I agree with this cavalry portion of his analysis, but I disagree with his analysis of the use of the infantry.

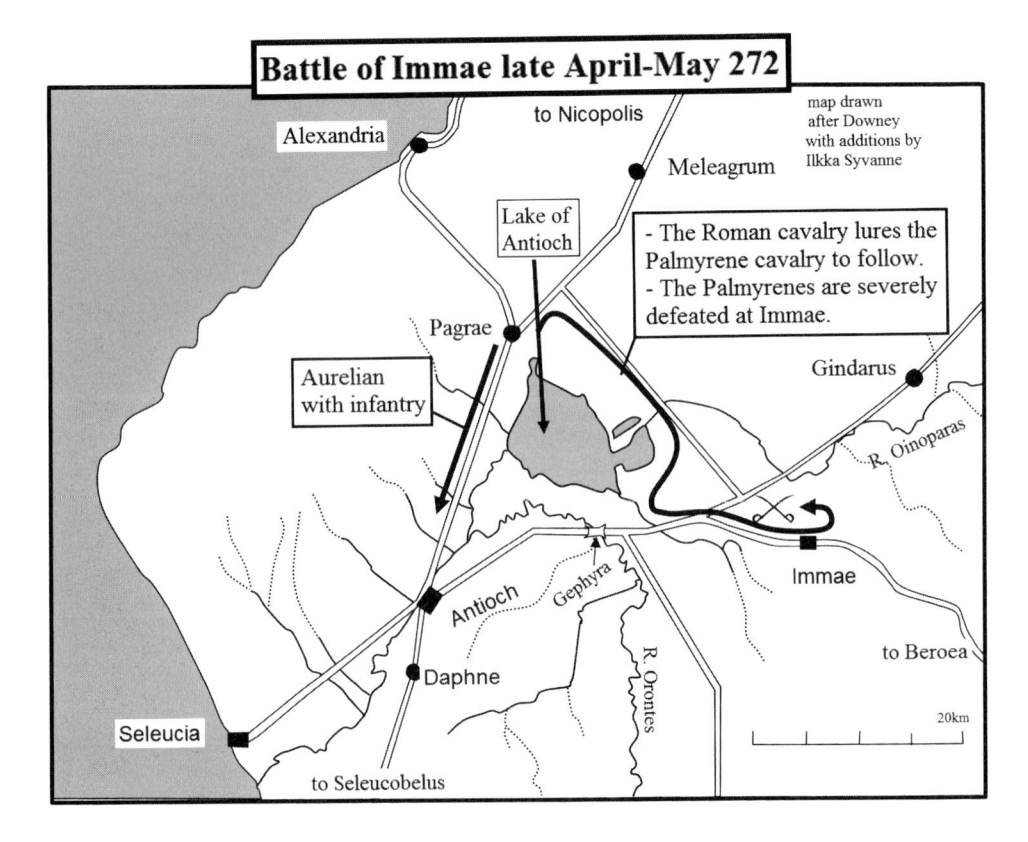

Battle of Immae late April-May 272

map drawn after Downey with additions by Ilkka Syvänne

- The Roman cavalry lures the Palmyrene cavalry to follow.
- The Palmyrenes are severely defeated at Immae.

On the basis of the planned attack against the city of Antioch from two directions, it is clear that the infantry was approaching along the Pagrae–Antioch road and the cavalry along the Beroea–Immae–Antioch road. And where would the infantry forces have become separated from the cavalry? There are two possibilities. Firstly it is possible that the infantry did accompany the cavalry along the eastern road leading from Pagrae to the Antioch–Gindarus road, and that it then stayed behind while the cavalry advanced further, and when the Palmyrenes then swallowed the bait they marched between Orontes and Lake Antioch to the Pagrae–Antioch road. Secondly, and this is the more likely alternative, the infantry and cavalry forces separated at Pagrae so that Aurelian dispatched his cavalry to the east to lure the Palmyrene cavalry into the deadly pursuit while he marched his infantry along the Pagrae–Antioch road while his cavalry forces led the Palmyrenes eastward to their destruction at Immae.

According to Vopiscus (Aurel. 25.1), Aurelian used the vision of Apollonius of Tyana and his promise of clemency very effectively for propaganda purposes when entering the cities of Antioch and Daphne. In short, the policy of promising forgiveness to all in the name of Apollonius was very successful. The Christians were not alone in their promise of forgiveness to those who had sinned against God.

It is probable that the above-mentioned incident in which the Christians demanded the ousting of the Bishop of Antioch, Paul of Samosata, took place at this time that Aurelian reached the city. Aurelian's response was that the bishops of Italy and the city of Rome decided who held the building (church), which meant the eviction of Paul from his see. Aurelian undoubtedly thought that this was the best decision he could make because Paul was a supporter of Zenobia, and because this confirmed the superior position of the bishops of Rome and Italy over the provincial bishops.[12]

6.3.5. The Battle of Daphne in late April-May 272

After settling matters at Antioch, Aurelian began a pursuit of Zenobia. The Palmyrenes however had posted their forces above the hill overlooking the suburbs of Daphne. Zosimus is the only source that has preserved any details of this and it is once again worth quoting him:

When this was known to the fugitives, they returned in crowds, and were kindly received by the emperor, who, having arranged affairs in that city, proceeded to Emesa. Finding that a detachment [*a moira, which could mean specifically a detachment of ca. 3,000 men, or any larger detachment/division of soldiers, the latter of which is probably meant here because the terrain requires a large force*] of the Palmyrenians had possession of a hill above the suburbs of Daphne, thinking that its steepness would enable them to obstruct the enemy's passage, he … commanded his soldiers to march with their shields in *testudo/synaspismos* formation both in width and depth, as to keep off any darts and stones that might be thrown at them [*'tois stratiôtais evekeleusata sunaspismenois kai puknê têi falaggi tên pros to orthion anabasin poioumenois ta te belê kai tous oloitropous'; this text means that the shields were placed rim-to-boss both in width and in depth, which was the offensive version of the* testudo/foulkon/synaspismos *order used by the infantry*].

As soon as they had ascended the hill and were on equal terms with their adversaries, they put them to flight in such disorder that some of them fell from the precipices and were dashed in pieces, and others were slaughtered in the pursuit by those that were on the hill, and by those that had not ascended it [*the implication being that Aurelian had sent some of his forces to the flanks of the enemy formation so that some of the enemy forces were fleeing towards these units posted on the lower ground. My suggestion is that this means primarily those who would have formed the western wing of the Roman infantry in the ravine*]. Having gained the victory, they crossed the river and marched on with great confidence in the success of the emperor, because he was

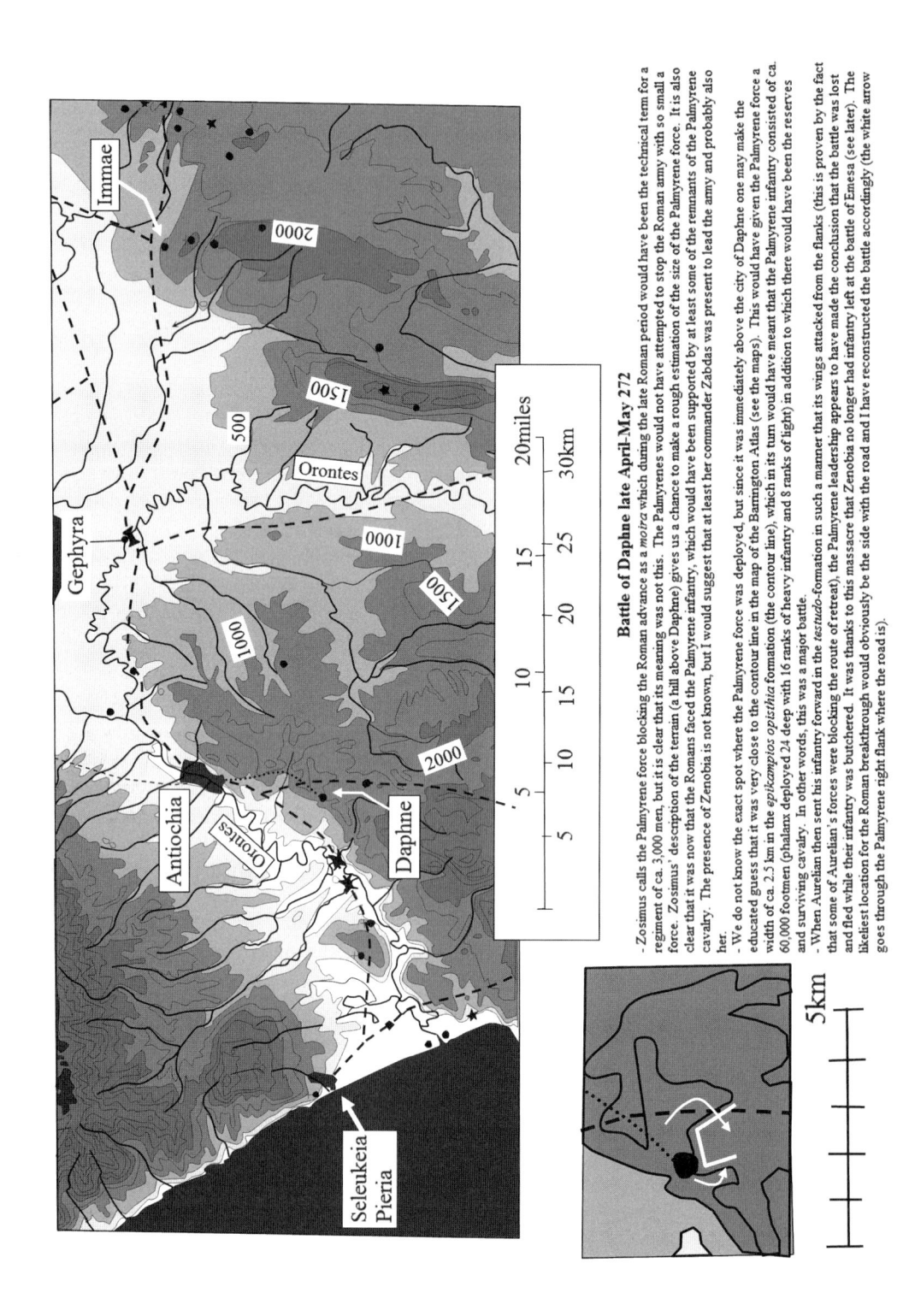

Battle of Daphne late April-May 272

- Zosimus calls the Palmyrene force blocking the Roman advance as a *moira* which during the late Roman period would have been the technical term for a regiment of ca. 3,000 men, but it is clear that its meaning was not this. The Palmyrenes would not have attempted to stop the Roman army with so small a force. Zosimus' description of the terrain (a hill above Daphne) gives us a chance to make a rough estimation of the size of the Palmyrene force. It is also clear that it was now that the Romans faced the Palmyrene infantry, which would have been supported by at least some of the remnants of the Palmyrene cavalry. The presence of Zenobia is not known, but I would suggest that at least her commander Zabdas was present to lead the army and probably also her.

- We do not know the exact spot where the Palmyrene force was deployed, but since it was immediately above the city of Daphne one may make the educated guess that it was very close to the contour line in the map of the Barrington Atlas (see the maps). This would have given the Palmyrene force a width of ca. 2.5 km in the *epikamptos opisthia* formation (the contour line), which in its turn would have meant that the Palmyrene infantry consisted of ca. 60,000 footmen (phalanx deployed 24 deep with 16 ranks of heavy infantry and 8 ranks of light) in addition to which there would have been the reserves and surviving cavalry. In other words, this was a major battle.

- When Aurelian then sent his infantry forward in the *testudo*-formation in such a manner that its wings attacked from the flanks (this is proven by the fact that some of Aurelian's forces were blocking the route of retreat), the Palmyrene leadership appears to have made the conclusion that the battle was lost and fled while their infantry was butchered. It was thanks to this massacre that Zenobia no longer had infantry left at the battle of Emesa (see later). The likeliest location for the Roman breakthrough would obviously be the side with the road and I have reconstructed the battle accordingly (the white arrow goes through the Palmyrene right flank where the road is).

liberally entertained at Apamea, Larissa, and Arethusa [*I have accepted here Ridley's emendation p.16 for the lacuna*]. [Zosimus 1.52.1–52.3, 1814 tr. possibly by J. Davis, p.26 with some changes and additions.]

The Palmyrenes clearly had the advantage of the terrain on their side, but it was thanks to the superior fighting quality and morale of the Roman infantry, who assumed the rim-to-boss formation for the attack, that this was not enough to secure them victory.

6.3.6. Battle of Emesa in about May-early June 272

Once the Palmyrene infantry had been butchered, Aurelian continued his march in the footsteps of Zenobia. Zenobia, however, had not been idle. She had assembled a new, more than 70,000 strong, force of cataphracts and other cavalry in the city of Emesa apparently by uniting the remnants of her forces with reinforcements brought from all of the outlying garrisons and from Palmyra which was roughly 150 km from Emesa. The withdrawal of these garrisons in what had formerly been part of the Roman Empire ensured the desertion of all of these areas to the Roman side. The Palmyrene strategy was to post their cavalry forces in a location that favoured the use of cavalry.

It is probable that Aurelian marched along the road Antioch–Apamea–Larissa–Epiphaneia–Arethusa–Emesa. Saunders (p.219) is correct to point out that at this stage Aurelian's main strategic objective was to destroy the Palmyrene field army so that it would be possible to besiege the city of Palmyra. Aurelian was therefore quite prepared to meet the enemy on their chosen battleground. He knew how to counter their advantages. While en route to Emesa, Aurelian would have received the surrender of most of the coastal region up to Egypt because the news of his victory and the reconquest of Egypt would have travelled fast. As usually suggested, it is probable that the Roman legions and other units which were posted in Syria, Palestine, Mesopotamia and Osrhoene deserted to his side at this time. The legions, or rather their core units, in this area included *III Gallica*, *IV Scythica*, *XVI Flavia*, *X Fretensis*, *I Parthica* and *III Parthica*. The problem with this is that it is possible that at least some of these units had already been transferred to the west before this, for example during the reigns of Valerian and Gallienus, so these, or detachments from these, would already have accompanied Aurelian. However, as stated, if the headquarters and other core units had remained behind in their main bases, it is very likely that these now joined Aurelian.

The list of enemies defeated by Probus while a commoner in Vopiscus (*HA Prob.* 12.4) includes the Parthians and Persians. This suggests that Aurelian and Probus united their forces before the siege of Palmyra, but it is quite possible that they united even before this. Therefore, the reconquest of Egypt cannot have taken long to achieve. This also implies that Probus was able to bring back the forces which he had taken with him and possibly also some parts of the remaining garrison forces in Egypt and north of it as reinforcements for Aurelian. The legions in Egypt, Syria Palaestina and Arabia included *II Traina* (Alexandria), *X Fretensis* (Jerusalem) and *III Cyrenaic*a (Damascus, but this legion was probably destroyed in 270). It is likely that at least the *X Fretensis* was present at the next battle.

106   Aurelian and Probus

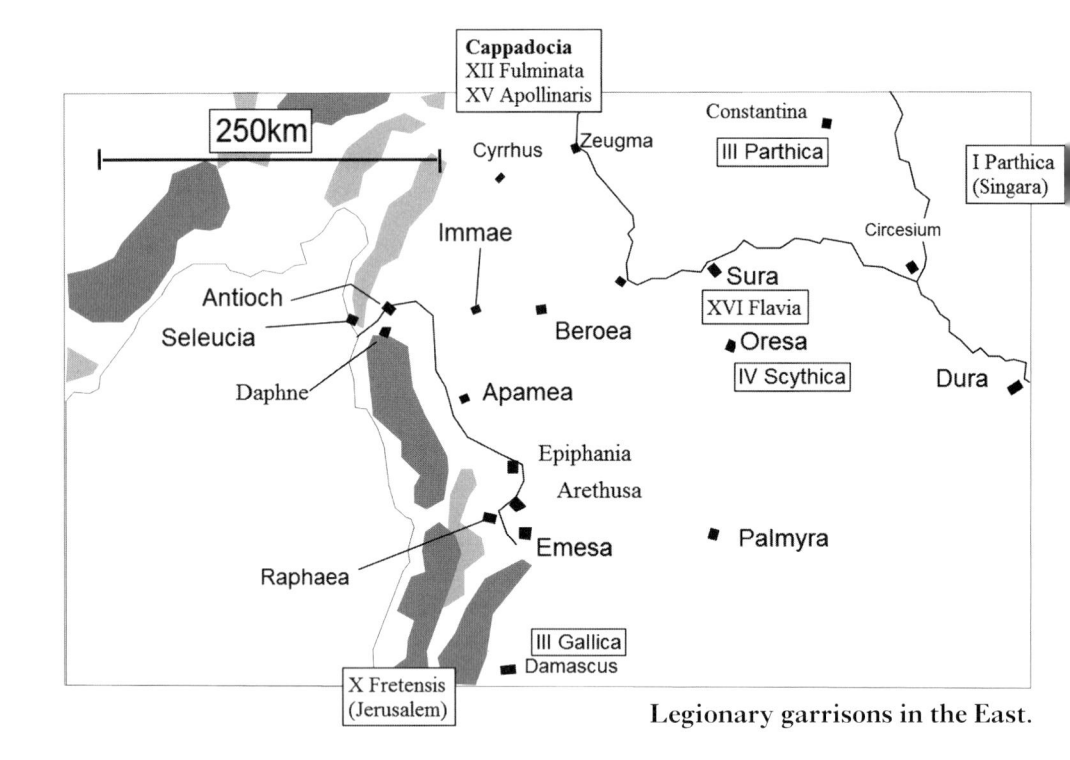

Legionary garrisons in the East.

Having gained the victory [*at Daphne*], they marched on with great satisfaction at the success of the emperor, who was liberally entertained at Apamea, Larissa, and Arethusa. Finding the Palmyrene army [*tôn Palmurênôn stratopedon*] drawn up before Emesa, amounting to more than seventy thousand men [*plêthos hepta muriadôn*], consisting of Palmyrenes and others, he opposed to them the Dalmatian cavalry [*Dalmatôn hippoi*], the Moesians and Pannonians [*Musois kai Paissin*], and the Celtic legions of Noricum and Raetia [*kai eti ge Nôrikois kai Rhaitois, haper esti Keltika tagmata*], and besides these the imperial bodyguards [*hoi tou Basilikou telous, in this case probably meaning the Praetorian Guard just like the telê from Asia would mean legions, see below*] selected man by man, the Mauritanian horse [*Maurousia hippos*], and Asian forces from Tyana, Mesopotamia, Syria, Phoenicia, and Palestine, all men/legions of acknowledged valour; the Palestinians besides other arms wielding clubs and staves/maces/cudgels [*kai apo tês Asias hai te apo Tuanôn dynameis kai ek tês mesên tôn potamôn kai Syrias kai Foinikês kai Palaistinês telê tina tôn andreiotatôn hoi de apo Palaistinês pros têi allêi hoplisei krunas kai rhopala epeferonto*]. [Zosimus 1.52.2–52.3, English tr. possibly by J. Davis in 1814, p.26 with some changes and additions.]

The list of units under Aurelian gives us some important clues regarding the composition of the forces and the events preceding it. Firstly, it proves that Aurelian was accompanied by the western units, Dalmatian and Moorish cavalry and imperial bodyguards when he entered Asia Minor. The inclusion of men from Tyana suggests that Aurelian had

Coin of Gallienus. Source Bernoulli. 'Gallienus Licinianus … was well grown in stature and valiant, with a dark skin, curly hair, a bushy beard, a good nose, and large eyes; he was magnanimous and he favoured the Blue faction.' Malalas 12.27, tr. by Jeffreys, Jeffreys and Scott, p.163.

Coin of Claudius. Source Bernoulli. 'Claudius Apollianus … had a broad face, a slightly upturned nose, greyish eyes, fairish hair, a twisted mouth and a slight lisp; he was magnanimous and he supported the Green faction.' Malalas 12.28, tr. by Jeffreys, Jeffreys and Scott, p.163.

Coin of Quintillus. Source Bernoulli. 'Quintillian … was of medium height, slender, with a long face, a long nose, dark skin, straight hair, good eyes and both his hair and beard were grizzled.' Malalas 12.29, tr. by Jeffreys, Jeffreys and Scott, p.164.

Coins of Aurelian. Source Bernoulli. 'Aurelian, the warrior … was tall, slender, slightly bald, with small eyes and completely grey hair; he was magnanimous and quick moving. He wore a diadem decorated with a star.' Malalas 12.30, tr. by Jeffreys, Jeffreys and Scott, p.164.

Coin of Tacitus. Source Bernoulli. 'Tacitus Augustus … was of medium height, slender, slightly bald and eloquent, with short, completely grey hair and a delicate nose; he was sensible.' Malalas 12.31, tr. by Jeffreys, Jeffreys and Scott, p.164.

Coin of Florianus. Source Bernoulli. 'Florianus Augustus… was short and fat, with receding hair, fair-skinned, with wine-coloured eyes, a slightly upturned nose, and greying hair and beard; he was an extremely sharp man.' Malalas 12.32, tr. by Jeffreys, Jeffreys and Scott, p.165.

Coin of Probus. Source Bernoulli. 'Aelius Probus… was of medium height, with a large belly and straight, closely cropped hair, a bushy beard, dark skin, a ruddy complexion, good eyes and was very learned; he favoured the Green faction.' Malalas 12.33, tr. by Jeffreys, Jeffreys and Scott, p.165.

Coin of Carus. Source Bernoulli. 'Carus … was short, with a good chest, fair skin, with straight greying hair, greyish eyes, a broad face, a good nose and thick lips; he was arrogant.' Malalas 12.34, tr. by Jeffreys, Jeffreys and Scott, p.165.

Nineteenth century photos of the siege of Verona in 312 in the Arch of Constantine depicting Constantine the Great and his soldiers. Note the different types of equipment depicted. There are soldiers without armour or helmet, the Moorish or Blemmye archers, soldiers with the muscular armour, soldiers with the pseudo-Attic helmets and soldiers with other types of helmets. Note in particular the two unarmoured soldiers with horned helmets depicted below, which Speidel (2004, 47ff.) identifies with the *Cornuti* who belonged to the *auxilia palatina* units in the *Notitia Dignitatum* (dated turn of the fifth century). This is a good example of what types of troops came into use during the latter half of the third century when the Romans started to recruit ever increasing numbers of barbarians.

A nineteenth century photo of the siege of Verona in the Arch of Constantine depicting the defenders serving under Maxentian. Note the use of hand-thrown stones when needed. Note the types of helmets used and the round shields. Most of these helmets probably depict the so-called ridge helmets.

Left and below: 19th century photos of the Battle of the Milvian Bridge in 312 in the Arch of Constantine depicting the moment when the cavalry of Constantine the Great had forced the cavalry of Maxentius into the Tiber. Note the pseudo-Attic helmets used by the cavalry of Constantine and by the Praetorian cavalry of Maxentius. Maxentius's Praetorian cavalry uses the typical equipment that had been in use ever since the days of Septimius Severus when the sources mention that the Praetorians typically wore the scale armour. Note also how the cavalry of Constantine wears no armour. This appears to have been the standard solution adopted by Constantine the Great to increase the speed of his cavalry attack, and one may assume that he was not alone in his thinking because for example Aurelian exploited the lightness of his cavalry forces against the Palmyrene cataphracts at the battle of Immae in 272.

Coins of Aurelian. (*Photo by author* (*British Museum*))

Coin of Probus. (*Photo by author* (*British Museum*))

Coin of Carus. (*Photo by author* (*British Museum*))

Coin of Diocletian. (*Photo by author* (*British Museum*))

Bust of Claudius or Aurelian as suggested by White (Brescia). (*Picture © Giovanni Dall'Orto at Wikipedia*)

Bust of Probus? (Brescia). (*Picture © Giovanni Dall'Orto at Wikipedia*)

Bust of Probus? (Brescia). (*Picture © Giovanni Dall'Orto at Wikipedia*)

A typical Germanic horseman.

Below right: A Roman auxiliary soldier of Germanic origins. The shield emblem is borrowed from the *Notitia Dignitatum* (turn of the fifth century). In other words the man belongs to the *Cornuti seniores*, Auxilia Palatina, *Magister Peditum Praesentalis*, *Numeri intra Italiam* (west). I have here made the educated guess that this unit may already have been in existence during the late third century. He is equipped with a *spatha*-sword, shield, and a short version of the *hasta*, or with a *lancea* meant for thrusting and throwing. Note the horned helmet, which is taken from the Arch of Constantine. This type of helmet was undoubtedly used also for head butts. Compare with the Germanic warrior (an Alaman) shown on the left. As far as the equipment is concerned there was no real difference between these two groups of soldiers because both were recruited from Germanic tribesmen and both groups had access to the same types of equipment.

A typical Germanic footman.
Drawn after a re-enactor photo.

Coins of Aurelian. Photos by author (British Museum). Note how different the profile is in these and in the above coins. This shows why it has been impossible for historians to identify Aurelian securely from the extant busts.

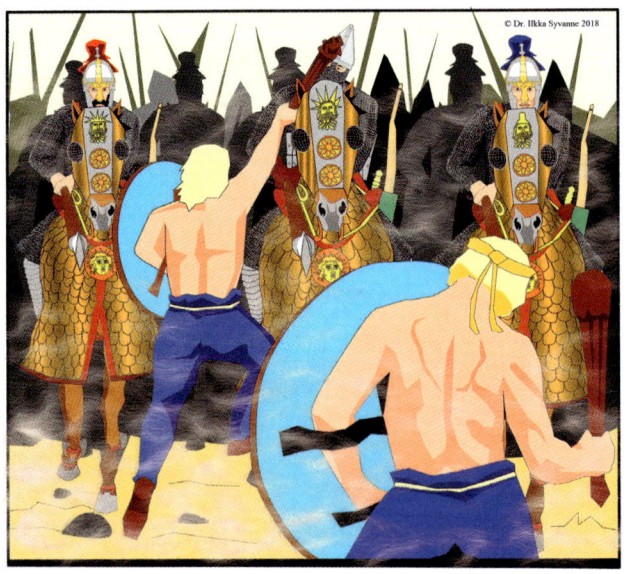

Germanic clubmen attack Palmyrene cataphracts at the battle of Emesa in 272.

An unidentified person in the collection of British Museum according to A.H. Smith (catalogue number 1953). I would suggest that it is possible that this head represents the emperor Carus because it certainly resembles some of his coins.

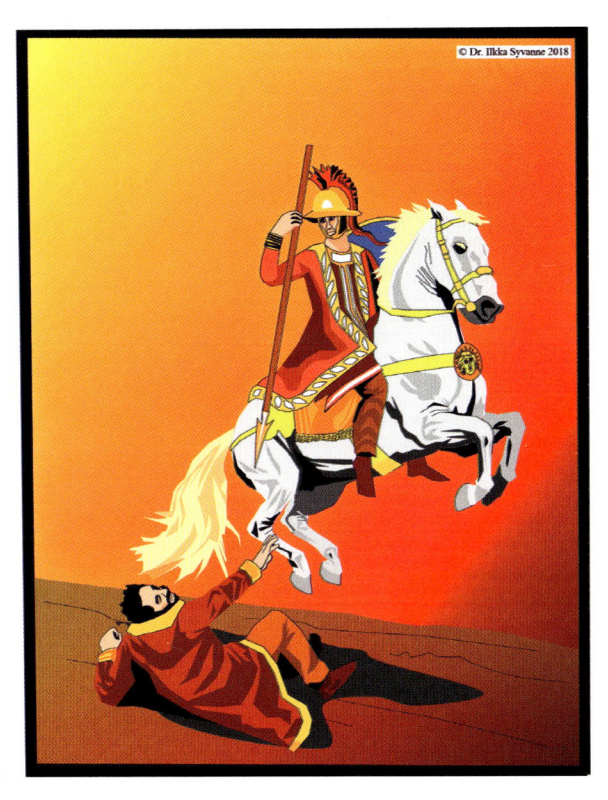

A Palmyrene horseman spearing a Persian nobleman who has fallen off his horse. The figure is based on a mosaic which shows a Palmyrene god with a flying horse spearing a lion. I have interpreted the flying winged horse here as a horse performing the croupade manoeuvre, because this shows the horse in the exact same position vis-à-vis the ground as is depicted in the mosaic. The spear-armed horseman is interpreted here to be the same as the so-called *hippakontistai* (spear-armed horsemen who used their spears for throwing and thrusting) of the Greek military theory. It is quite probable that the Palmyrenes also employed this type of non-armoured cavalry and not only cataphracts and mounted archers. Note how this horseman uses both Greco-Roman (e.g. the helmet) and Parthian/Persian (e.g. the coat) style equipment.

Praetorian cavalry performing feigned flight. Such a scene could have happened for example if the Praetorian cavalry was deployed alongside the rest of the cavalry at the battle of Immae in 272. The equipment is based on the fact that the Praetorians are known to have used predominantly scale armour from the reign of Septimius Severus onwards and on the Praetorian cavalry depicted in the Arches of Constantine and Galerius. In the former the Praetorian horsemen wore scale armour all the way down to the ankles and used pseudo-Attic helmets, while in the latter the scale armour was shorter and the helmet was the segmented helmet depicted in this image. The spears in this image are placed between the rider's leg and horse.

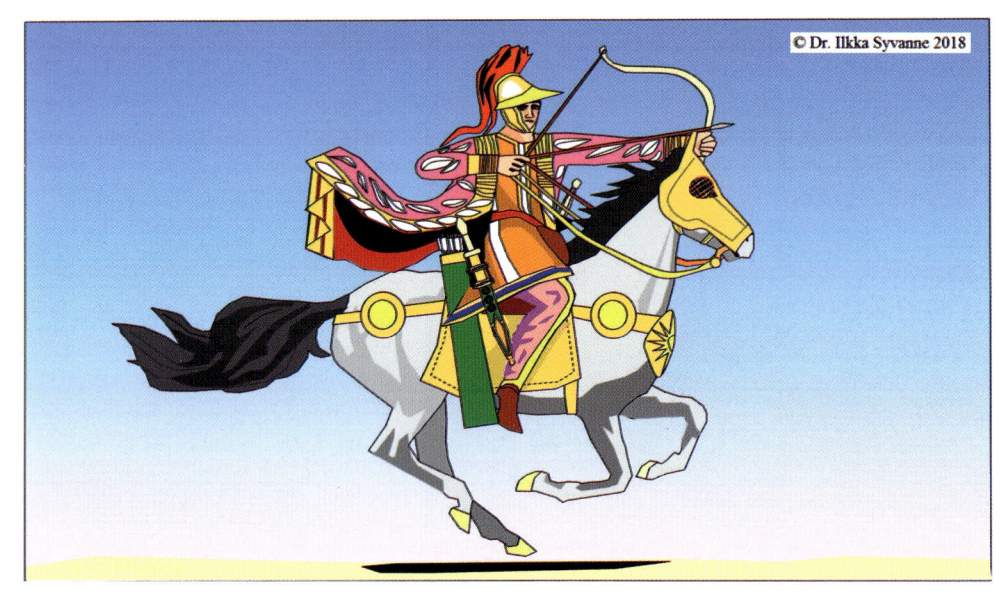

A Palmyrene mounted archer. The image is based on a mosaic preserved in Palmyra. Note the mix of Greco-Roman and Persian influences.

The Duel Betwen Probus and Aradio in AD 269
(Vopiscus, *Historia Augusta*, Probus IX.1-2)

Vopiscus fails to give any details of the duel other than that Probus saved the city of Carthage, and won the duel against Aradio and honoured him with a mighty tomb because he had been a brave man. Therefore, the above should be seen as an artistic impression of the fight. In this case I have used the imperial coinage of Probus (and other emperors) as a source of inspiration so that I have depicted Probus with the *aegis*-cloak and spear. This would have been fighting in the heroic mould with the *aegis* serving as the only form of protection. The drawings of the coins on both sides show what type of equipment would have been worn in this case. The profile of Probus has been taken from one of his coins. Note, however, that it varies from one coin to another, and that Probus was only a *dux* in AD 269 and not yet emperor.

drawn after Cohen

drawn after Cohen

Bust usually identified as Probus, but could equally well be Claudius. He definitely looks like the two busts identified as Claudius II located at Brescia. (*Source: Wikimedia Commons, public domain. Coloured by author*)

A cataphract armed for both long and close distance combat. The man belongs to a unit recruited from the Parthians.

Author's drawing depicting the head of an unknown late third century emperor at Metropolitan Museum. Nose and a part of the ear and cheek have been restored to the image. The likeliest candidates for the emperor would be Claudius, Aurelian, Probus and Carinus, but Aurelian would be the most likely of these. It is because of this that I have coloured the hair and beard grey.

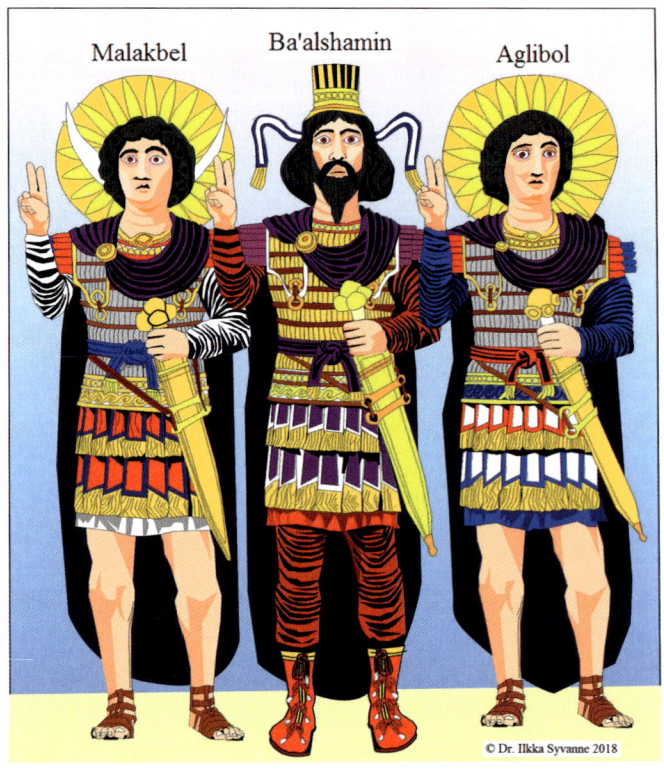

Top: Three Palmyrene gods in lamellar armour, first century AD (Louvre, author's drawing and restoration). I have left the physical characteristics as in the original with the exception that I have added the legs and some missing body parts or equipment. It is probable that similar types of Greco-Roman armour and equipment continued to be used in Palmyra also in the third century. After all, the Palmyrenes continued to serve in the regular Roman forces. In short, as far as equipment is concerned, the Palmyrenes were the equals of the Romans of Aurelian. It is also clear that the Romans could use similar gear even if the use of lamellar was rare for the Romans before the fifth century.

Left: A heavily equipped Roman front-rank fighter. The shield emblem has been borrowed from the *Notitia Dignitatum* and represents the *Ioviani*. I have here made the educated guess that this unit was already in existence during this period because it subsequently became the favourite unit of Diocletian. It is probable that he would have commanded this unit, whatever its name was before his own reign, as *comes domesticorum* who was the commander of the so-called *protectores*. See my biography of *Gallienus* with *MHLR* series for additional details.

This illustration depicts two Roman horsemen from the unit *Equites V Dalmatae* at the battle of Immae, shooting backwards at the pursuing Palmyrene cavalry. It makes the assumption that the Dalmatian cavalry already had the same names as in the *Notitia Dignitatum* and that Aurelian had not yet legislated against the use of white shoes by men.

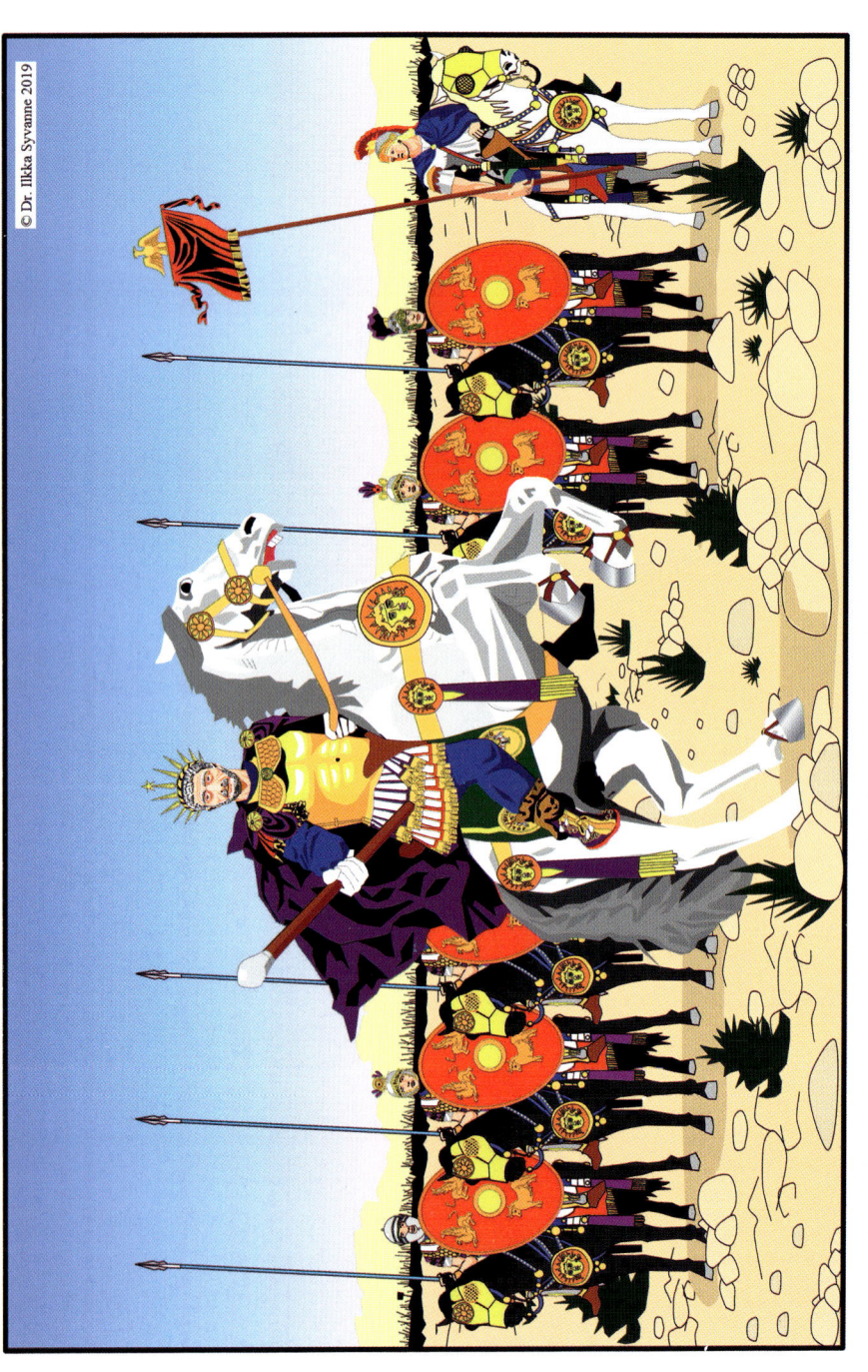

Aurelian with his retinue at the Battle of Emesa in about May–June 272. He is in front of his infantry to observe the progress of the cavalry battle so that he can make adjustments to his infantry formation behind him, if there is a need for this. With the exception of the man on the left, the retinue wears equipment shown in the so-called Trajanic reliefs of the Arch of Constantine. The drawing of Aurelian is based on the assumption that the head of the unknown late third century emperor at the Metropolitan Museum would represent Aurelian, and on the description of Aurelian's appearance in Malalas.

A Roman cavalry officer leading a cavalry attack. Note the spears and two dragon-standards in the background. The officer wears the gem-studded Berkasovo-helmet, which was undoubtedly worn only by men of some status. He uses a mace to direct the men. Some historians consider the mace to have been a status symbol for the officers, but this is inaccurate because the maces and clubs were also used by rank-and-file soldiers against heavily armoured *cataphractarii/clibanarii*. The mace has been borrowed from a statue of Constantine the Great.

Above: One of the presumed busts of Claudius II at Brescia. The identification with Claudius is presumably based on the strong chin if he was an ancestor of Constantius I, but the same argument can also be used for the support of his brother Quintillus. The photographer Giovanni Dall'Orto suggests also the possibility that this man could be Probus. This is quite possible. In my opinion, even Aurelian could be considered on the grounds of the man's age. (*Picture © Giovanni Dall'Orto at Wikipedia*)

'Aurelian, the warrior … was tall, slender, slightly bald, with small eyes and completely grey hair; he was magnanimous and quick moving. He wore a diadem decorated with a star.' Malalas 12.30, tr. by Jeffreys, Jeffreys and Scott, p.164. The drawing is based on the bust of Aurelian in Duruy and on my interpretation of the likely structure of the diadem if it was based on the rays of the *Sol Invictus*. He wears the *aegis* shown in his coin. Aurelian has just killed a person who had transgressed military discipline. This makes the assumption that Aurelian did not only like to watch executions and torture, but that he also sometimes participated in them; all sources are unanimous in their condemnation of his personal cruelty. He was a bloodthirsty ruler with perfect military skills – a man necessary for his times.

Above Left: 'Aelius Probus … was of medium height, with a large belly and straight, closely cropped hair. a bushy beard, dark skin, a ruddy complexion, good eyes and was very learned; he favoured the Green faction.' Malalas 12.33, tr. by Jeffreys, Jeffreys and Scott, p.165. The head is borrowed from one of the presumed busts of Probus found at Brescia. The body is just an educated guess of how he might have looked if he had a large belly as stated by Malalas. The gladiators preferred to have fat around their body to protect their vital organs against stabbing and cuts and it is possible that Probus had fattened himself for the same reason, because Probus was in the habit of fighting duels. The papyrus roll in his right hand is meant to show that he was a learned man.

Above right: A legionary in readiness to fight against infantry. The equipment was used during this period, but the shield emblem and unit *Prima Iulia Alpina* have been taken from the *Notitia Dignitatum*. I have speculated that it is possible that the Alpine units were created under Gallienus, but readers are still advised that this is purely speculative. The same concerns the colour scheme. The helmet is a ridge helmet. He wears scale armour and is equipped with a sword (*spatha*), a *spiculum/pilum* and two harpoon javelins.

Below: The two presumed busts of Claudius II at Brescia. See also previous comments. The other possible candidates for these busts are Quintillus, Aurelian and Probus. Whoever he was, these two busts clearly depict the same man. (*Picture © Giovanni Dall'Orto at Wikipedia*)

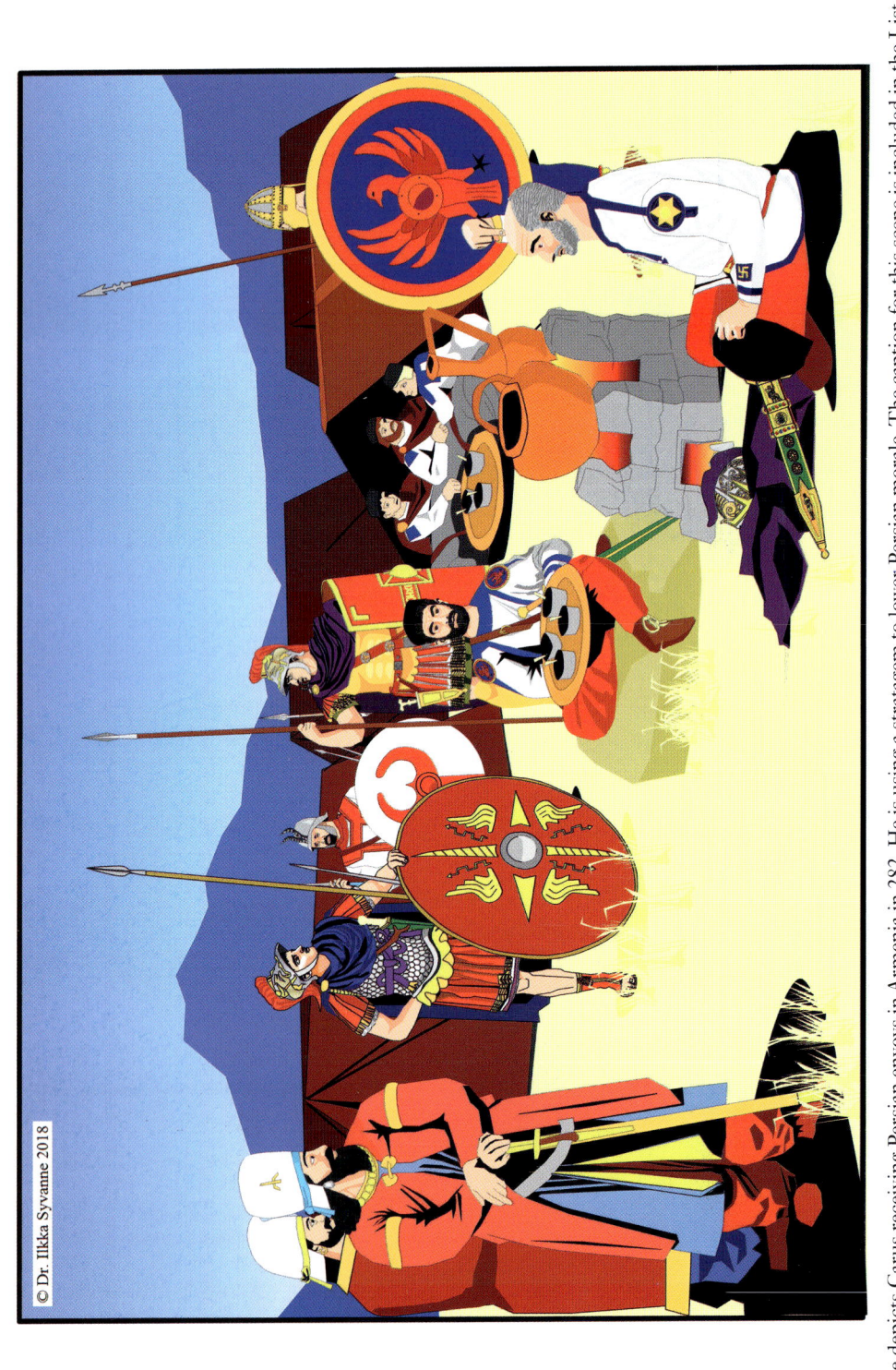

This scene depicts Carus receiving Persian envoys in Armenia in 282. He is using a stratagem to lower Persian morale. The caption for this scene is included in the List of Plates.

Top left: Germanic club-bearers in the Column of Trajan (18th century drawing)
Top centre: Germanic club-bearer in the Column of Theodosius I (no longer extant, drawing by Menestrier).
Top right: Gravestone of Aurelius Alexianus of Sparta, Member of Caracalla's Spartan cohort ca. 212-217. (drawing by Syvanne after Cowan/Richardson)

added to their number the citizen militia of Tyana or some unit or units that had been posted there previously of which we know nothing. If the Tyanans mean the citizen militia then Aurelian had clearly felt that it was worthwhile to bolster the numbers of his army even with militia forces. The men from Mesopotamia, Syria, Phoenicia, and Palestine would probably be the units that joined his army in the aftermath of the battles of Immae and Daphne, but it is of course possible that detachments from these units would already have been present when he entered Asia Minor. Regardless, it is still likely that at least the garrison forces from these units deserted Zenobia and joined Aurelian when he marched south. The most problematic portion of Zosimus's description is his reference to the Palestinians who wielded clubs. These could be Germans, enrolled into a unit that originated from Palestine, a detachment of which had been sent west during Gallienus's reign, as suggested by Speidel (2004, 95), or they could be men who belonged to a unit posted in Palestine like, for example, *legio X Fretensis*, or simply local Palestinians who had been enrolled into a native unit of clubmen similar to the Germanic units of club-bearers. Speidel's suggestion is probably the best of these because Roman works of art prove that the Germanic club-bearers were in existence at least from the reign of Trajan up to the reign of Theodosius I. It is in fact probable that the Romans distributed these Germanic club-bearers to all units that they thought fit, so that there were detachments of Germans attached to several legions. These Germans were the true specialists of anti-cataphract warfare. However, on the basis of the existence of other units of club-bearers, it is clear that the Germanic club-bearers were not the only such group serving in the Roman army, even if they are probably the most famous, hence it is also possible that the Palestinians were indeed Palestinians or members of the *legio X Fretensis*.[13]

108 Aurelian and Probus

We should assume that Aurelian received reinforcements from at least seven eastern legions (it is possible that he received reinforcements from an even greater number) and their support units so that his infantry contingent would have reached the figure of at least 100–110,000 men and his cavalry the size of 35,000 men. It is clear that the Palmyrenes were heavily outnumbered, but they would still have had an advantage in the number and quality of cavalry.

> At the commencement of the engagement/battle, the Roman cavalry decided to retreat, lest the Palmyrenes, who had the numerical superiority and superior ability to manoeuvre, should by some way be able to encircle the Romans. But the Palmyrene cavalry pursued them so fiercely, though their ranks were broken [*this implies that the pursuit was conducted with as great a speed as possible by using the irregular order called in Romano-Celtic parlance droungos*], that the event was quite contrary to the expectation of the Roman cavalry. For they were pursued by an enemy much their superior in strength, and therefore most of them fell. The foot had to bear the brunt of the action. Observing that the Palmyrenes had broken their ranks when the horse had commenced their pursuit, they wheeled about [*the verb Zosimus uses is sustrefō; Ridley and Pachoud (conversion) translate it as wheeling about; however, the verb has also other meanings which include notably massing/rallying together; both are possible in this case*], and attacked them while they were scattered and out of order. Upon which a massacre ensued, because the one side fought with the usual weapons, while those of Palestine brought clubs and staves against corselets of iron and bronze [*tois sidêrôi kai chalkôi tethôrakismenois. On the basis of this it is impossible to determine which kind of armour the Palmyrenes wore. My best educated guess is that it was a combination of chain mail made of iron, and of the plate with segmented armour made out of bronze.*] The chief cause for the flight of the Palmyrenes was this strange attack with clubs, and in their flight they trampled each other while also being killed by the enemy; the field was filled with dead men and horses, while the few that could escape took refuge in the city. [*In other words, whatever was left of the Palmyrene cavalry fled inside Emesa; this implies that the entire Palmyrene force consisted of cavalry.*] Zenobia was not a little disturbed by this defeat, and therefore consulted on what measures to adopt. It was the opinion of all her friends that it would be prudent to relinquish all pretensions to Emesa, because the Emesenes were disaffected towards her and friendly to the Romans [*Aurelian's favouritism of Sol Invictus undoubtedly had a role in this*]. They advised her to remain within Palmyra, and when they were secure in that strong city, they would deliberate at leisure on their important affairs. This was no sooner proposed than done, with the concurrence of the whole assembly. Aurelianus, upon hearing of the flight of Zenobia, entered Emesa, where he was cordially welcomed by the citizens, and found a treasure which Zenobia could not carry along with her. [*The ability of Zenobia to flee without being harassed by the Romans implies once again that the entire Palmyrene force consisted of cavalry. It is otherwise quite difficult to see how the Romans would not have harassed the enemy or prevented its flight, because it was not in the Roman interest to allow Zenobia to escape or to allow the enemy to reach much stronger Palmyra with its garrison.*] [Zosimus 1.53.1–54.2, English tr. possibly by J. Davis in 1814, p.26–7 with some changes and additions.]

The following account of Flavius Vopiscus of the battle of Emesa gives us some important details that are missing from Zosimus, namely the use of supernatural visions to encourage the men in the middle of the battle. In this case Aurelian appears to have claimed to the soldiers that either Apollonius of Tyana or the *Sol Invictus* appeared in the sky (or somewhere else) at the very moment the Roman cavalry was about to collapse. It was this vision, and apparently the steadiness of the infantry and the above-mentioned attack by the club-bearers, that encouraged the cavalry to reform and attack against their pursuers with the result that the Palmyrenes lost the battle.

> After the taking of Tyana, Aurelian marched towards Antioch; proposing to all that submitted to him, indemnity for what was past. At the village of Daphne, which is near Antioch, he gave the enemy a little blow, and came to that city. It is supposed the precepts of the venerable Apollonius had made an impression upon him; for he used his vision here with great humanity and clemency. The next battle was a general one, and for no less than the empire. It was fought at the city of Emesa in Phoenicia against the Queen Zenobia and Zabdas her general. Aurelian's horse were spent, and ready to run, when some divine form suddenly appeared to them [*this is likely to be Apollonius of Tyana again, although in light of the subsequent visit to the Temple of Heliogabalus, Sol Invictus would appear at least as likely. What is particularly notable about these policies is that they mirrored the policies of Caracalla who had also paid particular homage to Apollonius of Tyana apparently for the same purpose, and we should not forget the family connection of Caracalla with the Temple of Heliogabalus. It is possible or even probable that Aurelian imitated Caracalla also in this and not only in the reform of his coinage (see later). Note the similarity with the visions of Constantine the Great in Gaul and just before the battle of the Milvian Bridge in 312. It is more than likely that Constantine the Great modelled his visions after the example shown by Aurelian, although Aurelian was by no means the first Roman or Greek commander to use such visions*], and encouraging them on to the charge, they took the example of the foot, who all the while stood firm, till at last they put both Zenobia and Zabdas to flight, and obtained a most accomplished victory. Emesa readily yielded to the conqueror; who no sooner entered into it, but he went to the Temple of Heliogabalus/Elagabalus to pay his vows according to the common duty. [*Note the dedications made to the family god of Caracalla and Elagabalus. It is by no means impossible that Aurelian idolized Caracalla because he also followed his monetary scheme. One can even think that the abandonment of Dacia was modelled after Caracalla's abandonment of the conquest of his father in what is today Scotland.*[14]] But there he witnessed again the same divine form that he had seen supporting him in the battle. Wherefore, he founded there temples and dedicated great gifts. He founded also a Temple to the Sun at Rome of extraordinary magnificence. [Flavius Vopiscus, *Historia Augusta, Aurelian* 25.1–6, tr. by John Bernard, 223–4 with changes, emendations and corrections.]

Earlier examples of using the supernatural to uplift the morale of the army can be found for example from the *Stratagems* of Frontinus. It is clear that Aurelian was quite familiar with this side of military leadership. Frontinus's *Stratagems* (1.9.10) include for example the ruse which was employed by Pericles to encourage the Athenians in battle while discouraging the enemy.[15] He noted a dense and dark grove consecrated to Pluto which was visible to both armies. He placed a tall man dressed in purple robes on a chariot drawn by white horses in this grove who then drove forth from the grove when the signal for the battle was given and shouted that the gods were helping the Athenians. As a result of this, the enemy fled. Frontinus's suggestion (1.9.13, tr. by C.E. Bennett, 77) was that 'This sort of stratagem is to be used not merely in cases when we deem those to whom we apply it simple-minded,[16] but much more when the ruse invented is such as might be thought to have been suggested by gods.' We do not know whether Aurelian had read Frontinus's treatises, but he was certainly familiar with the concept of manipulating the soldiers through the gods. In this case it is possible that Aurelian saw a particular formation of clouds or that he had placed some man in the wagons (if these followed to the battlefield as is probable in this case) or some other place like among the infantry which he then claimed to be the vision of the god declaring his support for the Romans. For this to have been effective, Aurelian must have communicated his idea in advance to his closest officers and heralds who must have joined the shouting. One possibility is that Aurelian combined the above-mentioned godly vision with the stratagems (e.g. Frontinus, *Stratagems* 2.11) in which the commander claimed that the other troops had already achieved a victory, which in this case could have been that Aurelian claimed to the cavalry and that the god had already given victory to the infantry which was fighting well unlike the cavalry.

The Battle of Emesa in May–early June 272 (see map)
1) Aurelian approached the Palmyrene army located at Emesa from the direction of Arethusa.
2) Aurelian's plan appears to have been to lure the Palmyrene cavalry to pursue his cavalry behind the Roman infantry so that it could be entrapped between the infantry phalanx and wagon train.
3) It is therefore probable that Aurelian deployed his ca. 100–110,000 footmen so that the heavy infantry was deployed 16 ranks deep and light infantry 8 deep and that he was able to form double phalanxes. The second phalanx would have faced towards the rear to enable it to attack the enemy cavalry. The light-armed would have retreated between its files to form themselves up in the hollow between the two phalanxes. The length of the infantry line would therefore have been about 5.5 km. The shortness of the line would have served as a bait for the enemy cavalry to outflank the Roman infantry.
4) It is probable that the battle was actually fought closer to the city of Arethusa than the city of Emesa, because the Palmyrene cavalry would have wanted to deploy itself on the wider area between the rivers. Furthermore, subsequent events make it clear that the battle was fought so far away from the city of Emesa that the Romans were unable to take it with a pursuit of the fleeing enemy cavalry. It is also clear that the Palmyrenes managed to outflank the Romans which also means that the Romans could not have rested their flanks against the rivers. If the Palmyrenes deployed their forces in two lines of five parts (outer left, left, centre, right, outer right) each line deployed five deep in the Persian manner, then the length of their array would have been ca. 7 km, and they would have outflanked the Romans significantly. If they were deployed as a double line of rhomboids (128 men, 15 wide, 16 ranks deep), the length of the line would have been ca. 8.2 km which would have outflanked the Romans even more.
5) The Roman cavalry was deployed in front of the infantry to lure the Palmyrenes to follow it. In spite of the large size of the cavalry force (likely to be about 35,000 horsemen), it is probable that it was not deployed according to the Italian Drill array, but in the same way as Arrian had deployed his forces

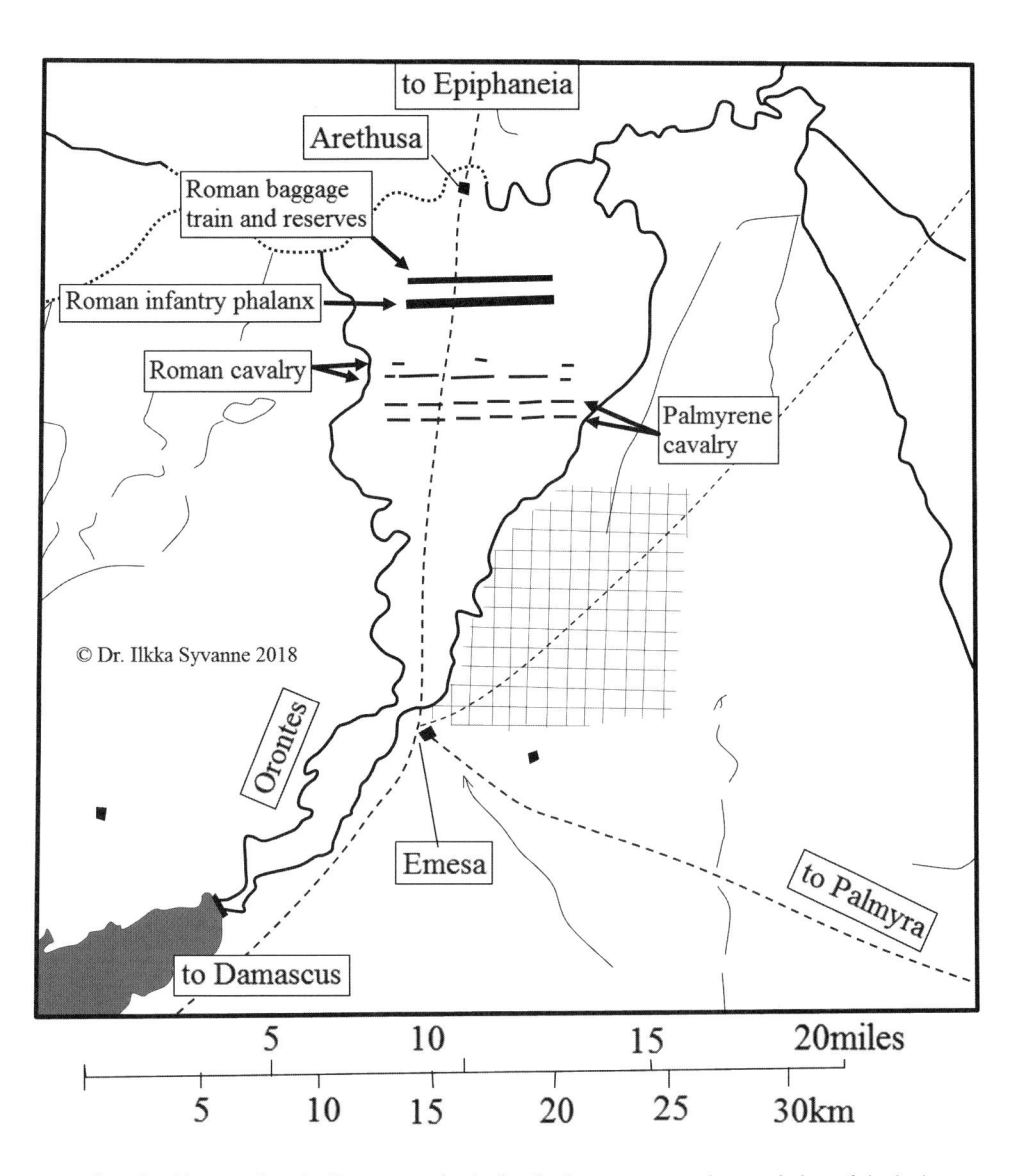

against the Alans so that the Roman cavalry had only three reserve units consisting of the legionary cavalry placed on the wings and the cavalry commander's personal retinue. If the reserves consisted of ca. 5,000 men then the width of the Roman cavalry line would have been roughly 7 km if deployed four deep and ca. 6 km if deployed five deep, the former being more likely in this case.

6) The Roman cavalry feigned flight to lure the Palmyrene cavalry to pursue up to the Roman infantry phalanx into the trap prepared for them.
7) The Palmyrene cavalry pursued so eagerly that the Roman cavalry was routed and unable to reform behind the infantry phalanx.
8) Aurelian uplifted morale with a stratagem which consisted of some sort of divine apparition that together with the example shown by the infantry, caused the cavalry to regroup and reform itself against the enemy.
9) The entrapped Palmyrene cavalry was destroyed in the trap between the infantry, baggage train, reserves and reformed cavalry.

112 Aurelian and Probus

Stoneman (pp.171–2) has aptly compared Aurelian's use of the vision with that of Constantine the Great to improve the morale of his soldiers. In Aurelian's case it was *Sol* (the equivalent of the Christian God) and Apollonius of Tyana (the pagan Christ) that he used to boost the morale of his men, while in the case of Constantine the Great it was the Christian God and Jesus Christ. They knew full well the motto that in combat there are no atheists. The use of religion was therefore a good way to improve the morale of the men. This does not preclude the possibility that Aurelian and Constantine both believed in their gods. It is entirely possible for a man to be a devout believer while using his religion as a means to influence the thinking of others. We simply do not know what their private thoughts were – all we have left is traces of their use of religion as means of manipulation, which is not enough to make any definite conclusions regarding their private beliefs and thinking. It would of course be easy to claim that the *Historia Augusta* is a later fabrication, but the circumstantial evidence speaks for its veracity. Furthermore, as I have shown above, this was certainly not the first instance of the Roman or Greek commanders exploiting the superstitious beliefs of their men for their own benefit.

We are now in a position to reconstruct the main features of the battle of Emesa. Firstly, the entire Palmyrene army of more than 70,000 men consisted solely of cavalry, most of which would have been fully armoured cataphracts. This is proven by the inability of the Romans to catch the remnants of the fleeing enemy force after the battle. In contrast, the Roman army was a combined and joint force with all arms of service present; it is likely that there were even contingents drawn from the navy whose duty it was to operate siege equipment.[17]

Secondly, the Roman battle formation had to be such that the Roman cavalry could withdraw with relative ease after it had reached safety. This precludes the double phalanx and the hollow square/oblong formations. The likeliest arrays would be the lateral phalanx and a variation of the *epikampios opisthia* in which the flank units of the lateral phalanx were refused.

The third clue is the use of the verb *sustrefō* by Zosimus for the infantry manoeuvres. Ridley and Paschoud translate this as wheeling, but the verb has other meanings too, like

antistomos difalangia

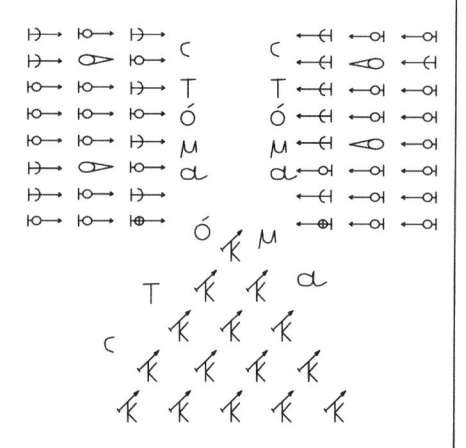

The reconstruction is based on the *antistomos*-formation in the Interpolated Byzantine Recension of Aelian (Codex Burney folio 19r, p.38) shown on the left

file-leader (*lochagos*); a misleading term since in all of the diagrams the *lochagos* is clearly a higher ranking officer (probably a *falangarchēs* or in some cases the *kerarchēs* or even *strategos/hypostrategos*) usually posted in the front centre or in the front right flank of the formation; in Roman usage this means probably a tribune.

spear-bearing (*kontos*-bearing) heavy infantryman (*hoplitēs kontaratos pezos*); *kontos* was a c. 3.74 m long (cavalry) spear that could be used for both thrusting and throwing.

targeteer or light-armed slinger (*peltastēs ē sfendonētēs psilos*); the 10th c. AD infantry peltast seems to have been a javelin thrower.

archer (*psilos toxotēs*)

horseman with a spear (*kaballarios kontaratos*)

ςτομα (stoma in Greek; note that the S doesn't conform with the standard practice and suggests that it had been copied from the ancient original diagram) = the face/front of the battle array coil into a mass, to rally, form a solid body, to turn all together, and so forth. Rallying or massing together would tell us nothing about the tactics adopted. In the *Greek-English Lexicon of Liddell and Scott* the noun *sustrofē* is equated with the Latin *globus* and with the winding into a ball or rolling up together. My own educated guess is that the verb meant all of these at the same time, so that some units wheeled to attack (e.g. the reserve units) while other units in the phalanx formed double fronts (the so-called *amfistomos phalanx / orbis*, which could be thought of as a ball or as a separate *globus* if it was separated from other units) so that their rear halves could face the cavalry behind them, and in some cases two units formed a united formation so that one unit wheeled to form a rear for the other, and in some other cases double-fronted units or united units divided to form a double phalanx so that the rear portion could attack the enemy cavalry behind them. If the Romans used the *epikampios opisthia*, then the flank units could have wheeled to form a longer line while attacking the enemy cavalry. However, the use of the standard lateral phalanx would appear likelier in this case. I would also suggest that it is probable that some of the units in the front line wheeled backwards when the Roman cavalry and the pursuers approached to form openings for these to pass into what was called in military theory *antistomos difalangia*. This is the manoeuvre described in *Aelian's military treatise* (Devine ed. 37.3) and in the *Byzantine Interpolation of Aelian* (Devine ed. 40.1–6, Dain ed. E1–5) which was to be used when enemy cavalry charged in wedge formation. The idea was to put the attacking enemy between two infantry 'phalanxes' (meant to be taken figuratively) when it entered the opening. This was one of the standard tactics used to negate the effects of the enemy charge. See the illustration overleaf.

My educated guess on the basis of the above is that the likeliest combat formation for the Romans in this battle is the standard lateral phalanx. It is also probable that wagons would have accompanied the army so that these were placed behind the infantry phalanx. When the army was arrayed in this manner, the standard procedure was to place some units of cavalry and infantry in reserve and among the wagons and to spread the *carroballistae* (limbered horse-drawn artillery carts) throughout the length of the baggage train for the protection of the rear. As noted above, the best evidence for the use of the standard lateral phalanx is that once the Roman cavalry had reatreated there still existed the danger that it would continue its flight. The *epikampios opisthia* formation would have made the retreat and the pursuit of the Roman cavalry more difficult. The second piece of evidence is that after the retreat the Roman cavalry and the Palmyrene pursuers were in such a position that the Roman infantry had to manoeuvre to face and attack the pursuers most of whom were presumably in the area between the phalanx and the line of wagons.

In sum, Aurelian seems to have used his cavalry force as a vanguard with the intention of tiring the enemy cavalry with a long retreat. This time this failed, for two reasons. The distance was apparently too short and the Palmyrene cavalry abandoned their order and charged at a gallop after the Romans, who in their turn appear to have maintained cohesion by cantering, with the result that the Palmyrene cavalry caught up with the Roman cavalry and routed it and most of the Roman cavalry fled around the flanks to the empty space between the phalanx and wagons, as combat doctrine dictated, while other units probably fled through the phalanx proper because the enemy pursued them too fast so that the Romans opened up routes for this with the *antistomos difalangia* manoeuvre or even by opening up the files. The use of the *antistomos difalangia* manoeuvre had the

An illustration of the way how the left flank Romans could have caught the Palmyrene cavalry inside a trap by using the wheeling

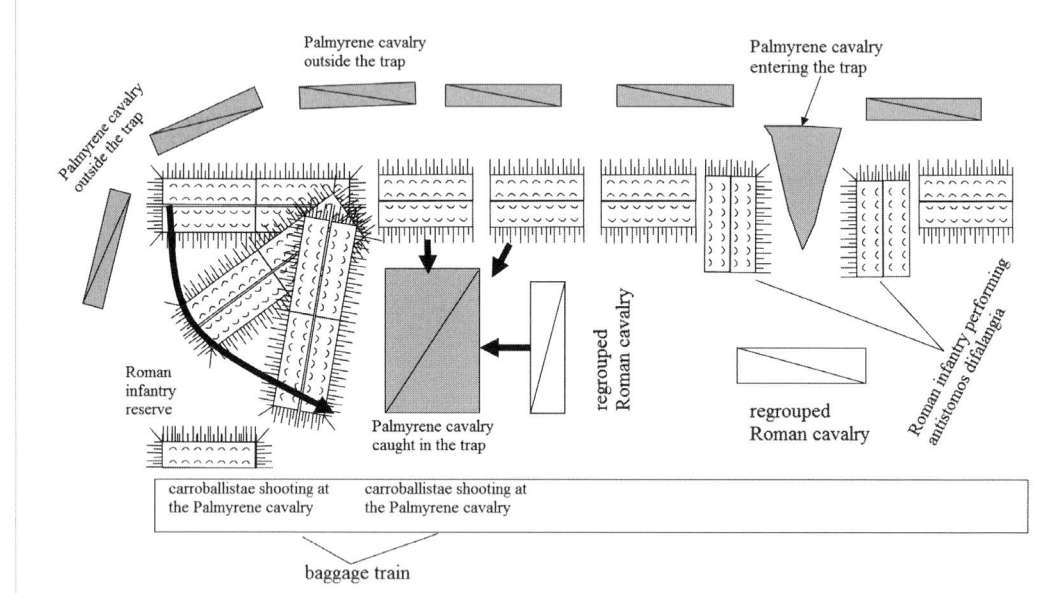

[Diagram labels: Palmyrene cavalry outside the trap; Palmyrene cavalry entering the trap; Palmyrene cavalry outside the trap; Roman infantry reserve; Palmyrene cavalry caught in the trap; regrouped Roman cavalry; regrouped Roman cavalry; Roman infantry performing antistomos difalangia; carroballistae shooting at the Palmyrene cavalry; carroballistae shooting at the Palmyrene cavalry; baggage train]

added tactical advantage of placing the Palmyrene pursuers between two Roman infantry units that could then annihilate the pursuers. Once the Roman cavalry was behind the phalanx, the idea was to rally and reform, or at least to dismount and form a front against the pursuers. This time, however, the Palmyrenes had pursued too hotly and the rallying proved difficult. [18]

It was in this situation that Aurelian played his trick of introducing a vision which rallied the cavalry which then joined the infantry forces in fighting the disordered Palmyrene cavalry. It would be tempting to connect this vision with the heroics of the Palestinian club-bearers so that the man in the vision would have been Hercules with a club, but the fact that Aurelian paid his respects to the god in the Temple of Heliogabalus immediately after entering Emesa suggests that the man/god in the vision was Apollonius of Tyana or the *Sol*. The likeliest trick that Aurelian could have used would have been to dress someone in the required attire in a chariot to show himself somewhere in the baggage train where he would have been visible to all those horsemen who would have sought to continue their retreat. In the meantime, the different infantry units of the phalanx would have preformed all of the above-mentioned combat manoeuvres, as dictated by the situation, to protect themselves and/or to attack the enemy either behind or in front of them. When the rallied cavalry then joined the infantry, the Palmyrenes had lost the battle. It is clear that most of the Palmyrene cavalry that had entered the empty space behind the phalanx would have been annihilated.

Furthermore, it is quite probable that the infantry units posted at both extremes of the phalanx would have formed double fronts after which these would have wheeled inwards towards the centre. See the diagram. This would have created a massive killing zone for all of the Palmyrene cavalry units that were caught between these units and the rallied

Battle of Emesa 272
The likely battle formations and tactics
(not in scale)

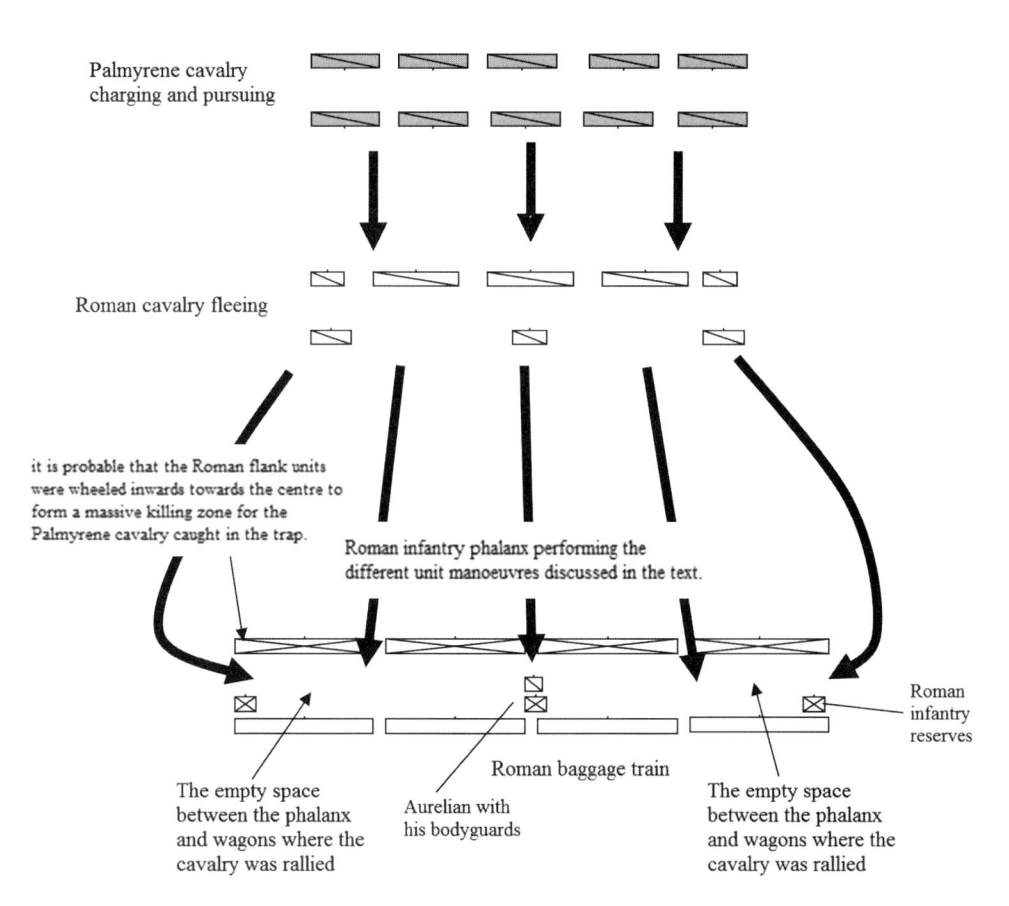

Palmyrene cavalry charging and pursuing

Roman cavalry fleeing

it is probable that the Roman flank units were wheeled inwards towards the centre to form a massive killing zone for the Palmyrene cavalry caught in the trap.

Roman infantry phalanx performing the different unit manoeuvres discussed in the text.

Roman infantry reserves

The empty space between the phalanx and wagons where the cavalry was rallied

Aurelian with his bodyguards

Roman baggage train

The empty space between the phalanx and wagons where the cavalry was rallied

cavalry. It is tempting to think that this would have been Aurelian's plan all along so that the enemy would enter the killing zone, but there exists the problem of the need to use the supernatural vision to rally the horsemen. However, there is one possible explanation for this, which is that when the Roman cavalry reached its intended place behind the infantry it could not rally according to the plan because the Palmyrene cavalry had pursued too hotly, and it was because of this that Aurelian needed his trick. Regardless, it is still clear that the combined arms approach proved its effectiveness once again against cavalry-based enemy as it had so often done since the days of Alexander the Great.

6.3.7. *Siege of Palmyra in about June-July 272*[19]
Despite what Zosimus states (see below), Aurelian did not attempt to give a hot pursuit of Zenobia but allowed her to flee to Palmyra. Having served in the east, Aurelian was well aware of the hazards of the desert.[20] He knew he had to collect adequate supplies and conclude alliances with the local Arabs and Bedouins to enable him to march his army to Palmyra, which was about 150 km from Emesa, a march of four to six days for infantry,

and then to besiege it. This was a major undertaking. It was not an easy task to besiege a city in the middle of a desert at the hottest time of the year, mid-July, which on top of it all had an abundant supply of water while the besiegers did not. Aurelian had to organize a relay of supply trains, which brought to his army food, fodder and wine, and he needed plenty of camels. This stage in the preparations receives only scanty attention in the *Historia Augusta* (Aurel. 26.1) and Zosimus (54.2). Zosimus's account is of greater value because he notes that the nearby peoples provided an abundance of supplies for Aurelian. This means that Aurelian had managed to form alliances with the caravan traders and Bedouins who not only provided supplies but also the supply trains which transported the necessities for the Roman army. This was a major undertaking because everything had to be transported across the desert for the massive Roman army.

Modern historians have compounded the problem by making the wrong conclusion regarding the alliance structure prevailing in the desert.[21] They have placed the incident between Zebba and Jadhima of the Tanukh to have taken place during the reign of this Zenobia, because Zebba is the Arabic form of Zenobia. On the basis of this, all have come to the conclusion that the Arabic allies of Aurelian must have been the Tanukh while those who harassed Aurelian during the march must be some other Arabs. The evidence has been misplaced solely on the basis of the name. The actual text (al-Tabari i.768–9) places the event before the rise of Ardashir which took place in 224. In short, when the *Historia Augusta* (*Aurel.* 26.1, 27.5) states that the Roman army was harassed by the brigands of Syria (*latronibus Syris…latrones Syri*) during the march to Palmyra, we should interpret this to mean the Christian Tanukh Arabs of Syria and not the other way round. According to Vopiscus, the brigands of Syria attacked Aurelian's army frequently during the march and caused him much harm. The Arab allies of Rome would have been the Arabs and Bedouins who had previously been in a dominant position in Syria before…

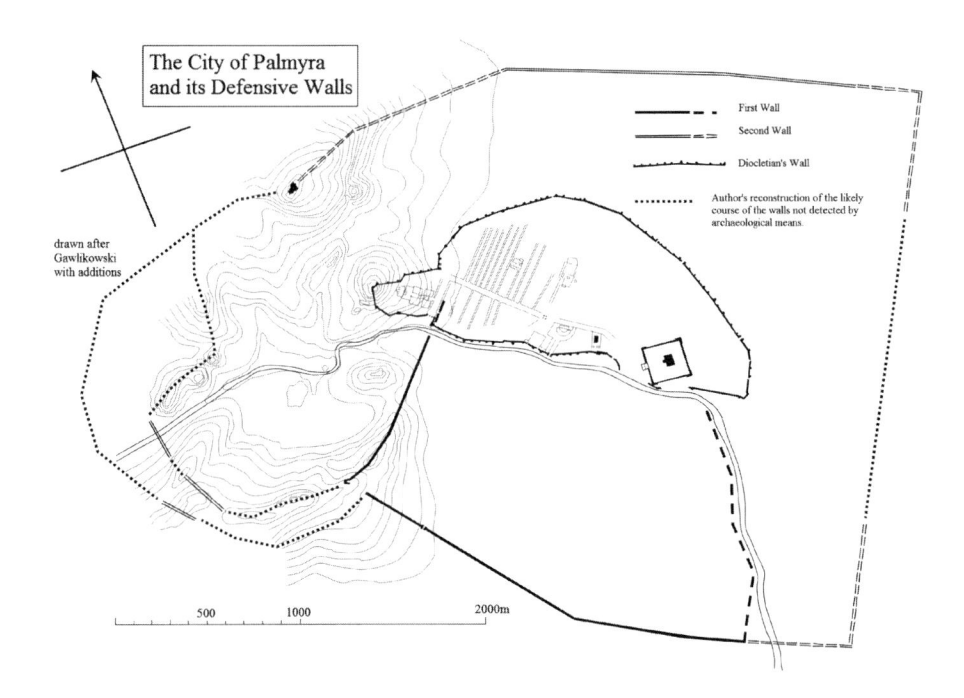

... the migration of the Christian Tanukh to Roman Syria. The last mass migration of the Tanukh to this area took place in ca. 226 when Ardashir conquered al-Hira, but this was only a portion of the large Tanukh tribal confederation because others remained under the Nasrid Tanukh ruler of al-Hira who was a vassal of Persia. The reason why I consider the Tanukh of Syria to have been the brigands of Syria is that the Tanukh were in Roman Syria at this time, they were Christians, and Zenobia was known for her favourable attitude towards them and Jews. As we shall see, now that Persia and Palmyra were allies, all of the Tanukh were fighting for Zenobia.[22]

The two best sources that we have of the siege of Palmyra are the texts of Vopiscus and Zosimus. Vopiscus's (*HA Aurel* 26.1ff.) text misplaces the order of events, but provides some very important pieces missing from Zosimus. Stoneman (p.175–6) and White (99) discuss the letters included in Vopiscus referring to this siege because these provide us with important details of the siege even if both question the veracity of the letters. White (99) and Saunders (237–8), however, note quite correctly that an extant fragment of Peter the Patrician[23] confirms the exchange of letters. Saunders is correct to point out that the exchange of letters belongs to the preparatory stage of the siege and not to the period after Aurelian had already begun it. In other words, Aurelian tried to persuade Zenobia to surrender in return for amnesty so that he would not have to undertake the difficult siege. The offering of terms of surrender was one of the standard procedures of the besiegers of antiquity before attempting an actual siege.

Aurelian, the Emperor of the Roman World, and the Protector of the East, to Zenobia, and those in arms with her. That which I require you now to do by my letter, you ought assuredly to have done of your own volition. I order you to surrender,

The ruins of Palmyra as seen by Wood in 1753.

and I promise you your lives with impunity: You Zenobia and your children shall only be obliged to lead your lives there where I with the advice of the most noble Senate shall place you. Your jewels, silver, gold, silks, horses, and camels must be disposed of to the exchequer at Rome. The people of this country of Palmyra shall be preserved in their rights. [Flavius Vopiscus, *Historia Augusta, Aurelian 26.7–9*, tr. by Bernard, p.225.]

Zenobia receiving this letter, wrote him back an answer, which was more haughty and more proud indeed than the conditions of her fortune required… Her letter was this. Zenobia the Queen of the East, to the Emperor Aurelian. No man ever before you desired what you do by a letter. Bravery is the way to effect whatever is to be done in war. You propose my surrender as if you can be ignorant that the Queen Cleopatra [*Zenobia claimed to be a descendant of Cleopatra and sometimes used the name*] chose her death rather than to live whatever quality under Augustus. Persian helpers are marching to assist us, and we are now expecting them. The Saracens [*Roman sources usually call the Arabs of al-Hira with this name and these are undoubtedly meant here*] are for us. The Armenians are for us. The Syrian robbers have beaten your army Aurelian already [*The Tanukh of Syria*]. What then will become of you when that force arrives, which is expected by us from all parts?… Zenobia dictated this letter herself in the Syriac language; Nicomachus says that he translates it out of that language into the Greek; the other letter of Aurelian was sent in Greek. [*According to the HA 33.3, Aurelian had Longinus executed later as the man who had counselled Zenobia in this letter, but at the same time the author claims that Longinus was actually not responsible for its contents because Zenobia had written the original in Syriac.*] Aurelian…was angry and immediately ordered his army and officers upon general assault. [Flavius Vopiscus, *Historia Augusta, Aurelian 27.1–28.1*, tr. by Bernard, p.225 with changes and comments.]

The above would have been the initial stage of the siege when Aurelian attempted to convince Zenobia to surrender without a fight. When this failed he ordered the general assault which is described in the following quotes.

But in the siege of Palmyra, his [*Aurelian's*] person was so far in danger that he received a flight shot of an arrow [*Aurelian must have attempted to encourage his men to assault the place in order to be wounded. The fact that Aurelian was already a middle-aged man means that the wounding was a more serious health hazard than it would have been for a young man in the prime of his life*] and the hot work that he met with is very plainly confessed by himself in a letter to Mucapor thus. 'Those at Rome deride my expedition and cry I make war against a woman; as if I had to do with none but Zenobia, and that she opposed me upon her own strength. But the case is the same, as if the war was with a man; …It cannot be expressed what showers of arrows, darts, and stones she sends us; and how prepared she is for her defence here? There is no part of the wall that is not planted with two or three batteries. She throws fire at us out of her engines. [*In short, it was not the walls that discouraged the Romans, but the mural artillery and archery.*] In fine, she fights not like a woman, but with the audacity of a man in despair. However… the gods… will still assist the Roman Empire.' [Flavius Vopiscus, *Historia Augusta, Aurelian*, 26.1–6, tr. by Bernard, 224–5 with changes and comments.]

He then marched immediately to Palmyra, which he invested on every side, while his troops were supplied with provisions of every kind by the neighbouring country. Meanwhile the Palmyrenes only derided the Romans, as if they thought it impossible for them to take the city; and one man in particular spoke in very indecent terms of the emperor's own person. Upon this, a Persian who stood by the emperor said, 'If you will allow me, sir, you shall see me kill that insolent soldier;' to which the emperor consented, and the Persian, placing himself behind some other men that he might not be seen [*in other words, he hid behind shields or mantlets*], shot at the man while in the act of looking over the battlements, and hit him while still uttering his insulting language, so that he fell down from the wall before the soldiers and emperor. [Zosimus 1.54.2–3, English tr. possibly by J. Davis in 1814, p.27–8 with some changes and additions.]

Saunders, White and Southern all analyze the defences of Palmyra on the basis of the archaeological finds of Gawlikowski. These prove that the walls that existed during the reign of Zenobia had been built between the late first century BC and first century AD. The size and structure of these walls varies from one place to another so that in places it was 5 metres high and 2.4 metres wide with a stone base, while in others it was made of mortar and stones with a thickness of c. 4 metres and c.5–6 metres high; in other places it was only ca. 1.7 metres thick. There were also no towers and fortified gates and similar features to improve the defences. This means that the walls were not built to withstand a major attack by the Romans or Persians. No traces of the wall have been found in some areas, but I would not preclude their existence on the basis of this because the Romans did not just charge into the city. Similarly, the archaeologists have found no traces of any Roman siege works or camps. On the basis of this, most modern researchers have made the assumption that Aurelian did not attempt to assault or besiege the place in earnest but only at a distance to starve the defenders into submission. Saunders' suggestion is that Aurelian placed his fortified camp at Ain El Baida, a day's march from the city, and that the Romans kept the city under guard from this distance.[24]

I agree with this general assessment, but with the caveat that it is still very likely that the Romans did actually attempt to assault the place when they began the siege. The information in the *Historia Augusta* (Aurel. 26.1–6) and Zosimus (54.2–3) is explicit that Aurelian attempted to conquer the city with an assault but then cancelled the attempt due to the effective protective fire of the Palmyrene mural artillery; hence he settled on the use of the siege at a distance as has been suggested by modern research. It was because of this that the soldiers exchanged missiles with the forces posted on top of the parapets. Furthermore, to be wounded by an enemy arrow Aurelian must have attempted to encourage his men to assault the city by leading from the front despite being already 57 years of age (he would be 58 in September). In short, it was not the height or strength of the walls that discouraged Aurelian, but the very effective use of mural artillery and archery which prevented the Romans from approaching to the distance where they could have broken through the walls. These artillery pieces were likely the handiwork of the philosopher Longinus who was certainly familiar with these devices.

It was then, after Aurelian had come to the conclusion that it would be too costly to assault the place when it was protected by such effective artillery, that he formulated a new plan. He placed his marching camp further away and then posted guards and pickets close to the city to keep it from getting supplies and to make certain that the defenders would be unable to make sorties out of the city without notice. It is clear that Aurelian also posted guards and spies further out so that he could prevent the arrival of the expected help from the Persians, Armenians and Saracens. Moreover, subsequent events prove that he had dispatched operatives and spies among these groups to enable him to subvert and defeat their attempts. In other words, I do not accept the opinion of Saunders and others[25] that the Romans would have defeated the Persians in Mesopotamia or in other places. My view is that we should accept what the *Historia Augusta* states, namely that the Persians, Armenians and Saracens attempted to bring relief for the city of Palmyra and that it was Aurelian with his forces that made these attempts futile.

It would have been after this initial assault had failed that Aurelian resorted to the use of the siege at distance to starve the enemy into surrender and it was also during this period that Aurelian prevented the relief forces from reaching the city of Palmyra. The following quote from the *Historia Augusta* describes this stage of the conflict:

> He [*Aurelian*] intercepted the relief force which had been sent to her [*Zenobia*] by the Persians. The Saracens and the Armenian troops he brought to his own side partly by bribery and partly by the force of his arms. [Flavius Vopiscus, *Historia Augusta*, *Aurelian*, 28.2, tr. by Bernard, 224–5 with changes and comments.]

The above account, subsequent information in the *Historia Augusta* (*Aurel.* 28.4–5, 29.2, 33.2, 33.4), and Sextus Aurelius Victor's reference to victory over Persia (35.1) and the assumption of the titles *Parthicus/Persicus maximus* in 272, prove that Aurelian defeated the Persian relief force in a battle or ambush. This is not surprising because he was aware of its approach – after all, if the contents of Zenobia's letter are correct, she had even warned him of their approach. Furthermore, as discussed above, the combined arms approach gave Aurelian a distinct advantage over the Persian cavalry force. The list of captives present in the trumph of Aurelian in 274 (*HA Aurel.* 33.4, see the quote later) proves that the Persian effort was not some half-hearted effort to save their ally but a real major campaign against the Romans, which is also proven by the inclusion of Armenians and Saracens. Besides the Persians, Armenians and Saracens, the list of captives included Indians, Bactrians, and Iberians (Georgians who would have come in the same force with the Armenians). The case for the presence of the Indians in the Persian army is uncertain, because it is possible that these captives were obtained from the rebel Firmus's army. But the Bactrians came from the east and the Persians possessed territories with Indians in the east with the implication that they could also have been sent west. The definite presence of Bactrians and the likely presence of Indians means that the Persians sent units against Aurelian that were drawn from their easternmost regions. It is also possible that there were Chinese units present in the Persian armies at this time because the Armenian historian Moses Khorenatsi refers to them.[26] The information regarding the Armenians and Saracens is more difficult to analyze due to the lack of details. I would suggest that Aurelian corrupted the Armenians with the help of Tiridates/Trdat who was the legitimate Armenian king and who at this time must have been serving in the Roman army on the basis of Armenian sources.[27] I would suggest that it is very likely that the Persian defeat had actually resulted from the defection of the Armenians to the Roman side and that it was because of this that the list of prisoners also included Iberians and Armenians. The case for the Saracens of al-Hira is more complicated. The reference to the use of force of arms may suggest that Aurelian employed the services of other Arabs and Bedouins so that he was able to ambush the Saracens and thereby force them to accept either the alliance, or die fighting. It is also possible that the Saracens formed one of the contingents accompanying the Persians so that it would not have been only the Armenians who betrayed the Persians but also the Saracens. On the other hand, Malalas (12.30) claims that Aurelian made Arabia into a province. He claims that this area had previously been controlled by the barbarian Saracens who were relatives of Odaenathus. This does suggest the likelihood that Aurelian or one of his generals together with the Arab and Bedouin allies had conducted a campaign against these Saracens and that Aurelian did add their territories to the Roman Empire at this time. The fact that the Tanukh of Syria had apparently been allies of Zenobia may also have worked to Aurelian's advantage in this situation because the Tanukh of al-Hira under the Nasrids undoubtedly saw the Syrian Tanukhs (which supported Zenobia) as their tribal enemies because they had fled from their territory. The defeat of the Persian relief army and the alliances with the Armenians and Saracens were major achievements. The consequences of this victory make it one of the most important military victories ever achieved by the Romans against the Sasanians because the Sasanian removal of forces from the east led to a series of troubles that effectively removed the Sasanian threat at least until 284. The Palmyran situation was now hopeless. With his Saracen helpers Aurelian controlled all routes leading into Palmyra so that he was able to starve them.

As noted above on the basis of *Historia Augusta* (*Prob*. 12.4), Probus was present in these actions, and since he was probably a commander of the *protectores* he undoubtedly played a significant role at least in the clandestine operations that brought about the desertion of the Armenians and Arabs to the Roman side.

The following quote from Zosimus proves that in the end the Palmyrenes were brought to their knees by a lack of provisions, and shows what they attempted to do to solve it:

> The besieged however still held out in the hopes that the enemy would withdraw for want of provisions, and persisted in their resolution until they were themselves without necessities. They then called a council, in which it was determined to flee to the Euphrates, and request aid of the Persians against the Romans. Having thus determined, they set Zenobia on a female camel, which is the swiftest of that kind of animal, and much more swift than horses, and conveyed her out of the city… Aurelianus was much displeased at the escape of Zenobia; and therefore exerted all his industry to send out horsemen in pursuit of her. They succeeded in taking her, as she was crossing the Euphrates in a boat, and brought her to Aurelianus. [*Zenobia's ability to flee means that after the initial assault had failed, the Romans had merely formed a cordon of guards further away to prevent the arrival of supplies. The flight and capture of Zenobia is also confirmed by the HA Aurel. 28.3–4.*] Though much pleased at this sight, yet being of an ambitious disposition, he became uneasy

at the reflection that in future ages it would not rebound to his honour to have conquered a woman. Meantime some of the Palmyrenes that were shut up in the town, resolved to expose themselves courageously, and to hazard their being made captives in defence of their city, while others on the contrary employed humble and submissive gestures from the walls, and entreated pardon for what was past. The emperor accepting these tokens, and commanding them to fear nothing, they poured out of the town with presents and sacrifices in their hands. Aurelianus paid due respect to the holy things, received their gifts, and sent them away without injury. But having made himself master of this city, with all the treasure it contained, he returned to Emesa, where he brought Zenobia and her accomplices to a judiciary trial. Zenobia coming into court pleaded strongly in excuse of herself, and produced many persons, who had seduced her as a simple woman, and among the rest Longinus [*the famous philosopher*], whose writings are highly beneficial to all lovers of learning. Being found guilty of the crimes laid to his charge, he received from the emperor sentence of death, which he bore with so much courage as to console his friends who were much concerned at his misfortunes. Several besides Longinus suffered upon the accusation of Zenobia. [Zosimus 1.55.1–56.3, English tr. possibly by J. Davis in 1814, p.27–8 with some changes and additions.]

The city of Palmyra therefore negotiated its surrender. The priests of Bal appear to have been active during these negotiations because there exists an inscription which commemorates the role of one such priest in August 272. In fact this has been used to date the surrender of Palmyra precisely to August 272, but this is not conclusive because the dedication would obviously have been made after the siege. Aurelian looted the treasure and left Sandario with 600 archers as a garrison inside the city and then marched to Emesa. Presumably at the same time as he did this Aurelian also made Marcellinus commander of the whole eastern frontier with the title *praefectus Mesopotamiae rectorque Orientis* so that he was also responsible for the supervision of Palmyra. I would suggest that it is probable that Aurelian also either captured or demolished the artillery pieces that had caused him so much trouble in the initial stages of the siege. The victory was celebrated in coins with the legends *restitutor orientis* and *pacator orientis*. One extant inscription also gives Aurelian the title *Palmyrenicus maximus*, and the *Historia Augusta* gives him the cognomens *Armeniacus* and *Adiabenicus* apparently thanks to the fact that he managed to convince the Armenians to desert to his side.[28]

It is not known when Aurelian received the Persian envoys who brought him gifts (royal chariot and purple cloak) from the King of Kings and presumably begged for peace. It is possible that this took place already during the siege, or while Aurelian was still at Palmyra, or when he had reached Emesa, or after it in 272. The *Historia Augusta* (*Aurel.* 28.4) suggests that Aurelian dealt with the Persian, Armenian and Saracen matter immediately after having captured Zenobia, but this could obviously refer to any period relatively soon after the capture. At this time, both parties saw the conclusion of peace preferable, the Persians because Shapur I had either died or was in his deathbed, or because his son Hormizd I had to march to the east against the Hephthalites or Sogdians who had invaded. Aurelian in his turn still needed to restore Gaul back to the Empire and may already have faced the invasion of the Carpi (Free Dacians) in the Balkans.[29]

I would suggest that it is probable that it had been Shapur I who had dispatched the relief force against Aurelian and that he had done this by removing forces from the east (Indians and Bactrians included in the list of captives) with the result that the Hephthalites and/or Sogdians had invaded, which in its turn required the attention of the new ruler Hormizd I. The circumstantial evidence therefore suggests that the victory achieved by Aurelian over the Persians was one of the greatest in the annals of Roman history. Aurelian definitely deserved his title *Parthicus/Persicus maximus* which he took in 272. However, the peace which was now concluded appears to have been based on the maintenance of the status quo, because Armenia remained in Persian hands. The only real change appears to have been the fact that the Armenian and presumably also Persian deserters stayed in the Roman army and that the Saracens became clients of Rome. As we shall see, Aurelian had no intention of keeping his word to the Persians but planned to invade Persia at the first opportunity.

The Palmyrenes were put on public trial once the army reached the city of Emesa. Flavius Vopiscus (*HA Aurel.* 33) and Zosimus both note how Zenobia excused herself by accusing the others and in particular the philosopher Longinus of the advice that had led to the revolt. She did everything in her power to save herself and her sons, and in fact it is possible that she had been instructed to do so because Aurelian wanted to save her life. The list of other men of importance who were executed is not known, but one may suspect that these would have included at least Zabdas and Zabbai (known only from an inscription) and possibly also Timagenes if he had managed to flee from Egypt. Aurelian spared the lives of Zenobia and her sons so that they could be paraded in a triumph. Flavius Vopiscus's account proves that this was not approved of by the soldiers who demanded that Zenobia should also be executed. According to Vopiscus (*HA Aurel.* 30.6ff., 33), Aurelian wanted to save Zenobia for two reasons. She and her husband had saved the east for the Romans during the reigns of Gallienus and Claudius, and he wanted to parade her before the Roman people in a triumph. I would suggest that it is also probable that Aurelian felt that he owed a personal debt to Zenobia for her role in the conquest of the east in his name while Quintillus was still the official emperor. However, there is an even likelier reason for Aurelian's willingness to forgive Zenobia, which is that he appears to have fallen in love with her daughter whom he actually then went on to marry in 274. A fuller discussion follows later. It is also possible that the difference in the treatment of surrendered enemies and others after the siege of Tyana was at least partially the result of the influence of Probus who rejoined Aurelian at the time of the siege of Palmyra. After this, Probus appears to have accompanied Aurelian on all of his campaigns so that one may accept Vopiscus's claim (*HA Prob.* 8.1) that Probus was the man who influenced Aurelian to be more lenient.

I would connect the problematic fragment (Banchich ed. frg. 196) of Peter the Patrician, which refers to an unknown military mutiny under Aurelian, with the dissatisfaction of the soldiers over the fact that Zenobia was not executed. This fragment claims that when Aurelian faced this mutiny he stated to the soldiers that they were mistaken if they thought that it was in their hands to decide who would be the emperor. Aurelian stated God had given him the purple which was in his right hand and that God had determined what would be the duration of his reign. After this Aurelian punished fifty instigators of the revolt. Banchich notes that it is impossible to determine when this took place and that it is possible that Peter has confused Marcus Aurelius with Aurelianus. Watson, however, connects this with the coins that were struck from the summer of 271 until 273 with various references to Jupiter. The most poignant of these were the legends Iovi Conservatori and Iovi Conser included in billon radiates. These coins were primarily minted for the soldiers and the message was that Aurelian was Jupiter's chosen one. If one then accepts this interpretation and puts it in the order of extant fragments it becomes apparent that the mutiny took place after the siege of Palmyra but before the end of the year 273.[30] My educated guess is that the mutiny took place as stated above. The other possible date for the revolt would be the time when Palmyra surrendered and Aurelian prevented its sacking by the soldiers. After all, he had promised that the soldiers would be free to pillage the barbarians and now when he prevented even this some of the soldiers were ready to mutiny. However, the fact that Aurelian had looted the treasury makes this alternative less likely than a mutiny at a time when Aurelian refused to kill Zenobia.

The punishment of the ringleaders of the mutiny could be thought of as another good example of Aurelian's so-called cruelty, but when one takes into context all of these references in the sources to Aurelian's harshness it becomes apparent that Aurelian was actually not cruel at all. Aurelian punished corruption, crimes, treachery, false accusers/informers, revolts, and senatorial conspiracies with a very firm hand, but this was absolutely necessary if he wanted to make the Roman administrative and military apparatus work for the benefit of the Roman commonwealth. Furthermore, it was necessary to punish with stern measures. The *Historia Augusta* claims that Aurelian falsely accused many senators of conspiracy and that he punished them with undue harshness. This is likely to be just another example of the pro-senatorial stance in this source. It is more than likely that Aurelian punished the culprits justly for their despicable behaviour. Aurelian was clearly a disciplinarian who demanded by-the-book behaviour from officials and soldiers, but considering the behaviour of the period, this was necessary. This can be contrasted with his clemency towards the cities of the east, Zenobia and her children, and towards Tetricus and his family (see later). It is clear that Aurelian always made calculated decisions about which was the best policy to follow in each circumstance. He always sought to punish corruption and crimes just as he punished any signs of disobedience in the army with harsh measures, but at the same time he showed clemency when he considered it beneficial for the Roman commonwealth. He was not a really harsh man, but a man who sought to rule with justice to correct the abuse of power. This, however, does not mean that he did not have a cruel streak in him. The sources make it clear that Aurelian enjoyed the watching of torture and bloodshed much too much for this to be acceptable even for Romans of the period and that he also sometimes killed persons in anger as happened at Tyana. Regardless, it is still clear that his policies were good for the Roman Empire.[31]

Eutropius (9.14) described Aurelian as a man who was always severe because he put to death even the son of his own sister (see later), but at the same time he described him as a reformer who reinstated military discipline and removed dissolute manners. Sextus Victor Aurelius (35.7) in his turn described Aurelian as a man who sought to prevent greed, embezzlement and extortion in the provinces, which was contrary to the customs in the military from whose ranks he came. This may refer to the rampant corruption in the military of his own day, but it is probable that the same was also true in the chaotic third century. Aurelian would have none of that but restored order and discipline in the military forces. In the words of the *Historia Augusta* (*Aurel.* 37.7, tr. by Magie, p.269): 'Now whatever crimes there were, whatever guilty plans or harmful practices, and lastly, whatever plots – all these Aurelian purged away throughout the entire world.'

According to Malalas (12.20), Aurelian then marched to Antioch. He placed Zenobia on a dromerary camel and paraded her to demoralize all possible remaining supporters of her and of Palmyra in the area between Emesa and Antioch. At Antioch he first watched the chariot races after which he brought Zenobia on the dromerary to the circus for all to gaze. Then he placed Zenobia in chains on top of a structure for three days that all would get the opportunity to see her humiliation. Aurelian called this a triumph.

It is possible that we should connect the letter of Aurelian to the Roman Senate and people by Trebellius Pollio (*HA Tr.* 30.4ff.) with this triumph at Antioch. This letter claims that Aurelian defended his decision not to execute Zenobia to the senators because he had heard that there were men who thought that Aurelian's decision to parade Zenobia in a triumph was unmanly and reproachable because she was a woman. As usual, historians have dismissed this letter as fictitious, but its contents do fit the circumstances. The soldiers had not accepted the decision not to kill Zenobia and Aurelian had indeed paraded Zenobia in a triumph before he had reached the city of Rome. I would suggest that it is possible that the letter is genuine and even if it is not it is still likely that it preserves the contents of the real letter sent by Aurelian to defuse the situation in Rome. The contents also suggest a well working network of spies that had informed Aurelian of the dissatisfaction among the conservative elements. According to Aurelian, these persons should keep the venom of their own tongues to themselves. Zenobia was a worthy opponent who had kept the east intact for the Roman Empire. It was Aurelian who chastised the conservatively thinking upper class figures of the Senate for their lack of understanding.

Malalas (12.30) includes a reference to a riot of the *monetarii*, who demanded back their customary rights at the moment when Aurelian was about to leave the city of Antioch. The angry Aurelian punished them. There are three possible occasions for this. The first would of course be the first time Aurelian entered the city after the battle of Immae in 272, but this is very unlikely because at that stage Aurelian is claimed to have

Left: Coin of Aurelian (source: Cohen)

Right: According to Strada (Lyon 1555, 162), this is a coin of Firmus located in Mantua. In my opinion the provenance of the coin is uncertain at best.

shown clemency towards all, as was his policy. The second would be when Aurelian was returning from Palmyra, which is already quite plausible because Aurelian was now free to curb corruption – the so-called customary right of the *monetarii* – just like he had done when he reached Rome in 271. If this trouble took place now, it would explain why it was necessary for Aurelian to reach Antioch on the double the next year when Palmyra revolted again. The third occasion would be during the return trip from Egypt in 273, if those historians who claim that Aurelian began his monetary reform in late 273 are correct. I would suggest that this rioting took place in 272.

According to Zosimus, Aurelian now continued his journey.

> Aurelianus marched towards Europe, carrying with him Zenobia, her son, and the rest of the confederates of this rebellion. Zenobia is said to have died, either of disease, or want of food, but the rest were all drowned in the strait between Chalcedon and Byzantium. [Zosimus 1.59, English tr. 1814, pp.29–30 with some changes by author.]

Most historians are of the opinion that this account of Zosimus is false because most sources state that Zenobia was paraded in the triumph of Aurelian in the city of Rome, and because her descendants lived in Rome in the next century. I agree with this view. For further details, see the discussion later in the context of the events of the year 274.

Two horsemen from the Helena Sarcophagus with two helmeted heads from the same monument. All of the horsemen in this work of art are depicted without armour and therefore they belong to the category of unarmoured cavalry (*afraktos*). Some of these are depicted with shields, while others are depicted without shields. In Greek military theory the *afraktoi* consisted of the *doratoforoi* (spear-bearers), *kontoforoi* (*kontos*-pike-bearers) and *akrobolistai* (skirmishers armed with bows, javelins, swords and/or axes depending on the subtype). This class of unarmoured Roman cavalry has not received the attention it deserves. On the basis of the fact that it is depicted in the Arch of Constantine (see pp. 12, 14 with Plates) and Sarcophagus of Helena, it is clear that it formed the main striking force of Constantine the Great. Furthermore, it is very likely that it had an important role already during the wars of Gallienus and Aurelian. The former is known to have used the unarmoured Moors as his elite cavalry (Syvänne, Gallienus, 72-5). It is similarly quite clear that the vast majority of Aurelian's cavalry was lightly-equipped at the battle of Immae (see pp.99-103). The types of helmets depicted in the Sarcophagus also merit special attention because these types of helmets have not received the attention they deserve. Note also the use of saddles with low cantle and front pommel, which always formed an alternative for the horned saddles. For an analysis of saddles, see Gawronski.

Chapter Seven

The Wars against the Palmyrene Rebels, Carpi and Firmus of Egypt in 272–3

7.1. Introduction to the Problems in Dating and the Consensus View

Dating has been relatively secure up to the fall of Palmyra thanks to the existence of coins and papyri which have enabled historians and numismatists to put the events into their rightful places. However, from this date onwards dating is insecure. It is often impossible to date events even to the right year with any uncertainty. I will offer in the following discussion two alternative timelines with all of the uncertainties included. I will first give the usually accepted sequence of events, after which I will present my alternative timeline for the wars that took place after August 272 but before October 273.

It is usually suggested that when Aurelian had finished the war against Zenobia he marched to Europe in the same year and that he then fought a war against the Carpi who had invaded and defeated them in a battle somewhere between Carsium and Sucidava, after which he settled the Carpi as farmer-soldiers in Thrace. Saunders dates this war to January/early 273. Watson dates the campaign to the winter of 272/3. White dates the Balkan campaign to the period late November 272 to January 273. Southern and Homo suggest the end of 272 and the beginning of 273. Cizek dates the wars against the Carpi, and the revolt of Palmyra and Firmus, to take place during the period after July 272 but before the end of 272. Therefore, with the exception of Cizek the historians are roughly unanimous in their dating. In my opinion Cizek's timetable is too tight. All historians are also united in their view that it was after the Carpic war that Aurelian marched against the Palmyrenes who had revolted again and after that against the rebels in Egypt. With the exception of Cizek, all other historians place these campaigns to take place in 273.[1]

7.2. My Theory Regarding the Sequence of Wars between August 272 and the end of 273

Now I will present my theory, which is based on the apparent back and forth travels of Aurelian in both Zosimus and *Historia Augusta*. I will now also present the evidence for each of the wars in greater detail.

The only two narrative sources for the war against the Carpi in the Balkans after Palmyra had been captured are the *Historia Augusta* (*Aurel.* 30.4–5) and Aurelius Victor (39.43). The former merely states that after Aurelian had subdued the East, he returned to Europe where he defeated the Carpi. The latter merely states that Aurelian had settled some Carpi on Roman soil. In addition to this, there exists a restored inscription[2] which refers to a battle which Aurelian fought in the area between Carsium and Sucidava, and we also know that Aurelian received the title *Carpicus maximus* before 17 October 273 when it is included in a papyrus. Taken together this means that Aurelian defeated the Carpic invaders and then settled some of them somewhere in the Balkans probably as *laeti* farmer-soldiers.[3] The list of captured enemies in the *Historia Augusta* (*Aurel.*, 33.4) refers also to the Roxolani (white Alans, a Sarmatian tribe), which may mean that they took part in this invasion, but most scholars, Saunders included, dismiss this because of the source. My learned opinion, however, is that it is very likely that the Roxolani did indeed take part in this campaign. The above evidence therefore dates the war to the period after the capture of Zenobia but before 17 October 273.[4]

Let us now return to Zosimus and the *Historia Augusta* which, when read carefully, seem to refer to two separate instances in which Aurelian was forced to return to the east.

Zosimus, *Nea Historia*

> Aurelianus marched towards Europe, carrying with him Zenobia, her son, and the rest of the confederates of this rebellion. Zenobia is said to have died, either of disease, or want of food, but the rest were all drowned in the strait between Chalcedon and Byzantium. (This account, which precedes the return against the Palmyrenes, does not actually state that Aurelian crossed the straits, but states merely that the Palmyrenes were drowned in them.)
>
> [Zosimus 1.59, English tr. 1814, pp.29–30 with some changes by author.]

Vopiscus, *Historia Augusta*

> The peace of the east being established, Aurelian returned to Europe a conqueror. He defeated the Carpi and when the Senate in his absence gave the title *Carpicus*, he sent as a jest to the Senate the message [*I would suggest that this absence was caused by the revolt of Firmus in Egypt*] that they might as well call him *Carpiculus* because *carpisculum* is a kind of boot. To him the *cognomen* appeared ignoble because he was already called *Gothicus*, *Sarmaticus*, *Armeniacus*, *Parthicus* and *Adiabenicus*.
>
> [Vopiscus, *HA Aurel.* 30.4–5, tr p.228 by Bernard but with many changes and additions.]

Zosimus, *Nea Historia*

> When Aurelianus was on his way to Europe [*I have changed the translation here on the basis of the Paschoud edition/translation p.52 because it is more accurate than either of the English translations. The original Greek text suggests as stated in the French translation by Paschoud that Aurelian had not yet reached Europe before he returned. See also above.*] he was informed by a messenger that a party he had left at Palmyra, having won over Apsaeus, the principal author of all that was past, was tampering with Marcellinus, whom the emperor had appointed governor of Mesopotamia and of the east, to assume to himself the imperial robe. Under the pretence of taking time for deliberation, he delayed them so long that they again importuned him repeatedly. He was forced therefore to frame ambiguous answers to their demands, until he had given notice to Aurelianus of their design. In the meantime the

Palmyrenes, having clothed Antiochus in purple, continued to Palmyra. Aurelianus, being informed of this, hastened into the east, without any preparation, and arriving at Antioch, surprised all the people, who were then attending a horse-race, and were astonished at seeing him. From thence he proceeded to Palmyra, which he took and razed without a contest, but not thinking Antiochus worthy of being punished, on account of the meanness of his condition, he dismissed him.

[Zosimus 1.60.1–61.1, English tr. 1814, p.30 with some changes and additions by author.]

After this action, he speedily reduced the Alexandrians, who were disposed to a rebellion, being already in commotion. (This does not include any referrals to a new march to Europe or a war against the Carpi, but all the same it is likely that Aurelian was indeed in Thrace at the time he learnt of the Egyptian revolt.)

[Zosimus 1.61.1, English tr. 1814, p.30.]

Vopiscus, *Historia Augusta*

It is rare, and a hard thing for the Syrians to keep their faith. No sooner was Aurelian employed about the affairs of Europe, but the Palmyrenes, who had so very lately been beaten and crushed, broke out into another rebellion. They killed Sandarion, whom he [*Aurelian*] had left Governor of Palmyra, and six hundred archers that were in garrison; designing to set up one Achilleus [*Antiochus in Zosimus*], a kinsman of Zenobia, as emperor anew. But Aurelian, who was always prepared, returned from Rhodope [*this referral would mean that Aurelian had already reached Europe when he learnt of the revolt, but the information in Zosimus suggests otherwise. It is therefore possible that Vopiscus has confused the two separate occasions when Aurelian returned east*] and punished them by destroying the city as they deserved.

[Vopiscus, *HA Aurel.* 30.4–5, tr p.229 by Bernard but with many changes and additions.]

Secure now therefore of the state of the east, he returned again to Europe; and with his accustomed bravery he defeated all the roving enemies. While Aurelian was active in Thrace and Europe, there arose in Egypt a certain Firmus, [*this places Aurelian in Thrace when the revolt took place*] who not setting himself up as an emperor [*In the HA FSPB 1ff. Vopiscus claims that he was a usurper after all, contrary to the claims of Aurelian who just called him a bandit.*], pretended to make that province rather a free-state. Aurelian made no delay to oppose this evil. Nor did his wonted success abandon him. For he presently recovered Egypt again.

[Vopiscus, *HA Aurel.* 32.1–3, tr p.230 by Bernard but with many changes and additions.]

He [*Firmus*], then seized the imperial power in opposition to Aurelian with the purpose of defending the remainder of Zenobia's party. Aurelian, however, returning from Thrace defeated him [*This means that Aurelian was in Thrace when he heard of the revolt.*] [Vopiscus, *Historia Augusta*, *FSPB* 5.1, tr. by Magie p.395 with my comment.]

On the basis of the above, I would suggest that Aurelian had reached Chalcedon when he heard of the revolt of Antiochus at Palmyra from Marcellinus and that it was because of this that he drowned most of the Palmyrene prisoners in the straits between Chalcedon and Byzantium. Aurelian did not want to be slowed down by prisoners. The march from Emesa to Chalcedon could easily have taken seventy days for Aurelian to complete because he was in no hurry.[5] If Palmyra was conquered in late June or early July, then one may make the guess that Aurelian could have reached the city of Chalcedon in mid-October if he spent the whole of July in settling the pressing matters in the east. It would not have taken that long for Aurelian to learn of the revolt because according to Procopius (*Anecdota* 30.1ff.) the couriers could be expected to travel at a speed of 200–250 miles a day,[6] which means that if Marcellinus had sent the message from the city of Antioch it would have reached Aurelian in three days.

Once Aurelian had learnt of the revolt, he acted with great determination. He reached the city of Antioch faster than the news of his arrival reached the city. This means that Aurelian probably prevented the movement of postal couriers for security reasons and that he probably left infantry marching behind while he advanced with the cavalry on the double, and it means that he had a very well organized security apparatus for this to be possible. Zosimus's text does not state what the status of the city of Antioch was when Aurelian reached it. My suggestion is that it was still in Roman hands so that the reason for Aurelian's speed was the danger that the Antiochenes could join the Palmyrenes, especially so if the above-mentioned revolt of the *monetarii* had been crushed just recently as I have suggested above.

After this, Aurelian would probably have waited for his infantry forces to arrive. With forced marches it would have been possible for the cavalry to reach Antioch in 15 to 18 days and the infantry 30 to 38 days. In other words, Aurelian and his cavalry forces would have been at Antioch before the end of October while his infantry would have reached it by about mid-November. Since the sources claim that Palmyra was now conquered and then razed to the ground without trouble, I would suggest that Aurelian had previously removed the pieces of mural artillery that had caused him so much trouble. As discussed above, the walls were no obstacle. It is also likely that the defenders would have been quite demoralized to see their conquerers before them so quickly.

According to Vopiscus (*HA Aurel.* 31.4–32.1) Aurelian destroyed the city and ordered his soldiers to kill women, children, old men and peasants, and the leader of the revolt Antiochus/Achilles was pardoned because of his insignificance. However, there may have been another reason for this: that he was a relative of Zenobia. If Aurelian intended to marry Zenobia's daughter, which according to Zonaras (12.27) he did, there was every reason to pardon this man – and my suggestion is that this was indeed the reason. On the basis of the letter from Aurelian to Cerronius Bassus (unknown) included in this text, Aurelian had put a time limit on the butchery so that there would remain some people to inhabit the place. The text, however, states that most of the population was put to the sword to serve as a warning example for the few remaining. The letter also claims that the Temple of the Sun, which had been pillaged by the eagle-bearers of the Third Legion and by the *vexilla*-bearers, the *draco*-bearers, buglers and trumpeters, was to be restored to its former condition by using the booty previously captured from Palmyra which was under the control of Bassus. It is obviously impossible to verify the veracity of this letter, but its contents would fit the circumstances. The rebels needed to be made a warning example of, while Aurelian still wanted to promote the cult of the Sun throughout his Empire. According to the *Historia Augusta*, Aurelian then marched back to Europe where he crushed the roving enemies, who must be the above-mentioned Carpi possibly with the Roxolani. If we assume that Aurelian left some of the forces that had already previously been left with Marcellinus, he would not have needed to stay long in the Palmyra-Emesa region. Allowing for regular marching speed, Aurelian would have reached Byzantium in January 273. Consequently, I would suggest that Aurelian engaged the Carpi and Roxolani in the winter-spring of 273 and that he then returned to the East to crush the revolt of Firmus.

It is unfortunate that we do not know what type of enemy the Carpi represented for Aurelian, because there are no extant descriptions of their fighting tactics. However, we can make some educated guesses on the basis of what were the fighting tactics of the Dacians (the Carpi were the so-called Free Dacians) and what type of tactics one would expect in this location. One would expect the Carpi to have possessed both cavalry and infantry and that they did not wear much protective equipment, so their forces could be considered to have been lightly equipped as far as their mobility is concerned. Most of the infantry would have consisted of spearmen and javelineers who also carried shields. Similarly, most of the cavalry would have consisted of spearmen. In addition to this, they would naturally have had some foot archers and mounted archers. In fact the inclusion of the Roxolani and the location suggests that the Carpi may have possessed Sarmatian-style cavalry of their own, so these would not have consisted solely of the allied Roxolani. We should also expect that the Carpi employed shield-wall phalanxes and close order units for combat when they decided to engage the enemy in a pitched battle, and in this case they apparently fought a pitched battle which they lost. The location given by the above inscription suggests the likelihood that Aurelian forced the invaders against the river Danube so that they were forced to fight. This in its turn suggests the possibility that the invaders consisted solely of cavalry whose only intention was to raid and then flee in the Sarmatian manner before the Romans could mount a response. Whatever their tactics, the Carpi were still by Roman standards only a barbarian horde and nothing more. The history for the wars between the Carpi and the Romans was one-sided. The Romans defeated the Carpi repeatedly from the reign of Philip the Arab (*Philippus Arabs*) onwards until they simply disappear from the sources.

The revolt of Egypt took place probably some time during the spring of 273. The above account has already made it clear that the rebels in Egypt consisted primarily of those who had previously supported Zenobia and Palmyra, and that the leader of the revolt was Firmus. On the basis of the list of captives in Aurelian's triumph, Firmus's allies may have included Indians, so it is possible that the revolt was timed according to the monsoon winds. So Firmus decided to revolt in support of the Palmyrenes in June/July 272 and dispatched his ships to India in July 272 bearing the news of the catastrophe that had hit Egypt and Palmyra, and these ships reached India by early September 272. They would have returned with the contrary monsoon winds, so they could have started their return journey at the earliest in November/December 272 or at the latest in January 273, and they would have reached the Red Sea ports at the latest in February 273. If so, then when the ships brought Firmus an affirmative answer to his suggestion of forming a grand alliance, he would have finished his final preparations for the revolt, so the actual revolt would probably have taken place in about March 273.

Left: Coin of Zenobia
Right: Coin of Aurelian
(source: Cohen)

The reason for the revolt is obscure, but in my opinion the likeliest reason is just the rebellious spirit of the Egyptians against the Romans at this time. It was because of this that Timagenes and others like him had joined the Palmyrenes. This was not the only revolt in Egypt during the tumultuous third century and more were waiting over the horizon. The Egyptians were clearly dissatisfied with their Roman rulers. The best evidences of this are the two revolts of Egypt that took place in 294–98. The fact that there were usurpations and revolts all around must have encouraged everyone who had anything against anyone to act. It was the spirit of the age. There must also have been commercial reasons for this because the leader of the revolt was a merchant and he was supported by his foreign trading partners. These commercial connections had clearly been established during the Palmyran interlude of 270–72. If my suggestion regarding the alliance structures and the influence of monsoon seasons is correct for the timing of the revolt, then Firmus and other Egyptians who supported the Palmyrenes had decided to revolt against the Romans immediately after the Romans had regained control of Egypt under M. Aurelius Probus. It was only thanks to the time it took to form the alliances that the revolt was delayed until the spring of 273.

The identity of the rebel leader has been considered suspect solely on the basis of the fact that the name comes from the *Historia Augusta* so it is claimed to be a forgery or a mixup with the prefect/*corrector* Claudius Firmus who is known to have been in charge of Egypt in 274.[7] This, however, does not take into account the actual text of the *Historia Augusta* which quite clearly separates three different persons with the name Firmus from each other. Vopiscus (*HA FSPB* 3.1) states in no uncertain terms that there were three different men called Firmus, one of them prefect of Egypt (presumably the *corrector* of Egypt Claudius Firmus who was in office in 274), another *dux limitis Africani* and also proconsul, and the third who was the friend and ally of Zenobia. In short, Vopiscus did not have any trouble in distinguishing between the men with the same name unlike most modern historians.

According to Vopiscus, the third Firmus was a swarthy huge man with prominent eyes and curly hair. He was known to eat a huge amount of meat and to be a real powerhouse. He was known for his publicity stunts which included the holding of an anvil on his chest while in a crab position, swimming among crocodiles, driving an elephant and the riding of hippopotami and ostriches. According to Vopiscus (*HA FSPB* 4.3–4), Firmus was able to outdrink Aurelian's *duces* in drinking contests and also the *vexillum*-bearer Burburus who was particularly well known for his ability to withstand wine. This is a nice vignette to the lifestyles of the period soldiers which is also known from other sources. Soldiers have always been known as heavy drinkers, because this is one of the means by which they can alleviate their stress, and there is nothing incredible or unbelievable in this statement. This incidental reference is also valuable for another reason, which is that it shows Firmus at his best. He lulled the Roman officers in charge of the defence of Egypt into a drunken stupor while he undoubtedly milked every piece of information he could out of them. This was first rate intelligence gathering. It was probably largely thanks to this that he was able to overcome the Roman garrisons protecting Egypt. Once in power, he immediately put a stop to the grain shipments to the city of Rome (*HA FSPB* 5.4). It made it absolutely necessary for Aurelian to crush the revolt promptly.

According to Watson (p.135), Aurelian set up a supplementary mint at Tripolis (Tripoli in northern Lebanon) in or about late summer 273. It is unfortunate that we do not know the exact date for the opening of this mint. All that is known with certainty is that it was opened in 273. Watson suggests that the intention may have been to give the soldiers a reward in the form of a donative to celebrate the victory over Palmyra or to encourage the troops to fight with greater eagerness against the enemies in Egypt. It is also possible that the opening of this new mint is connected with the previously mentioned punishment of the *monetarii* of Antioch.

Flavius Vopiscus offers us valuable information in a roundabout way regarding the commercial and military aspects of Firmus's policies in two places: *HA Aurel.* 33.4–5 and *FSPB* 3.1ff. The latter states that Firmus was a rich merchant who kept a close relationship with the Blemmyes (subjects of Aksum at this time), Saracens and Indians and often sent merchant vessels to India. The former contains a list of captives in Aurelian's triumph which includes Egyptians, Blemmyes, Aksumites, Arabes Eudaemones (Arabs of Aden who would be the Yemenites), Saracens and Indians.[8] All of these were nations along the Red Sea route to India and on the basis of the fact that they were captives it is clear that they were allies of Firmus. When these two lists are combined with the letter of Aurelian to the Roman people included by Vopiscus (*HA FSPB* 5.3–6, esp.5.3), it becomes clear that the vast majority of Firmus's forces consisted of his barbarian allies, because the text claims that he rose in revolt with the barbarians and gathered together the remaining supporters of Zenobia. This means that his forces consisted of quite a mix of different nationalities, all with differing fighting tactics. One may assume that Firmus' allies arrived both on land and on ships in about February/March 273 while the remaining supporters of Zenobia launched their attack from the inside so that Firmus surprised the Romans completely.

In short, I would place the beginning of the revolt roughly to the period February/March 273. All of the nations mentioned are known to have fought by using close order formations, but by Roman standards all of these were lightly equipped (mostly without armour and equipped only with shields, javelins, spears, swords and bows) and poorly organized, so that in all known instances the Romans were able to defeat them with far fewer men than their enemies had.[9] They cannot have posed any serious threat to the elite forces that Aurelian brought to the scene. It is because of this that the war assumed an 'I came, I saw, I won' (*veni, vidi, vici*) character.

If the revolt took place in March, the news of the revolt could have reached Rhodope in nine to ten days in ships, or by land in about the same time. Let us assume that Aurelian was at Rhodope when he learnt of the revolt of Firmus, because this is where the *Historia Augusta* claims Aurelian was when he learnt of the Palmyran revolt. As I have hopefully shown above, this is likely to be a mistake for the location where Aurelian learnt of the revolt of Firmus because Zosimus clearly states that Aurelian had not crossed into Europe when he learned of the Palmyran revolt. It would have taken about ninety days for Aurelian to reach Egypt if he began his march at Rhodope. However, we should add to this figure the time it took for Aurelian to complete the reorganization of the defensive structures in Thrace in the aftermath of settling the Carpi and the time it took for him to organize supplies and ships for the campaign against Egypt. These could have easily taken a whole month, but obviously one cannot know this for certain. If one adds a month to the figure then Aurelian would have reached Egypt in about June-July 273. If Aurelian used a fleet, then he could have reached Alexandria in 10 days in favourable winds and in 19–20 days in unfavourable winds.[10] It is unfortunate that we do not know what means Aurelian used to reach Egypt. One thing, though, is certain, which is that it involved the use of the fleet because in all cases Aurelian would have needed a fleet to transport his supplies and to place the city of Alexandria under siege if that were necessary.

We do not know any details of the military action that took place in Egypt beyond the fact that Aurelian routed the enemy and gained a complete victory with relative ease. Vopiscus (*HA FSPB* 5) claims that there were some who claimed that Aurelian had Firmus strangled, but at the same time he claims that Aurelian's letter to the people of Rome stated otherwise. The main purpose of the letter appears to have been to calm down any possible disturbances in Rome by convincing the populace that the grain supply would soon return to normal. This indeed would have been a convincing reason for the writing of such a letter once Aurelian had possession of the city of Alexandria with its courier ships. According to the same letter, Aurelian had captured Firmus who was then tortured and killed. Considering Aurelian's famed cruelty it is probable that he watched and supervised the torture and killing just as he did when he punished his slaves (*HA Aurel*. 49.3–5) – or perhaps he even participated in it.

The Egyptians were also punished for their revolt. Aurelian increased the tax on them by increasing the amount of grain they were required to contribute to Rome. Egyptian revenue in kind, in glass, papyri, linen and hemp were also to be paid to the city of Rome. He appointed additional boatmen on the Nile in Egypt and also on the Tiber in Rome. The Tiber was dredged and its banks supported to ease the transport of supplies along it to the city of Rome. The *Historia Augusta* does not specifically state that these would also have been paid for by the Egyptians, but this is more than likely because the addressee of Aurelian's letter in the *Historia Augusta* is *praefectus annonae* Flavius Arabianus (otherwise unknown). Aurelian also demolished the walls of Alexandria and separated a large part of Bruchium from the city as a punishment. The idea was to prevent the occurrence of similar revolt in the future.[11]

As noted above, there is every reason to believe that Aurelian's joking letter to the Senate, which referred to the granting of the title *Carpicus* to him, could actually be correct. Aurelian was indeed absent from Rome at the time the Senate gave him the title because the earliest known specimen of the title *Carpicus maximus* can be found on a papyrus dated 17 October 273. This may even mean that Aurelian was still in Egypt, making arrangements in the area including the improvement of the communications along the Nile. The sequence of letters from Egypt to Rome mentioned by the *Historia Augusta* would probably have been that the first letter was the letter to the populace meant to calm fears of famine followed up by the other two letters (the *Carpicus* letter to the Senate and the organization of grain supplies for the *praefectus annonae*).

Aurelian could even have conducted a punishing expedition south along the Nile and/or along the Red Sea against the Blemmyes and Aksumites (Ethiopians/Eritreans), and it is also possible that the Meroites were used as allies during such a campaign. If Aurelian punished the Saracens of the Arabian Peninsula and the Yemenis (Arabs of Aden/Arabia Felix), this would have required a naval campaign, and so would the attack against the Axomitae/Aksumites who were opposite the Yemenis. The fact that these nations had provided military support for Firmus would have made a punishing expedition necessary. The list of nations in the *Historia Augusta* (*Aurel.* 41.10), which worshipped Aurelian as a god in 275, proves that some sort of punishing expeditions were probably conducted, but by whom is not known. The worship of Aurelian as a god should be interpreted as a payment of tribute (i.e. protection money) in the form of gifts to the emperor god so that the nature of these payments as a tribute could be veiled as a worship of a god. The list in question mentions the Saracens, Blemmyes, Axomitae (Ethiopians/Eritreans), Bactrians, Seres (Chinese), Hibernians (Georgians), Albanians of Caucasus, Armenians and the peoples of India.

In the case of Bactrians and Chinese it is clear that Aurelian did not conduct any punishing expeditions against them. The best educated guess for their inclusion would be that these had sent some gifts to Aurelian (which could be interpreted as worship) in an effort to form an alliance with him in a situation in which the new Persian ruler Hormizd was fighting somewhere close to Bactria – unless of course the worshippers in question were the prisoners taken from the Persian army. In fact, I would suggest that in the case of the Chinese it is likelier that they meant the captured soldiers because China would be too far away for them to ask Aurelian to ally with them unless there was some unknown war between the State of Western Jin and Persia in Central Asia. However, in the case of the tribute paid by the Armenians, Georgians, Albanians, and Saracens, it is clear that their aim would have been to convince Aurelian to liberate them from the Persian yoke. If this is the case, and I would suggest that it was, then their joint effort appears to have paid dividends, because Aurelian was on his way against Persia when he was killed in late 275. The reason for the tribute paid by the Indians could be the same, but in this case it is possible that the Romans did make a show-of-the-flag expedition there too because they certainly did that during the reigns of Constantine the Great and Constantius II with the same result, which was the payments of tribute to the Romans.[12]

The Saracens (Kinda?), Blemmyes, Aksumites and Yemenis would of course have paid their tribute as a result of having been punished by the Romans because of their support of Firmus. All these nations would have been under the Aksumites at this time, which is proven by the information provided by the *Monumentum Adulitanum II* and the information provided by Vopiscus (*HA Aurel.* 33.4–5; *FSPB* 3ff.). The list of peoples paying tribute to Aurelian suggests that the Romans conducted a major joint and combined operations campaign along both shores of the Red Sea so that they were able to liberate the Arabs, Kinda and Blemmyes from the Aksumite yoke. In other words, the

136 Aurelian and Probus

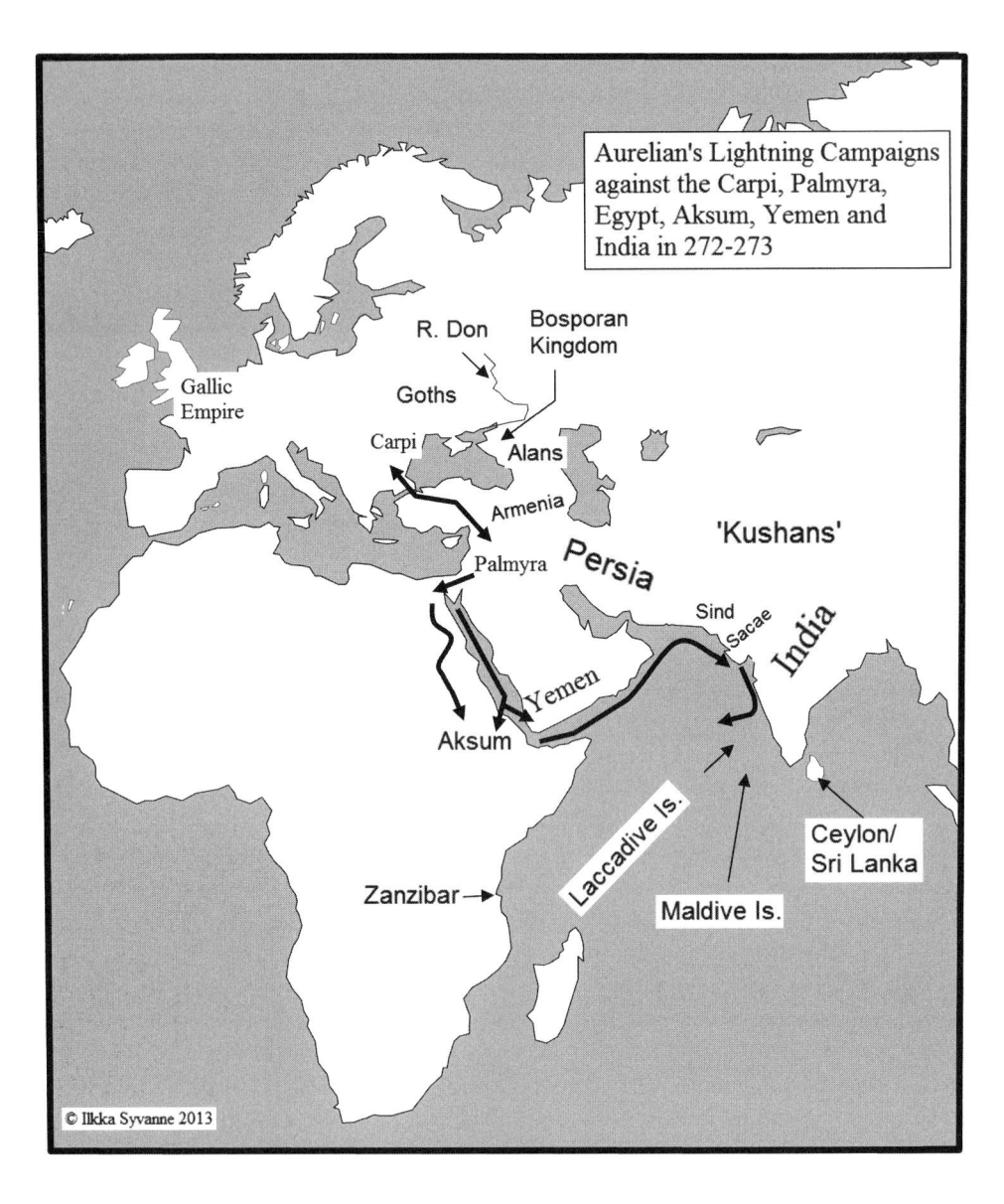

Aurelian's Lightning Campaigns against the Carpi, Palmyra, Egypt, Aksum, Yemen and India in 272-273

support the Aksumites gave to the Palmyrenes proved very costly for them and resulted only in their own subdual by the Romans. On the basis of the above and Vopiscus (*HA Prob*. 17.1) and Zosimus (1.71.1) it is clear that the Aksumites lost control of the tribes that they subdued so that we find for example the Blemmyes operating independently during the reign of Probus.

It is not known whether Aurelian participated in any of these probable punishing expeditions, but he easily could have. He could even have sailed to India and back if he began his journey in July 273 and returned back in February 274. This would still have left him plenty of time to crush Tetricus in 274. However, I would suggest that he did not join any such show-of-the-flag expedition because the *Historia Augusta* shows him reorganizing shipments of grain from Egypt to the city of Rome. Furthermore, it would be quite incredible if the sources had left such a spectacular adventure unmentioned, on top of which it would have been very irresponsible for the emperor to conduct such a campaign in a situation in which he had not subdued the Gallic Empire. However, I would not entirely rule out the possibility that he could have joined a punishing campaign against the Blemmyes, Saracens, Axomitae and Yemenis, because such an expedition from Alexandria along the Nile and Canal of Trajan and the Red Sea up to Aden and then back would have encompassed ca. 3,500 nautical miles which could have been covered in favourable winds with an average rowing speed of 5 knots in 30 days, and in unfavourable winds in 90 days plus whatever fighting and negotiations there were – and we should remember that it is very unlikely that the winds would have been unfavourable constantly, so the entire expedition could have easily been performed within 90 days. If the Romans dispatched a show-of-the-flag expedition to India, its ships would have continued from Aden to India while the rest of the fleet would have turned back. In short, there was plenty of time for such a campaign to take place after June-July 273. Regardless, I am still of the opinion that if this punishing expedition took place, as is very probable, then it would have been conducted by some *dux* or *duces* rather than by the emperor himself because it is once again difficult to see how the sources could leave Aurelian's participation unmentioned. Furthermore, none of the other known campaigns in this area were conducted by the emperors themselves, with the exception of Septimius Severus who was planning to invade Axum/Aksum before he cancelled the campaign thanks to the outbreak of a pestilence.[13]

7.3. The Financial Reform of 273–4[14]

It is possible that Aurelian started his famous reform of the monetary system while in Egypt because the Alexandrian mint started to issue new reformed coins in the autumn 273. The defeat of Palmyra and the revolt in Egypt enabled Aurelian to instigate the next stages in his financial reforms which had undoubtedly been suggested by his 'financial minister' Sabinus who also transferred the principal mint of the Empire from Milan to Ticinum at the same time. The most important portion of the reform was the improvement of the quality of the coins to the standard it had been under Caracalla. In fact, Watson suggests that Aurelian and his advisors may have used the monetary system of Caracalla as their model when they reformed the coinage. The second portion of the reforms was the making of tax gathering more efficient.

Alaric Watson is undoubtedly correct in suggesting that even if it is obvious that Aurelian wanted to root out corruption and loved law and order for their own sake, his primary intention was to keep his armies paid, fed, housed and ready to fight. He was a military man who understood that if he wanted to have a well functioning military he needed a well functioning economy in which taxes were efficiently gathered for use by the army.

The exact timing of the reform is contested; some historians claim that it started in the autumn of 273 while others place it in the next year; the latest date for the reform would have been the end of August 274. The fact that the Alexandrian mint started issuing coins in autumn 273 that reflect the reforms that became apparent later in other mints, suggests that the earliest date is to be preferred.

138 Aurelian and Probus

At the heart of the reform was the improving of the standardization of the coins. The silver content in the coins was raised five per cent on average while the range of variance in their size and content was reduced significantly. Aurelian recalled the old debased silver coins and replaced them with these newly issued improved coins. The tighter control exercised by Aurelian is apparent from the fact that with the exception of Lyon all mints followed these standards and also followed the centralized coin designs that Aurelian used in his propaganda. The quality of gold coins was also improved so that the weight of the *aureus* was increased to 6.6g, which had also been the standard under Caracalla. The improved quality of the silver and gold coins also meant that the minting of bronze coins became once again affordable – the debasing of silver coins had made bronze coins next to useless for commercial purposes. The state now introduced three denominations of bronze coins; these once again resemble those in use under Caracalla.

The aim was to restore the trust of the people, merchants and soldiers in the quality and value of the coins issued by the state so that commercial transactions would not be hindered. By and large this appears to have worked because the major problems with inflation took place only later under the tetrarchs when Diocletian famously tried to correct the situation with his price edict. The reform, however, was still not a great success because the improved quality coins were too valuable for daily transactions and

Roman horseman in the Museum of Naples.
(source: Duruy)

the state and the cities did not issue enough bronze coins. This was particularly true in Gaul where the pre-reform coinage remained the preferred form of payment. It is therefore not surprising that the Lyon mint continued to mint below-standard coins. The other result of this was the increase in the numbers of forged coins which were minted to look like the older coins. Newly issued coins restored the credibility of the currency, but they did not put a stop to inflation largely thanks to the fact that daily commercial transactions continued to be made with the older debased coins.

The presence of the Chinese forces in the Persian army makes it possible that the mail and scale hoods visible in the paintings of Dura Europos could have been borrowed from the Chinese.

Chinese horseman from the Dunghuang painting (first half of the fourth century). Aurelian and the Romans faced Chinese cavalry in the Persian army so that they could have easily encountered similarly equipped Chinese in combat. Note the clear Central Asian influence on the equipment.

Chapter Eight

Aurelian in the West 274–5

8.1. The Return to the West in spring 274

The exact date of the reconquest of Gaul is not known with certainty and we also do not know what route Aurelian took when he marched to Gaul. Saunders (251ff.) offers a detailed discussion of the chronological problems. At the root of the problem is the inscription which calls Aurelian *restitutor orbis*[1] with the dating *tr p IIII* (tribunician powers four years) *cos III* (consul three times). There is no universal agreement regarding the exact dating of these offices: some claim that *tr p IIII* ended in 9 December 273, while Saunders claims that the *dies imperii* system dated the tribunician powers IIII to the year August 273 to August 274. Saunders is correct to note that on the basis of the normal marching speed of the army the latter system is to be preferred. However, if Aurelian started his return march in July 273, then the other earlier alternatives would also become possible. Regardless, in this reconstruction I follow Saunders' basic argument which is that the reconquest took place either in August 274 or before it. The reason for this is that it is probable that Aurelian tarried for a while in Egypt, as discussed above. However, there is one difference in our interpretation. He places the decisive battle at Durocatalaunum to have taken place in late April 274 while I prefer to place it to the summer 274, as does Watson (p.93). Saunders' date, however, is still quite possible.

The narrative sources do not offer us much evidence regarding the route Aurelian took when he left the east. Zosimus (1.61.2) states that Aurelian returned to Rome where he celebrated a triumph. Vopiscus (*HA Aurel.* 32.3) implies that Aurelian marched straight to Gaul. Zosimus's account has usually been dismissed because Vopiscus (*HA Aurel.* 34.2–3), Victor (35.5),[2] Eutropius (9.13), and Jerome (263 Olympiad) state that both Zenobia and Tetricus were paraded in the triumph of Aurelian. Saunders is of the opinion that the *Historia Augusta* is to be preferred in this case for this reason so that Aurelian would have marched along the Danube to the Catalaunian Fields where he engaged Tetricus's forces in combat. This would have been the most direct route and it would also have enabled Aurelian to inspect the frontier during his march. However, I agree with Watson (83, 93, 243) that it is entirely possible that Aurelian visited Rome before he marched against Tetricus in Gaul. It is also entirely possible that Aurelian would have paraded Zenobia twice before the Romans in triumph – after all he had already paraded her in triumph in the east. Watson, however, suggests that the triumph was delayed to take place only after the Gallic campaign, which is also possible, but I prefer to follow Zosimus here. Zosimus (1.61.2) also claims that it was then that Aurelian started the construction of the new temple of Sol where he placed the statues of *Sol* and *Belos* – one may assume that it would also have had a statue of Apollonius of Tyana, as implied by the previous account. Zonaras

(12.27) also places Aurelian's marriage to the daughter of Zenobia (Ulpia Severina) to take place before the Gallic campaign, which is therefore to be preferred to the possibility that it took place after it. Aurelian's presence in Rome suggests also that he presided over the reform of coinage while there because the reformed coins had already been issued at Alexandria, even if Zosimus (1.61) states that it took place only after the Gallic campaign.

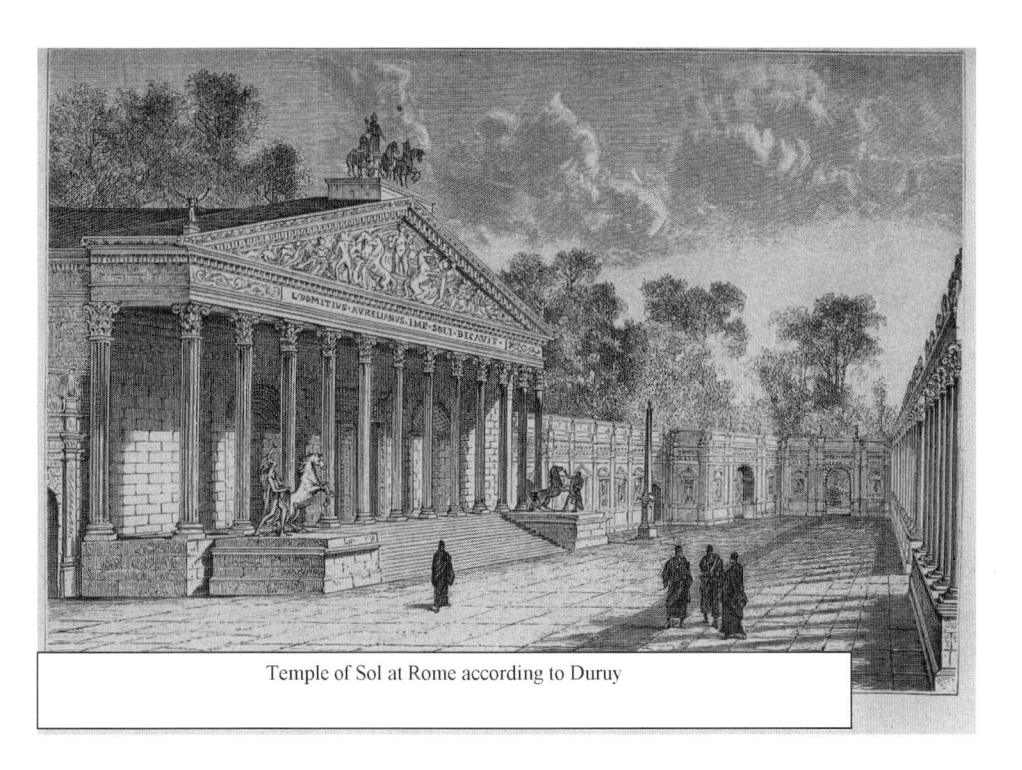

Temple of Sol at Rome according to Duruy

8.2. Aurelian's Marriage with Ulpia Severina, his Augusta and Domina

On the basis of the extant coins it has long been recognized that Aurelian married a lady called Ulpia Severina and that she received the titles *Augusta* and *Domina* to correspond with Aurelian's *Augustus* and *Dominus* immediately after her marriage in 274. The first known coins depicting Severina as *Augusta* were minted at Alexandria in August 274, followed after that by the other mints still in operation in 274. The origins of this Ulpia Severina has caused plenty of speculation. Most historians consider her to be some unknown lady from the Danubian regions on the basis of the name Ulpia because the name Ulpius was popular in the Balkans thanks to its connection with the emperor *Ulpius Traianus* (Trajan). However, it has also been suggested that she would be related to Ulpius Crinitus of the *Historia Augusta*, who claimed to be a descendant of Trajan, but most of those who dismiss *Historia Augusta* as a source, like for example Watson, dismiss this as worthless speculation. Another theory is that she was a daughter of none other than Zenobia, because Zonaras (12.27) claims that Aurelian married Zenobia's daughter while he married the rest of her daughters to other distinguished Romans. This is not as easy to dismiss because it does not come from the hated *Historia Augusta*.[3]

Regardless, Saunders dismisses this theory on the grounds of her nomenclatura because as a daughter of Odaenathus she should have had the nomen Septimia and not Ulpia.[4] In my opinion this is inconclusive because people of the time are known to have changed their names when it became advantageous to do so and in the case of Zenobia's daughter there certainly would have been quite pressing reasons for a change of name. And why the name Severina? One possible answer could be that Aurelian wanted to return the Roman Empire to the golden age of the Severans. In short, in my opinion we should trust what Zonaras states. There was no reason for him to lie about this. The claim also receives support from the fact that Aurelian pardoned Zenobia and her relatives.

Coins of Severina. Source: Cohen. Note the coins which bear AUG instead of AUGG, which have been used to prove that Severina acted as a dowager during the interregnum.

It is curious that Aurelian married so late in life. He was about 59 or 60. The usual suggestion is of course that Aurelian married for dynastic reasons, to procreate offspring. This he certainly did. It is unfortunate that we do not know if he was a widower or whether he kept mistresses. It is possible that as a soldier he had visited the brothels or had kept concubines with the result that he never married, but this would have been quite contrary to his character. It is also possible that Aurelian was one of those manly military men who just did not know how to behave among women, with the result that he did not feel any great desire to marry one. It would also be possible to speculate that he had not married because he was bisexual or gay, but this speculation is probably the least likely because at least the Christian sources, which had every reason to hate him, would not have kept silence about it had it been so. In short, the silence of the sources allows many different speculations, but ultimately it is clear that we just do not know anything about Aurelian's personal life before the marriage.

According to Flavius Vopiscus (*HA Aurel.* 42.1–2), Aurelian had a daughter who survived him. It is usually assumed that Aurelian must have sired her with Severina, but this is by no means certain. Aurelian was 59/60 and Severina must have been in her teens or just past her teens. If the account of the *Historia Augusta* (*Aurel.* 42.1–2) is correct, then it is likelier that the daughter was the love child of some earlier relationship, because Vopiscus claims that her grandson was the proconsul Aurelianus who lived in Sicily. This is obviously not conclusive because Roman history was full of examples in which the career paths and age requirements for various posts were overlooked for political reasons. It is possible that the daughter was indeed the offspring of Severina. This receives support from the otherwise inexplicable execution of the son and/or daughter of Aurelian's sister. This son could have expected to succeed Aurelian, and if Severina had become pregnant, this dream might have evaporated into the wind. It appears certain that Zenobia's children survived to produce offspring as several independent sources mention the existence of her descendants in Rome,[5] and I would include Severina as one who could have given birth to these.

8.3. The reconquest of Gaul in summer 274

The sources for the reconquest are bare in their details. The Greek sources, Zosimus (1.61.2), Syncellus (AM 5764), and Zonaras (12.27), state in the briefest possible way that Aurelian reconquered Gaul from the insurgents. The Latin sources add to this some important pieces of information. Sextus Aurelius Victor (35.3–4) states that when the Germanic invaders had been driven out of Gaul, the legions had been destroyed because their general had betrayed them. This suggests a possibility that the local governor Faustinus had cooperated with the Franks. The reason for this was that Tetricus was being attacked by his soldiers because the governor (*praeses*) Faustinus had corrupted them. It was then because of this that Tetricus had sent a letter to Aurelian in which he begged for Aurelian's protection. Tetricus stated that he had drawn up his army in combat formation only for the sake of appearance and that he would betray his army during the combat. Consequently, he surrendered to Aurelian immediately when he approached. Eutropius (9.13.1), *Historia Augusta* (*Tr.* 24.2–3, *Aurel.* 32.3–4), Jerome (263 Olympiad) and Orosius (7.23) also state that Tetricus feared his own soldiers, abandoned them and surrendered out of his own free will to Aurelian. The location of the battle, Durocatalaunum (Châlons-sur-Marne/Champagne), has been preserved by Eutropius and *Panegyrici Latini* (8(5)4.3). The latter mentions the massive carnage which took place at Durocatalaunum. Jordanes (*Romana* 290) agrees because according to him Tetricus betrayed his own army among the Catalauni.

We are now in a position to reconstruct the principal features of this war. The Germans had invaded Gaul either in 273 or 274, but had been defeated by Tetricus. However, it was then that Faustinus had raised a revolt at Trier (Victor 35.4, Polemius Silvius 521–522) with the result that Tetricus was fearful of his own men. He communicated his fears secretly to Aurelian who duly marched to Durocatalaunum in 274. It was then that Tetricus sent a second message to Aurelian which stated the above. Then when the armies were about to engage in combat, Tetricus abandoned his army with the result that Aurelian basically massacred the disordered force. It is also probable that Tetricus would have purposefully arrayed his army in such a manner that it was easy to destroy.[6]

144   Aurelian and Probus

Left: Coin of Tetricus. Right: Tetricus with his son.
Source: Cohen.

Aurelian duly took Tetricus and his son Tetricus II, who had been made a co-emperor by Tetricus I, prisoners to be paraded in the triumph. However, Aurelian pardoned both and even made Tetricus either *corrector Lucaniae* or *corrector totius Italiae*.[7] This was in striking contrast to the treatment of Heraclammon at Tyana. Aurelian had either changed his mind about the best policy to be followed or he just wanted to reward Tetricus for the services he had given Rome by protecting Gaul against the barbarians just as he rewarded Zenobia with her life for the services she had done on behalf of Rome – or perhaps Aurelian just felt sympathy with the troubles Tetricus had with his unreliable soldiers. It is likely that this was one of the instances in which Probus influenced the policy decisions of Aurelian because as supreme commander of the *protectores* it is likely that Probus was in charge of clandestine operations such as these would have been. And why did Aurelian massacre the Gallic army in a situation in which the Roman Empire needed every soldier it had? In my opinion, it was because Aurelian as soldier-emperor felt that the worst offence the soldiers could make was to rebel against their commanding officer. He had no use for such soldiers and had them all killed.[8]

Now he had Faustinus at Trier (*Augusta Trevorum*) to deal with. Trier was close by so it did not take long for Aurelian to engage his next opponent after the massacre at *Durocatalaunum*. It has been suggested on the basis of the statement of Polemius Silvius (521–2), who claims that Faustinus was a usurper under Aurelian, that Aurelian did not face him now but later in 275 during his second Gallic campaign. This is possible, but I would suggest that there is actually no discrepancy in the sources when we remember that after the surrender of Tetricus, Faustinus would indeed have been a usurper under Aurelian. In fact, the following text of Zosimus proves this to be the case:

> After these successes he easily defeated and punished Tetricus and other insurgents [*it is this 'allous epanastantas' that proves the existence of other rebels after Tetricus had been subdued*] in a manner they deserved. [Zosimus 1.61.2, my free translation based on Paschoud, Ridley and Bernard.]

Even if not mentioned by the sources, it is probable that Aurelian conducted a very short punishing expedition across the Rhine to chastise those who had previously attacked and supported Faustinus. This receives support from the text of Vopiscus (*HA Probus* 12.3) which states that Probus defeated the Franks in the pathless marshes. It is quite possible that this incident took place now. If so, then it is possible that Probus served under Aurelian during this campaign or that Aurelian had placed Probus in charge of the expedition. The subsequent triumph at Rome includes Franks and Germans among the captives. These must have been the allies of Faustinus, and the Celts, Franks and Germans that Postumus and Victorinus had enrolled into their army during the reign of Gallienus (*HA Gall.* 71, *Tr.* 6.1–2), and possibly also tribal warriors who would have been captured during the punishing expedition, if that is what Aurelian did. It is probable that at least some of these Germanic soldiers and units survived the massacre at Durocatalaunum and the subsequent defeat of Faustinus because these were not present in those massacres to become the *auxilia palatina* units of the late Roman period.

After this Aurelian restored the defensive structures in the area and fortified at least the city of Dijon. He also built a city called *Aureliani*, which is now known as Orléans. In addition to this, Aurelian closed the Mint of Trier so that it could not be used to obtain the support of the Rhine army in the manner Faustinus had used it. The Lugdunum (Lyon) Mint was also reopened and White suggests that it was placed under the control of Probus. The restoration of Gaul into the Roman Empire was celebrated with the titles *restitutor Galliarum*, *restitutor libertatis* and *restitutor orbis*. In addition to this, the inscriptions show Aurelian with the title *Britannicus maximus* which was usually awarded for conquest. It is clear that if Aurelian had wanted to cross the Channel he could have easily done so and it is because of this that it is possible that he did. However, there is no definite evidence for Aurelian's presence on the island and it may be that he received the title as a result of the surrender of the island. However, in light of the evidence I would not preclude the possibility that Aurelian did conduct a campaign in person.[9]

8.4. The Triumph at Rome in 274

After the conquest of Gaul the whole Roman Empire stood united under Aurelian. It was now the time to celebrate the achievement in grand style. Aurelian was now the *restitutor orbis* and *pacator orbis*. The titles were advertised on coins and inscriptions with good reason. The following description of the triumph in the *Historia Augusta* is the only one that describes the triumph of Aurelian in any great detail and is therefore included here.

> The peace of the west did conclude with Aurelian the entire master of all the Roman world. Every part of it now was reduced to him; and so he took his way to the city of Rome, to celebrate a solemn triumph, at once over Zenobia and Tetricus, that is, the east and west.
>
> It will not be amiss to know the manner of the triumph of Aurelian; for it was a very noble one. There were three chariots of state, worthy of the magnificence of the greatest kings. The first was the chariot of Odaenathus, curiously wrought and distinguished with silver, gold, and jewels. The next was an equally fine chariot which had been given to Aurelian by the King of Persia. The third was Zenobia's chariot, which she had made for herself, in hopes to make her entrance into the city of Rome with it; nor was she mistaken. For she did so, but it was as a captive, and both her and her chariot were led in triumph. [*Festus 24.1 also notes that Zenobia was led captive in front of the chariot.*] There was a fourth chariot drawn by four stags supposed to be the chariot of the King of the Goths. In this chariot Aurelian rode

146 Aurelian and Probus

Aurelian's Deus et Dominus coin which celebrates him as RESTITUTOR ORBIS. Source: Cohen

Coin of Aurelian, the *Invictus Augustus*, with the RESTITUTOR ORBIS reverse. Source: Cohen

to the capitol to sacrifice there those stags, which he had captured with the chariot and he had vowed to the most excellent and most mighty Jupiter. These chariots were preceded by twenty elephants, and two hundred tamed wild beasts of several kinds out of the countries of Libya and Palestine; all which Aurelian gave afterwards away to private citizens so that the feeding of these would not burden the privy purse. There were four tigers, and also giraffes, elks and other such animals. There were 800 pairs of gladiators. There followed the captives of the barbarian nations: Blemmyes, Axomitae [*Aksumite Ethiopians*], Arabes Eudaemones [*Arabs from Arabia Felix/Aden*], Indians, Bactrians, Hiberians [*Iberians/Georgians*], Saracens and Persians every one with their offerings; there were also Goths, Alans, Roxolani, Sarmatians, Franks, Suebians [*Iuthungi*], Vandals and Germans [*presumably the Alamanni*] all prisoners with their hands bound. There were also with them those men of Palmyra that were left alive, and also Egyptians because of their revolt. There were ten women captives led in the like manner, who had fought in male clothing and had been captured among the Goths when many others like them had been killed at the same time. These were called Amazons in a placard in the same manner as other placards were carried before all showing the name of each nation. Then came Tetricus, well dressed in a scarlet robe, yellow tunic, and Gallic trousers. By him marched his son, whom he had declared joint emperor with him in *Gallia*. And next marched Zenobia. She was adorned with jewels, and her chains were of gold, the weight of which was borne by others. The crowns of the vanquished nations were displayed and carried in the procession. Then marched the people of Rome, with all the *vexilla*-standards of the collegia and camps [*vexilla collegiorum atque castrorum: the collegia should be translated to mean the military associations known as collegia (sing. collegium) which met in the scholae (schools, sing. schola). The vexilla of the castra would presumably mean the cavalry standards belonging to the regular cavalry.*],[10] the *cataphractarii milites* [*The cataphracts appear to have always held a special place in Roman triumphs after they had been introduced into the Roman army. The reason for this was undoubtedly their awesome appearance which was expected to make an impression on the audience. It is no wonder that modern audiences are also captivated by these.*], wealth of the kings, all the army [*omnis exercitus: this presumably means both the regular cavalry and infantry or just infantry because the cataphracts had marched earlier*], and then the Senate, but the Senate was a little sad because senators were also led in triumph [*Tetricus*]… It was almost the ninth hour of the day before they reached the Capitol and very late when they arrived at the Palace. The following days were spent in the pleasures of the plays of the stage, races of the circus, wild-beast hunts, fights of the gladiators and encounters of the galleys [*naval battles, naumachiae*].[11] [Flavius Vopiscus, *Historia Augusta, Aurelianus* 22.4–24.6, tr. by Bernard, 231–3 with emendations, corrections, comments and changes.]

Most of the historians dismiss the list of the captives included in this triumph solely on the basis that it is included in the *Historia Augusta*. However, as discussed above, this is the wrong way to approach this source. There should always be specific reasons for the dismissal of evidence. In this study this list is given the attention it deserves. The list is a very valuable piece of evidence because it allows us to reconstruct some of the missing pieces from the puzzle by showing what nations were allied with the enemies of Aurelian in each instance.

The Blemmyes, Axomitae [*Aksumite Ethiopians*], Saracens (Kinda), Arabes Eudaemones [*Arabs of Aden*] and Indians were probably the allies of Egyptian rebels led by Firmus. In other words, Firmus and his Palmyrene allies had the backing of most of the peoples of the Red Sea route to India. With the addition of these allies, the size of Firmus's army was undoubtedly considerable even if it consisted primarily of masses of lightly equipped tribal warriors and citizen militia. It is probable that the Bactrians, Hiberians [*Iberians/Georgians*], and Persians, and probably also at least some of the Saracens (al-Hira) and Indians were captured at the time when Aurelian defeated the Persians in 272. The Palmyrenes would also have been captured during the same campaign. Of these, the case for the presence of Indians in the Persian army is not known with certainty because these may also have been present in the rebel Firmus' army. One possibility is of course that there were Indians in both armies, because the Persians certainly possessed territories with Indians in the east. The Alans would probably have fought with the Goths so that both were captured at the same time in 271 when Aurelian defeated Cannabaudes. The 'Amazon' women captives are likely to have consisted of the Alans, serving under the Goths, but one cannot entirely rule out that these were really native Goths. The Sarmatians and Vandals were naturally captured when they invaded in 271. The Suebians would be the Iuthungi and possibly also the Marcomanni, while the Germans would be the Alamanni, but the list includes also some problematic names. These are the Franks and Roxolani Sarmatians (White Alans). It has been suggested that the Roxolani fought with the Carpi in 273 (see above), but it is of course possible that they would have fought with the Goths in 271 because they inhabited the area controlled by the Goths. The most problematic are the Franks. The only sensible solution to their inclusion in 274 is that Tetricus and Faustinus had employed these as allies or as elite forces later known as the *auxilia palatina*. This is actually very likely in light of the fact that Postumus had enrolled large numbers of these into his army. This would also explain why Tetricus had so much trouble with his soldiers and why he was so eager to betray them to Aurelian, and it would add still another reason besides disobedience to the list of reasons why Aurelian would want to massacre them.

The inclusion of the *vexilla* of *collegia* and *castra* is also important because it clearly refers to the military *collegia* which assembled in the meeting halls called schools (*scholae*) as I have already postulated several times and probably also to the *vexilla* of the regular cavalry posted in the *castra* (their castles/garrisons). It stands as still another proof that the *scholae* units were created probably by Septimius Severus at the turn of the second century AD.

8.5. Aurelian in Rome in late 274–early 275

It was presumably during Aurelian's longest stay in the city of Rome that many of the policies and practices of his became evident to the population, and it is because of this that I have included a discussion of his habits and customs here.

According to the *Epitome de Caesaribus* (35.5), Aurelian was the first emperor to use the diadem and also used gems and gold on every piece of clothing contrary to the Roman custom. This could be interpreted as an example of Aurelian's hostility towards the conservative senators demonstrated through clothes. It was the hated Gallienus who had previously used imperial costumes bristling with gems and gold. It could also be interpreted that Aurelian now wanted to be identified as *Dominus et Deus*, the titles which he used, to separate himself from the rest of the population. However, there are several problems with this. Firstly, Gallienus had already used gems on his clothing. Secondly, Jerome claims that it was Diocletian who introduced the diadem and gems into clothing. Thirdly, the image given by the *Historia Augusta* of Aurelian's policy towards clothing contains some contradictory material. Vopiscus implies the exact opposite when he states that Aurelian did not use clothing made of silk and planned to forbid the use of gold on tunics and leather and the use of silver for gilding. However, what is notable about this list is that Aurelian did not carry out his plans regarding gilding, so it is possible that he was just trying to please Tacitus, the future emperor, who had advised Aurelian to adopt these policies. Furthermore, the fact that Aurelian did not wear silk does not preclude the use of the jewels and other items of luxury to make his position as emperor visible to the subjects. The refusal to use silk can also be seen merely as a measure meant to save money. Aurelian forbade men from using boots of purple, wax-colour, white, or ivy, while he allowed this for women. However, refusing to allow men to wear purple boots supports the view that Aurelian wanted to restrict this right only for the emperor. Gallienus on the other hand had been famous for using effeminate boots, and this was now forbidden to men other than the emperor. Then there is the problem of what would be the implications for the fact that Aurelian's slaves were dressed just as they had been when Aurelian was a commoner. In my opinion this does not mean that Aurelian would not have wanted to separate himself from the commoners, but rather that he did not want his slaves to assume too important a position in relation to the free population.[12]

The image which arises from this is that Aurelian was a military man who was frugal with money, but who still wanted to stress his own superior position as emperor through clothing. The measures that forbade the wearing of certain types of footwear were clearly meant to separate Aurelian from his subjects as *Dominus et Deus*. Therefore, regardless of the circumstantial evidence preserved by the *Historia Augusta*, I would suggest that the *Epitome* is likely to be correct in its statements and that Aurelian dressed as described, at least on formal occasions and on military campaigns, to separate him from his subjects and soldiers/officers. He was a man of lowly origins who needed pomp and royal regalia to separate himself from his subjects who he wanted to look at him with awe and respect.

The above-mentioned policies, however, were not extended to cover the clothing worn by women or soldiers. Aurelian allowed matrons to dress in purple, unlike his own imperial slaves; he allowed his soldiers to have clasps of gold (previously silver); and he allowed soldiers to have tunics with one to five bands of embroidery. These measures were clearly meant to flatter the soldiers while also showing to the conservatively minded senators that matrons and soldiers were held in high esteem by the emperor. It did not matter that the matrons wore purple, because women could not become emperors.

Aurelian made plans to improve the living standards of the populace by building a public bath in the Transtiberine district and by building a forum at Ostia. One of his unfulfilled plans was to give the populace of Rome free wine – after all, his one weakness was red wine and he wanted others to share it. The plan was to buy land in Etruria for the purpose of settling the families of the slaves captured in war so they would plant the hills with vines to make wine for Romans. Aurelian had also prepared vats, casks, ships and the labour needed for this project, but the plan was opposed by the *praefectus praetorio* who managed to change Aurelian's mind by saying that after that he should also give the populace chickens and geese. Aurelian settled on a watered-down version of his plan, storing wine belonging to the privy purse in the porticos of the Temple of the Sun so that the populace could buy it at subvented price. One intention would therefore have been promotion of the worship of the *Sol*. Aurelian distributed largesse among the populace three times (presumably when he visited the city of Rome) and on one of those occasions his gifts consisted of white tunics with long sleeves. This gift is reminiscent of the handing of the *Caracallus*-cloaks to the populace by Antoninus Magnus, better known as Caracalla. Aurelian was also the first emperor to hand over handkerchiefs to the populace which they waved when they wanted to show their approval. It was for good reason that the populace loved him while the senators feared him.[13]

According to Vopiscus, Aurelian disliked to reside in the Palace of Rome and preferred to live in the Gardens of Sallust or the Gardens of Domitia. He built a 1,000 ft long portico in the Gardens of Sallust where he and his horses exercised daily even though he was not in good health. This suggests several things. Aurelian disliked the pomp of the palace and it is therefore probable that he dressed in eastern pomp merely because it was the wise course to take. He needed splendour, ceremony and titles to stress his divine right to rule over his subjects, which included the nobles and senators. The evidence suggests that Aurelian was a soldier who liked to take physical exercise. He rode daily even though he was in poor health, and at 60 years old, with his health deteriorating, he still tried to postpone the inevitable by training as hard as he could. Perhaps it was because of this that he built a portico which offered him at least some protection against the elements in the winter of 274–5. Aurelian's lifestyle was very Spartan. His only amusements were to watch the performances of actors and one gourmand who could eat vast amounts of food and drink red wine. The fact that Aurelian's banquets consisted mainly of roasted meats mean that he and his men were on a high-protein diet with low carbohydrate intake. This was good for muscles, but otherwise potentially dangerous. However, the fact that Aurelian liked red wine worked to his advantage because it protected his arteries against the worst effects of the high protein diet. Notably none of the sources suggests that Aurelian had any heart problems. However, his meat-heavy diet and the fact that he used riding as his principal form of physical exercise does suggest another possibility which is that he suffered from gout. Vopiscus gives us a description of how Aurelian treated himself when he was ill. He claims that Aurelian never summoned a physician but in most cases cured himself by abstaining from food. Modern medicine would not recommend this approach, but it might have been beneficial for Aurelian for another reason which is that he did not trust his life in the hands of the doctors who could after all be working for someone else.[14]

On the basis of the *Historia Augusta*, it is possible that there was a senatorial revolt or conspiracy during Aurelian's last stay in Rome which involved the killing of his sister's son and/or daughter. It is not known why Aurelian would have killed his sister's son, but the likeliest reason is that he acted as a figurehead ruler in a senatorial conspiracy. One can imagine that if the children of Aurelian's sister were expecting to succeed Aurelian they would have felt cheated when Aurelian then married Severina, and if she then became pregnant, then the relatives could have thought that it was now or never. The killing of the daughter of the sister, if it took place, could be connected with a sexual relationship or marriage with a man of senatorial background for the possible purpose of usurpation.[15]

8.6. The Beginning of the Year 275: The Preparations for the Eastern Anabasis

The evidence for the events of the year 275 is by far the worst we have of this period. Aurelian's plan for the year appears to have been to force the Goths to provide soldiers for his planned invasion of Persia after which he would have marched against the main foe (see below), but before this could take place fate intervened. The year began with yet another war in Gaul and Raetia. According to the *Historia Augusta* (*Aurel.* 35.4–5), Aurelian marched to Gaul and delivered the Vindelici (of the city of *Augusta Vindelicum*/ Augsburg in Raetia) from a barbarian siege, after which he returned to Illyricum to begin a war against the Persians. In other words, at the time of the troubles in Gaul and Raetia, Aurelian was already in Illyricum making preparations for the forthcoming war against the Persians. Zonaras (12.27) states that after his triumph Aurelian pacified the restless Gauls for the second time. Zosimus (61.2) in his turn notes that Aurelian subdued Tetricus and other rebels after his triumph at Rome (see above) with the implication that there were presumably other insurgents in Gaul after Tetricus had surrendered.

When all of these pieces of evidence are taken together it becomes probable that there was a new revolt or invasion in Gaul either in late 274 or in early 275 and that Aurelian marched there to crush it. It is possible that this revolt was a usurpation attempt by Faustinus in Trier, because Polemius Silvanus (p.521) claims that he was a usurper under Aurelian, but it is also possible that the Faustinus incident had already taken place in 274. The latter is more likely. What appears probable is that Aurelian did indeed march first to Gaul as stated by the *Historia Augusta* and Zonaras and that he strengthened his army with forces usually posted in Raetia. So, my suggestion is that Aurelian marched from Illyricum through Raetia to Gaul and took most of Raetia's garrison forces with him. When this was noticed by the neighbouring Alamanni, they exploited the opportunity, invaded, and put *Augusta Vindelicum* under siege. In the meantime however, Aurelian had crushed the revolt, after which he marched at the double to *Vindelicum* where he defeated the barbarians once again. Saunders dates this war to late winter/early spring 275, but this is probably too early in light of the fact that Aurelian was already in Illyricum making preparations for the forthcoming Persian war. My suggestion is that the campaign took place in spring/late spring.[16] It was only after this that Aurelian was free to implement his own plans for the year.

The *Historia Augusta* (*Aurel.* 44.3–5) includes a claim that Aurelian consulted the Druid priestesses in Gaul and asked whether power would remain in the hands of his descendants. If there is any truth to this claim, it is clear that this must have happened after the birth of the daughter and it is therefore likelier that it took place (if it did) during the second Gallic campaign. Vopiscus claims that the Druids answered that the descendants of Claudius would inherit power and that their prediction was proven correct by the fact that Constantius was now the emperor. The inclusion of Constantius in this context makes the consulting of the priestesses very suspect, but I would add to this the fact that Aurelian was a son of a priestess and therefore a man who knew how the answers to the questions of believers were answered by priestesses. In short, it is unlikely that Aurelian would have earnestly asked such advice. There is one exception to this, which is that it is possible that Aurelian could have asked such advice in the expectation that the priestesses would publicly declare that his descendants would rule the Empire – the idea being the reinforcement of his rule in the eyes of the populace. The priestesses would not have given Aurelian the kind of answer claimed by Vopiscus. They would have known what to tell the emperor.

On the basis of the extant sources, Aurelian appears to have continued his march to the Balkans immediately after he had defeated the invaders at Vindelicum. Flavius Vopiscus (*HA Aurel.*35.4–5) states that Aurelian returned to Illyricum, where he had prepared an army which was large/powerful while not being too large, and then declared war on the Persians. According to Malalas (12.30) and Jordanes (*Romana* 291), Aurelian then began another war, but they do not state against which enemy. Zonaras (2.27) on the other hand states that when Aurelian was directing his army against the Scythians (i.e. Goths), he was killed while at Heraclea in Thrace. According to Syncellus (AM 5764), Aurelian was killed after having attacked the Scythians (Goths).

The above conflicting information regarding the target of Aurelian's planned attack has naturally divided historians. Some are of the opinion that Aurelian's plan was to invade Persia, while others, like Saunders (267ff.), think that Aurelian's plan was to attack the Goths. Those who support the Persian war think that Aurelian wanted to invade either Armenia or Mesopotamia because these were in Persian hands. The former is true, but the latter was already in Roman hands. Watson and White have suggested that it is possible to reconcile the sources if one thinks that Aurelian fought a campaign against the Goths in the summer of 275, after which he planned to march against the Persians in the autumn of 275. Watson however still considers it unwise to trust the *Historia Augusta* in this case and states as his final conclusion that the evidence remains inconclusive because of this.[17]

I disagree. As already discussed, the *Historia Augusta* is just as relevant as a source as the other ones. The claim that Aurelian's goal was to attack Persia is backed up by circumstantial evidence. It is probable that Aurelian's goal was to install Trdat/Tiridates on the Armenian throne because this would have returned the situation to the state that it had been under Caracalla and before him. However, it is possible that Aurelian had even more grandiose plans; the situation for a full scale invasion of Persia was very opportune because ever since the death of Hormizd I in ca. 273 the new Persian King of Kings Bahram I had been fighting against 'the kings of the east'.[18] The period from 272 onwards until at least 287 was among the darkest in the annals of Sasanian Persia. Hormizd I (ca. 272–3) had spent his entire short reign in the east fighting against the Hephthalites/Sogdians, who had presumably exploited the transferral of forces to the west against Aurelian in 272, and then his successor Bahram I (ca. 273–6) spent most of his reign in the east, and then his successor Bahram II (ca. 276–93) did the same.[19] Note also the quite apparent diplomatic activities that preceded this campaign against Persia which I mentioned in the context of Aurelian's Egyptian campaign. The campaign against the Scythians (Goths) was done to force them to join his campaign force. This is proven by the *Historia Augusta* (*Tacitus* 13.2–3). According to this text, when Tacitus began his reign, the Goths[20] informed him that they had assembled for a war against the Persians because Aurelian had commanded them to do so. There is nothing strange about this. The Romans had collected Goths for their wars against the Persians ever since the days of Septimius Severus and Caracalla.[21] Gordian III and Valerian had done so, and Galerius, Constantine and Constantius II were to do so after Aurelian.[22] This was one of the standard operating procedures of Roman strategy against the Persians. Gothic cavalry lancers were particularly useful and effective against Persian cavalry. Furthermore, the Romans needed to bolster the numbers of their horsemen if they wanted to be able to face the Persians on equal terms. Combined arms tactics required enough horsemen to work. The horsemen were needed not only for reconnaissance, pursuit and protection of the flanks of infantry, but also to tie up enemy cavalry in one place so that the Roman infantry would be able to reach it in combat.

It was not fated for Aurelian to invade Persia.

8.7. The Project to Persecute the Christians

According to Eusebius, Jerome, Orosius, Lactantius and Syncellus, just before his death Aurelian had sent orders to begin a persecution of Christians. If this is true, and there is every reason to believe it is, then Aurelian would have come to the conclusion that there were Christian fifth columnists within Roman society who posed a potential danger to his project to unite the Romans behind *Sol Invictus* and its Messiah Apollonius of Tyana, and other gods whose images Aurelian used in his propaganda. The other possibility, which does not preclude the previous one, is that Aurelian considered the Christians to be common criminals who were to be punished for their failure to show him and the gods proper respect – after all Aurelian was a person who was merciless towards those whom he considered corrupt and/or criminal. In my opinion it is also possible that Aurelian considered Christianity to be a threat to military discipline because the Christian soldiers could not be motivated to fight with the same trick that Aurelian had used to motivate the soldiers at Emesa.[23] Later Christian sources give a long list of names of those who became martyrs during the persecution launched by Aurelian, but modern historians have quite rightly considered these to be later fabrications because the above-mentioned sources clearly state that Aurelian died before the intended persecution began[24]. Regardless, it is still possible, as suggested by Alaric Watson, that some scattered persecutions were already launched during the lifetime of Aurelian but not any wide-scale persecution. I would also suggest an alternative interpretation for the lists of martyrs, which is that they did not die as a result of the intended persecution of Christians because it was never launched, but as a result of some other action taken against either criminals or other enemies, and were later converted into martyrs by Christian authorities because the killed persons were Christians. Regardless, it is still clear, as the previous research has shown, that most of the persons mentioned as martyrs for Aurelian's reign were actually killed under other emperors like Marcus Aurelius whose name resembled Aurelianus.[25]

It should be noted though, that had Aurelian's project been put into effect it would probably not have brought the 'Christian menace' [26] to an end because all persecutions appear to have just strengthened Christianity and the resolve of its followers. The reason for this was the cult of martyrdom and the promise of eternal life to those who died as martyrs. It was Constantine the Great who finally recognized that it was easier to join the Christians rather than fight against them.

8.8. The assassination of Aurelian in the summer of 275

The principal features of the assassination of the great soldier emperor Aurelian are well known and discussed by several historians, but there are still some unanswerable questions, one being the exact timing of his death. The following analysis is based on the original and secondary sources so that all of the main problems and suggestions are included. It is based on the conclusions already made, but still makes some new observations.[27] This includes the naming of the units which carried out the murder.

The basic details for the death of Aurelian are as follows. Aurelian threatened to punish one of his trusted freedmen called Eros for some unknown offence. Vopiscus calls him with the name Mnestheus, but it has long been recognized that Vopiscus did so probably intentionally because this word had been derived from the Greek *menutes*, which meant a *notarius*. This man was a *domesticus* and *notarius secretorum* and he had been used as a trusted secretary and spy/informer by Aurelian. The likely reason for the threat was that this Eros had taken bribes from the officers who had been guilty of embezzlement and extortion in the provinces, because Aurelius Victor connects the murder with Aurelian's policy of punishing soldiers who were guilty of this. Aurelian must have realized that his trusted informant had been taking bribes and that he had hidden from him the cases of corruption among the officers. Perhaps Aurelian purposely cultivated a reputation for cruelty in the manner suggested by Machiavelli (*Prince*, 17), but in this case Eros was able to turn this reputation against Aurelian.

Rightly fearing for his life, Eros forged letters in which Aurelian ordered the execution of several tribunes. The tribunes in question must be the tribunes of the *protectores*, who could actually be very high ranking individuals acting as generals as the leading figure in the plot is known to have been. This individual was the *dux* Mucapor, of Thracian origins. There is no doubt that the plotters consisted of the imperial bodyguards because Zosimus (1.62.2) calls these '*tôn doruforôn*'. With the exception of Paschoud, the *doryforoi* have been translated as praetorians, but at this time in history the men in question must have belonged to the *protectores domestici*.[28] They included many friends of Aurelian who knew from personal experience Aurelian's strong hatred of corruption and his quick violent temper when he faced such situations. Eros then showed the forged list to the men, which included his own name. The plot to kill Aurelian was formed hastily and without much planning because the conspirators did not have anyone to put on the throne as a successor for Aurelian. The only reason for the murder was that the men on the list feared that the quick temper of the emperor would be brought down upon them. The plot was apparently formed at Heraclea/Perinthus.

Flavius Vopiscus (*HA Tac.* 2.4–6) summarises the circumstances in which the murder took as follows:

> Aurelian, as I have shown in the previous book, was killed by the treason of a despicable slave and stupidity of the officers (because these believe any lies if these are told to them when they are angry, being usually drunken and at best usually without good counsel), but all these persons being returned to their senses, and severely denounced for their folly by the army, the question was immediately raised, who of them, if any, should be chosen as emperor. [*It is ironic that a man who loved wine was killed by a party of drunkards.*] The army, which was used to set up emperors hastily, in their hatred against those [*officers*] present, sent to the Senate the letter, which I have already presented in the previous book [*Vita of Aurelianus*], in which they asked the Senate to choose the prince from among its ranks. But the Senate knew that the princes chosen by them do not always please the army and they referred the choice back to the army. This was repeated so many times that six months passed [*before Tacitus was elected*]. [Tr. by Bernard (252–3) with several changes and emendations by Ilkka Syvänne which are partially based on the edition/translation of Magie (298–9).]

The important point in the above discussion is that it implies that the officers were fooled to murder Aurelian when they were in a drunken state. This reference to the drinking habits of the officers and soldiers is also confirmed by so many independent sources that it must be true. It was thanks to this that Eros was able to convince the officers that they faced the danger of execution.

When Aurelian then continued his journey from Heraclea/Perinthus towards Byzantium with the purpose of crossing to Asia to begin his long planned campaign against Persia, the tribunes and the *protectores* with the the *dux* Mucapor at their head attacked and killed Aurelian at a place called Cenophrurium. Aurelian was 61 years of age at the time of his death. This is yet another instance of the imperial bodyguards murdering their emperor, but in this case the reason for it was probably the craziest ever in the annals of Roman history. The murder is described as follows by Zosimus:

> During his stay at Perinthus, now called Heraclea, a conspiracy was thus formed against him. There was in the court a man named Eros, whose office was to carry out the answers of the emperor. This man had been for some fault threatened by the emperor, and put in great fear. Dreading therefore lest the emperor should realize his menaces by actions, he went to some of the guard, whom he knew to be the boldest men in the court; he told them a plausible story, and showed them a letter of his own writing, in the character of the emperor (which he long before learned to counterfeit), and persuading them first that they themselves were to be put to death, which was the meaning expressed by the letter, he endeavoured to prevail on them to murder the emperor. The deception worked. Observing Aurelianus to go out of the city with a small retinue, they ran out upon him and murdered him. He was buried on the spot with great magnificence by the army in consideration of the great services he had performed, and the dangers he had undergone for the good of the public. [Zosimus 1.62, English tr. 1814, pp.30–31.]

When the conspirators realized their horrible mistake and what Eros had done, they and the other members of the army built a tomb for the great emperor and erected a temple on the spot. Eros, the man who had caused the death of Aurelian, was tied to a stake and exposed to wild beasts. These events were then recorded in marble statues and on columns in honour of the deified Aurelian.[29]

According to Aurelius Victor (36.2), the *dux* Mucapor delivered the actual killing blow, which may mean that the other conspirators held Aurelian in place so that Mucapor could kill the emperor with greater ease. We do not know the exact timing of the murder of this great emperor. On the basis of an inscription at Rome dated 25 April 275 Aurelian was still alive roughly at that date, which serves post quam for the date of murder. Coins were minted in the name of Aurelian and Severina with the regnal year seven, which means that Aurelian was recognized at Antioch after 29 August 275. The last papyrus dated 19 October 275 refers to the seventh year of Aurelian's reign, which implies that he was recognized as emperor in Rome roughly in mid-September. The first known papyrus to name Tacitus as emperor dates from 9 May 276. However, as stated by Saunders, the fact that inscriptions give Tacitus two tribunician powers suggests that he must have become emperor before 10 December 275.[30]

The problem is complicated by the fact that three Latin sources (*HA Tac.* 2.6; Aurelius Victor 35.9–36.1; *Epitome* 35.10) state that there was a six to seven month interregnum before the new emperor was chosen. On the basis of the above information this would be impossible. It has therefore been suggested that Severina acted as a sort of regent during this period to retain the loyalty of the soldiers in the absence of an emperor. Evidence for this has been the odd coins of Severina with the legend *concordiae militum* on the reverse, which was not used by empresses. The coins minted at Alexandria which acknowledge Severina as sole *aug.* (*concordia aug.* = only one augusta) rather than *augg.* (as it was during the lifetime of Aurelian) have been rightly used for the same purpose. This evidence, however, is controversial because it is entirely based on guesswork. It is still entirely possible that these coins were minted during her husband's lifetime. On the basis of the papyri, inscription and coins, most historians are of the opinion that the interregnum was much shorter than the six/seven months claimed by the Latin sources and rather suggest that Aurelian died in about August/September 275 and that the interregnum lasted at most about two months. Saunders' suggestion is that the length of the interregnum in the Latin sources resulted from a misunderstanding so that the six-month reign of Tacitus became the length of the interregnum.[31] This is an attractive suggestion, but the evidence used to counter the six/seven month interregnum is actually not conclusive because it is possible that Aurelian continued to be officially recognized during the chaotic and exceptional situation, so it was because of this that the name of Aurelian was still found in papyri as late as 19 October 275. This would date the murder of Aurelian roughly to May/June 275 so that Severina would have served as a dowager empress after that. It

Aurelian according to Duruy

is certain that there was an interregnum, but whether it was short as suggested by the inscriptions and papyri, or whether it was six or seven months long as suggested by the Latin sources, is uncertain. In sum, in light of the extant but uncertain evidence, August/September 275 remains the likeliest time for the murder of Aurelian and that the interregunum lasted not more than two or three months; but it is entirely possible that the Latin sources are actually correct. The question remains unsolvable unless new evidence surfaces, for example as a result of archaeological finds.

And what was the role of Probus in these events? Vopiscus claims that some time during his reign Aurelian appointed Probus commander of the Tenth Legion just as Claudius had previously appointed Aurelian as its commander to signal that he would be the intended successor.[32] I have already pointed out in my biography of Gallienus that it is probable that this Tenth Legion was one of the late Roman elite legions, the likeliest candidates being *Ioviani* and *Herculiani*, and that the commander of these elite units would have probably been *comes domesticorum peditum* if the *protectores* were divided into infantry and cavalry as they were at the time when the *Notitia Dignitatum* was written at the turn of the fifth century, or that the commander was simply *comes domesticorum* if the *protectores/domestici* were not divided. The latter alternative is more likely because Vopiscus clearly states that the position was the highest in the army. The other possible titles for the commander of this unit would have been *magister officiorum* or *magister peditum*. The existence of the *magister officiorum* and *comes domesticorum* can be deduced from the sources for the reigns of Gallienus and Diocletian, and similarly the title of *comes domesticorum* can proven to have existed under Carus, Numerianus and Carinus because it was the title held by Diocles/Diocletian. The key point here is that Aurelian appears to have appointed Probus as the supreme commander of all of the *protectores/domestici* units either as *magister officiorum* or as *comes domesticorum*, and it was the members of these units that carried out the murder and were later present in Syria where Probus served as a general. Does this mean that he was one of the conspirators? In light of the evidence this seems very unlikely. None of the sources claim that Probus would have had any responsibility for the murder. Tacitus appointed Probus general, which is unlikely to have happened if he was one of the conspirators. Probus then went on to kill all of the remaining conspirators once he had become emperor. In sum, Probus was not one of the conspirators even if the murder was carried out by the officers and soldiers serving under him.

Chapter Nine

Aurelian, the Man with Perfect Ability in War[1]

It has long been recognized that Aurelian was one of the greatest emperors that Rome ever had and I fully agree with this view. Aurelian had unified the Empire by crushing Palmyra and the Gallic Empire. He had also rationalized the borders by abandoning Dacia. Its inhabitants were resettled south of the Danube to replace the population lost as a result of the massive barbarian invasions that took place between 249 and 272. In short, at the time of his death, the Roman Empire was once again the most powerful empire on earth and it was thanks to his efforts that this was the case.

Aurelian has rightly been recognized as a particularly gifted military commander and great soldier emperor. He had defeated a succession of invaders so that he had secured the borders. He had defeated the barbarians along the Rhine and Danube frontiers. He had defeated the Arabs, Armenians, Persians, Palmyrenes, Egyptians, Aksumites, Blemmyes and Yemenites, and he had defeated Roman usurpers and possibly even some enemies in Britain and India. When Aurelian was killed, he was on his way to exact vengeance on the Persians. The timing was opportune because Aurelian could expect the Armenians to desert en masse to his side because his army included the legitimate Armenian king with his followers and because Persia was badly weakened by its own civil war. It is very probable that Aurelian's own devastating victory over the massive Persian army in 272 had contributed to this because the Persians had massed together a huge army by withdrawing large numbers of units from their eastern territories with the result that it caused them gigantic problems when Aurelian then annihilated these forces. This is one of the most crushing defeats the Romans ever inflicted on Persia and its consequences paralyzed all Persian operations in the west until at least 284. It was only bad luck that prevented Aurelian from finishing his long and illustrious career with at least a partial conquest of Persia.

Admittedly Aurelian had suffered one very serious defeat/setback at the battle of Placentia, but he also showed his superb leadership qualities after this by retaining control of his forces so that he was able to wrest a victory from the jaws of defeat – perhaps it was largely thanks to his fame for cruelty that this was possible. On top of this, he followed up his success by ruthlessly crushing all the usurpers that had exploited the situation. He certainly lived up to his fame.[2] Aurelian knew how to retain the loyalty of his troops under the most demanding conditions and how to uplift morale with stratagems.

Aurelian was as skilled in regular warfare as he was in guerrilla warfare. He was also an accomplished diplomat and user of stratagems, as his policies towards Palmyra, the Gallic Empire, Armenia and Arabic tribes prove. It is also of note that none of the sources ever claim that Aurelian faced logistical troubles or that he ever had trouble paying his soldiers. He knew that the army marched on its stomach and he knew how to keep his men happy. The best proof of his skill as a military commander is that he was able to defeat every type of enemy there existed at the time.

The reconquest of Palmyra brought him and the Roman Empire great wealth, but Aurelian did not use this money for his own agrandisement. He did build a magnificent temple for *Sol Invictus* in the city of Rome, but its main purpose was to unite the people behind his rule and was thus beneficial for the security of the state. Aurelian was frugal with his own expenses, so he was able to spend more money on the people and army to obtain their goodwill. The extra taxes imposed on Egypt and other resources were used for the wellbeing of the common people of Rome and not on massive useless building projects the only purpose of which would have been to aggrandize the ruler. In short, he used the taxes for the benefit of the state and not for his own benefit. Aurelian curbed corruption with a harsh hand, which, despite what the pro-senatorial sources state, was very beneficial for the wellbeing of the state and its inhabitants, and in its turn brought more tax income to state coffers thanks to the economic growth it permitted. Coin reform was not a complete success, because Aurelian did not mint enough coins of lower denominations, but it was still a great success in another sense. It restored the faith of the populace and foreigners in Roman coinage. It was thanks to Aurelian's enlightened economic policies, provisions given to the populace and the curbing of corruption that Aurelian was quite rightly loved by the Roman people, while the Senate feared him – corrupt senators had every reason to fear him as did corrupt officers. It was indeed this enlightened but harsh policy which Aurelian practised against corrupt officials that brought his life to an untimely end.

Coins of the great Roman emperor Aurelian by Cohen

Chapter Ten

Tacitus 275–6[1]

Coin of Tacitus celebrating his Gothic victory. The cos II (2nd consulship) depicted in this coin has been used to calculate the length of his reign. (source: Cohen)

10.1. The Interregnum lasting two to three months, or six to seven months

Several sources confirm that the idiotic murder of an able emperor angered the soldiers to such an extent that they refused to choose the successor for Aurelian from among the officers present and delegated the matter for the Senate to decide.[2] It was thanks to this that an interregnum followed, which may have lasted two months but might have lasted as long as seven months. It is possible that Severina served as a dowager during this period so the soldiers were kept pacified. Whatever the truth, it is still clear that the army gave the Senate powers which it had not had for ages. The Senate was hesitant to play the role that it had been given so it threw the ball back into the army's corner. The authenticity of the following quotes from Vopiscus is suspect, but they still give us some idea of the kind of discussions which must have taken place at this time and so it is worthwhile to quote them at length:

> The army, who used to set up emperors hastily, hated those who had a hand in the murder of Aurelian, and who at the same time were present, ...sent to the Senate

the letter… that the Senate would choose an emperor from their own ranks. But the Senate knew that the emperors chosen by them do not always please the army, and they remitted the choice to the army again. This was repeated so often… from one another that six months elapsed. [Vopiscus *HA Tac.* 2.5–6, tr. by Bernard, 253–, with emendations, corrections and additions.]

Upon the 7th day of the Calends of October [*25 Sept 275. It has long been recognized that this date may actually be the date Aurelian was murdered rather than the date of Tacitus's accession to power, but one cannot know for certain. It is possible that the dating of the early reign of Aurelian is off because the exact dating of the death of Claudius is uncertain*] …Velius Cornificius Gordianus, the consul, spoke thus to them: Fathers of the Senate… we must now… choose an emperor without whom the army cannot well subsist longer… there is a necessity which obliges us to it besides. For the Germans have broken into the quarter on the side of the Rhine, and have seized for themselves strong, famous, rich and powerful cities. And though there is nothing mentioned of any motions of the Persians, yet you may easily imagine how light-minded the Syrians are, …What shall I say to you of Africa, of Illyricum, of Egypt, and the armies in all those parts? How long do you think they can subsist without an emperor? …Either the army will accept him whom you shall choose, or themselves will choose another, if they refuse him. [Vopiscus *HA Tac.* 3.2ff., tr. by Bernard, 253–4, with emendations, corrections and additions.]

Tacitus was the first of the consulars with the right to voice his opinion first. But as he was about to speak, all the Senate prevented him and cried: 'We salute Tacitus, our emperor…' Tacitus answered: 'I am astonished, Fathers of the Senate, that in the place of the most valiant Aurelian you are willing to make such an old man emperor [*Tacitus was 75, but at 61 Aurelian with his ailing health had not been a young man either*]. How am I fit with the limbs which you behold to throw the dart and the spear, and to clash the shield, and to ride without ceasing as an example to the soldiers [*This refers to the fact that as senator Tacitus did not possess any military experience*]; … Can you believe that the army will approve of an old man to be at the head of them?' …The Senate returned him these acclamations: 'Trajan came pretty old to power.' This was repeated ten times. 'And Hadrian came old to power.' This was repeated ten times. 'Antoninus Pius came to power old.' This was repeated ten times… 'Who governs better than a man of years?' This was repeated ten times. 'We make you an emperor, not a soldier.' This was repeated twenty times. … 'The Gods save you, our emperor Tacitus.' [Vopiscus *HA Tac.* 4.1ff., tr. by Bernard, 254–6, with emendations, corrections and additions.]

They all were asked their opinions. The next to Tacitus was Maecius Faltonius Nicomachus [*otherwise unknown*]… he addressed them as follows: '… We have chosen a person of an advanced age to be our emperor, and who will watch over us all like a father. Nothing from him that is immature, that is unadvised, that is ill, is to be feared. We may promise ourselves a reign of all sobriety, all gravity, and nothing cruel…' Tacitus was extremely moved… They went from thence unto the Field of

Mars; where Tacitus, having placed himself upon the tribunal, Aelius Cesettianus [*otherwise unknown*], the Prefect of the City, spoke thus: 'Most venerated soldiers and fellow citizens, you have here the emperor chosen by the Senate at the request of the army.' [*The soldiers present would have consisted of the soldiers garrisoned in the city of Rome. These included at least some members of the Praetorians, urban cohorts, frumentarii, equites singulares augusti, and aulici/scholae/protectores. The implication is that members of the imperial bodyguard units and urban cohorts who had been left behind in Rome confirmed the choice of the Senate because these were untarnished by the murder which had been committed by the other bodyguards who had followed Aurelian.*] [Vopiscus *HA Tac.* 5.3ff., tr. by Bernard, 256–9, with emendations, corrections and additions.]

The above account is consistent with the other information that we have and could easily be true, but there are two problems with it. Firstly, the source is the *Historia Augusta* which has dated the events in a way that most historians do not accept. Secondly, Vopiscus offers an alternative version to that which he had already given, as follows:

It is not here to be omitted what several writers have written that Tacitus was absent in Campania when he was named emperor… For as soon as the rumour had broken out that he was the person to be elected emperor, he retired and lived at his house at Baiae for two months. [*This could be used as proof that the interregnum was actually six to seven months long, and why Tacitus was able to claim tribunician II powers – this implies the assumption of power before 10 December 275 – while he would have become de facto emperor only in 276.*] But they fetched him from thence again, and he was present at this Act of the Senate… Tacitus next went to the army. … *praefectus praetorio* Maecius Gallicanus [*otherwise unknown*] spoke as follows: "My most venerated fellow-soldiers, the Senate had given you the emperor whom you desired…" Then Tacitus … promised them a bounty and the donative [*In other words, this version claims that the ultimate decision was put in the hands of the soldiers left in the city of Rome who were not tarnished by the murder, but in this case it is the Praetorian Prefect who took the lead and not the City Prefect. One possible way to reconcile these two sources is that both prefects actually spoke for the same or different audiences because the Urban Cohorts were no longer in the same camp with the Praetorians after 270. Zonaras 12.28 provides a similar account by stating that Tacitus was at Campania and was only then brought to the city of Rome to take power*]. [Vopiscus *HA Tac.* 7.5ff., tr. by Bernard, 259–60, with emendations, corrections and additions.]

10.2. The Reign of Tacitus

The reign of Tacitus meant a break in the line of the Illyrian soldier emperors which had resulted from the rise of the Illyrians under Gallienus. Tacitus appears to have had Italian roots, but as a rich senator he had estates not only in Italy, but also in Numidia and Mauretania. In light of his background, it is not surprising that his reign signalled a break in the general pattern of history. Vopiscus describes Tacitus as a conservative senator who restored to the Senate some of its traditional powers. This has been questioned by most modern historians, but the main reason for that appears to be their hypercritical attitude towards the *Historia Augusta*. In my opinion, the fact that the numismatic and epigraphic evidence contains evidence that supports Vopiscus's claims proves otherwise. The coin legends prominently include *clementia temporum* and some of the coins also revived the SC (*senatus consulto*) which signalled authorization by the Senate. Tacitus revived the use of *genius senatus* in his inscriptions and did not take the title *deus et dominus natus* and did not issue any coins depicting *Sol Invictus*, which signalled a clear break with his predecessor. Most importantly, some inscriptions call him *auctor verae libertatis* (originator of true liberty) and some coins *restitutor rei publicae* (restorer of the state).[3] Taken together there is every reason to believe that the information in Vopiscus is correct. The following quotes contain the principal claims of Vopiscus regarding the domestic policies of Tacitus during his short reign. Vopiscus began his account of the reign with a description of Tacitus's speech to the Senate after he had been confirmed by the soldiers posted in the capital:

> … that he resolved to set up a statue of Aurelian in gold in the capitol, with others of silver in the House of the Senate, in the Temple of the Sun, and in the Forum of Trajan. [*This was meant to please the army and other supporters of Aurelian.*] The silver ones were dedicated, but the golden one was not. In the same speech he promised that if any person publicly or privately adulterated silver with brass, or gold with silver, or brass with lead, it should be a capital offence including the loss of property. Also that slaves should not be witnesses in cases of capital offence against their masters even in cases of treason. [*This was particularly pleasing for the senators after the purge of the Senate under Aurelian.*] He obliged all persons to have pictures of Aurelian [*to please the army and other supporters of Aurelian*]. He ordered a temple to be built where they should set up the statues of such of the deified emperors as had reigned well. … In the same speech he desired the consulship for his brother Florianus [*he was a half-brother*], but the Senate could not grant it, because all the consuls… had already been appointed by the Senate. [Vopiscus *HA Tac.* 9.1ff., tr. by Bernard, 260–61, with emendations, corrections and additions.]

> He turned his private fortune, which was worth 280,000,000 sesterces, over into the exchequer, and the money which he had in his house he used for the pay of the soldiers. [*There is no doubt that this was very enlightened policy. Tacitus gave out of his own free will money to the soldiers that very few rich senators were prepared to do. However, this was also undoubtedly quite necessary in the circumstances for the purpose of gaining the loyalty of the army, and one may therefore suspect that this was a PR stunt.*] He wore the same togas and tunics as he did when he was a private man. He forbade brothels in the city of Rome, but this could not be maintained for long [*This is a good indication of the conservative nature of Tacitus. On the basis of this and other period information it is probable that there was a strong conservative block among the senators at this time. It is therefore not surprising that they reacted with such hostility against the libertarian ways of Gallienus. See my biography for further details. The fact that the brothels were soon reopened is a good indication of how impossible it was to maintain such a ban. There have always been and always will be brothels regardless*

of what the conservatively minded person thinks]. He ordered the baths to be shut up before candle-light… He acknowledged Cornelius Tacitus, the writer of the Augustan History, as his relation [*modern historians consider this to be false on the basis of the respective gentes, but I would not preclude the possibility that it is true. It is possible that names had been changed, or someone had been adopted into a new family, or that someone had been born out of wedlock etc*] and ordered it placed in all libraries… He forbade men from wearing garments made entirely of silk [*This resembles the attitude of Aurelian towards silk clothing, and one wonders whether Tacitus was the man who had advised Aurelian in this*]. He ordered his house levelled and a public bath built in its place at his own expense… The estates which he had in Mauretania, he assigned to the repairs of the Capitol. [Vopiscus *HA Tac.* 10.1ff., tr. by Bernard, 261–2, with emendations, corrections and additions.]

He lived a very sober life; never in a whole day did he drink a pint of wine, and many times…. A single cock, a swine's jowl and some eggs sufficed for his banquet. He indulged passionately with greens, especially lettuce, which was served in abundance… He loved bitter foods, seldom bathed [*conservatives clearly considered bathing as an effeminate luxury, also pointing out how often the hated Gallienus bathed. See my Gallienus*], and was all the stronger because of it in his old age. He delighted himself with curious glassware. He only ate dry bread seasoned with salt and the like. He loved fine marble, stately buildings, and hunting. His table was coarse… He forbade his wife to use jewels and clothes with gold stripes. For it was he who had advised Aurelian to forbid the same, and to forbid the gilding of rooms and leather… [*This is interesting, because according to Vopiscus Aurelian had planned to implememt this but had failed to carry it out in practice. The gilding of leather would presumably mean the gilding of leather armour.*] As old as he was, it is a wonder that he was able to read very tiny letters and he read or wrote something every night, excepting the day after the Kalends of a month. [Vopiscus *HA Tac.* 11.1ff., tr. by Bernard, 262–3, with emendations, corrections and additions.]

The above shows well how conservatively minded Tacitus was and it is therefore not surprising that he was also similarly conservative in his stance towards the position of the Senate in society. After all, he had been a rich senator without any real power for most of his life and it is not surprising to find him correct this situation. Even if Tacitus built a public bath for the people, it is still clear that he did not feel any real sympathy towards the common man. Tacitus's conservatively minded policy was rather to protect the commoners from their own vices. He did not attempt to gain their goodwill with handouts like Aurelian did. The following quotes from Vopiscus shows the two principal features of this policy:

The great joy of the Senate to regain the power of choosing the emperor was such as I cannot fail to mention. They ordered public processions to be made upon it, … they wrote to their relatives, and not only to their relatives but also to strangers, and letters to the provinces so that all their allies and all nations knew that the Roman commonwealth had been restored… and that the Senate chose the emperor… and made the laws, the barbarian kings brought their entreaties to the Senate, and war and peace was to be treated by the authority of the Senate… All appeals from the proconsuls and regular judges were to be presented to the Prefect of the City… The right of creating proconsuls, and ordering proconsular provinces is remitted to us [*the Senate*]; and the appeals of all magistrates… are returned into the hands of the Prefect of the City of Rome… [*This means that Tacitus would have restored the command of the soldiers to the senators and also that the provinces were subjected to the rule of the Senate, while judicial appeals were to be made to the Prefect of the City.*] Tacitus scarcely gave the people of Rome largesse in all his six months of rule [*This in contrast to Aurelian*]. [Vopiscus *HA Tac.* 12.1ff., 16.1ff. tr. by Bernard, 262–3, with emendations, corrections and additions.]

The above implies that foreign policy and governing of the provinces were returned into the hands of the Senate, and that Tacitus had restored command of the armies also to the senators. All of these claims have been questioned by modern historians.[4] In light of what I have stated above I would suggest that it is more likely that Vopiscus is correct about Tacitus's policies rather than not. The inscriptions calling Tacitus *auctor verae libertatis* (originator of true liberty) and coins calling him *restitutor rei publicae* (restorer of the state) are particularly relevant in this case. In fact, the nomination of Maximinus in charge of Syria could even be a proof of this if Zosimus's (1.63.2) '*ten Syrias archên*' is interpreted to mean *dux* or *corrector* in charge of the Syrian section of the frontier. In light of the above it is not surprising that the equestrian officers formed a conspiracy against Tacitus. He would not have been liked by the populace either because he failed to bribe them. Nevertheless, the shortness of his reign makes it difficult to be certain what his policies were. All that we have are the comments of Vopiscus and the few extant inscriptions and coins.

In short, the evidence for the reign of Tacitus is full of uncertainties. Tacitus was an old and respected senator who became an emperor at the ripe old age of 75. He did not possess any military experience and needed to learn military matters fast if he wanted to retain the trust of the soldiers. There exists possible evidence for this stage of Tacitus's career if Modestus's treatise (supposedly written for none other than Tacitus) is accepted as genuine and not as a fifteenth century forgery based on Vegetius. In light of the internal evidence, it is entirely plausible that the treatise is genuine, and I have therefore included an analysis of its contents in Appendix 1, but one cannot know for certain. If the treatise is genuine it is of particular note that the cavalry was apparently reattached to the legions either by Claudius or Aurelian. This conclusion receives support from the resulting strength of the legionary cavalry detachment, which was 726 horsemen plus supernumeraries. The increased cavalry numbers would have resulted from the distribution of Gallienus's enlarged cavalry army back into the legions. In light of the subsequent diminished role of the cavalry under the late Roman emperors, this seems quite probable. The second important point is that one of the previous emperors (either Septimius Severus or one of his successors) had created a new type of legion with new combat tactics based on the use of phalanxes with unit depths of six ranks by adding light-armed soldiers to its strength. However, in practice, unit organization remained the same because the six-rank array consisted of four heavy footmen and two light-armed footmen just as it had been before. If there was any real difference with the previous practice it was probably the posting of the light-armed between the ranks of the heavy-armed, but one wonders whether even this was in any way a new solution never before used. The importance of the missile arm had also increased in contrast to the previous period. If the short treatise was indeed written for Tacitus as a summary of the art of war, then he had use for it soon, as the following quotes from Zosimus prove.

Tacitus had three problems in his hands: 1) What to do with the murderers of Aurelian?; 2) How to deal with the invasion of Franks, Alamanni, Iuthungi and others?; 3) How to deal with the barbarian allies, the Goths and Heruls, which Aurelian had summoned for the Persian war because these appear to have revolted in the meantime? Tacitus decided: 1) to punish the murderers immediately; 2) to send a commander to take charge of operations against the Franks, Alamanni, Iuthungi and others; 3) to take care of the Goths and Heruls in person. Tacitus combined the first and third tasks because both lay in the east. It was also of utmost importance to be present in person as emperor where the conspirators were so that the person who ordered the execution would possess enough authority to carry out the punishments.

Vopiscus claims that at the very beginning of his reign Tacitus appointed Probus as *dux totius orientis* (general in command of the entire east), that he sent a letter in which he confirmed the appointment, and that he appointed Probus to be his co-consul for the coming year, 277. The appointment entailed the bribery of Probus with five-fold rations and the doubling of military insignia. I would suggest that Vopiscus has preserved for us the way in which Tacitus dealt with the commander of the *protectores*, which was to promote him to a higher rank so that he could be separated from the bodyguard units that had served under him. It is by no means impossible that Tacitus could have discussed in the Senate the possibility of nominating Probus as successor of Aurelian before his own nomination as emperor. After all, Probus was the supreme commander of the *protectores* and had apparently had a role in the punishment of Eros and then in the consulting of the Senate after that. It was of the utmost importance to make certain that Probus would not attempt to usurp power now that Tacitus had been nominated.[5]

If Vopiscus (*HA FSPB* 7.2) is correct in his claim that Aurelian had previously nominated Saturninus the Moor as supreme commander of the eastern forces with orders never to visit Egypt, then it is clear that Probus had been nominated as a successor to his friend Saturninus in this position. If true, we do not know what Saturninus's reaction to this was, but at least his replacement by Probus would explain why he later rebelled against Probus, even if both men had been close friends previously. The nomination of Saturninus back to the same command by Probus could have been seen as a veiled insult by Saturninus if he was that type of a man.

According to Aurelius Victor (p.36) and Vopiscus (*HA Tac*. 13.1), Tacitus's first action was to torture to death all those who had a hand in the murder of Aurelian. Mucapor, the *dux* who had given the killing blow, was singled out for a special torture. These statements are slightly misleading in the sense that Tacitus actually did not kill all of the conspirators now, but apparently only those whom he found present in the army assembled by Aurelian. According to Zosimus (1.65.1), there were still conspirators alive in the east at the time of Tacitus's death. They must have continued their march to the eastern front in preparation for the campaign against Persia just like the Goths and Heruls who were in Asia Minor. We do not know where Mucapor and the other conspirators were when Tacitus had them killed, but one may guess that it was somewhere close to the Hellespont or Bosporus. After the murderers had been punished, Tacitus proceeded against the

Goths and Heruls who were ravaging Asia Minor, in all probability because the Romans had failed to keep them happy with gold and silver during the interregnum. The Goths raided Pontus, Cappadocia, Galatia, and Cilicia. Tacitus appears to have divided the army assembled in the east into three separate armies. One of these was placed under his relative Maximinus who took charge of Syria. The second of these was given to his half-brother Florianus, who had also been appointed as Praetorian Prefect. Tacitus took charge of the main army in person so that he and his brother Florianus conducted a joint campaign against the Goths and Heruls with the result that they defeated the 'barbarian invaders' with relative ease.[6]

> Upon his [*Aurelian's*] death the empire fell into the hands of Tacitus, in whose time the Scythians crossed the Palus Maeotis, and made incursions through Pontus even into Cilicia, until he opposed them. Partly in person, and partly by Florianus, the prefect of the court, whom he left in commission for that purpose, this emperor completely routed and destroyed them. He himself was going into Europe, but was thus circumvented and killed [*which implies that Tacitus had left the mopping up of the enemy forces to Florianus*]. He had committed the government of Syria to his cousin Maximinus, who treated the nobility of that country with such austerity, that he caused them both to hate and fear him. Their hatred became so excessive, that at length conspiring with the murderers of Aurelianus, they assaulted Maximinus, and having killed him, fell on and slew Tacitus also as he was upon his departure. [Zosimus 1.63.1–2, English tr. 1814, p.31 with some changes and additions by author.]

John of Antioch (Roberto ed. frg. 239) and Zosimus both state clearly that Tacitus was killed by the assassins of Aurelian because they feared his relative Maximinus. Zonaras (12.28) states that the soldiers killed Maximinus because he behaved harshly and then Tacitus because they feared he would punish them for killing Maximinus. This implies that Maximinus had been delegated the task of purging the army from the conspirators, but that the conspirators hit first by assassinating both Maximinus and Tacitus. This is not surprising because the conspirators had included many men belonging to the imperial bodyguard units which after all were responsible for security and intelligence gathering. I would also suggest that Probus was part of the conspiracy against Maximinus and Tacitus from the start because the nomination of Maximinus would have meant the demotion of Probus from the position into which he had been appointed at the beginning of Tacitus's reign. In other words, once Probus had been separated from most of his subordinates and had moved to Syria, Tacitus felt strong enough to remove him from his post by appointing Maximinus as his replacement. This did not suit Probus and the *protectores* which he had taken with him to the east. The presence of these *protectores* in the east means that Probus had thought it necessary to take some of them with him when he had marched to Syria to assume command of the eastern armies. This was a wise decision. It is likely that the assassination of Tacitus was carried out by the *protectores* who had served under Probus. These men were special operatives for whom such missions came naturally. It is not a coincidence that we find Ammianus Marcellinus and ten other *protectores domestici* under Ursicinus carrying out a similar operation at the behest of Constantius II in 355.[7] Tacitus was probably killed on 7 June 276.

10.3. Tacitus as Emperor

Tacitus was a true blast from the past. He was conservative by nature and therefore the ideal candidate to those in the Senate who yearned for the glory days of the Roman Republic. Tacitus did not let down his supporters, but thanks to the fact that he was killed in a military conspiracy his influence ended with his own death. All his so-called reforms were duly cancelled when Probus became emperor, so his only lasting legacy was the defeat of the Goths. The war in Gaul was a disaster because the invaders were able to conquer sixty major cities; it is clear that Tacitus was en route to Gaul at the time of his murder. After Tacitus's reign the soldiers would no longer make the mistake of delegating the choosing of the emperor to the Senate. It was now the time of the soldiers.

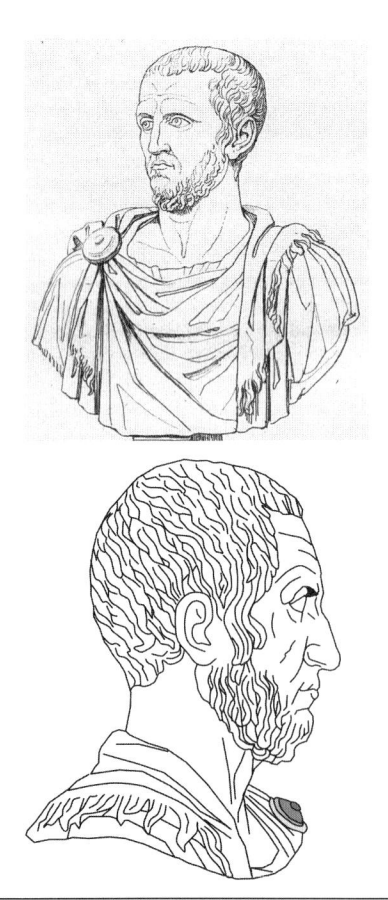

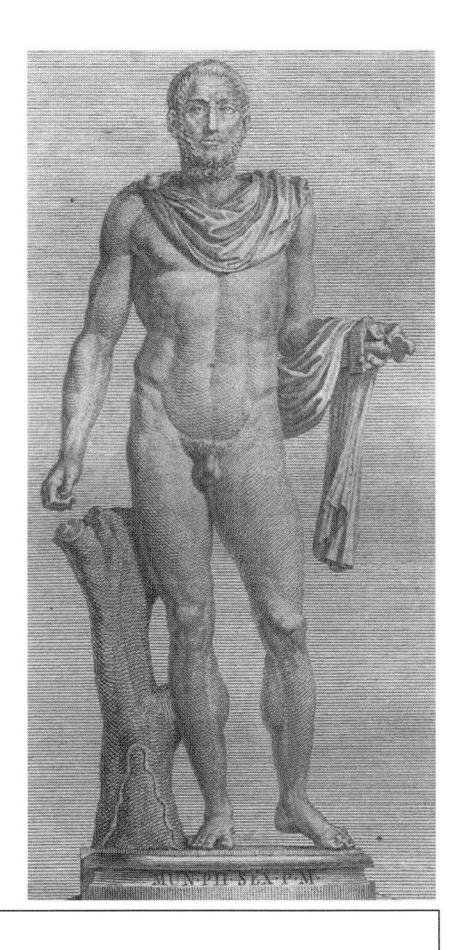

Top left: A bust of Tacitus at Louvre (source: Piranesi, 1805).
Below left: A bust of Tacitus at Louvre. (drawn after Bernoulli).
Right: A statue of Tacitus. Despite his 75 years of age, he was in tip top physical condition. (source: Visconti).
- Piranesi, Benoulli and Visconti identify these as Macrinus, but most modern historians consider these to represent Tacitus.
- "Tacitus Augustus … was of medium height, slender, slightly bald and eloquent, with short, completely grey hair and a delicate nose; he was sensible." Malalas 12.31, tr. by Jeffreys, Jeffreys and Scott p.164

Chapter Eleven

The Struggle for Dominance: Probus vs. Florianus[1]

Left: Bust of Probus according to Duruy.

Right: The so-called bust of Probus according to Bernoulli.

When the news of the murder of Tacitus was brought to his half-brother Florianus he claimed the right to succeed him. The soldiers accompanying him and the soldiers posted in the west supported Florianus's nomination and he was also confirmed in his post by the Senate. So he became the legitimate emperor.

Coin of Florianus (source: Cohen)

The nomination of Florianus was unacceptable for the ambitious Probus and his friends. The following quote from Vopiscus gives us a good indication of how Probus and his supporters manipulated the soldiers to nominate Probus as emperor:

> When the news came of the death of Tacitus, the Forces in the East were for preventing those in Italy [*This would be the field army that had been brought from the west and now served under Florianus, but it is also possible that it merely refers to the Praetorians who did not belong to the protectores that had served previously under Probus*] and also to prevent the Senate from appointing an emperor for a second time [*In other words, Probus and the soldiers did not want to see another Tacitus on the throne*]. The question was whom they should choose. The tribunes [*These would probably be the tribunes who belonged to the protectores who stage-managed the nomination process*] addressed the soldiers, maniple by maniple on the parade-ground saying that we must choose one who is a man of courage, goodness, modesty, clemency and probity. This was repeated so often by everyone and everywhere until they all shouted out 'Probus Augustus, may the gods serve you!' [*The word probity used here (probum) meant that the soldiers should choose Probus, which the soldiers understood readily after it was repeated often enough so that then all shouted together 'Probus'.*] Then they ran and erected a tribunal of turf and Probus was proclaimed emperor and decked with a purple robe which they took from a statue in the temple and from there he was carried to the Palace [*This would presumably be the Palace at Antioch*], he all the while moving against his will and drawing back and often saying to them 'This is not convenient for yourselves. You will not do well under me. I cannot bring favours to you!' [*This was merely a feigned show of reluctance.*] [Vopiscus, *HA Prob.* 10.1ff. tr. by Bernard, 283–4, with emendations, corrections and additions.]

Probus and his accomplices had stage-managed Probus's nomination. He and his friends were vehemently opposed to the policies followed by the Senate and their emperor Tacitus. They certainly did not approve that Florianus would succeed his half-brother. It was the time to put an end to the pretensions of the Senate. Now the Roman Empire and its armies were divided so that Probus possessed Egypt, Phoenicia, Syria and Palestine, while Florianus possessed the area from Cilicia as far as Italy and the Hesperiae, as Zonaras put it at 12.29. The best description of the resulting power struggle is by Zosimus:

> A universal civil disturbance arose now, those of the east choosing Probus emperor, and those at Rome Florianus. The former of these governed all Syria, Phoenicia, Palestine, and Egypt; but the latter was in possession of all the countries from Cilicia to Italy; besides which the homage of all the nations beyond the Alps, the Gauls, Spaniards, Britons, and Africans was paid to him. When both therefore were ready for war, Florianus came to Tarsus, resolving to encamp there, leaving his victory over the Scythians at the Bosphorus unfinished, by which he gave them an opportunity of recovering themselves and returning home, though he had cut off their retreat. Probus protracted the time, because he came with less preparation for a battle. By these means it came to pass that the weather, being exceedingly hot, a pestilential

disorder broke out amongst the troops of Florianus, most of whom were Europeans, and consequently unaccustomed to such excessive heat, by which many were taken off. [*This implies that Probus possessed enough men to block the route from Florianus's army and that he preferred to reduce the enemy through delay. The outbreak of pestilence among the enemy may imply that Probus resorted to the use of bacteriological warfare, for example by introducing bacteria into the water or food sources.*[2]] When Probus understood this, he thought it a proper time to attack the enemy. The soldiers of Florianus, attempting what exceeded their strength, fought some slight skirmishes before the city, but nothing being done worthy of notice, some of the troops of Probus deposed Florianus. [*This means that the soldiers of Florianus were unable to break out from the siege.*] Having performed this, he was kept in custody for some time, until his own soldiers said that it was the will of Probus that he should share his empire. Florianus therefore assumed the purple robe again, until the return of those who were sent to know the true resolution of Probus. On their arrival they caused Florianus to be killed by his own soldiers. [Zosimus 1.64.1–4, English tr. 1814, p.31–2 with some changes, emendations and additions by author.]

It is very likely that the letter of Probus to the *praefectus praetorio* Capito, which is included by Vopiscus, belongs to this place and it may quite well be accurate in its contents too. Vopiscus therefore gives us an important clue of how Probus managed to convince the soldiers of Florianus to change sides.

> As I have never coveted the Empire so I have taken it upon my will. It is a most insidious thing and yet it is not free for me to help myself. I must act the part which the soldiers have imposed upon me. I beseech you Capito [*otherwise unknown*] to enjoy with me the state in safety and provide grain and provisions and necessities for the soldiers. [*This implies that Probus had subjected the soldiers of Florianus to hunger by isolating them at the city of Tarsus and that he promised to provide supplies for the soldiers through Capito.*] I for my part, if you take the care that all things are done well, shall be glad to have no other prefect than you [*This implies that Probus promised to Capito that he would be allowed to keep his position if he betrayed Florianus.*]. [Vopiscus, *HA Prob.* 10.6–7 tr. by Bernard, 284–5, with emendations, corrections and additions.]

I would therefore suggest that Probus, as the better commander, managed to isolate Florianus and his men in the city of Tarsus with the result that Florianus's army was subdued through the combination of famine and pestilence. When the situation became intolerable Probus approached Capito through a letter and managed to convince him to switch sides with the promise of giving the soldiers provisions while Capito would be allowed to keep his office. On the basis of Zosimus this worked initially, but some of the men who had accepted Probus's terms changed their minds once the supplies had been delivered to them, and in fact it is possible they had planned this all along by pretending to agree with Probus. This, however, proved impossible in the circumstances, so Florianus was killed by those of his men who rather sided with the winner Probus.

172 Aurelian and Probus

Probus and Florianus ruled together for about 2 months and 20 days, which means that Probus was able to defeat his enemy with relative ease thanks to his far superior military skills.[3]

Now that Probus had managed to get rid off Florianus, the next stage consisted of obtaining the approval of the other armies and the Senate. It was because of this that Probus assumed a conciliatory tone at the very beginning of his reign towards the Senate and it is because of this that I find Vopiscus's description of Probus's conciliatory tone towards the Senate at the very beginning of his reign credible:

> Fathers of the Senate, It was right that you gave the world the emperor last year and from your own ranks because you are and always will be the sovereigns of the world. I wish that Florianus had waited for the same again from you and that he had not claimed to himself the Empire as if it was his inheritance, … but he having seized it on his own hand, and the army having deferred it to us, and the wiser soldiers having punished him for usurping power, I refer myself fully to the command of your excellencies to judge whether I deserve to be the emperor [*If this letter preserves the real contents of Probus's message it was indeed conciliatory and absolved the Senate from the guilt of having nominated Florianus as emperor. This is by no means impossible.*] [Vopiscus, *HA Prob.* 11.1ff. tr. by Bernard, 285, with emendations, corrections and additions.]

The Senate's decrees confirming the victor of the civil war as emperor were suitably humble and flattering if we are to believe Vopiscus, and there is no reason to think that it would not have been so even if it is uncertain whether the actual contents of the decrees and speeches of the Senate are accurate.

> The consul Aelius Scorpianus said to them, 'Conscript fathers, You have heard the letter of Aurelius Valerius Probus. What do you say about it?' They cried: 'The gods save the emperor Probus. You have been long a worthy, brave, just, and good commander and general… you are Franciscus, Gothicus, Sarmaticus, Parthicus and you are all things [*This list implies that Probus was present in most of the campaigns of Aurelian. As commander of the protectores it is not surprising that he would have been close to his emperor and friend Aurelian*]. … Then Manlius Statianus, who was the eldest senator spoke thus: 'Fathers of the Senate, Thanks to the immortal gods and above the rest to Jupiter the Best [*Iovi Optimo*]… we have no want now of either Aurelian, or Alexander Severus, or the Antonines, or Trajan, or Claudius. We have all things and all their virtues in this one princeps, the knowledge of war, clemency, good life, exemplary way of guiding the commonwealth, and assurance of every virtue. What part of the world is there to which he has not made known his victorious arms? Witness the Marmaridae defeated on African soil; witness the Franks, whom he overthrew in their impassable marshes; witness the Germans [*presumably the Iuthungi*] and Alamanni, whom he repulsed from the banks of the Rhine. What shall I say about the Sarmatians, Goths, Parthians and Persians, and Pontus? The trophies of Probus flourish everywhere. [*The list of enemies defeated includes all those*

defeated under Aurelian plus the Marmaridae under Claudius and the victory in Pontus against the Goths under Tacitus. Probus was clearly present in most of the major actions.] It would be too long to tell how many kings of great nations has he put to flight, and how many commanders he killed with his own hand [*This implies that Probus also challenged other enemy commanders besides the mention of Aradio in Africa on page 60. After the reign of Caracalla, there appears to have been quite a few commanders who challenged the enemy leaders to duels. Another example of this is the challenge to a duel presented by Gallienus to Postumus. For this, see my bio of Gallienus.*]; and how many arms he captured without help as a commoner… Therefore, Fathers of the Senate, I decree to him the titles of Caesar and Augustus, and I add thereto the proconsular power, the reverential title of Father of Our Country, the chief pontificate, the right to make three proposals to the Senate, and the tribunician power.' They cried, 'We all, all say the same!' [*In other words, the Senate confirmed Probus as emperor, with the traditional powers.*] [Vopiscus, *HA Prob.* 11.5–12.8. tr. by Bernard, 286–8, with emendations, corrections and additions.]

Vopiscus claims that Probus then sent as an answer to the Senate the following letter:

Probus having received this Act of the Senate sent a second letter to them by which he permitted them to be judges of appeals, to create proconsuls, and to create legates with proconsular powers [*These have been claimed to confirm the power to nominate military commanders to the Senate, but the matter is more complicated than that.*], to give the governors the rights of *praetor* [*This merely confirmed the traditional rights of the governors to be judges*], to confirm by Special Decree of the Senate the edicts made by himself. [Vopiscus, *HA Prob.* 11.5–12.8. tr. by Bernard, 286–8, with emendations, corrections and additions.]

Most modern historians consider the above-mentioned granting of proconsular powers to the Senate to mean the return of military commands back to the senators and therefore to be unhistorical just like the previous return of these powers by Tacitus (*HA Tac.* 19.2–4). The reason for this is that there is, according to the majority view among historians, no definitely credible evidence for this, but as always this is a matter of opinion and not a fact.[4] However, I would not preclude the possibility that this return did actually take place. There is evidence for senatorial military commands because Syria Coele had a senatorial proconsul whose name was Saturninus (the usurper), but on the basis of the sources it had been Probus who had nominated him.[5] This is actually not surprising because it had always been the emperor who decided who would be in which position ever since the reign of the first emperor Augustus. There are three possible ways to reconcile the return of military commands and the current state of evidence for this. Firstly, it is possible that Probus did indeed initially confirm the decisions made by Tacitus so that he was able to ensure smooth succession to power and that he later removed this right from the Senate. Secondly, it is possible that Probus did indeed grant proconsular powers back to the Senate, but we cannot confirm this from the other sources because of some historical accident; even in this case the change would have been merely a cosmetic one because the Senate would not have dared to appoint anyone proconsul without the prior approval of the emperor. Thirdly, it is possible that military and civilian powers had already been divided so that proconsular power in this case actually meant only civilian powers while command of the armies was in the hands of the *duces* (dukes) and *comites* (counts) because this phenomenon was already visible under Gallienus. Whatever the truth, the extant evidence suggests that the senators did not receive back the right to military commands, at least in the case of individual units posted along the borders.

The evidence for the relationship between Probus and the Senate is scarce, but it is known that it was generally a good one because the heavily pro-senatorial sources are full of praise for Probus. We know that Probus's reign meant a return to the days of Aurelian in most respects because his reign was military in nature. He favoured the army and used military themes in his propaganda coins and once again started to use the *dominus et deus* title previously used by Aurelian. The best explanation for the discrepancy is that Probus was wise enough to pay lip service to the Senate by involving it in his decisions somehow even if it was he who made the decisions in practice just like it had been from the reign of the first emperor Augustus onwards. None of the sources claim that Probus was particularly cruel towards anyone as Aurelian had been, with the implication that he presumably did not launch witch hunts to find traitors among the senators as Aurelian did. All sources basically praise him for his fairness. For example, Zosimus (1.71.4) calls him a good and just ruler. As noted by Kennedy (235–6), if there was one fault in Probus, it was his misplaced trust in his subordinates. In sum, it is clear that Probus was able to maintain a good working relationship with the Senate throughout his reign thanks to his wise treatment of the senators.[6]

Once securely in power, Probus's next object was to get rid off the murderers of Aurelian. Zosimus gives us the best description of how this was achieved. It is once again a good example of the military skills of Probus, who knew how to lure his enemies into a trap:

> Probus, having thus gained the empire, marched forward, and performed a very recommendable action for the public good, as a prelude to what he should afterwards do. For he resolved to punish those who had murdered Aurelianus, and conspired against Tacitus [*This appears to hide the truth that Probus was himself the man who had murdered Tacitus and who had also been the overall commander of the men who had murdered Aurelian. The principal reason for this conclusion is that his elevation to power was clearly stage-managed with the implication that he was the man behind the plot*]; though for fear of an insurrection he did not openly execute his design, but planned a company of men, in whom he had confidence, at a convenient post, near to which he invited the murderers to a feast. Coming there in expectation of being entertained at the emperor's table, Probus ascended into a balcony from whence he could view the action, which he gave a signal to his men to perform. As soon as they received it, they fell on the murderers in their defenceless state, and left only one of them alive, whom he caused afterwards to be burnt alive, as a very dangerous criminal. [*It seems probable that this man was a very high-ranking officer in the protectores and therefore one of the principal plotters. According to Zonaras 12.29, Probus rebuked the murderers first, and only then had them all killed. If this is true, then the murderers were simply apprehended first in the ambush and executed only after*

this.] [Zosimus 1.65.1–2, English tr. 1814, p.32 with some changes and additions by author.]

This is a good example of first rate generalship by Probus. It would have been foolish for him to have given his enemies any chance of resisting. The 'Illyrian Military Mafia' had now regained power in a manner befitting a mafia boss. This time they intended to retain it and not repeat the mistake of handing it over to the Senate again.

Some coins of Probus drawn by Beger (1696) and Cohen. Note the religious propaganda (*Sol Invictus*, *Iovi Cons.*), which shows continuity from the reign of Aurelian.

Bahram II receiving the submission on the Segestani according to Rawlinson

Chapter Twelve

Probus the Fireman

12.1. The Gothic and Armenian Wars in 276–8

On the basis of the title *Gothicus*, which Probus is attested to have possessed by 277, we know that Probus's first war was against the Goths in about 276/7. These would have been the very same enemies against which he, Tacitus and Florianus had fought in the spring of 276. And where was this war fought? The usual assumption is that it was fought in Asia Minor, but I would suggest that it was actually fought in Thrace. The reason for this conclusion is that since Florianus had blocked the route of retreat from the Goths with his army on the Bosphorus, it is probable that his withdrawal from there to fight against Probus had allowed the Goths to cross the Bosphorus into Thrace so that they were pillaging it at the time Probus began his march west.

Probus's march to the west is confirmed by coins bearing the text adventus and the laws preserved in the *Justinian Code*, which place Probus in Cyzicus and then in the Balkans at Serdica, Sirmium and Siscia. The date for his stay at Sirmium is 5 May 277, which would imply that the war and reorganization lasted quite a while.[1] Probus would therefore have first marched to the naval headquarters of the *Classis Pontica* at Cyzicus probably with the intention of using its naval resources for the shipping of his forces to the European side of the straits. We should not forget that Probus had previously commanded the naval expedition to retake Egypt from the Palmyrenes. He therefore knew well how to use naval forces for amphibious and naval operations and also for the provisioning of armies in the field. It is therefore not surprising that his first object was to make certain that the naval resources in the region were used in support of his land campaign.

The only sources which describe the Gothic war of Probus are Armenian and Georgian and these describe the war only because the Armenian hero Trdat/Tiridates the Great had an important role in it. These sources are: Agathangelos (1.2, 37ff., p.53ff.); Moses (2.79); and the *Georgian Chronicles* (pp.80–81). The following discussion is based on these as well as on my *Military History of late Rome Volume 1*, and has some new conclusions.

According to Agathangelos (p.39), the ruler of the Goths assembled an army to fight against the ruler of the Greeks who was none other than the emperor Probus. This implies that the Gothic and Herul fugitives had managed to cross into Thrace and from there to the Danube where they would have met their brethren, and that the Gothic king, who had dispatched these forces previously to support Aurelian, had now assembled a fresh force with which he had invaded Thrace in revenge for the treatment the Goths had received. The Gothic king challenged Probus to a duel, presumably because Probus was well known for his skills as a duellist, but unfortunately for Probus his days as a duellist appear to have been in the past because Agathangelos states that he was at the time weak in bodily strength. According to Malalas (12.33, tr. by Jeffreys, Jeffreys and Scott p.165),

'Aelius Probus … was of medium height, with a large belly and straight, closely cropped hair, a bushy beard, dark skin, a ruddy complexion, good eyes and was very learned; he favoured the Green faction.'

Probus was only 44 years old at the time, but the reference to the large belly could suggest that he had allowed his physical condition to deteriorate. Furthermore, Agathangelos states in no uncertain terms that he was now simply too weak to fight. However, on the basis of later references to Probus's personal bravery in war (see later), it would seem that this only applied to the winter of 276/7; the implication is that Probus was just suffering from some illness/flu during the winter season and that it was this that prevented him from fighting the duel. It is also quite easy to explain why Probus would have had a big belly: he could have done as the gladiators and added extra girth around his waist for extra protection against cuts and thrusts. A big belly does not mean that the man would not have been fully fit and ready to fight; consider modern sumo wrestlers. According to Agathangelos, Probus was also unable to bring the enemy to a decisive battle because the Goths refused to fight a pitched battle with armies deployed for combat, army opposing army. This means that the entire Gothic army consisted of cavalry and that the Gothic ruler was a true expert in this style of fighting. The fact that Probus was also a learned man means that he was well versed in the history of warfare and all aspects of the art of war – the ability of the Gothic king to avoid all the snares set up by his skilled enemy shows that he was a very able commander.

It was then that the *comes* Licinius (the future emperor) and the exiled Armenian king Trdat/Tiridates came to the rescue. These two men were friends because Trdat had been educated in the household of Count Licinius. According to both Agathangelos and Moses, Tiridates was an expert martial artist. Moses goes on to claim that Trdat had defeated in a boxing match the boxing champion Clitostratos of Rhodes, whose favourite technique was the neck grip, and that he had also defeated Cerasos of Argos in like manner. In addition to this, Tiridates drove chariots in competitions. He was a man with capital letters just like Probus. Agathangelos's account (39–42) implies that the war between the Goths and Probus lasted for a significant amount of time because he not only states that Probus was unable to force the enemy to fight a decisive battle, but that he was also forced to issue an order that all available forces were to be marched immediately to his assistance. It was these reinforcements that included Licinius and Tiridates. When these two men and their forces had reached the city (Serdica?) where Probus was, the gates had already been locked so that there was not enough forage available for the horses of their vast army. The implication of this is that the reinforcements consisted primarily of cavalry, which Probus needed sorely for the purpose of forcing the cavalry-based enemy to fight a battle. It was then that Tiridates gave a demonstration of his strength. He saw a walled pen with a great pile of hay, and then climbed the wall after which he threw heaps of hay to the troops together with the guards and donkeys, and then climbed back.

Licinius could hardly believe his eyes, and when the gates of the city were opened in the morning, Licinius went to meet Probus. It was then at a meeting of officers that Licinius learnt from Probus that the king of the Goths had challenged Probus to a duel. Licinius had a solution to the problem. He suggested that Tiridates fight in disguise against the king of the Goths, and when Tiridates was brought before Probus, he agreed to the plan. The personal appearance of Tiridates must have been quite imposing.

Next morning, the Romans dispatched Tiridates, robed in imperial garb to fight the agreed duel. Tiridates and the Gothic king whipped the flanks of their horses and charged at a gallop against each other. It was Tiridates who gained the upper hand. He tilted the king onto the ground, seized him and brought him before Probus. It is very unfortunate that the sources fail to tell us what happened next. However, we can make some educated guesses based on what we otherwise know. On the basis of the *Georgian Chronicles*, the Romans exploited the capture of the Gothic king by attacking the enemy, which was routed. See below. It is likely that the Gothic King was ruler of the Greuthungi Goths, because the invaders were from Lacus Maeotius (the Sea of Azov) and they subsequently withdrew past the Bosporan kingdom. It is also very likely that the victory in the duel enabled Probus to conclude a treaty with the captured king, most probably a treaty of friendship and alliance with the Goths, so that they would become Roman allies (*foederati*). They were apparently initially attached to the Roman army because Vopiscus (*HA Prob.* 18.1–2) claims that Probus settled the captured Greuthungi as allies in the Balkans only after he had concluded peace with the Persians. This actually makes a lot of sense. The Greuthungi Goths had been originally summoned to fight against the Persians because as cavalry lancers they were particularly effective against them, and Probus therefore kept the Goths with him until the time when he knew that the Goths were no longer needed against the Persians. In sum, the Armenian sources imply that the Gothic war lasted for so long that Probus was forced to summon reinforcements, which in its turn would mean that it is possible that Probus indeed reached the city of Sirmium very close to the date 5 May 277, when the *Justinian Code* states he was there.

If the Gothic king concluded the alliance, which I suggest he did on the basis of Vopiscus's account, this did not concern all of the Greuthungi Goths because we know from the other sources that the last remnants of these Gothic forces were destroyed by Tejran, King of the Bosporans. It was he who intercepted and massacred the survivors so that Probus was able to strike coins with *Victoria Pontica* (this refers to Probus's success as a general) and *Victoria Gothica* (which refers to Probus's success during his reign).[2]

Agathangelos's account of the subsequent exploits of Tiridates is important because it enables us to reconstruct events in the east from 277 onwards. According to him, the grateful emperor rewarded Tiridates with a great army, which Tiridates then used for the invasion of Armenia. Tiridates defeated the Persians in a pitched battle in about 277/8 so that the surviving Persians were forced to flee back to Persia.[3] The principal reason for this success was that the Persians were unable to concentrate their forces against him in a situation in which most of their forces were in the east fighting against the rebel Hormizd and because the nomads had broken through the Darubend/Darbend Gate (see below). It has been suggested that Probus was able to claim the title *Persicus Maximus* on 21 October 279 largely thanks to the efforts of Tiridates, but in this study I am making the claim that it is probable that Probus had a personal role in these events, which will be analyzed later in the right context.[4]

It is thanks to the *Georgian Chronicles* (pp.80–81) that we know why Narses, the High King of Armenia, failed to block the invasion of Tiridates in 277/8, and other things which took place not mentioned by the Armenian sources. This text proves that the Khazars, an anachronistic term which may mean the proto-Turks or proto-Huns, or some other nomadic group, tried to force their way through the Derbend Pass as they had done before. This text claims that the nomads were opposed by Mihran/Mirian, who is actually to be identified with Narses because the *Georgian Chronicles* are in the habit of hiding the client status of Georgia (Georgia means at this time its eastern portion which was called Iberia while its western portion Colchis was under Roman rule) and its ruler to the Armenians and Persians. An account of the Gothic invasion follows this, which in all its principal elements is the same as that preserved by the Armenian sources. The *Chronicles* state that when the Goths invaded, the Roman emperor assembled his army and marched against the invaders. The Gothic king proposed a duel. The emperor disguised Tiridates as himself and dispatched him against the Gothic king. Tiridates then duly captured the king and the Romans routed the Goths. This account implies that the Romans attacked the Goths after their king had been captured. Most of these defeated Goths would presumably have fled only to be butchered later by the Bosporans close to their homes.

The *Chronicles* once again note that Tiridates was given Roman troops, but adds at the same time that Tiridates was crowned king of Armenia and sent to Armenia. Tiridates then expelled Mihran's (i.e. Narses') soldiers and Persian governors from Armenia. On the basis of Moses (2.91) it is possible to calculate that Tiridates was crowned king of Armenia in about 278, which corresponds nicely with the timeline I have suggested here. The situation changed when Narses and Mihran/Mirian had defeated the nomads so that he was able to turn his forces against the Armenian king. We do not know when this happened, but one may presume that it was in about 278. To be able to crush the Armenians, Narses ordered the Persian nobles to bring reinforcements from Persia. These reinforcements included a relative of Narses who bore the name Peroz. Narses dispatched this Peroz to reinforce Mihran/Mirian in Georgia/Iberia. The *Chronicles* claim that Mihran/Mirian gave this Peroz his own daughter as wife together with the strategically important land in Georgia/Iberia called Xunan. Now the Persians outnumbered the Armenians so that Tiridates was forced to resort to guerrilla warfare. This enabled Tiridates to avoid defeat by prolonging the war. It was during the following years that Tiridates increased his already great renown as a duellist – he was possibly the best duellist of his day.

12.2. The Campaigns in Gaul, Germania, Illyricum, and Thrace in 277–8

Probus could not rest on his laurels after the Gothic victory because the invasion of Gaul, which had begun during the interregnum, had resulted in the loss of sixty or seventy major cities in the area. The Romans were in deep trouble. Therefore, once the campaign against the Goths was finished, Probus marched to Sirmium, where he is attested to be 5 May 277, after which he continued his journey to Siscia, which he would have reached about mid-May. The probable route to Gaul would then have taken him to Emona, Aquileia, Patavium (Padua), Genua, Mutina (Modena), Placentia (Piacenza), Forum Iulii (Fréjus), Aquae Sextiae (Aix-en-Provence) and Arelate (Arles), and from there to Lugdunum (Lyon), which he would have reached towards the end of September or beginning of October. Historians have speculated that Probus would have visited Rome briefly on the basis of the ADVENTUS coins, which he could have easily done by taking a small detachment of cavalry with him while the rest of the army continued its march towards Gaul. If Probus did this, as is probable, he would have continued from Aquileia to Ravenna, Ariminum (Rimini), Fanum (Fano), and Reate (Rieti), to Rome, which would have taken about nine days after which he would have returned back north via the route which connected him with the forces sent in advance. The problem with this is that there is no definite evidence for the visit to Rome at this time so it is quite possible that Probus marched straight to Ludgunum where he is known to have minted ADVENTUS coins with him riding a horse towards the end of 277. However, I am still inclined to accept the view that Probus made a short visit into the city of Rome to secure his own position. This would not have taken many days to accomplish and it would have kept the senators happy – and we know that the senators were happy under Probus's rule.[5] The march from the south of Gaul northwards was a logistically sound decision because it enabled the shipping of supplies from the Mediterranean along the Rhône for the army.

The subsequent campaign to regain possession of Gaul from the invaders and its follow-up campaign in Germania is described by two sources, Vopiscus and Zosimus, but Vopiscus places it in its right place at the very beginning of the reign of Probus while Zosimus places it after the revolt of Saturninus, which probably took place either during the Gallic campaign or right after it. The following discussion presents the evidence first and then the conclusions, but it is necessary to point out at the beginning of the analysis that Probus divided his huge force so that he gave his generals the task of defeating the Franks while he himself took on the task of defeating the Alamanni and other Germanic tribes or tribal confederations. This becomes apparent when one compares the accounts and it has also been recognized in the previous research.[6]

ADVENTUS coin of Probus (source: Cohen)

12.2.1. The Gallic Campaign in 277

In the next place he set out with a huge army [*cum ingenti exercitu*] for Gallia, which first fell into confusion after the death of Postumus, but was overrun by the Germans after the death of Aurelian. He fought there several so great and successful battles that he recovered 60 noble cities which had fallen into the barbarian hands and recovered all the booty… While they were roaming up and down along our bank or rather throughout all Gallia, he slew 400,000 of them [*This figure is usually considered inflated, like the similar figures for the Goths and their allies for the reigns of Gallienus and Claudius, or the Helvetii against Julius Caesar,*[7] *or the numbers involved in the great barbarian migrations of the fifth century. In my opinion it is probable that Probus's forces did not kill all of these, but rather that the 400,000 represents the entire armed strength of all of the invaders raiding Gaul, or alternatively the total number killed during the fight in Gaul and the subsequent invasion of enemy territory. It is consistent with all of the previous instances in which great masses of barbarians invaded Roman territory. It is quite easy to believe that when the Franks, Alamanni, Iuthungi, Burgundians, Vandals, Longiones and others invaded en masse that their overall numbers could easily approach 400,000, and the barbarians, who were unskilled in besieging, certainly needed huge numbers of soldiers to be able to take 60 major cities in Gaul which were protected by garrisons, citizen militia and walls at this stage of history. It is therefore not surprising that Probus needed the huge army mentioned to deal with this trouble.*] and the remainder he drove back beyond the river of Neckar and Alba [*This is usually identified with Swabian Alb/Jura in modern Swabia. This is the area between the Neckar, Danube and the Black Forest which is located to the west of Alb. Swabia comes from the tribal name Suebi/Suevi, which formed at this time a part of the Alamannic Confederacy. However, Bernard, who translated the text in the seventeenth century, identified Alba with the river Albis, today called the Elbe. Considering the terminology used by Vopiscus – ultra Nicrum fluvium et Albam removit – this is a sensible conclusion. In light of the number of kings and the use of the Neckar, the Alamanni were the more likely target of Probus's operations, so the Alba is probably the Swabian Alb. But on the basis of Zosimus's text it is actually more likely that Alba would be the Elbe because Probus continued his march eastwards where he defeated the Burgundians and Vandals both of whom were located close to the Elbe. Since it is impossible to know for certain what Vopiscus meant, I have here given both alternatives.*] and he took as much booty as the barbarians had taken from the Romans. Besides this, he built opposite the Roman cities on barbarian soil forts [*castra*] in which he placed garrisons. He assigned fields, barns, houses and magazines of grain for all the forces which he placed on the other side of the Rhine. Heads of the barbarians were brought to him daily at the price of one *aureus* [*gold coin*] apiece, and he did not stop fighting until nine minor kings [*reguli*] threw themselves at his feet and from whom he received hostages first and then corn, cows and sheep. Some say he commanded them not to use swords again because they could now rely on the protection of Rome in case they needed to be defended. It seemed that this could not be achieved unless the Romans advanced the frontier to cover the whole of Germania as a province. However, he severely punished those, with the approval of the minor kings, who did not return the booty as promised. He also took 16,000 recruits who were scattered throughout the provinces and incorporated into the *numeri* and *milites* of the limes-frontier [*i.e. among the so-called frontier troops which were called limitanei, which at this time consisted of legions and their auxiliary forces.*] in groups of 50 or 60 men[8] saying that the assistance of the barbarian auxiliaries must be felt rather than seen. [Vopiscus, *HA Prob.* 13.5ff. tr. by Bernard, 289–90, with emendations, corrections and additions.]

Auxiliaries bringing heads for the emperor Trajan in the Column of Trajan. Drawing by Bellori.

Praetorians bringing heads in the Arch of Constantine. Drawing by Bellori.

The granting of one gold *aureus* for each head brought by the soldiers by the emperor Probus was an old and tried method to encourage the soldiers in their duty. Headhunting made the soldiers eager to fight and kill for two reasons. It enriched them and the trophies in the form of heads were proofs of their manhood in the eyes of other soldiers. The use of this method to encourage the men to do their duty proves quite nicely how well-versed Probus was with the ways of fighting.

He sent the following letter to the Senate. Fathers of the Senate, I give thanks to the immortal gods that they approved and justified your judgment in your choice of me. All that broad and extended country of Germany is subjugated. Nine minor kings of different tribes have humbled themselves and prostrated themselves at my feet, or should I say at your feet. Now they all plough and plant for you, and serve against the enemies of the interior… 400,000 of the enemies are slain; and 16,000 other with their arms have come into our service. Seventy noble cities [*note the discrepancy of 60 vs. 70 cities, but it of course possible to think that the 70 cities would include the cities liberated in Agri Decumates*] are recovered out of the slavery of the enemy and all Gallia is entirely liberated… The fields of Gallia are ploughed with the cattle of the barbarians, and the German beasts yield their captive necks to our yokes. All their sheep graze now upon our pasture, the flocks of the tribes nourish our troops, and the herds of their horses are now bred for our horsemen, and our barns are full of their corn… It is our wish, Fathers of the Senate, that you appoint a new governor for Germania [*The subsequent revolt of the military commanders left in charge of Gaul proves that this governor of Germania was not in charge of military forces. In other words, the details that we have imply that the civilian and military duties in the provinces were already separated in most cases*.] [Vopiscus, *HA Prob.* 15.1ff. tr. by Bernard, 290–91, with emendations, corrections and additions.]

Probus the Fireman 183

Having performed these affairs as I have related, Probus obtained several victories over the barbarians in two different wars; in one of which he himself commanded, but left the other to the conduct of his lieutenant. Perceiving that it was necessary to assist the cities of Germany which lay upon the Rhine, and were harassed by the Barbarians, he marched with his army towards the river. When the war began there, a grievous famine prevailed throughout the surrounding country; but a heavy shower of rain and corn fell together, so that in some places were great heaps of it made by its own descent. [*If true, I would suggest a natural explanation for this miracle would be that there were great heaps of grain on the ground because the fleeing barbarians had abandoned them when the Romans approached, and that Probus then claimed that this had resulted from a miracle to encourage the men in the same manner that Aurelian had encouraged his men with visions. It is of course quite possible that the whole thing had been stage-managed from the start. The other natural explanation would of course be a powerful storm which had raised grain into the air which would then have dropped, but this sounds too good to be true. The third natural explanation is that Zosimus or his source has mistaken the rain miracle of Marcus Aurelius to have taken place under Marcus Aurelius Probus. This is probably the likeliest alternative.*] At this prodigy, all were so astonished that at first they dared not touch the corn to satisfy their hunger; but being at length forced to it by necessity, which expels all fear, they made bread of it, which not only allayed their hunger, but enabled them to gain the victory with great ease. The emperor terminated several other wars, with scarcely any trouble; and fought some fierce battles, first against the Longiones, a German nation [*belonging to the Alamanni*], whom he conquered, taking Semno [*possibly after the Semnones, a tribe which belonged to the Alamannic confederacy. He would have been one of the nine minor kings mentioned by Vopiscus.*] their general, and his son, prisoners. These he pardoned upon submission, but took from them all the captives and plunder they had acquired, and dismissed, on certain terms, not only the common soldiers, but even Semno and his son. Another of his battles was against the Franks, whom he subdued through the good conduct of his commanders. [Zosimus 1.67.1–1.68.1, English tr. 1814, p.32–3 with some changes and additions by author.]

The above quotes make it obvious that Probus's plan for the campaign season of 277 was to divide his massive army into two army groups so that his generals (possibly Proculus and Bonosus) were in charge of liberating the north of Gaul from Frankish hands while Probus himself liberated central Gaul, the upper reaches of the Rhine and Raetia from the Alamanni. One may make the educated guess that Probus's generals and Probus both had a minimum of about 70,000 men for them to be able to defeat the enemies they faced. It is probable that the Alamanni were supported by the Burgundians and Vandals because Probus campaigned against them next year. The principal reason for the troubles was that the abandonment of *Agri Decumates* during the reign of Gallienus had left a gaping hole in the Roman defensive structures. In other words, the first stage of the operations consisted of pushing the invaders away from Gaul and from the establishment of the beachheads on the other side of the Rhine frontier.

The accounts of Zosimus and Vopiscus make it clear that Probus and his generals soundly defeated their enemies and forced them across the Rhine so that Probus pushed the enemy past even the Neckar and received the surrender of nine minor kings. It is probable that one of them was King Semno (after Semnones, a part of the Alamannic confederation) mentioned by Zosimus.

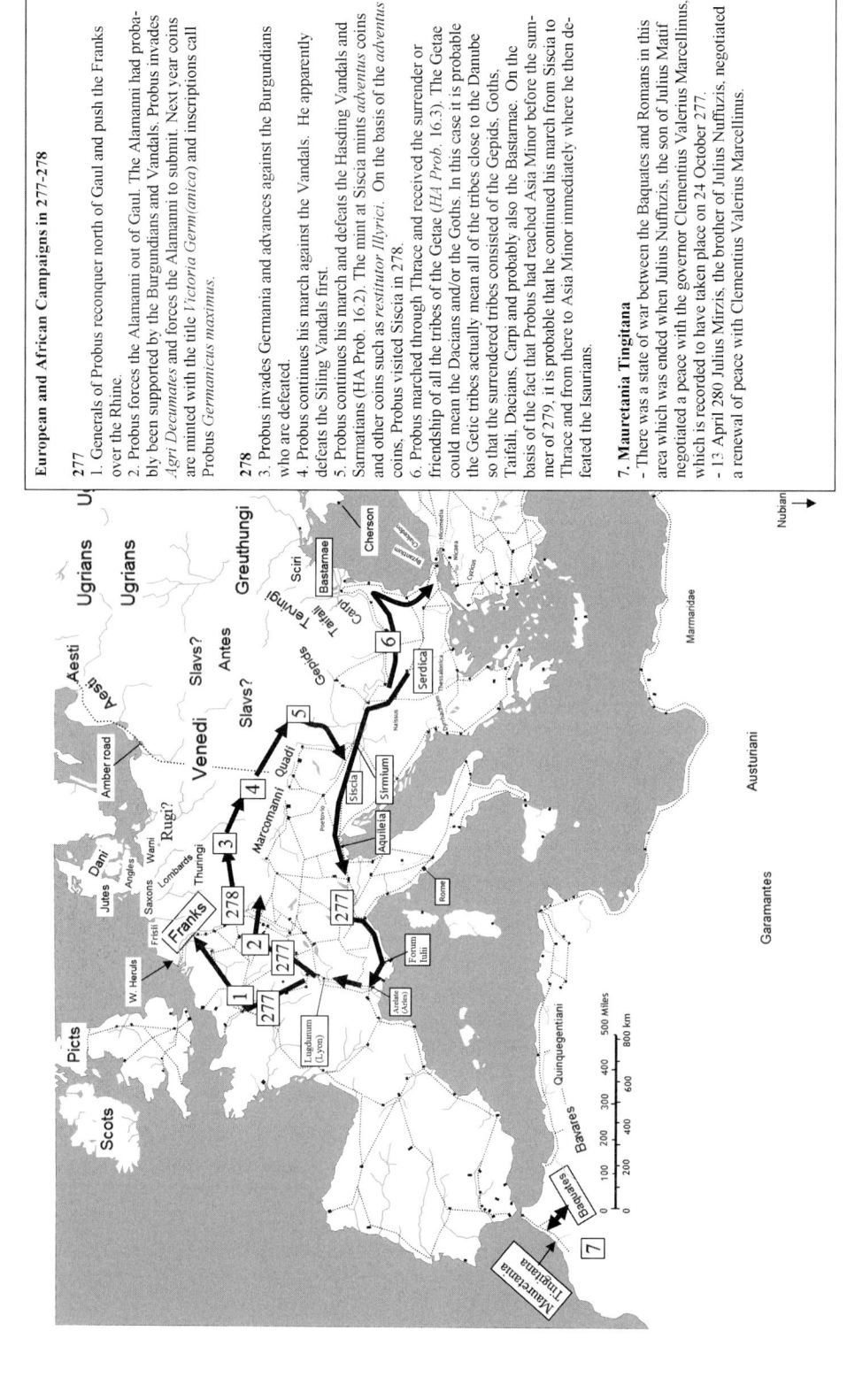

European and African Campaigns in 277-278

277

1. Generals of Probus reconquer north of Gaul and push the Franks over the Rhine.
2. Probus forces the Alamanni out of Gaul. The Alamanni had probably been supported by the Burgundians and Vandals. Probus invades *Agri Decumates* and forces the Alamanni to submit. Next year coins are minted with the title *Victoria Germ(anica)* and inscriptions call Probus *Germanicus maximus*.

278

3. Probus invades Germania and advances against the Burgundians who are defeated.
4. Probus continues his march against the Vandals. He apparently defeats the Siling Vandals first.
5. Probus continues his march and defeats the Hasding Vandals and Sarmatians (HA Prob. 16.2). The mint at Siscia mints *adventus* coins and other coins such as *restitutor Illyrici*. On the basis of the *adventus* coins, Probus visited Siscia in 278.
6. Probus marched through Thrace and received the surrender or friendship of all the tribes of the Getae (HA Prob. 16.3). The Getae could mean the Dacians and/or the Goths. In this case it is probable the Getic tribes actually mean all of the tribes close to the Danube so that the surrendered tribes consisted of the Gepids. Goths, Taifali, Dacians, Carpi and probably also the Bastarnae. On the basis of the fact that Probus had reached Asia Minor before the summer of 279, it is probable that he continued his march from Siscia to Thrace and from there to Asia Minor immediately where he then defeated the Isaurians.

7. Mauretania Tingitana

- There was a state of war between the Baquates and Romans in this area which was ended when Julius Nuffuzis, the son of Julius Matif negotiated a peace with the governor Clementius Valerius Marcellinus, which is recorded to have taken place on 24 October 277.
- 13 April 280 Julius Mirzis, the brother of Julius Nuffuzis, negotiated a renewal of peace with Clementius Valerius Marcellinus.

Probus the Fireman 185

Shapur I
It is possible that the helmet is a Roman helmet so that the coin would depict a trophy
(source: Rawlinson).

Hormizd I
(source: Rawlinson)

Bahram I
(source: Rawlinson)

Bahram II
(source: Duruy)

Narses
(source: Rawlinson)

Column commemorating the victories of Probus possibly over the Alamanni found at Merten near Metz. Restored drawing by Duruy.

These victories enabled Probus to demand and obtain the booty back, together with hostages, grain, cows, sheep, and 16,000 barbarian recruits which were distributed in groups of 50 and 60 along the frontiers. See Appendix 2. Probus also restored the borders by building *castra*-forts (consisting mostly of the so-called *quadriburgia*) on both sides of the Rhine and presumably also along the Danube, because the borders facing the *Agri Decumates* required the building of forts along the entire length because the previous line of forts was now in barbarian hands. The Alamanni were naturally forced to become allied *foederati*, but Probus and the Romans could not put too much trust in their loyalty, as was also noted in Vopiscus's account. The soldiers who were settled on the frontiers were given farms, store-houses, homes and rations of provisions to support them. At least at this stage of his career Probus's policy was not to enlarge the Empire in the west but to provide it with better defensive structures. He fortified both banks of the Rhine so that the outpost forts on the barbarian side provided intelligence of enemy activities, acted as staging posts for operations into the enemy territory, and acted as the first line of defence against any possible barbarian aggression. In light of Probus's future actions it is possible that this formed only the first stage in Probus's plans which would have been to conquer the whole of Germania.

As I have noted previously, most of these new forts followed the so-called Tetrarchic model so that the forts were smaller and better protected than previously. These forts were typically square in shape (*quadriburgia*); walls were thick; barracks were placed against the walls; and the towers projected outside from the walls. The purpose was to make these forts more defensible than had been the case with the typical Principate fortresses. However, the term 'Tetrarchic fort' is highly misleading, because modern research has proved that this type of defensive structure had been in existence since the late second century (Le Bohec, 2006, 98ff.) with the implication that Probus was following up a quite old and traditional model.[9]

It is also probable that Probus created the so-called *Barcarii* (*ND Occ.* 35.32) on the Lake Constance at this time as suggested by Reddé (p.630) and it is similarly possible that he created the Fleet of Lake Como. The events of the reigns of Gallienus and Claudius would have shown that there existed a need for such naval units in case the enemy managed to penetrate Roman defences. As I have noted previously, it is clear that Probus's strategy along the Rhine frontier set a precedent for his successors to follow.[10]

It is thanks to an extant inscription that we know that there was also trouble in Mauretania Tingitana in 277. It proves that the Baquates had revolted and ravaged Mauritania Tingitana, but the local governor was able to force them to sign a peace treaty in 277. But the fact that the peace had to be concluded again in 280 means that the Baquates resumed their raiding afterwards. The evidence clearly shows that the Roman forces, which consisted of auxiliary forces, proved quite adequate for the task at hand.[11]

12.2.2. The Campaigns in Germania, Illyricum and Thrace in 278

> He made war on the Burgundi and Vandili. [*This makes it very likely that the Burgundians and Vandals had joined the Alamanni in their invasion of Gaul.*] But seeing his forces were too weak, he endeavoured to separate those of his enemies, and engage only with a part. [*If the Burgundians and Vandals had united their forces,*

this would not be surprising, because according to Jerome a.373 and Cassiodorus 1119, in 373 the Burgundians were able to provide the Romans with 80,000 mercenaries and one should add to this figure those who were left behind to protect their homes. The Vandals possessed at least the same number of men. In short, if the Burgundians and Vandals united their forces, they could have had 200,000–300,000 men. However, let us assume that they did not unite their forces, but fought two separate wars. Even in this case Probus would have faced enemy forces consisting of about 100,000–150,000 men in each case. In either case it is not surprising that Probus resorted to the use of the stratagem, of luring the enemy to cross the river, which is likely to have been either the Elbe or one of the rivers close to it.] His design was favoured by fortune; for the armies lying on both sides of the river, the Romans challenged the Barbarians that were on the further side to fight. This so incensed them, that many of them crossed over, and fought until the Barbarians were all either slain or taken by the Romans; except a few that remained behind, who sued for peace, on condition of giving up their captives and plunder; which was acceded to. But as they did not restore all that they had taken, the emperor was so enraged, that he fell on them as they were retiring, killed many of them, and took prisoner their general Igillus. [*It is possible that this was only an excuse for the attack because after all Zosimus was using Roman sources. It is entirely plausible to think that Probus actually ate his words and attacked the enemy for a second time unexpectedly. In other words, I would consider it is quite possible that Probus resorted to the use of a second stratagem to finish the job.*] All of them that were taken alive were sent to Britain, where they were settled, and were subsequently very serviceable to the emperor when any insurrection broke out. [*The sending of the Burgundians to Britain was a wise move because it isolated the barbarians from their countrymen and basically forced them to fight for the Romans in their new alien surroundings.*] [Zosimus 1.68.1–3, English tr. 1814, p.33 with some changes and additions by author.]

From Gallia he went into Illyricum, on his way to which he so secured and established the peace of Raetia as not to leave the least suspicion of any danger. [*This would presumably refer to the campaigns against the Burgundians and Vandals, because Probus had already pacified the Alamanni during the previous campaign. What is notable about Vopiscus' account in this case and after is that he referred constantly to the territory in Roman hands when the actual fighting was conducted north of it.*]. In Illyricum he so severely beat the Sarmatians and other tribes [*In light of Zosimus' text it is probable that Probus continued from the lands of the Siling Vandals straight to the lands held by the Hasding Vandals and Sarmatians so that Probus actually attacked the enemies from an unexpected direction, possibly when they had returned from Illyricum which they had apparently pillaged. The other tribes would therefore include at least the Hasdings, but may also have included the Quadi and some Dacian groups and others.*] that he so easily recovered all the spoil which they possessed that it seemed like there was no fighting. He carried his arms into Thrace, where all the Getic tribes either became allies or submitted to him because they were frightened by his fame. [*This presumably implies that Probus marched along the Danube River in a show-of-the-flag campaign and received the submission of the tribes north of it. The other possibility is that Probus crossed the Danube and then marched along it on enemy soil to make the case even more pressing, because in the above instances Vopiscus had clearly referred to fighting* north of Roman territory when he referred to a specific locale within the Roman territory. However, in the accompanying map on page 184 I have still reconstructed Probus's route south of the Danube, but readers should keep their minds open also to the other option.] Then he went into the east. [Vopiscus, *HA Prob.* 16.1–3, tr. by Bernard, 291–2 with emendations, changes and comments.]

The Germanic campaign of Probus was an unprecedented success for the times and it is not surprising that Vopiscus's account of Probus's life is basically a panegyric. The Romans had not conducted a raid so deep into Germania after the reigns of Caracalla and Maximinus Thrax. The only comparable invasion of enemy territory in the past was that by Caracalla; he defeated all of the tribes from the mouths of the Rhine and Elbe up to the mouth of the Danube, and Probus achieved almost the same with his two year campaign when he also defeated the Sarmatians and subdued the Getic tribes. Probus' campaign in the area can therefore be called a true triumph, and I would suggest that it was only after this triumph had been accomplished that he sent the letter (which is possibly fictitious, but undoubtedly based on some letter of Probus which he sent to the Senate to announce his great victories). According to Vopiscus, Probus killed about '400,000' Germanic invaders and drove all the rest back over Niger (Neckar) and Alba (Elbe). It is the figure of 400,000 and the Elbe which suggests that the announcement was only made after the second campaign had been accomplished. Probus would also have deserved the title of *Magnus* (the Great) added to his other titles. Obviously his successes owed everything to the sometimes frantic efforts of his two great predecessors, Gallienus and Aurelian, but this does not diminish his achievements.

12.3. The Campaigns of 278–9

The events and whereabouts of Probus after early 278 are controversial and there exists no consensus view among historians regarding this.[12] The view adopted here is that Probus followed up his campaigns in Germania, 'Illyricum' and 'Thrace' with a campaign in the east. And why did Probus not complete the conquest of the Germanic territories at this stage? There were three reasons for Probus to march to the east immediately. The first of these is that the Blemmyes had invaded Egypt and threatened the important taxes that were earmarked for Rome. The second is that Probus had received the news of the impending Persian invasion in a situation in which Narses as the Great King of Armenia, had managed to force Tiridates on the defensive (see above). The third is that the Isaurians had also revolted; but this problem was handled en route to Egypt and was of secondary importance in comparison with the other problems, the most important of which was naturally the state of war with Persia. Regardless, the Isaurians were to be the first enemy Probus faced in 278 while en route to Egypt.

12.3.1. The Isaurian War in 278
In 278 Probus faced a serious revolt in Isauria. There are three sources for this war: 1) Zosimus, who provides the most detailed account; 2) Vopiscus (*HA Prob.* 16.4–17.2); 3) An inscription from Cremna, which is dated securely to between the summer of 278 and the beginning of 279 so that the likeliest date is the summer or autumn of 278. The

siege has been thoroughly analyzed by Stephen Mitchell and his team and the following discussion is entirely based on this study.[13]

Mitchell provides a full text, translation and analysis of the inscription, which dates the war. On the basis of this inscription we know that the man in charge of the siege of Cremna was Terentius Marcianus, *vir perfectissimus, praeses provinciae Lyciae Pamphyliae* (governor of the province of Lycia and Pamphylia). The campaign also took place between summer 278 and the end of 278 before Probus became consul for the third time in the beginning of 279. This means that Probus had continued his march from Siscia immediately, through Thrace where he had received the surrender of the Getic tribes, after which he had marched against the Isaurian rebels.

The details in the *Historia Augusta* and Zosimus differ. According to the former, the rebel in Isauria was called Palfuerius and Probus defeated him in person and liberated Isauria and Pamphylia before continuing his march to the east. According to the latter the rebel was called Lydius and he was then besieged at Cremna by Probus' generals. Some historians consider Lydius and Palfuerius to be one and the same man while others consider these to be two different rebels who revolted in the same area against the Romans. The question is ultimately unsolvable but the details in the sources are not entirely irreconcilable because it is possible that Probus defeated Lydius/Palfuerius first and then left the conduct of the siege of the defeated enemy for Terentius Marcianus to finish when he marched forward against the more important enemies.

> Then he went into the east and while he was on his way, he captured and slew a robber of great power called Palfuerius, and thereby set free the whole of Isauria and restored obedience towards the laws of Rome among the tribes and cities. And when he had done that, he said that it was a country in which it was easier to drive the bandits from one place to another than extirpate them. Therefore, in order to get rid of them, he settled his veterans on private holdings in all those places which were difficult of access on condition that their sons should be sent to the army at the age of eighteen so that they would not became bandits. [Vopiscus, *HA Prob.* 16.4–6, tr. by Bernard with some major changes and emendations.]
>
> The wars upon the Rhine being thus terminated, a circumstance happened in Isauria which should not be omitted. There was an Isaurian named Lydius, who had been a robber from his youth, and with a gang like himself had committed depredations throughout Pamphylia and Lycia. This gang being attacked by the soldiers, Lydius, not being able to oppose the whole Roman army, retreated to a place in Lycia called Cremna, which stands on a precipice, and is secured on one side by large and deep ditches. Finding many who had fled there for refuge, and observing that the Romans were very intent on the siege, and that they bore the fatigue of it with great resolution, he pulled down the houses, and making the ground fit for tillage, sowed corn for the maintenance of those that were in the town. But the number being so great that they were in need of much more provisions, he turned out of the place all that were of no service, both male and female. The enemy, perceiving his design, forced them back again; on which Lydius threw them headlong into the trenches that surrounded the walls, where they died. Having done this, he constructed a mine, from the town beyond the enemies' camp, through which he sent persons to

steal cattle and other provisions. By these means he provided for the besieged for a considerable time, until the affair was revealed to the enemy by a woman. Lydius, however, still did not despond, but gradually retrenched his men in their wine, and gave them a smaller allowance of corn. But this not answering the end, he was at length driven to such straights, that he killed all that were in the town, except a few of his adherents, sufficient as he thought to defend it, and some women, whom he ordered to be in common among them all. [*On the basis of this it is very unlikely that Lydius and his men would have been locals because it is difficult to see how the men would have agreed to such an order if their families were in the city. This means that Lydius had been forced to seek a place of refuge in Cremna after he had been defeated in battle.*] But when he had resolved to persevere against all dangers, there happened at length this accident. There was with him in the town a man who was expert in making engines, and in using them with such dexterity, that when Lydius ordered him to shoot a dart at any of the enemy, he never missed his aim. It happened that Lydius had ordered him to hit a particular person, whom either accidently or on purpose he missed, for which he stripped and scourged him severely, and, moreover, threatened him with death. The man was so exasperated on account of the blows he had received, and so affrighted at the menaces, that he took an opportunity to steal out of the town; and falling in with some soldiers to whom he gave an account of his actions and sufferings, he showed them an aperture in the wall, through which Lydius inspected all that was done in their camp, and promised them to shoot him as he was looking through it in his usual manner. The commander of the expedition on this took the man in his favour; who, having planted his engine, and placed some men before him that he might not be discovered by the enemy, took aim at Lydius as he looked through the aperture, and with a dart shot him and gave him a mortal wound. He had no sooner received this wound, than he became still more strict with some of his own men. Having enjoined them upon oath never to surrender the place, he expired with much struggling. [*The defenders did not keep their oath, but surrendered.*] [Zosimus 1.69–70, English tr. 1814, p.33–4 with some changes and additions by author.]

Mitchell and his team have conducted thorough archaeological work on the city of Cremna and have analyzed the finds in detail. It is thanks to this research that we are now in a position to know that the Romans used a double siege wall with turrets/towers placed on prominent rocky outcrops. The idea was to isolate the defenders completely with these two walls. The east wall opposite the city was constructed stronger 1.8–2 metres wide and 2–2.5 metres high with several turrets/towers, while the rear facing wall was 180–280 metres west of the former and not more than one metre thick. This has led Mitchell and his team to speculate that the idea behind the building of the west wall was that two walls made the blockade more effective and that the building of it kept the men busy. In their opinion it was not strong enough to have been built as a protection for the rear. This is a possibility, but I would not preclude a purely defensive purpose either, because an even smaller obstacle would have sufficed to keep the Roman army secure from fast surprise attacks.

The archaeological finds suggest that the Romans used three different methods of attack against the city: 1) stones shot by ballistae/catapults/*onagri*; 2) an assault mound brought close to the city; 3) undermining of the wall below tower 5 of Cremna.

Archaeological finds prove that the Romans used the siege mound, and that it is also likely that they had used the city aqueduct both for the purpose of aiding the approach close to the wall and also to provide secure foundations for the mound. The finds have similarly demonstrated that the Romans concentrated their stone throwers, ballistae, slingers and archers against the spot in the wall opposite their siege mound, which is only natural. See the map drawn after Mitchell *et al*. The defenders built a more modest counter-mound opposite the Roman one, but it is not certain whether it would have been big enough to counter the Roman assault mound if the siege had not ended in surrender. Mitchell has noted that the Roman siege mound had reached to within 20 metres of the wall by the time the siege ended. On the basis of this he speculated that it was the imminent approach of this mound to the wall that precipitated the surrender rather than the death of Lydius. This is probably taking the evidence a bit too far because it is clear that the death of the leader was actually the cause of the surrender, as stated by Zosimus. Had Lydius survived, there is every reason to believe that the defenders would have fought to the bitter end – which was fast approaching. But it is clear that the city would have fallen when the siege mound reached the wall. It was only a matter of time.

Towers 5 and 6 of Cremna and the intervening curtain wall show heavy damage and emergency repairs. This section is right opposite the Roman siege mound and it is possible that the damage was caused by the siege engines brought on top of it, but it is also possible, as Mitchell *et al* note, that some of the damage was caused by artillery pieces placed just north of Roman turrets 5 and 6, which would have been used to protect the workers and engineers when the mound was being built.

Mitchell *et al* also suggest it is probable that the Romans attempted to undermine tower 5, because there are signs of such work, but the disturbance of the site during the 1960s makes it impossible to prove without a doubt. The location of this mine would have been conveniently protected by the Roman mound right next to it. It would have been easy to sap the ground underneath tower 5 when the workers and engineers were simultaneously protected by the sheds and also by the covering fire of the artillery pieces, archers, and slingers on the mound.

Mitchell and his team have found several 25 kg (1 talent) balls on the site, which was the standard size shot for the Roman stone throwers (both for the catapult/*ballistae* and *onagri*), but they have also found one 102 kg and one 135 kg stone ball on the site. Mitchell *et al* have speculated that these large shots may have been rolled downhill by the defenders, even if the sources also include information that the Romans used such stones in exceptional circumstances. My suggestion is that the latter is true in this case because the siege lasted quite a while and Romans would have wanted to resort to such extraordinary measures.[14]

The damage done to the wall of Cremna proves that the Roman stone throwers who shot 25 kg stones caused serious damage to towers 9 and 10 of Cremna and the section of the wall between them. This damage would have been caused by the *onagri* placed near turret 4, which was only 130 metres from the wall and therefore within the effective range of the stone throwers.

Siege of the City of Cremna in 278

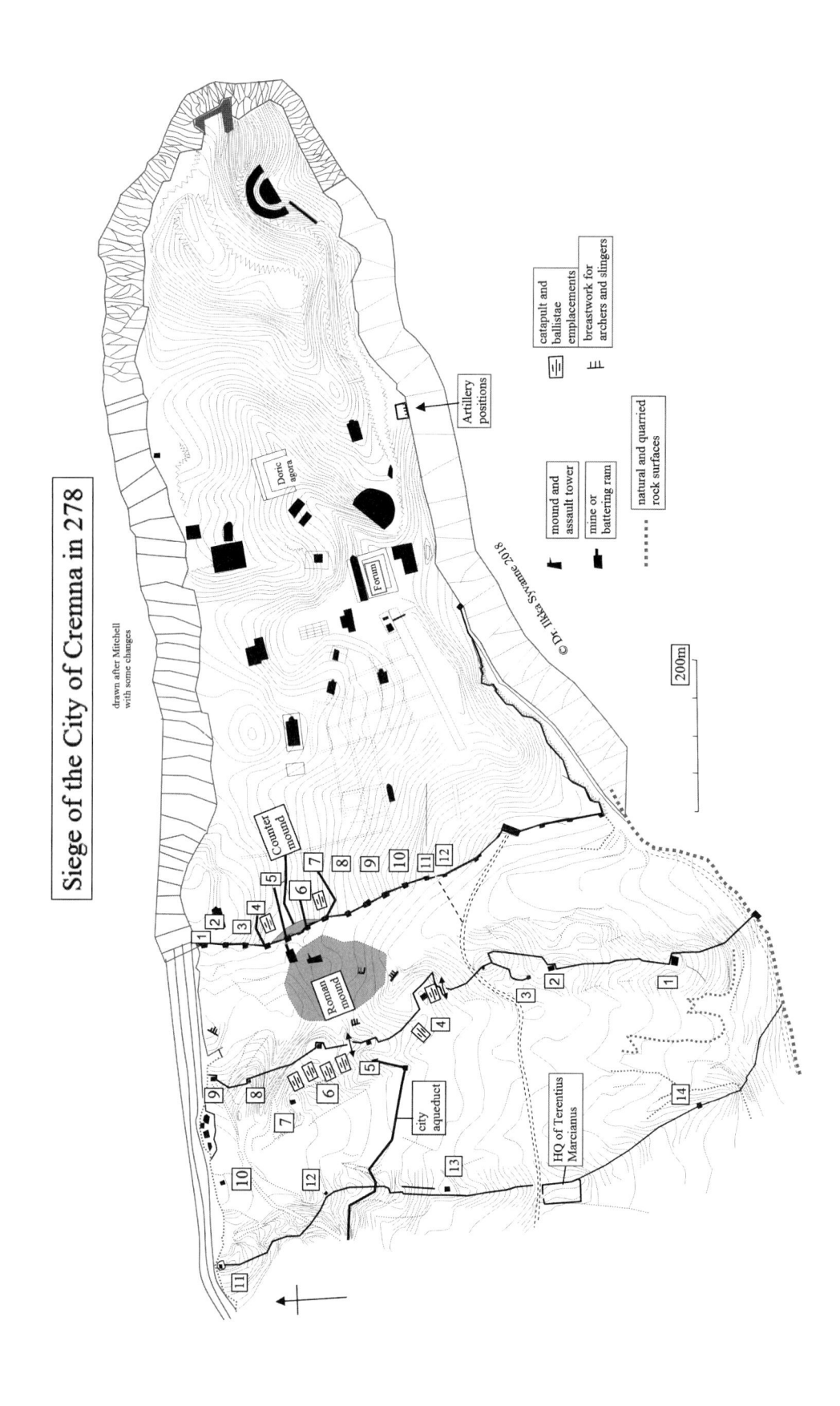

drawn after Mitchell with some changes

Doric agora

Forum

Artillery positions

Counter mound

Roman mound

city aqueduct

HQ of Terentius Marcianus

© Dr. Ilkka Syvänne 2018

200m

catapult and ballistae emplacements
breastwork for archers and slingers
mound and assault tower
mine or battering ram
natural and quarried rock surfaces

The attached map of Cremna and its siege works is entirely based on Mitchell's study.

Once the revolt was over it was time to ensure peace. Vopiscus states that Probus sought to do this by settling veterans with their families in the strategically most important places, such that their livelihoods were secured, and their sons were required to perform military service when they reached the age of 18. There is no definite evidence for this outside Vopiscus, but in my opinion it is likely that he has preserved for us one of the means Probus adopted for pacification of this dangerous region of Pamphylia, Pisidia, and Isauria, which the sources call collectively Isauria. There is no doubt that Probus was a well-read man and knew that the Romans had used such methods in the past.

This was standard policy adopted by Republican-era Romans and also by Augustus after conquering new territory, namely the creation of colonies of settlers to secure conquered territory. Mitchell *et al* note that Diocletian reorganized this territory and it was then that three new legions, *I, II, III Isaura*, appear in the sources. Mitchell presumes that these legions were recruited and deployed in this area for the purpose mentioned by the *Historia Augusta*.[15] This is a good example of the legions raised in the third century becoming visible only under the Tetrarchs.

12.3.2. The Wars against the Blemmyes and Persians in 278–9

As noted above, it is probable that the counter-offensive of Narses against Tiridates posed a threat to Roman territory. On the basis of the *Georgian Chronicles* (p.81),[16] we are fortunately in a position to reconstruct the strategy adopted by Probus in this situation. Once he had defeated the Isaurians and had left the siege of Cremna to Terentius Marcianus, he dispatched reinforcements to Tiridates while he himself continued his march to Egypt, if we are to believe Vopiscus, but there is a discrepancy between Vopiscus and Zosimus which may be very significant for the analysis. It is possible that Probus actually marched against the Persians and left the campaign against the Blemmyes to his generals.

According to the *Georgian Chronicles*, Narses and his subordinate Mirian, King of Georgia, had previously forced Tiridates on the defensive after they had received reinforcements from Persia. Now that Probus sent reinforcements to Tiridates, it was the turn of Narses to flee Armenia. Then the Persians received new reinforcements with the result that Tiridates was forced to retreat. According to the *Chronicles*, this situation persisted for years so that whenever Tiridates received reinforcements, the Persians were forced to retreat and vice versa.

Agathangelos leaves out the setbacks and merely states that once Tiridates had regained his kingdom he went to the province of Ayrarat where he wintered in the city of Valarshapat in the East of Armenia. After this, Tiridates spent his whole reign devastating the Persian kingdom and the land of Asorestan. He threw his enemies into disarray and exacted vengeance against the Persians. Agathangelos claims that Tiridates ravaged many regions of Syria, which presumably refers to the fighting against the rebel Saturninus (see later), that he destroyed many Persian armies and obtained a huge amount of booty. Agathangelos states that Tiridates became the commander of the Roman cavalry, which presumably means that Tiridates was simultaneously King of Armenia and Roman *magister equitum* just like we find many foreigners to be in the Roman army in the following century. It was then in this dual position that Tiridates defeated many armies of the 'Huns' (presumably meaning the Alans and other nomads) and conquered many regions of Persia.[17]

The problem with Agathangelos's account is that it leaves out all the setbacks and fails to give any timeline for the events. I would suggest that it is possible that Tiridates received the Roman title during the reign of Probus. He had definitely received this title by the reign of Carus because it was then that Tiridates is known to have accompanied the Roman army during its campaign against Persia (see later). Despite its uncertainties and the leaving out of setbacks, it is still clear that Agathangelos's account confirms what the *Georgian Chronicles* state, namely that Tiridates and the Romans were able to force the Persians out of Armenia in 278/9.

There remains the problem of what Probus did during this Armenian war. At the heart of the problem are the conflicting statements in Vopiscus and Zosimus regarding Probus's role in the Egyptian campaign and it is therefore worthwhile to quote both:

Ptolemais in Thebais, having revolted from the emperor, commenced a short war. Probus, by the good conduct of his generals, compelled both that place and its allies the Blemmyes to surrender. [*This account implies in no uncertain terms that the enemies were defeated by Probus' generals. However, it is possible that there is actually no contradiction in the sources if we assume that Probus achieved his success with his generals and not through them. Zosimus's account also implies that the Egyptians had revolted and had called in the Blemmyes to assist them. In such situations it was typical for the emperor to take charge of the campaign in person, but in this case I am inclined to accept the literal meaning of the language used by Zosimus.*] [Zosimus 1.71.1, English tr. 1814, p.34 with some changes and additions by author.]

He reduced unto peaceable subjection all the parts of Pamphylia, and the other provinces adjoining Isauria, and so followed his journey into the east. He conquered the Blemmyes of whom he sent some prisoners to Rome, who were a wonderful spectacle for the amazed people of Rome. The cities of Coptos and Ptolemais in Egypt he liberated from the barbarian yoke, and restored them to the Roman laws. He achieved such fame with this that the Parthians sent ambassadors to him and confessed their fear and sued for peace. [*This account implies that Probus was personally in command of the campaign, but, as said, Zosimus's account contradicts this.*] He received the envoys very arrogantly and then sent them back home with worse thoughts than they had before. He refused the presents, which they brought him from the king, and wrote thereupon a letter to Narseus: [*Narses, the Great King of Armenia. This has falsely been used as evidence of forgery by Vopiscus, because the king of kings at this time was Bahram II. This fails to take into account the division of powers in the Persian realm at this time. On the basis of all of the extant sources, it is clear that the defence of the western border of Persia was at this time in the hands of Narses, because Bahram II, the king of kings, was fighting in the east against Hormizd and his allies*] 'All that you have will be mine; I wonder therefore that you should think to gratify me with such a handful of things. Keep all things that you take such a pleasure for yourself for the time being. If we want them, we know how to get them.' This letter was a matter of great concern for Narseus, especially as it was accompanied by the news of the recovery of the cities of Coptos and Ptolemais from the Blemmyes, and the putting of those to the sword who before this had made themselves the terror of nations. After the peace with Persia was made, Probus returned to Thrace. [Vopiscus, *HA Prob.* 17.1–18.1, tr. by Bernard, 292–3 with emendations, changes and comments.]

To summarize, the above account provides us with conflicting information regarding the whereabouts of Probus. On the basis of Zosimus it is probable that the Egyptians of the cities of Coptos and Ptolemais had actually revolted against Roman rule and called in the Blemmyes as their allies rather than the other way round. The obvious reason for such hostility towards Roman rule would be the taxes imposed by Aurelian for Egypt, but this was just the latest incident in a long succession of grievances and revolts against the Romans beginning with the reign of Gallienus. It is clear that the Egyptians were at this time very dissatisfied with the Roman rule and this hostility did not end with the reign of Probus.

I would also suggest that it is likely that Probus did indeed leave the campaign against the Egyptian rebels and their Blemmye allies to his generals, as stated by Zosimus, because there was a much more pressing danger in the form of the war with Persia. However, if the revolt of Saturninus is dated to the years 278/9, then Probus would have taken care of this personally after which he would have sent his generals to Egypt while staying in Syria to protect it against the Persians. Vopiscus (*HA Prob.* 18.4–5, 19.1–20.1[18]) also clearly implies that the revolt of Saturninus took place before the revolts in Gaul, but in this study I have adopted the view that it is more likely that the revolt of Saturninus took place later in 280. The fact that Vopiscus fails to give the revolt of Saturninus any role in the events of the year 278/9 when Probus was said to have fought against the Isaurians and Blemmyes supports this conclusion. The revolt of Saturninus would surely have been of greater importance than either of these in a situation in which the Romans and Persians were at war; hence my conclusion.

It is probable that one of the commanders of the Egyptian campaign was Saturninus the Moor. I would also suggest that it was after the Egyptian campaign and peace with Persia that Probus nominated Saturninus as supreme commander of eastern forces probably with instructions not to visit Egypt because this area would have been left outside his jurisdiction just as before under Aurelian.[19] The idea behind such an order would of course be that Egypt was considered the personal domain of the emperor. Furthermore, it is clear that Probus understood well that any potential usurper in the east would require the riches of Egypt for him to be able to revolt. Therefore, it was in his interest to forbid his military commanders in the east from entering Egypt because this could have given them local connections in Egypt that they could have used in case of revolt. Vopiscus (*HA FSPB 7.1*) claims that Saturninus was a native of Gaul, but I agree with the majority view that Zosimus (1.66.1) is right to call him Saturninus the Moor. The reasons for my readiness to accept Zosimus's statement are: 1) Probus's other close friend was Victorinus the Moor (Zos. 1.66.2); 2) Probus had in all probability once been a commander of the Moorish bodyguard cavalry.[20] This means that Probus promoted his former comrades, subordinates and friends to higher positions. Saturninus the Moor, like Victorinus the Moor, were such men.

The title Probus gave Saturninus on this occasion has been a source of disagreement. Jordanes (*Roma* 293) calls Saturninus *magister militum*. Jerome/Hieronymus (Chron. 281/265th Olympiad) calls him *magister exercitus*. Zosimus (1.66.1) calls him *tēn Syrias archēn* implying some sort of governorship of Syria. Vopiscus (*HA FSPB* 7.2) claims that Aurelian appointed him *dux limitis Orientis*. It is possible that Aurelian did indeed nominate Saturninus to a command in the east, and that Probus then gave him the same post, possibly with a grander title. The titles referring to the position of *magister* are usually considered anachronistic, but as I have shown in the previous studies and in this study there is every reason to believe that the Romans had already started to use the title *magister* for their higher-ranking military commanders during the third century, well before its supposed reappearance under the Tetrarchs. The reason for such a grandiose title would of course have been that Probus wanted to reward his loyal friend well so that he would stay loyal to his emperor.

The main problem with the above reconstruction is that none of the sources, including the *Georgian Chronicles* and Agathangelos, states that Probus led a campaign against the Persians in person. The only evidence for it is circumstantial, namely that Probus was not apparently present at the siege of Cremna nor was he fighting against the Blemmyes, but he still received the title *Persicus maximus* and *Medicus maximus* both of which are attested in papyri in 279 and 280.[21] Furthermore, the *Georgian Chronicles* clearly state that the Romans sent reinforcements to Tiridates and that it was thanks to these that Tiridates forced the Persians away from Armenia. I would suggest that Probus led these forces in person and that the Georgian and Armenian sources, which are in the habit of hiding the Roman role in their victories, hide the fact that the man responsible for the great victory was none other than Probus. This leaves the problem of why this is not mentioned in the Roman sources. This is inexplicable, but it might be explained by the fact that none of them pays any attention to Armenian matters so none even mentions the sending of Tiridates with Roman forces to retake Armenia. It is inherently more likely that Probus received the titles *Persicus maximus* and *Medicus maximus* as a result of some military action rather than as a result of merely concluding a peace with Persia.

And why was Probus ready to conclude such a peace in a situation in which he had the upper hand, as is so well attested by the possibly fictitious letter included by Vopiscus? The reason for this would be the revolt of Proculus and Bonosus in Gaul, Spain and Britain, which must have taken place in about 279. However, if the revolt did not take place then, the other alternative is that Probus was planning to continue his unfinished campaign in Germania. Conversely, why were the Persians ready to conclude the peace with Probus in 279? The reasons for this are simple. Firstly, Bahram II was still fighting against his brother Hormizd in the east and this was more threatening to the very existence of the Sasanian realm than a war with Rome. Secondly, the Romans and Armenians had already defeated Narses and forced him to evacuate Armenia and now that the Persians had learnt of the crushing of enemies in Egypt, they had every reason to fear that Probus would conduct the next major invasion into Persian territory proper this time, strengthened with forces that had previously fought in Egypt. It is probable that the Persians were unaware of the revolts in Gaul (if these took place in 279) because they were ready to conclude peace now, but this of course is an argument from the silence of the sources.

It is not known how the two superpowers dealt with the Armenian question now. The only thing certain is that Tiridates retained at least the possession of the western portion of Armenia, because the Romans marched through it in 283 and it was then clearly in Armenian hands (see later). Yet, it is possible that Tiridates actually retained all of Armenia, because the Persians had been driven out, but it is equally possible that the peace with Persia was bought with concessions so that the Romans withdrew their forces from Armenia, and left it for Tiridates and Persians to fight it out to decide who would be the master of the Armenian Highlands. The titles Probus received and the possibly fictitious letter in the *Historia Augusta*, however, suggest that Probus had the upper hand in the negotiations, so it is likelier that the Persians conceded the whole of Armenia to the Armenians and that it was because of this that the Romans then withdrew their forces from there. Ultimately this question remains unsolvable unless some new evidence for the period resurfaces. From the Roman point of view the most important point was that the peace with Persia released forces for the campaigns against the usurpers in the west so that the next mission for the fireman Probus was to quell the fires raging in the west. Subsequent events prove that Probus had no intention of honouring the peace agreement with Persia. His only intention was to buy a temporary peace for the purpose of crushing the usurpers and then continue his campaign against the Persians at the first opportunity. One may imagine that the Persians had no intention of honouring their word either, but had just bought enough time to finish the civil war in the east. Thomas Artsruni (p.121) states that the war between the Armenians with Roman support and the Persians lasted until the reign of Probus, who finally concluded a peace with them. This statement suggests that the two empires were at peace from 279 until 283.

12.4. The Refugee Problem in the Balkans in about 279

En route to crush the usurpers in Gaul or to continue his unfinished campaign in Germania, Probus had to deal with the sudden refugee problem in the Balkans. According to Vopiscus, the Bastarnae and many other tribes including the Gepids, Greuthungi, and Vandals asked to be resettled on Roman soil. This suggests that there existed some sort of pressure behind these tribes in the *barbaricum* which made mass migration to Roman territory preferable. The Greuthungi however may have been the *foederati* of Probus which he had obtained in 277 and who now wanted similar terms as the rest of the tribes. I have suggested in an appendix to *Britain in the Age of Arthur* that it is possible that this pressure in the *barbaricum* was caused by Odin and his folk who were migrating from what is today Russia into what is today north Germany, Denmark and Sweden.[22] The Bastarnae remained loyal to Probus, but unfortunately for him the rest of the tribes and the Franks, who had either been settled in this area in 278, now all revolted when Probus was fighting against the rebels in Gaul. The settlement of these barbarians on Roman soil must have taken place in the summer to early autumn of 279.

> After the peace with Persia, Probus returned again into Thrace; where upon the lands of the Roman Empire he planted 100,000 Bastarnae, who all kept their faith with him; but others of the barbarian nations whom he transplanted in great numbers in like manner, that is the Gepids, the Greuthungi [*the largest of the Gothic*

confederacies], and the Vandals, all these broke their faith, and while Probus was fighting against the tyrants [*This means that the barbarians revolted when Probus was fighting against Proculus and Bonosus.*], they rose against him and overran the entire world on foot or in ships and damaged the reputation of Rome until Probus overcame and defeated them several times and only a few lucky ones returned home to enjoy their joy of managing to escape from the hands of Probus. [*This means that after Probus had crushed the rebels in Gaul he did not continue operations against the remaining rebels in Britain but rather marched against the barbarians in the Balkans.*] And these were the exploits of Probus among the barbarians. [Vopiscus, HA Prob. 18.1–3, with emendations, changes and comments.]

He likewise left in Thrace the Bastarnae, a Scythian people, who submitted to him, giving them land to inhabit there; on which account they observed the Roman laws and customs. But the Franks having applied to the emperor [*This suggests that the Franks had until then served as foederati and now sought the same terms as had been granted to the Bastarnae*], and having a country given to them, a part of them afterwards revolted, and having collected a great number of ships, disturbed all Greece; from whence they proceeded into Sicily, to Syracuse, which they attacked, and killed many people there. At length they arrived in Africa, whence though they were repulsed by a body of men from Carthage, yet they returned home without any great loss. [Zosimus 1.71.1–2, English tr. 1814, p.34–5 with some changes and additions by author.]

The coins such as shown above were often used when the loyalty of the soldiers was suspect. It was then that the emperors usually felt it was necessary to advertise the loyalty of the armies. (*Source: Beger, 1696*)

In sum, it is probable that when Probus was en route to Gaul, he faced a sudden refugee crisis in the Balkans, which he solved by settling the refugees on Roman soil. The Bastarnae remained loyal, but the rest did not (see pp.207–208). Zosimus's text proves that the Franks had until then served as *foederati* and that they demanded and got the same terms as the Bastarnae. It is also probable that the Greuthungi who were settled in the Balkans now were actually the Gothic *foederati* obtained in 277, and it would not be too far fetched to think that even the Vandals would have served in the same capacity until then and that all of these groups now demanded the same terms as had been given to the Bastarnae, and which were duly granted. The case is less certain for the Gepids, but it is similarly plausible to think that Probus could have had Gepids among his army as a result of the treaties conducted in 278. And if the Franks, Greuthungi, Vandals and Gepids were *foederati*, why was Probus now ready to settle them in the Balkans when there was an urgent need for soldiers for the war against the usurpers in Gaul or for the continuation of the war against the tribes of Germania? My suggestion is that Probus settled all of these nations in the Balkans as *laeti* (enemies who had been defeated, but who were given land in return for military service) so that he was able to transfer the local higher quality regular forces into his army. It is also clear that if the Goths, Vandals and Gepids had been intended for use against the Persians, they were no longer needed, and it would not have been wise to use the Franks against their fellow tribesmen present either in the usurpers' army (if they had already rebelled) or against the native armies across the Rhine if Probus intended to conquer the whole of Germania up to the Elbe. Whatever the plans of Probus were at this stage, it would seem probable that it was now that Saturninus the Moor revolted and put a stop to all of these. The other alternative is that Saturninus revolted only later in about 281 so that Probus was forced to march there in that same year. However, I have here adopted the former alternative as more likely even if the latter cannot be ruled out.

12.5. The Revolt of Saturninus the Moor in about 279–80

We do not possess any definitely secure information of when Saturninus revolted and how Probus dealt with this. In this study I have adopted the view that it took place approximately in 279–80.[23] According to Zonaras (12.29), Probus trusted his friend Saturninus so blindly that when the news of the revolt was brought to him he disbelieved it and punished the messenger. According to Vopiscus (HA FSPB 71.ff.), Saturninus was declared an emperor when he visited Egypt after which he returned to 'Palestine' and presumably went from there to Syria where the other sources claim that he was

Left: A coin of Saturninus drawn by Strada (1555) in the collection at Mantua. Provenance of the coin is uncertain.

Right: A coin of Probus by Cohen

either building a New Antioch or repairing the old one (e.g. Syncellus AM 5770; Jordanes *Rom.* 293). In my opinion the visit to Egypt was part of a planned usurpation and that Saturninus was not made an emperor against his own wishes as claimed by Vopiscus. It is clear that Saturninus visited an area which was not under his own jurisdiction to secure Egypt and its resources behind his revolt, and that his plan was to withhold grain and other shipments to cause trouble for Probus in Rome.

It is usually assumed that Vopiscus and Zosimus offer conflicting evidence for the course of the war against Saturninus, but on closer look there is actually no definite reason to think so, as the following analysis will show, even if the evidence remains open to many interpretations:

> His other troubles were such as he suffered from the attempts of particular ambitious subjects who were for setting themselves as emperors, one of whom was Saturninus, who usurped the Empire in the east, and who engaged Probus in several battles till Probus by his known gallantry overcame him [*This implies that Probus had improved his physical shape after 277 so that he was able to fight in battles again. The big belly was apparently not an obstacle for this. Rather it protected his vital organs from killing blows*], and with the same conquest established such a firm peace in the east that not a mouse dared to stir more there. [Vopiscus, *HA Prob* 18.4, tr. by Bernard with emendations, changes and comments.]

> This Saturninus was set up in the time of Probus and killed against his wishes. For Probus wrote several kind letters to him and promised a pardon, but the soldiers who were about him would not believe it. So the party of Probus, which was sent against him, besieged him in a castle/fortification [*castrum*] and killed him sadly even though Probus did not desire it. [*In Zosimus's version Saturninus was killed by his own soldiers so there is a discrepancy here.*] [Vopiscus HA *FSPB* 11.2–3, tr. by Bernards with emendations, changes and comments.]

> While Probus was thus employed, Saturninus, a Moor, the most familiar friend of the emperor, and for that reason entrusted with the government of Syria, threw off his allegiance, and rebelled against the emperor. When Probus learnt of this, he resolved to punish him [*The verb used, metrechomai, is problematic because it can be used to mean to attack/go after, or to avenge/punish. The 1814 version translates the clause 'to frustrate his designs' while Ridley translates it as to punish and Paschoud translates it that Probus planned to confront that attack. I have adopted in this study the translation of Ridley mainly because it reconciles the two sources with each other*], but was anticipated by the soldiers in the east, who destroyed Saturninus and all his associates. [Zosimus 1.66.1, English tr. 1814, p.32 with one change and comment by author.]

At the root of the problem therefore is how one translates one verb in Zosimus. If it is translated that Probus intended to attack Saturninus, but Saturninus was killed by his own soldiers before this, it is in conflict with the text of Vopiscus which refers to fighting before the killing. However, if it is translated that Probus intended to punish

Saturninus, but Saturninus' own soldiers killed him before this, it does not conclusively preclude the existence of fighting before this took place, even if it still leaves that option also open. In other words, it is also possible to interpret even the latter translation in two different ways. In this study I have adopted the translation which refers to the intended punishment because it reconciles all of the sources with each other, most importantly because Vopiscus is not the only ancient source which refers to the fighting between Probus and Saturninus before the killing of Saturninus. The *Epitome* (37) and Jordanes (*Rom.* 293) also state that Probus defeated Saturninus. Jordanes adds the detail that Saturninus was killed at Apamea. Orosius (7.24) states that Probus fought two bloody civil wars (one against Saturninus and another against the Gallic usurpers), and that Saturninus was defeated and captured. The *Epitome*, Jordanes and Orosius therefore confirm the account of Vopiscus with the implication that we should interpret the text of Zosimus in the manner I have done here. The only discrepancy that remains relates to the identity of the killers of Saturninus. One may assume that Zosimus has actually used such a source that has purposefully hidden the assassination of the usurper by Probus's own men, but obviously one cannot entirely preclude the possibility that Saturninus' own men would have attempted to save themselves with their desperate action when it became apparent that their cause was hopeless.

My reconstruction of the course of the revolt is therefore as follows. It is probable that Saturninus usurped power when Probus was in the Balkans in 279, or at the latest in early 280, so that he was immediately forced to return to Asia Minor and march against the usurper. Probus and Saturninus then fought several battles in which the forces of Saturninus were bested in bloody battles. According to Vopiscus, the bravery of Probus was one of the reasons for his successes. It is probable that the above-mentioned battles of Tiridates in Syria, mentioned by Agathangelos, took place now so that Tiridates served as Roman *magister equitum* for Probus.

Probus is claimed to have been unwilling to have his old friend Saturninus killed despite his betrayal, and it was because of this he offered a pardon. If Proculus and Bonosus had revolted by then in Gaul, as is quite probable, the main purpose of offering terms would have been to end the war as fast as possible. However, it is quite probable that this was meant only as a ruse from the start so that Probus would not have to fight against the usurper. Vopiscus's text at least makes it clear that Saturninus' men did not believe Probus's promises. It was thanks to this that Probus was forced to fight a series of bloody battles and then send a detachment of soldiers to pursue Saturninus, which then managed to force him to seek shelter from the city of Apamea, where he was then killed by the soldiers sent by Probus or by his own men. However, if Vopiscus is correct in his statement that Probus had not wanted to kill his old friend then it is possible that Probus was actually angry over the killing and disobedience and that this played a role later when Probus disciplined his men with menial labour which led to his own demise. However, I would rather suggest that, in light of the fact that Aurelius Victor (37.2–3) likened Probus to the treacherous Hannibal, that Probus had planned to have his disloyal friend killed from the start and had just attempted and failed to achieve this through a stratagem.

The war against Saturninus was probably over by about April-May 280 so that Probus was able to march against the usurpers Proculus and Bonosus in Gaul, which he would have reached in about September-October. The fighting against Saturninus had undoubtedly caused casualties so that he was forced to leave some of his men behind.

12.6. The Revolts in Gaul, Spain and Britain crushed in about 280–1

We do not know when Probus reached Italy and Gaul, but one may assume that he invaded the south of Gaul in about September-October 280. He began his campaign by securing the south just as he had done before in 277. This made logistical sense because it was possible to ship supplies along the Rhône from the Mediterranean for the army. The only description of the resulting fighting comes from the pen of Vopiscus. It is thanks to him that we know the reasons for the sudden revolts. The commanders who revolted shared one thing in common which was that both suffered from personal weaknesses which united them in vice in a situation in which both knew Probus's reputation for being a disciplinarian in the mould of Aurelian so both feared punishment if Probus learnt of their failures.

The other pretenders were Proculus and Bonosus at the city of Colonia in Gaul [*Cologne*] and they claimed for themselves all of Britain, Spain, and Further Gallia [*The fact that Britain joined this revolt was to cause Probus trouble when the barbarian foederati revolted in the Balkans. This text also suggests that Proculus and Bonosus cooperated and revolted together, with the implication that both must have exchanged messages before they declared themselves emperors. Eutropius's text 9.17 and the Epitome 37 suggests the same because these stated that Proculus and Bonosus usurped power together at Agrippina*], but these were defeated with barbarian help... All the Germans refused to assist Proculus when he asked for their help, preferring to serve under Probus rather than under Bonosus and Proculus. After this, as a reward Probus permitted to all Gallia, Spain, and Pannonia the right of planting vines and the making of wines. He set his own soldiers upon digging the Mountain Almus, which is by the city of Sirmium in Illyricum [*in the province of Lower Pannonia*], and he planted it himself with chosen vines. ...

Proculus was a native of Albingauni in the Maritime Alps. He was a nobleman, but his ancestors had been great robbers so he was very rich in cattle and slaves and all things that could be got by such means. It is said that at the time he took upon him the Empire he armed 2,000 of his own slaves. He had a masculine wife called Samso as wife and she drove him into the madness of usurping power. Her name was originally Vituriga. They had a son called Herennianus... It cannot be denied but that Proculus was an extraordinary and brave man although also accustomed to a life of robbery and he always passed his life under arms. He had commanded many legions as tribune in the course of which he had done actions of great valour. ... 'From Proculus to Maecianus his kinsman, Greetings, I have taken captive 100 virgins from Sarmatia, ten of which I lay in one night, and all of them I made women in the course of fifteen days.' As is obvious he boasted about a foolish and very licentious deed reckoning it a fine thing that was otherwise a crime. However, even with his military honours he still lived a life of depravity and lustfulness. He always acquitted himself with great courage so that the people of Lugdunum, who appeared to have been harshly treated by Aurelian and who feared Probus, solicited him to declare himself emperor. Onesimus tells us... that he was made an emperor as a result of a game of 'Brigands' in a banquet [*According to Magie/HA pp.408–9, the game of Brigands resembled chess but with thirty pieces on each side*]. ...One of the company who wanted to show himself witty saluted him as emperor... Regardless, Proculus showed himself beneficial for the Gauls because he defeated with glory the Alamanni, who were at that time still called Germans, even if it was in the manner of a brigand that he fought always. [*This suggests that Proculus disliked open battles and preferred to use ambushes and surprise attacks.*] Regardless, Probus forced him to flee to distant lands so that he sought aid from the Franks whom he pretended to be his ancestors, but Probus defeated and slew him because the Franks betrayed him as was their custom to do with laughter. ...

Bonosus was a Spaniard by origin but descended from a Briton father and Gallic mother. His father was a rhetorician..., or as I have found from others, grammarian [*paedagogi litterarii*]... He served first among the front ranks [*inter ordinaries: this means he was either a decanus or a centurion, the latter being more likely*], and then in the cavalry. Next he commanded the *ordinarii* [*duxit ordines, meaning either that he rose to the position of centurion or that he became the highest ranking centurion, namely primus pilus, the latter being more likely*], after which he became tribune [*The tribunes could be commanders of legions or even higher ranking commanders when they were members of the bodyguards. I would suggest that the tribuneship in question meant a rise to the command of some unit of bodyguards.*] and then *dux limitis Raetici* [*general in charge of the Raetian Limes/Raetian Frontier.*]. No man ever drank like Bonosus. The emperor Aurelian said often of him that 'He was born to not to live, but to drink', but he still held him in high honour because of his ability in war. ... It happened at one time that the Germans had burnt the Roman galleys on the Rhine. He feared that he might be punished for this neglect and usurped power. He held this position longer than he deserved before he was finally defeated by Probus after a long and hard fight, after which he hanged himself. [*This suggests that Bonosus and Proculus possessed some loyal soldiers who put up a stiff fight despite the fact that the Franks betrayed them with a laughter. The decisive battle or battles took place close to Cologne, on the basis of Aurelius Victor 37.3; Epitome 37; Eutropius 9.17; Orosius 7.24.*]... He left two sons and a wife. The sons Probus forgave. The wife he obliged by giving her a pension for life. For besides that she was a woman of wit and merit, ... she was a princess of royal Gothic blood, and one whom the emperor Aurelian had purposefully married to Bonosus that through her and him he might the better penetrate into all the affairs of the Goths... 'From the emperor Aurelian to Gallio Avitus, greetings. I wrote to you previously about the Gothic noblewoman at Perinthus... I wish that Hunila be married to Bonosus.' [*This letter may once again be fictitious, but I would still suggest that it contains the truth so that it was really Aurelian who married the Gothic princess to Bonosus, as claimed by Vopiscus, for the intelligence-gathering reasons mentioned.*] [Vopiscus HA Prob. 18.5–8, FSPB 12.1–15.10, tr. by Bernard with emendations, changes and comments.]

He likewise suppressed an insurrection in Britain, by means of Victorinus, a Moor, who had persuaded him to confer the government of Britain upon the leader of the insurgents. Having sent for Victorinus, and chosen him for his consul, he sent him

204   Aurelian and Probus

Coin of Bonosus according to Cohen.

Drawings of coins by Strada (1555) in a collection located at Mantua.

Left: Coin of Proculus.
Right: Coin of Bonosus

Provenance of the coins is uncertain at best.

to appease the disturbance; who, going presently to Britain, took off the traitor by a stratagem. [Zosimus 1.66.2, English tr. 1814, p.32 with some changes and additions by author.]

The above accounts suggest strongly that the two usurpers Proculus and Bonosus cooperated with each other and that their usurpation was a premeditated move by both men. The reference to the dissatisfaction of the inhabitants of Lugdunum (Lyon) as a result of their punishment by Aurelian is symptomatic of the trend in Gaul. The Gauls had first created their own Gallic Empire under Postumus and were still dissatisfied with the central government, and were also to be so in the near future when the so-called Bacaudae emerged in Gaul under the Tetrarchs. It is possible or even likely that Proculus and his ancestors had been the precursors of these bandits so that they had operated on both sides of the law simultaneously. The likely reason for Proculus's usurpation was that as a famous robber he feared the punishment of these actions. The likely reason for the usurpation of Bonosus was his neglect of duty as a result of which his fleet (presumably the fleet of the Rhine) had been destroyed by barbarians. The torching of the Roman fleet and the defeat of the Alamanni by Proculus suggest that Gaul did not enjoy a state of peace even after the campaigns of Probus in 277–8. In the case of Proculus's action against the Alamanni there is another possibility – because it took place only after the usurpation – which is that these had been incited to invade Gaul by Probus while he was still in the east or in the Balkans. Both men had personal weaknesses: Proculus was a robber and rapist while Bonosus was a drunkard, which undoubtedly endeared the men to each other as so often happens with men of such character. These persons always consider upright men like Aurelian or Probus as posing a potential danger to their very existence.

Probus's campaign clearly progressed so that he approached Lugdunum from the south along the Rhône so that his army was supplied by the fleet. When Probus reached the vicinity of Lugdunum, he inflicted a serious defeat on Proculus who duly fled north to join his comrade-in-arms Bonosus. Bonosus and Proculus both called the Franks to their assistance, but it is uncertain whether the Frankish betrayal of the usurpers took the form of denying them help or of betraying them in the middle of a battle that took place near Cologne. The battle itself appears to have been hard-fought – although it is possible that there were actually a series of battles because Orosius (7.24) specifically refers to a series of great battles. This could mean that the single battle near Cologne lasted for several days or that the decisive battle in front of it was preceded by a series of battles which forced the usurpers to seek shelter from Cologne while vainly asking the Franks to assist them. The other possibility is that the series of battles actually means only two battles, the first one in which Proculus was defeated by Probus and the second in which Probus defeated both usurpers. It is impossible to know for certain which alternative would be correct. All we know is that there were at least two battles and that the decisive battle took place near Cologne.

Unfortunately for Probus the battle near Cologne did not end the war, because Zosimus (1.66.2) and Zonaras (2.29) both refer to the revolt of the governor of Britain. According to both, Probus blamed his friend Victorinus the Moor for this because he had recommended him for the post of governor of Britain. It is uncertain whether this man was a new separate usurper as usually thought, who usurped power soon after Proculus and Bonosus or after their defeat, or whether this was Proculus who is not listed among the killed. We know from Vopiscus that the usurpers were able to flee because Bonosus was able to hang himself after the battle. This means that Proculus could have fled to Britain. Britain was one of the provinces which joined the rebels Proculus and Bonosus when they declared themselves emperors, and Britain was still in revolt after they had been defeated at Cologne. On the basis of the statements of Zosimus and Zonaras, I would suggest that the governor of Britain was not Proculus, but a supporter of him and Bonosus, and that he declared himself emperor after his friends had been defeated. Could this man be the otherwise elusive Silbannacus?[24] There was no chance that this problem could have been solved fast by purely military means because the Franks had burned the Rhine Fleet which meant that Probus would have been forced to build a new fleet or transfer it from the Mediterranean to be able to ship his men across the Channel. In short, the crushing of Britain would have taken a major effort and Probus did not have the time for that because the barbarian *laeti* in the Balkans had revolted. It is also possible that the revolt of Saturninus the Moor took place at this time, making it all the more urgent for Probus to march east.

In these circumstances Probus accepted Victorinus the Moor's advice that he should be sent to Britain to correct his mistake. Therefore Victorinus pretended to be a fugitive in fear for his life, and fled to Britain where his story was believed by all thanks to the reputation of Probus. Consequently, Victorinus was able to assassinate the usurper during the night and return the island to the fold of the Roman Empire. One wonders whether the barbarian settlers previously sent to the island by Probus had a role in this. This had been a very bold special operation to kill a usurper. When Victorinus then returned on board ship Probus was there to greet him. Victorinus had thrown his military belt into the sea and when he approached Probus beltless this led Probus to make the hasty conclusion that Victorinus had failed, so he flew into a rage. Victorinus, however, calmed his friend soon enough with his words. Victorinus asked to be relieved of his duties and asked his friend to allow him to retire. Probus duly gave his friend Victorinus gifts and granted his wish of being allowed to retire. Victorinus clearly had a conscience. The killing of a friend had not been an easy task.[25]

This time Probus sought to secure the peace through enlightened economic policies. He allowed the Gauls and Spaniards to grow vines and produce wine so that they could earn an income. The readier availability of cheap wine would also have led to greater consumption of wine in general which would have made the people happier. The export of this wine abroad would also bring economic benefits for the Empire. The policy of promoting the production of wine and its ready availability for the population followed up the policies adopted previously by Aurelian and can be seen as a continuation of them.

It is probable that the war in Gaul with its sideshow in Britain lasted from about September/October 280 until about January/February 281, but it could have taken until about April/May 281 for the situation to be solved. However, if Probus crushed Saturninus only later in 281, then the events described here took place one year before.

12.7. The Crushing of the Revolts in the Balkans in about 281–2

After this, Probus marched back to the Balkans against the *foederati/laeti* who had revolted (see pp.197–9). If Probus began his journey back to the Balkans in about February 281, he would have reached the theatre of operations by about the beginning of June, or at the latest in September if the crushing of the revolts in the west took longer. It is actually very likely that Probus conducted a winter campaign, because most of his soldiers originated from the Balkans and it would have been relatively easy for him to convince them to fight for their families. In fact, it is possible that it was because of this that Probus was forced to prioritize the war in the Balkans, as he had done in 278, even when the wars in the west had been left unfinished.

On the basis of Vopiscus and Zosimus, it is clear that Probus defeated the enemies on land in several battles so that the remnants of these forces were more than happy to flee back to their territories north of the Danube. The war against the barbarians would probably have lasted from about June 281 until about September/October 281, or from about September 281 until about January/February 282. The former is more likely on the basis of the coins and medallions that date Probus's triumph at Rome.

Probus enlarged the same project of promoting the growing of wine to cover also the Balkans for the same reasons as he did this in Gaul and Spain. This policy undoubtedly entailed the export of wine to the barbarians, which was good for the economy of the Empire and its border regions. The Franks, however, conducted an epic campaign in the Mediterranean and were able to reach their compatriots north of the mouth of the Rhine. What followed after this depends on how one interprets the evidence regarding the revolt of Saturninus and is therefore open to many views. It is therefore possible that it was only now that Probus advanced against Saturninus so that the campaign in the Balkans would have taken place in 281 and the war against Saturninus in 281–2. However, on the basis of the coins and medallions which date the triumph of Probus, this is less likely than the version I have given above.

12.8. The Triumph at Rome in about 281–2

The only description of the Triumph which Probus had in Rome in about 281/2 comes from the pen of Vopiscus:

> Coming to Rome, he entertained the people there with public games and pastimes in a manner which was most magnificent. Besides he gave them largesses. He celebrated a triumph for his conquest of the Blemmyes and the Germans [*It was not usually considered proper to celebrate a triumph against any other but foreign foes*] which had throngs of men [*drungi/droungoi*] from all nations with up to fifty men [*note that in this case the drungus/droungos means a group of up to fifty men with the implication that in irregular combat order the men could have been similarly deployed into small groups of up to 60 men; see Appendix 2*] in each marched before in triumphal procession… In the circus wild-beast hunt… the whole circus was turned into a forest… Next appeared three hundred couple of gladiators amongst which were several of the Blemmyes which had been led in triumph, several Germans and Sarmatians and also some Isaurian bandits. [Vopiscus, *HA Prob.* 19.1–8, tr. by Bernard, 295–6 with emendations, changes and comments.]

The date of the triumph can be counted from the medallions and coins dated to the years 281 and 282. The two medallions from 281 and 282 have obverse legend *Gloria orbis* and the reverse legend *invictus Probus p. f. aug*. Other coins which date from the triumphal celebrations have the legends *pacator orbis, ubique pax* and *victorioso semper*. On the basis of the coins dated *tr. p.V cos. IIII* and *tr. o. VI cos V*, it has been suggested that the triumphal celebrations began after July 281 and ended before July 282. The existence of large numbers of medallions supports the claims of Vopiscus that Probus distributed largesse during his Triumph.[26]

An incident took place in Rome while Probus was there to celebrate his triumph. It is described as follows by Zosimus:

> This circumstance likewise happened during the reign of Probus. Eighty gladiators conspiring together, and having killed their keepers, ran out into the city, and plundered all in their way, many other persons, as is usual in such cases, without doubt mixing with them. But the emperor sent a party and suppressed them. When Probus, who was a brave and just prince, had done this… [Zosimus 1.72.2, English tr. 1814, p.35.]

208 Aurelian and Probus

Coin depicting the triumph of Probus. (source: Cohen)

Coins of Probus advertising his victories and manly qualities and the benefits that this brings for the Romans. (sources: Beger 1696 and Cohen)

This incident in question was evidently of little importance, but it shows nicely how the emperor could be forced to act as police chief when residing in Rome. The duties of the emperor were manifold.

12.9. The Assassination of Probus in August-September 282

In 282 Probus marched from Rome to the Balkans to begin the final preparations for war against the Persians which had been on the books ever since 275. The situation remained opportune because the Persians were still engaged in civil war.

> After these things, as Probus was preparing for a war with Persia and was on the march through Illyricum, the soldiers treacherously plotted together and killed him. The reasons for the murder were these. First because he never let them be

idle because he employed them in many works and said that soldiers ought not to eat bread for nothing. He added to this the remark that he hoped in a short time he would make it so that the state should have no need of soldiers. With this he intended to say that … the Romans shall reign universally and possess everything in safety… There shall be no more wars… the Roman laws and their magistrates shall prevail… When he came to Sirmium, desiring to enrich and enlarge his native place, he set several thousand of his soldiers to drain the marsh which was to be done by constructing a great canal with outlets flowing into the Save, and so the ground would become of use to the people of Sirmium. [*According to Aurelius Victor 37, the winter rains had damaged the reservoirs and canal and it was because of this that Probus put his soldiers to work. According to Eutropius 9.17, Probus planted vineyards on Mount Alma near Sirmium and on Mount Aureus in Moesia Superior and was then killed in the Iron Tower at Sirmium. This implies that Probus also ordered other works to be done in the Balkans besides the building of the canal just before he was killed.*] The fatigue of this piece of work enraged the soldiers so that they assaulted him, and as he fled for safety into an iron tower, which he had built there to serve as a watch tower, they killed him in the fifth year of his reign. However, afterwards, the army built for him a mighty tomb on a large mound whereon was carved an inscription: 'Here lies the emperor Probus, who was a man of probity, and conqueror of all barbarian nations, and the conqueror of pretenders too.' … he finished so many wars in so many parts of the world unaided that it is a wonderful thing… He did many valiant deeds with his own hand. [*This implies that Probus continued to fight duels as emperor and that he also took part in combat to encourage his men.*] He trained many of the famous *duces*: Carus, Diocletian, Constantius, Asclepiodotus, Hannibalianus, Leonides Cecropius, Pisonianus, Herennianus, Gaudiosus, Ursinianus and all the others whom our fathers have admired. [Vopiscus, *HA Prob.* 20.1–22.3, tr. by Bernard 296ff. with emendations, changes and comments.]

When Probus was still at Sirmium, Carus revolted between 29 August and 13 September 282. The exact reason for the usurpation is unclear. A fragment of Peter the Patrician has preserved for us the reason that Carus gave to the soldiers. On the occasion of Carus' proclamation, he stated that he had come to the throne to correct the ills caused by the Persians, but this is obviously only the official version, meant to gain the support of the soldiers.[27] The real reason would have been Carus' personal ambition and the situation was now opportune. Instead of leading the army against Persia, Probus had forced the soldiers to perform civilian duties, on top of which he had insulted them with statements that there would be no need for soldiers in the future – a statement which can be found in Vopiscus and Aurelius Victor (37.3) and Eutropius (9.17) and is therefore likely to be true. It is probable that Probus's intention was not to insult the soldiers but to encourage them. Subsequent events make it clear that Carus knew how to please the rank-and-file and how to act as their comrade-in-arms, and this was certainly one of those instances. Carus clearly contrasted himself with the disciplinarian Probus who put the men to perform menial work – work fit for slaves and not for soldiers. The following events also prove that Carus' words were not exaggerated – he was an able commander who exacted revenge against the Persians. This gives some credence to the expected impact of the above statement. The soldiers apparently knew that Carus was an able commander and their comrade-in-arms who could be expected to lead them to success against the Persians.

The principal reasons for the success of the usurpation were clearly Probus's poorly timed actions and careless words. They made him hated among the rank-and-file and they began to prefer Carus over Probus. Carus, despite being ten years older than Probus, was still in tip top physical shape. However, the fact that Vopiscus credits Probus with personal bravery for this period of his rule proves that he was also strong. Probus continued to be a man who put his life on the line for his soldiers. Regardless, it is still possible to think that his obese appearance might have angered the soldiers in a situation in which Probus demanded physical labour from them. In any case, the likeliest reason for the murder of Probus is simply his ill-timed and thoughtless disciplining of soldiers with menial work which was made worse by his thoughtless words in a situation in which they expected to be led against the Persians. It is strange that he forced his men to do this in a situation in which the Persians were fighting a civil war and the time was ripe for an invasion. There are three possible ways to explain his behaviour. It is possible that the disobedience of the soldiers previously during the last stages of Saturninus' revolt had angered Probus so that when the area of Balkans was in need of large scale improvements he decided to put the soldiers to work as a form of disciplining them, but I would still suggest that Probus did not want to punish the soldiers for the murder of Saturninus because it had been his plan all along even if the sources whitewash him from all the guilt. The second alternative is that Probus felt it necessary to use the soldiers in this manner for the benefit of the civilians, which indeed seems likely. The third of the possible reasons would have been to mislead the Persians who were probably expecting the Roman invasion. Postponing the invasion would have caused the Persians to relax. Furthermore, it is possible that Probus thought that the best time to invade Persia was the winter season when his European soldiers would not need to be acclimatized and when the Romans would also be able to avoid the season when mosquitoes and other nasty insects bothered the men the most. I would suggest that both the second and third of the alternatives played a role in Probus' planning. He intended to delay the invasion until winter and ordered the men to perform menial work for the benefit of the civilians so that they would not grow lazy in the meantime. This, however, was a grave mistake because the soldiers expected to be led against the Persians.

A fragment of Peter the Patrician (Banchich frg. 197) has preserved for us important details of the beginning of Carus' revolt and Probus' reaction to it. According to this text, when Probus heard of the plans of Carus to revolt, he assembled a council to discuss what to do with him. The only one who spoke was *chiliarchos* (probably *tribunus militaris*) Martinianus who stated that Probus' hesitation was bringing ruin and that he should act immediately and declare war against the tyrant. On the basis of an extant inscription, this Latinius Martinianus was *vir egregious* and *procurator Augusti*.[28] The fragment suggests that the principal reason for the success of Carus was Probus' initial hesitation of what to do. It was this that sealed his fate. In this case, he clearly had good intelligence of what was afoot thanks to an efficient intelligence/security apparatus, but failed to act. When Probus finally decided to do something it was too late. It is clear that Probus's position at the time of Carus' usurpation was very weak because he had managed to enrage his soldiers with his thoughtless words. Although, I would suggest that it is quite probable that Probus's statement had been taken out of context, if he ever even said such things. I would suggest it is quite possible that Carus skillfully twisted Probus' originally innocent public statement that the soldiers would not be needed in the future into something that angered them, and the henchmen of Carus then 'stirred the pot' to prepare the ground for his well planned usurpation.

According to John of Antioch (Roberto ed. frg. 243), the forces posted in Raetia and Noricum declared Carus emperor, and when Probus dispatched an army against Carus, it deserted to his side, and when the others learnt of this, they killed Probus. Zonaras (12.29) claims that Carus was reluctant to become an emperor and asked Probus to relieve him from office before the soldiers forced him to become emperor, but that Probus refused and the soldiers forced Carus to become their emperor. Probus then dispatched an army against Carus, but it deserted to Carus' side. When the bodyguards of Probus learnt of the desertion, they killed their emperor. It is possible that Zonaras is correct in stating that Carus was reluctant to become an emperor and knew the mood of the soldiers so well that he wanted to be removed from office, but it is even more likely that this was just an excuse put forth by Carus later and that he had actually formed a well orchestrated plot to usurp power.

According to Vopiscus (*HA Prob*.24.1ff.), the descendants of Probus fled from Rome after his death and settled near Verona and Lakes Benacus and Larius (Garda and Como) where they lived in a quiet and unassuming way. If true this was certainly the right thing to do in a situation in which they could have otherwise been seen as a threat to those in power. The Senate and people reacted to the killing of Probus with mourning and fear. Vopiscus also claims that when they were informed that his successor was Carus, who was known as a good man, but who had Carinus as son, they feared the future.

Left: A coin of Probus. The text on the reverse depicts Probus as a man really well. He was an honourable man. (Source: Cohen).

Below: Two coins of Probus. The one on the left celebrates his martial qualities by connecting him with Mars Victor and the one on the right celebrates the eternal city. (Source: Beger 1696).

Chapter Thirteen

Probus. The Military Intellectual

The following quotes from Sextus Aurelius Victor and Eutropius are the best descriptions we possess of Probus as a soldier emperor and commander:

> Probus… was almost a second Hannibal because of his great knowledge of warfare and versatile training of the soldiers and his toughening of the young recruits. [Aurelius Victor 37.2, tr. by H.W. Bird, p.41.]

> Probus… a man rendered illustrious by the distinction which he obtained in war. He recovered Gaul, which had been seized by the Barbarians, by remarkable successes in the field. He suppressed, in several battles, some persons that had attempted to seize the throne, … He was a man of spirit, activity, and justice, equalling Aurelian in military glory, and surpassing him in affability of manners. [Eutropius 9.17, tr. by John Selby Watson, p.522.]

This and the descriptions of military action prove that Probus was a true master of warfare, who knew history and military science and how to use this knowledge for the benefit of the Roman Empire. However, he was not merely a bookworm, but an experienced veteran of several wars by the time he became emperor. It comes as no surprise therefore that he was the man who trained the most illustrious *duces* of the era, as was stated by Vopiscus (*HA Probus* 22.3). According to him, these men consisted of Carus, Diocletian, Constantius, Asclepiodotus, Hannibalianus, Gaudiosus, Ursinianus (Ursinus?) and others. In short, both Aurelius Victor and Vopiscus credit Probus with the improvements of the Roman forces that enabled them to secure the Empire in the coming years so that Constantine was able to launch a series of offensives to expand the Empire.

The military campaigns prove the above to be true. Probus always knew how to fight in the most advantageous manner regardless of the enemy, and he indeed defeated every type of enemy that existed. He was unfortunate in his choice of officers because he clearly should not have put any trust in their loyalty. Bonosus, Proculus, Saturninus and Carus all betrayed their master. It is impossible to say how much of this was his own fault. What is certain is that the strict discipline he instituted for the army did have its consequences just like it had during the reign of Aurelian. It is clear that his fame as a disciplinarian caused the Gallic usurpations. It is clear that his strict discipline improved the combat performance of the army, but at the same time it also caused the revolt that ultimately led to the murder of Probus. Both great soldier emperors, Aurelian and Probus, were killed because they were disciplinarians. In the case of Probus it is likely that he was primarily responsible for his own fate. In contrast, Aurelian was not directly responsible for the fate he suffered.

Of note is also the fact that Aurelius Victor compared Probus with Hannibal who was well-known for his merciless cruelty. Machiavelli (*Prince*, 17) claims that it was thanks to this cruelty that Hannibal was able to retain control of his soldiers, who never mutinied as a result. Indeed it is possible to think that Probus could have modelled his approach to the army after that of Hannibal and Aurelian; but if this is the case, then it backfired badly.

It is also clear that Probus made several mistakes in his military appointments because so many revolted against him. These men were undoubtedly able generals, but not worth the trust Probus placed in them. As noted by Kennedy (235–6),[1] if there was one fault in Probus, it was that he was too trusting towards his subordinates, especially Carus. There is no doubt that Probus was a good and loyal friend, but that some of his so-called friends betrayed this trust.

The reference to the personal interest of Probus in the training of soldiers and recruits suggests that he sought to make his army as versatile as possible. The idea was to make the Roman army suitable for all types of war that one could imagine, and on the basis of the military successes of Probus and his successors, he achieved his aim. The Roman army was prepared to meet any challenge the enemies threw at them. The reference to the training of soldiers and recruits also implies that Probus was the man who raised many of the units that appear during the so-called late Empire, which was after all only two years away at the time of his death. In short, Probus was the man who probably created the late Roman army which is visible to us only in the post-284 sources. He was the man who contributed most to the successes achieved by these forces. It is also very likely that the military equipment that is so familiar to us from this period was already standard issue during his reign so that all new units raised by him were equipped with it. The next emperor Carus wore the *pilleus Pannonicus* (round fur hat) with the implication that this had already been introduced as a standard piece of equipment.

On the civilian side of life, Probus' greatest achievements were entirely based on his military successes. The most important of these was that he managed to keep the Empire together despite the centrifugal forces. It was thanks to this that he was able to make improvements in the economy, the most important of which was the growing of wine in Spain, Gaul, Pannonia and Moesia. This undoubtedly proved very beneficial for the economic wellbeing of all these areas. It was safer to drink wine than water and it was also a great service to all future generations who love to drink red wine as I do. In religion Probus was a traditionalist, but thanks to the fact that he did not launch any persecutions, society as a whole was united in plurality. The use of military forces for the persecution of religious or ethnic minorities when they did not pose any threat would have been a waste of resources and detrimental to the fabric of society. The fact that none of the sources mentions any conflict between Probus and the Senate means that Probus was also wise enough to avoid conflicts with the senators even if he still made it clear that he was *deus et dominus* whose decisions were not to be challenged. This means that he paid proper respect to the Senate and did not seek conflict with it. However, it is probable that the killing of Tacitus and Florianus was already sufficient as a precedent that the senators understood not to challenge his position which in turn meant that Probus had no need to chastise the Senate as had been the case under Aurelian.

In short, Probus would certainly deserve the title Great added to his name, but we should still not forget that his fame as a commander and his great military exploits were made possible by the efforts of Gallienus and Aurelian who formed the foundation for the rise of the Roman Empire back to the position it had held under Caracalla. It is clear that the three greatest military emperors of the third century after Caracalla were Gallienus, Aurelian and Probus – all operated in very different circumstances and all had different personalities, but all were great military leaders in their own ways. Also, all were killed by their own men just on the brink of their greatest successes. It was thanks to Gallienus, Aurelian and Probus that Constantine the Great became possible.

Coins depicting Probus either with the *Aegis* chest piece or with the *Aegis* cloak
Drawn after coins available online

Bahram II (276-293) or Bahram IV (388-399). Drawing by Ilkka Syvänne 2009.

Chapter Fourteen

The Reigns of Carus (282–3), Carinus (282–5) and Numerianus (282–4)

Coins of Carus depicting him as *deus et dominus* and as victorious ruler. One of the coins depicts him at the very beginning of the reign together with his son Carinus. Source: Cohen. The *divo* coin (source: Beger 1696) was struck after his death.

14.1. Carus the Man

> Carus was a mediocre man, who is to be ranked with the good rather than the evil rulers [*principes*, *princes*]; and he would have been a much better ruler, had he not left Carinus as his heir. [Vopiscus, *Historia Augusta*, Carus 3.5.]

This is the rather harsh judgment of Flavius Vopiscus of Syracuse in the *Historia Augusta*. The main reason for this characterization is that the text was written when Diocletian was still alive so it was necessary to disparage his enemies as much as possible.[1] As I shall show, Carus was an able military commander and it was probably only because his reign was cut so short that the sources do not give us a better image of him. Vopiscus (*HA Prob.* 22.3) also preserves material which shows the above incorrect because the name of Carus is included among the great *duces* schooled by Probus. Similarly, Zonaras (12.30) states that Carus was a Gaul who was a brave man and who excelled in warfare. And what was the primary mission of a good emperor in the eyes of the soldiers and populace? It was to be an outstanding military leader. In short, there is no doubt that Carus was a very able military commander, but the hostile sources are still correct in their criticism of his son Carinus – he was a man who aroused hatred by his sexual habits and arrogance and this obviously casts a shadow on his father as well.

Marcus Aurelius (Numerianus?) Carus was probably a native of Narbonensis, but it is also possible that he was of Illyrian stock so that he was born either in the city of Rome, or in Milan, or in Illyricum. The *Historia Augusta* (Carus 4.3) claims that one source has him born of Carthagian/Punic stock in Illyricum. The same source, however, makes it clear that Carus wanted everyone to see him as a native Roman. We know next to nothing about his career before his rise to power. The *Historia Augusta* (Probus 22.3; Carus 4.6, 5.4) merely states that Carus held various civil and military positions and was at one time a *proconsul Ciliciae* and a *dux* under Probus before being appointed *praefectus praetorio* by Probus. So Carus was exceptionally well qualified to be emperor. He had experience of both civilian and military matters. The above also makes it probable that the Illyrian faction may have temporarily lost its grip on power, but the situation was not to last for long.[2]

According to Malalas (12.34), Carus was a haughty short man with a good chest, fair skin, straight greying hair, greyish eyes, a good nose, thick lips, and a broad face. Malalas also claims that Carus was 60 and a half years old at the time of his death, which would mean that he was 58 or 59 on his accession to power. He had three children and at least one grandchild. This would place the date of Carus's birth to the year 223/4. On the basis of the coins, the description seems accurate enough, but one should add to this the fact that Carus was also showing the signs of typical male balding. He was clearly a mature man.[3]

14.2. The Wars against the Sarmatians, Quadi and Franks/Alamanni in 282

Unlike his immediate predecessors Carus was in the happy position to have a fully grown son, a younger son and a daughter. The eldest of his sons, Carinus, could be left in charge of the west while Carus would finally put into effect the long-planned campaign against Persia. It was because of this that Carus made his sons M. Aurelius Carinus and Numerianus his co-rulers as Caesars, the latter of whom was too young to rule and was therefore taken along to the east to learn the art of soldiering. Numerianus was married to the daughter of the new praetorian prefect Aper to secure his support for the throne. This repeated the administrative solution of the emperors Valerian and Gallienus during the years 253–60. The general assumption is that Carus did not visit Rome to secure his position, but left it to his son Carinus who was then made *Augustus* of the West in early 283.[4]

However, Malalas (12.34) and Zonaras (12.30) include confused but roughly similar accounts according to which Carus subjugated Caria (this is located in south-west Asia Minor and is clearly a mistake for something else), made a campaign against the Persians, constructed a fortress city on the *limes* called Caras (usually identified with Carrhae, but this must be a mistake), returned to Rome and then advanced against the Huns, and was killed at the age of 60 and a half. If the return to Rome and then against the Huns (these could be the Sarmatians and Quadi) is a mistake for the situation immediately after the death of Probus, then it is possible to think that Malalas and Zonaras have placed the sequence of events in the wrong order so that Carus would have first visited Rome to secure the support of the Senate after which he would have returned back to the Balkans to fight the Huns, and only after that against the Persians. This would actually be quite probable because it would not have taken long for Carus to visit Rome if he used a relay of horses. By doing so he would have secured his position among those whose opinions mattered while it would also have given him the chance to secure the West for his son Carinus.

The sources offer information of the Sarmatian war very sparingly. All that we have to go on are the *Historia Augusta* and the coins which depict Numerianus as *Augustus* (i.e. in 283) with the legend *Triunfu. Quadro(rum)* that has Carus and Numerianus in a *quadriga* (four-horsed chariot) with an attendant Victory and captives, and that all three emperors assumed the title *Germanicus Maximus*.[5]

The Sarmatians are claimed to have been emboldened to invade Roman territory thanks to the death of Probus. They probably sought more payments. Probus, however, had assembled the army in readiness in the Balkans for the forthcoming Persian war so the Romans were ready to receive them. According to Vopiscus, Carus crushed the Sarmatians in a few days when they threatened to invade not only Illyricum but also Thrace and Italy and thereby freed the provinces of Pannonia from fear. Vopiscus claims that Carus killed 16,000 Sarmatians and took captive 20,000 of both sexes. The inclusion of women does not mean that the Sarmatians would have been accompanied with their families, because the Sarmatians and Alans both had women warriors. The fact that Carus was able to defeat the Sarmatians so decisively presumably in a battle suggests considerable military skills because as cavalry the Sarmatians usually withdrew rather than faced the possibility of defeat. The implication is that Carus was either able to force the enemy against some terrain obstacle like a river, mountain or swamp, or that he managed to encircle the highly mobile enemy forces with cavalry of his own. Presumably at least some of the defeated force was able to flee, so the enemy force likely numbered more than 36,000.[6]

The question of who fought against the Quadi is also problematic. It is possible that they fought alongside the Sarmatians, or that they fought a separate campaign. If the latter is true, then it is possible they were defeated by Carus in a separate action, or that they were defeated by another army under the nominal command of Numerianus (and it was because of this that coins were later struck in his name) so that some other more experienced man (e.g. Diocletian or Aper) was the de facto commander or that this army was under Carinus. However, the fact that all three emperors, Carus, Carinus and Numerianus, took the title *Germanicus maximus* suggests that this campaign was conducted by Carus in person and that his sons got the title thanks to the efforts of their father.[7]

Coin commemorating the victory of Numerianus over the Quadi.
Source: Duruy.

After the Sarmatian problem had been dealt with and Carinus had taken charge of the forces in the West, Carus launched the long planned invasion of Persia. Carinus (Aurelius Victor 38.2; Nemesianus, *Cynegetica* 63ff.) was placed in command of the forces in Gaul and he achieved a number of successes against the barbarians along the Saône and Rhine rivers. In other words, the death of Probus resulted in similar problems also in the West. The probable enemies in these areas were the Franks and Alamanni. However, it has also been claimed that Carinus continued his father's campaign against the Quadi when the latter marched to the east, and that Carinus then advanced all the way to Britain, presumably achieving the above-mentioned successes in Gaul en route. Carinus defeated some enemies and/or invaders in Britain (the possible candidates are local rebels, the Irish Scotti, the Picts and the Saxons), which enabled him and his brother Numerianus to take the title *Britannicus maximus*. Carinus was clearly well-schooled by his father in the military arts.[8]

14.3. The Persian Campaign in 282–4[9]

The commander-in-chief of the force invading Persia was naturally Carus himself while his son Numerianus was taken along to learn the art of soldiering and generalship. The other commanders included at least the *praefectus praetorio* Aper, the *comes domesticorum* Diocles (the future emperor Diocletian), *comes* Licinius (the future emperor), and the King of Armenia Tiridates/Trdat once the Romans were able to unite their forces with him.

The extant sources suggest that Carus's campaign started with an advance into Armenia, undoubtedly to support Tiridates/Trdat against the Persians so that he would be able to obtain their services for the main advance along the Tigris to Ctesiphon. The addition of the super-heavy Armenian cavalry cataphracts was of the greatest importance for the success of the campaign. The situation for the invasion was opportune because Bahram II was still fighting against his brother Hormizd in the east. The three sources which suggest invasion through Armenia as the likely route taken by Carus are Synesius (*de regno*, PG 66. 1081ff.), Moses Khorenatsi (3.79, Thomson tr. p. 227), and Sidonius Apollinaris (*Carm.* 23.91–6). Both Synesius and Moses are problematic as sources because these provide a confusing account of the campaign and also claim that Carinus was present, but this does not remove the likelihood that both are correct to include the advance into Armenia and the use of Armenians as allies because this is also confirmed by Sidonius Apollinaris (*Carm.* 23.91–6). The name of Carinus in Synesius is easy to dismiss as a mistake for Carus. The accounts which suggest an initial advance into Armenia are Synesius and Sidonius. The following contain the translations of the relevant parts of Sidonius by W.B. Anderson (*Sidonius. Poems and Letters*, 2 vols., Loeb 1935–36, p.289) and Synesius by Fitzgerald in Dodgeon and Lieu (REF1, pp.119–21) with my comments inside parentheses:

Sidonius:

Who shall leave unmentioned the campaign against Persia or the victorious warfare of Carus, our prince and the marching of Roman legions over Niphates [*a mountain in Armenia*] at the time when the Emperor was overwhelmed by lightning and a life that was itself like lightning met its end?

Synesius:

…a certain monarch of those days was leading an expedition against the Parthians, who had behaved towards the Romans in an insulting manner. Now they had reached the mountain frontiers of Armenia, before entering enemy country, he was eager to dine, and gave orders to the army to make use of the provisions in the supply column [*this means that Carus prevented the soldiers from using local Armenian resources because this could have angered their ally*], as they were now in a position to live off the neighbouring country should it be necessary. He was pointing out to them the land of the Parthians. …an embassy appeared from the enemy lines, …it turned out somehow that the king was dining… Such a thing did not exist at that time as the Guards' regiment [*Doryforoi meaning the spear-bearers/bodyguards, which is translated by Fitzgerald as the Guards' regiment*], a sort of picked force detached from the army itself, of men all young, tall, fair-haired and superb [*this is slightly misleading because there certainly were several different units of bodyguards in existence, but these were naturally composed of veterans of proven fighting quality and not of young men*].

[*Bodyguards*] equipped with golden shields and lances… Here, in contrast, every phalanx doing its duty, was the guard of the king and the kingdom. And these kings held themselves in simple fashion, for they were kings not in pomp but in spirit,… it was in such guise… that Carinus [*actually Carus*] was seen by the embassy. A tunic dyed with purple was lying on the grass, and for repast he had a soup of yesterday's peas, and in it some bits of salted pork…

…he did not spring up, nor did he change anything; but called out to these men from the very spot and said that he knew that they had come to see him, for that he was [*Carus*], and he bade them to tell the young king… that unless he conducted them wisely, he might expect that the whole of their forest and plain would be in a single month barer than the head of [*Carus*]. …he took off his cap [*pileus, likely to be the pileus Pannonicus, a round fur cap with a round top*], and showed his head, which was no more hairy than the helmet lying at his side [*i.e. it is probable that the plume of the helmet had a few feathers/horsehairs as was the hair on Carus's head; it is unlikely the helmet would have had no plume*]… if they were hungry to attack the stew-pot with him, but if not in need, he ordered them to depart at once… when these messages were reported to the rank-and-file and to the leader of the enemy,… shuddering and fear fell upon every one at the thought of fighting men such as these, whose very king was neither ashamed of being a king, nor being bald, and who, offering them a stew-pot, invited them to share his meal. And their… king arrived in a state of terror and was ready to yield in everything.

The above account includes several important nuggets of evidence. Firstly, it suggests that Carus advanced through the mountains of Armenia and that he maintained strict control over his army; he did not allow his men to live off the land while they were on the friendly territory. Secondly, it proves that the Persians were aware of the Roman plans and tried to defuse the situation through negotiations. Thirdly, it proves that Carus was a wise commander who sought to endear himself with the rank-and-file soldiers by dressing and eating like them. Basically he did what all good Roman commanders had always done, which was to behave like a comrade-in-arms with the soldiers. This is what Trajan, Septimius Severus, and Caracalla had done.[10] Malalas (12.34) claims that Carus was an arrogant man, but this account proves that Carus was not arrogant towards his own men, only against the enemy and/or the Senate. Fourthly, Carus was wise enough not to be easily detectable; he was able to blend in with his men. This made it difficult for the enemy or assassins to target him.[11] Fifthly, the eating of the soup with the common soldiers was not only a good way to show camaraderie but it was also a good way to avoid being poisoned.[12] Sixth, the account suggests that Carus advanced through Armenia to the Tigris and then along it to Ctesiphon and that the Roman army later retreated along the Euphrates (Moses 3.79). This is the very same route that Galerius was to use in 297.[13] On the basis of this, it is more than likely that Galerius imitated Carus. Seventh, it is very likely that Carus was using one of the standard stratagems of antiquity, which had been used by Scipio Africanus and which was also included in the collection of Stratagems of Polyaneus (8.8). Scipio did not execute three Carthagian spies who had been found inside his camp, but allowed them to go around his army so that they could witness the very high quality of his forces and thereby take the discouraging message back to their army. The same type of stratagem can also be found in the *Stratagems* of Frontinus (4.7.7) where it is the consul Valerius Laevinus (280 BC) who allowed the enemy spy to inspect his camp. Carus allowed enemy envoys to wander in his camp, evidently unattended because it was he who shouted and called them to meet him. The idea was to show the Persians how confident he was of his own success and how well drilled his veteran force was. He undoubtedly expected this to lower the enemy's morale, and on the basis of what the text states this seems to have been its effect.

The use of such a stratagem by a student of Probus is not surprising even if it is strange to call the 60-year-old Carus a student of Probus who was after all ten years younger than him, but we should still do so because it is clear that Probus had indeed schooled all of his *duces* in the art of war thanks to his great knowledge of warfare and thanks to his personal experience of combat under Valerian, Gallienus, Claudius and Aurelian.

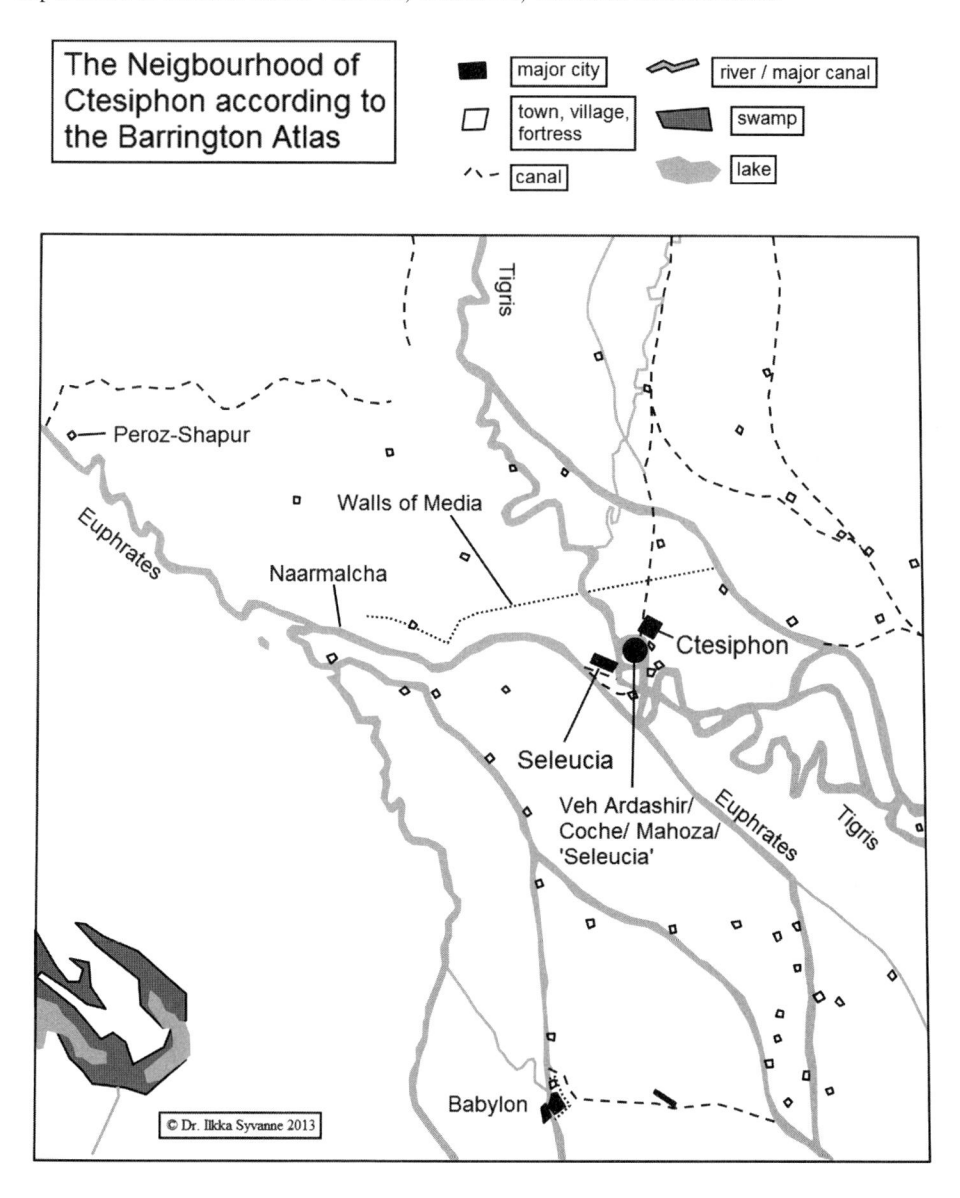

According to the *Historia Augusta* (*Carus* 8.1ff.), Carus conquered Mesopotamia without opposition because the Persians were fighting a civil war, but there are other accounts which suggest that there were also battles. In my opinion, these accounts can be reconciled. The version provided by *Historia Augusta* refers to the general situation in which the Persians lacked adequate resources to oppose the invasion because Bahram II was fighting against his brother, while those accounts that mention the battles refer to the fighting that took place when local forces attempted to oppose Carus and prevent the capture of the Persian capital and the other surrounding cities. The fact that the besieging of Ctesiphon, Coche and Seleucia and the crossing of the rivers required boats or ships suggests the likelihood that Carus launched a fleet along the Tigris (or Euphrates?) or that his forces carried ship/boat-building materials for this purpose. Furthermore, the successful siege operations prove that Carus' army carried with it all the siege equipment necessary for the taking of such large well-fortified cities. The initial preparations for the war and sieges would obviously have been made already under Probus, but it is still clear that as Praetorian Prefect of Probus, Carus was also involved in the process. Clearly Carus was acutely aware of all the aspects of warfare, from preparations and logistics to the actual prosecution of the war.

According to Aurelius Victor (38.3), Carus routed the Persians when he passed beyond Ctesiphon. This would suggest that the Persians did not give battle against Carus before he besieged Ctesiphon and presumably also Coche (Veh Ardashir). However, it is possible that this battle took place when Carus was besieging Seleucia (the original Greek city) on the other side of the Tigris, which he then levelled so thoroughly that it was still in ruins when Julian passed through it in 363. In other words, the Persians resorted only to harassment when Carus besieged Ctesiphon and Coche/Veh Ardashir, and engaged Carus after he had turned around to penetrate Persian territory even deeper or when he besieged Greek Seleucia. The last of these is the likeliest in light of Zonaras's text. It means that Carus was able to capture both the original Ctesiphon and the new city built by Ardashir I which was called Coche or Veh Ardashir, and possibly also Greek Seleucia while the Persians only harassed his forces. Zonaras's account (12.30) proves that the Persians fought a battle against the Romans when the Romans were in the area between the Euphrates and Tigris presumably when they besieged Greek Seleucia. According to Zonaras, Carus had encamped his army in a hollow that enabled the Persians to direct a river through a canal into this encampment. Carus, however, attacked and put the Persians to flight – in other words, this time the Persians chose to fight. It is possible to think that this was the same battle that was mentioned by Aurelius Victor to have taken place when Carus had advanced beyond Ctesiphon, but it is also possible that Victor's battle is an entirely separate battle which took place when Carus, being advised to do so by Aper, decided to advance deeper into Persian territory so that he turned around back to the Tigris and then possibly across. The conquest of Ctesiphon together with the two other cities enabled Carus to assume the title *Persicus maximus*.

According to most of the sources, once Carus had decided to continue his campaign against the Persians, he encamped on the Tigris, but the stories do not tell us on which side of the river. The claim of Nemesianus (*Cynegetica* 63ff.) that Carus and Numerianus captured the heartland of Persia and the ancient fortresses of Babylon should be interpreted as a symbolic reference to the Persian heartland around Ctesiphon (rather

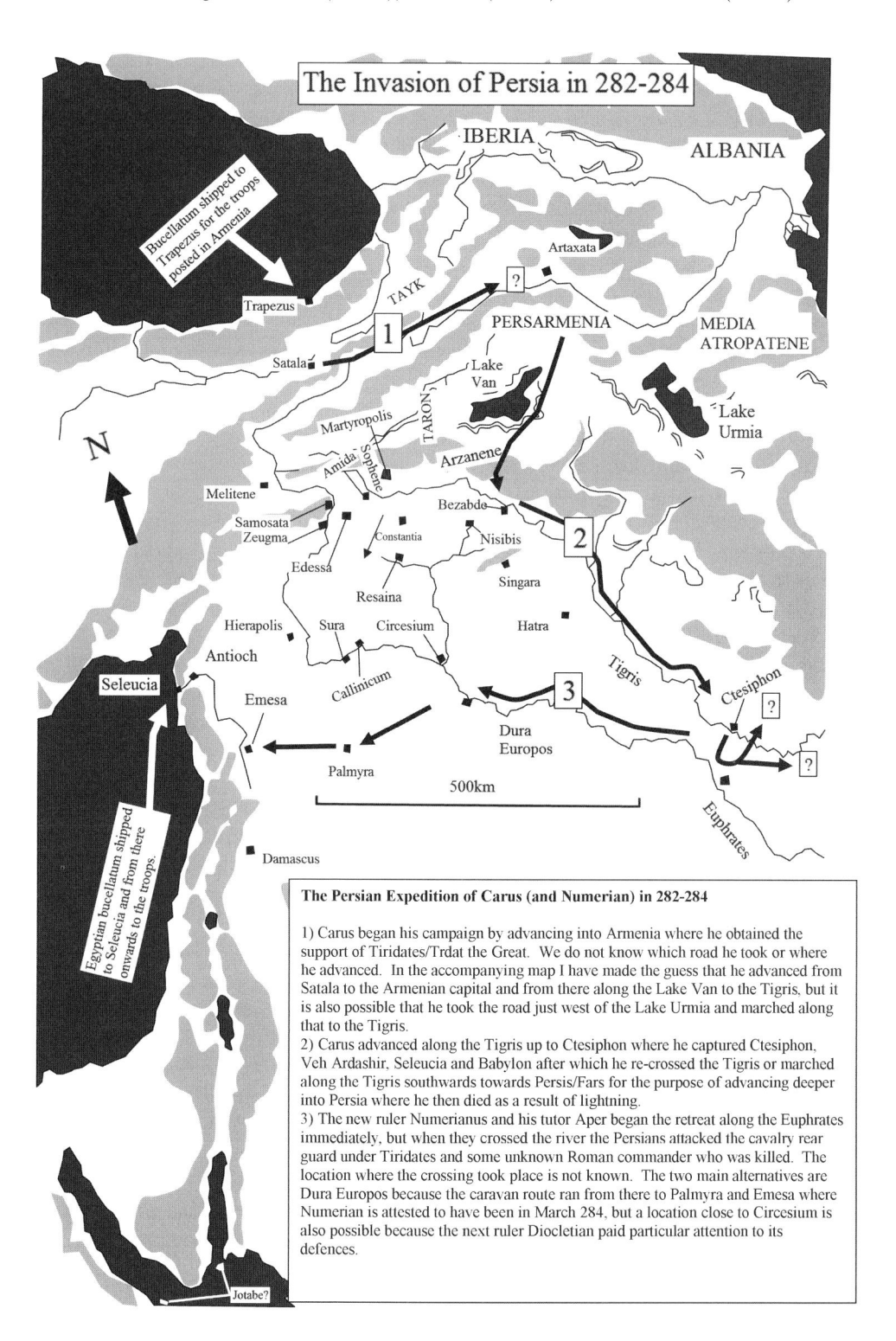

The Reigns of Carus (282–3), Carinus (282–5) and Numerianus (282–4) 223

The Invasion of Persia in 282-284

The Persian Expedition of Carus (and Numerian) in 282-284

1) Carus began his campaign by advancing into Armenia where he obtained the support of Tiridates/Trdat the Great. We do not know which road he took or where he advanced. In the accompanying map I have made the guess that he advanced from Satala to the Armenian capital and from there along the Lake Van to the Tigris, but it is also possible that he took the road just west of the Lake Urmia and marched along that to the Tigris.

2) Carus advanced along the Tigris up to Ctesiphon where he captured Ctesiphon, Veh Ardashir, Seleucia and Babylon after which he re-crossed the Tigris or marched along the Tigris southwards towards Persis/Fars for the purpose of advancing deeper into Persia where he then died as a result of lightning.

3) The new ruler Numerianus and his tutor Aper began the retreat along the Euphrates immediately, but when they crossed the river the Persians attacked the cavalry rear guard under Tiridates and some unknown Roman commander who was killed. The location where the crossing took place is not known. The two main alternatives are Dura Europos because the caravan route ran from there to Palmyra and Emesa where Numerian is attested to have been in March 284, but a location close to Circesium is also possible because the next ruler Diocletian paid particular attention to its defences.

than in Persis/Fars) and the region around Babylon – and it is indeed likely that Carus had visited Babylon before turning back to the Tigris. Most of the stories relate that when Carus had begun his advance deeper into Persia he became bedridden in his tent as a result of some illness. Then a thunderstorm hit the Roman camp, but what happened after that is controversial. Most of the sources state that lightning hit the emperor and killed him, while other sources state that he had already died of disease and it was then that some of his *cubicularii* burned the tent, or that the tent was burned as a result of the lightning.[14]

Obviously, historians have always suspected that the emperor had been assassinated which was then covered up by the burning of the tent. If this is the case, then a likely reason would be that the flooding of the Roman camp caused a shortage of fodder and supplies, and when the emperor then decided to push ever deeper into the Persian territory, because he had been advised to do so by *praefectus praetorio* Aper, the soldiers and officers became restless, which was then exploited by the assassins.[15] The likeliest culprit would of course be Aper himself, because it is easy to see that he could have advised such a course of action to make Carus' position untenable. Aper could have foreseen a possibility of ruling through Numerianus. The other possible culprit would be the *comes domesticorum* Diocles/Diocletian, but his role in this would be less likely.

In light of the extant evidence, death by lightning appears to be the likeliest alternative and not far-fetched as often assumed. People do die every day from being struck by lightning. The Roman sources appear to have been eager to prove that the emperor could not have died as a result of a thunderbolt because this could be interpreted as evidence that the gods opposed the Roman aim to advance further than Ctesiphon. In fact, Aurelius Victor (38.3–5) even claims that Carus was deservedly killed by a bolt of lightning because he had overlooked the oracles which stated that he should not advance any further than Ctesiphon. The superstitious could see the death by a thunderbolt as a sign of the wrath of the gods and it was in the interest of most to disclaim it; and when we find so many sources stating this and the *Historia Augusta* so eager to disapprove it, it must be true. Furthermore, it is unlikely that Carus would have been unaware of the importance of logistics in a situation in which he had a long career behind him in civil service and in the military and in a situation in which he had also been personally in charge of supplies. On top of it all, the above-mentioned quote from Synesius proves that Carus was an expert in logistical matters. It is also very unlikely that the succession of Numerianus as emperor would have been so smooth had there been a conspiracy against Carus. In short, it is likely that Carus died as a result of a lightning bolt, which frightened all superstitious men senseless, hence the need to cover it up with a story of illness. The burning of the tent and corpse ensured that the tell-tale signs of a lightning bolt could not be seen.

The death of the emperor was a disaster. Numerianus was declared *Augustus*, but Aper was the de facto ruler. The Romans started their retreat from Persian territory immediately. The likeliest reasons for this are: 1) the manner of the death of Carus frightened the superstitious; 2) the youth and inexperience of the new emperor failed to garner him enough support to continue the campaign. The details of what happened after this are not known with certainty because most of the sources that describe the events that took place after the death of Carus have confused the reign of Numerianus with the

Coin of Numerianus
(source: Cohen)

disastrous reign of Valerian so that these sources falsely claim that the Persians defeated Numerianus, captured him and then flayed him. The sources which have confused the evidence include Malalas, *Chronicon Paschale*, and Zonaras.[16] Then there are sources which merely state that when Carus had died Numerianus decided to end the campaign and retreat, and that it was during the retreat that Numerianus started to suffer from an eye ailment which enabled the Praetorian Prefect Aper to kill him in his litter, and that this murder was punished by Diocletian who was then declared emperor. The sources which include this account are Aurelius Victor, *Historia Augusta*, *Epitome de Caesaribus* (Pseudo-Victor), and Syncellus. The Armenian tradition as preserved by Moses (3.79, Thomson tr. 227) tells still another story. According to him, Ardashir, together with the Arabs of Mesopotamia, gave a second battle against the Romans on both sides of the Euphrates so that Carus was killed at Rinon. Moses also claims that Carinus, accompanied by Trdat/Tiridates, had advanced into the desert against Kornak and was likewise killed, together with his army. Trdat, whose horse was wounded, could not flee, so he was forced to swim across the Euphrates to join his own army where Licinius was. As is clear, this account is full of incorrect claims. Regardless, I would still suggest that Moses has preserved one important detail missing from the other sources, which is that there was a successful Persian attack against the Roman cavalry rearguard led by Tiridates/Trdat when the retreating Roman army was crossing the Euphrates during which some unknown Roman commander died.

The place where the Euphrates was crossed is not known. The two likeliest places are Circesium and Dura Europos, because a major road ran through both to Palmyra and then to Emesa where Numerianus is attested to have been in March 284.[17] If the crossing took place at Circesium, then this would have been the likeliest reason for Diocletian's subsequent decision to fortify Circesium (Amm. 23.5.2). If he had witnessed the crossing, this could have been the reason. It was undoubtedly wise to have a well-fortified place with artillery pieces in this place for the protection of Roman armies crossing the river. However, any locale south of Circesium where the Euphrates could be bridged would suit the description given above. The march across the desert actually proves that the Romans did possess plentiful supplies. The defeat of the Roman rear guard cannot have been significant because Diocletian still possessed large enough an army to engage simultaneously the forces of Carinus and the invaders from the north in 284–285 and then force the Persians to sign a humiliating peace treaty in about 286–287. It is probable that most of the casualties were suffered by the Armenians. Cavalry rearguards typically consisted of 1,000–3,000 men at most with the implication that even if the Persians would have annihilated the entire force, which is unlikely, the casualties suffered by the Romans would have been insignificant in comparison with those suffered by the Persians when they had lost three major cities with their populations.

14.4. Carus, the Promising Reign Cut Short by a Lightning Bolt

It is impossible to say what were the long term aims and policies of Carus as his reign was cut so short. However, something can be said. Carus clearly aimed to create a dynasty and he had copied the solution that had been adopted earlier by Valerian with Gallienus so that he divided the Empire between two *augusti*, one of whom ruled the west and the other east, but obviously so that Carus was the senior *Augustus*. We do not know whether Carus had plans of making his other son Numerianus also *Augustus* as Septimius Severus had done with Caracalla and Geta. The second of his aims was evidently the ever elusive conquest of Persia.

Carus was undoubtedly treacherous towards his emperor and a devious man, but the military campaigns prove that Carus was an expert in military matters – perhaps partly because he knew how to betray trust and how to mislead the enemy – and it is clear that he was a suberb general. Carus crushed the Sarmatians and Quadi. He conquered the Persian heartland and took three major cities. He inflicted a serious defeat on the Persians in at least one battle and caused massive economic damage to the Persians. The conquest of Ctesiphon with the other surrounding cities was the first great Roman success after the disasters of the reign of Valerian. Odaenathus had advanced twice into this same area as a Roman general, but his achievements were not thought to have been Roman achievements. Aurelian had inflicted a crushing defeat on the Persians and Armenians which had neutralized the Persians as a military threat until about 284, thanks to the chaos it had caused in the east of Persia, but he had not invaded Persia and had not conquered Ctesiphon, Coche and Seleucia, and neither had Probus – although it had been Carus who had prevented the latter. Therefore it is clear that it was finally the achievements of Carus that washed away the shame of Valerian in Roman eyes. His great victory, however, was marred by the manner of his death. The death by thunderbolt was a sign of the anger of the gods.

The legacy of Carus was mixed, but it was not his fault that he died as he did. The other poisonous part of his reign was that he left the Empire in the hands of his son Carinus, whose sexual behaviour was disapproved of by almost everyone, most importantly by the officers of his bodyguard. This, however, would not have been a problem had the eastern army stayed loyal to him.

14.5. Epilogue: Numerianus, Carinus, and the Rise of Diocletian in 283–5[18]

When the Roman army left the city of Emesa and marched northwards, the emperor Numerianus died. The sources claim that Aper murdered him, or that he died as a result of some unknown illness which affected his eyes. Prefect of the Praetorian Guard and father-in-law of the Emperor Numerianus, Aper decided to hide the death from the troops until Carinus could assume control of the army. The corpse of Numerianus was placed in a covered litter, but when the Roman army was approaching the city of Nicomedia on 20 November 284, the soldiers noticed a strong stench coming from the litter. When they connected this with the fact that they had not seen Numerianus for days, they became suspicious. Aper attempted to reassure the soldiers that there was nothing amiss, but some soldiers, which I have speculated in the *Military History of Late Rome Volume 1* to have been the *protectores domestici* serving under Diocles, forced their way through the guard and found Numerianus dead within. The soldiers duly arrested Aper and pitched a marching camp on the spot. They also set up a tribunal for a general assembly/council of the army. All the men knew that Aper would be punished and a new emperor would be chosen, which would mean the distribution of money to the soldiers. The assembly of officers chose Diocles, the *comes domesticorum*, as their new emperor, which the soldiers confirmed with shouts of 'hail *Augustus*!' Then Diocles stepped onto the tribunal. One of the officers theatrically asked, 'How was Numerianus killed?' which Diocles answered by drawing up his sword and pointing it at Aper. After this, Diocles shouted that it was Aper who had engineered Numerianus's murder, and stabbed him with the sword. This was the beginning of the reign of Caius Aurelius Valerius Diocletianus Augustus.

Coins of Carinus depicting him as *Caesar* and then as *Augustus* with his father and then finally as *Augustus* together with Numerianus. (Source: Cohen)

As I have noted in my *Military History of Late Rome Volume 1*, the above story of Aper's guilt seems quite far-fetched and must have been concocted by Diocles. Aper had nothing to gain from such an action, unlike Diocles. In my opinion, it is quite possible that the *comes domesticorum* Diocles had murdered Numerianus and that Aper's praetorians had failed to prevent it. It was then when the death had been covered up that Diocles was finally obliged to order his men to force their way into the litter so that he could overthrow Aper. This is obviously speculation, but at least it would reconcile the sources. Whatever the truth, the Illyrian Mafia was now on its way to regaining its dominant position; but there was still one obstacle left to remove. This man was Carinus and it was not an easy matter to defeat him, because he was an expert military commander.

As noted above, Carinus had not rested on his laurels while his father had campaigned in the East. Carinus had restored the Rhine Frontier and also achieved some significant military success in Britain as a result of which he and his brother were able to take the title of *Britannicus Maximus* in 284. The personal behaviour of Carinus, however, undid all of his great military achievements. When Carinus became emperor, he immediately killed those of his former classmates who had teased him at school. In addition to this, he put to death many senators with spurious accusations in order to get their money. But the most dangerous of Carinus's actions was his seduction of the wives of many nobles and officers. This undermined the loyalty of the men who held his life in their hands.[19]

The *Historia Augusta* (Car. 16) gives us a long list of the faults of Carinus, which has usually been doubted, but in light of what happened the list is not necessarily a complete fabrication. This account adds to the list of vices the corruption of youths of the same sex. This is suspect in light of the fact that the other sources fail to mention this, but cannot be entirely ruled out. Flavius Vopiscus claimed that Carinus allowed his sexual vices to influence his choice of officeholders. He chose one of his doorkeepers as new City Prefect of Rome, and killed the Prefect of the Praetorians and replaced him with Matronianus, who was one of his clerks and an accomplice and assistant in his debaucheries. Vopiscus also claims that Carinus wrote haughty letters to the Senate in which he threatened to confiscate their property and give it to the city mob. He also alleges that Carinus married and divorced so often that he had nine wives altogether, on top of which he is claimed to have divorced one while she was pregnant. This statement has been doubted because the coins show only one wife, Magnia Urbica *Augusta*, but in my opinion this is not conclusive. He could have easily married other women before he became *Augustus*. Carinus filled the palace with actors, harlots, pantomime players, singers and pimps, and granted favours to the basest of persons. Vopiscus attests that Carinus appointed a man to sign the state papers on his behalf, and never came forward to meet the prefects or consuls. The luxurious lifestyle of Carinus manifested itself in clothing (jewels on shoes, jewelled clasps and belts) and banquets and baths. What is notable about the last is that the cooling of baths is claimed to have been done with snow, which suggests that snow was put in storage under ground during winter for later use – this was a wise practice. It is impossible to be certain whether these claims are correct because Vopiscus was at pains to present Carinus in the worst possible light, but it is certain that at least in one case the claims are not correct. Vopiscus claims that Carus would have forbidden Carinus to appear in public as a consul. This is certainly incorrect, as is noted by Magie in his translation (p.441), because Carinus was *consul ordinarius* with his father in 283 – unless of course this refers to the situation after mid-283. According to Vopiscus, it was then because of these excesses that Carus stated that Carinus was no son of his. This has obviously been doubted, with very good reason, because the same text claims that Carus intended to kill and replace his son Carinus with Constantius, the governor of Dalmatia, but the only definitely improbable part of this is the name of the replacement. It is not impossible that Carus was angry over the behaviour of his son and that he intended to replace him with his other son Numerianus. However, I would still put this in the category of likely fabrications of the *Historia Augusta* meant to please Diocletian and Constantius Chlorus.

Whatever the truth behind the reaction of Carus when he learnt of the foolish behaviour of his son Carinus, it is clear that Carinus was guilty of at least some serious excesses because all sources refer to them. This gave Diocletian the chance to undermine Carinus's position among the senators and soldiers – as a former officer in charge of imperial security Diocletian knew how to do this. He would have known personally many of the officers belonging to the *praetoriani, frumentarii,* and *protectores domestici*, and these were undoubtedly quite prepared to desert their emperor just as the former *protector* Constantius was. However, Diocletian's principal object appears to have been to influence the senatorial class, because he abolished the *frumentarii* (Aur. Vict. 19.44), the group of people the senators feared most. In truth, Diocletian did not abolish the secret service, but only changed its name. Henceforth they were called *agentes in rebus* (general agents).

It was therefore largely thanks to Carinus's own personal behaviour that he fell into trouble. The death of Numerianus and the usurpation of Diocletian caused others to rise against their hated ruler. Thanks to the discrepancies in the sources we do not know how many of these there were. We do know that there was at least one usurpation, by M. Aurelius Iulianus against Carinus in Italy and Pannonia, but it has also been suggested that there were two simultaneous usurpations by similarly named men. According to the latter version, *corrector* Sabinus Julianus usurped power in Italy (*PLRE1* M. Aur. Sabinus Iulianus 24) and was then defeated near Verona. The second of the revolts would then have been by *praefectus praetorio* Sabinus Julianus in Italy (*PLRE1* Sabinus Iulianus 38) who was then defeated in Illyricum. It is impossible to know for certain which of the versions is correct even if in my opinion a single person named Sabinus Julianus would seem far more likely than two. Whatever the truth, the crushing of the revolt or revolts took several months so that Carinus achieved his first victory near Verona in 284 and then a second in Illyricum in 285. He was clearly a superb general.

Diocletian's plan was to attack the victor of the conflict between Carinus and Sabinus Julianus so that he would face a weakened foe. Consequently, the engagement between Carinus and Diocletian took place only when Carinus had defeated Julianus and had advanced against his next foe Diocletian. The armies of Carinus and Diocletian then faced each other across the River Margus in Moesia in the spring of 285 somewhere between the Mons Aureus and Viminacium. It is probable that Carinus's army outnumbered Diocletian's because Diocletian had been forced to leave a field army under Constantius in Asia Minor to fight against the northern invaders who had passed through the Caucasus, but this is not known with certainty. Whatever the truth, the winner of the battle was the militarily gifted Carinus, but then when he was pursuing the defeated foes, his officers assassinated him because he had ravished their wives. One of the men who betrayed Carinus was certainly his Praetorian Prefect Aristobulus who was not only kept in office by Diocletian but was also nominated as consul with Diocletian for the year 285. On the basis of this, it is clear that Aristobulus and his Praetorians were the ones who killed Carinus. Carinus was very foolish to keep men like Aristobulus among his bodyguards. It should have been self-evident for Carinus that he should not have kept close to his person such armed men whose wives he had seduced (or raped?) – he more than deserved his fate if for no other reason than stupidity.

The new ruler, Diocletian, was to become one of the greatest Roman emperors, but unlike his predecessors, his solution was not to keep power in his hands alone but to divide it between four emperors, the reason for this being that he did not have a son. For this and other events of the so-called late Roman period, see my book series *Late Roman Military History* vols. 1–7.

However, without the hard efforts of Gallienus, Aurelian and Probus, there would not have been any Roman Empire left for Diocletian and Constantine the Great to transform into what is today called the Late Roman Empire. Gallienus survived the storm and created the army that was to restore the Empire. Aurelian united the breakaway regions and Probus secured the achievements of Aurelian and created the late Roman army and its officer cadre.

Diocles (Diocletian/Diocletianus) according to Duruy.

Carinus according to Duruy after M. Aur. Carinus Capitole salle des Empereurs no70.

Appendix I

Modestus, Vegetius, and the Late Third Century Army

A. The Military Treatise of Modestus to Tacitus

There exists a military treatise by Modestus, which is addressed to the emperor Tacitus. The author of this treatise is usually thought to be have used Vegetius's *Epitome of Military Science* as a source, or alternatively it is thought that it is a fifteenth century forgery,[1] but this view is not shared by all historians and it is because of this that I have included a discussion and analysis of it here.

Its authenticity receives support from the circumstantial evidence. Firstly, Tacitus was a man who did not possess any military experience, so he would certainly have needed such advice as Modestus's treatise offers. Secondly, the text is not an exact carbon copy of Vegetius,[2] so it is possible that both authors have used the same source or sources for their text. Thirdly, it is possible that Vegetius has used Modestus as one of his sources.

My purpose is to offer a possible glimpse into the state of Roman military science as it stood at the beginning of Tacitus's reign by offering a description and analysis of the material included by Modestus with the assumption that it is a genuine treatise and not a forgery. If the legions (the so-called *Parthica* legions) as described in Modestus and Vegetius were created under Septimius Severus as I have suggested in my biography of Caracalla, it is possible to think that the legionary tactics and equipment that these two treatises describe were also used during the third century.

The standard modern edition of Modestus is 'Modesti libellus de vocabulis rei militaris ad Tacitum Augustum (Estudio de la transmission manuscrita y edición crítica)' by Tomás Gonzales Rolan and Ana Moure Casas, in *Filologia Clasica* Vol. XX (1986–7), Universidad Complutense Madrid, and it is this edition which is used here. The following discussion concentrates only on the main points.

The correspondences between Modestus and Vegetius have been analyzed often and the following list is from Rolan and Casas (p.289):

Modestus	Vegetius
1.1–2	2.1.5–13
1.2–3	2.1.2–8
2	1.1.26
3	2.2
4	2.4
5	2.6
6	2.7
7	2.8

8	2.9
9	2.13
10	2.14
11	2.15
12	3.14
13–15	2.16–18
16	2.22
17	3.8
18	3.16
19	3.24
20	3.17
21	3.26
22	3 praefatio, 14–18
23	1.28

B. The Basic Components of the Roman Armed Forces

Modestus began his treatise (1.1–3) with the standard definitions of what constituted the Roman military forces. It consisted of three basic elements which were: cavalry (*equites*), infantry (*pedites*) and navy/fleets (*classes*). The cavalry consisted of the *alae* (wings), *vexillationes* (detachments) and *equites legionarii* (legionary cavalry). A comparison with the sixth century author Lydus (*De Magistr.* 1.46) suggests the probability that the cavalry *alae* (*ilai*) consisted of 600 horsemen and the *vexillationes* of 500 horsemen. Lydus does not include *equites legionarii* separately but includes cavalry units called *turmae*, which consisted of 500 mounted archers. It is therefore possible that Lydus's *turmae* are actually the units of legionary cavalry, which consisted of smaller 32-horsemen (plus one *decurio*) units which were also called *turmae*. The *alae* would presumably have been the cavalry units of the regular auxiliary forces, while the *vexillationes* would have consisted of native/tribal units of cavalry that had been enrolled into the army.[3] The infantry consisted of legions (*legiones*) and auxiliary forces (*auxilia*) so that the latter consisted of the *socii* (allies) and *foederati* (treaty-based allies). The division of *auxilia* into two types of forces is valuable because it suggests that the units of *socii* were probably the regular auxiliary units while the *foederati* were primarily treaty-based tribal forces which could be based either inside the Roman Empire (as soldier-farmers in return for military service) or as allies outside the borders in return for payments.

C. The Combat Formations

The *tirones* (recruits) were to be trained to fight in a single line (*simplex acies*), double line (*duplex acies*), *acies quadratum* (hollow square) and *triangulum/cuneus* (triangle/wedge). This suggests that the standard battle formations at this time were the single phalanx, double phalanx and hollow square/oblong formations and that the wedge was the standard tactical formation which was used to break through enemy formations. The manoeuvres used in the forming of these arrays would also have enabled the use of other combat formations and manoeuvres and one may assume that these were also known and used even if they were not included in this list of training manoeuvres by Modestus, because we know they were used during the reign of Aurelian. Regardless, the list (2.1–2) given by Modestus here is still valuable because it gives us the likely standard combat formations used at the time. It is also valuable for another reason. It gives us the basic combat manoeuvres that the Romans expected their legionary infantry to be able to use, because Modestus describes only after this (3.1–2) the way in which the *auxilia* were to be used. According to Modestus, the auxiliary forces were to be used only as light-armed forces (*levis armatura*) for the legions, because these forces came from different places and had different habits so they did not have the same discipline, equipment and way of fighting. The *auxilia* were never to form the principal fighting force of the army. It was an auxiliary service as the name implies. The information that Modestus provides (p.4) of the size of the ideal army is antiquated because he states that all authors agreed that each consul was never to lead more than two legions reinforced with auxiliary forces against an enemy. The above is basically the same as in Vegetius 1.26.

The Standard Legionary Combat Formations in 275 according to Modestus

The legionary structure and its combat formation, to be found in Vegetius (2.6), is also partially antiquated. However, there are some significant differences between these two accounts. I will begin with Modestus's version (5.1–7.3) after which I will elaborate the differences and conclusions.

D. The Old Style Legion and its Ten Cohorts

The legion consisted of ten cohorts. The first cohort consisted of 1,105 footmen and 132 horsemen, so it had more men than the other cohorts. The men of the first cohort were considered to be of higher quality than the others because it was in charge of the legionary eagle standard (the *aquila* carried by the *aquilifer*) and the imperial standard depicting the emperor (the *imago* carried by the *imaginifer/imaginarius*). It was called *cohors milliaria* (milliary cohort) because of its size. The first cohort was placed on the right wing of the first line. The cohorts from the second to the tenth, all had 560 footmen and 66 horsemen, and were therefore called *cohors quingentaria* (quingentarian cohort). The order of cohorts in the first line from right to left were one to five, and in the second line from six to ten. The third cohort was to consist of stronger men because it stood in the centre and likewise the fifth was to have energetic soldiers because it was on the left flank. The sixth cohort was to consist of solid young men (*iuniores*) because it was behind the first cohort and therefore guarded the standards. The eighth was to have spirited men because it stood in the centre and the tenth was to consist of aggressive warriors because it held the left flank. The total number of men in a legion was therefore 6,105 and 726 horsemen. There were never to be fewer soldiers than this in a legion, but it was acceptable to have a larger force by adding other milliary cohorts to it. This last instruction allowed the commander to compose a generic legion out of legionary detachments, which was stronger than the regular legion.

The above text is basically the same as in Vegetius (2.6), but there are discrepancies in the figures. In Vegetius the cohorts second to the tenth had 555 footmen and 66 horsemen each while in Modestus's version they had 560 footmen and 66 horsemen each. This discrepancy can be explained by adding to the figure of 555 the supernumerary standard-bearers, heralds and musicians for a total of 560 men. In fact, Modestus's own figures are off in this respect because he claims that the total size of the force was 6,105 footmen and 726 horsemen when in reality with 560 footmen his total should be 6,145 footmen and 726 horsemen. In other words, the total 6,105 that Modestus gives is based on the same figure as in Vegetius, namely 555 footmen per cohort, and it becomes the 6,145 only when it is counted as 560 footmen.

E. Centurions

Modestus (6.1–7.3) and Vegetius (2.7–8) also give us similar but still slightly different versions of the legionary centurions. I will begin with Modestus's version.

The *primus hastatus*, who commanded 200 men, was located in the second line. However, as we shall see from Vegetius's text he was actually one of the commanders of the first cohort. The *princeps* of the first cohort commanded 150 men. Ten centurions were in charge of the first cohort.[4] In addition to these, there were centurions who commanded single centuries which were now called *centenarii*. Each of the second to the tenth cohorts had five centurions so that the total number of centurions was 55. Since the cohorts two to ten made up 45 centurions it is clear that the first cohort must have had 10 centurions.[5]

Vegetius (2.8) gives a different rundown. According to him, the first cohort was led by the following five men: 1) *primus pilus/primus princeps* who commanded four centuries; 2) *primus hastatus* who commanded two centuries making altogether 200 men in the second battle line. He was also known as the *ducenarius*; 3) the *princeps* of the first cohort who commanded one and a half centuries making 150 men; *secundus hastatus* commanded also 150 men; *triarius prior* commanded 100 men. The rest of the cohorts were commanded by centurions now called *centenarii*, five each so that there were altogether 55 centurions. In other words, Vegetius's text implies that the above-mentioned five higher ranking centurions of the first cohort would probably be part of the 10 centurions that are required for the first cohort for the total of 55 centurions per legion.

These versions are irreconcilable, but if one still tries to reconcile them then one may assume that it is possible that Vegetius has included extra officers for the first cohort because the first reference to the practices of the period occurs in the context of *primus hastatus*, who were called *ducenarii*, and that both authors have made the mistake of placing this officer in the second battle line (*ducebat in acie secunda*) unless the implication is the *primus hastatus* was actually an officer who commanded also at least one century placed behind him in the sixth cohort. My suggestion, however, is that the *primus hastatus* and the *princeps* of the first cohort were just higher ranking centurions so that they received salaries commensurate with the number of men officially under their command. The reasons for the conclusion that the numbers of men commanded by the higher ranking centurions refer to the pay grade are: 1) it is impossible to reconcile the commands of 200 men and 150 men with each other unless the centuries in question were divided accordingly; 2) both texts claim that there were 55 centurions altogether. The other possibility is that Vegetius is correct and that the five higher ranking centurions were just centurions who received higher pay according to the official number of men under them. In light of the evidence, it is actually likelier that Vegetius is correct to include the other ranks so that one may assume that Modestus (if he was the author) either made omissions or his treatise was later carelessly copied so that some sections were lost.

F. Rank-and-file structure

The legionary rank-and-file organization in both Modestus (7.3; 9.) and Vegetius (2.8) is the same. Both state that the centuries were organized into units of tens commanded by *decani* (sing. *decanus*) and that the *decani* were also called *caput contubernii*. The ten-man group was also called *contubernium* (tent group) or *manipulus* (maniple). From other sources, we know that the fighting component of the *contubernium* consisted of eight men with the implication that the two extra men per ten-man group were one *tiro*-recruit and one servant, but it is also possible that the two extra men per file/tent-group were light-armed men so that we should add to these figures the servants and recruits.

G. Higher Ranks

The higher command structure of the legion (Modestus 6, 8) was as follows. The *legati* (sing. *legatus*) of the emperor had been in charge of the legions and auxiliaries, but their duties were overtaken by the time of Modestus by the *magistri militum* (Masters of Soldiery) who belonged to the *illustres*-rank. Each of these commanded not only two legions but more legions. The *magistri* referred to by Modestus are not necessarily anachronistic for this era thanks to the changes instituted by Gallienus (see my bio of him). The *praefectus legionis* was the successor of the *legatus* because he was in charge of the legion. The tribunes, centurions and soldiers followed his orders. The tribunes performed judiciary functions on his behalf. Arms, horses, clothes and food supplies were the responsibility of the *praefectus legionis*, as were discipline, punishment and exercises of the infantry and cavalry. Below the legionary prefect served the *tribunus maior* who was appointed by the emperor. As noted in the text, the tribune (i.e. the *tribunus maior* who was usually a member of the imperial bodyguard) could also be used as acting commander of the legions instead of the prefect. The *tribunus minores* (sing. *tribunus minor*) received their position by being promoted through the ranks. *Ordinarii* were those who commanded the first units in battle (*ordines*). The list of ranks is basically the same as in Vegetius (2.7, 2.9) but omits the discussion of *praefecti castrorum* and *praefecti fabrorum* included in Vegetius (2.10–11).

H. Standards and NCOs

Modestus (9–10) states that each legion had an eagle standard (*aquila*) carried by *aquilifer*, each cohort had a *draco*-standard carried by a *draconarius*, and each century had a *vexillum*-standard. Each century was commanded by a centurion, now called *centenarius*, who had a helmet with a crosswise plumed silver crest. The soldiers could therefore recognize their century both from the *vexillum* and the crosswise plumed helmet of their centurion. The centurions were required to be robust and of the right stature and were also to be good throwers of *hasta*-spear and missiles. The centuries consisted of the ten-man *contubernia* under their *decani*, which were also called *manipuli* (maniples).

The 32-horseman *turmae* (sing. *turma*), each under its *decurio* (so that there were 2 x 32 horsemen plus two *decuriones* per standard cohort) formed the basic component of the legionary cavalry. The *decurio* was to be agile, good at mounting his horse, dressed in *lorica*-armour (body armour, cuirass) and fully equipped with weapons. He was expected to be a good horseman, good with the *contus*-spear and a good archer. He was also expected to be able to teach all the necessary cavalry skills to his own *turma*. The key point here is the expectation that all legionary horsemen were expected to be both lancers and mounted archers – a requirement which can be found in Arrian (*Techne Taktika* 34.1–44.2; *Ektaxis kata Alanon*) which confirms that the Romans continued to attach great importance to the versatility of their cavalry forces.

The above information is basically the same as in Vegetius (2.13–14), but Modestus omits some of the material contained in Vegetius.

I. The old legionary combat formation used by old style legions

Modestus (11–14, 18–20) includes two basic variants of the combat tactics, which can also be found in Vegetius (2.15–17, 3.14–17, 3.24). The first of the battle arrays was the old standard legionary *duplex acies* for one legion, the principle of which could be easily extended. Note however that the above-mentioned training scheme suggests that this was not the only type of combat formation that Modestus and Vegetius expected the old style legions to be able form. They were also expected to be able to fight as a single phalanx, hollow square/oblong and wedge.

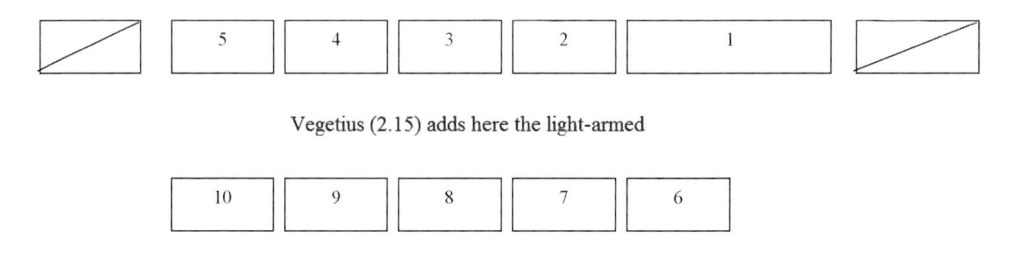

| / | 5 | 4 | 3 | 2 | 1 | / |

Vegetius (2.15) adds here the light-armed

| 10 | 9 | 8 | 7 | 6 |

Vegetius (1.20, 2.16) adds here the *triarii* who could be interpreted as reserves

The first line consisted of cohorts 1–5 with cavalry placed on the flanks. The *ordinarii* and other officers (*caterique principales*), who fought in the first line in front of and among the standards (*signa*), were called as *principes*. They were considered to be heavy-armed (*gravis armatura*), equipped with helmets (pl. *cassides*, sing. *cassis*), cataphract-armour (sing. *catafracta*, pl. *catafractae*), shin-guards (pl. *ocreae*, sing. *ocrae*), *scutum*-shields (pl. *scuta*), longswords (*gladios maiores, spathae*), shortswords (*gladios minores, semispathae*), five darts (*plumbatae*) placed behind the *scutum*-shield, and two missiles/javelins (*bina missilia*), one long and one short. The long missile had a triangular iron head nine inches long with a shaft (*hasta*) five and a half foot long. It used to be called *pilum* (heavy javelin), but was now called *spiculum*. This was designed to pierce the *scuta* of the infantry and the *loricae* of the cavalry. The short javelin had an iron head five inches long and a shaft of three and a half feet long. It used to be called *vericulum*, but its new name was *verutum*. Modestus omits here the references to the light-armed (*levis armatura/ferentarii/ exculcatores: armaturae, sagittarii, funditores, tragularii*) behind the first line, which can be found in Vegetius (2.15).[6] Vegetius is probably correct to add these to the formation, but obviously the light-armed would not have been part of the legionary array proper but a separate force of light-armed under their own commanders, which according to Modestus would have consisted of the *socii* and *foederati*. It should be noted however that legionaries were trained to use all of the weapons mentioned so it was possible to use the legionaries in like manner when deemed necessary. The second line consisted of cohorts 6–10 and was called the *hastati*. These were armed in the same manner as the first line.

Vegetius (1.20, 2.16) adds to this list the antiquarian *triarii* as a third line behind the second line. It is impossible to know whether this existed or not, but it is possible to reconcile this by assuming that the *triarii* would have been separate reserves, for example among the baggage train or in front of a marching camp that the Romans used as required by the situation. Vegetius (3.17) and Modestus (20) state that there were always to be *subsidia* (reserves, sing. *subsidium*) infantry and cavalry behind on the flanks and middle, which may be the meaning here. It should be noted however that the extant evidence for Roman battle arrays suggests that there were usually no extra reserves for the *duplex acies* because the second line in itself was usually considered as a reserve, and it is therefore quite possible that Modestus did not in fact make an omission here.

J. The New Legionary Array (my theory: created by Septimius Severus)

The second of the variants (Modestus 12–14) was a single line consisting of six ranks (*ordines*), which presumably had cavalry wings (Modestus 18), and reserves of cavalry and infantry behind (Modestus 20). This is the most problematic piece in both Modestus (12–14) and Vegetius (3.14–17) because it is difficult to reconcile with the other information that we have of Roman battle arrays. My educated guess, however, is that it was used by the Parthian legions that had been formed by Septimius Severus, and probably by other new legions that were raised after his reign. We have no concrete evidence for this structure outside Modestus and Vegetius, on top of which there is the problem of what was the size of the file/tent-group (*contubernium*) if it consisted only of six men when it had previously consisted of ten men out of which eight men were designated for combat duties. Does this mean that the tent-group still remained the same, but so that only six men out of it were placed in the battle line, the rest being placed among the baggage and/or in the reserves? In my opinion, if the array reflects the truth in any way, we should interpret the six-man file to have consisted of one half of the *contubernium* so that it had four legionaries plus the two light-armed who would not have been part of the heavy infantry *contubernium*. Two such files would therefore have made up one traditional eight-man *contubernium* of heavy-armed (plus the recruit and servant left behind in the camp) and half of a *contubernium* of the light-armed.

K. The New Infantry Phalanx

The Stonewall (Murus), the Heavily-armed (Gravis Armatura)

1) The first rank (*ordo*) consisted of men the ancients called the *principes*. Modestus describes their equipment only later and these references make it clear that the men wore at least cataphract-armour, helmets, *scuta, spathae, lanceae* and *spiculi*.
2) The second rank consisted of the best soldiers otherwise called *hastati* who were equipped with cataphract-armour, and *spiculus*-javelins or *lancea*-spears. Vegetius (3.14) states that in the second line were the cataphracted *sagittarii* (archers) and the best men armed with *spiculi* or *lanceae*.
   – The omission of the archers in the second rank in Modestus actually makes sense in light of the description of how the two front ranks fought, but I would not completely preclude the possibility that there could have also been men armed with bows because Syrianos Magistros (*Peri Strategias* 36) states that when the infantry faced cavalry the first two ranks were to shoot straight at the horses while the rest behind were to shoot at an angle. However, in light of the description of the way in which the first and second ranks fought (Modestus 12.6 and Vegetius 3.14), it is still likelier that Modestus's omission is more accurate. Vegetius could easily have mixed the second and third ranks in his description. The interval between ranks one and two was six feet so that they could throw their spears with greater ease.
   – The soldiers of these two ranks consisted of heavily equipped mature men who were confident and experienced. They stood like a *murus* (stonewall) in place and neither gave ground nor pursued the enemy, and fought with *pila* (sing. *pilum*).

The Light-armed (levis armatura/ferentarii)

3) The third rank consisted of the mobile armed men, of young *sagittarii*, and of good javelineers, which the ancients called *ferentarii*.
4) The fourth rank consisted of the very mobile shield-bearers (*scutati expeditissimus*),[7] young archers, and of those who were armed with javelins or *martiobarbuli/mattiobarbuli* (lead-weighted darts) which were also called *plumbatae*.
   – the third and fourth ranks were called light-armed (*levis armaturae*) and they always advanced in front of the battle array to provoke the enemy with javelins and arrows. If the enemy fled, they and the cavalry pursued them. If the enemy forced them back, they fled through the first and second lines and assumed their previous positions. The first and second lines fought with *pila*. Modestus has here only the javelins (*prima autem et secunda acies cum ad pila, ut dicitur, ventum fuerit, totum sustinent bellum*) to mean the mêlée, but Vegetius includes the fuller version with swords included (*prima autem et secunda acies cum ad spathas et ad pila ut dicitur, ventum fuerit, totum sustinent bellum*) which is of course more accurate as it means that the fighting was done with javelins and swords by the first and second lines

Appendix I 239

who then sustained the fight. Modestus, however, adds a problematic instruction at 14, which states that *levis armaturae/ferentarii* and *sagittarii* and *funditores* (slingers) provoked the enemy in front of the first and second *acies*. The problem with this is that Modestus (and Vegetius) places the slingers at the fifth rank (see below). This same instruction can be found in Vegetius 2.17 in the context of the old legionary structure with cohorts so it is possible that Modestus has placed it in the wrong context. My suggestion is that both versions of Modestus are correct so that the fifth rank could be used either in front of the first rank or alternatively as a support force for the sixth rank if the enemy threatened from behind. I suggest that it was up to the commander to decide whether to send men from the fifth rank forward (see next) at the same time as the third and fourth ranks (the so-called light-armed) advanced to skirmish, or to keep them where they were.

The Fifth Rank
5) The fifth rank consisted of the *ballistarii/balistarii* (probably users of *manuballista* or *arcuballista*), *funditores* (slingers), *tragularii* (in this case probably users of *tragula*-javelin), *fustibalatores* (staff-sling users). The young recently recruited fighters who did not possess shields were posted in this rank so that they used either hand-thrown stones or javelins. Vegetius (3.14) has basically the same list, but he elaborates the material by stating that in the fifth rank were placed the *carroballistae* (horse-drawn carts with *ballistae*), *manuballistarii*, *fundibalatores*, and *funditores*. In other words, Vegetius understood the *ballistarii* to be artillerymen using the *carroballistae*. Similarly, Vegetius understood the *tragularii* to be the *manuballistarii* of his own day. It is therefore quite possible that both were working from the same source so that Vegetius has elaborated the text on the basis of the terms used during his day. If we assume that Vegetius was correct in his interpretation, then the use of the drawn artillery carts would mean that the fifth rank was not a real rank of soldiers in the traditional sense. However, in my opinion it is clear that Vegetius's elaborations are incorrect, and he also proves this to be the case when he explains the distances between the ranks and files (3.15) which clearly prove that we are here dealing with a real fifth rank. Vegetius states in that section that each file in the formation occupied three feet and each rank occupied six feet plus one additional foot so that the depth for six ranks was 42 feet. In short, we should rather accept what we find in Modestus's text so that the *ballistarii* of Modestus's time did not mean the artillerymen of Vegetius's day, but rather the crossbowmen equipped with the *arcuballistae* or *manuballistae* while in this case the *tragularii* meant the javelin-throwers which would be otherwise missing from the list of skirmishers. The lightly-equipped fifth rank belonged to the 'heavy-armed' because they are not included among the light-armed (the third and fourth ranks) by Modestus and Vegetius. This text is also valuable for another reason. It shows where the Romans placed their recruits (the *tirones*) when they were included in the battle array.

The Sixth Rank = Heavy Infantry Reserve
6) The sixth rank consisted of strong soldiers who were equipped with *scutum* shields and every type of defensive and offensive equipment. The ancients called these *triarii*

and formed the 'last rested reserve'. In my opinion it is clear that this posting of the *triarii* as the last rank made the formation two-fronted so that it was possible to face enemies from the front and behind simultaneously. In short, the *triarii* did not only form the 'last reserve' as stated by the sources but also a second front towards the rear when needed and probably in such a manner that the fifth rank would have served as its light-armed in such case.

Equipment worn by the front-rank fighters, signiferi and centurions
Modestus (13) continues the account by stating that all those in front of the standards (Vegetius 2.16 elaborates by calling these *antesignani*) and the *signiferi* wore less armour and wore helmets covered with bearskins to frighten the enemy. The centurions wore cataphract armour, *scuta*, and helmets with silver crosswise crested plumes.

L. The Tactics for the New Phalanx

Modestus (14) describes how the above array was to be used but he has taken it from the section (in Vegetius 2.17) which describes the old-style legion so it is possible that he has made a mistake. This adds to the list of skirmishers (ranks three and four) also the slingers. It is quite possible that this was so because it would be odd if the Romans had not used their slingers in front of their array like they used the other light-armed men. This section states that the first, second, and sixth ranks stayed in their place while the *ferentarii, levis armaturae* and *sagittarii* and *funditores* advanced in front to provoke the enemy. The *funditores* meant only a part of the fifth rank, and since it is known that the slingers needed room to operate it is indeed quite understandable if these were sent separately from the rest. Regardless, I would still suggest that it is possible that the entire fifth rank could also be sent forward to skirmish at the same time as the third and fourth ranks, if the commander so desired. If the enemy forced the light-armed back, they retreated behind the first and second ranks and these stood like a wall against the enemy. The pursuit of the enemy was once again to be performed by the light-armed and cavalry.

M. Diverse instructions
After the above, Modestus included (15–17) diverse instructions before he returned to tactical issues (18–20) presumably meant to be used with the six-ranks formation.

The first of these general instructions (15) is that the shields of every cohort were to be painted with different colours and that each soldier was to have his name, cohort and century painted on the inside of the shield. This enabled the soldiers to recognize each other with greater ease and is the same as in Vegetius 2.18.

The second (16) is that each legion was to have *tubicenes* (trumpeters using the *tuba* straight trumpet), *cornicenes* (cornet players using the *cornu*-horn made from the horns of the wild ox), and *bucinatores/buccinatores* (horn players after the curved *bucina* military horn/trumpet). The *tubicenes* called the soldiers to battle and it also called them to retreat. The *cornicenes* sounded signals to the standard-bearers but not to the soldiers. In short, the soldiers were ordered by the *tubicenes* and the standard-bearers by the *cornicenes*. The *bucinatores* sounded their horn to signal *classicum*, which was a fanfare used to announce capital punishment or the presence of the emperor. When the soldiers were to go to guard duty (*ad vigilias*) or to build *agrarias* (outpost of the camp), or for military exercises, or for any assignment outside, this was announced by the *tubicenes*; and its ending was also announced by the *tubicenes*. The *cornicenes* ordered the standard-bearers either to move or to halt. In sum, the officers used these musicians to order the soldiers to fight, halt, follow, or to return as needed. This is the same as in Vegetius 2.22, but Vegetius also includes a fuller discussion of the different ways to command the soldiers at 3.5 which is not specifically included in Modestus. However, Modestus still refers to, or implies the use of, all of these (voice, horns, standards, plumes) in his treatise.

The third (17) concerns guard duties in the camp. Each of the centuries was to detail four footmen and four horsemen for guard duty during the night. Guard duty for each group of guards lasted for four hours and the 'night' was divided into four parts. The guards were dispatched to their duty by the *tubicenes* and then recalled to their tents by the *cornicenes*. This instruction is included in a longer discussion of the organization of marching camps by Vegetius 3.8. In Modestus it follows logically after the previous discussion of the ways in which the horns/trumpets were used, and it is therefore possible that this piece of information had originally been included in a treatise which dealt with all of the different uses of the horns/trumpets which has been retained in Modestus, but placed elsewhere by Vegetius.

N. The New Phalanx in Combat

Both Modestus (18) and Vegetius (3.16) naturally place the cavalry on the flanks as most ancient military treatises did. The *loricati* (armoured horsemen) and *contati* (those carrying *contus*) were placed next to the infantry. The *sagittarii* and others who did not carry armour were posted further out. The stronger ('*fortioribus*') cavalry protected the flanks of the infantry, while the faster ('*velocioribus*') and lightly-equipped ('*expeditis*') were to scatter and disorder the flanks of the enemy formation. The *dux* (general) was also required to know which cavalry unit to place against which enemy *drungus* (a throng meaning irregular array) or *globus* (a crowd meaning a detached unit). The reason for this was that certain types of troops were better against certain types of troops than others. Vegetius 3.19 equates *globus* with *drungos* so it was probably the same type of array. If the Roman cavalry was inferior to the enemy, Modestus instructed the commander to place mobile infantry equipped with light shields and trained for this duty among the cavalry. The name for these was the *velites*. The *velites* were used in such a manner that one young soldier, who was a good runner and equipped with a light shield, sword and javelins/missiles, was placed between two horsemen. This is basically the same as in Vegetius 3.16 even if there are some slight differences in the way the sentences are structured.

Modestus follows this with a description of how to fight against elephants (19), which is essentially the same as the latter half of Vegetius's chapter 3.24 even if the latter is longer and slightly different. If one speculates about the inclusion of this at this place, it is possible to use it as a proof of the accuracy of Modestus's treatise because such a summary as Modestus claims to have made for Tacitus would definitely have been required information for the inexperienced Tacitus, because at the time of his death Aurelian had been on his way against the Persians who used elephants. It is quite plausible to think that Modestus's treatise was written before it became apparent that the first enemies which Tacitus had to deal with were the Goths and Heruls which Aurelian had assembled against the Persians, and even then the instruction of how to fight against elephants would not have been out of place because Probus was subsequently forced to deal with this question immediately after assuming power and was also planning to begin the long planned campaign against the Persians when he was murdered. The above instructions for the use of cavalry units against detached enemy cavalry *drungi* and *globi* would also fit the circumstances in which the fight was to be conducted against the Persians.

The information about the elephants in warfare is as follows. The elephants frightened the enemy with their size, horror of their trumpeting (*barritus horrore*), and by the novelty of the spectacle. Pyrrhus, Hannibal, Antiochus and Jugurtha had used them against the Romans. The Romans had devised several different means against the elephants as a result. The first was to cut off the trunk with a sword as had been done by a centurion from Lucania. The second was to use cataphracted horses to draw a war chariot and place

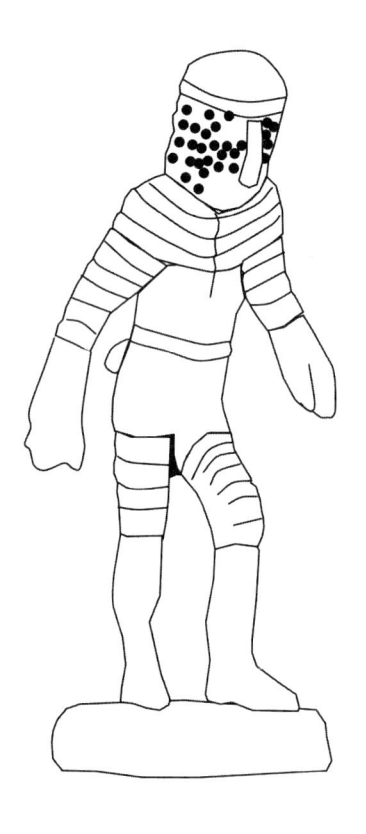

Fully Armoured gladiators.
Left: a drawing by Duruy of a relief depicting a gladiator now at the Louvre, which Carter identifies as an 'arbelas' gladiator who was armed with a knife and *arbelos* (semi-circular shoe-maker's knife). The original image in the Louvre has a visible trace of *arbelos* on the left hand which is not visible in Duruy's drawing, but I have restored it with a line to the image. **Right**: Author's drawing of a bronze figurine from Vertigny, which is usually identified as *crupellarius*. It is possible that Modestus and Vegetius meant soldiers equipped like these gladiators with the addition of spikes against the elephants.

clibanarii (heavily-armoured men) armed with *sarissae* (very long spears – *longissimos contos*) and use them to thrust into the elephant. The third was to send cataphracted legionaries (*cataphractos milites*) with iron barbs attached to their arms, helmets and shoulders so that the elephants were unable to seize them with their trunks. The implication is that these soldiers also wore armour on their arms (*manicae*?) and probably also on their legs, so they may have looked like the gladiator *crupellarius* or '*arbelas*' or medieval knight with the addition of spikes.

The fourth method, the use of *velites* against the elephants, was the principal tactic that had been used by the ancients. The *velites* were young, lightly-equipped, agile men, mounted on horses armed with javelins. They were therefore much like the eleventh century peltasts who were infantry in antiquity but light-armed horsemen in the eleventh century (see Syvänne, 2010). The *velites* rode their horses back and forth alongside the elephants and peppered them with *lanceae* (a lance with two variants, long and short), or *maiora spicula* (heavy javelin). The reference to a long *spiculum* is interesting because it suggests that there existed also a longer variant of the *spiculum/pilum*, which can possibly be equated with a cavalry spear but with the likely difference that these two types had a different point. These were at their best used in quantity, thrown in volleys simultaneously at the elephant. The fifth tactic was to use slingers and staff-slingers. These killed the Indos[8] who drove/rode the elephants and the men in the towers. The sixth tactic was to open up the formation (*agmen*) of legionaries to allow the elephants pass through, after which they were surrounded from all sides with a *globus* so that the *magistri militum* (masters of soldiers)[9] could capture the elephants with their drivers. Vegetius adds here a seventh tactic which was to use the *carroballistae* behind the battle line to transfix the elephants with their missiles. This is consistent with the above where Vegetius has these *carroballistae* in the fifth line while Modestus does not. It is not certain whether the omission by Modestus was purposeful or just accidental because we know that the Romans did use *carroballistae* as part of their battle line during the third century, so it would have been quite possible to use them in the manner described by Vegetius. One possibility is that Modestus assumed that this knowledge was not necessary, because the *carroballistae* crews, when present, would have targeted the elephants anyway without having been ordered to do so. Modestus described only how to use the six ranks of the phalanx with their cavalry wings against the elephants.

Modestus (20) like Vegetius (3.17) stated that the *dux* posted chosen footmen and horsemen with extra *vicarii*, *comites* and *tribuni* behind the *acies* to the wings and the centre as reserves. In other words, the 'real last reserve' was not the sixth rank *triarii*, but these. If the enemy attacked vigorously the reserves were to rush forward to block it. The *cuneus* (wedge) and *forfex* (pincer) arrays were formed by using the reserves behind for this purpose. If the Romans had few men, it was necessary to make the reserve stronger. Modestus omits the discussion of the *serra* (saw) array and the use of the *globi* against *globi*, which are mentioned by Vegetius. Similarly, Modestus does not include any discussion of the different unit tactics (*serra, globus/drungos, cuneus, forfex, orbis*)[10] nor of the seven different battle formations (lateral phalanx/rectangle, right oblique, left oblique, forward angled array, forward angled array with light infantry posted in front, right wing sent in advance to outflank, and use of terrain) included in Vegetius 3.19–20.

O. Security and Secrecy

Modestus (21) includes two instructions on how to prevent the enemy from learning what the Romans had planned. Enemy spies/scouts (*exploratores*) inside the camp were to be captured by calling all men inside the tents. The commander was to deliberate matters with many in councils, but to keep the number of trusted men small. This meant that the enemy got several possible versions if discussions leaked, but not the real decisions because the number of trusted men remained small. The list selects only two examples from a large number of maxims included in Vegetius 3.26.

P. The Reason for the Writing of the Treatise

Modestus (22) states that as ordered by the invincible emperor his intended purpose was to write a treatise based on scattered ancient authors and that he had done that as well as his modest talents allowed. This was a standard topos among this class of authors and is the same as can be found in Vegetius (*3 praefatio*) but with the difference that Vegetius has much longer discussion.

Q. Military Art, the Forgotten Art?

Modestus (23) ends his treatise with a general discussion of military art. According to him, the passion for war and the lands which produced the Lacedaemonians, Athenians, Marsi, Samnites, Peligni and Romans still produced strong men. He also stated that Epirotes were at one time powerful, and that the Macedonians and Thessalians had defeated the Persians so that they marched to the borders of India. The Dacians, Moesians, and Thracians were always so warlike that the fables told that Mars was born among them. Modestus commiserated that it would take too long to enumerate the strengths possessed by all of the provinces, and that the long peace had caused men to turn to civilian professions and forget the practice of military training. The interesting point here is which nations Modestus names. They are all territories located in Italy, Greece and Balkans. The implication is that the treatise, which Modestus (and Vegetius, see below) had used for this, was probably written during the reign of Gallienus because it was during his reign that these areas formed the only source of recruits for him. It is also probably not a coincidence that the text refers to the pagan god of war Mars.

The above is basically the same word for word as the middle portion of Vegetius 1.28, but again Vegetius has a longer discussion. Vegetius also promotes the training of native recruits in the same context because it was cheaper to the train one's own men rather than to pay foreigners to fight. It is probable that this is a later addition of Vegetius which refers to the problems of his own day when the Romans did indeed pay foreigners to fight on their behalf.

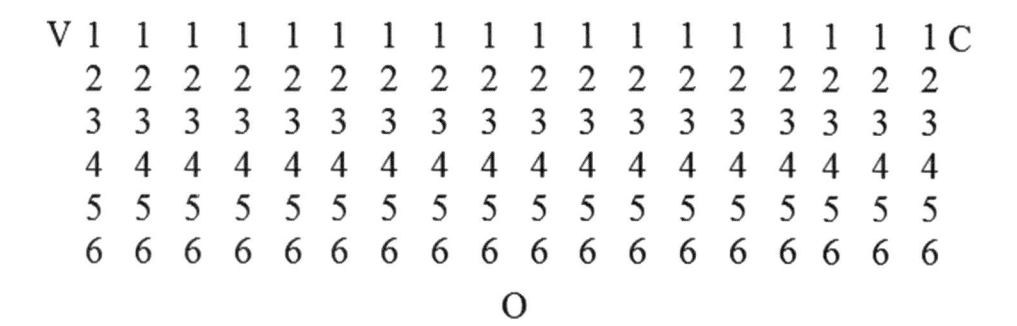

```
V 1  1  1  1  1  1  1  1  1  1  1  1  1  1  1  1  1  1 C
  2  2  2  2  2  2  2  2  2  2  2  2  2  2  2  2  2  2
  3  3  3  3  3  3  3  3  3  3  3  3  3  3  3  3  3  3
  4  4  4  4  4  4  4  4  4  4  4  4  4  4  4  4  4  4
  5  5  5  5  5  5  5  5  5  5  5  5  5  5  5  5  5  5
  6  6  6  6  6  6  6  6  6  6  6  6  6  6  6  6  6  6
                           O
```

The Principal Roman Combat Formations according to Modestus in ca. 275

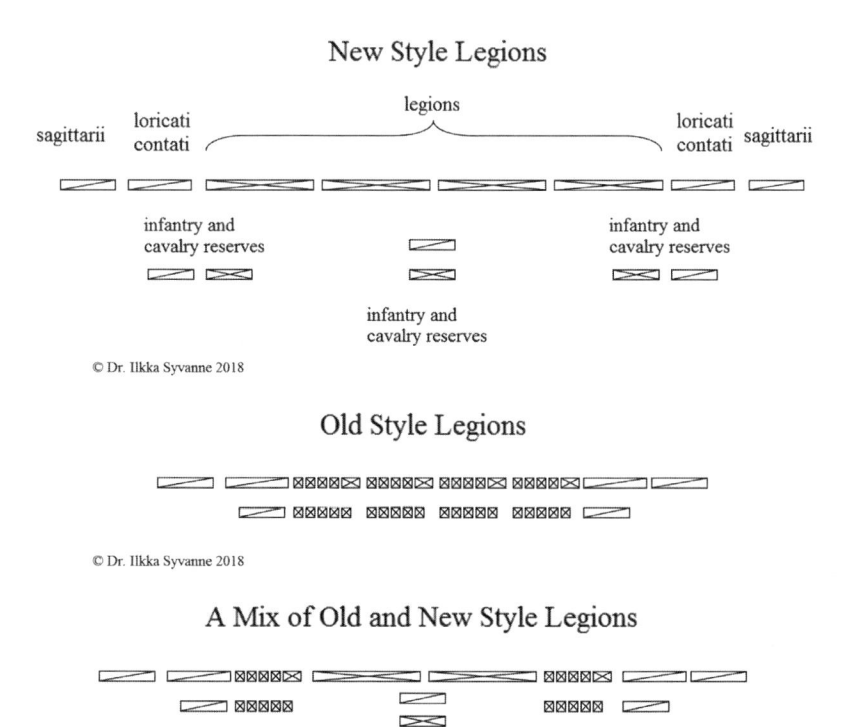

New Style Legions

sagittarii | loricati contati | legions | loricati contati | sagittarii

infantry and cavalry reserves

infantry and cavalry reserves

infantry and cavalry reserves

© Dr. Ilkka Syvanne 2018

Old Style Legions

© Dr. Ilkka Syvanne 2018

A Mix of Old and New Style Legions

R. Unit Organization for the New Legions

The above discussion has referred to the new type of legion which was deployed as a phalanx of six ranks for combat, which I have speculated to have been introduced by Septimius Severus for his Parthian legions on the basis of the unit structure.

The basic building block of this legion remained the same as before. It was the century, but its strength had been changed to suit the new tactical concept. We can calculate its strength by dividing the figures 555 (Vegetius) and 560 (Modestus) by five (the number of centurions). As noted above, Modestus's figure includes the supernumerary men so that the division should be made according to Vegetius's figure. This gives each century 111 men. The organization behind this is that there were 108 legionaries deployed six deep (18 files x 6 ranks = 108) plus *optio* (second-in-command), *vexillarius* (standard-bearer with *vexillum*; could also be called *signifer* carrying a *signum*) and centurio for a total of 111 men. Even if the basic structure of the file in combat had remained practically the same as before,[11] these numbers actually imply one major change, namely that now the light-armed had been added to the legionary numbers whereas in the past these had previously been separate and classed as auxiliary forces. The attached diagram gives one possible way the soldiers (numbers 1–6 show ranks), *vexillarius* (V), *optio* (O) and *centurio* (C) could have been deployed for combat.

The cohort formed the next unit size. It consisted of the above-mentioned centuries for 555 men with the NCOs. We should add to this figure *tubicen*, *cornicen*, *draconarius*, *vicarius* (second-in-command to *tribunus*) and *tribunus* for a total of 560 men. I would suggest that the *bucinatores* were not included in the regular cohortal structure because they were needed only on very special occasions. The milliary cohort would have had 1,110 men plus the supernumeraries.

The legionary cavalry in its turn probably consisted of 22 *turmae* of cavalry for 704 horsemen plus 22 decurions, 10 musicians, 5 standard-bearers, and 5 centurions for a total of 746 horsemen.

The legion consisted of the above-mentioned cohorts and of the milliary cohort so that the total size for the legion was 6,100 footmen plus the supernumeraries and 726 horsemen plus the supernumeraries. With four legions the battle array envisaged by Modestus would have looked something like in the attached diagram. The above also explains why we find heavy-armed legionaries deployed three deep in Josephus (e.g. BJ 2.173, 5.130–1) in a situation in which the *contubernium* (tent-group/file) consisted of eight soldiers, one recruit and one servant, as dictated by the size of the tent. The reason for this was that the Romans trained a third or fourth of their recruits to fight with the bows. In those situations in which we find the Romans using three deep or six deep formations of heavy-armed legionaries, they used the missing numbers of legionaries as archers. In other words, the three heavy-armed legionaries and one archer would have made up a half-file/half-tent-group, and the six heavy-armed legionaries and two archers, the entire fighting component of the file/tent-group.

Appendix II

The Problem of Third Century *Drungus/Droungos* as a Military Unit

The word *drungus/droungos/drouggos* could mean different things in the sources of various eras. It could mean an irregular order adopted by any unit (including both infantry and cavalry), or it could mean a very specific type of unit, or it could be used as a synonym for names of units, as it was later used for example by the sixth century *Strategikon* (2.2.1–3), by Leo the Wise (e.g. 4.44) and *Sylloge Tacticorum* (e.g. 35.2) in the tenth century. However, there seems every reason to suspect that the word could be used in similar manner also in the third and fourth centuries on the basis of Vopiscus's references to units with this generic term.

Flavius Vopiscus (*HA Probus* 13.7, 19.2) has two references to the unit called *drungus* (*droungos*), which meant an irregularly formed unit – a throng. In the first instance Probus took from the defeated Germans 16,000 *tirones* (recruits) who were distributed among the *numeri* and *milites* of the *limites* (frontiers) in groups of fifty or sixty men. In this case the *numeri* can mean the irregularly organized national *numeri* or any auxiliary unit, but the former is more likely because after the granting of citizenship to the freeborn men by Caracalla the auxiliary units came to consist solely of citizens and could therefore be considered as Roman soldiers. The *milites* would traditionally be interpreted to mean the legions but considering the time period I would suggest that in this case it means both legions and auxiliary units. The problem with this is that Vopiscus fails to specify whether the recruits consisted of cavalry or infantry, or both. I would suggest both.

In the latter instance Probus paraded in his triumph barbarians (included Germans and Blemmyes) in groups that had up to fifty men each. In this case it is clear that the size of the *drungus* was not uniform, and that the men walked on foot.

On the basis of the above, I would suggest that the *drungus* was any irregular throng of men and that the word could be applied equally to any unit that assumed an irregular order or which was irregular in size. In Vopiscus's vocabulary the *drungus* meant a small throng of up to fifty men, or alternatively about fifty or sixty men. The word could also be applied to units of foot and horse. It is possible that the fifty-man units were cavalry units (e.g. 10 files 5 ranks) while the sixty-man units were infantry units deployed in the manner specified by Modestus, but this is pure speculation.

Meanings of terms changed later because the sixth century *Strategikon* (2.2.1–3) already connects the *droungoi* with the larger units called *moirai* (1,000–3,000 men) and *mere* (3,000–6,000/7,000 men) rather than with the smaller units that had at most 50 or 60 men as in Vopiscus's text. This may mean that the *droungos* was smaller than the *moira* with the implication that it could be identified with the *tagma/bandon* of 200– 400 men, but this is uncertain because the *Strategikon* fails to state this clearly. The important points in the *Strategikon* at 2.2.1–3 are that the *moirai*, *mere* and *droungoi* were all expected to be flexible in size and that the *droungos* was now a larger unit than it had been previously. By the tenth century the *drungus/droungos* was a synonym for the units called *chiliarchia* or *moira*, which were not to possess more than 3,000 men each. However, the word still retained the meaning that the unit was arrayed in irregular order. The *droungos/chiliarchia/moira* consisted of units variously called *tagmata* (sing. *tagma*), *banda* (sing. *bandon*), or *allagia* (sing. *allagion*) as it was called in the *Sylloge Tacticorum*. The ca. 6,000-strong divisions (Roman legions or *catervae*) were then called *mere* (sing. *meros*) or *tourmai* (sing. *tourma*). The *meros* consisted of three *droungoi/moirai* and were not to have more than 6,000 men (Leo) or 9,000 men (*Sylloge*). Note that the *turma/tourma* was no longer the small 30–32 horseman cavalry unit of earlier times. This clearly reflected a tendency to inflate the terms, because the *turma* was already identified with the 500-man unit of mounted archers in sixth-century Lydus's *De Magistratibus* (1.16), which in its turn used much earlier texts as its sources. It is therefore not surprising that the meaning of *droungos* was similarly inflated. At the time of the writing of the *Sylloge* (the date is contested, but it was in the tenth century), the infantry *tagmata/banda* consisted of 200–400 men, while the cavalry *banda/allagia* consisted of at least 50 men or at most 350–400 men. This would mean that at that time the 50-man units were identified with cavalry and that they were no longer called *droungos*. By then the *droungos* was a unit consisting of 1,000–3,000 men.[1]

In sum, I would suggest that in practice the Romans were employing smaller units of flexible size and organization called *drungi/droungoi* because their size varied and they were formed by choosing a suitable number of men from existing units or detachments. The most natural way for this would have been to divide the existing larger units into smaller throngs, for example because the unit was no longer close to its paper strength as a result of illnesses or injuries or for some other reason. Later Roman military treatises such as the sixth century *Strategikon* and the much later Leo's *Taktika* and *Sylloge Tacticorum* specifically refer to this when they state that the size of combat units varied according to the availability of men. The *Strategikon* also notes that the depth of the cavalry unit depended on its quality. The better the quality, the shallower the formation; it varied from five to ten men. Even though this instruction is first found in the *Strategikon*, it is clear that the Romans had always followed this same policy. The depths of the units, including both infantry and cavalry units, had always been varied according to the quality and size of the force.[2]

Notes

Chapter 1
1. In some cases I have left sources unmentioned in the footnote because their information (with a reference to the source) has been included in the secondary source mentioned in the footnote.

Chapter 2
1. See Syvänne MHLR vols.1–2.
2. Syvänne, *Caracalla*, 35ff.; with Syvänne, *Gallienus* (still forthcoming at the time of writing).
3. Syvänne, 2011; Syvänne, *Gallienus*.
4. Greco-Roman military theory had several names for the *duplex acies* depending on which direction the phalanxes faced. The *diphalangia amphistomos* had two phalanxes facing opposite directions. The *diphalangia antistomos* had two phalanxes facing each other. The *diphalangia homoistomos* had two phalanxes facing the same direction. The *diphalangia heterostomos* had two phalanxes facing different directions. As is obvious, the terms allow different interpretations and have also been differently interpreted in the treatises, but it is not necessary to analyse these in this case because the main point here is that the two phalanxes could be used to face different directions as needed.
5. The following discussion is based on: Zahariade (2011), D'Amato (2009b), Rankov, Reddé (highly recommended), Pitassi (2009, 2011), Bounegru and Zahariade (Danubian Fleets), Starr, and Syvänne (2004, 2013–14, *MHLR vol.1, Caracalla*).
6. Commodus is credited with the founding of the fleets *Classis Nova Libyca*, and *Classis Africana* to protect the grain shipments from Egypt, but some historians suspect their existence. The existence of the *Classis Mauretanica* is also contested because some historians believe these ships to have been detachments drawn from other fleets.
7. Research paper/presentation held at Norfolk in 2014; Herodian 2.14. 6–7; Starr (1943 with 1960); Paulus in *Digest* 49.18.5 (Levick 2, p.75).
8. This is based on Syvänne, 2004 and my presentations 2013–14 with *MHLR Vol.1*; Pitassi.
9. A fuller discussion with sources in Syvänne, 2016 and *Caracalla*.
10. Syvänne, 2011; *Gallienus*.

Chapter 3
1. Sources collected in PLRE1, Aurelianus 6; Cizek, 11–12.
2. Sources, analysis and comments in: the PLRE1 Aurelianus 6, Cizek, 12–13.
3. *HA Aurel.* 5.3ff., 6.1ff., 7.3ff.,
4. *HA Aurel.* 8.1ff.
5. No such legion is known, but since the evidence for the third century is so poor one cannot exclude the possibility that such a legion existed. As tribune Aurelian would have been the acting commander of the legion (i.e. *praepositus*). He would have been the *tribunus maior* of Modestus and Vegetius. See Appendix 1. It is also likely that Aurelian would have been a member of the imperial bodyguards when assigned to such command.
6. Magie (HA 3, p.214) notes that none of the five third legions is known to have possessed the cognomen *Felix*, but it is nevertheless entirely plausible that such a legion existed. One of the existing legions could have obtained this title or one of the newly recruited third century legions (we do not know the names of all of these) could have held the title.

7. It is more probable that the reconnaissance was conducted with cavalry which could flee if necessary.
8. Maximinus Thrax is claimed to have held the same position just before he murdered Alexander Severus in 235.
9. *HA Aurelian* 8–15. The author claims that Aurelian acted as deputy (*vicar*) for generals (dukes i.e. *duces*) and tribunes on about forty occasions and in addition held very many commands as a general and tribune. The *HA* also claims that Aurelian saw service both in Gaul and Illyricum. In the latter case, he is supposed to have acted as a deputy to Ulpius Crinitus *dux* of Thrace and Illyricum during his medical leave. In addition, the *HA* contains a letter supposedly sent by Valerian to Gallus in which he states that he had left his (grand)son (Saloninus) Gallienus to the care of Postumus, because he considered Aurelian much too stern and harsh and therefore not suited to accompany the merry making Gallienus. If there is any truth in this, this sequence of events would suggest that Valerian had left Postumus with Gallienus to act as his advisor. It would also suggest that Valerian appointed Aurelian as a deputy general of Crinitus in 255 or 256. During Crinitus's absence in 255 Aurelian distinguished himself with the result that when Valerian returned to Byzantium in 255, he ordered Crinitus to adopt Aurelian as his son and appointed Aurelian to the positions of consul and inspector of all army camps, the latter being the same position that Maximinus Thrax is also supposed to have held as a reward and from which position he rose to become the emperor after the murder of Alexander Severus. White (50ff.) also believes that Crinitus was a real person, but dates the events differently.
10. When the *consules ordinarii* were asked to resign after six months by the emperor, he replaced them with the *consules suffecti*. This was a means which the emperors used to bribe people with the consular honour.
11. Full argumentation for this and the offices can be found in Syvänne, *MHLR* vol.1 and *Gallienus*.
12. Magie in his edition of the *HA* (*Probus* 3, Loeb ed. p.341, n. 4) suggests that the name of the sister is fictitious on the basis of the name or that she was a half-sister. Considering the period practice of taking new names when assuming imperial office, I would not preclude the possibility that she was a full sister, but it is not impossible that she could have been a half-sister. After all, it was not uncommon for women to die when giving birth to a child.
13. Sources collected in the PLRE1, Delmatius 1, Probus 3.
14. Magie (*HA*, p.342, n.1) notes in his edition/translation that it is possible that Artabassis Syrus is an error for the Armenian Artavasdes, but in my opinion this is unlikely on the grounds that Artavasdes/Artavazd the Mandakuni or Mamikonean fled to the Roman territory only in about 260/1. See my arguments in *MHLR Vol.1*, *Gallienus* and Syvänne & Maksymiuk, 2018. On the basis of Kerdir's inscription (the so-called KKZ) it is clear that Shapur I needed to conquer Armenia, Iberia/Georgia and Albania in about 260. This is also confirmed by the *HA* (*Val*. 1.1.ff.), which lists these areas as independent from Persia. My educated guess is that Khosrov the Great had been murdered in about 256/7 by Persian special operatives after which the new regent Artavazd allied himself with Shapur I only to change his alliance back to the Roman side by about 259.
15. *HA, Probus* 5.1ff.
16. *HA, Probus* 6.1ff. Syvänne, *Gallienus*.
17. The following chapter on enemies is based on Syvänne *MHLR Vol.1* and *Caracalla*.
18. The *Georgian Chronicles* (pp.80–1 see with Syvänne *MHLR Vol.1*) specifically claim that the Khazars (anachronistic term which either means some nomadic group or the Alans) were in the habit of attacking the Derbend Pass at this time, which may suggest some Roman diplomatic efforts in the area against the Persians.
19. The evidence is collected in Banchich (Zonaras 12.25, pp.114–16), Bray (239ff.), Cizek (22–3) and Geiger (173ff.). The following account is based on these and Syvänne, *Gallienus*.

Chapter 4

1. In general for the reign of Claudius see Syvänne *Gallienus* and Southern (2001, 108–10). Note, however, that my reconstruction of Claudius' reign differs from all other accounts because I date the events differently. The account provided here is also slightly different from the one that I give in *Gallienus*.
2. Based on my biography of Gallienus.
3. The *HA Claud.* 4.3 includes a letter to the Senate. The letter is probably fabricated, but it is still clear that Claudius initially sent only a letter and his henchmen to Rome to secure the backing of the Senate in a situation in which he still needed to defeat Aureolus.
4. Zonaras 2.25, *HA* (*Gall.*, esp. 14–15); Aur. Vict. 33. See the summary of the various later versions in Zonaras/Banchich pp.114–16.
5. A complete analysis of the sources and the campaigns are offered by Syvänne, *Gallienus*. In other words, I go even further in the reconciliation of Gallienus than Alföldi.
6. Aurelius Victor 33, Eutropius 9.9; *HA Tr.* 3–8, 24; PLRE1 for other sources. For other interpretations, see Potter (263–4) and Drinkwater (1987, esp. 23–36, 148ff.) with Syvänne, *Gallienus*.
7. Zonaras (12.26) has preserved us an incident which took place when Claudius was in Rome. It was then that Claudius gave the order that nobody was entitled to receive the property of another as a gift from the emperor. As a result of this, an old woman approached the emperor and noted that Gallienus had confiscated her property and had given it as a present to Claudius. Claudius duly returned her property. The incident proves two things: Claudius was not incorruptible; Claudius had some sense of justice left in him and it is quite possible that he sought to correct the abuse of power when he was in the position to do so.
8. Potter, 265.
9. *HA Claud.*; *Aurel.*; *Probus* esp. 5.5ff. ; Syvänne, *MHLR vol.1* (165–7, 179–81, 189), *Caracalla* (Index under *Aulici*), and *Gallienus*.
10. If there is any truth to this story, one could argue that it was actually this Claudius who stopped the purge of Gallienus's relatives and friends and not the real Claudius! However, it is still more likely that it was the real Claudius who did this because the soldiers demanded it. On the basis of this, it would also be possible to argue that the *HA* has dated the usurper to the wrong reign so that Censorinus and Urbanus would have been usurpers during Aurelian's reign in 271. Censorinus's use of the name Claudius (Claudus) could be seen as a gesture to seek support from those who had supported Claudius and Quintillus.
11. The claimed career of Censorinus in the *HA* (TR 33) is of interest because it gives a possibility of making one additional speculation, which is to suggest a possible collusion with Aurelian. It claims that Censorinus had not only served as praetorian prefect twice, but also that he had held the post of extraordinary envoy to the Persians. When we remember that Aurelian had also served as an envoy (*Aurel.* 5.5–6) to the Persians, it becomes possible to think that these two men knew each other and could have cooperated against Claudius. The likeliest date for such a collusion is the year 270 when the sources make it clear that Aurelian was not doing anything worthy of note against the invaders in the Balkans. It should be noted, however, that this is mere speculation based on the uncertain evidence presented by the very unreliable source.
12. The letter from Claudius to Aurelian included in the *HA* (*Aurel.* 16.1–17.4, letter in 17.1–4).
13. Dexippus fr. 6; See the analysis in Drinkwater, 2007, 73–5.
14. Capture of Narbonensis and Spain in Drinkwater, 1987, 36, 120. The name Gratianopolis is later and dates from the period of the reign of Gratian in the fourth century.
15. HA Tr. 6; Aurelius Victor 33.2.
16. For a full analysis, see Syvänne, *Gallienus*.
17. On the basis of earlier research, which in its turn is based on the Arabic traditions preserved by al-Tabari, Al-Yaqubi. Ibn al-Athir amd al-Nuwairi, Stoneman (156–7) suggests the

252 Aurelian and Probus

possibility that Zenobia (Zabba/Zebba) could have used a ruse to kill the sheik of the Tanukh Arabs called Jadhima in order to gain control of the desert region up to al-Hira. The whole account is completely ludicrous and is solely based on the fact that Zabba/Zebba of Palmyra is the Arabic version of Zenobia. It has long been recognized that the story of Zabba/Zebba of Palmyra contains fabulous legends, but several previous researchers have still quite mistakenly placed the events mentioned in this tradition occurred during the reign of the famous Zenobia. The account in question is preserved in detail in al-Tabari (i.750–71), but for some unknown reason the previous researchers who accept the above have failed to take into account the timeline given by al-Tabari. He states (i.768–71) in no uncertain terms that Zebba and Jadhima both lived just before the rise of the Sasanians under Ardashir I and Shapur I. In other words, this Zenobia/Zebba of Palmyra lived during the period before the year 224/226.
18. Details of the minting of various coins here and below are referred to in Watson, 221–3.
19. *Legio VI Ferrata* was posted at Legio-Kefar Otnay (Caparcotna), but it disappears from the sources in ca. 260 and it is possible that it was destroyed together with Valerian's army in ca. 259/60 (or during the usurpation of the Macriani, my comment). See Farnum, 20. However, in my opinion, it is possible that a new legion was raised to replace it during the 260s which could have been one of the newly raised third century legions which we know nothing about unless it is included in the *Notitia Dignitatum* (turn of the fifth century).
20. HA Claud. 11.1; Zosimus 1.44; Malalas 12.28; Watson, 60–4; Southern, 2008, 106–7.
21. For the trade and trade routes, see Southern (2008, 24–33); Stoneman, 31ff., 53.
22. This is my interpretation for what happened.
23. The terms I have used come from Greek/Byzantine military theory and their inclusion in this discussion is entirely my own. For other analyses of the Palmyran military, see Southern (2008, 24–6), Nicolle (22–41). Nicolle considers the role of the mounted archers to have been of greater importance than that of the cataphracts, but I disagree because the sources make it quite clear that most of the combat cavalry consisted of these and that they were the most fearsome force wielded by the Palmyran state.
24. Stoneman, 121ff. with indexes on the men named.
25. Stoneman, 129ff.
26. Stoneman (146–51) collects the evidence. He does not accept the traditional interpretation, but may be correct in stating that the appeal to Aurelian was already done in 270.
27. Stoneman, 123ff.
28. See e.g. *PLRE1 Probus 3, Probus 5*.
29. For a fuller analysis of the Moorish tribes and their ways of fighting, see Syvänne *MHLR* vol.1.
30. The official marriage status was probably that of concubine/mistress with the emperor so as not to upset Roman customs, but opinions differ on this point and it is also probable that the Marcomanni saw the marriage as real.
31. Dexippus fr. 6; See the analysis in Drinkwater, 2007, 73–5.
32. *Epitome de Caesaribus* 34.2; Watson, 43.
33. Potter, 263–4; Watson 44.

Chapter 5
1. The *HA Aur.* 18.1 states that Aurelian served as commander of all cavalry under Claudius. The evidence for the position of Aurelian under Claudius is collected by Saunders p.134ff. For the titles, see my *MHLR Vol.1* and *Caracalla*. However, as noted above, it is actually possible that Aurelian had the title *tribunus et magister officiorum*.
2. This chapter is based on Saunders (137ff.), but unlike him I accept the traditional sequence of events and would not consider it impossible for Quintillus to have ruled for 77 days.
3. The *HA (Claud.* 12) claims that some of the surviving Goths tried to seize Anchialus and Nicopolis when they retreated northwards, but were then defeated by the valour of the

provincials. In other words, Vopiscus claims that the locals managed to defeat the retreating Goths at a time when Aurelian had withdrawn his forces and marched to Sirmium to declare his bid for power. This is a good example of the tendency of *Historia Augusta* to whitewash all of the failures that took place under Claudius and Aurelian. Ammianus (31.5.16) states in no uncertain terms that the Goths pillaged both Anchialus and Nicopolis at this time. The other possibility is that this failure took place in 269 and was the reason why Claudius had urged Aurelian to improve his performance and why he had intended to send his brother with reinforcements to the Balkans only to change his mind later so that he marched there in person. See *HA, Claud.* 17 with Syvänne, *Gallienus*.
4. For the coins and papyri, see Watson 60–4, 221–3. Note, however, that my reconstruction of the events differs completely from the one adopted by him and others in suggesting an alliance between Aurelian and Zenobia against Quintillus.
5. The information concerning the dating, minting and papyri is in Watson, 60–4, 221–3. See also Southern 2008, 112–15.
6. The date of November is from Watson, 62.
7. For a completely different reconstruction of the early wars of Aurelian against the Iuthungi, Vandals, Alamanni and others, see Watson, 48ff. We reconstruct the campaigns in a completely different order and manner. In my opinion, he places the campaign of the Iuthungi mentioned by Dexippus's fragment in the wrong context by connecting it with the campaign in which Aurelian suffered a defeat at Placentia in 271.
8. This emendation was made for the first time by Valesianus.
9. See the forthcoming Syvänne (*Gallienus*) with Zon. 12.26.
10. Saunders (169ff.) reconstructs Aurelian's march in such a manner that he would not have reached Aquileia before turning northwards to catch the retreating invaders. This is a distinct possibility.
11. At this time, after the reign of Gallienus, the field army was divided into separate cavalry and infantry corps. The most important reasons for this conclusion are: 1) The existence of a separate cavalry commander implies the existence of a separate infantry commander; 2) the sources (e.g. Zos. 1.45) show the cavalry and infantry operating independently of each other, with the implication that these had separate command structures. For additional info, see Syvänne (*MHLR Vol.1* with the forthcoming *Gallienus*).
12. Müller FHG 682ff.; Dindorf HGM 190ff. As noted, Watson interprets the evidence differently.
13. For the various views, see: Drinkwater (2007, 73–5); Saunders 163ff; White 65 ff.
14. The connection between the myriads of killed Alamanni with this campaign was first made by Saunders (p.171). The reason for my educated guess that Aurelian used cavalry for the ambush is that I interpret the use of the word *peraioû* (to carry over, convey to the opposite bank) in this context not to mean the carrying of the Roman attack over to the other side of the Danube, but to mean the throwing of the Iuthungi back over the river with a cavalry attack. The best evidence for this is that the Roman army was deployed on one side of the river as a crescent when the Iuthungi envoys came to meet Aurelian. The other reasons for this conclusion are: 1) Aurelian had previously served as *hipparchos*; 2) the Roman army was deployed as a single crescent on both sides of Aurelian when the Iuthungi envoys came to meet him and all of the leading officers are claimed to have stood beside their horses; 3) the Iuthungi envoys stressed the mounted fighting qualities of their horsemen (*hippomachia*); 4) it would have been difficult to overtake the retreating Iuthungi with infantry forces and then bypass them to place an ambush on the opposite bank of the Danube, whereas it would have been relatively easy for a cavalry force to mount a pursuit during which they would have been able to bypass the enemy which was encumbered with infantry and spoils of war and place an ambush on the opposite bank.
15. For the use of similar practices to receive enemy embassies under Constantius II, see Syvänne *MHLR Vol.1*.

16. For a fuller discussion, see the forthcoming Syvänne, *Gallienus* with Syvänne *MHLR Vol.1*.
17. I do accept Drinkwater's (2007, 73–5) suggestion that the Iuthungi had previously been allowed to settle inside the Roman Empire by Gallienus and had received subsidies in return for defence of their lands somewhere in Pannonia.
18. Drinkwater interprets this to mean undiluted members of the warrior band, but I am inclined to agree with those historians who think that this refers to racial purity. This would certainly not have been the only instance of such behaviour among the Germanic peoples. It is not without reason that there was a distinction between the Alamanni (all-men) and '*katharos*' Iuthungi (young ones), and between the Bastarnae (bastards with mixed Celtic and German lines) and Sciri (pure ones, the pure-bred Germans).
19. In short, I do not accept Drinkwater's (2007, 77) claim that the Iuthungi army would have consisted simply of bands of young warriors. Would the emperor himself have taken the field with his field army, if the enemy consisted only of a few thousand raiders? Wouldn't it have sufficed for him to let his generals handle such minor threats? Furthermore, could the numerous generals of the third century (namely those that were given command of entire sections of frontiers with the title of *dux*) have usurped power if they had only a few thousand men at their disposal? On the contrary, it is clear that the generals had large armies that allowed them to face the even larger enemy forces; the downside was that this also enabled them to usurp the throne. Most importantly, would there have been any need for the large-scale fortification programme (including the rebuilding of the walls of Rome), if the enemy consisted only of small numbers of raiders? Obviously not, because if this had been the case then even citizen militias would have been able to deal with them.
20. The timing of the events in Watson, 48–9.
21. Zonaras 12.26–7; most of the sources collected in Bancich, Zonaras, 59–60, 116–25; Banchich, Peter, 127.
22. Translations of the original texts conveniently in Banchich, 60, 124.
23. Saunders 173–5.
24. For Aurelian's anti-corruption policies and other policies meant for the upkeep of the public morals, see e.g. *HA Aurel*. 36.1ff., 37.7, 38.2ff., 39.3ff. 49.3ff. The sequence in which these measures were introduced is not clear, but it is likely that Aurelian would have started his legislative reforms early on with those measures which corrected the abuse of power under Gallienus. Gallienus's colossal project was cancelled by Aurelian: *HA Gall*. 18.2ff.
25. This is the strategy that was later recommended by Vegetius, Maurice's *Strategikon* and Phocas' *De Velitatione*. See Syvänne (2004) with forthcoming Nikephoros II Phokas.
26. Dexippus, *Skythika* fr. 7; Zosimus 1.48.
27. Dexippus, *Skythika* fr. 7; Zosimus 1.48–9. For the mistakes of Gallienus, see the forthcoming Syvänne, *Gallienus*.
28. The discussion is based on *HA Prob*. 6.5–6 and my biography of *Gallienus*.
29. Dexippus, *Skythika* fr. 7; Zosimus 1.48–9.
30. Peter the Patrician Banchich frg. 193 = *Anon. Cont. Dio, Müller FHG 4*, p.197.
31. Epitome 35.2 claims that the battle of Placentia was a victory for Aurelian, but this is clearly a mistake.
32. See my *Gallienus*.
33. Epitome 35.3; Llewellyn; Watson, 52; White, 76. Domitian the Second was probably the gifted general of Gallienus who contributed greatly to the victory of Aureolus over the Macriani in 261.
34. See the discussion in Llewellyn. Note however that my interpretation differs from that proposed by Llewellyn.
35. Since the two other usurpers, Septimius and Domitianus, can be located to Dalmatia and Gaul repectively, it is clear that Urbanus must have been at Rome.

36. The fact that Aurelian subsequently tried to establish the sun god as supreme god and used the Apollonius of Tyana as a Christ-figure for this religion suggests a cynical readiness to use religious concepts to promote unity within the empire. On the basis of this, it might be plausible that he could have sent the abovementioned letter to appease the traditionalists at Rome. On the other hand, the punishment Aurelianus unleashed against the senators at Rome when he finally arrived and the subsequent establishment of the sun god and Apollonius of Tyana might also be seen as his reaction against the old religion with its foolish consultings of the Sibylline Book. It would also have represented his rather desperate attempt to subvert the growing power of Christianity with a competing god and new Christ-figure acceptable to most pagans.
37. HA Aurel. 18.3–6.
38. Dio Cont. fr.10.4; Epitome 35.2; HA Aurelian 18.6ff, 21.5, 38.2–4, 39.8; Watson, 50–2; White, 81–2.
39. Zosimus 1.49.2; Epitome 53.3; Watson, 52; Llewelyn.
40. For Aurelian's supposed cruelty, see Watson, 159ff.; Allard 2006b; White, 75–7.
41. Most of the Praetorians would have been with Aurelian, but it is still clear that a detachment of the guardsmen would have remained in the city itself. These would have been quite ready to join their comrades in Aurelian's army and fight against the usurpers.
42. HA 21.5ff.; Zosimus 1.49.2; Victor 35; Epitome 35.4; Eutropius 9.14; Amm., 30.8.8. Watson 162, 223.
43. Watson, 133.
44. In this case, the *militia* suggests the troops in the emperor's presence (i.e. Praetorians); *riparienses* frontier troops posted alongside the rivers (i.e. the Danube); *lembariarii* (after *lembos* - boat/ship) suggests either mariners/marines posted alongside the rivers (i.e. the Danube) or the mariners/marines of the regular sea-going navy, which in this case would have presumably meant detachments from the fleets of Ravenna and Misenum posted in Rome (note the location of their headquarters on the accompanying map); the *castrensiani* suggests troops posted in frontier forts; the Dacians were either regular troops posted in the province of Dacia or Dacian conscripts, the former being the more likely alternative. The list of troops suggest that Aurelian deployed specialist infantry corps used to fighting on the streets, rivers and hills. In other words, troops most suited to fighting in the streets of Rome that included all of these variants.
45. HA 21.5ff.; Zosimus 1.49.2; Victor 35; Epitome 35.4; Eutropius 9.14; John of Antioch Roberto ed. frg. 236.
46. The following discussion and the images of the wall are based on Nick Field's study of the walls (esp. 23ff.)
47. HA Aur. 21.9, 35.1–2, 45.4–5, 48.1;
48. In other words, the effect would have been akin to a tax reduction in a modern society. Another good example would be the US system in which bankrupt individuals would regain their credit after some years have passed since their bankruptcy. This is one of the reasons for American economic dynamism which is missing from Europe, where the debts often stay on the records until paid in full, the latter of which makes most individuals quite reluctant to even attempt to improve their position in society.
49. *HA Aurel.* 39.3–4.
50. Watson, 127–35.

Chapter 6
1. HA Aur. 22, Prob 9 (esp. 9.5);
2. HA Aur. 22; Amm. 31.5.17.
3. It was probably then that Constantius, the father of Constantine the Great, met Helena, the mother of Constantine, at Drepanum in Bithynia. Constantine was born at Naissus on February 273. See Syvänne, 2015, 169–70 after Barnes.

4. Vopiscus's (HA Prob. 9.1–5) account of Probus' exploits in North Africa and Egypt is confused and it is probable that he has confused the two Probi with each other. Therefore it is possible that M. Aurelius Probus actually fought against the rebels in Carthage including the duel against Aradio in 271 and advanced from there to Egypt, but since Vopiscus claims that Probus advanced from Libya, where he had fought against the Marmaridae, to Carthage, I have here adopted the view that these events probably took place in 269, just as the instance in which Probus was almost taken prisoner by the Palmyrenes would have taken place in 270 so that the return with reinforcements would have taken place in 272. Regardless, the state of the evidence is such that it is possible that the campaign in Carthage could have taken place in 271 and the reconquest of Egypt in 272.
5. Peter the Patrician, Banchich frg. 194 = *Anon. Cont. Dio FHG 4*, p.197.
6. Southern 2008, 134–5.
7. Saunders, 208ff.
8. Saunders (214ff.) suggests that Egypt surrendered when the news of the Palmyrene defeat at Immae was brought there and that the Romans reached it via land. He also does not accept that M. Aurelius Probus would have had any role. I agree with the usual view that Probus was in charge of the operation and that the conquest was probably an amphibious operation while it is not impossible that Probus was actually advancing from Carthage.
9. *HA Probus* 9.5; Cizek, 106; Watson 69–71, 223–4; Southern 2008, 115, 131–3. My interpretation of the campaign of M. Aurelius Probus in Egypt in 272 is that it is only the last mentioned part of the text of the *HA, Probus* 9.5 that belongs to the reign of Aurelian and that the incident in which Probus fought so carelessly actually belongs to the period when he fought under Tenagino Probus. I do not accept the claims put forward by some historians that there would not be any shred of evidence for fighting in Egypt (e.g. Southern p. 132 refers to Hartmann's similar arguments). The shred of evidence is in the *Historia Augusta*, but of course these historians do not accept this as a valid source to be used.
10. Saunders (212ff.) places the battle of Immae to late April/May, but prefers late April. Either way it was easily warm enough if the wind blew in the right direction because the climate was warmer during the Imperial period – even in our less warm climate the weather can get hot if the wind blows from the right direction.
11. See e.g. Southern 2008,135–8; Watson, 73–4; White, 93–5. Stoneman includes a neutral comment regarding Downey's reconstruction (170) but does not endorse it.
12. See above with White, 95–6.
13. For an analysis, see Syvänne 2004 with Syvänne *MHLR Vol.1*, 314–5.
14. For a fuller analysis, see my *Caracalla*. Caracalla kept the southern portion of the conquests, but apparently gave the northern portion of it back in return for formal recognition of Rome's superior position so that these tribes became Roman allies.
15. Frontinus (*Stratagems* 1.9.8ff., 2.4.18) lists a number of instances of the use of the supernatural which had been used by commanders in the past and this is only one example. The religious practices of others could also be used. See e.g. Frontinus 2.1.16–17. Frontinus (1.12) wisely also included examples of how to dispel fears inspired by omens. It is likely that Aurelian was familiar with similar methods.
16. This referred to the barbarian troops of Sertorius who manipulated the barbarians by using a white deer as a means of obtaining 'prophecies'.
17. See the units listed in Pseudo-Hyginus's treatise.
18. *Aelian* (Devine ed. 37.3); *Byzantine Interpolation of Aelian* (Devine ed. 40.1–6, Dain ed. E1–5); *Strategikon* 12.1.7.307ff., 12.2.13.
19. Saunders puts the end of the siege at August 272, but it is quite probable that it ended before as suggested by Cizek (111–114).
20. A good description of these can be found in Stoneman (172–3) and in Saunders (222ff., esp. 229ff.). Stoneman, however, puts the distance between Emesa and Palmyra at 140 km, while Watson puts the distance about 160 km. Consequently, there is no agreement regarding the

distance: all are within the range 140–160 km, which is a march of four to six days in desert conditions for infantry and baggage train. The reason for the differences in the distances is that they were measured differently in different geographical works. These differences are listed in Saunders p. 230 n. 260. The following list emends the km figures, but it is possible that his miles should be emended. The shortest old estimate for the distance from Emesa to Palmyra is 80 miles, while the modern estimates vary from 88 miles to c.97/8 miles (155–157 km, 144 km in Saunders) up to 111–112 miles (178–180 km, 165 km in Saunders). The differences in estimates are therefore significant. White (98–9) states that the distance was 80–90 miles (130–145 km). For a general discussion of how the Romans organized their water supplies for their campaigns, see Syvänne, 2006.

21. E.g. Stoneman 173; Southern 2008, 140–1; Watson, 76; White, 98.
22. Tabari i.768ff., i.821ff.
23. Banchich Frg.195, Anon. Cont. of Dio, Müller FHG 4, p.197.
24. Gawlikowski; Saunders, 224ff.; Southern 140ff.; White, 99ff. On the basis of the finds, Southern (140ff.) claims that the walls did not surround the entire city, so she claims that there was no real siege at all.
25. See Saunders, 216ff.
26. Moses 2.78. Of note is also the claim that the Seres (i.e. the Chinese) revered Aurelian as god in the *HA Aurel.* 41.10. This is obviously suspect, but all the same it is quite probable that the fame of Aurelian reached China either via Persia or via the Red Sea route, or rather that the Seres in question were Chinese soldiers now in Roman custody.
27. Agathangelos (37) and Moses (2.79) with Syvänne *MHLR vol.1*. According to Moses (2.81), a Chinese refugee called Mamgon, who is claimed to have belonged to the imperial family of China, was sent to Armenia by Shapur I at the same time as Tiridates was returning to Armenia in 277. Mamgon chose not to fight against Tiridates, but Tiridates did not use him against the Persians. However, he gave Mamgon and his entourage a place to settle and a stipend to support his followers. For Mamgon and the Chinese connection see Moses 2.81, and for an analysis of the circumstances of his arrival, see Syvänne and Maksymiuk, 104. Did these Chinese bring with them the knowhow to build trebuchets, which probably made an appearance in Roman armies soon after this if we take fourth century heavy ammunition as evidence? There is obviously no need for this assumption because the Greeks and Romans certainly knew the mechanical principle as they used cranes. In sum, the evidence that we have suggests the likelihood that there were Chinese units in the Persian army at this time and that then as a result there were also some Chinese prisoners in the Roman army. The State of Wei and its successor Western Jin were neighbours of Persia in Central Asia and it is quite easy to see that it was possible for the Chinese to flee to Persia and vice versa. In fact, the son of the last Sasanian ruler fled to China. Conditions prevailing in China after the fall of the Han Dynasty in the third century would certainly have been such that there could have been a continuous string of refugees fleeing towards the west and the safety provided by the Persian Empire. A good summary of Chinese history at this time can be found e.g. in Lewis (31ff.).
28. *HA Aurel.* 33; Saunders, 239ff. PLRE1 Marcellinus 1.
29. *HA Aurel.* 28.4, 29.2, 33.2; al-Thalibi pp. 498–9. For the circumstances, see Syvänne *MHLR vol.1* 169ff. with Syvänne & Maksymiuk (108–9). The time of the death of Shapur I is not known with certainty. Estimates vary from 270 until 273. I and Maksymiuk prefer 272.
30. Banchich in *The Lost History of Peter the Patrician* (p.131) and Watson (186–7).
31. Examples of 'cruelty': HA Aurel. 6.3–8, 8.1–4, 16, 23.4–5, 31.1ff., 32.1ff., 36.1ff., 37.4, 37.7, 38.2ff., 39.2ff., 39.8ff., 40.2, 44.2, 45.1, 47.1ff, 49.3ff.; Epitome 35.4; Eutropius 14; Sextus Aurelius Victor 35.7ff. My interpretation of the evidence is basically the same as that adopted by White (75–7). That Aurelian liked to be present when people were tortured presages similar instances that took place under the Tetrarchs when they and their guests could be having banquets while people (e.g. Christians) were tortured in their presence. For this, see Syvänne, *MHLR vol.1*. The times were violent.

Chapter 7

1. Cizek, 113–17; Homo, 108–15; Saunders 243ff.; Southern 2008, 152ff.; Watson 80ff.; White, 105ff.
2. The inscription (CIL III 12456) which mentions a battle along the lower Danube in Dobruja between Carsium and Sucidava reads as follows: *[I(ovi) O(optimo)… gratum referens quod i]mp(erator) Aure(ianus) vicit [reginam Ze]nobiam inviso[sque tyrannos et Carpos inter Ca]rsium et Sucid[avam delevit] Duros[torum] Aurel[ianum].* Saunders notes that most historians associate this inscription with Aurelian's Carpic war, but at the same time he correctly notes that the crucial word *Carpos* is a restoration and the evidence is therefore uncertain.
3. Who exactly were the *laeti* is not known, but it is probable they were defeated enemies handed over to the Romans by the defeated tribe who were then settled on Roman soil as farmers and soldiers, while the *foederati* (allies) were defeated tribes settled on Roman soil in their entirety.
4. Saunders 243–4.
5. Saunders (p.242) calculates that the journey of ca. 916 miles from Emesa to Byzantium took about 70 days.
6. In the early fifth century the courier (*agens in rebus*) Palladius (Socrates 7.18–19 with the PLRE1 Palladius 5) was able to carry the most important messages from the eastern front to the capital in three days and then back to the eastern front also in three days. See Syvänne, 2016.
7. Saunders, 250–1, Watson 82; White, 107–8. Watson claims that a person who swims among crocodiles, rides ostriches, drinks huge amounts of wine and gets people to strike an anvil balanced on his chest while he was in the crab position is scarcely a credible historical figure. In my opinion this is too restricted a view of what people do to get the attention and adoration that they crave. I see no reason to disbelieve the account because of this. People have done far stranger things to obtain followers. Contrary to majority opinion Stoneman (178–9) considers Firmus to have been a historical figure, but his interpretation of the papyri which call Firmus *epanorthotes* (corrector) is challenged by others. Southern (2008, 155–6) remains non-committal about the historicity of Firmus presumably in an effort to avoid criticism, but she at least notes that the *HA* did separate three different men with the same name Firmus.
8. The fact that the *HA* separates the Aksumites/Axomitae from the Indians means that the latter signifies the real India. The sudden emergence of the Blemmyes and Aksumites at this stage as supporters of Zenobia's party should be connected with the events described by the so-called *Monumentum Adulitum II* (translation in Burstein 101–4). Hatke's (37–66) analysis proves that it describes the conquest of the western shore of the Red Sea (the eastern desert with the Blemmye tribes of Atalmo, Beja and Tangaites) up to Roman Egypt, and the conquest of the eastern shoreline from the Gulf of Aqaba up to the land of the Sabaeans (this included the defeating of the Arabitae, which I interpret to be Arabs of Arabia Felix, and the defeating of the Cinaedocolpitae, which I interpret to be the Kinda) by some unknown Aksumite ruler during the period c.200–270. Hatke quite correctly notes that at this stage the Aksumites did not invade the territory held by the Meroites/Kushans, which took place in the following century. I would date the Aksumite conquest of the eastern desert roughly to the period 259–270 on the basis of the information included in the *HA*. The earliest date for the Aksumite advance up to the borders of Egypt would be around 259–61 because it was in about 261 that the Prefect of Egypt Aemilianus usurped power and then advanced against the barbarians whom he forced to retreat (*HA Thirty* 22.6). The problem with this is that the text does not identify who the barbarians were. It is possible that they were the Blemmyes or some other barbarian tribe. If they were the Blemmyes then one can think that the Aksumites subdued them on behalf of Rome. We are on firmer ground for the period after 270. It was then that the Aksumites and Blemmyes were fighting on behalf of Zenobia (*HA Aurel.* 33.4–5; *FSPB* 3ff.). On the basis of this I would suggest that the Aksumites probably conquered the eastern desert regions with the western and eastern shorelines of the Red Sea during the 260s possibly on

behalf of Rome. It was thanks to this that the Palmyrenes and their supporters in Egypt sought and obtained help from both the Blemmyes and the Aksumites.
9. For a detailed analysis of these different types of enemies, see Syvänne *MHLR* vols. 1–2 with *Caracalla*.
10. Sailing/rowing speeds are based on Casson's estimates (281–99).
11. HA Aurel. 45, 47; Ammianus 22.16.15.
12. For Roman strategy when dealing with Parthians/Persians, see Syvänne *MHLR* vol.1 290–1, 337–9, *Caracalla*. The Romans operated in Indian waters also later, see Syvänne *MHLR vol.2*.
13. Syvänne *Caracalla* 227–31 with Dio 76.13.1. It is of course possible to think that Aurelian could have sought to outdo Septimius Severus and did indeed conduct the campaign against the Blemmyes, Saracens, Yemenis and Aksumites in person because Aurelian sought a return to the golden age of the Severans at least in his monetary policies. Regardless, a campaign by some general is more likely.
14. Based on Watson 128–42.

Chapter 8

1. For an analysis of the term *restitutor orbis*, see Valérie Allard 1.
2. Strictly speaking Victor mentions only Tetricus present in the triumph.
3. This brings up the methodological question: Why do those who dismiss the *HA* as worthless not treat Zonaras or any other texts which they claim to include falsifications or errors in the same manner? If the same problems are present in these other sources, shouldn't these too be dismissed as worthless. And vice versa if these other sources are accepted as valid for argumentation, why not the *HA*?
4. See the various theories in: Saunders, 262ff.; Southern 2008, 160–1; Watson, 113; White, 117–18. The PLRE1, however, has Severina as *Augusta* from 270 until 275.
5. Southern (2008, 160–1) lists the sources which mention the descendants of Zenobia. Southern, however, does not accept the claim that Aurelian would have married Zenobia's daughter.
6. In other words, I do not agree with Watson's analysis (93–5) but agree with White (112–3) that Tetricus and his staff betrayed their army to be butchered.
7. For the sources, see PLRE1 Tetricus1 and Watson 95, 246.
8. I therefore disagree with White (113) who thinks that the massacre was unintentional because Aurelian would have wanted to pardon those men just like Tetricus because they were needed. In my opinion the massacre was intentional because Aurelian did not need such men.
9. White 112–14.
10. See Syvänne, *Gallienus*.
11. Bernard (p.232) translates *opes regiae* as train of the court, while Magie translates it as wealth of the kings on the basis of the meaning of Ops as goddess of plenty. Both are possible.
12. Epitome 35.5; HA Aurel. 35.4–36, 46, 49.7ff., HA Tac. 10.4, 11.6.
13. HA Aurel. 45, 47–8, 50.
14. HA Aurel. 49–50.
15. HA Aurel. 36.3, 37.4, 39.8–9, 42.1–2, 50.5; Eutropius 9.14; Epit. 35.9.
16. Watson (101–2) suggests that the *HA* refers loosely to Gaul when it describes the barbarian invasion of Raetia, or alternatively that the invaders reached Gaul too, or that Aurelian marched to Raetia via Gaul. However, I am inclinded to agree with Saunders' (258, 265–7) speculation that the rebels in Gaul could have been supporters of Faustinus in Trier while the attackers in Raetia consisted of barbarians (Alamanni). However, in other details my reconstruction differs from that adopted by Saunders. Cizek (190–2) and White (142–3) suggest that there was a rebellion at Lugdunum because the silver coins were not up to the new standard, but offers other alternatives. For my view, see the text.
17. Cizek, 192–6; Saunders 267ff.; Watson, 102–3; White, 143. It should be noted that the argument regarding the order of the cities in different sources regarding the place where

260 Aurelian and Probus

Aurelian was subsequently murdered is not relevant because those that name Byzantium/Constantinople first wrote in Constantinople so they naturally saw things from their own perspective.
18. One would like to know whether Aurelian had had a role in this fight between the kings in the same manner as Caracalla had had when he encouraged Artabanus to begin his civil war against Vologaesus. See Syvänne, *Caracalla*.
19. See Syvänne *MHLR vol.1* with Syvänne and Makzymiuk (2018), 109ff.
20. Saunders' claims (269ff.) that this should be dismissed on the grounds that the *HA* states that the Goths in question were the Maeotidae (Goths of the Sea of Azov) is false. He is mistaken here because the fact that the Bosporans later engaged the retreating Goths proves that the *HA* is correct.
21. See Syvänne, *Caracalla*. Caracalla, however, was not even the first emperor to employ Goths in the army because Maximinus Thrax (half-Goth, half-Alan) was already enrolled in the bodyguards of his father Septimius Severus.
22. See Syvänne *Gallienus* for the use of Goths by Valerian. See Syvänne *MHLR vols.1–2* for the use of Goths under Galerius, Constantine and Constantius II. Constantine the Great actually concluded an alliance treaty with the Tervingi Goths which required them to contribute soldiers to the Romans when this was required. Julian was the first Roman ruler who did not understand the importance of this. He dismissed the barbarian helpers, although he still appears to have had some left in his army thanks to the policies of Constantius. The treaty relationship between the Romans and Goths was broken by Valens in the most foolish manner.
23. Christians could be motivated to fight with tricks, as Constantine the Great was to prove, but they could not be motivated with sights of the *Sol* or Apollonius of Tyana.
24. Jordanes Romana 290 states that Aurelian launched a persecution, but Eusebius is a period source and his view is to be preferred in this case because he did not have any reason to lie about this.
25. Eusebius *HE* 7.20–22; Lactantius 2.14–21; Orosius 7.23; Syncellus AM 5764; Homo 375–7, Watson, 198–202.
26. This would have been the general view of the Roman authorities towards what at the time was considered a strange cult which was alien to Roman culture.
27. The analysis of the murder is based on the following sources. Greek sources: Zosimus 1.62; Zonaras 12.27; Leo Grammaticus (also known as Symeon Magister), p.79; *Consularia Constantinopolitana* p.229; John of Antioch Roberto ed. frg. 238; Syncellus AM5765; Malalas 12.30; Cedrenus, p.455; Scutariotes/Synopsis Sathas p.39. Latin sources: Victor 35.8; Eutropius 9.15.2, Epitome 35.8, Lactantius 6; *Chronica Urbis Romae* p.146; Jordanes *Romana* 291; Jerome 263 Olympiad 260/2290/223c; *HA Aurel* 35.5, 36.4–6. Secondary sources: Homo, 322–6; Saunders, 273–80; White, 144–7, 153–5; 195–207; Watson, 104–7; Banchich, 122–5.
28. It is not surprising that the corrupt persons would have consisted of the officers of the bodyguards because Zonaras's text (12.26) proves that this corps was already corrupt under Gallienus because Claudius (who was the commander of this unit, see my *Gallienus*) had been guilty of at least one such instance.
29. Vopiscus *HA Aurel.* 37.1–4.
30. Saunders, 276–280; White, 153–155; Cizek, 203–206; Watson, 104–116.
31. *Ibid.*
32. *HA Prob.* 6.5–7.

Chapter 9
1. These are Orosius's words (7.23).
2. It should be kept in mind that it was and is very rare even for great military commanders to have an unblemished war record with no losses. It is because of this that we should not judge Aurelian too harshly by the one defeat that he had. After all, he was able to rectify the situation after his mistake.

Chapter 10
1. This and the following chapters build upon my earlier study of the reigns of Tacitus, Florianus and Probus in the *MHLR* (vol.1, 171ff.), and include new material.
2. Aurelius Victor 36; *HA Tac.* 1.1–7.7; Zonaras 12.28.
3. E.g. McMahon, Tacitus. Translations of the terms are by McMahon.
4. See e.g. McMahon, Tacitus.
5. HA Prob. 7.1–5.
6. Syncellus AM5765; John of Antioch Roberto ed. frg. 239: Tacitus defeated the Maeotidae and was on his way back to Europe when he was killed in a conspiracy. The reason for this was the nomination of Maximinus as governor of Syria. The assassins of Aurelian killed Maximinus and then Tacitus.
7. See Syvänne, *MHLR vol.1*, 335–6. The man murdered was Silvanus.

Chapter 11
1. This and subsequent chapters are based on my earlier study of the reign of Probus and his successors (*MHLR vol.1*, 171ff.), but includes plenty of new material.
2. For a fuller discussion, see Syvänne, 2004 with Syvänne, Water and Caracalla.
3. John of Antioch, Roberto ed. frg. 240, Zonaras 12.28; Aur. Vict. 37.1.
4. See e.g. the list of opinions in McMahon, Tacitus n.29.
5. See later. Kreucher (202–12) lists the known governors of the provinces including Saturninus (p.207).
6. Kennedy, 231–6; Kreucher, 187ff.

Chapter 12
1. Kreucher, 136–7. Kennedy (219) suggests in his thesis that the date in the *Justinian Code* is likely to be mistaken as are so many other dates in it, but on the basis of the Armenian and Georgian sources I agree with Kreucher that it is more than likely that the date is correct.
2. See Kazanski & Mastykova, 52–3.
3. Agathangelos 46–7.
4. We know that Probus had achieved some military success against the Persians by 21 October 279, because the title *Persicus Maximus* has been found on a papyrus bearing that date. The date and analysis of the role of Tiridates in these events can be found in Kreucher (158–61) and in Syvänne *MHLR vol.1*, 173.
5. Kreucher, 136–9.
6. For example by Kennedy, 220.
7. According to Julius Caesar (*Gallic War* 1.29), his description of the size of the army of the Helvetii was based on the register of the soldiers written in Greek. The list separated the children, old men, women and warriors from each other so that out of the entire force of 368,000 persons about 92,000 were able to bear arms. When one remembers that the Helvetii were just a small force in comparison with the large third century tribal confederations (note e.g. the size of the Iuthungi force), it is clear that a combination of these could easily put to the field as many as 400,000 warriors so that e.g. the Franks would have invaded with ca. 100,000 men, the Alamanni with 100,000 men, the Iuthungi with 100,000 men, the Vandals with ca. 50,000 men, the Burgundians with 80,000 and so forth.
8. The figure of 60 men is consistent with the six ranks formation included in Modestus (see Appendix 1), while the figure of 50 is consistent with the cavalry units (e.g. 10 files, 5 ranks). See the discussion in Appendix 2.
9. Syvänne, 2015, 175.
10. Syvänne, 2015, 175.
11. Syvänne, 2015, 175; Kreucher, 144–5; PLRE1 Clementius Valerius Marcellinus, Julius Nuffuzis, Julius Matif.

12. At the heart of the dating problems is the dating of the revolt of Saturninus the Moor, because the different ancient historians and chroniclers provide us with conflicting evidence about its date. Zosimus dates the revolt to the beginning of Probus' reign, but as already discussed he has placed the events in the wrong order. Jerome (Hieronymus) dates the revolt to 281 (but his dates are one year too late) while Syncellus dates it to the sixth year of Probus' reign (282). Vopiscus (*HA Prob.* 18.4–5, 19.1–20.1) also clearly implies that the revolt of Saturninus took place before the revolts in Gaul. If the revolt is to be dated early to the reign of Probus then it would probably have taken place in about 278 with the implication that Probus marched east to crush the rebel in 278/9. But if it is to be dated later it is likely that it would have taken place in about 279–280 or 280–281. In the former case Probus would have been forced to abandon his planned campaign in Germania or against Proculus and Bonosus and then campaign against Saturninus in about 280. The third alternative is that Saturninus revolted at about the same time as the barbarians in the Balkans so that Probus continued his campaign from the Balkans to the east in 281. In this study I have decided to adopt the view that Saturninus revolted in about 279–280 and was the reason why Probus did not continue from the Balkans to Gaul in 279, but turned back to the east and only then marched against Proculus and Bonosus in 280. The analysis of the evidence can be found in: Kreucher, 172ff. (dates the revolt to the year 281); Kennedy, 224 (dates it to 279); Syvänne, 2015, 175 (dates it to 279, but places the campaign in different context) and the sources and discussion in this book. Kreucher notes that Jerome has misplaced the events by one year so that the actual date he referred to would be 280.
13. This chapter is entirely based on Mitchell, 177–217, and the original sources mentioned. The other studies that I have used in this chapter are Kennedy (223–4) and Kreucher (150–5).
14. I suggested in 2004 that it is possible that the Romans were already using the trebuchet by the late Roman period but with the caveat that it was also possible to shoot these extra heavy pieces of ammunition with the older artillery pieces. Regardless, it is clear that the references to super heavy ammunition multiply after the third century, which means that it is possible that the Chinese prisoners captured from the Persian army (see the narrative) could have been responsible for the introduction of the trebuchet at this time.
15. Mitchell, 217.
16. The *Georgian Chronicles* falsely refers to the man who attacked Tiridates with the name Mirian (the King of Georgia/Iberia) whereas in truth Mirian would have been a subordinate of the Great King of Armenia Narses. Narses was the second most important man in Persia right after the king of kings Bahram II who was fighting against another brother of his in the east called Hormizd. I have here adopted the solution of calling Mirian of the *Chronicles* almost always with the name of Narses. However, it is still clear that the real Mirian did participate in these operations, but only as a subordinate of Narses.
17. Agathangelos (122–132).
18. In the former case Vopiscus places the revolt of Saturninus to take place before the revolts in Gaul while in the latter case Vopiscus states that the next project of Probus after the Triumph at Rome was to march against the Persians, which means that he no longer had to deal with Saturninus in 282. However, if the revolt of Saturninus was ended in the manner as described by Zosimus (see later) even the second of Vopiscus's statements can be explained away.
19. According to Vopiscus (*HA FSPB* 7.2), it had been Aurelian who had nominated Saturninus as supreme commander of the eastern forces and that he had forbade Saturninus from visiting Egypt, but from the other sources it becomes apparent that Saturninus was also in this position under Probus.
20. It is of course possible that Zosimus has created a doublet between the names in 1.66.1–2, but in light of the fact that Probus was definitely the commander of the Moorish bodyguard cavalry at one point in time of his career makes it more than probable that Probus promoted his former comrades and friends to high positions.
21. The titles in Kennedy (225–6) and Kreucher (158–161).

22. The reason for this conclusion is that according to the extant sources four generations separate Odin from Horsa and Hengist, and that it was during this period that we see the mass migration of the Goths and others towards the Roman territories in 267 onwards and then the mass migration of the Franks, Alamanni, Burgundians, and Vandals. It is also at the end of this period that we see the so-called Saxons starting their raids at about the same time as Odin and his folk would have reached the north of Germany and Denmark. The first version of this appendix has been available online since 2016 at academia.edu so that everyone can check up why I have suggested this. The monograph *Britain in the Age of Arthur* has not yet been released by the publisher (Pen & Sword) at the time of writing.
23. See Kennedy, 224–5; Kreucher, 172–7; and above. Aurelius Victor (37.3) dates the revolts of Saturninus and Bonosus and Proculus to take place simultaneously, which would make it possible that the revolt of Saturninus took place in about 279–280.
24. All that we know is that there exist two coins which prove that at some unknown point in time in the third century there existed an otherwise unknown usurper Silbannacus who minted coins. See my biographies of *The Reign of Emperor Gallienus* (2019) and *Gordian III and Philip the Arab* (2021).
25. The sources are collected and translated by Banchich/Zonaras, pp.128–9.
26. Kennedy, 228–9.
27. Peter the Patrician Banchich frg. 197–8 = *Anon. Cont. Dio Müller FHG 4*, p.198 with the comments of Banchich p.131–2. For good examples of the effective use of disinformation and propaganda in the past see Syvänne, 2011, Caesar vs. Pompey, and *Caracalla*. Carus was certainly not the first Roman to use these.
28. Peter the Patrician Banchich frg. 197 = *Anon. Cont. Dio Müller FHG 4*, p.198 with the comments of Banchich p.131.

Chapter 13
1. Kennedy, 235–6.

Chapter 14
1. As stated in the beginning of the book, I will use the *HA* despite its general unreliability. In other words, I do not follow the absurd practice of either dismissing its evidence completely or the practice of frowning on it as a source after which it is still used because it is the only source for many events.
2. The sources are collected in the PLRE1 Carus. See also Leadbetter 1–3.
3. Leadbetter 1–3.
4. Carinus made *Augustus* early in 283 in Leadbetter 1 and Leadbetter 2.
5. Leadbetter 1–2; Comment on the coins of Numerianus by Magie in the *HA Carus* pp.426–7.
6. *HA* Carus 8.1ff., 9.4.
7. *HA* Carus 8.1ff., 9.4; Leadbetter 1–2.
8. Leadbetter 2 with Nemesianus.
9. The sources are usefully collected in REF1, 111–121 with endnotes that add references to other sources.
10. See my *Caracalla* for the effects of this behaviour.
11. It is for the same reason that modern day officers do not wear signs of their position in the field and why their subordinates are forbidden to salute them while on a campaign. The idea is to make it difficult for enemy special forces to target the commanders.
12. See also Syvänne, *Caracalla*.
13. See Syvänne and Maksymiuk, 2018, 124–6.
14. See the various versions preserved in REF1, 112ff.
15. For a similar situation facing Julian, see Syvänne *Desperta Ferro* 2015, MHLR vol.2, 94–112.
16. I have discussed this matter with Katarzyna Maksymiuk in the *Military History of Third Century Iran* (115–6) in which we decided to adopt a compromise position. However, since

17. Numerianus at Emesa in March 284 in Leadbetter 3.
18. This chapter is based on my *Military History of Late Rome vol.1* (177–90), but adds some new material which is missing from that book. The *Military History of Late Rome* also includes material which I have not included in this book.
19. Eutropius 9.19; Epitome 38.7; Zonaras 12.30.

Appendix 1

1. See e.g. Rolan and Casas, esp. 306ff.
2. The text of Vegetius used here is: *Flavius Vegetius Renatus, Epitoma Rei Militaris*, edited with an English translation by Leo F. Stelten (New York 1990).
3. The late Roman *Notitia Dignitatum* includes among the *vexillationes* units which have tribal names such as the *Mauri, Taifali, Marcomanni, Parthi, Dalmatae, Persae* etc. The problem with this is that the *vexillationes* also include units that cannot be securely placed in the 'tribal' category, but it is of course possible that the units were promoted or transferred from one section to another in the late Roman hierarchy because the cavalry *vexillationes* ranked highest.
4. This is my interpretation of the problematic sentence: '*Sic decem centurionibus regebatur quibus…*' which has usually been emended on the basis of Vegetius 2.8 as follows: '*Sic decem centuriae cohortis primae a quinque ordinariis regebatur*,' meaning that the ten centuries of the first cohort were commanded by five men called *ordinarii*.
5. This is the reason why I accept the edition of Rolan and Casas rather than the emended text.
6. The light-armed *levis armatura/ferentarii* were at the time of Vegetius called *exculcatores*. The *armaturae* were men equipped with *plumbatae, gladii* and *missilia* like most of the forces of Vegetius's day. The *sagittarii* were archers. The *funditores* were slingers equipped with slings or *fustibali* (staff-sling). The *tragularii* were equipped with crossbows that were either called *manuballistae* (hand-*ballistae*, presumably torsion-powered crossbows) or *arcuballistae* (bow-*ballistae*, presumably regular crossbows).
7. Alternative translations would be: 1) of the lightly-equipped shield-bearers; 2) of the men equipped with a light shield. *Scutati expeditissimus* allows many interpretations because soldiers described as *expediti* in the sources could mean regular legionaries without baggage or regular legionaries equipped as light infantry, and one can also think that the *scutati expeditissimus* would refer to the weight of the *scutum*-shield.
8. The Rolan & Casas edition (p.318) has *destinatis illos*, but the *destinatis Indos* of Vegetius is more likely.
9. Vegetius has *magistri* but not *magistri militum*.
10. Saw (*serra*) was a formation in which units advanced and retreated like a saw. The *globus/drungus* was a separate detachment operating independently. The *orbis* was a unit or units facing two or all directions, the equivalent of the *amfistomos difalangia* of Greek military theory. The wedge (*cuneus*) was used to break through enemy arrays, while the pincer (*forfex*) was used to counter the wedge.
11. There is evidence for the use of legionaries as light infantry from the Republican era so the inclusion of these in the battle array was not new. Furthermore, there is also evidence for the use of extra-large legions like this one from that era too. Regardless, it is clear that Septimius Severus (if he created these legions) increased the overall size of the legion with additional light-armed men because before this the legionaries had just been seconded as light-armed when there was a need for this. For Republican-era use of legionaries as light infantry, see Syvänne, 2011.

Appendix 2

1. Leo, *Taktika*, 4.43–9; *Sylloge* 35 (esp.35.2); Syvänne, 2004.
2. See e.g. Syvänne, 2004, 2011.

Bibliography

Primary sources online:
Ammianus, Anonymous Continuator of Cassius Dio/Peter the Patrician, Arrian, Cedrenus, Chronicon Paschale, De velitatione bellica, Epitome de Caesaribus (Pseudo-Aurelius Victor), Eusebius (Church History), Dexippus, Eutropius (Breviarum), Rufus Festus (Breviarum), Historia Augusta, Jerome, Jordanes (Getica, De summa temporum/Romana), Julian the Apostate, Lactantius, Malalas, Orosius, Petrus Patricius, Strategikon (Maurice), Leo Grammaticus/Symeon, Syncellus, Synopsis Chronike, Tacitus, Aurelius Victor, Vegetius, Zonaras, Zosimus.

All of the abovementioned sources are available on the Internet. The sources for Rome's eastern wars have been conveniently collected in translation in Dodgeon and Lieu (=REF1), and most of the rest have now been conveniently collected and translated by Banchich and Lane 2009, and Banchich 2015.

Select Sources
Agathangelos, *History of the Armenians*, tr. and comm. by R.W. Thomson. New York (1976).
Artsruni, Thomas, *History of the House of the Artsrunik*, tr. and comm. by Robert W. Thomson, Detroit (1985).
Banchich, Thomas M. (2015), *The Lost History of Peter the Patrician*, Routledge, Abingdon-on-Thames (2015).
—— (2002), 'Marcus Aemilius Aemilianus (ca. July–ca. September, 253),' in *De Imperatoribus Romanis*.
Le Bohec, Yann (2006), *L'armée romaine sous le Bas-Empire*. Paris.
Bounegru O. and Zahariade M. (1996), *Les Forces Navales du Bas Danube et de la Mer Noire aux 1er-VIe Siècles*. Oxford.
Bray, John (1997), *Gallienus. A Study in Reformist and Sexual Politics*, Kent Town South Australia.
Burstein, Stanley ed. (1997 and 2009), *Ancient African Civilizations Kush and Axum*. Princeton.
Carter, M. (2001), 'Artemidorus and the ΑΡΒΗΛΑΣ Gladiator', in *Zeitschrift für Papyrologie und Epigraphic 134*, 109–15. I owe a reference to this source to the comments of Andrei Sandu in Facebook.
Casson, Lionel (1971/1995), *Ships and Seamanship in the Ancient World*. Princeton.
Cizek, Eugen, (2004), *L'empereur Aurélien et son temps*. Paris.
Downey, G. 'Aurelian's Victory over Zenobia at Immae, A.D. 272', in *Transactions and Proceedings of the American Philological Association*, Vol. 81 (1950), pp. 57–68.
Drinkwater, John F. (2007), *The Alamanni and Rome 213–496 (Caracalla to Clovis)*, Oxford UP.
—— (1987) *The Gallic Empire. Separatism and Continuity in the North-Western Provinces of the Roman Empire A.D. 260–274, Historia, Zeitschrift für alte Geschichte, Einzelschriften* Heft 52, Stuttgart.
Fields, Nick (2008), *The Walls of Rome*. Oxford.
Gawlikowski, M. (1974), 'Les défenses de Palmyre', *Syria 51*, 231–42.
Gawronski, Radoslaw Andrzej (2018), *Roman horsemen against Germanic tribes. The Rhineland frontier cavalry fighting styles 31 BC-AD 256*. Warsaw.
Geiger, Michael (2nd ed. 2015), *Gallienus*. Peter Lang Edition.

Georgian Chronicles, *Rewriting Caucasian History. The Medieval Armenian Adaptation of the Georgian Chronicles. The Original Georgian Texts and The Armenian Adaptation*, tr. R.W. Thomson. Oxford 1996.

Hatke George (2013), *Aksum and Nubia*. New York.

Historia Augusta, *Scriptores Historiae Augustae*, 3 vols., tr. by D. Magie. Loeb 1921–32; *The Lives of the Roman Emperors*, 2 vols. tr. by John Bernard. London 1693.

Homo L. (2004), *Essai sur le Règne de l'Empereur Aurélien (270–275)*, Paris.

Kayumov, Ildar, 'Μονάγκων and onager' in the *Proceedings of the XXIII Limes Congress in Ingolstad* 2015 and PowerPoint presentation of the same both of which should be available online at academia.edu the time of the publication of this monograph.

Kennedy, Myron Leo, *The Reign of the Emperor Probus 276–282 A.D.*, A Thesis submitted to the Graduate Faculty of the University of Minnesota, June 1952.

Kreucher G. (2003), *Der Kaiser Marcus Aurelius Probus und seine Zeit*. Historia Einzelschriften 174. Stuttgart.

Leadbetter William,

Leadbetter 1: Carus, in *De Imperatoribus Romanis* website, updated 11 Sept 2001

Leadbetter 2: Carinus, in *De Imperatoribus Romanis* website, updated 11 Sept 2001

Leadbetter 3: Numerianus, in *De Imperatoribus Romanis* website, updated 11 Sept 2001

Leo, Taktika, Dennis G.T. (2010/ revised ed. 2014) *The Taktika of Leo VI*. Washington DC; Haldon J.F. (2014), *A Critical Commentary on the Taktika of Leo VI*. Washington DC.

Levick B. (1985), *The Government of the Roman Empire. A Sourcebook*. Beckenhamn and Sydney 1985.

Lewis, Mark Edward (2009), *China Between Empires. The Northern and Southern Dynasties*. Cambridge and London.

Machiavelli, Niccolo, *The Prince*, English tr. by George Bull, London (1981).

Maksymiuk, see Syvänne

Malalas, *The Chronicle of John Malalas*, tr. by E. Jeffreys, M. Jeffreys and R. Scott with others. Melbourne (1986). Contains both the Greek and Slavic versions in English.

McMahon, Robin Tacitus (275–276 AD), in *De Imperatoribus Romanis* website updated 2 February 2000.

Mitchell, Stephen (1995) with Sarah Cormack, Robin Fursdon, Eddie Owens and Jean Öztürk. *Cremna in Pisidia*. London.

Modestus, 'Modesti libellus de vocabulis rei militaris as Tacitum Augustum (Estudio de la transmission manuscrita y edición crítica)' by Tomás Gonzales Rolan and Ana Moure Casas, in *Filologia Clasica* Vol. XX (1986–87), Universidad Complutense Madrid.

Moses Khorenatsi, *History of the Armenians*, tr. R.W. Thomson. Cambridge and London (1978)

Nicolle D. (1991/2001), *Rome's Enemies 5. The Desert Frontier*. Oxford.

Peri Stratêgias/Peri Strategikes = 'The Anonymous Byzantine Treatise on Strategy', ed. and tr. George T. Dennis, *Three Byzantine Military Treatises* (CFHB XXV, Washington DC, 1985), 1–135.

Pitassi M. (2011), *Roman Warships*. Woodbridge and Rochester.

—— (2009), *The Navies of Rome*. Woodbridge and Rochester

Polemius Silvius, in *MGH AA Chron. Min.1*, p.511ff. (available online).

Polyaenus, *Stratagemata*, several editions available online together with at least one French translation. The best edition and translation, however, modern one by Peter Krentz and Everett L. Wheeler, *Polyaneus Stratagems of War*. 2 vols. Chicago 1994.

Potter, David S., *The Roman Empire at bay AD 180–395*, Routledge, London and New York 2004.

Rankov B. (1995), 'Fleets of the Early Roman Empire, 31 BC–AD 324', in *The Age of Galley*, Ed. R. Gardiner, Consultant Ed. J. Morrison. London, 78–85.

Reddé M. (1986), *Mare Nostrum*. Paris and Rome.

REF1 = *The Roman Eastern Frontier and the Persian Wars* (AD 226–363). A Documentary History, compiled and edited by Michael H. Dodgeon and Samuel N.C. Lieu, London and New York 1991.

Saunders, Randall Titus, *A biography of the emperor Aurelian (A.D. 270–275)*, a doctoral Dissertation University of Cincinnati (1991).
Saxer, Robert (1967), *Untersuchungen zu den Vexillationen des römischen kaiserheeres von Augustus bis Diokletian. Epigraphische Studien 1*. Köln, Graz.
Smith, A.H. (1904), *A Catalogue of Sculpture in the Department of Greek and Roman Antiquities. British Museum vol.III*. London.
Southern P. (2008), *Empress Zenobia. Palmyra's Rebel Queen*. London and New York.
—— (2001), *The Roman Empire from Severus to Constantine*. London and New York.
Starr C.G. (1943), 'Coastal Defense in the Roman World', in *The American Journal of Philology*, 56–70.
Stoneman R. (1992), *Palmyra and its Empire. Zenobia's Revolt against Rome*. Ann Arbor.
Strategikon, *Das Strategikon des Maurikios*, ed. G.T. Dennis, German tr. by E. Gamillscheg. Vienna 1981; *Maurice's Strategikon*, tr. by G.T. Dennis. Philadelphia 1984.
Sylloge Tacticorum, Sylloge tacticorum *quae olim 'Inedita Leonis tactica' dicebatur*, (c.AD 950) ed. Alphonse Dain, Paris (1938); English translation *A Tenth-Century Byzantine Military Manual: The Sylloge Tacticorum*, tr. by Georgios Chatzelis and Jonathan Harris. Birmingham (2017). Ilkka Syvänne's view is that this treatise was written in 904.
Syvänne, Ilkka, (2019) forthcoming *Britain in the Age of Arthur*. Pen and Sword, Barnsley.
—— (2019) *The Emperor Gallienus. The Apogee of Roman Cavalry*. Pen & Sword, Barnsley.
—— (2018) *A Military History of Late Rome 361–395*, Pen & Sword, Barnsley.
—— (2017), *Caracalla. A Military Biography*. Pen & Sword, Barnsley.
—— (2016) 'The Eyes and Ears: The Sasanian and Roman Spies AD 224–450', *Historia i Swiat 2016*, Based on research paper of *The 8th ASMEA Conference*, Washington DC, 2015. Written with the generous support of the ASMEA Research Grant.
—— (2015) *A Military History of Late Rome 284–361*, Pen & Sword, Barnsley 2015.
—— (2011) 'The Reign of Decius 249–251', in *Slingshot* May 2011, 2–8.
'La campaña de Juliano en Persia (363 d.C.). Un análisis crítico', *Desperta Ferro* 2015.
A research paper 'Duel for Power. Caesar vs. Pompey 49–48 BC', *Historicon 2011*.
'Water Supply in the Late Roman Army', in *Environmental History of Water*, Eds. Petri S. Juuti, Tapio S. Katko and Heikki S. Vuorinen, IWA Publishing. London 2006, Chapter 6 (pp.69–91).
—— (2004) *The Age of Hippotoxotai. Art of War in Roman Military Revival and Disaster (491– 636). Acta Universitasis Tamperensis 994*, Tampere University Press. Tampere.
Syvänne Ilkka and Maksymiuk Katarzyna (2018), *The Military History of the Third Century Iran*. Siedlce.
Vegetius, *Flavius Vegetius Renatus, Epitoma Rei Militaris*, edited with an English translation by Leo F. Stelten (New York 1990).
Victor/Aurelius Victor, several Latin texts and translations available online. The English translation used here is: *Liber de caesaribus of Sextus Aurelius Victor*, tr. by H.W. Bird, Liverpool UP (1994).
Watson, Alaric, (1999), *Aurelian and the Third Century*. London and New York.
White, John F. (2015), *The Roman Emperor Aurelian. Restorer of the World*. New Revised Edition. Barnsley.
Williams A., Edge D., Capwell T., "An Experimental Investigation of Late Medieval Combat with the Couched Lance", in *JAAS 2016*, 1–16.
Zonaras, (2009), *The History of Zonaras from Alexander Severus to the Death of Theodosius the Great*, tr. by T.M. Banchich and E.N. Lance. Intr. and comm. by T.M. Banchich. London and New York. Greek txt: PG and CSHB both available from the web.
Zosimus, *Nea Historia*: *Zosime, Histoire Nouvelle*, tr. and ed. Paschoud. Budé Paris. 1971–89 4 Vols.; A dated English translation by unknown hand (possibly J. Davis) *The History of Count Zosimus Sometime Advocate and Chancellor of the Roman Empire*, (London 1814); The latest English translation is *Zosimus. New History*. tr. by R.T. Ridley. (Melbourne 1990).

Index

Abrittus, battle of, 3
Achilles/Achilleus, Palmyran usurper, 129–30
Aden, *see* Yemen
Adiabene (Persian/Armenian province), *Adiabenicus* (Roman title), 99, 122, 128
Administration (Roman), 124, 217
Adrianople, *see* Hadrianopolis
Aemilianus, L. Mussius, usurper, 258, 265
Aemilia, Via (road), 83
Africa (with North Africa), ix, 3, 22, 52, 59–61, 64, 67–8, 92, 94, 132, 161, 170, 172–3, 198, 249, 256, 265
  see also Egypt, Blemmyes, Aksum, Mauretania
Africanus, *see* Scipio
Agens vice rationalis, acting head of treasury, 89
  see also Sabinus
Agentes in Rebus, general agents, secret service, 229, 258
  see also Frumentarii, Intelligence gathering, *Peregrini*
Agriculture, *see* grain, wine
Agri Decumates, Upper Germany, Baden-Württeberg, Germany, 182–3, 186
  see also Raetia
Aksum, Axum, Aksumites, Axomitae (Ethiopians), ix, 25, 54, 68, 133, 135–7, 146–7, 158, 258–9, 265–6
Alamanni, Germanic tribal confederacy, ix, 3–4, 36, 38, 41, 48, 50–1, 61, 63, 69–73, 75–6, 78–83, 146–7, 151, 166, 172, 180–7, 203–204, 216, 218, 253–4, 259, 261, 263, 265
  see also Iuthungi, Scythians
Alans/Ossetes, Sarmatian tribal confederacy, 21, 40–1, 77–8, 111, 128, 146–7, 194, 217, 250, 260
  Ektaxis kata Alanon, 21, 111, 236
  see also Sarmatians
Alba, 181, 188
  Elbe, Albis, 181, 187–8, 199
  Swabian Alb, 181
Alba Longa/Albanum, city, Latium, Castel Gandolfo, Italy, 5
Albania, Albanians (located roughly in modern Azcrbaijan), 41–2, 135, 250

Albinus, Ceionius (probably Marcus Nummius Celonius Annius Albinus who in his turn may be identical with Nummius Albinus) Urban Prefect in 256, 32
Alexander the Great, king of Macedonia, i, 115
Alexander Severus, 15, 250, 267
Alexandria, city, Egypt/Alexandrians, 22, 67–9, 99, 105, 129, 134, 137, 141, 155, 172
  Classis Alexandriana, 22
Allies Roman (contingents provided by allies also known as *Foederati*/Federates or *symmachiarii*), *see also* Laeti
Ambassador, embassy, envoy, viii, 31, 66, 71–5, 92, 95, 122, 194, 219–21, 251, 253
  see also Diplomacy
Ambushes, surprise attacks, ix, 15, 24–5, 32–3, 66, 68–71, 79, 120–1, 129, 133, 174, 190, 203, 253
  see also Stratagem
Ammianus Statilius, Prefect of Egypt, 99
Anchialus, city, 50–1, 64, 252–3
Ancyra, Galatia city, Ankara, Turkey, 53, 95–6
Antioch, city, 53, 59, 94–6, 98–103, 105, 109, 125–6, 129–30, 133, 155, 170, 200
Antiochus the Great, Seleucid king, 242
Antiochus, *see* Achilles
Antoninus, usurper, *see* Uranius
Antoninus Gallus, 31–2
Antoninus Magnus, *see Caracalla,* 149
Antoninus Pius, emperor (138–161), 161, 172
Apamea/Apameia, city, 59, 105–106, 201
Aper, Praetorian Prefect, 217–18, 222, 224–5, 227–8
Apollonius of Tyana, miracle-worker, pagan Christ, 30, 96–8, 101, 103, 109, 112, 114, 140, 152, 255, 260
  see also Sol
Apsaeus, Palmyrene noble, 128
Aquae Sextiae (Aix-en-Provence), city, 179
Aquila, aquilifer, 8, 233, 236
Aquileia, city, Italy, 64–6, 69–70, 75, 93, 179–80, 253
Aquitania, 49

Index 269

Arabia/Arabs/Saracens, Bedouins, 32, 35–6, 41–2, 53–6, 99, 105, 115–16, 118, 120–3, 131, 133, 135, 137, 146–7, 158, 225, 251–2, 258–9
  see also Palmyra, Persians, Yemen, Tanukh, Kinda
Arabianus, Flavius, 134–5
Archemporos, synodiarches, 54
Archers, archery, *sagittarii, hippotoxotai*, vii, 8–9, 12, 21, 38–40, 42–3, 54–6, 87, 101, 118–19, 122, 129, 131, 191, 232, 236–41, 246, 248, 252, 264, 267
Ardashir I, Persian ruler (ca. 224–240/3), i, 116–17, 222, 225
(in truth Narses), 252
Arelate (Arles), city, 179
Arethusa, city, 105–106, 110
Aristobulus, Praetorian Prefect, 229–30
Aristocracy, 49, 84
Arithmoi, arithmos, 19, 21, 73
  see also Bandon, Tagma, Numeri
Armenia/Armenians, *Armeniacus* (Roman title), viii, 21, 32, 36, 41–2, 54–6, 118, 120–3, 128, 135, 151–2, 158, 176–9, 188, 193–4, 196–7, 218–20, 225–6, 250, 257, 261–2, 265–6
  see also Tiridates
Army, see Military
Arrian / Arrianos, 13, 21–2, 110, 236, 265
Artabanus, Parthian ruler, 260
Artabassis Syrus (possibly to be identified as Aravasdes), 35, 250
Artavasdes, Armenian regent, 250
Arthur, king, 197, 263, 267
  see also *Syvänne, Britain in the Age of Arthur*
Asclepiodotus, *dux*, 209, 212
Asia, province of Asia, Asia Minor, Central Asia, 3, 28, 53–5, 58, 94–6, 99, 106–107, 135, 154, 166–7, 176, 201, 217, 229, 257
Assassins, assassination, murder, poison, 4, 26, 36, 43–6, 48–50, 52, 61, 70, 97, 153–7, 160–2, 166–9, 174, 201, 205, 208, 210, 212, 220, 224–5, 227–9, 242, 250, 260–1
  see also Stratagems
Atheist, 112
Athletes, boxing, boxers, wrestling, pancratium/pankration, 31, 177
  see also Martial Arts
Athens, Athenians, city in Greece, 110, 244
Attalus, king of the Marcomanni, 61
Attitianus, quartermaster, 49
Augsburg (Augusta Vindelicum), 150
  see also Battles/Sieges
Augustus, title, 66–7, 84, 99, 118, 141, 170, 173–4, 193, 217, 224, 226–8, 263, 267

Emperor Octavian (BC 27–AD 14), 118, 174, 193
Aulici (Corporis in Aula, Protectores, Scholae/Ostensionales, Scutarii, Collegia, Domestici) (imperial bodyguards), viii, 3–5, 7, 26, 34, 49–50, 64, 72, 77, 95, 121, 144, 146–8, 153–4, 157, 162, 166–7, 170, 172, 174, 218, 224, 227–9, 251
  see also Bodyguards, Comes, Lions
Aurelian, Lucius Domitius Aurelianus, emperor (270–275), vi–vii, ix, 1–3, 22, 28–36, 43–5, 47–52, 53–5, 59, 61, 63–167, 172–4, 176, 181, 183, 188, 194–6, 202–206, 212–14, 220–1, 226, 230, 233, 243–4, 249–62, 265–7
  career as commoner, 29–36, 43–5, 47–52, 53–5, 59, 61, 63
  usurpation and early reign, 63–74
  against Sarmatians, Alans and Vandals, 74–8, 145–8
  against Alamanni, Iuthungi, and Marcomanni, 69–73, 78–83, 145–8
  against three usurpers, Senate and mint workers, 80–6
  building of Aurelian Walls, 86–8
  against Goths, 92–4, 145–8, 150
  against Zenobia, 92–123, 145–8
  against Persians, Armenians and Tanukh Saracens of Syria and al-Hira, 118–23, 145–8, 150–2
  mutiny of the army, 123–4
  triumph at Antioch, 125
  riot of the *monetarii* of Antioch, 125–6
  against Achilles and Palmyrene rebels, 127–31
  against the Carpi, 127–31, 134
  against Firmus, the Kinda Saracens, Yemenites, Aksumites and Indians, 127–37, 145–8
  marriage with Ulpia Severa, daughter of Zenobia, 141–3
  Aurelian's daughter, 142–3
  triumph at Rome, 140, 145–8
  against Tetricus, 140, 143–4
  against usurper Faustinus, 143–5, 148, 150–1, 259
  against Franks, 144–5
  victory in Britain, 145
  against rebels and invaders in Raetia and Gaul, 150–1
  plan to persecute Christians, 152–3
  religious policies and use of religion, 30, 74, 79, 82, 96, 98, 108–109, 112, 114, 140, 149, 151–3, 159, 163, 183, 255–6, 260
  Apollonius of Tyana, 30, 96–8, 101, 103, 109, 112, 114, 140, 152

assassination of Aurelian, 153–7, 181
Aurelian as emperor, 158–9
monetary reform, coins, 3, 84, 89–90, 96, 109, 125–6, 130, 133, 137–41, 159, 259
internal policies, 89–90, 123–6, 134–5, 137–42, 148–50, 204
see also against usurpers, against Zenobia, against Firmus, against Tetricus
Aurelius, Marcus, emperor, 38
Aureolus, *hipparchos*, rebel and usurper, 3–4, 43–8, 61–3, 251, 254
Auxilia/Auxiliaries, vii, 4, 6–9, 12, 21–2, 28, 32, 35, 54–5, 72–3, 94–5, 145, 148, 182, 186, 232–3, 235, 246–7
see also Allies, *Laeti*

Babylon, city in Egypt, ix, 67–9
Babylon, city in Mesopotamia, 222, 224
Bacaudae/Bagaudae, bandits, 204
Bahram I, ruler of Persia (ca. 273–6), 152
Bahram II, ruler of Persia (ca. 276–93), 152, 194, 196, 219, 222, 262
Balkan, Balkans, ix, xviii, 3, 28–33, 35–6, 43–6, 49–52, 62, 64, 70, 90, 92–4, 122, 127–8, 141, 151, 176, 178, 197–9, 201–202, 204–210, 217, 244, 251, 253, 262
see also Illyricum, Thrace, Dacia, Pannonia, Moesia
Ballista, Balista, general and usurper, 3
Ballistae/Carroballistae/Arcuballista/ Manuballista, Ballistarii, 7–8, 15, 24–5, 85–8, 113, 191, 239, 243, 264
Bandits, brigandage, robbers, rogues, 116–18, 129, 189–90, 202–205, 207
Bandon (pl. *banda*), 19, 21, 247–8
Baquates, Moorish / Berber tribe, 186
Barbarians, 3, 8, 35, 43, 45–6, 50, 60, 62–3, 68, 71, 74–7, 79, 83, 87, 89, 92, 96, 121, 124, 131, 133, 144, 146, 150–1, 158, 164, 166–7, 181–3, 186–7, 194, 197–8, 202, 204–206, 209, 212, 218, 247, 256, 258–60, 262
see also Alamanni, Iuthungi, Bactrians, Georgians, Blemmyes, Burgundians, Carpi, Germans, Franks, Goths, Heruls, Quadi, Bastarnae, Peuci, Sciri, Sarmatians, Roxolani, Alans, Indians, Marcomanni, Arabs, Moors, Vandals, Yemen
Bassus, Cerronius, (unknown, could be Pomponius Bassus PUR in 270–71 cos. 259, 271 or L. Caesonius Ovidius Manlius Rufinianus Bassus PUR ca. 285), 130
Bastarnae / Bastarni, mixed tribe, 33, 36, 39, 197–9, 254

Battle, Battles, naval battles, vii, ix, 2–3, 12–13, 15–16, 20–2, 24, 38, 40, 42–3, 47–8, 55–6, 60–1, 66–9, 70–3, 75–6, 79, 83, 92, 94, 98–115, 120–3, 125, 127, 131, 140, 143–5, 147, 158, 170–1, 177–8, 181–6, 193–7, 200–201, 203, 205–206, 212, 217, 222, 225–6, 229–30, 232, 234–40, 243, 246, 254, 256, 258 264
Battles of,
Abrittus in 251, 3
Aemilianus vs. Barbarians in 261, 258
Alexandria(?), Tenagino Probus vs. Timagenes in 270, 68
Augsburg (Augusta Vindelicum) in 275, 150
Aurelian vs. Cannabaudes in 271, 92
Aurelian vs. Carpi in 273, 127, 131, 258
Aurelian vs. Persians, Armenians and Saracens in 272, 120–3
Aurelian vs. Sarmatians in 271, 76
Aurelian vs. Vandals in 271, 75
Aureolus vs. Macriani in 261, 254
Babylon in Egypt in 270, ix, 67–9, 256
Carthage (M. Aur. Probus possibly with Tenagino Probus against rebels in 270), 60–1
Carus vs. Sarmatians in 282, 217
Carus vs. Persians in 282–4, 222, 225–6
Catalaunian Fields in 274, *see Durocatalaunum*
Cologne (Probus vs. Proculus and Bonosus) in 280–1, 203, 205–206, 212
Cyrene (Tenagino Probus vs. Marmaridae in 269–70), 60–1
Danube in 270, 70–3,
Daphne in 272, ix, 103–105, 107
Durocatalaunum in 274, 140, 143–5
Eben-Ezer fresco, 56
Emesa in 272, vii, ix, 16, 22, 55, 94, 98, 105–15
Fanum Fortunae (Fano) in 271, 83
Immae in 272, vii, ix, 99–103, 107, 125, 256, 265
Lake Garda in 269, *see* Verona in 269
Margus, River in 285, 229–30
Milvian Bridge in 312, vii, 12–13, 109
Placentia in 271, ix, 79–82, 158, 254
Pontirolo, Bridge near Milan, a battle or two battles in 268, 43, 47–8
Probus vs. Florentianus in 276, 170–1, 212
Probus vs. Goths in 277, 177–8
Probus vs. Alamanni in 277, 181, 183
Probus vs. Burgundians, Vandals and others in 278, 184–6
Probus vs. Isaurians in 278, 190, 212
Probus vs. Persians in 278–9, 193–7
Probus vs. Saturninus in 279–80, 200–201, 212

Index 271

Probus vs. Proculus in 280–281, 203, 205–206, 212
  see also Battle of Cologne
Probus' generals vs. Franks in 277, 181, 183
Probus' generals vs. Blemmyes in 278–9, 193–7
Tejran vs. Goths, 178–9, 260
Ticinus, Ticinum in 271, 83
Tiridates vs. Persians in 277/8, 178
Verona in 269, 61–2, 71
Berbers, *see* Moors
Beroae, city in Syria, 101–102
Bisexual, 142
  see also Sex
Bithynia, Bithynians, province and area, 53, 94–5, 255
Black Sea, 39
Blemmyes (modern Beja tribe), 25, 54, 67–8, 133, 135–7, 146–7, 158, 188, 193–6, 207, 247, 258–9
Bodyguards / Bodyguard (word), 4–7, 26, 34, 36, 42, 44–5, 47–8, 72, 76–7, 94, 106, 154–5, 162, 166–7, 195, 203, 211, 219, 226, 230, 235, 249, 260, 262
  see also Aulici, Equites Mauri, Equites Singulares Augusti, Evocati Augusti, Praetoriani, Urbaniciani, Frumentarii, Peregrini, Vigiles, Intelligence Gathering, *Statores*
Bonosus, *dux* and usurper, xi, 2, 92–3, 183, 196, 198, 201–205, 212, 262–3
Borani, tribe in the Black Sea area, 25
Border, *see* Limes
Bosporans, Bosporus (Kingdom in the Crimea and Caucasus), 39–40, 178–9, 260
Bosporus, Straits of, 166
Bostra, city, 53, 55
Brigandage, *see* Bandits
Britain/Britannia, 22, 145, 158, 170, 187, 196–8, 202–206, 218, 228, 263, 267
Burgundians/Burgunds/Burgundi, Germanic tribe, 36, 181, 183, 186–7, 261, 263
Byzantium, city (Constantinople, Istanbul), ix, 33, 35, 90, 93–5, 126, 128, 130–1, 154, 250, 258, 260
  meeting at Byzantium, 33, 35, 250

Caesar, *see* Julius Caesar
Caesar, title, 99, 173, 217
Caesarea, city, 1
Callinicus of Petra, historian and sophist, 59
Callistus, *see* Ballista
Cannabaudes, Cannabas, Gothic king, 92, 147
Capito, Praetorian Prefect, 171
Cappadocia, province and area, 96, 167

Caracalla, emperor (211–17), 30, 36, 66, 96, 109, 137–8, 149, 152, 173, 188, 214, 220, 226, 231, 247, 249–52, 256, 259–61, 263, 265, 267
  for further details, see Syvänne, *Caracalla*
Caras, city, 217
Carinus, M. Aurelius Carinus, emperor (283–285), v, 2, 157, 211, 215–20, 225–30, 263, 266
Carpi, a tribe (probably Free Dacians, but Germanic origin has also been suggested), v, ix, 36, 39, 93, 122, 127–9, 131, 134–5, 147, 258
  see also Dacia, Goths, Decius
Carrago, see Wagon Laager, Fortifications
Carrhae, Mesopotamia city, Haran, Turkey, 217
Carroballistae, see Ballistae
Carthage, city, Tunis, Tunisia, Carthagians, 5, 60, 92, 94, 198, 216, 220, 256
Carus, M. Aurelius Numerius Carus, Praetorian Prefect, emperor (282–283), v, vii–viii, 2, 157, 194, 209–13, 215–26, 228–9, 263, 266
  usurpation against Probus, 209–11
  wars against the Sarmatians, Quadi, Franks and Alamanni, 216–18
  Persian war, 218–26
Castra, fort, camp, 6–7, 146–8, 181, 186, 200, 235, 255
  see also Fort, Praefectus castrorum, Wagon Laager
Castrensiani, frontier troops, 84, 146–8, 181, 186, 255
  see also Limes
Cataphractarii (*Equites Cataphracti*) / *katafraktoi*, cataphracts, vii, 8, 16, 21, 32, 37, 39, 41–2, 55–6, 80, 100–101, 105, 107, 112, 139, 147, 219, 237–8, 240, 242–3, 252
  see also Archers, Cavalry, Clibanarii, Parthia, Armenia, Oshroene, Contarii
Cataphracts, *see Cataphractarii*
Cavalry (word), vii, x, 3–4, 6–9, 12–13, 15–17, 19–22, 28, 31–5, 37–45, 49, 55–6, 60, 64, 70–3, 76–80, 83, 94–5, 100–103, 105–106, 108–15, 120, 130–1, 147–8, 152, 157, 165, 177–8, 180, 193, 195, 203, 217, 219, 225–6, 232, 235–8, 240–3, 246–8, 250, 252–3, 261–2, 264–5, 267
  see also Cataphractarii, Archers, Legions, *Auxilia, Aulici, Praetoriani, Equites, Equites Singulares Augusti, Clibanarii, Contarii, Equites Mauri*, Armenia, Persia, Goths, Sarmatians, Alans, *Turma, Droungos*, Palmyra
Cecropius/Ceronius, Commander of the Dalmatian cavalry and murderer of Gallienus, 44–5
Cecropius, *dux* schooled by Probus, 209

Celts, Celtic, inhabitants of Gaul, and soldiers of Gaul, Raetia and Noricum, 106, 108, 145, 254
    see also Bastarnae, Gaul
Censorinus, usurper under Claudius II, 50, 251
Central Asia, *see* Asia
Century, *centuria*, centurion, *centenarii*, v, 6–9, 203, 234–6, 240–2, 245–6, 264
Cerasos of Argos, boxing champion, 177
Chalcedon, city, 95, 126, 128, 130
Chariovistus (Chariovistus?), Germanic leader, 32
Chicken, 149
    see also Grain, Fleets, Supply, Cows, Pigs, Sheep
China, Chinese, 120, 135, 257, 262, 266
    see also Silk Route
Christians, Christianity / Christ, Jesus, 44, 59, 103, 112, 116–17, 142, 152–3, 255, 257, 260
    see also Apollonius of Tyana, Sun, Paul of Samosata, Zenobia
Cilicia, Cilician Gates, 95, 99–100, 167, 170, 216
Circus Factions / Chariot Races (Blues and Greens), Citizenship, citizen, citizens of cities, 34, 177
City Prefect, see *Praefectus Urbi*
Civilian police/ paramilitary forces/ militia / including officials and corporations often used as militia, 4–5, 7, 26, 208
    see also Urbaniciani, Vigiles, Statores, Stationarii, Beneficiarii, Intelligence Gathering
Classis, Classes, see Fleets
Claudia, sister of Probus, 34
Claudius II, M. Aurelius Valerius Claudius, emperor (268–270), claimed to be an ancestor of Constantine the Great, v, vii–viii, 2–4, 34, 36, 43–54, 59, 61–71, 82, 84, 89, 92, 123, 151, 157, 161, 165, 172–3, 181, 186, 221, 251–3, 260
Cleopatra, Egyptian queen, 59, 118
    see also Zenobia
Clibanarii, 243
    see also Cavalry, *Cataphractarii, Contarii*, Mounted Archers
Clitostratos of Rhodes, boxing champion, 177
Coche, Veh Ardashir, Persian city, 222, 226
Cohort, 5–8, 15, 35, 86, 162, 233–7, 239–40, 246, 264
Cohortes Urbanae, see Urbaniciani
Collegia, see Aulici
Cologne (Colonia Agrippinensis), city, 202–203, 205
Comes (companion, count, general), comites, *comes domesticorum equitum / peditum*, viii, 3–4, 26, 49, 64, 157, 174, 177, 218, 224, 227–8, 243

Commodus, emperor (180–192), 249
Consilium (Emperor's Council), *see* Council
Constance, Lake, 186
Constantine the Great, emperor, vii, 9, 12–13, 44, 46, 52, 62, 96, 109, 112, 135, 152–3, 212, 214, 230, 255, 260, 267
Constantinople (Byzantium), city, *see* Byzantium
Constantius I (F. Val. Constantius I), protector, governor, *dux*, emperor (292–306), 44, 46, 151, 209, 212, 229, 255
Constantius II, emperor (337–361), 135, 152, 167, 253, 260
Consul, consulship with proconsul, 33, 49, 140, 161, 166, 172, 189, 203, 220, 228, 230, 233, 250
Contarii, kontoforoi (*contus*-bearers), *contus*, 21, 39–40, 55, 236, 241
    see also Cavalry, *Cataphractarii*, Spearmen, *Hasta*
Contubernium, contubernia, a file/tent group of eight soldiers, one recruit (*tiro*) and one servant, 6, 235–8, 246
    see also Decanus
Corn, *see* Grain
    see also Fleets
Corporis in Aula, see Aulici
Council (Emperor's private *Consilium*), 74, 210, 244
Council of officers (Military), 44, 74, 210, 227, 244
Council, Church, 59
Council, Palmyrene, 121
Cows, 33, 181, 186
    see also Grain, Fleets, Supply, Sheep, Chicken, Wine
Cremna, city, *see* Siege of Cremna
Cremona, city, 78
Crete, 94
Crinitus, Ulpius, *dux*, 32–3, 141, 250
Crocodiles, 132, 258
Ctesiphon, Persian capital, Iraq, viii, ix, 219–20, 222, 224, 226
Cuneus, *see* Wedge
Customs, *see* Trade
Cyrene, Cyrenaica, Pentapolis, 60
    see also Legions, *legio III Cyrenaica*
Cyzicus, city and naval base, 95, 176

Dacia/Dacians/Getae (when not Goths), Roman provinces, general area, Dacian soldiers and peoples, 29, 36, 39, 41, 64, 84, 93, 109, 122, 131, 158, 187, 244, 255
    see also Balkans, Carpi, Goths, Illyricum, Thrace

Index

Dalmatia, province and area, 229, 254
  see also Equites Dalmatae
Dalmatius/Delmatius, Maximus, father of Probus, 34
Danube, river and frontier, 33, 35, 41, 70–1, 76–7, 92–3, 131, 140–1, 158, 176, 181, 186–8, 206, 249, 253, 255, 258, 265
  see also Balkans, Illyricum, Thrace
Daphne, city, ix, 98, 103, 106–107, 109
  see also Battles
Decanus, decani, 6–7, 203, 235–6
  see also Contubernium
Decius, emperor (249–251), 3–4, 15, 28, 35, 267
  see also Syvänne, *Gallienus* (pp.29–36) with Syvänne, *Gordian III and Philip the Arab*
Decurio, Decurions, cavalry, 7–8, 232, 236, 246
Diocletian, (Diocles / C. Aur. Val. Diocletianus) *Comes Domesticorum*, emperor (284–305), vii–viii, 49, 138, 148, 157, 193, 209, 212, 216, 218, 224–30
Diplomacy, diplomat, 28, 54, 58, 60, 67, 152, 250
  see also Ambassador
Domestici, see Aulici
Domitia, Aurelian's sister, 80
Domitia, Gardens of, 149
Domitian I, Domitianus I, emperor (81–96), 80
Domitianus II, usurper under Aurelian, 80–3, 254
Domitianus, *dux* under Gallienus, possibly to be identified with the usurper, 80, 254
Domitilla, wife of Domitian I, 80
Domna, *see* Julia Domna
Draconarius, draconarii, draco, 7–8, 130, 236, 246
Droungos, drouggos, droungoi, drungus, v, 16, 19, 22, 108, 207, 247–8
Duces, see Dux
Duke / Dukes, *see Dux*
Dura Europos, Coele Syria city, Syria, 13, 54–6, 225
Dux (general), *duces*, duke, 3, 32–3, 43, 48, 52–3, 132–3, 137, 154–5, 165–6, 174, 196, 203, 209, 212, 216, 221, 241, 243, 250, 254
Ducenarius, 7, 58–9, 234
Dynastic succession, dynasty, 142, 226, 257, 266

Egypt / Egyptians, v, ix, 6, 34, 53–5, 58–61, 64–9, 77, 89, 92, 94–5, 99, 105, 123, 126–9, 131–5, 137, 140, 146–7, 152, 158–9, 161, 166, 170, 176, 188, 193–6, 199–200, 249, 256, 258–9, 262
  see also Alexandria, Blemmyes, Aksumites, Moors, Arabs, Firmus, Tenagino Probus, M. Aur. Probus, Saturninus, Fleets, India, Yemen

Elagabalus, Heliogabalus, emperor (218–222) and sun god, 30, 99, 109, 114
  see also Sun, Apollonius of Tyana
Elbe, *see* Alba
Elephant / Elephants, 16, 31, 42, 132, 146, 241–3
Emesa, Homs, Syria, vii, ix, 16, 22, 30, 55, 94, 96, 98, 101, 103, 105–106, 108–10, 112, 114–15, 122–3, 125, 130–1, 153, 225, 227, 256–8, 264
  see also Battle of Emesa
Emona, city, 78, 179
Envoy, *see* ambassador
Epidemics, plagues, 62
Epiphaneia, city, 105
Equestrian Order / Equestrians / Upper Classes, 3, 7, 165
  see also Senate
equites, cavalry in general, 3–4, 9, 34, 49, 51, 64, 72–3, 93, 232
equites cataphractos/cataphractarios, see cataphracts 32
equites of Gallienus (Gallienus' cavalry *tagmata*), 3–4, 34–5, 49, 64, 72–3, 193, 201
equites singulares Augusti /Germani, 4, 26, 72, 95, 162
  see also Aulici, Bodyguards, Lions, *Praetoriani*
Equites Dalmatae, vii, 44–5, 80, 94, 106, 264
Equites Mauri, (elite imperial cavalry bodyguards, and mixed infantry and cavalry *Numeri*), 36, 72, 80, 94, 106, 195, 262, 264
  see also Bodyguards, Moors, Saturninus, Victorinus, Probus
equites singulares, (elite cavalry auxiliaries protecting commanders), 7, 22
  see also pedites singulares, Bodyguards
Eros (Mnestheus), Aurelian's secretary and killer, 153–5, 166
Eruli, *see* Heruls
Ethiopia, Ethiopians, *see* Aksum
Etruria, 149
Euphrates, river, 121, 220, 222, 225
Evocati / Evocati Augusti, (veterans called back into service and bodyguards of the emperor), 4–5, 26
  see also Aulici, Bodyguards

Factions, *see* Circus Factions
Fanum, city, 83, 180
Faustinus, usurper, 143–5, 148, 151, 259
Felicissimus, treasurer and rebel, 84
Felix, *see* Legions
Firmus, Claudius, Prefect / *Corrector* of Egypt, 132, 258
Firmus, *dux limitis Africani*, 132, 258

Firmus, usurper in Egypt under Aurelian, v, ix, xi, 2, 120, 127–9, 131–5, 147, 258
Flaccinus, Valerius, *see* Valerius
Fleets (navy, naval, ships, shipping, galleys, vessel, vessels, *classis/classes*), ix, 4–5, 22–5, 28, 33, 35, 38–9, 42, 55, 64, 67–8, 92, 94–5, 99–100, 112, 131, 133–5, 137, 147, 149, 176, 180, 186, 198, 200, 200–206, 222, 232, 249, 255, 265–6
  see also Tenagino Probus, M. Aur. Probus, Praetorian Fleets, Misenum, Ravenna
Florianus, M. Annius Florianus, half-brother of Tacitus, emperor (276), v, vii, 163, 167, 169–72, 176, 213, 261
Foederati (Federates), *see* Allies
  see also Laeti, Auxilia
Fortifications / Fortresses / Forts / Fortified Camps / Walls, ix, 15–16, 23, 25, 28, 33, 36, 38–9, 41–3, 58, 70, 75, 85–9, 97, 101, 118–19, 122, 130–1, 134, 145, 177, 181, 186, 189–91, 200, 217, 222, 225, 238, 240, 254–5, 257, 265
  see also Wagon laager, *Castra*, Phalanx, Sieges, *Ballistae*
Forum Iulii (Fréjus), city, 179
Francicus, title, 172
Franks, Germanic confederacy, 3–4, 25, 32, 36, 38–9, 41, 143–8, 166, 172, 180–1, 183, 197–9, 203, 205–206, 216, 218, 261, 263
Free Dacians, *see* Dacia, Carpi
Freedmen, 30, 153
Frontier, *see* Limes
Frumentarii (soldiers with logistical duties that also acted as postmen and spies), 4–5, 26, 162, 229
  see also Intelligence Gathering, *Peregrini, Aulici, Speculatores, Agentes in Rebus*

Galatia, 53, 95, 167
Galerius, emperor (293–311), viii, 87, 152, 220, 260
Gallia, *see* Gaul
Gallia Narbonesis, *see* Gaul
Gallicanus, Maecius, Praetorian Prefect, 162
Galliena, female cousin of Gallienus?, 61
Gallienus, P. Licinius Egnatius Gallienus, emperor (253–268), vii, xi, 2–7, 15, 23, 28–9, 31–6, 43–50, 52–4, 61, 63, 70–5, 77, 80, 82, 84, 89, 105, 107, 123, 145, 148, 157, 162–5, 173–4, 181, 183, 186, 188, 195, 214, 217, 221, 226, 230, 235, 244, 249–51, 253–4, 259–60, 263, 265, 267
  see also Syvänne, *Gallienus*
Gallus, Antoninus, *see* Antoninus Gallus
Garamantes, Berber tribe, 60

Gaudiosus, *dux*, 209, 212
Gaul, Gallia, Gallic Empire, Gallic, (roughly mod. France and Belgium) 3–4, 28, 32, 35, 43, 46–9, 51–2, 62, 64, 69, 72, 80, 83, 89, 94, 109, 122, 137, 139–41, 143–6, 150–1, 158, 168, 170, 179–83, 186–7, 195–9, 201–204, 206, 212–13, 216, 218, 250, 254, 259, 261–2, 265
  see also Celts, Postumus, Laelianus, Marius, Victorinus, Tetricus
Genetlius, sophist, 59
Genua, city, 179
Georgia, Iberia, Colchis, 40–2, 54, 120–1, 135, 146–7, 176, 178–9, 193–4, 196, 250, 261–2, 266
  see also Armenia, Persia and Syvänne, *MHLR Vol.1* (pp. 107–112)
Gephyra, place, 102
Gepids, Gepidae, Germanic tribe, 36, 197, 199
Germani, *see* equites singulares Augusti
Germanica, Classis, see Fleets
Germanicus Maximus, title, 62, 83, 217–18
Germans, Germanic peoples, Germanic auxiliaries and allies, Germania, vii, 4, 9, 32, 36–40, 48, 107, 143, 145–7, 161, 172, 179–83, 186, 188, 196–7, 199, 202–3, 207, 247, 254, 262–3, 265
  see also Alamanni, Chatti, Chauci, Franks, Goths, Marcomanni, Quadi, Vandals, Gepids, Saxons, Franks
Geta, emperor (211–212), brother of Caracalla, 226
Getae, *see* Carpi
Gladiator, 34, 42, 146–7, 177, 207, 242–3, 265
Gold / Gold content in coins and medallions, golden, 33, 35, 72, 74, 89, 118, 138, 142, 145–6, 148–9, 163–4, 167, 181–2, 219, 259
Gordian III, emperor (238–244), (for additional details, see the forthcoming Syvänne, *Gordian III and Philip the Arab*), 152
Gordianus, Velius Cornificius, consul, 161
Goths, Germanic tribal confederacy, Visi, Austrogothi, Tervingi, Greuthungi, Scythians (also called Getae in some sources), 3, 15, 25, 33–4, 36, 39–41, 43, 48, 50–2, 59, 61–4, 68, 70, 73, 77, 90, 92–5, 145–8, 150–2, 166–8, 170, 172–3, 176–9, 181, 197–9, 203, 242, 252–3, 260, 263
  see also Heruls, Scythians, Aurelian, Probus
Gothicus, title, v, 34, 46, 48, 62, 128, 172
Grain / Corn, 64, 66–8, 75, 92, 133–5, 137, 171, 181–3, 186, 189–90, 200, 249
  see also Fleets, Wine, Cows, Supply, Pigs, Chicken
Gratian, emperor (367–383), 251
  see also Syvänne, MHLR Vol.2

Greece, 198, 244
    see also Greeks, Balkans
Greeks, 7, 34, 40, 42, 44–5, 47, 58, 65, 109, 112–13, 118, 128, 143, 153, 176, 222, 252, 257, 260–1, 264, 266–7
Green Circus Faction, 34, 177
Greuthungi Goths, see Goths

Hadrian, emperor (117–138), 86, 161
    Mausoleum of Hadrian, Castel Sant'Angelo, 86
Hadrianopolis, Adrianople, city, 93
Haemus, Haemimontum, mountain range and mountain, 50
Haldagates, Germanic leader, 32
Hannibal, Carthaginian general, 201, 212–13, 242
Hannibalianus, *dux*, 209, 212
Hariomundus, Germanic leader, 32
Hasta, hastati, 7, 33, 35, 234, 236–8
    see also Spear, *Contarii*, Cataphract, *Lancea*, Javelin, *Xyston*
Heliogabalus, see Elagabalus
Hellespont, 166
Helvetii, Germanic tribe, 181, 261
Heraclea / Perinthus, 154–5
Heraclianus, Praetorian Prefect and conspirator, 43–5, 49, 51–4
Hercules, 114
Herculiani, see Legions
    see also *Aulici*, Bodyguards
Herculianus, see Heraclianus
Herennianus, *dux* under Probus (possibly *praefectus praetorio* under Diocletian), 209
Herennianus, son of Proculus, 202
Heruli / Heruls, Germanic tribe, 3, 12, 25, 33, 36, 39, 43, 51, 59, 63, 68, 166–7, 176, 242
    see also Goths, Germans
Hildomundus Germanic leader, 32
Hippomachia, cavalry battle, 73, 253
Hipparchos, 4, 64, 253
    see also Comes, *Magister*
Hippotoxotai (mounted archers), see Archers
Hippotoxotai, The Age of Hippotoxotai, monograph of Syvänne, 267
Hira, al, city (Tanukh Arabs), 117–18, 121, 147, 252
    see also Arabs, Tanukh
Hispania, see Spain
Homosexuals / Gays, see Bisexual
Hormizd / Hormozd I Ardashir, son of Shapur I, ruler of Persia (ca. 272–3), 122–3, 135, 152
Hormizd, brother of Bahram II, Persian rebel, 178, 194, 196, 219, 262
Huns, tribal confederacy, 178, 194, 217

Iberia (Caucasus), see Georgia
Illyricum, Illyria, Illyrians, area, Illyriciani, 5, 32, 35–6, 50, 62, 64, 80, 92, 94, 150–1, 161–2, 175, 179, 186–8, 202, 208, 216–17, 228–9, 250
    see also Balkans, Danube, Thrace, Dacia, Greece, Dalmatia, *equites Dalmatae*
Illyrian soldiers, Illyrian faction, 'Illyrian mafia', 5, 62, 162, 175, 216, 228
Imaginarii / imaginiferi, 8, 233
Immae, city, see Battle of Immae
Imperial Fleet, see Fleets, Praetorian Fleets
India / Indians, ix, 54, 120, 123, 131, 133, 135–7, 146–7, 158, 244, 258–9
Indian Ocean (mentioned or implied), 54, 133, 136–7, 147, 259
Infantry (word), viii, 4–6, 8, 13, 15–16, 21, 37–40, 42–3, 49, 51, 55, 60, 70–1, 76, 78–9, 100–103, 105, 108–15, 130–1, 147, 152, 157, 232–3, 235, 237–9, 241, 243, 247–8, 253, 255, 257, 264
    see also Legions, Allies, *Auxilia*, *Numeri*, Fleets
Ingenuus, general and usurper, 35
Intelligence gathering, information gathering, informers, informant, couriers, spying, spies, reconnaissance, reconnoitre, scouting, (words), 4, 7, 15, 24–6, 28, 32, 71, 84, 92–3, 97, 120, 124–5, 130, 133–4, 152–3, 167, 186, 203, 210, 220, 244, 250, 258, 267
    see also *Frumentarii, Peregrini, Praetoriani, Aulici, Evocati, Speculatores, Urbaniciani*, Ambushes, Diplomacy, Ambassador, Agentes in Rebus
Ioviani, see Legions
Iran, see Persia
Isauria / Isaurians, 188–9, 193–5, 207
    see also Palfuerius, Lydius, Marcianus, M. Aur. Probus, Cremna
Isaurae legions, see legions
Italy, Italian, Italians, 17, 22, 28, 43, 45, 48, 50–1, 61–2, 64, 66, 70–1, 73–6, 78, 83, 89, 92, 94–5, 103, 110, 144, 162, 170, 202, 217, 229, 244
Italian Drill, 17, 110
Itureans, auxiliaries, archers, 32
Iuthungi, see *Alamanni*

Jadhima, Tanukh sheik, 116, 252
Javelin, javelineers, 5–6, 8, 13, 21, 25, 38, 60, 131, 133, 237–9, 241, 243
    see also Pilum, Spears, Lancers, *Contarii*, Cataphracts
Judaea, province and area, 53
Judaism, Jews, 59, 117
Jugurtha, Numidian king, 242
Julia Domna, mother or stepmother of Caracalla, 59

Julian, emperor and usurper, 5, 46, 222, 260, 263, 265, 267
Julian Alps, 70, 75
Julius Caesar, Roman dictator, 181, 261
Julius Nuffuzis, Moorish chieftain, 261
Julius Matif, Moorish chieftain, 261
Julius Placiadianus, Prefect of Vigiles, 51, 83
Jupiter, 124, 146, 172

Khosrov the Great, King of Armenia (ca. 215–253/9), 250
see also Tiridates
Kinda Arabs, 135, 147, 258
see also Yemen
Koloneia, city, 95
Kontoforoi, see Contarii

Laelianus, Vipius Cornelius Laelianus (Lollianus), Gallic emperor (ca. 268/9), 48
Laeti, 8, 128, 199, 205–206, 258
see also Allies
Lancea, 238, 243
see also Spear, Lancers, *Xyston, Contarii, Hasta*, Javelin
Lancers, 21, 39–42, 56, 152, 178, 236
see also Cataphracts, Cavalry, *Contarii*
Larissa, city, 105–106
Lauriacum, city, 70
Legate, *legatus*, 6–7, 173, 235
Legions, legionaries, viii, ix, 3–8, 16, 21–2, 28, 32, 35, 42, 49, 53, 55–6, 72, 94–5, 105–108, 111, 130, 143, 157, 165, 182, 193, 202–203, 219, 231–49, 252, 264
legio I Italica, xii–xiii
legio I Adiutrix, xii–xiii
legio I Minervia, xii–xiii
legio I Parthica, xii–xiii, 6–8, 55, 105, 231
legio I Illyricorum, 94
legio I Isaura, 193
legio II Augusta, xii–xiii
legio II Adiutrix, xii–xiii
legio II Traiana, xii–xiii, 6
legio II Italica, xii–iii
legio II Parthica, xii–xiii, 4–8, 231
legio II Isaura, 193
legio III Felix, 32, 35, 130, 249
legio III Gallica, xii–xiii, 53, 55, 105, 130
legio III Augusta, xii–xiii, 130
legio III Cyrenaica, xii–xiii, 53, 105, 130
legio III Italica, xii–xiii, 130
legio III Parthica, xii–xiii, 6–8, 55, 105, 130, 231
legio III Isaura, 193
legio IV Scythica, xii–xiii, 55, 105

legio IV Flavia, xii–xiii
legio IV Martia, 94
legio IV Parthica (attested first under Diocletian, but may have been created by Alexander Severus), xii–xiii, 6–8
legio V Macedonica, xii–xiii
legio VI Gallicana, 32
legio VI Ferrata, xii–xiii, 55, 252
legio VI Victrix, xii–xiii
legio VII Macedonica (Claudia), xii–xiii
legio VII Gemina, xii–xiii
legio VIII Augusta, xii–xiii
legio X Gemina, xii–xiii, 49, 157
legio X Fretensis, xii–xiii, 49, 53, 55, 105, 107, 157
legio X Fortissimus Exercitus? (Ioviani?), 49, 157
legio XI Claudia, xii–xiii
legio XII Fulminata, xii–xiii, 55, 95
legio XIII Gemina, xii–xiii
legio XIV Gemina (Flavia), xii–xiii
legio XV Apollinaris, xii–xiii, 55, 95
legio XVI Flavia, xii–xiii, 55, 105
legio XX Valeria Victrix, xii–xiii
legio XXII Primigenia, xii–xiii
legio XXX Ulpia, xii–xiii
naval legions, 22–3
Ioviani, 49, 157
Herculiani, 49, 157
Lembariarii, 84, 255
Leonides, *dux*, 209
Licinius, Valerius Licinianus Licinius, *dux, comes* and emperor (311–323), 177, 218, 225
Limes, limitanei, limitis, frontier, border, 26, 28, 33, 38, 76, 84, 93, 122, 132, 140, 158, 165, 174, 181–3, 186, 194, 196, 203, 206, 217, 219, 228, 232, 244, 247, 254–5, 258, 265–6
Logistics, *see* Supply
Lollianus, *see Egnatius, Laelianus*
Longinus, philosopher and advisor of Zenobia, 58–9, 118–19, 122–3
Longiones, Germanic/Alamannic tribe, 181, 183
Lycia, province, 189
Lydius, Isaurian rebel, 189–91
see also Palfuerius
Lyon, Lugdunum, city, 5, 138–9, 145, 179, 202, 204–205, 259

Macedonia, Macedonian, 29, 244
Macriani, means in the text either only Macrianus Sr. and Jr., or collectively everyone involved in the usurpation including Quietus and Ballista, 3
Marcianus, *dux*, 43–5, 50

Marcianus, Terentius, governor, 189, 193
Magister Equitum, 3–4, 26, 49, 64, 193, 201
  see also *Hipparchos, Comes, Magister Officiorum,*
Magister Peditum, 4, 26, 157
  see also *Hipparchos, Comes, Magister Officiorum.*
Magister Militum, magister exercitus, 4, 26, 196
Magister Officiorum, Tribunus et Magister Officiorum, 4, 26, 34, 49, 157, 252
  see also *Hipparchos, Comes, Magister Equitum/Peditum,*
Magnia Urbica, wife of Carinus, 228
Mainz, city, 32, 48, 98
Maniple, *manipulus, manipuli*, depending on source a file or two centuries or units, 6, 77, 170, 235–6
Manlius Statianus, senator, 172
Marcianus, *dux*, plotter to kill Gallienus?, 43–5, 50
Marcianus, Terentius, *praeses*, 189, 193
Marcomanni, Germanic tribe, 36, 38, 61–3, 69, 75, 78–9, 82–3, 147, 252, 264
  see also Alamanni, Iuthungi, Goths, Scythians, Suebi
Marcus Aurelius, emperor, see Aurelius
Marius, M. Aurelius Marinus, Gallic emperor (ca. 269), 48
Marmaridae, Berber/Moorish tribe, 60, 172–3, 256
  see also Moors
Mars, Roman god of war and location in Rome, 162, 244
Martial Arts, 5, 177
  see also Athletes, Tiridates
Matronianus, Praetorian Prefect, 228
Mauretania / Mauritania / Mauritanians, 22, 162, 164, 186, 249
  see also Africa, *Equites*, Fleets, Moors
Maximian, emperor, 49
Maximinus Thrax, emperor (235–238; for additional details, see the forthcoming Syvänne, *Gordian III and Philip the Arab*), 74, 188, 250, 260
Maximus Dalmatius, see Dalmatius
Maximinus, relative of Tacitus, governor of Syria in 275/6, 165, 167, 261
Mediolanum, see Milan
Meros (pl. *mere*, military division, roughly the equivalent of legion 6,000–7,000 men), 8, 19, 247–8
Mesopotamia, province and area, Mesopotamians, 3, 32, 54–5, 105–107, 120, 122, 128, 151, 222, 225

Milan (*Mediolanum*), city, 3–4, 43, 46–50, 78–9, 89–90, 137, 216
Military, see Allies, Archers, *Auxilia*, Bodyguards, Cavalry, Infantry, Legions, *Numeri*, Fleets, Ambushes, Battles, Sieges, Intelligence Gathering, *Equites, Aulici*, Bodyguards, *Evocati, Stratores, Praetoriani, Urbaniciani, Vigiles*
Military equipment, see Chapter 2, Appendix 1, Legions, Archers, *Aulici, Auxilia, Numeri*, Civilian Police, Bodyguards, *Praetoriani, Cataphractarii*, Lancers, *Contarii*, Plates
Militia, see Civilian Police
Mint, mints, minting, 53, 64, 66–7, 69, 84–6, 89–90, 99, 124, 133, 137–9, 141, 145, 155–6, 159, 180, 252–3, 263
  see also Gold, Silver
Mirian, Mihran, Georgian king, 179, 193, 262
  see also Narses
Misenum, city, Italia (HQ of the Fleet of Misenum), 5, 255
  see also Fleets, Praetorian Fleets
Modestus, military theorist, v, 13, 165, 231–47, 249, 261, 266
Moesia, provinces and general area, Moesians, 22, 29, 35, 106, 209, 213, 229, 244
  see also Balkans, Illyricum, Thrace
Mogontiacum, see Mainz
Moira (pl. *moirai*, military division / regiment), 19, 103, 247–8
Moors, Moorish, Berbers, 36, 52, 60–1, 67–8, 80, 94, 106, 166, 195, 199–200, 203, 205, 252, 262
  see also *Equites Mauri*
Mounted archers, see Archers
  see also *Cataphractarii*, Cavalry, *Equites, Leones*, Oshroene, Armenia, *Parthia*
Mucapor, *dux*, murderer of Aurelian, 118, 154–5, 166
Murder, see Assassins
Mursa, city, 77–8
Mutina (Modena), city, 179

Naissus, city, 93, 255
Narbonensis, province, Gaul, 51–2, 62, 216, 251
Narses, The High King of Armenia (the de facto vice regent of Persia's Western border), the future Persian ruler (293–302), 178–9, 188, 193–4, 196, 262
  see also Mirian, Tiridates
Navy, see Fleets
Nicaea city, 95
Nicomachus, Maecius Faltonius, senator, 161
Nicomachus, historian, 59, 118
Nicomedia, city, 95, 227

Nicopolis ad Istrum, city, 32, 50–1, 64, 252–3
Nile, river, 54, 134–5, 137
Noricum, province and general area, 3, 94, 106, 211
North Africa, *see* Africa
  see also Egypt, Blemmyes, Aksumites, Moors
Notarii/notarius (secretary/notary), 7, 153
Notitia Dignitatum, 157, 252, 264
Numeri, Numerus (arithmos, arithmoi, katalogos, katalogoi), national *numeri*, units in general, 4, 6, 8–9, 72–3, 182, 247
  see also Arithmoi
Numerianus, M. Aurelius Numerius Numerianus, emperor (283–284), v, 2, 157, 215, 217–18, 222, 224–9, 263–4, 266
Numidia, 162
  see also Africa, Egypt, Aksum, Mauretania

Odaenathus, Septimius Odaenathus, King / Sheik of Palmyra, Roman *dux* (259/60–267), 52, 54, 58, 121, 142, 145, 226
  see also Zenobia, Herodes, Palmyra
Onager / Onagri, 7–8, 25, 85, 191, 266
  see also Ballistae, Stone Throwers
Orontes, River, 100–102
Oshroene, province and area, 55, 105
Ostensionales, see Aulici with Syvänne, Caracalla (p.37–8)
Ostia, city and harbour, 5, 87, 149

Pagrae, city, 100–103
Palfuerius, Isaurian rebel, 189
  see also Lydius
Palmyra, city, Palmyrans, v, vii, ix, 3–4, 46, 52–61, 63–4, 66–9, 80, 84, 89–90, 92–6, 99–03, 105–106, 108–34, 136–7, 146–7, 158–9, 176, 225, 252, 256–7, 259, 265, 267
  see also Odaenathus, Zenobia
Pamphylia, province, 95, 189, 193–4
Pannonia (general area) with provinces Pannonia Superior and Inferior, 5, 29, 34–5, 61, 75–6, 95, 97, 106, 202, 213, 217, 229, 254
  see also Balkans, Illyricum, Thrace, Moesia
Pannonicus, pileus Pannonicus, hat, viii, 5, 213, 220
Paramilitary forces, *see* Civilian Police
Parthia / Parthians, *see* Persia
  see also Legions (I, II, III, IV Parthica)
Parthicus, Parthicus Maximus, title, 53, 99, 120, 123, 128, 172, 178, 196, 222, 261
Patavium (Padua), city, 179
Paternus, Aspasius, *éminence grise*, 49
Paul of Samosata, Bishop of Antioch, 59, 103
Pavia, *see* Ticinum

Pedites (infantry), 232
  see also Infantry
Peregrini, Princeps Peregrinorum, 4–5, 26
  see also Intelligence gathering, *Frumentarii, Speculatores, Agentes in Rebus*
Pericles, Athenian statesman, 110
Persia, Persians, Parthia, Iran, viii, ix, 3, 31–2, 35–6, 40–3, 50–6, 58, 93, 95, 105, 110, 117–23, 135, 145–7, 150–2, 154, 158, 161, 166, 172, 178–9, 188, 193–7, 199, 208–10, 217–26, 241–2, 244, 250–1, 257, 259, 261–3, 266–7
Persicus, Persicus Maximus, *see Parthicus*
Peuci, Peucini, tribe, 33
Phalanx, shield-wall, murus, 15–16, 37–8, 60, 110–14, 131, 165, 219, 232, 236, 238–41, 242, 245, 249
Philip the Arab, (244–249) for further details, see forthcoming Syvänne, *Gordian III and Philip the Arab*), 131
Philippopolis, city, 93
Philosophy, 58–9, 97, 119, 122–3
Phocas, *see* Phokas
Phoenicia, Phoenice, provinces and area, 55, 106–107, 109, 170
Phokas, Nikephoros II Phokas, emperor (963–969), 254
  see also Syvänne, Nikephoros II Phokas
Pilum / spiculum, pila /spiculi (heavy javelin), 31, 38, 237–8, 243
  see also Javelin, *Lancea*, Lancers
Pipa, Pipara, daughter of Attalus, concubine of Gallienus, 44, 61
  see also Attalus, Marcomanni, Gallienus
Pisonianus, *dux*, 209
Placentia, (Piacenza), city, ix, 78–9, 158, 179, 253–4
Placidianus, Julius, Prefect of the *Vigiles*, 51–2, 62, 64
Plague, *see* Epidemics
Po, river, 70
Poetovio, city, 91
Pompey, republican era consul, 263, 267
Pontirolo, bridge, *see* Battles
Pontus, 22, 167, 172–3, 176, 178
Pontifex maximus, pontiffs, 30, 82, 173
Postumus, M. Cassianius Latinius Postumus, usurper, emperor in the Gallic Empire (260–268), 3–4, 31, 43, 48, 98, 145, 148, 173, 181, 204, 250
Praefecti/Praefectus legionis/Prefect(s) of the legions, 3, 6–7, 235
Praefectus Aegypti/Prefect of Egypt, 59, 132, 258
Praefectus Mesopotamiae rectorque Orientis, 122
Praefectus Annonae, 134–5
  see also Praepositus Annonae, Annona, Supply

Praefectus castrorum, 6–7, 235
Praefectus Fabrorum, 6–7, 235
Praefectus/Praefecti Praetorio (Praetorian Prefect(s), Prefect(s) of the Guard and acting Prefect), 26, 44–5, 49–50, 52, 149, 162, 167, 171, 216–18, 222, 224–5, 227–9, 251
Praefectus Urbi/ Praefectus Urbis Romae (Urban Prefect of Rome, Prefect of the City), 5, 26, 32, 162, 165, 228
  see also Urbaniciani
Praefectus vigilum/Prefect of *Vigiles*, 51
  see also Placiadianus
Praepositus / Praepositi (acting commanders for various purposes), 6–7, 249
Praetorian Fleets, Imperial Fleet (Misenum, Ravenna), 5, 22–3
  see also Misenum, Ravenna, Fleets
Praetoriani (Praetorians, Praetorian Guard), vii-viii, 4, 8–9, 26, 50, 72, 84, 94, 106, 154, 162, 170, 227–30, 255
  see also Praefectus Praetorio, Aulici, Bodyguards, Equites, Praetorian Fleets
Praetorians, see Praetoriani
Prefect of the City, see Praefectus Urbi
Prefect, see Praefectus
Princeps Peregrinorum, see Peregrini
Prisoners, captives, (capture of city = captives, slaves), 3, 31–3, 35, 41, 47, 52, 76–8, 82, 99, 101, 120–3, 127–8, 130–1, 133–5, 144–7, 149, 178–9, 182–3, 187, 189, 194, 201–202, 217, 222, 225, 243–4, 256–7, 262
  see also Slaves
Probus, Marcus Aurelius Probus (other versions: Aurelius Valerius Probus; Equitius Probus; Aelius Probus), emperor (276–282), i–ii, v, vii–xi, 1–3, 11, 28–9, 33–6, 45, 51, 59–61, 68, 77–8, 86, 91, 94–5, 99–100, 105, 121, 123, 132, 136, 144–5, 157, 166–214, 216–18, 221–2, 226, 230, 242, 247, 250–2, 256, 260, 261–2, 266
  early career until 276, 29, 33–6, 45, 59–61, 68, 77–8, 91, 94–5, 99–100, 105, 121, 123, 132, 144–5, 157, 166–8, 250, 256
  Probus vs. Florianus in 276, 169–74, 261
  Probus vs. Murderers of Aurelian in 276, 174–5
  Probus vs. Goths and war in Armenia in 276–8, 176–9, 261
  Campaigns in Gaul, Germania, Illyricum, Thrace in 277–8, 179–88, 247, 262
  Isaurian war in 278–9, 188–93
  Wars against the Blemmyes and Persia in 278–9, 193–7, 261
  Refugee problem in the Balkans in 279, 197–9

  The revolt of Saturninus the Moor in 279–80, 199–201, 262
  The revolts in the West in 280–1, 202–206, 262
  The revolts in the Balkans in 281–2, 206–207, 262
  Triumph at Rome in about 281–2, 207–208, 247
  The Assassination of Probus in 282, 208–11
  Probus the military intellectual, 212–4
Probus, Tenagino, general and admiral, 36, 51, 59–61, 63–4, 67–9, 256
Proconsul, see Consul
Proculus, *dux* and usurper, xi, 2, 183, 196, 198, 201–205, 212, 262–3
Protector / Protectores / Protectores Domestici, see Aulici
Provisions, see Supply
Puteoli, city, 5
Pyrrhus, King of Epeiros, 242

Quadi, Germanic tribe, 33, 35–6, 187, 216–18, 226
Quintillus, M. Aur. Claudius Quintillus, brother of Claudius II, emperor (270), vii, 50–1, 62, 64–7, 69–70, 73–4, 82, 89, 123, 251–3

Raetia, province, 3, 43, 51, 61, 71, 94, 106, 150–1, 183, 187, 203, 211, 259
  see also Augsburg, Alamanni, Iuthungi
Ravenna, city, Italy (HQ of the Fleet of Ravenna), 5, 22, 74, 180, 255
  see also Fleets, Praetorian Fleets
Reconnaissance, see Intelligence Gathering
Red Sea, 54, 131, 133, 135, 137, 147, 257–8
  see also Trade, Firmus, Zenobia
Regalianus, usurper in 258/9, 35
Rhine, river, 144–5, 158, 161, 172, 181, 183, 186, 188–9, 199, 203–206, 218, 228, 265
  see also Limes
Rhodanus (Rhone), river, 70, 180, 202, 205
Riparienses, 84, 255
Rome, city, Italy, capital, ix, 5, 26, 32, 47, 49–50, 61, 64, 66–7, 70, 73–6, 80, 82–6, 89–90, 92, 98–9, 103, 109, 118, 125–6, 133–5, 137, 140–1, 143, 145–6, 148–50, 155, 159, 162–3, 165, 170, 179–80, 188, 194, 200, 206–208, 211, 216–17, 228, 251, 254–5, 262, 265
Roxolani, Sarmatian tribe, 128, 131, 146–7
  see also Sarmatians
Ruse, see Stratagems

Sabinus, Gaius Valerius, 'financial minister' under Aurelian, 89, 137
Sabinus, Julianus (M. Aurelius Sabinus Julianus), usurper or usurpers in 284, 229

Sagittarii, see archers
Saloninus, P. Licinius Cornelius Saloninus Valerianus (Saloninus), second son of Gallienus and Salonina, 250
Saone, river, 218
Saracens, *see* Arabs
Sarmatians, ix, 3, 9, 31–3, 35–6, 39–41, 61–2, 69, 74–8, 92, 128, 131, 146–7, 172, 187–8, 202, 207, 216–18, 226
  see also Alans, Roxolani, Goths, Dacia
Sarmaticus, Sarmaticus Maximus, title, 69, 77, 128, 172
Satala, city, 95
Saturninus the Moor, usurper under Probus (not to be confused with the similarly named usurper under Gallienus), xi, 2, 36, 51–2, 61, 166, 173, 180, 193, 195–6, 199–201, 205–207, 210, 212, 261–3
Saxons, Germanic confederacy, 25, 36, 39, 218, 263
Scholae, see Aulici
Scipio Africanus the Elder, 220
Sciri, (pure = purebred), Germanic tribe, 36, 39
Scutarii, see Aulici
Scythian, Scythians, (often used to denote any Germanic tribe specializing in cavalry combat along the Danube frontier), 68, 71, 73–5, 151–2, 167, 170, 198
  see also Goths, Heruls, Iuthungi, Alamanni, Vandals, Sarmatians
Scythica, see Legions
Seleuceia/Seleucia/Seleukeia Pieria, city, Coele Syria, Maharacik, Turkey, 55, 100
Seleucia in Mesopotamia close to Ctesiphon, viii, 222, 226
Semno, Germanic chieftain, 183
Semnones, Germanic tribe, 183
  see also Alamanni, Suevi
Senate / Senators / Upper Class, 3, 7, 30–1, 33, 43–4, 46–7, 49–50, 63–4, 69–70, 73–4, 82, 84, 86, 118, 124–5, 128, 134–5, 147–50, 154, 159–66, 168–70, 172–5, 180, 182, 188, 211, 213, 217, 220, 228–9, 251, 255
  see also Equestrians
Septimius Severus. L. emperor (193–211), 6–7, 137, 148, 152, 165, 220, 226, 231, 237, 245, 259–60, 264
Serdica (Sofia), city, 90, 176
Severina, Ulpia, wife of Aurelian and daughter of Zenobia(?), 141–3, 150, 155–6, 160, 259
Severus, Alexander, *see* Alexander Severus
Sex, sexual behaviour, sex-slaves, concubines, brothels, mistress, whores, prostitutes, 44, 74, 142, 150, 163, 216, 226, 228, 252
  see also Bisexual

Shapur I, Persian ruler (ca. 240/3–272), i, xi, 3, 52, 122–3, 250, 252, 257
Sheep, 33, 181–2, 186
  see also Grain, Fleets, Supply, Prisoners, Chicken, Wine, Cows
Ships, *see* Fleets
Sicily, island, 143, 198
Siege Warfare, vii, ix, 6–8, 16, 25–6, 37, 42–3, 46–50, 87–8, 96–9, 105, 112, 115–24, 134, 150–1, 189–93, 196, 200–1, 222, 256–7
  see also Ballistae, *Onager*, Fleets
Sieges of,
  Apamea, 200–201
  Augsburg, 150–1
  Coche, 222
  Cremna, ix, 25, 188–93, 196, 266
  Ctesiphon, 222
  Mainz in 268, 48, 98
  Milan in 268, 43, 46–50
  Palmyra in 272, 105, 112, 115–24, 256–7
  Seleucia, Mesopotamia, 222
  Tarsus, 171
  Tyana, 96–9, 123
  Verona in 312, vii
  see also Battles and the names itself
Signiferi, 8, 240, 246
Silbannacus, usurper, 205, 263
Silk, Silk Route, 53–4, 89, 118, 148, 164
  see also China
Silver / Silver Content in Coins, 72, 84, 89, 118, 138, 145, 148–9, 163, 167, 236, 240, 259
Sirmium, city, Lower Pannonia, Srmska Mitrovica, Serbia, 29, 34, 62, 64–5, 93, 176, 178–9, 202, 209, 253
Singulares, governor's auxiliary bodyguards, 7, 22
  see also Bodyguards
Siscia, city, 64, 78, 93, 176, 179, 189
Slaves, 32–3, 134, 148–9, 154, 182, 202, 209
  see also Prisoners, Freedmen
Slingers, 5–6, 8, 25, 38, 191, 239–40, 243, 264
Sol, *see* Sun
Soldiers, *see* Allies, Archers, Javelin, Spearmen, *Auxilia, Aulici*, Bodyguards, Cavalry, *Contarii, Cataphracts*, Fleets, Infantry, Legions, *Praetoriani, Urbaniciani*
Spain, provinces, area, units, 3, 51–2, 61, 64, 196, 202, 206, 213, 251
Spear, spearmen, 5–6, 8–9, 13, 33, 35, 38–40, 42–4, 55–6, 60, 72, 131, 133, 161, 219, 236, 238, 243
  see also Javelin, *Contarii, Cataphracts*, Lancers, Legions, *Auxilia, Xyston, Lancea, Hasta*
Speculatores, 4, 7, 26

Spice Trade, 53–4
  see also Silk
Spying, *see* Intelligence Gathering
Stablesiani, 5
  see also bodyguards, *equites*
Statores military police / *Stator* / *Statores Augusti*, Emperor's military police, 4, 7, 82
Stone Throwers, 7, 25, 88, 191
  see also Ballistae, Onager
Stratores, see Stablesiani
Stratagems, ruses, viii, 43, 45, 48, 82, 109–11, 158, 187, 201, 204, 220–1, 252, 256, 266
  see also Assassins, Ambushes, Battles, Tactics
Strategikon (military treatise), 17, 19, 80, 247–8, 254, 256, 265, 267
Strategos, Strategoi, Palmyran, 54
Strategy (word), 28, 75, 83, 105, 152, 179, 186, 193, 254, 259, 266
  see also Stratagem, Diplomacy, Ambassador, Trade
Suebi / Suevi, Germanic / Alamannic tribal confederacy (means usually Iuthungi), 36, 69–70, 146–7, 181
  see also Alamanni, Iuthungi, Marcomanni
Sun (*Sol, Sol Invictus, Helios, Heliogabalus*), 30, 74, 96, 98, 108–109, 112, 114, 140, 149, 152, 159, 163, 260
  see also Apollonius of Tyana, Elagabalus
Supply, Logistics, Supply Depots/Hubs/Bases, Food, Fodder, Wine, Water, Oil, Supplying, Supplies, Provisions, 5, 15, 22–3, 25, 37, 42, 64, 66, 75–6, 89, 93–5, 115–16, 119–21, 126, 128, 134–5, 149–50, 158–9, 164, 171, 176, 180, 186, 189–90, 202, 205, 213, 219, 222, 224–5, 235, 257, 261, 267
  see also Grain, Wagons, *Frumentarii, Praefectus Urbi*, Sheep, Cows, Chicken, Pigs, Wine, Fleets
Surprise attacks, *see* Ambushes
Sword, swordsmen, *spatha, semispatha, gladius*, vii, 5–6, 8, 21, 31, 38, 42, 56, 101, 130, 133, 181, 195, 227, 237–8, 241–2, 264
Symmachiarii, 21
  see also Allies
Syracuse, city, 198
Syria, provinces and area, Syrians, 3, 22, 35, 53–5, 68–9, 100, 105–107, 116–18, 121, 129, 157, 161, 165, 167, 170, 173, 193, 195–6, 199–201, 261, 265
Syrianos Magistros (author of *Peri Strategias*), 238, 266

Tacitus, M. Claudius Tacitus, emperor (275–276), v, vii, 2, 36, 148, 152, 154–7, 160–70, 173–4, 176, 213, 231, 241–2, 261, 266

Tacitus, Cornelius, historian, 38, 164, 265
Tactics, Tactic (word), 6, 15–16, 21, 24, 38, 40–2, 60, 78, 83, 113–14, 131, 133, 152, 165, 231–2, 236, 240, 243, 245, 247–8, 267
  see also Ambushes, Battles, Sieges, Stratagems, Phalanx
Tagma, 19, 21, 106, 247–8
  see also Arithmoi, Bandon, Numeri
Taifali, Germanic tribe, 36, 264
Tanukh Arabs, (Syria and al-Hira), 116–18, 121, 252
  see also Arabs, Palmyra, Hira, Kinda
Taxes, tax, taxpayers, donativa, 23, 46, 133–4, 137, 159, 162, 188, 195, 255
  see also Trade
Tervingi Goths, *see* Goths
Tetricus I, Gallic emperor (270/1–274), 489, 124, 136, 140, 143–8, 150, 259
Tetricus II, son of Tetricus I, 144, 146
Theodosius I, emperor, 107, 267
Thessalians, 244
Thessalonica, city, 93
Thrace / Thracia, province and area, 33, 35–6, 50, 61, 64, 92–3, 127, 129, 134, 151, 154, 176, 179, 186–9, 195, 197–8, 217, 244, 250
  see also Balkans, Moesia, Illyricum, Pannonia, Dacia
Thuriangians, Germanic tribe, member of the Frankish Confederacy, 36
Tiber, river, 86, 134, 149
Ticinum, Pavia, 34, 83, 137
Timagenes, general of Zenobia, 58, 68–9, 123, 132
Tiridates / Trdat, king of Armenia (ca. 256–330), 120–1, 152, 176–9, 188, 193–4, 196–7, 201, 218–19, 225, 257, 261–2
Torture, 84, 124, 134, 168, 257
Trade, tolls, customs, caravans, 23, 53–4, 67, 116, 124, 252
  see also Taxes, Silk Route, Spice Trade, Supply, Firmus
Trajan, emperor (98–117), column, canal, forum, 9, 54, 60, 89, 107, 137, 141, 161, 163, 172, 220
Trassus, *dux*, 53
Trdat, *see* Tiridates
Tribunician powers, 140, 155, 162, 173
Tribunus, tribune, (often also a title preceding another title, or a tribune from the bodyguards used as commander of other units), 3–7, 32, 34–5, 43, 49, 96, 154, 170, 202–203, 210, 235, 243, 246, 249–50, 252
Tribute payments, 54, 73, 135
Trier, Treves, Augusta Trevorum, city, 143–5, 151, 259

Tripoli/Tripolis, city in Lebanon, 133
Turma / Tourma (unit of ca. 6,000 horsemen), 248
Turma/Tourma (unit of 500/512 horsemen), 232, 248
Turma (unit of 32–36 horsemen), 7, 9, 232, 236, 246, 248
Tyana, city,
see also Apollonius of Tyana

Uranius, Antoninus, usurper, 99
Urbaniciani (*Cohortes Urbanae,* Urban Cohorts, sing. *Urbaniacus*), viii, 4–5, 26, 86, 162
see also Praefectus Urbi
Urban Prefect, see *Praefectus Urbi*
Urbanus, usurper, 80, 82–4, 251, 254
Ursicinus, Ammianus Marcellinus' commander, 167
Ursinianus, (Ursinus?) *dux*, 209, 212

Vaballathus, Waballathus, L. Iulius Aurelius Septimius Vaballathus Athenodorus, son of Zenobia and Odaenathus, usurper, 53–4, 58–9, 66–7, 69, 84, 89, 99
Valens, emperor, 260
Valerian Sr. (Valerianus) emperor (253–259/60), father of Gallienus, 2–3, 28, 31–6, 50, 52, 105, 152, 217, 221, 225–6, 250, 252, 260, 264
Valerian (Valerianus), brother of Gallienus, 47
Valerius Flaccinus, kinsman of emperor Valerian, 35
Valerius Laevinus, consul 280 BC, 220
Valerius, Clementius Valerius Marcellinus, Roman governor, 261
Vandals, Germanic confederacy, ix, 36, 61–2, 69, 74–8, 92, 146–7, 181, 183, 186–7, 197–9, 253, 261, 263
see also Aurelian, Probus, Goths
Vegetius, military theorist, v, 7–8, 13, 15, 22, 165, 231, 233–46, 249, 254, 264–5, 267
Veh Ardashir, see Coche
Velites, 241, 243
Velitatione, de, 254, 265
Verona, city, vii, ix, 61, 63, 70, 78, 211, 229
see also Battles, Fortifications
Vexillationes (Vexillations = military detachments or cavalry units), Vexillarii (bearers of vexilla), Vexillum, Vexilla, 33, 51, 80, 130, 133, 146–8, 232, 236, 246, 264, 267
Via Egnatia, road, 93
Via Flaminia, 83

Vicar, vicarius, vicarii, 243, 246, 250
Victoria / Vitruvia, mother of the Gallic emperor Victorinus, 48–9
Victorinus the Moor, a friend of Probus, 36, 195, 203, 205–206
Victorinus, M. Piavonius/Piaonius Victorinus, emperor / usurper in Gaul (268/9–270/71), 48–9, 52, 145
see also Victoria / Vitruvia, Postumus
Vigiles, 4–5, 51
Viminacium, city, 229
Virunum, city, 70

Wagons, Wagon Laager, Wagon train, *carrago,* 28, 32, 37, 39, 110, 113
see also Ballistae, Fortifications, Supply
Wedge, *cuneus* (both infantry and cavalry versions), 8, 15–16, 22, 37–8, 113, 232, 236, 243, 264
see also *MHLR Vol. 1* (pp.246–8) and the forthcoming *Nikephoros II Phokas (912–969), The White Death of the Saracens* (forthcoming in 2021)
Wei, Chinese dynasty, 257
Western Jin, Chinese dynasty, 135, 257
Wine, 31, 92, 116, 133, 149–50, 154, 164, 190, 202, 206, 213, 258
see also Grain, Fleets, Supply, Sheep, Chicken, Cows

Xyston (spear), 72
see also Spearmen, *Contarii,* Cataphract, *Lancea, Hasta*

Yemen, Himyar, Sabae, Hadramaut, Arabes Eudaemones, Arabia Felix, Aden, ix, 133, 135, 137, 146–7, 158, 258–9
see also Arabs, Palmyra, Kinda, Tanukh

Zabba (falsely identified with the famous Zenobia), 252
Zabbai, general of Zenobia, 58, 123
Zabdas, general of Zenobia, 53, 58, 68, 100–102, 109, 123
Zenobia, Septimia, Queen of Palmyra, rebel, v, 1, 46, 51–5, 58–9, 63, 65–8, 77, 84, 89, 92, 97, 99–103, 105, 107–109, 115–33, 140–6, 252–3, 258–9, 265, 267
see also Palmyra, Battles of Immae, Daphne, Emesa, Siege of Palmyra